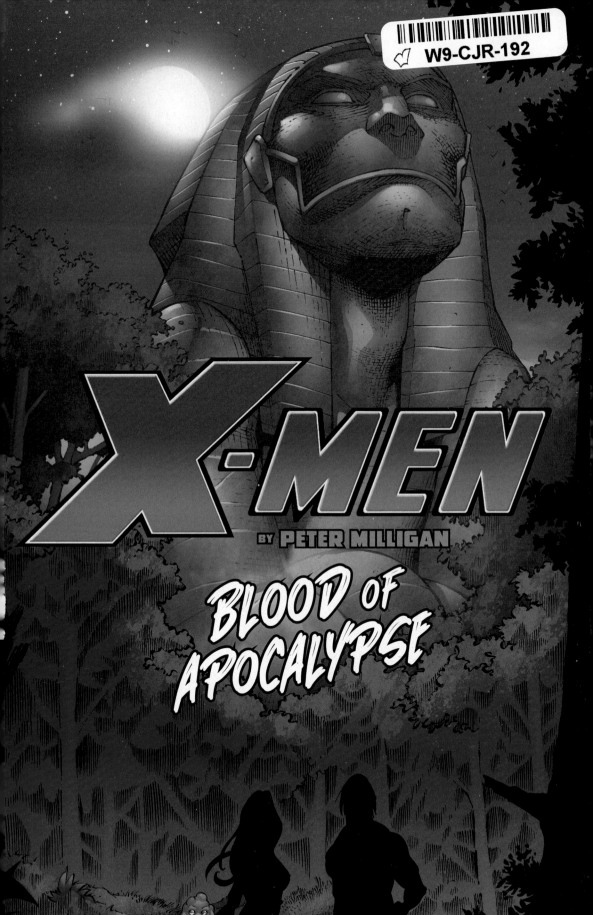

X-MEN

BY PETER MILLIGAN

BLOOD OF APOCALYPSE

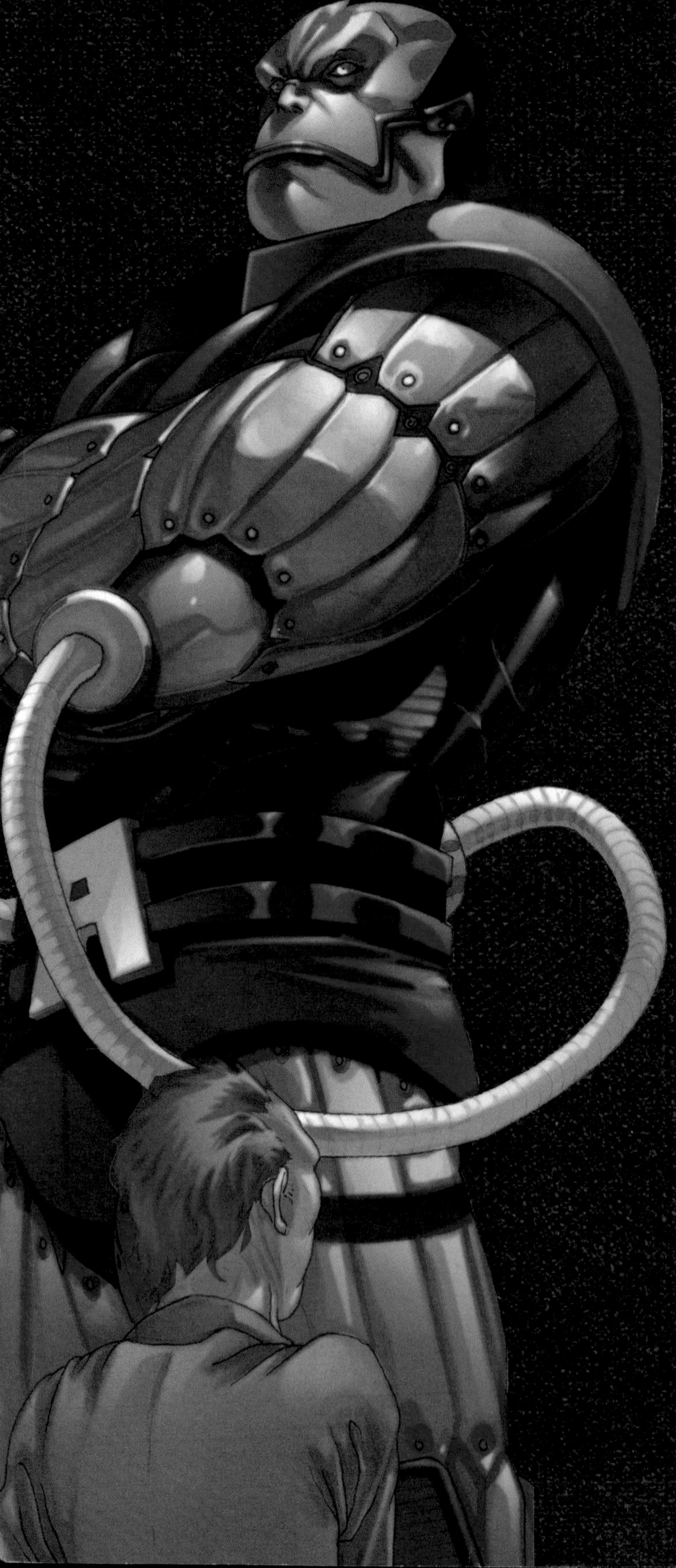

COLLECTION EDITOR: **Jennifer Grünwald**
ASSISTANT EDITOR: **Daniel Kirchhoffer**
ASSISTANT MANAGING EDITOR: **Maia Loy**
ASSOCIATE MANAGER, TALENT RELATIONS: **Lisa Montalbano**
VP PRODUCTION & SPECIAL PROJECTS: **Jeff Youngquist**
BOOK DESIGNER: **Adam Del Re**
SVP PRINT, SALES & MARKETING: **David Gabriel**
EDITOR IN CHIEF: **C.B. Cebulski**

X-MEN BY PETER MILLIGAN: BLOOD OF APOCALYPSE. Contains material originally published in magazine form as CABLE & DEADPOOL (2004) #26-27 and X-MEN (1991) #177-187. First printing 2021. ISBN 978-1-302-93090-5. Published by MARVEL WORLDWIDE, INC., a subsidiary of MARVEL ENTERTAINMENT, LLC. OFFICE OF PUBLICATION: 1290 Avenue of the Americas, New York, NY 10104.

Printed in Canada. KEVIN FEIGE, Chief Creative Officer; DAN BUCKLEY, President, Marvel Entertainment; JOE QUESADA, EVP & Creative Director; DAVID BOGART, Associate Publisher & SVP of Talent Affairs; TOM BREVOORT, VP, Executive Editor; NICK LOWE, Executive Editor, VP of Content, Digital Publishing; DAVID GABRIEL, VP of Print & Digital Publishing; JEFF YOUNGQUIST, VP of Production & Special Projects; ALEX MORALES, Director of Publishing Operations; DAN EDINGTON, Managing Editor; RICKEY PURDIN, Director of Talent Relations; JENNIFER GRÜNWALD, Senior Editor, Special Projects; SUSAN CRESPI, Production Manager; STAN LEE, Chairman Emeritus. For information regarding advertising in Marvel Comics or on Marvel.com, please contact Vit DeBellis, Custom Solutions & Integrated Advertising Manager, at vdebellis@marvel.com. For Marvel subscription inquiries, please call 888-511-5480. **Manufactured between 1/7/2022 and 2/8/2022 by SOLISCO PRINTERS, SCOTT, QC, CANADA.**

10 9 8 7 6 5 4 3 2 1

X-MEN
BLOOD OF APOCALYPSE
BY PETER MILLIGAN

CABLE & DEADPOOL
#26-27

Fabian Nicieza
WRITER

Lan Medina
PENCILER

Ed Tadeo
INKER

Gotham
COLORIST

PATCH ZIRCHER, UDON'S ALAN TAM & ROB SCHWAGER
COVER ART

X-MEN
#177-179

Peter Milligan
WRITER

Salvador Larroca
PENCILER

**Danny Miki &
Allen Martinez** with
Avalon Studios [#179]
INKERS

Liquid! [#177-178] &
Avalon Studios [#177 & #179]
with **Chris Sotomayor**
& **Tom Chu** [#178]
COLORISTS

SALVADOR LARROCA & LIQUID!
COVER ART

X-MEN
#180-181

Peter Milligan
WRITER

Roger Cruz
PENCILER

Victor Olazaba with **Don
Hillsman III** [#181]
INKERS

Liquid! [#180] & **Chris
Sotomayor** [#181]
COLORISTS

SALVADOR LARROCA & LIQUID!
COVER ART

X-MEN
#182-187

Peter Milligan
WRITER

Salvador Larroca
PENCILS/INKS/WASHES

Aron Lusen [#182-183] &
Jason Keith [#184-187]
COLORISTS

SALVADOR LARROCA & ARON LUSEN
COVER ART

X-MEN
#182-186 BACKUP STORIES

Peter Milligan
WRITER

Wil Quintana [#182 & #184-186]
& **Dave McCaig** [#183]
COLORISTS

**Aaron Lopresti &
Danny Miki** [#182];
Pasqual Ferry [#183];
**Clayton Henry &
Mark Morales** [#184];
**Paul Pelletier &
Dave Meikis** [#185];
**Casey Jones &
Vince Russell** [#186]
ARTISTS

VC's Cory Petit
LETTERER

Nick Lowe
ASSOCIATE EDITOR

Sean Ryan
ASSISTANT EDITOR

**John Barber &
Ralph Macchio**
CONSULTING EDITORS

Nicole Wiley Boose & Mike Marts
EDITORS

X-MEN CREATED BY **Stan Lee & Jack Kirby**

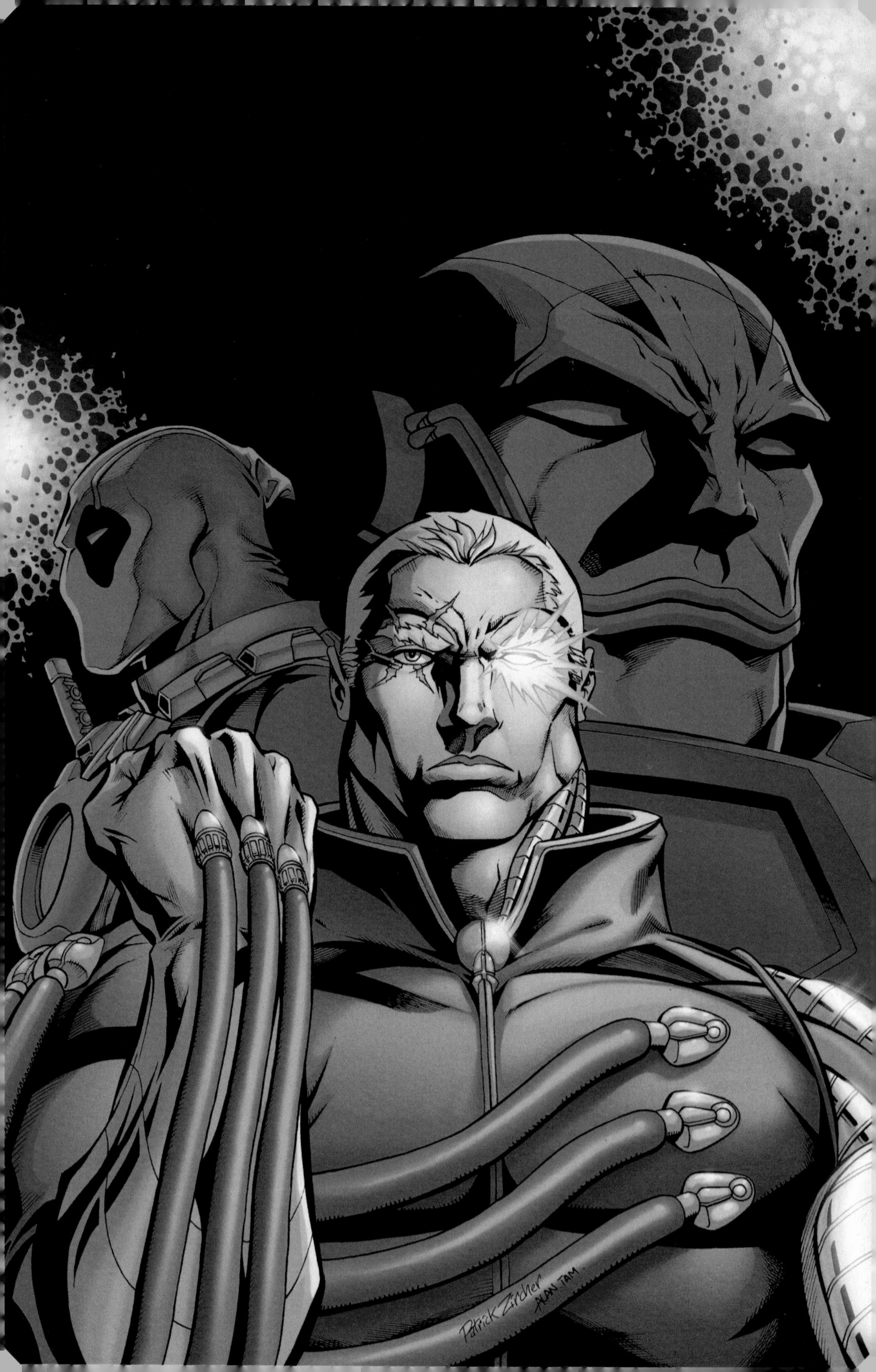
Patrick Zircher
ALAN TAM.

BORN AGAIN PART ONE WITH EYES CLOSED

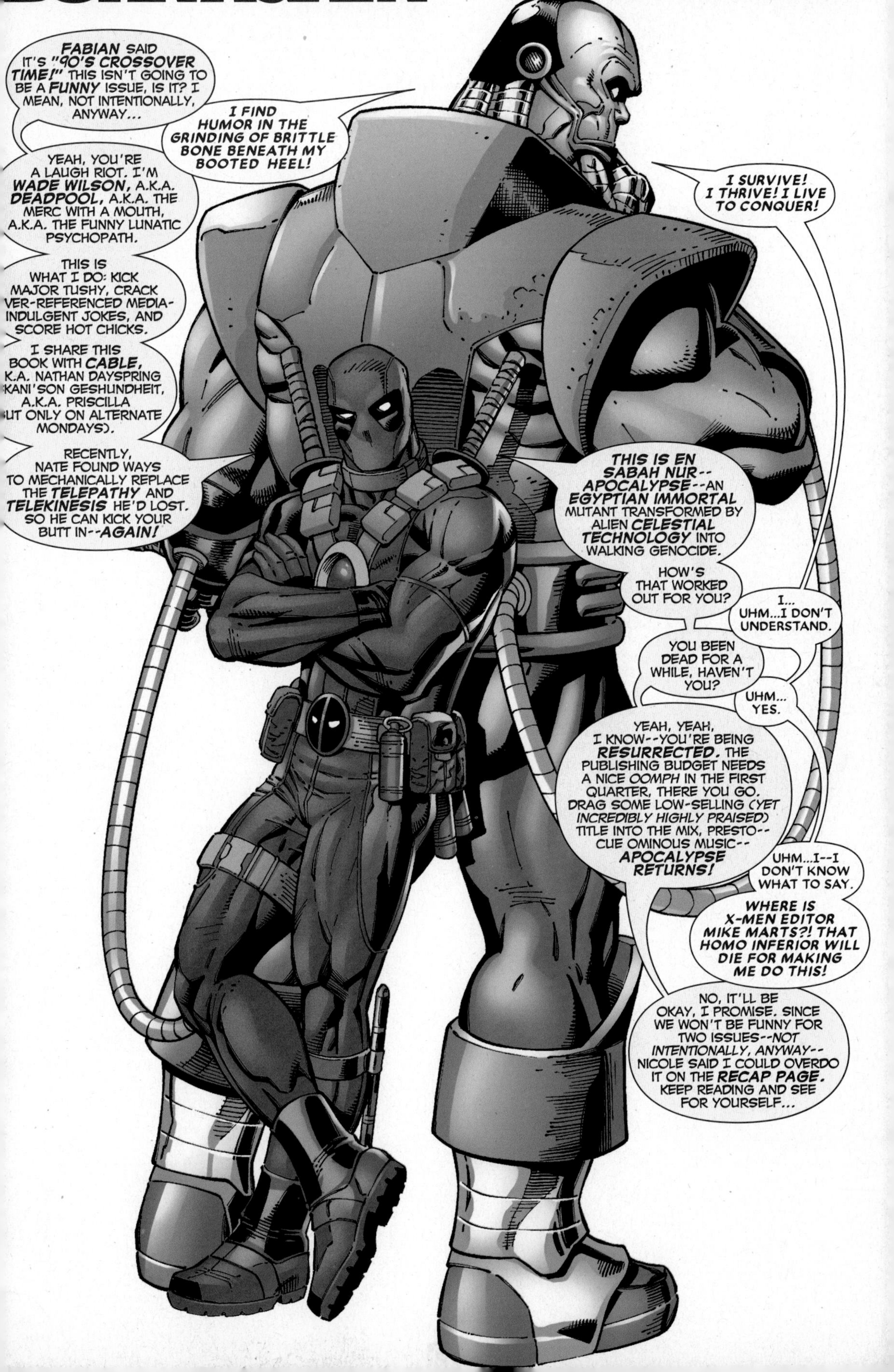

FABIAN SAID IT'S "90'S CROSSOVER TIME!" THIS ISN'T GOING TO BE A FUNNY ISSUE, IS IT? I MEAN, NOT INTENTIONALLY, ANYWAY...
I FIND HUMOR IN THE GRINDING OF BRITTLE BONE BENEATH MY BOOTED HEEL!
YEAH, YOU'RE A LAUGH RIOT. I'M WADE WILSON, A.K.A. DEADPOOL, A.K.A. THE MERC WITH A MOUTH, A.K.A. THE FUNNY LUNATIC PSYCHOPATH.
THIS IS WHAT I DO: KICK MAJOR TUSHY, CRACK VER-REFERENCED MEDIA-INDULGENT JOKES, AND SCORE HOT CHICKS.
I SHARE THIS BOOK WITH CABLE, K.A. NATHAN DAYSPRING KANI'SON GESHUNDHEIT, A.K.A. PRISCILLA UT ONLY ON ALTERNATE MONDAYS).
RECENTLY, NATE FOUND WAYS TO MECHANICALLY REPLACE THE TELEPATHY AND TELEKINESIS HE'D LOST. SO HE CAN KICK YOUR BUTT IN--AGAIN!
I SURVIVE! I THRIVE! I LIVE TO CONQUER!
THIS IS EN SABAH NUR--APOCALYPSE--AN EGYPTIAN IMMORTAL MUTANT TRANSFORMED BY ALIEN CELESTIAL TECHNOLOGY INTO WALKING GENOCIDE.
HOW'S THAT WORKED OUT FOR YOU?
I... UHM...I DON'T UNDERSTAND.
YOU BEEN DEAD FOR A WHILE, HAVEN'T YOU?
UHM... YES.
YEAH, YEAH, I KNOW--YOU'RE BEING RESURRECTED. THE PUBLISHING BUDGET NEEDS A NICE OOMPH IN THE FIRST QUARTER, THERE YOU GO. DRAG SOME LOW-SELLING (YET INCREDIBLY HIGHLY PRAISED) TITLE INTO THE MIX, PRESTO--CUE OMINOUS MUSIC--APOCALYPSE RETURNS!
UHM...I--I DON'T KNOW WHAT TO SAY.
WHERE IS X-MEN EDITOR MIKE MARTS?! THAT HOMO INFERIOR WILL DIE FOR MAKING ME DO THIS!
NO, IT'LL BE OKAY, I PROMISE. SINCE WE WON'T BE FUNNY FOR TWO ISSUES--NOT INTENTIONALLY, ANYWAY--NICOLE SAID I COULD OVERDO IT ON THE RECAP PAGE. KEEP READING AND SEE FOR YOURSELF...

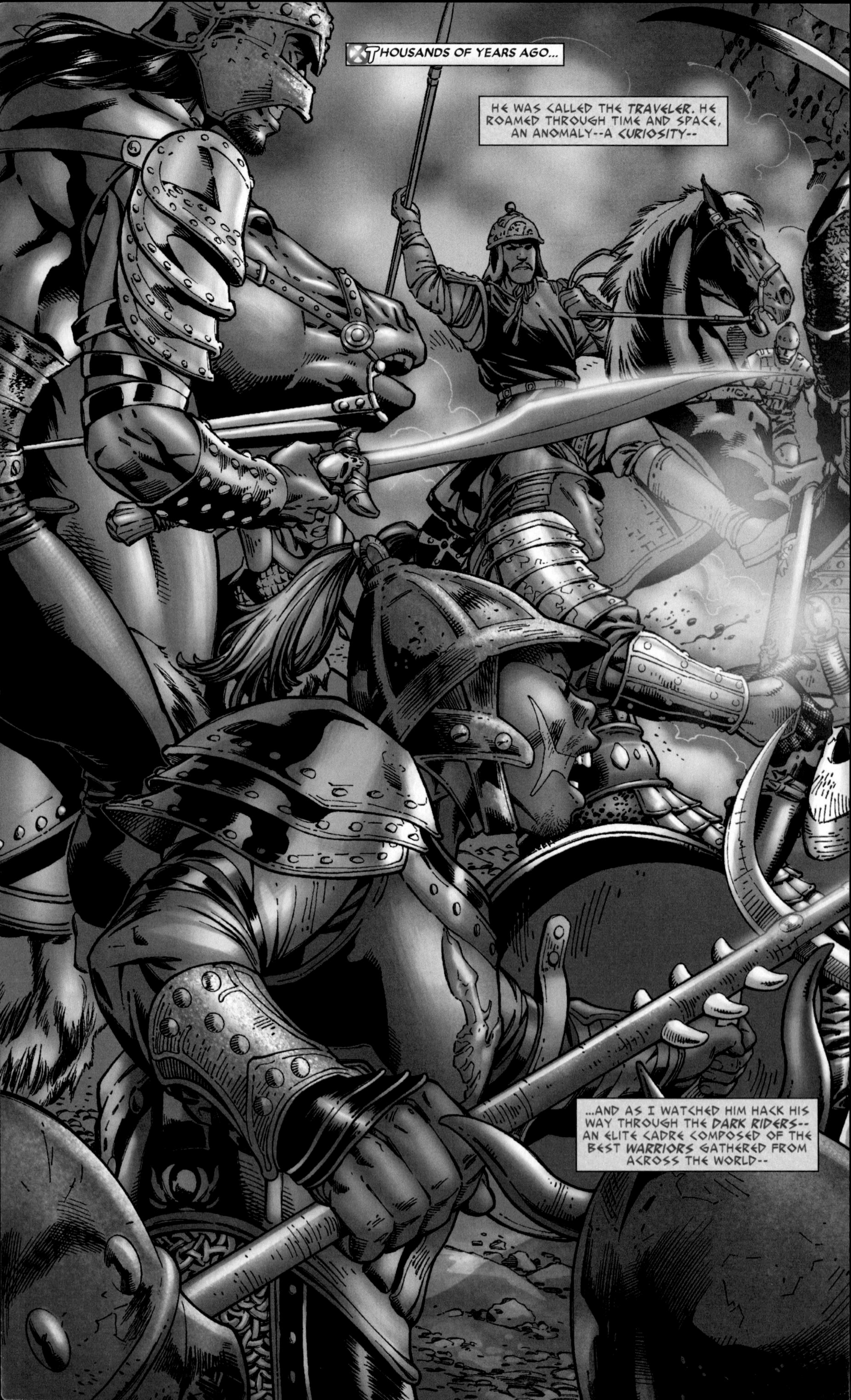
THOUSANDS OF YEARS AGO...
HE WAS CALLED THE TRAVELER. HE ROAMED THROUGH TIME AND SPACE, AN ANOMALY--A CURIOSITY--
...AND AS I WATCHED HIM HACK HIS WAY THROUGH THE DARK RIDERS--AN ELITE CADRE COMPOSED OF THE BEST WARRIORS GATHERED FROM ACROSS THE WORLD--

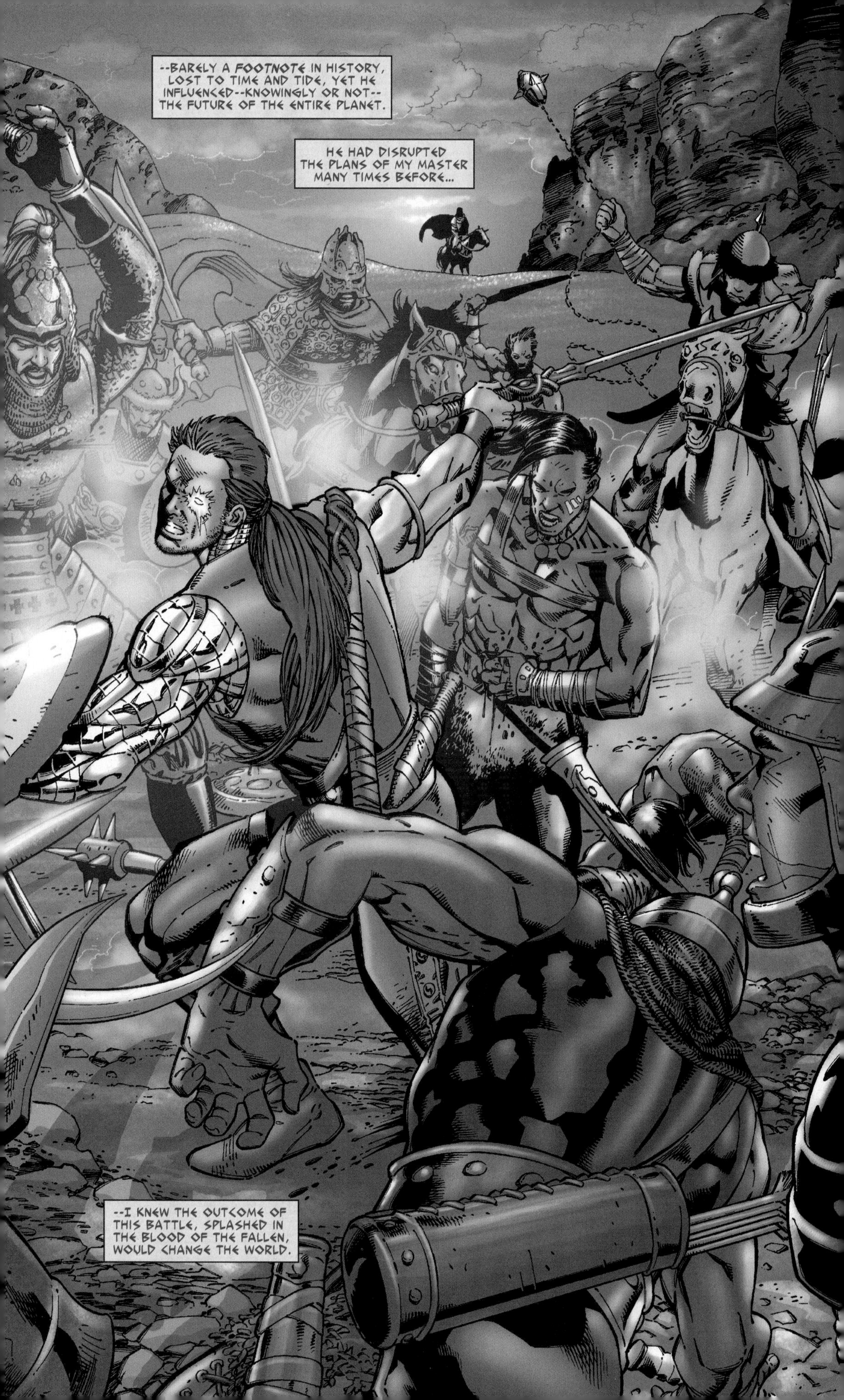
--BARELY A *FOOTNOTE* IN HISTORY, LOST TO TIME AND TIDE, YET HE INFLUENCED--KNOWINGLY OR NOT-- THE FUTURE OF THE ENTIRE PLANET.
HE HAD DISRUPTED THE PLANS OF MY MASTER MANY TIMES BEFORE...
--I KNEW THE OUTCOME OF THIS BATTLE, SPLASHED IN THE BLOOD OF THE FALLEN, WOULD CHANGE THE WORLD.

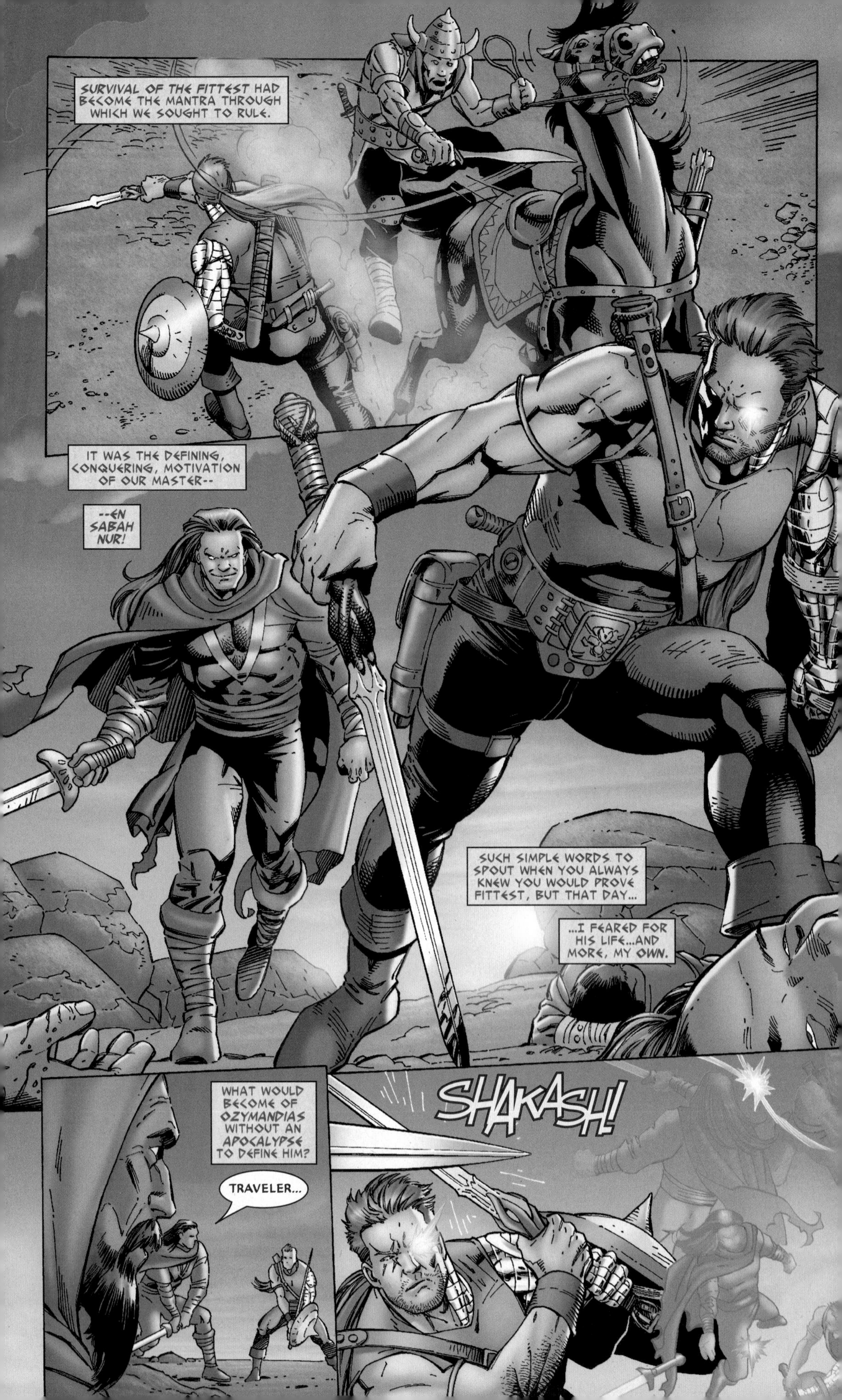
SURVIVAL OF THE FITTEST HAD BECOME THE MANTRA THROUGH WHICH WE SOUGHT TO RULE.
IT WAS THE DEFINING, CONQUERING, MOTIVATION OF OUR MASTER--
--EN SABAH NUR!
SUCH SIMPLE WORDS TO SPOUT WHEN YOU ALWAYS KNEW YOU WOULD PROVE FITTEST, BUT THAT DAY...
...I FEARED FOR HIS LIFE...AND MORE, MY OWN.
WHAT WOULD BECOME OF OZYMANDIAS WITHOUT AN APOCALYPSE TO DEFINE HIM?
TRAVELER...
SHAKASH!

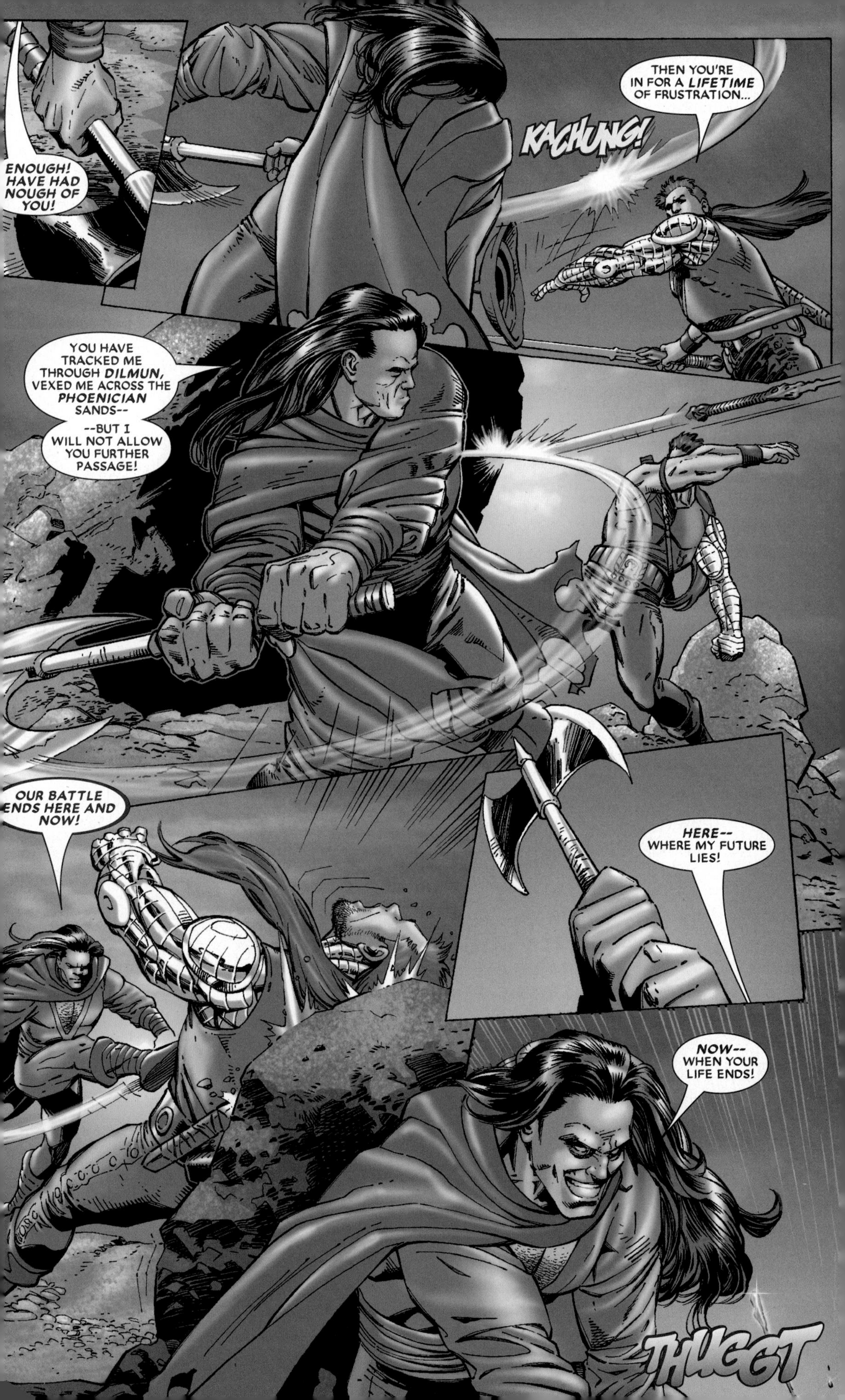
ENOUGH! HAVE HAD NOUGH OF YOU!
KACHUNG!
THEN YOU'RE IN FOR A LIFETIME OF FRUSTRATION...
YOU HAVE TRACKED ME THROUGH DILMUN, VEXED ME ACROSS THE PHOENICIAN SANDS--
--BUT I WILL NOT ALLOW YOU FURTHER PASSAGE!
OUR BATTLE ENDS HERE AND NOW!
HERE-- WHERE MY FUTURE LIES!
NOW-- WHEN YOUR LIFE ENDS!
THUGGT

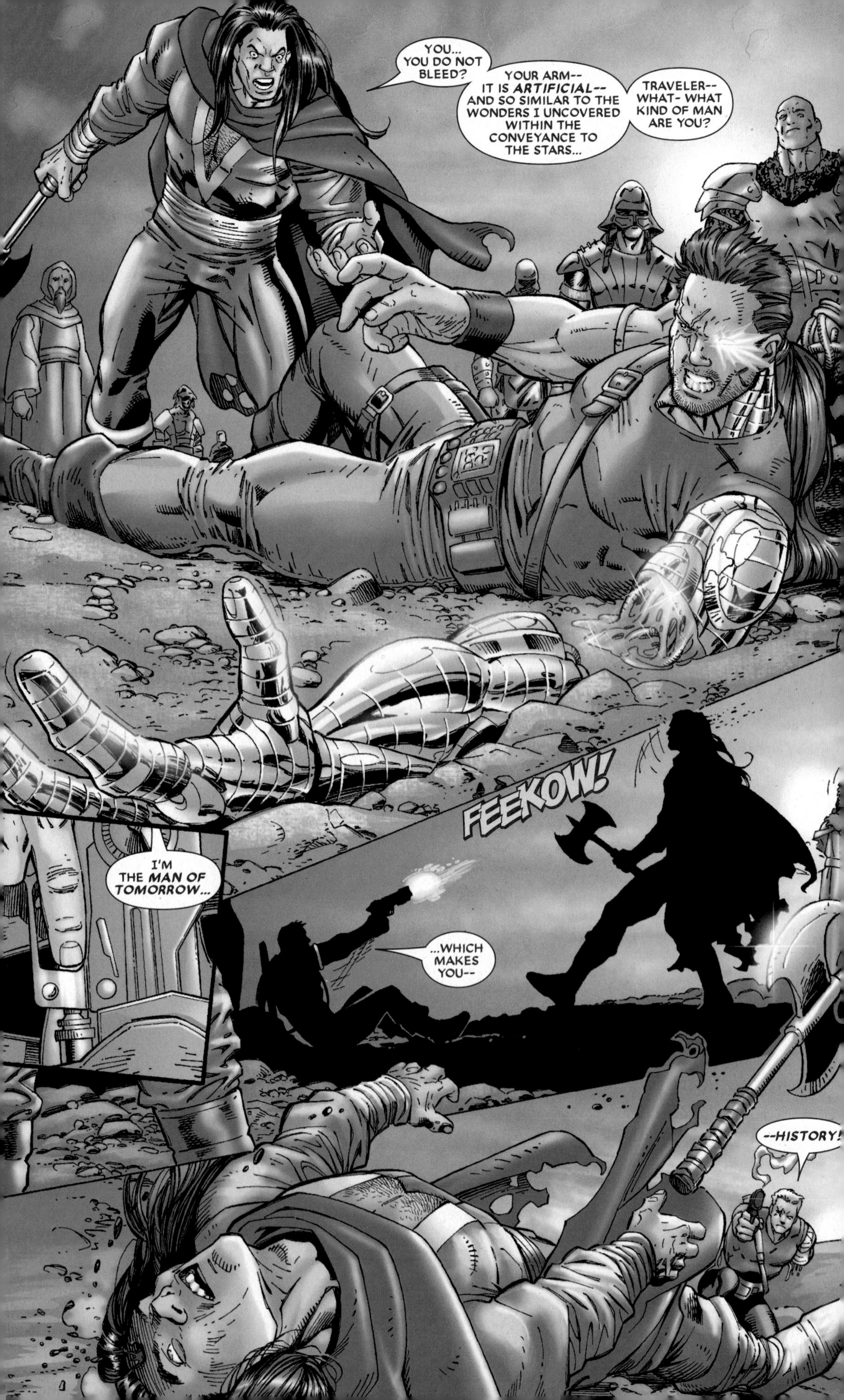
YOU... YOU DO NOT BLEED?
YOUR ARM-- IT IS ARTIFICIAL-- AND SO SIMILAR TO THE WONDERS I UNCOVERED WITHIN THE CONVEYANCE TO THE STARS...
TRAVELER-- WHAT- WHAT KIND OF MAN ARE YOU?
I'M THE MAN OF TOMORROW...
FEEKOW!
...WHICH MAKES YOU--
--HISTORY!

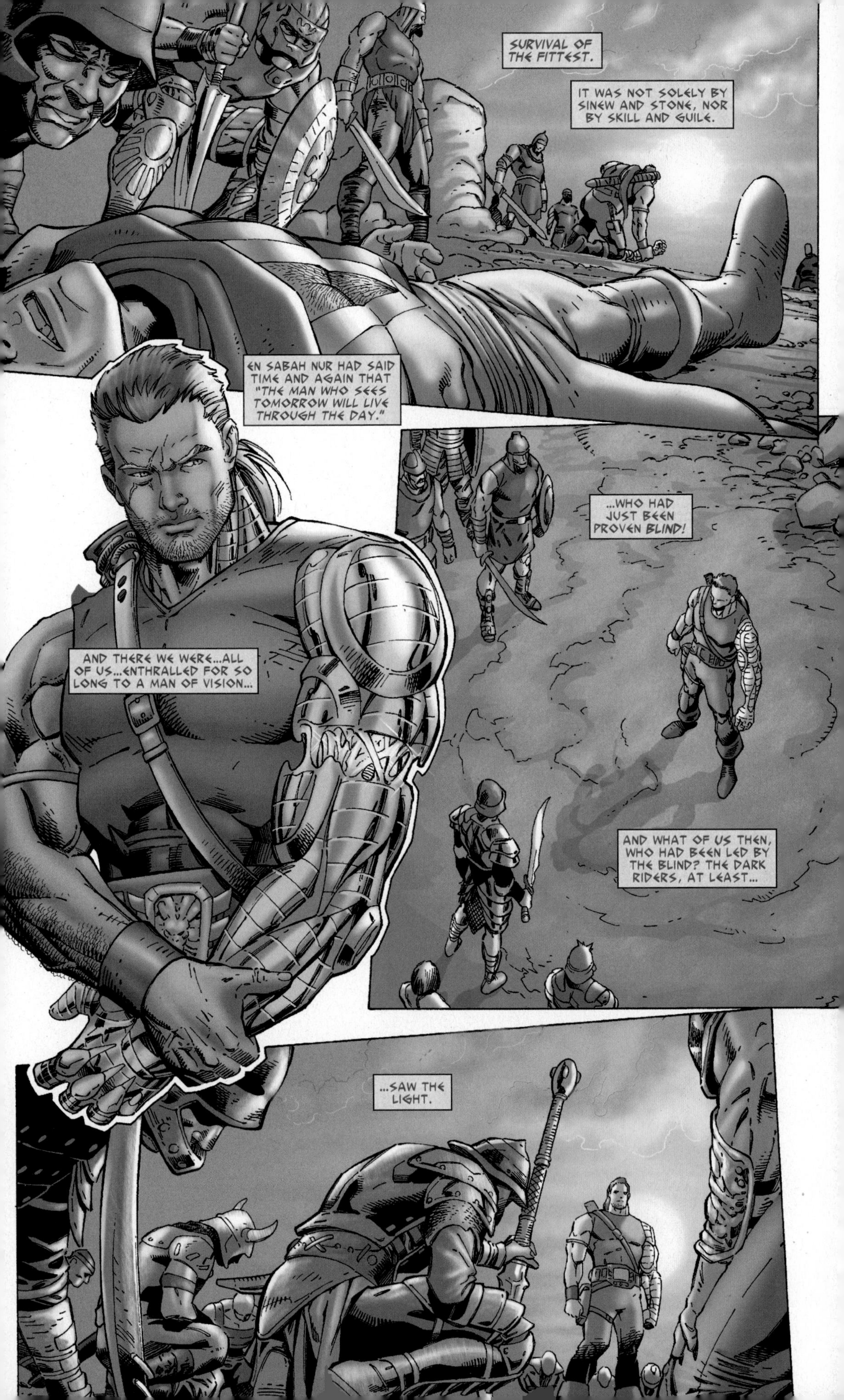
SURVIVAL OF THE FITTEST.
IT WAS NOT SOLELY BY SINEW AND STONE, NOR BY SKILL AND GUILE.
EN SABAH NUR HAD SAID TIME AND AGAIN THAT "THE MAN WHO SEES TOMORROW WILL LIVE THROUGH THE DAY."
AND THERE WE WERE...ALL OF US...ENTHRALLED FOR SO LONG TO A MAN OF VISION...
...WHO HAD JUST BEEN PROVEN BLIND!
AND WHAT OF US THEN, WHO HAD BEEN LED BY THE BLIND? THE DARK RIDERS, AT LEAST...
...SAW THE LIGHT.

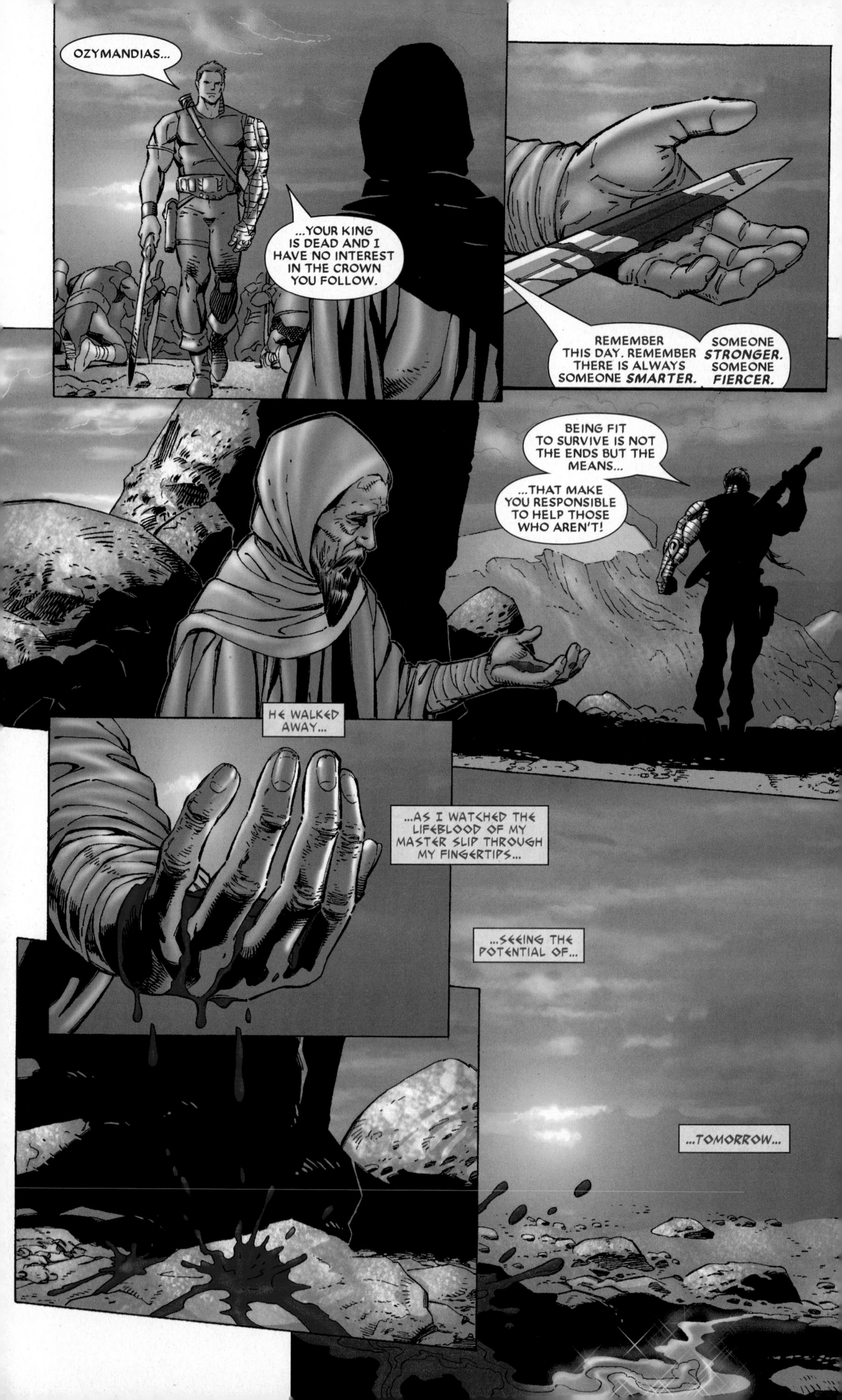

OZYMANDIAS...
...YOUR KING IS DEAD AND I HAVE NO INTEREST IN THE CROWN YOU FOLLOW.
REMEMBER THIS DAY. REMEMBER THERE IS ALWAYS SOMEONE SMARTER.
SOMEONE STRONGER. SOMEONE FIERCER.
BEING FIT TO SURVIVE IS NOT THE ENDS BUT THE MEANS...
...THAT MAKE YOU RESPONSIBLE TO HELP THOSE WHO AREN'T!
HE WALKED AWAY...
...AS I WATCHED THE LIFEBLOOD OF MY MASTER SLIP THROUGH MY FINGERTIPS...
...SEEING THE POTENTIAL OF...
...TOMORROW...

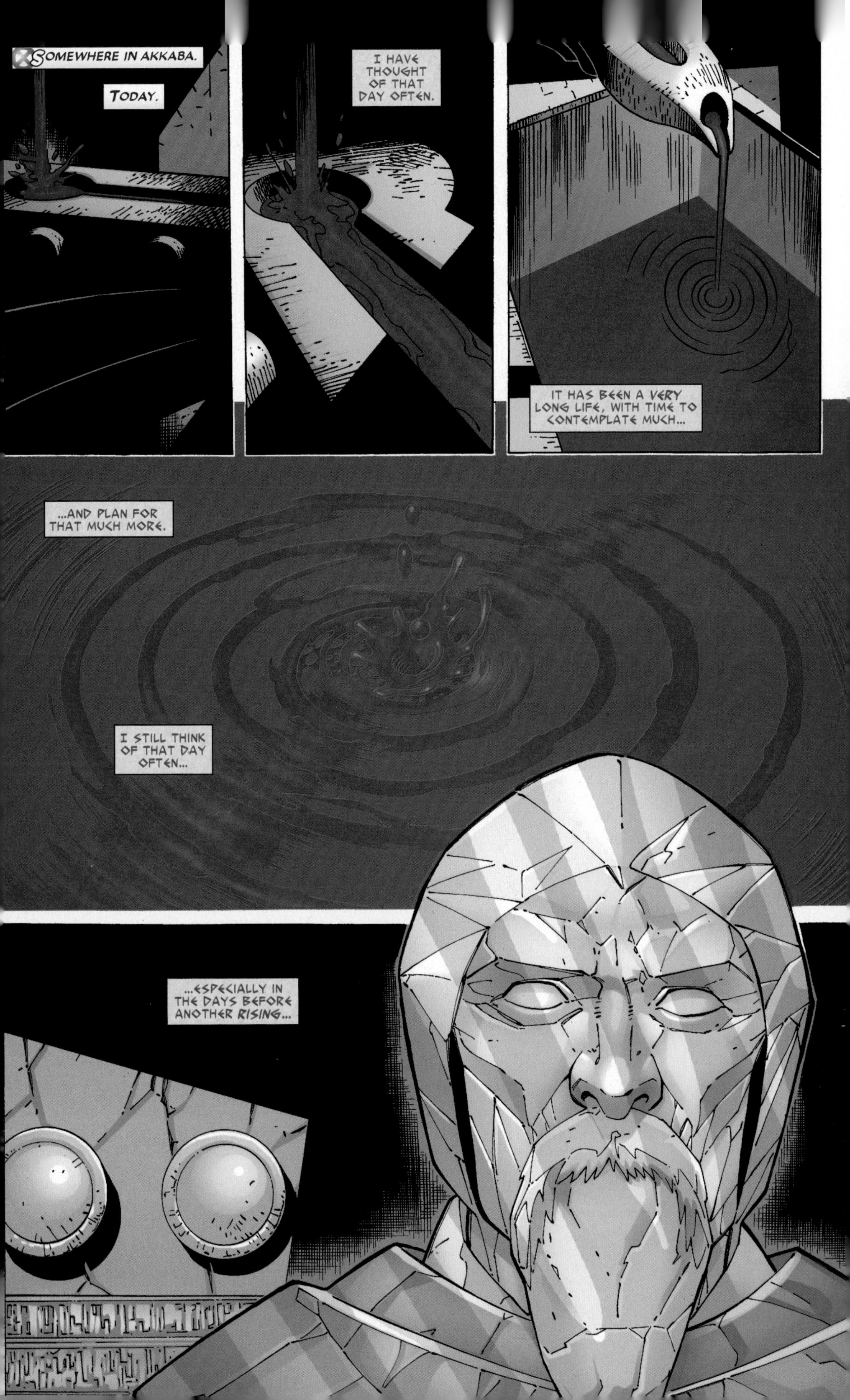
SOMEWHERE IN AKKABA.
TODAY.
I HAVE THOUGHT OF THAT DAY OFTEN.
IT HAS BEEN A VERY LONG LIFE, WITH TIME TO CONTEMPLATE MUCH...
...AND PLAN FOR THAT MUCH MORE.
I STILL THINK OF THAT DAY OFTEN...
...ESPECIALLY IN THE DAYS BEFORE ANOTHER RISING...

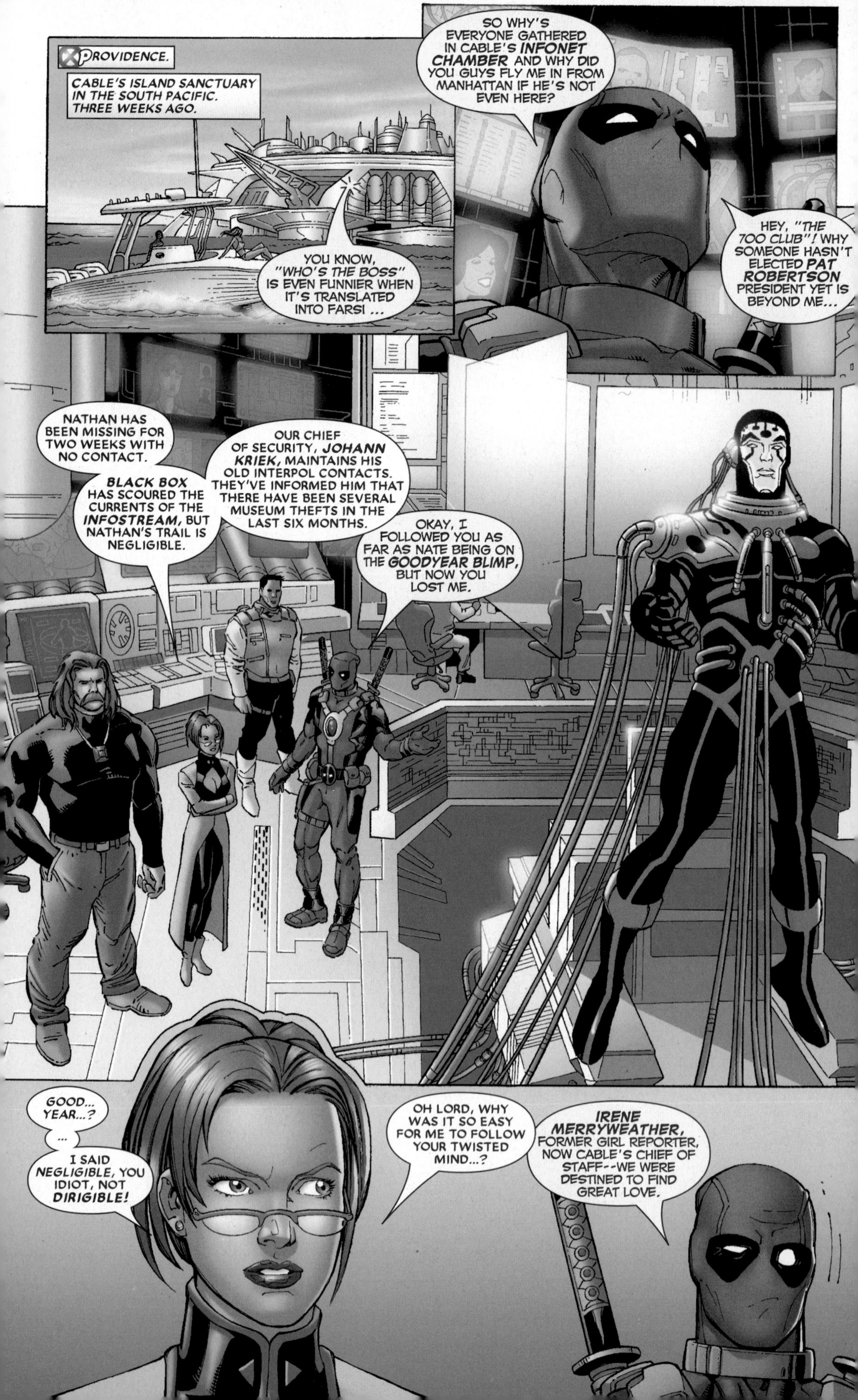
PROVIDENCE.
CABLE'S ISLAND SANCTUARY IN THE SOUTH PACIFIC. THREE WEEKS AGO.
YOU KNOW, "WHO'S THE BOSS" IS EVEN FUNNIER WHEN IT'S TRANSLATED INTO FARSI ...
SO WHY'S EVERYONE GATHERED IN CABLE'S INFONET CHAMBER AND WHY DID YOU GUYS FLY ME IN FROM MANHATTAN IF HE'S NOT EVEN HERE?
HEY, "THE 700 CLUB"! WHY SOMEONE HASN'T ELECTED PAT ROBERTSON PRESIDENT YET IS BEYOND ME...
NATHAN HAS BEEN MISSING FOR TWO WEEKS WITH NO CONTACT.
BLACK BOX HAS SCOURED THE CURRENTS OF THE INFOSTREAM, BUT NATHAN'S TRAIL IS NEGLIGIBLE.
OUR CHIEF OF SECURITY, JOHANN KRIEK, MAINTAINS HIS OLD INTERPOL CONTACTS. THEY'VE INFORMED HIM THAT THERE HAVE BEEN SEVERAL MUSEUM THEFTS IN THE LAST SIX MONTHS.
OKAY, I FOLLOWED YOU AS FAR AS NATE BEING ON THE GOODYEAR BLIMP, BUT NOW YOU LOST ME.
GOOD... YEAR...?
...
I SAID NEGLIGIBLE, YOU IDIOT, NOT DIRIGIBLE!
OH LORD, WHY WAS IT SO EASY FOR ME TO FOLLOW YOUR TWISTED MIND...?
IRENE MERRYWEATHER, FORMER GIRL REPORTER, NOW CABLE'S CHIEF OF STAFF--WE WERE DESTINED TO FIND GREAT LOVE.

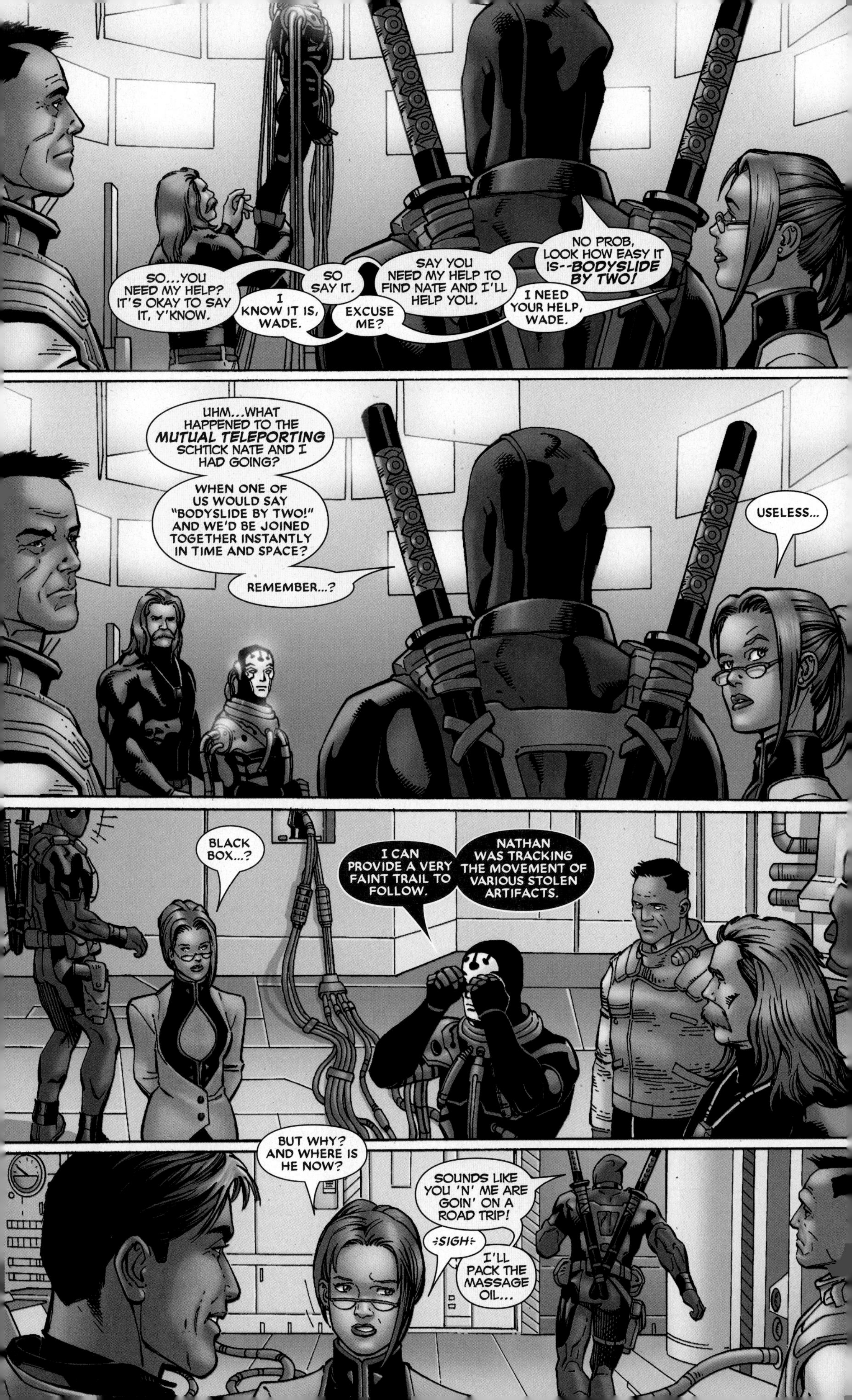
SO...YOU NEED MY HELP? IT'S OKAY TO SAY IT, Y'KNOW.
I KNOW IT IS, WADE.
SO SAY IT.
EXCUSE ME?
SAY YOU NEED MY HELP TO FIND NATE AND I'LL HELP YOU.
I NEED YOUR HELP, WADE.
NO PROB, LOOK HOW EASY IT IS--*BODYSLIDE BY TWO!*
UHM...WHAT HAPPENED TO THE *MUTUAL TELEPORTING* SCHTICK NATE AND I HAD GOING?
WHEN ONE OF US WOULD SAY "BODYSLIDE BY TWO!" AND WE'D BE JOINED TOGETHER INSTANTLY IN TIME AND SPACE?
REMEMBER...?
USELESS...
BLACK BOX...?
I CAN PROVIDE A VERY FAINT TRAIL TO FOLLOW.
NATHAN WAS TRACKING THE MOVEMENT OF VARIOUS STOLEN ARTIFACTS.
BUT WHY? AND WHERE IS HE NOW?
SOUNDS LIKE YOU 'N' ME ARE GOIN' ON A ROAD TRIP!
SIGH
I'LL PACK THE MASSAGE OIL...

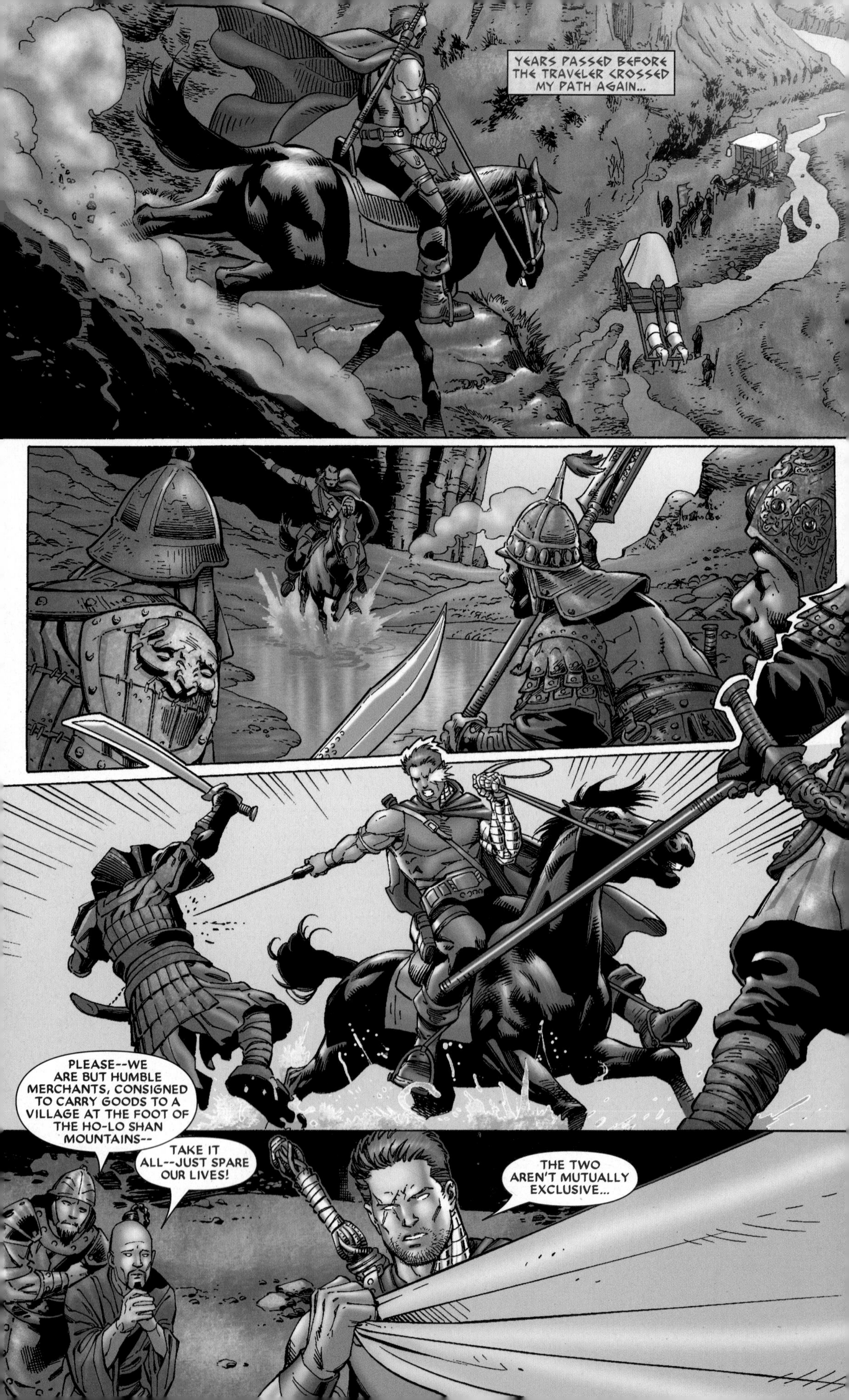
YEARS PASSED BEFORE THE TRAVELER CROSSED MY PATH AGAIN...
PLEASE--WE ARE BUT HUMBLE MERCHANTS, CONSIGNED TO CARRY GOODS TO A VILLAGE AT THE FOOT OF THE HO-LO SHAN MOUNTAINS--
TAKE IT ALL--JUST SPARE OUR LIVES!
THE TWO AREN'T MUTUALLY EXCLUSIVE...

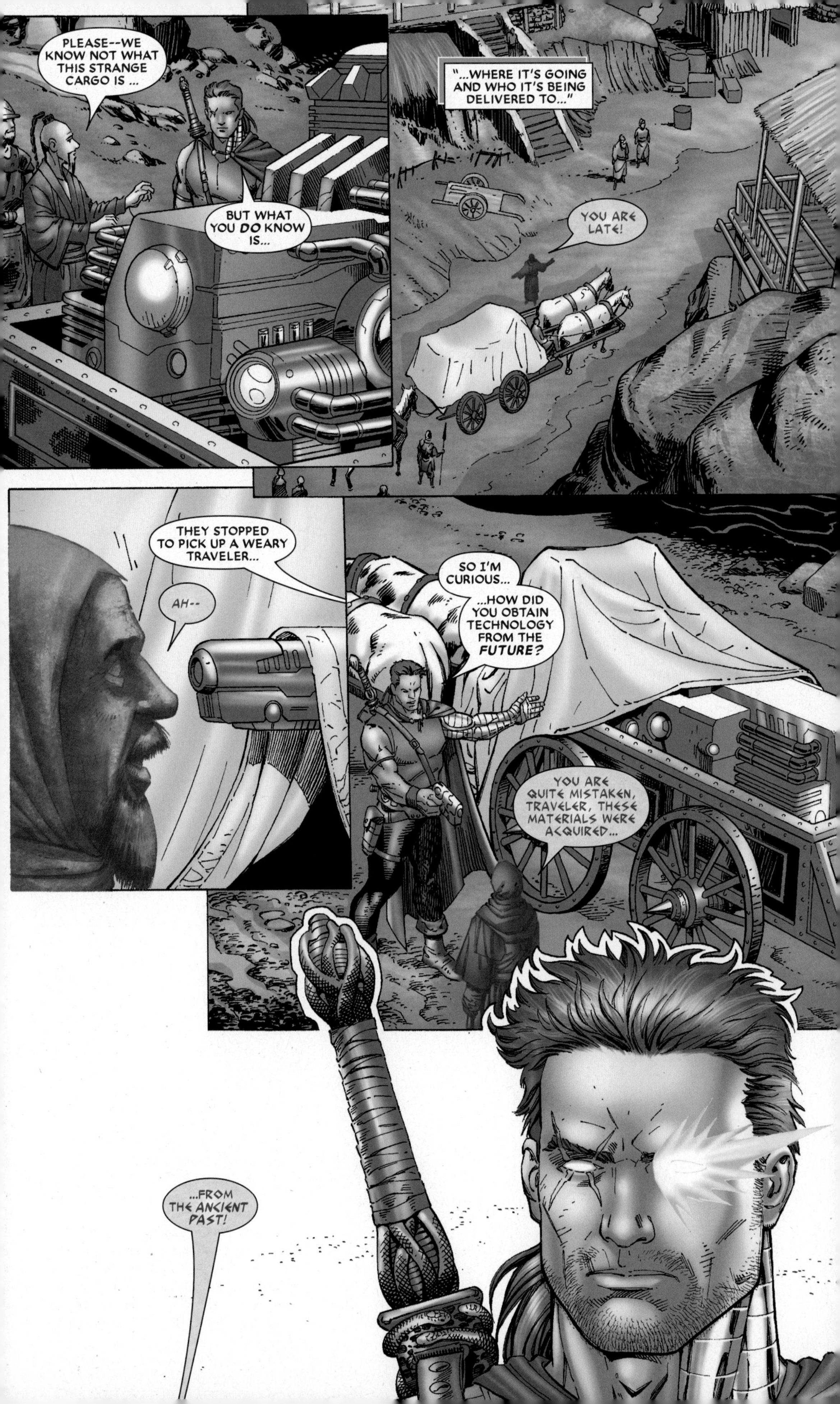
PLEASE--WE KNOW NOT WHAT THIS STRANGE CARGO IS ...
BUT WHAT YOU DO KNOW IS...
"...WHERE IT'S GOING AND WHO IT'S BEING DELIVERED TO..."
YOU ARE LATE!
THEY STOPPED TO PICK UP A WEARY TRAVELER...
AH--
SO I'M CURIOUS...
...HOW DID YOU OBTAIN TECHNOLOGY FROM THE FUTURE?
YOU ARE QUITE MISTAKEN, TRAVELER, THESE MATERIALS WERE ACQUIRED...
...FROM THE ANCIENT PAST!

HERE?

HERE. RIGHT...?

WE TRACKED A BLACK MARKETER SUSPECTED IN A MUSEUM THEFT THROUGH A RENTED TRUCK. THAT TRUCK'S ODOMETER READING ON CHECK-IN--

--TRIANGULATES TO A DIAMETER THAT--

JUST SHUT UP AND SAY "YES."

THIS MAKES NO SENSE. IF CABLE IS TEN STEPS AHEAD OF US, THEN WHY ISN'T HE HERE?

OR WHY IS THIS PLACE STILL STANDING?

I DON'T KNOW. ONLY ONE WAY TO FIND OUT.

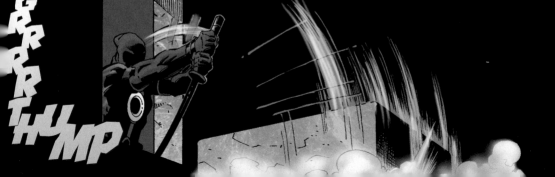

GRRRTHUMP

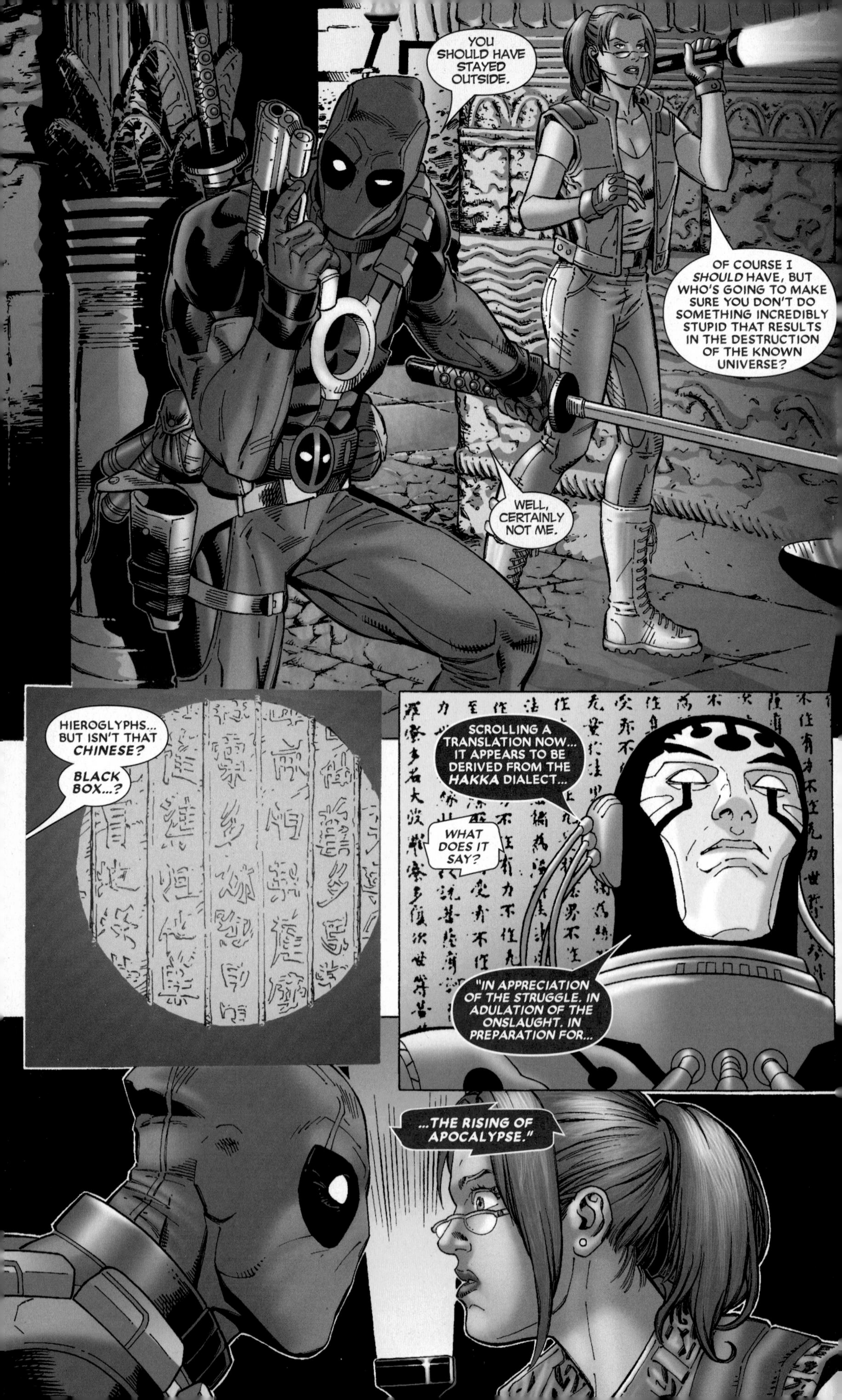

YOU SHOULD HAVE STAYED OUTSIDE.
OF COURSE I *SHOULD* HAVE, BUT WHO'S GOING TO MAKE SURE YOU DON'T DO SOMETHING INCREDIBLY STUPID THAT RESULTS IN THE DESTRUCTION OF THE KNOWN UNIVERSE?
WELL, CERTAINLY NOT ME.
HIEROGLYPHS... BUT ISN'T THAT *CHINESE?*
BLACK BOX...?
SCROLLING A TRANSLATION NOW... IT APPEARS TO BE DERIVED FROM THE *HAKKA* DIALECT...
WHAT DOES IT SAY?
"IN APPRECIATION OF THE STRUGGLE. IN ADULATION OF THE ONSLAUGHT. IN PREPARATION FOR...
...THE RISING OF APOCALYPSE."

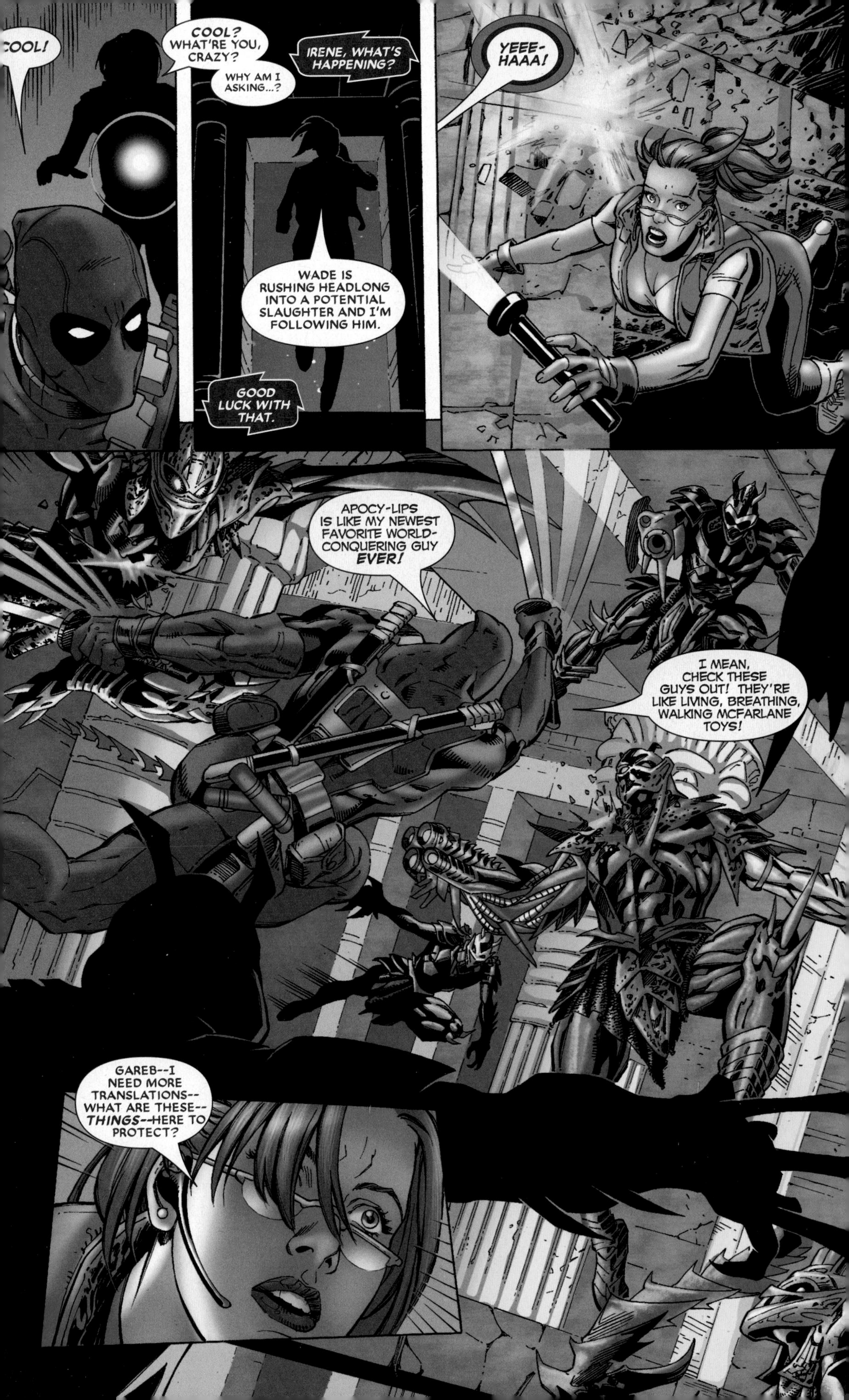
COOL!
COOL? WHAT'RE YOU, CRAZY?
WHY AM I ASKING...?
IRENE, WHAT'S HAPPENING?
WADE IS RUSHING HEADLONG INTO A POTENTIAL SLAUGHTER AND I'M FOLLOWING HIM.
GOOD LUCK WITH THAT.
YEEE-HAAA!
APOCY-LIPS IS LIKE MY NEWEST FAVORITE WORLD-CONQUERING GUY EVER!
I MEAN, CHECK THESE GUYS OUT! THEY'RE LIKE LIVING, BREATHING, WALKING MCFARLANE TOYS!
GAREB--I NEED MORE TRANSLATIONS--WHAT ARE THESE--THINGS--HERE TO PROTECT?

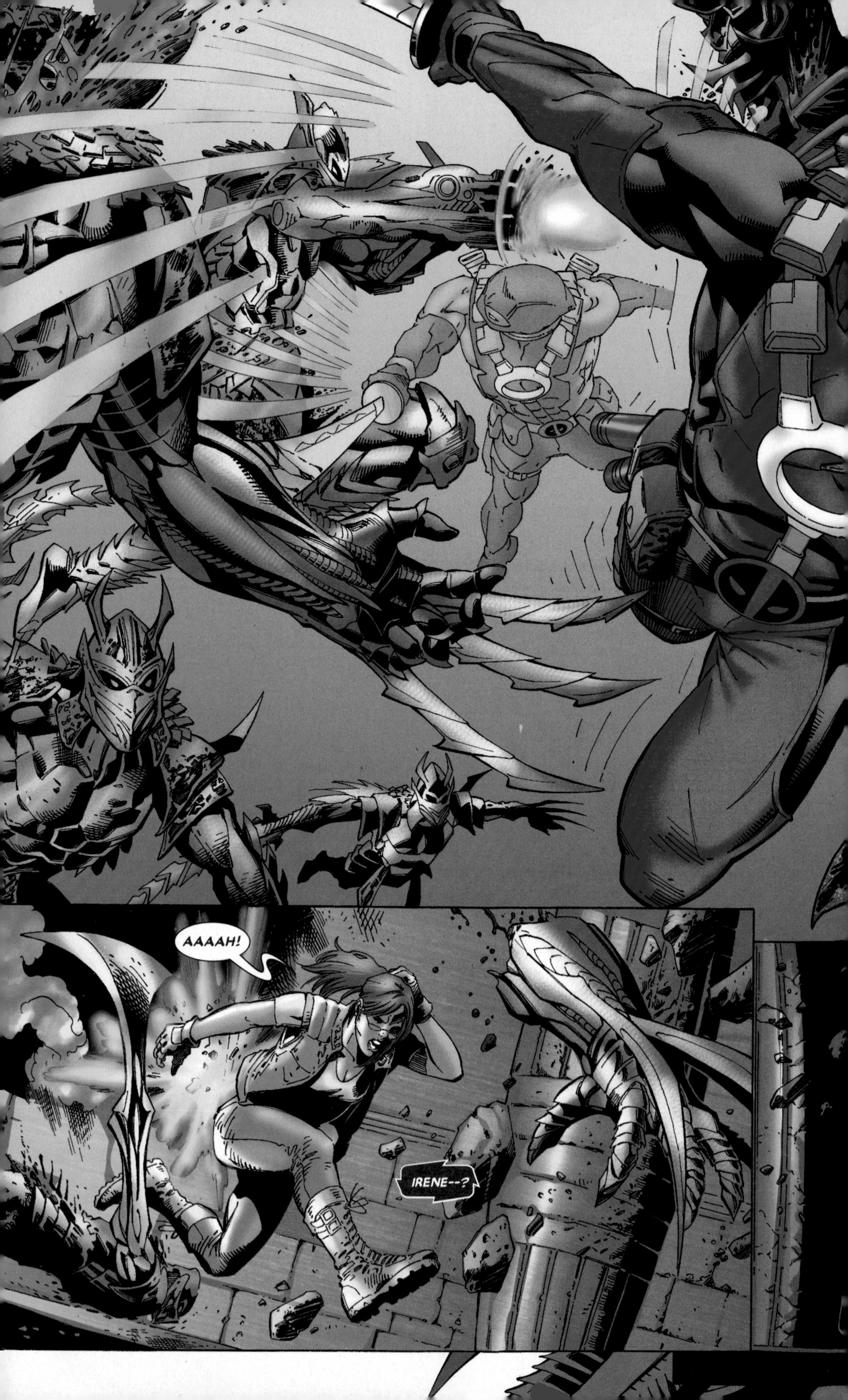
AAAAH!
IRENE--?

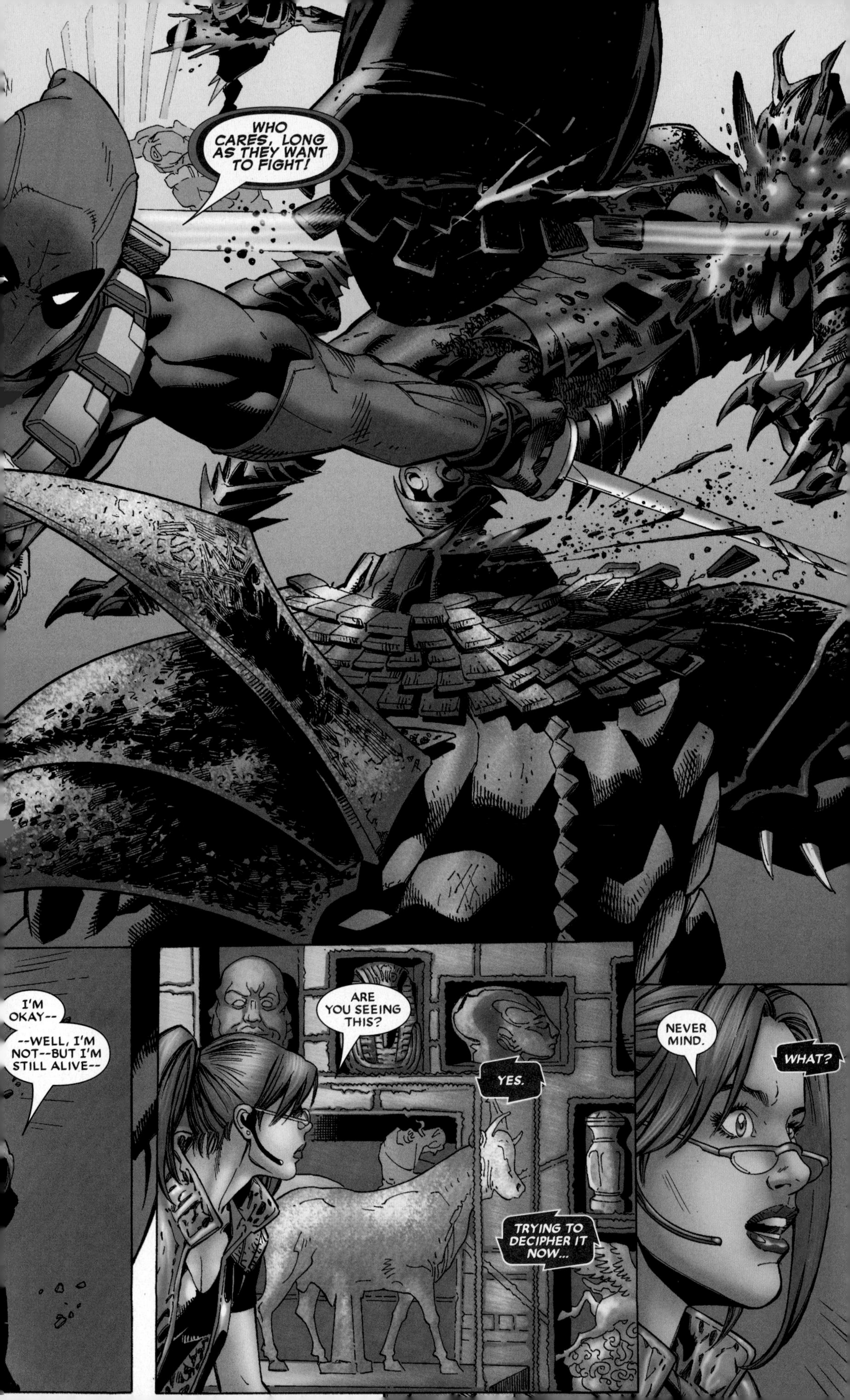
WHO CARES, LONG AS THEY WANT TO FIGHT!
I'M OKAY--
--WELL, I'M NOT--BUT I'M STILL ALIVE--
ARE YOU SEEING THIS?
YES.
TRYING TO DECIPHER IT NOW...
NEVER MIND.
WHAT?

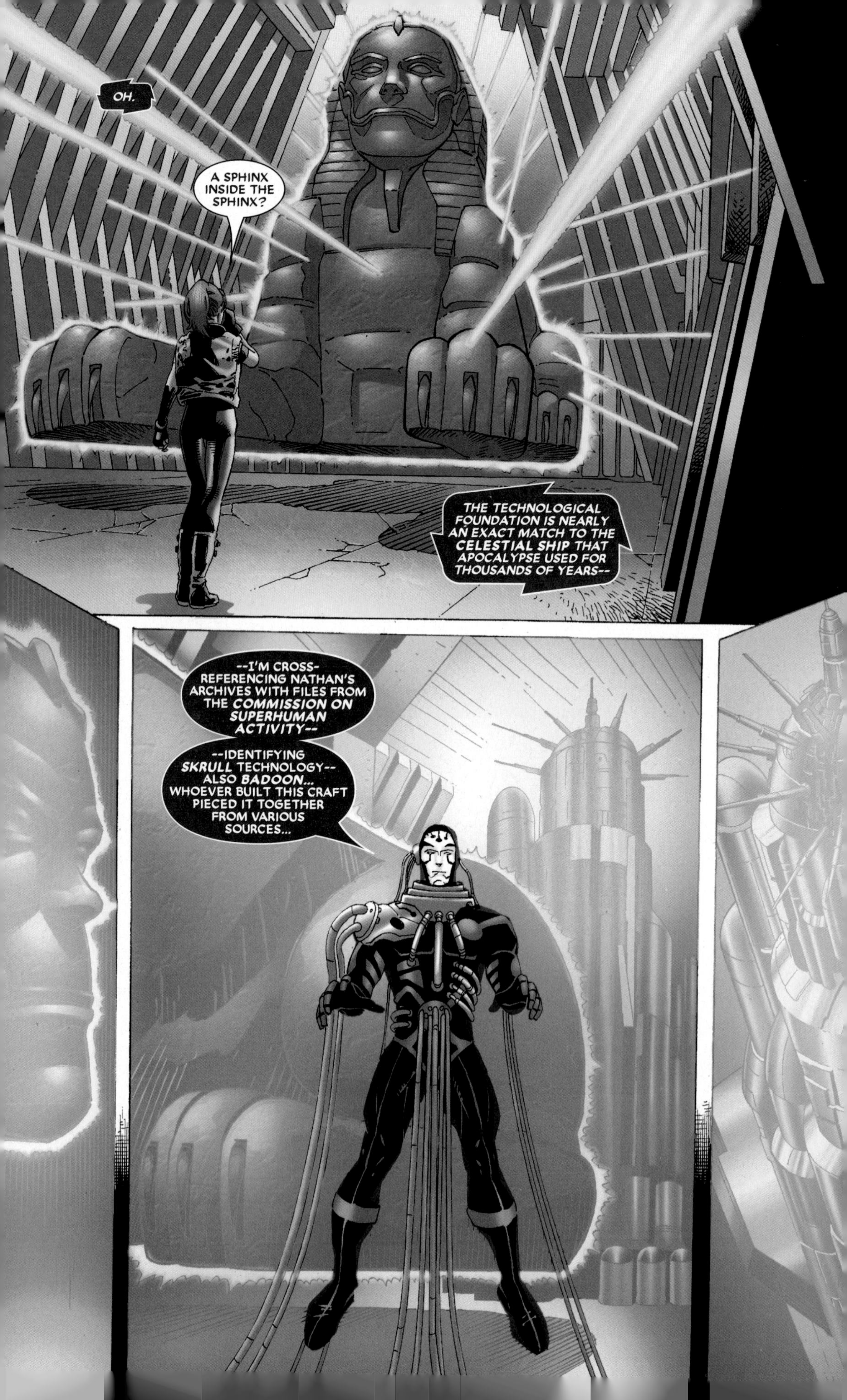
OH.
A SPHINX INSIDE THE SPHINX?
THE TECHNOLOGICAL FOUNDATION IS NEARLY AN EXACT MATCH TO THE CELESTIAL SHIP THAT APOCALYPSE USED FOR THOUSANDS OF YEARS--
--I'M CROSS-REFERENCING NATHAN'S ARCHIVES WITH FILES FROM THE COMMISSION ON SUPERHUMAN ACTIVITY--
--IDENTIFYING SKRULL TECHNOLOGY--ALSO BADOON... WHOEVER BUILT THIS CRAFT PIECED IT TOGETHER FROM VARIOUS SOURCES...

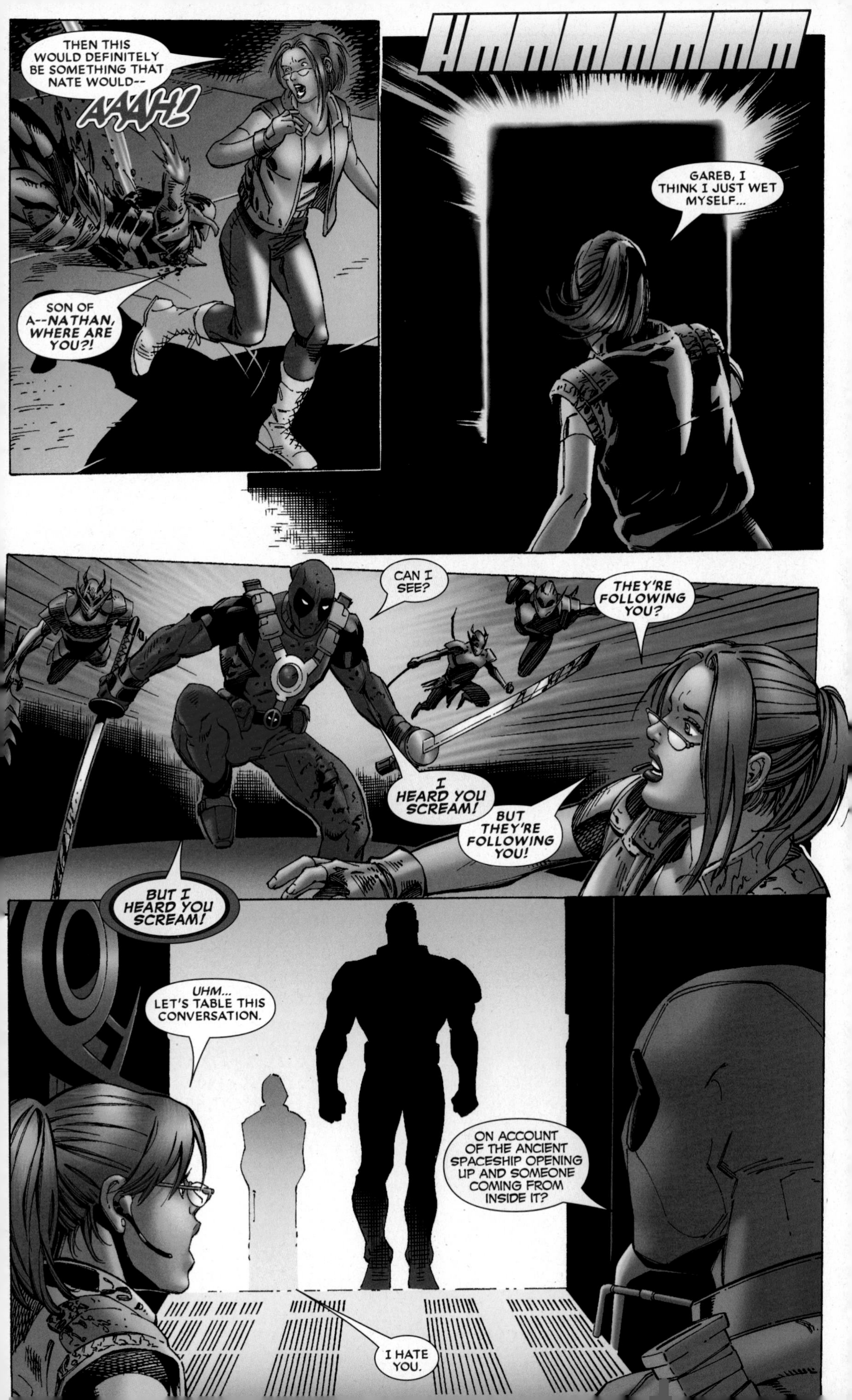

THEN THIS WOULD DEFINITELY BE SOMETHING THAT NATE WOULD--
AAAH!
SON OF A--NATHAN, WHERE ARE YOU?!
GAREB, I THINK I JUST WET MYSELF...
CAN I SEE?
THEY'RE FOLLOWING YOU?
I HEARD YOU SCREAM!
BUT THEY'RE FOLLOWING YOU!
BUT I HEARD YOU SCREAM!
UHM... LET'S TABLE THIS CONVERSATION.
ON ACCOUNT OF THE ANCIENT SPACESHIP OPENING UP AND SOMEONE COMING FROM INSIDE IT?
I HATE YOU.

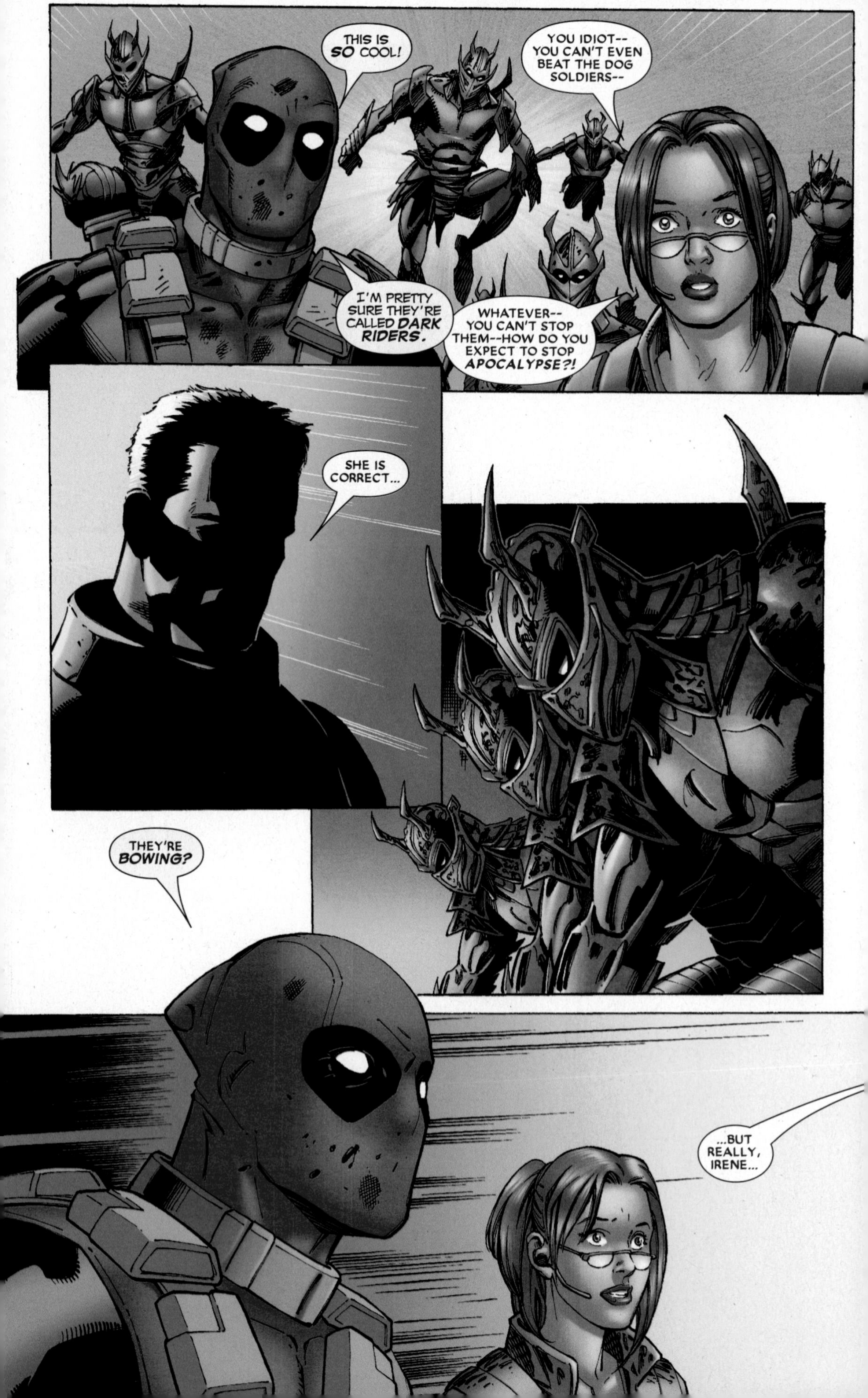

THIS IS SO COOL!
YOU IDIOT-- YOU CAN'T EVEN BEAT THE DOG SOLDIERS--
I'M PRETTY SURE THEY'RE CALLED DARK RIDERS.
WHATEVER-- YOU CAN'T STOP THEM--HOW DO YOU EXPECT TO STOP APOCALYPSE?!
SHE IS CORRECT...
THEY'RE BOWING?
...BUT REALLY, IRENE...

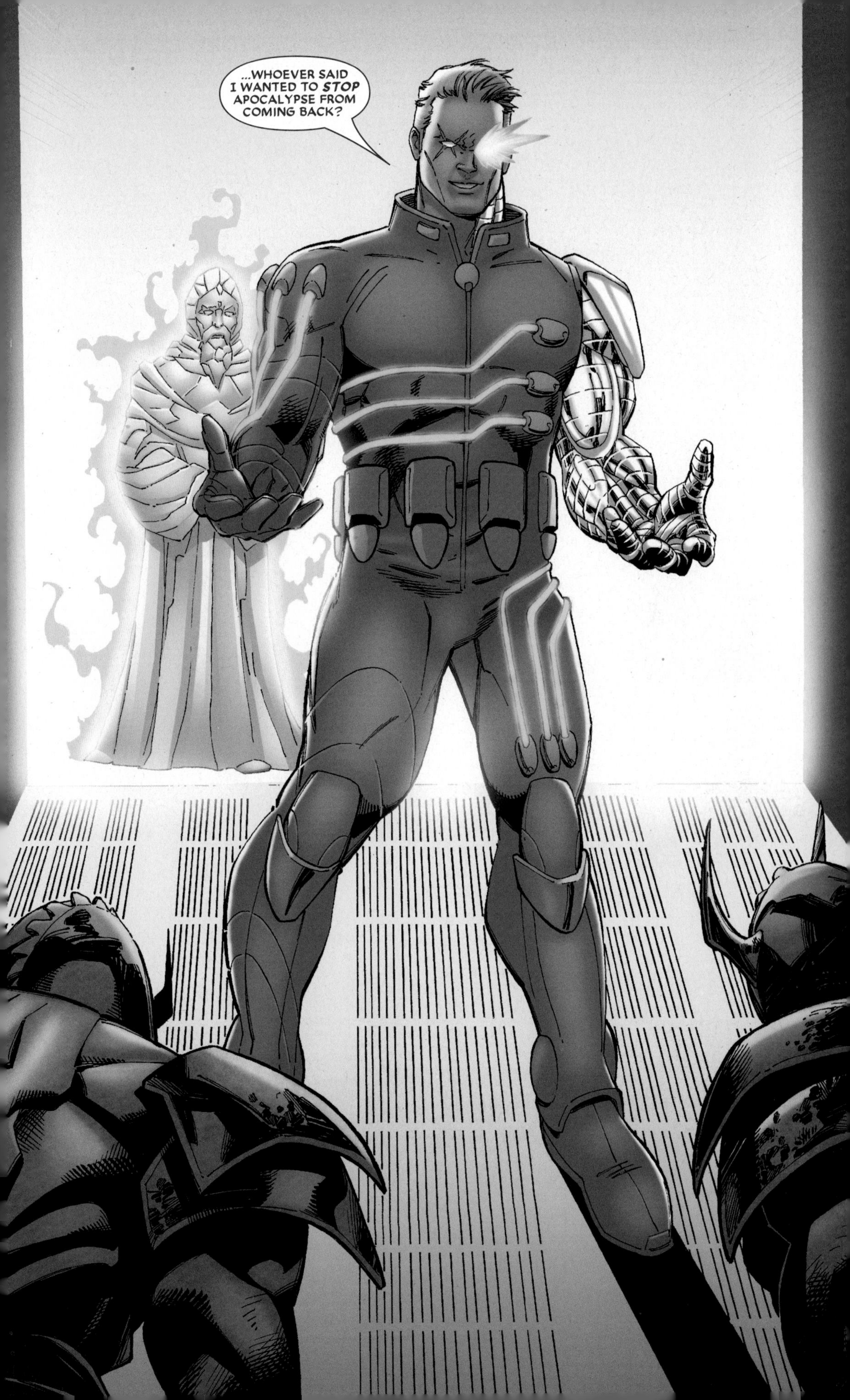
...WHOEVER SAID I WANTED TO STOP APOCALYPSE FROM COMING BACK?

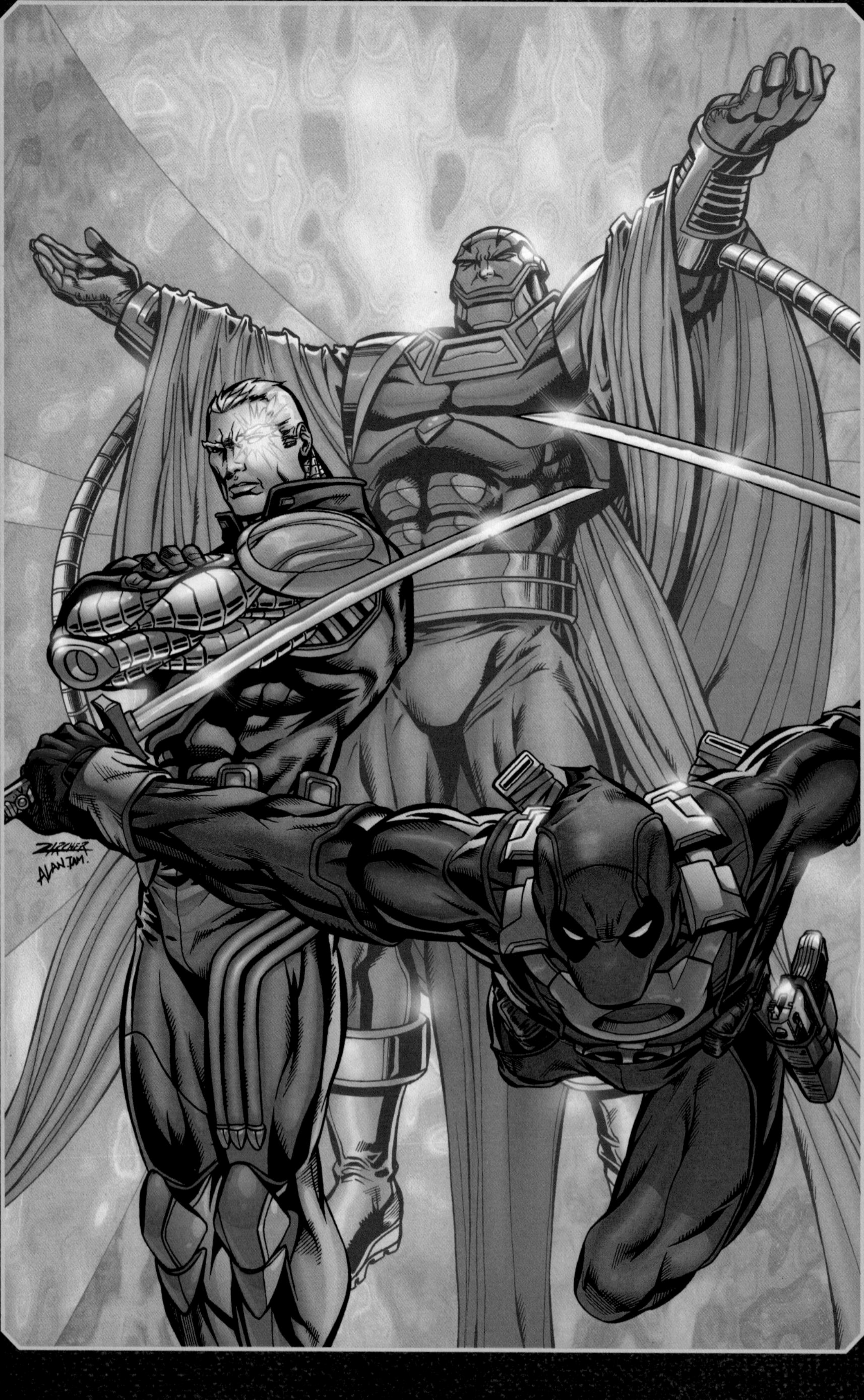
ZIRCHER
ALAN.JAM.

CABLE & DEADPOOL #27

BORN AGAIN PART TWO WITH EYES OPEN

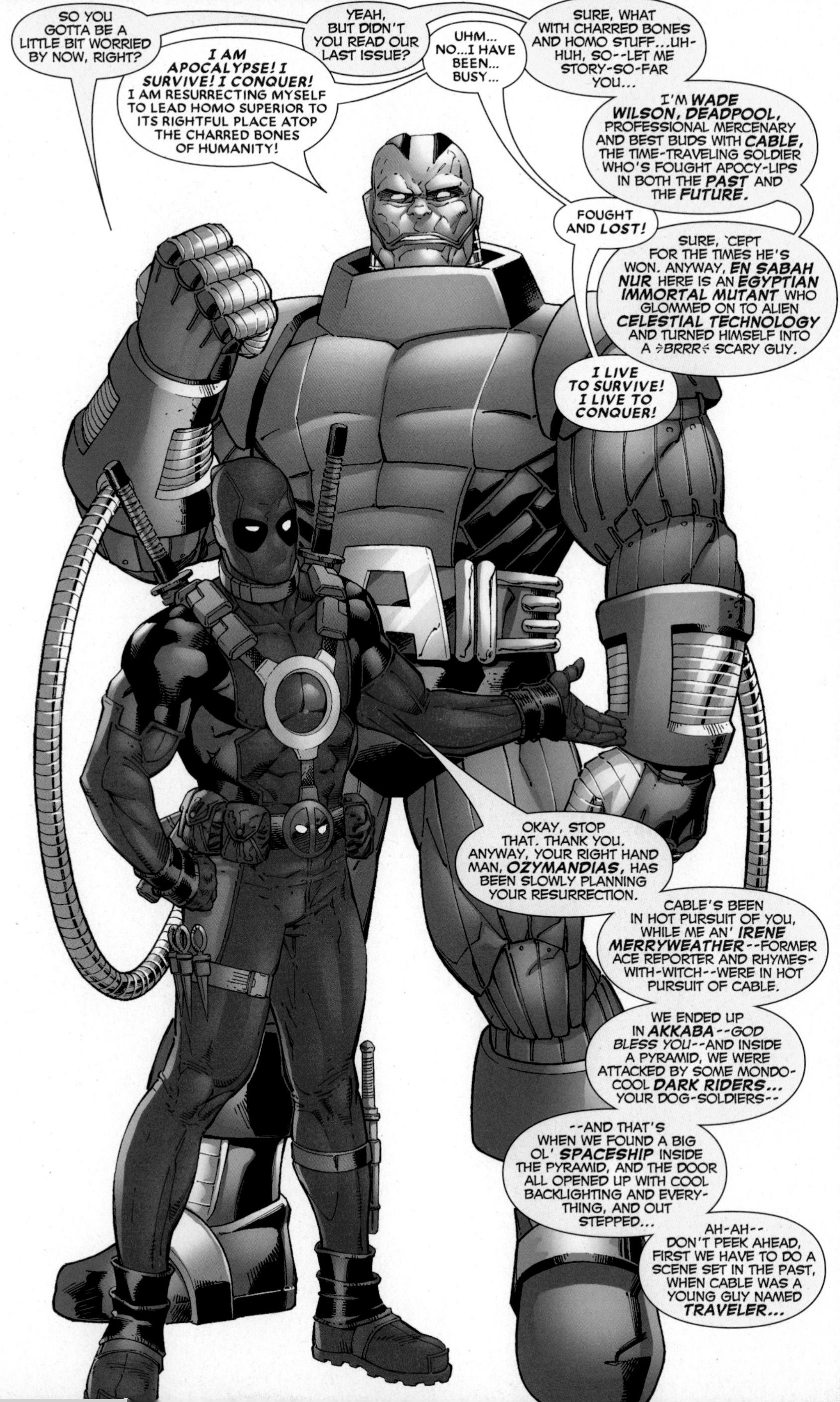

SO YOU GOTTA BE A LITTLE BIT WORRIED BY NOW, RIGHT?
I AM APOCALYPSE! I SURVIVE! I CONQUER! I AM RESURRECTING MYSELF TO LEAD HOMO SUPERIOR TO ITS RIGHTFUL PLACE ATOP THE CHARRED BONES OF HUMANITY!
YEAH, BUT DIDN'T YOU READ OUR LAST ISSUE?
UHM... NO...I HAVE BEEN... BUSY...
SURE, WHAT WITH CHARRED BONES AND HOMO STUFF...UH-HUH, SO--LET ME STORY-SO-FAR YOU...
I'M WADE WILSON, DEADPOOL, PROFESSIONAL MERCENARY AND BEST BUDS WITH CABLE, THE TIME-TRAVELING SOLDIER WHO'S FOUGHT APOCY-LIPS IN BOTH THE PAST AND THE FUTURE.
FOUGHT AND LOST!
SURE, 'CEPT FOR THE TIMES HE'S WON. ANYWAY, EN SABAH NUR HERE IS AN EGYPTIAN IMMORTAL MUTANT WHO GLOMMED ON TO ALIEN CELESTIAL TECHNOLOGY AND TURNED HIMSELF INTO A BRRR SCARY GUY.
I LIVE TO SURVIVE! I LIVE TO CONQUER!
OKAY, STOP THAT. THANK YOU. ANYWAY, YOUR RIGHT HAND MAN, OZYMANDIAS, HAS BEEN SLOWLY PLANNING YOUR RESURRECTION.
CABLE'S BEEN IN HOT PURSUIT OF YOU, WHILE ME AN' IRENE MERRYWEATHER--FORMER ACE REPORTER AND RHYMES-WITH-WITCH--WERE IN HOT PURSUIT OF CABLE.
WE ENDED UP IN AKKABA--GOD BLESS YOU--AND INSIDE A PYRAMID, WE WERE ATTACKED BY SOME MONDO-COOL DARK RIDERS... YOUR DOG-SOLDIERS--
--AND THAT'S WHEN WE FOUND A BIG OL' SPACESHIP INSIDE THE PYRAMID, AND THE DOOR ALL OPENED UP WITH COOL BACKLIGHTING AND EVERYTHING, AND OUT STEPPED...
AH-AH-- DON'T PEEK AHEAD, FIRST WE HAVE TO DO A SCENE SET IN THE PAST, WHEN CABLE WAS A YOUNG GUY NAMED TRAVELER...

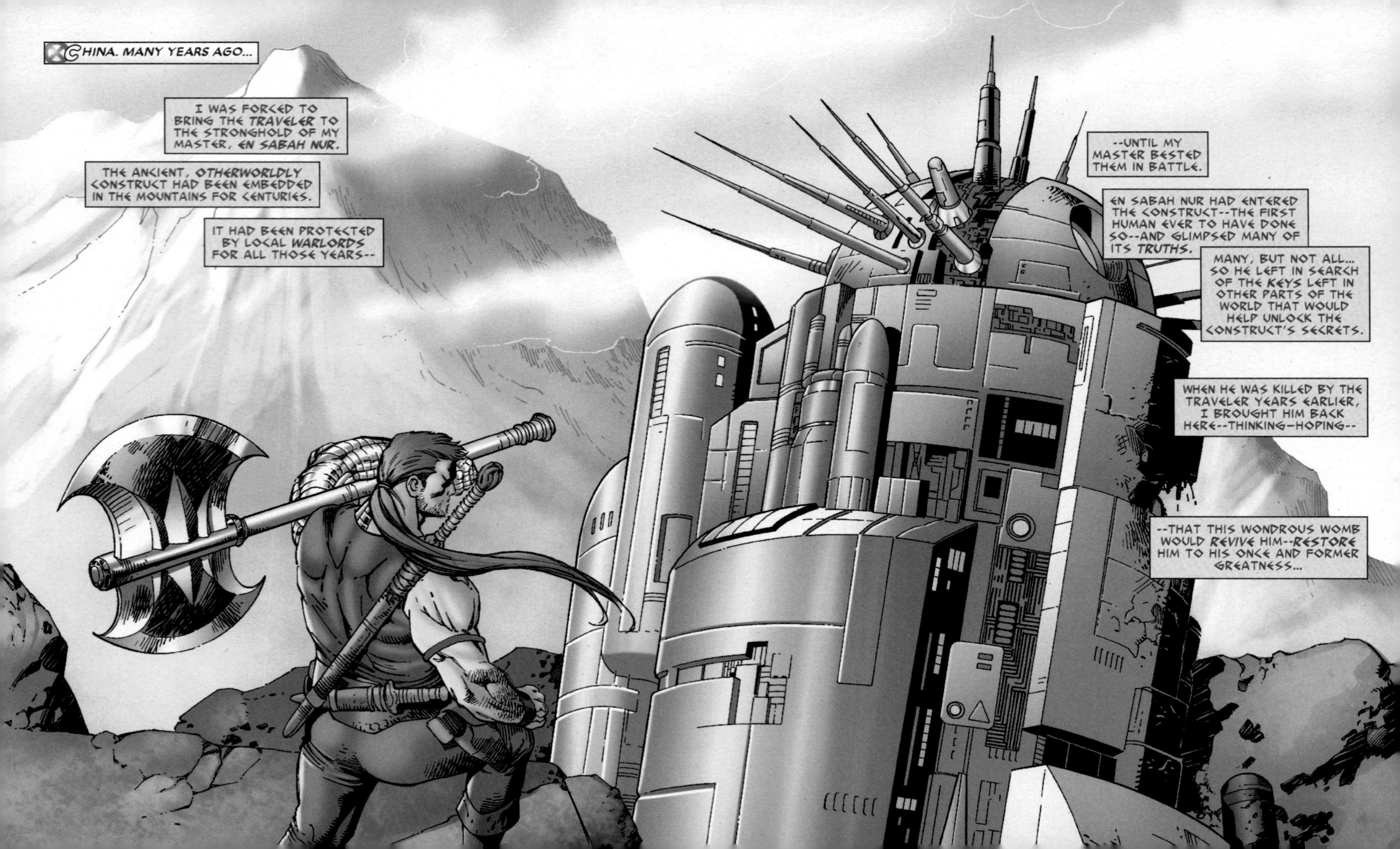
CHINA. MANY YEARS AGO...
I WAS FORCED TO BRING THE TRAVELER TO THE STRONGHOLD OF MY MASTER, EN SABAH NUR.
THE ANCIENT, OTHERWORLDLY CONSTRUCT HAD BEEN EMBEDDED IN THE MOUNTAINS FOR CENTURIES.
IT HAD BEEN PROTECTED BY LOCAL WARLORDS FOR ALL THOSE YEARS--
--UNTIL MY MASTER BESTED THEM IN BATTLE.
EN SABAH NUR HAD ENTERED THE CONSTRUCT--THE FIRST HUMAN EVER TO HAVE DONE SO--AND GLIMPSED MANY OF ITS TRUTHS.
MANY, BUT NOT ALL... SO HE LEFT IN SEARCH OF THE KEYS LEFT IN OTHER PARTS OF THE WORLD THAT WOULD HELP UNLOCK THE CONSTRUCT'S SECRETS.
WHEN HE WAS KILLED BY THE TRAVELER YEARS EARLIER, I BROUGHT HIM BACK HERE--THINKING--HOPING--
--THAT THIS WONDROUS WOMB WOULD REVIVE HIM--RESTORE HIM TO HIS ONCE AND FORMER GREATNESS...

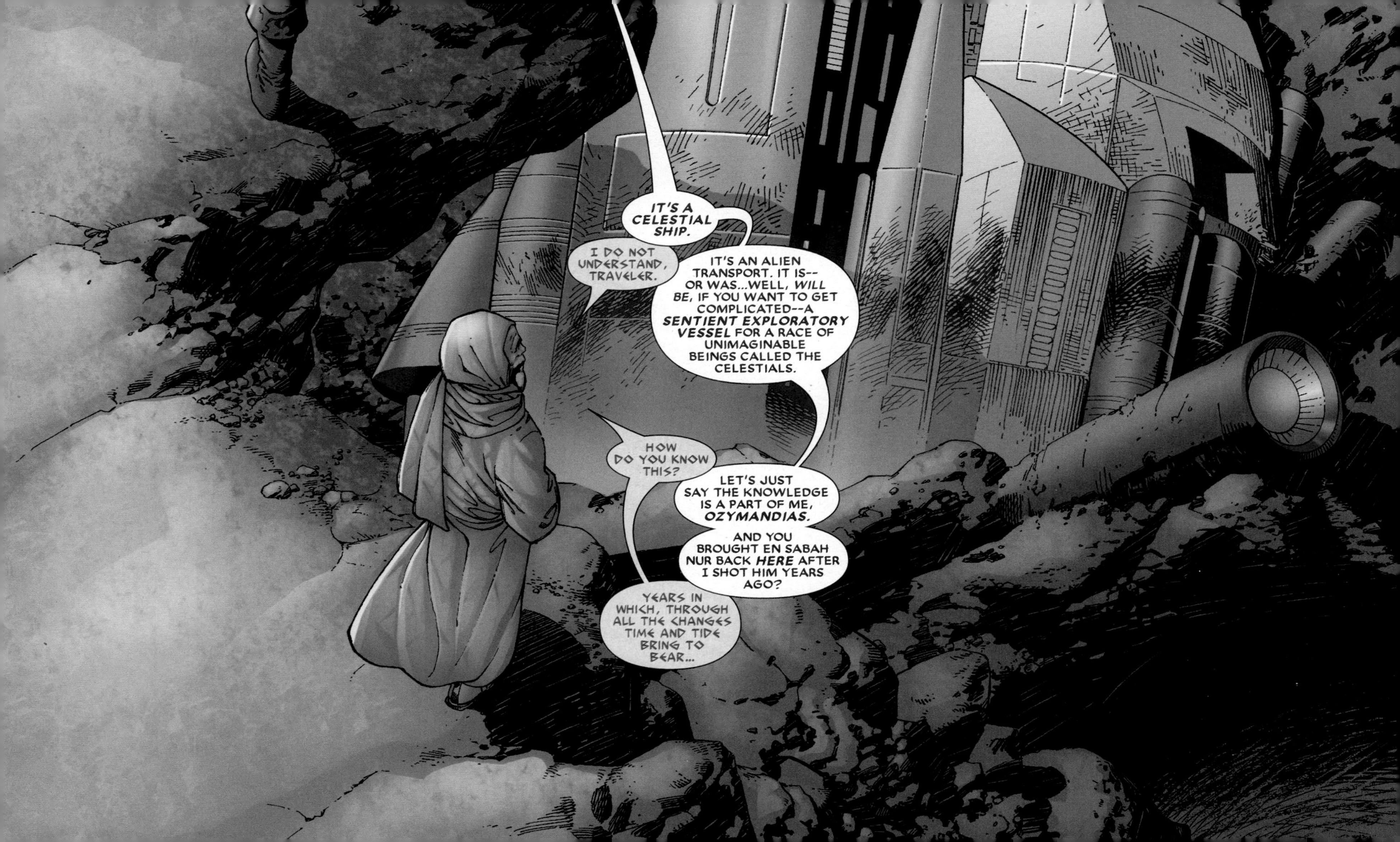
IT'S A CELESTIAL SHIP.
I DO NOT UNDERSTAND, TRAVELER.
IT'S AN ALIEN TRANSPORT. IT IS-- OR WAS...WELL, WILL BE, IF YOU WANT TO GET COMPLICATED--A SENTIENT EXPLORATORY VESSEL FOR A RACE OF UNIMAGINABLE BEINGS CALLED THE CELESTIALS.
HOW DO YOU KNOW THIS?
LET'S JUST SAY THE KNOWLEDGE IS A PART OF ME, OZYMANDIAS.
AND YOU BROUGHT EN SABAH NUR BACK HERE AFTER I SHOT HIM YEARS AGO?
YEARS IN WHICH, THROUGH ALL THE CHANGES TIME AND TIDE BRING TO BEAR...

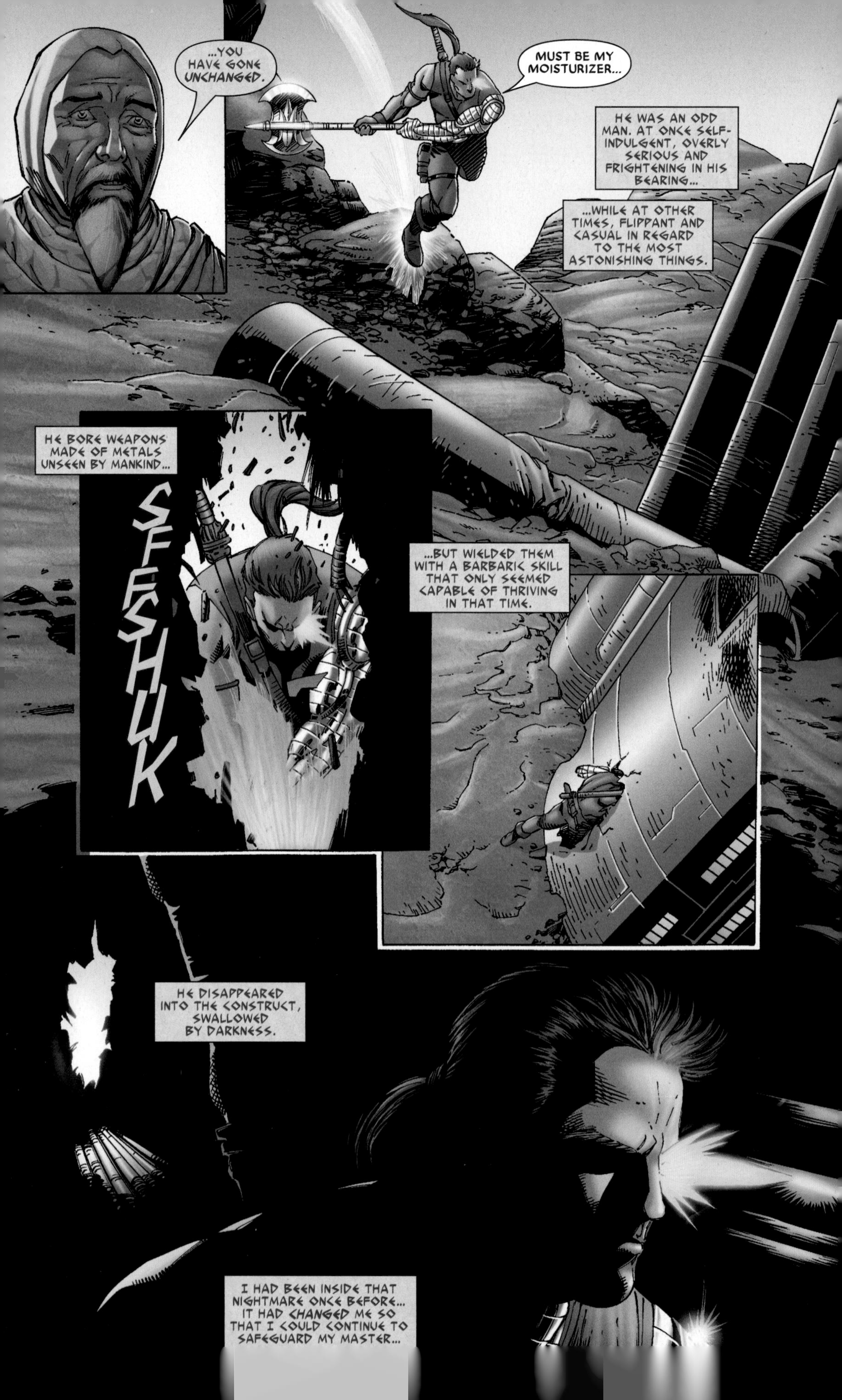
...YOU HAVE GONE UNCHANGED.
MUST BE MY MOISTURIZER...
HE WAS AN ODD MAN. AT ONCE SELF-INDULGENT, OVERLY SERIOUS AND FRIGHTENING IN HIS BEARING...
...WHILE AT OTHER TIMES, FLIPPANT AND CASUAL IN REGARD TO THE MOST ASTONISHING THINGS.
HE BORE WEAPONS MADE OF METALS UNSEEN BY MANKIND...
SFSHUK
...BUT WIELDED THEM WITH A BARBARIC SKILL THAT ONLY SEEMED CAPABLE OF THRIVING IN THAT TIME.
HE DISAPPEARED INTO THE CONSTRUCT, SWALLOWED BY DARKNESS.
I HAD BEEN INSIDE THAT NIGHTMARE ONCE BEFORE... IT HAD CHANGED ME SO THAT I COULD CONTINUE TO SAFEGUARD MY MASTER...

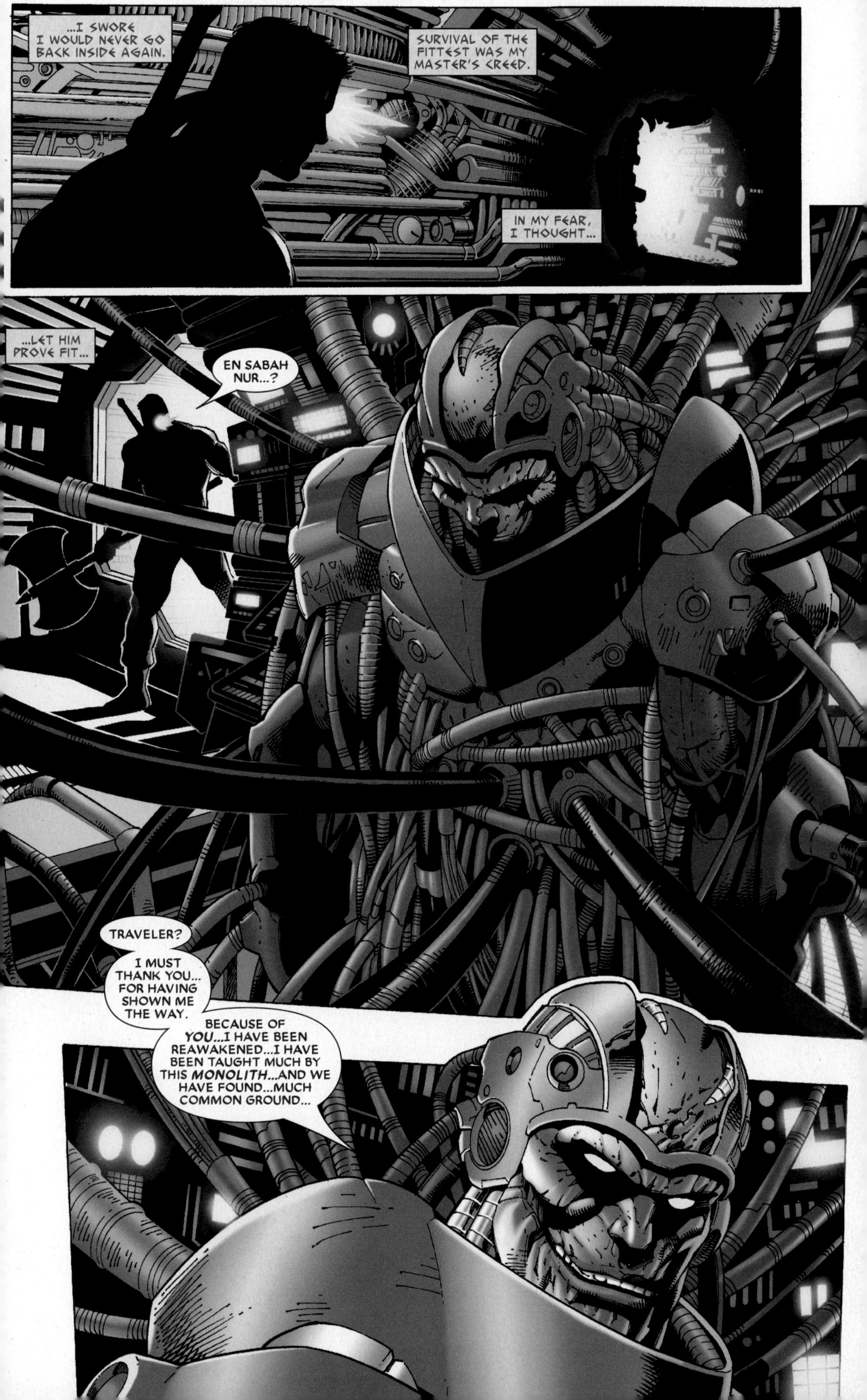
...I SWORE I WOULD NEVER GO BACK INSIDE AGAIN.
SURVIVAL OF THE FITTEST WAS MY MASTER'S CREED.
IN MY FEAR, I THOUGHT...
...LET HIM PROVE FIT...
EN SABAH NUR...?
TRAVELER?
I MUST THANK YOU... FOR HAVING SHOWN ME THE WAY.
BECAUSE OF YOU...I HAVE BEEN REAWAKENED...I HAVE BEEN TAUGHT MUCH BY THIS MONOLITH...AND WE HAVE FOUND...MUCH COMMON GROUND...

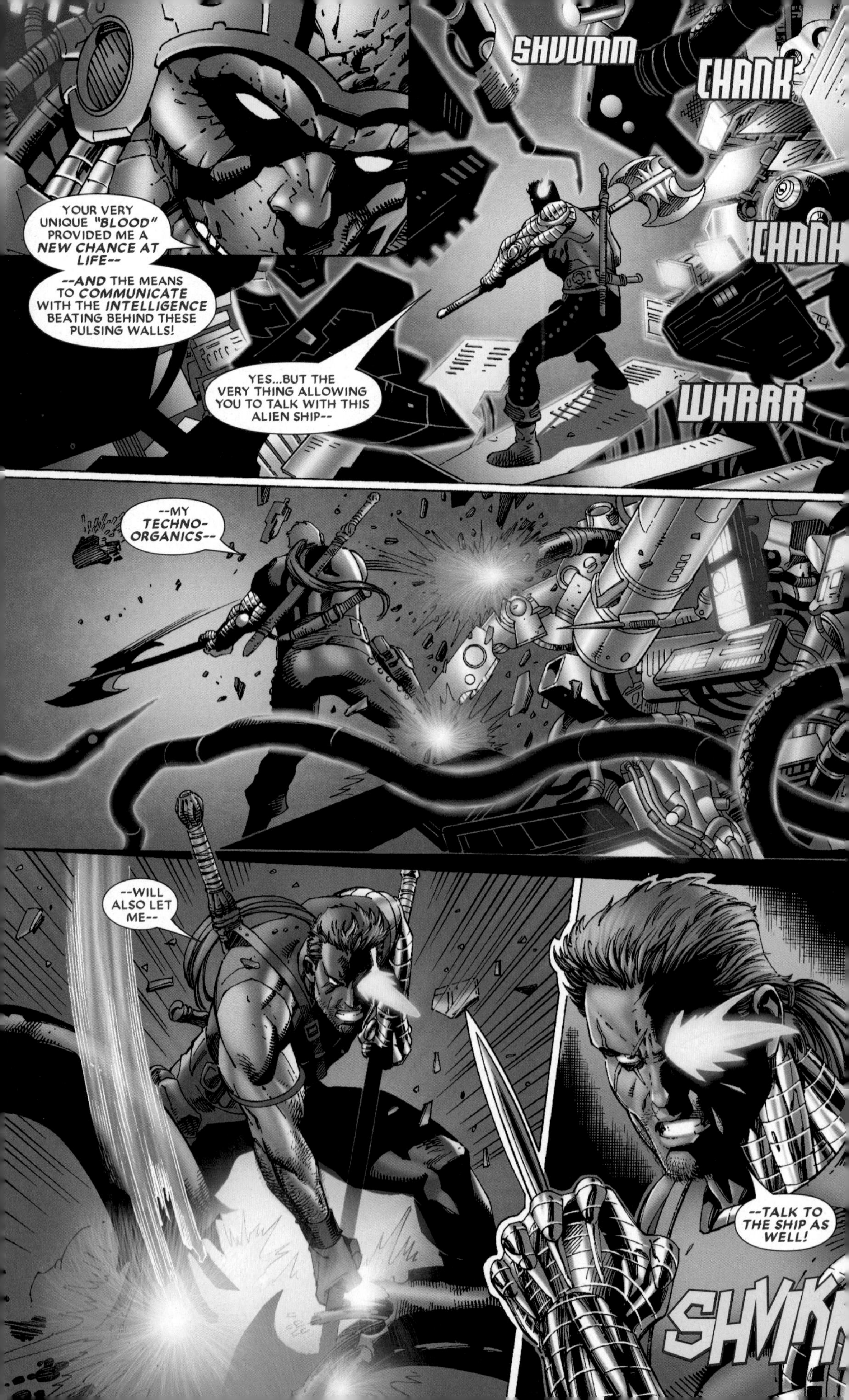
SHVUMM
CHANK
YOUR VERY UNIQUE "BLOOD" PROVIDED ME A NEW CHANCE AT LIFE--
CHANK
--AND THE MEANS TO COMMUNICATE WITH THE INTELLIGENCE BEATING BEHIND THESE PULSING WALLS!
YES...BUT THE VERY THING ALLOWING YOU TO TALK WITH THIS ALIEN SHIP--
WHRRR
--MY TECHNO-ORGANICS--
--WILL ALSO LET ME--
--TALK TO THE SHIP AS WELL!
SHVKK

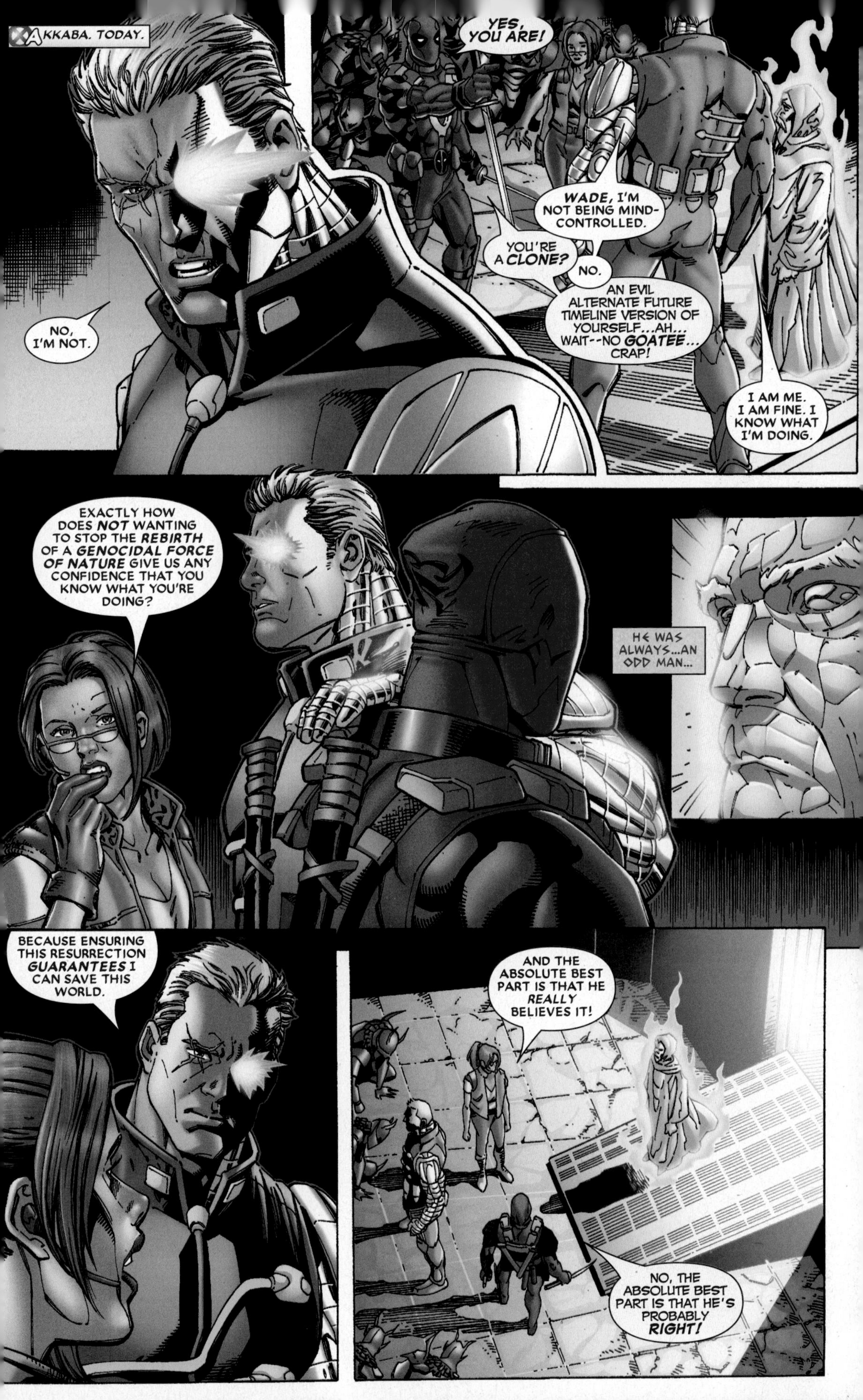
AKKABA. TODAY.
NO, I'M NOT.
YES, YOU ARE!
WADE, I'M NOT BEING MIND-CONTROLLED.
YOU'RE A CLONE?
NO.
AN EVIL ALTERNATE FUTURE TIMELINE VERSION OF YOURSELF...AH... WAIT--NO GOATEE... CRAP!
I AM ME. I AM FINE. I KNOW WHAT I'M DOING.
EXACTLY HOW DOES NOT WANTING TO STOP THE REBIRTH OF A GENOCIDAL FORCE OF NATURE GIVE US ANY CONFIDENCE THAT YOU KNOW WHAT YOU'RE DOING?
HE WAS ALWAYS...AN ODD MAN...
BECAUSE ENSURING THIS RESURRECTION GUARANTEES I CAN SAVE THIS WORLD.
AND THE ABSOLUTE BEST PART IS THAT HE REALLY BELIEVES IT!
NO, THE ABSOLUTE BEST PART IS THAT HE'S PROBABLY RIGHT!

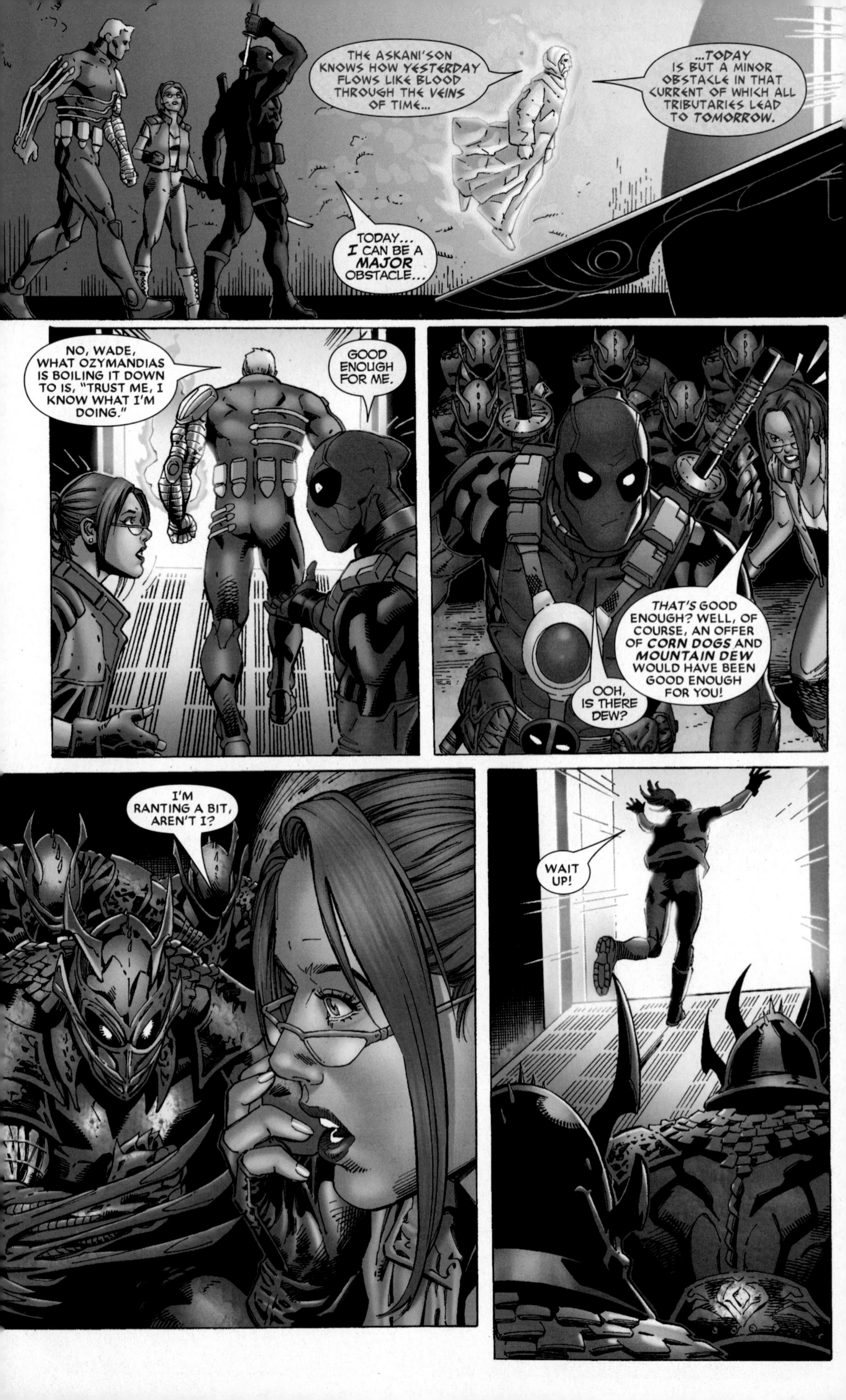
THE ASKANI'SON KNOWS HOW YESTERDAY FLOWS LIKE BLOOD THROUGH THE VEINS OF TIME...
...TODAY IS BUT A MINOR OBSTACLE IN THAT CURRENT OF WHICH ALL TRIBUTARIES LEAD TO TOMORROW.
TODAY... I CAN BE A MAJOR OBSTACLE...
NO, WADE, WHAT OZYMANDIAS IS BOILING IT DOWN TO IS, "TRUST ME, I KNOW WHAT I'M DOING."
GOOD ENOUGH FOR ME.
THAT'S GOOD ENOUGH? WELL, OF COURSE, AN OFFER OF CORN DOGS AND MOUNTAIN DEW WOULD HAVE BEEN GOOD ENOUGH FOR YOU!
OOH, IS THERE DEW?
I'M RANTING A BIT, AREN'T I?
WAIT UP!

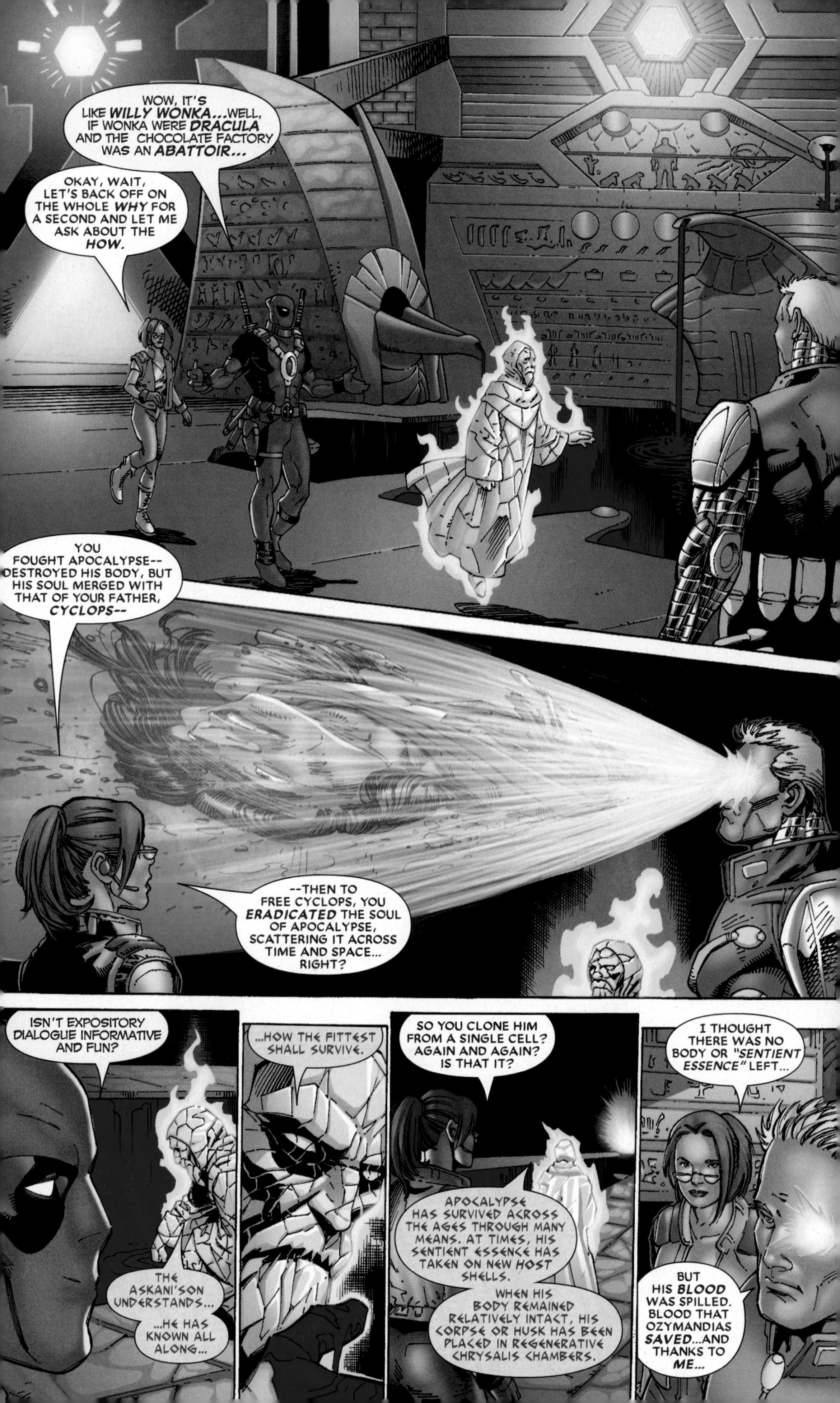

WOW, IT'S LIKE WILLY WONKA...WELL, IF WONKA WERE DRACULA AND THE CHOCOLATE FACTORY WAS AN ABATTOIR...
OKAY, WAIT, LET'S BACK OFF ON THE WHOLE WHY FOR A SECOND AND LET ME ASK ABOUT THE HOW.
YOU FOUGHT APOCALYPSE-- DESTROYED HIS BODY, BUT HIS SOUL MERGED WITH THAT OF YOUR FATHER, CYCLOPS--
--THEN TO FREE CYCLOPS, YOU ERADICATED THE SOUL OF APOCALYPSE, SCATTERING IT ACROSS TIME AND SPACE... RIGHT?
ISN'T EXPOSITORY DIALOGUE INFORMATIVE AND FUN?
THE ASKANI'SON UNDERSTANDS...
...HE HAS KNOWN ALL ALONG...
...HOW THE FITTEST SHALL SURVIVE.
SO YOU CLONE HIM FROM A SINGLE CELL? AGAIN AND AGAIN? IS THAT IT?
APOCALYPSE HAS SURVIVED ACROSS THE AGES THROUGH MANY MEANS. AT TIMES, HIS SENTIENT ESSENCE HAS TAKEN ON NEW HOST SHELLS.
WHEN HIS BODY REMAINED RELATIVELY INTACT, HIS CORPSE OR HUSK HAS BEEN PLACED IN REGENERATIVE CHRYSALIS CHAMBERS.
I THOUGHT THERE WAS NO BODY OR "SENTIENT ESSENCE" LEFT...
BUT HIS BLOOD WAS SPILLED. BLOOD THAT OZYMANDIAS SAVED...AND THANKS TO ME...

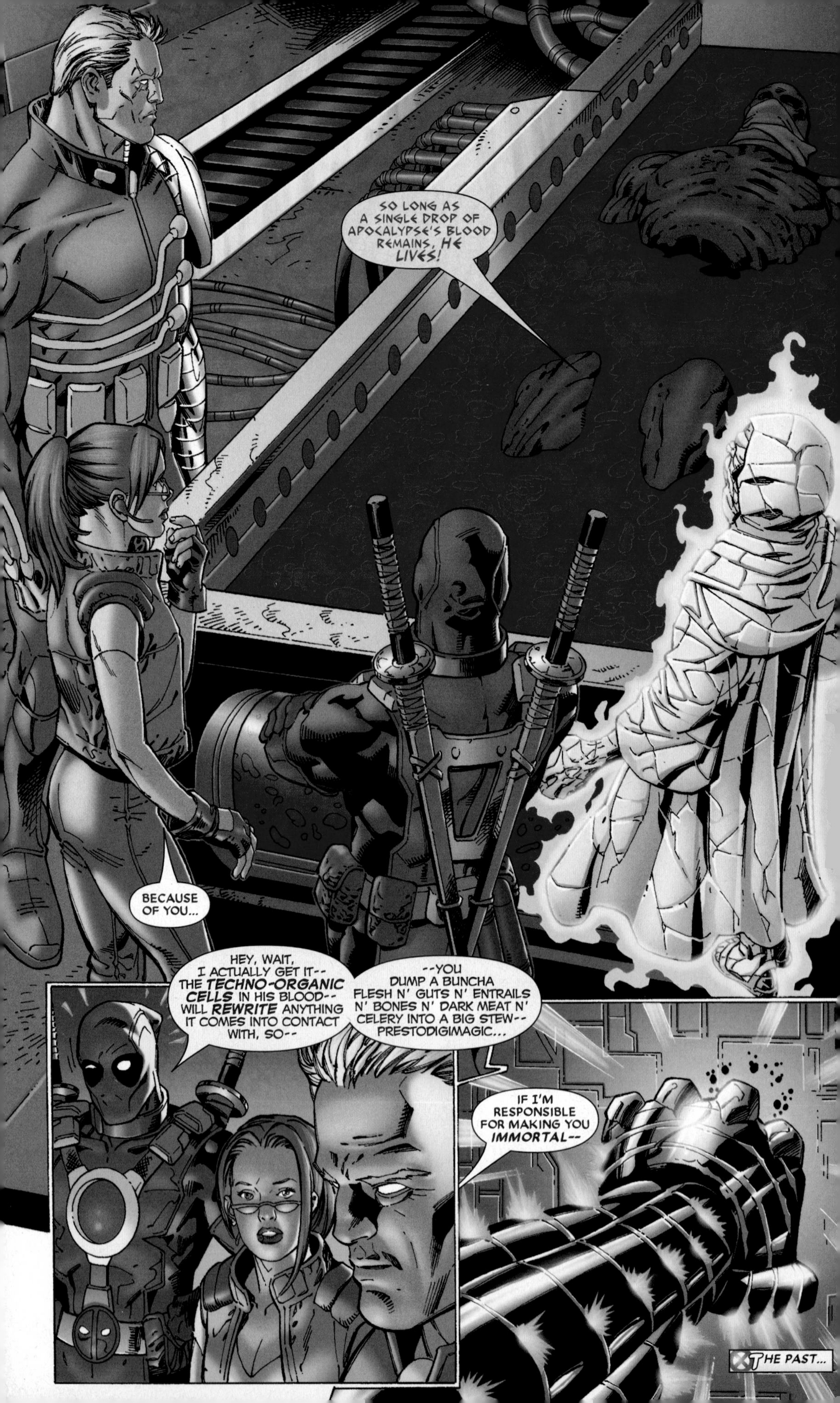
SO LONG AS A SINGLE DROP OF APOCALYPSE'S BLOOD REMAINS, HE LIVES!
BECAUSE OF YOU...
HEY, WAIT, I ACTUALLY GET IT-- THE TECHNO-ORGANIC CELLS IN HIS BLOOD-- WILL REWRITE ANYTHING IT COMES INTO CONTACT WITH, SO--
--YOU DUMP A BUNCHA FLESH N' GUTS N' ENTRAILS N' BONES N' DARK MEAT N' CELERY INTO A BIG STEW-- PRESTODIGIMAGIC...
IF I'M RESPONSIBLE FOR MAKING YOU IMMORTAL--
THE PAST...

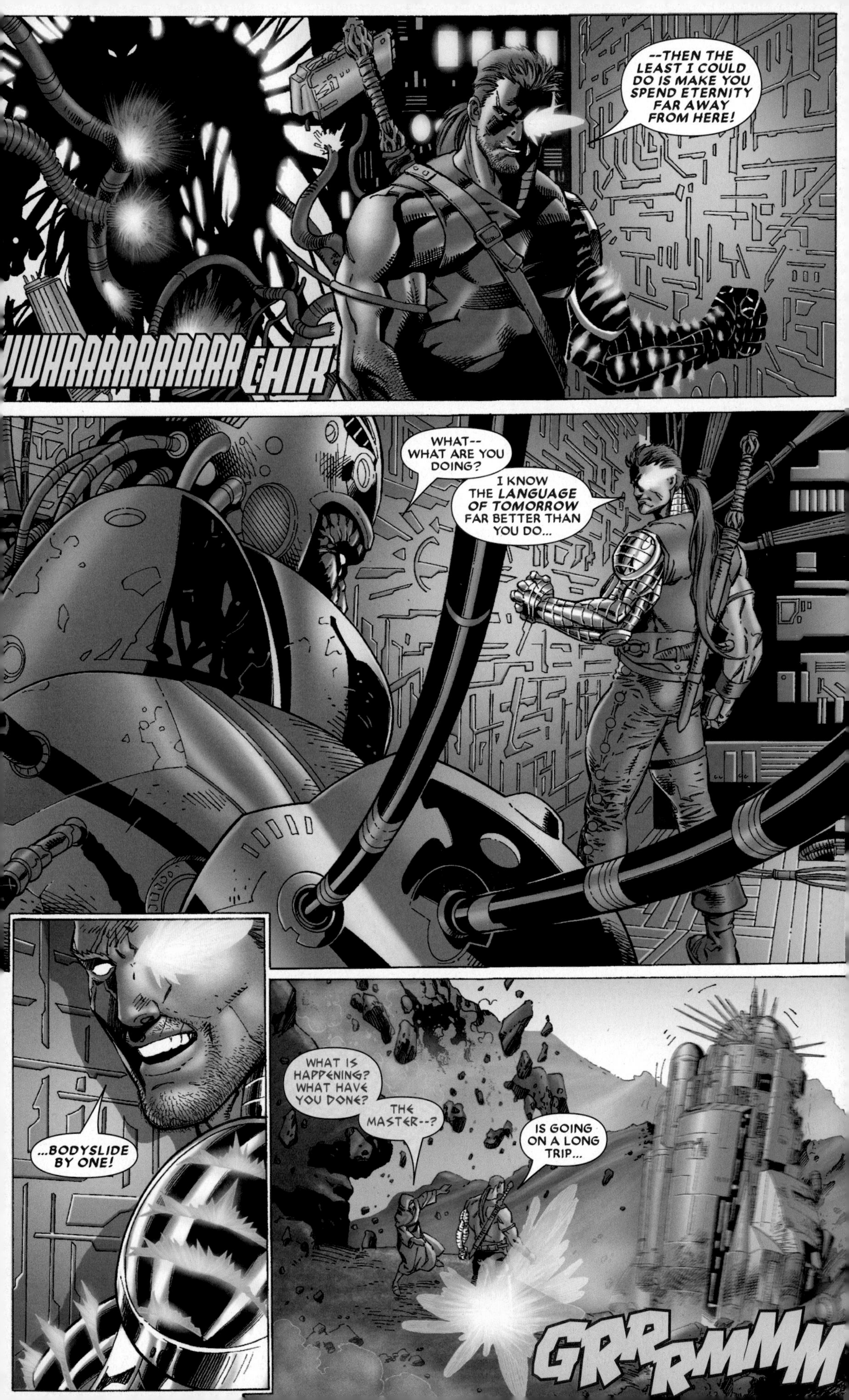
--THEN THE LEAST I COULD DO IS MAKE YOU SPEND ETERNITY FAR AWAY FROM HERE!
WHARRRRRRRRRRRCHIK
WHAT-- WHAT ARE YOU DOING?
I KNOW THE LANGUAGE OF TOMORROW FAR BETTER THAN YOU DO...
...BODYSLIDE BY ONE!
WHAT IS HAPPENING? WHAT HAVE YOU DONE?
THE MASTER--?
IS GOING ON A LONG TRIP...
GRRRMMMM

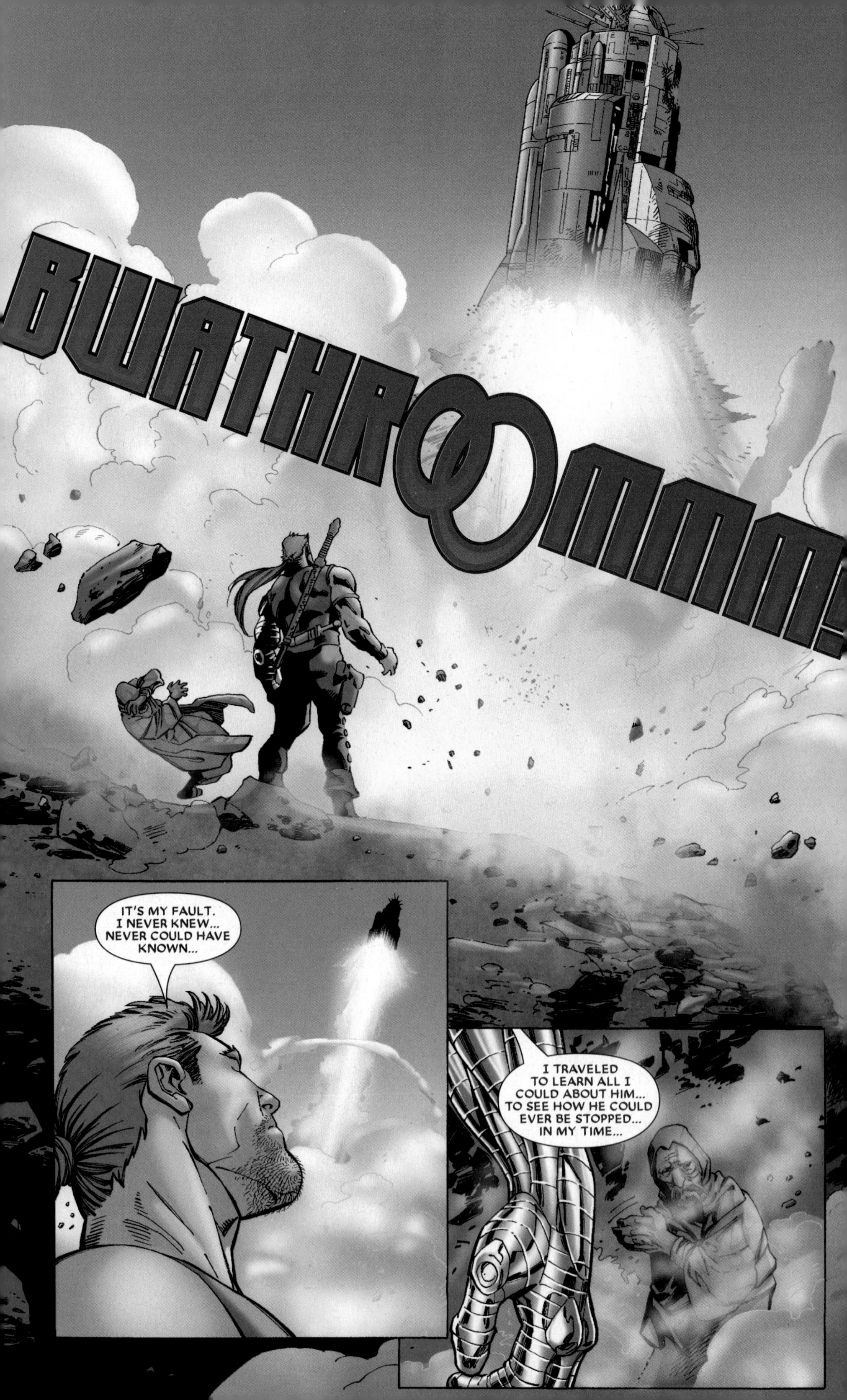
BWATHROOMMM!
IT'S MY FAULT. I NEVER KNEW... NEVER COULD HAVE KNOWN...
I TRAVELED TO LEARN ALL I COULD ABOUT HIM... TO SEE HOW HE COULD EVER BE STOPPED... IN MY TIME...

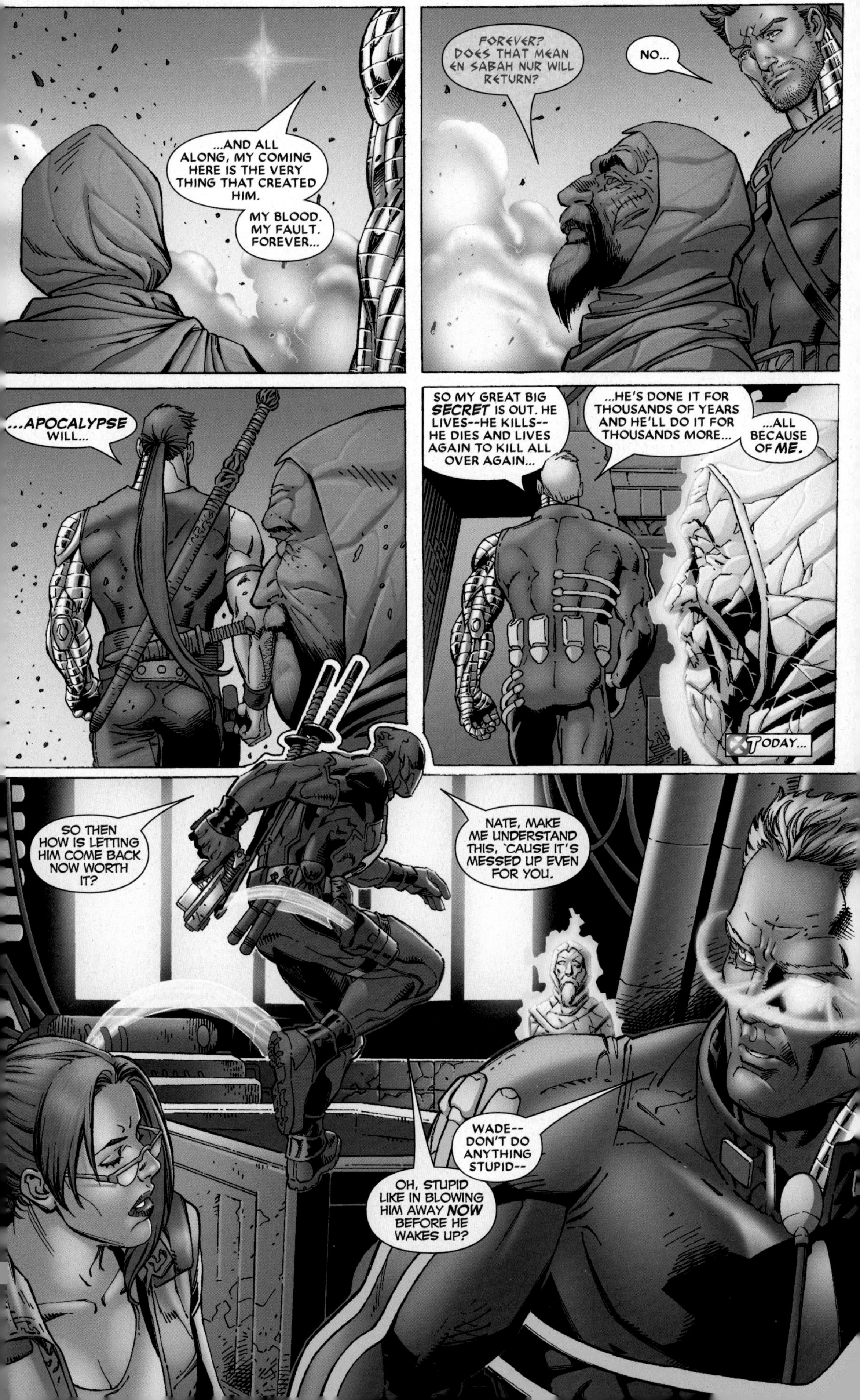

...AND ALL ALONG, MY COMING HERE IS THE VERY THING THAT CREATED HIM.
MY BLOOD. MY FAULT. FOREVER...
FOREVER? DOES THAT MEAN EN SABAH NUR WILL RETURN?
NO...
...APOCALYPSE WILL...
SO MY GREAT BIG SECRET IS OUT. HE LIVES--HE KILLS--HE DIES AND LIVES AGAIN TO KILL ALL OVER AGAIN...
...HE'S DONE IT FOR THOUSANDS OF YEARS AND HE'LL DO IT FOR THOUSANDS MORE...
...ALL BECAUSE OF ME.
TODAY...
SO THEN HOW IS LETTING HIM COME BACK NOW WORTH IT?
NATE, MAKE ME UNDERSTAND THIS, 'CAUSE IT'S MESSED UP EVEN FOR YOU.
WADE--DON'T DO ANYTHING STUPID--
OH, STUPID LIKE IN BLOWING HIM AWAY NOW BEFORE HE WAKES UP?

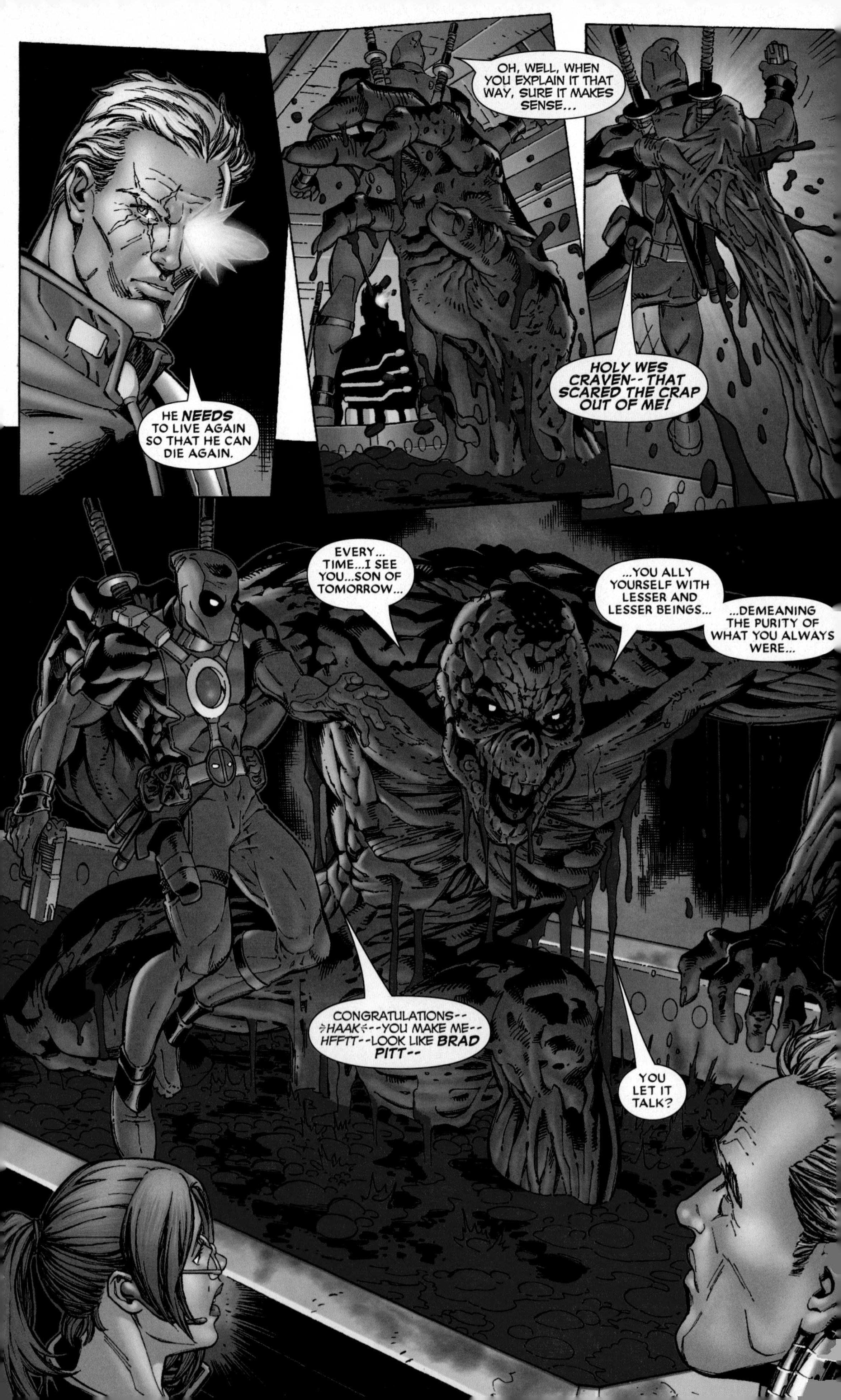

HE *NEEDS* TO LIVE AGAIN SO THAT HE CAN DIE AGAIN.
OH, WELL, WHEN YOU EXPLAIN IT THAT WAY, SURE IT MAKES SENSE...
HOLY WES CRAVEN-- THAT SCARED THE CRAP OUT OF ME!
EVERY... TIME...I SEE YOU...SON OF TOMORROW...
...YOU ALLY YOURSELF WITH LESSER AND LESSER BEINGS...
...DEMEANING THE PURITY OF WHAT YOU ALWAYS WERE...
CONGRATULATIONS-- *>HAAK<*--YOU MAKE ME-- *HFFTT*--LOOK LIKE **BRAD PITT**--
YOU LET IT TALK?

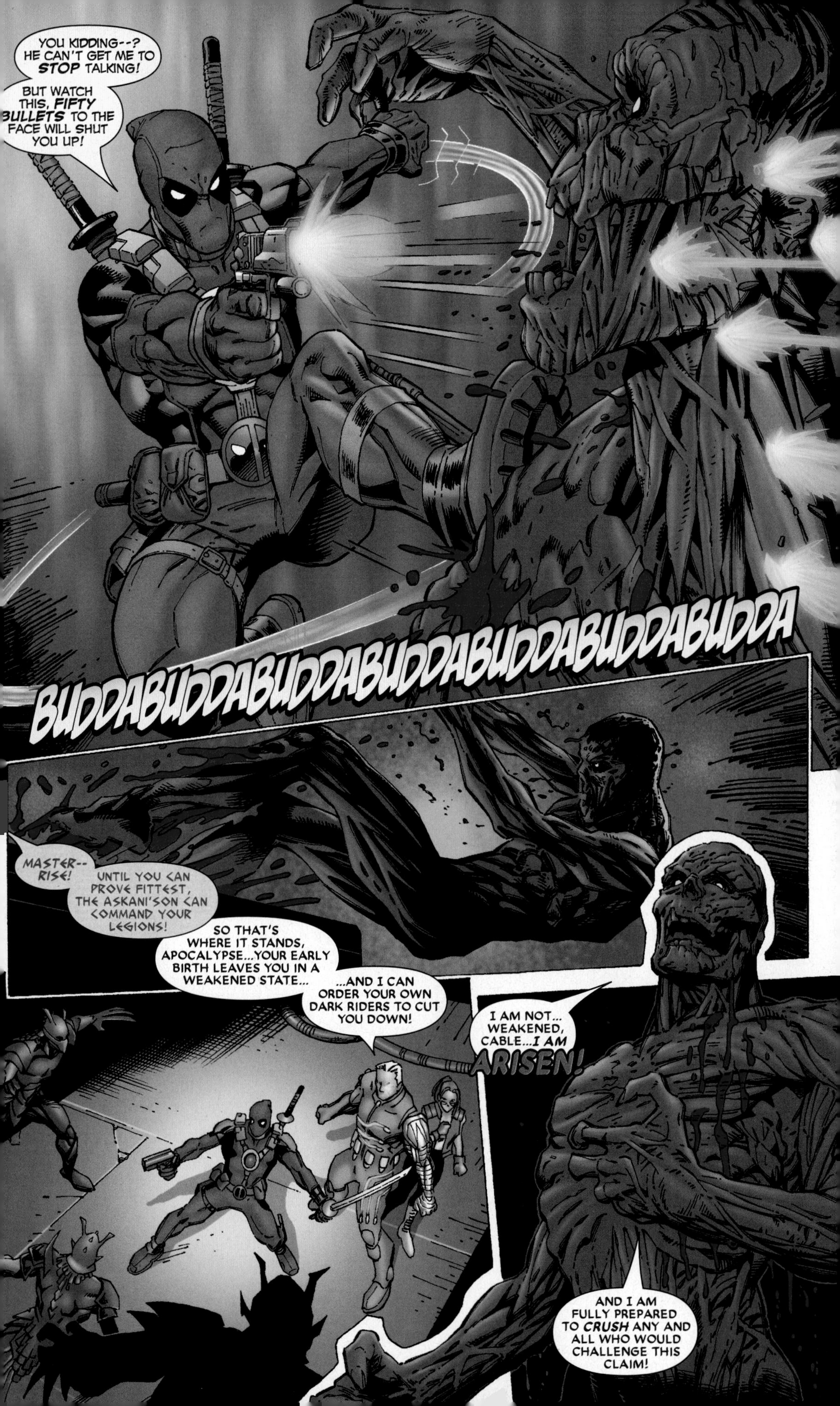

YOU KIDDING--? HE CAN'T GET ME TO STOP TALKING!
BUT WATCH THIS, FIFTY BULLETS TO THE FACE WILL SHUT YOU UP!
BUDDABUDDABUDDABUDDABUDDABUDDABUDDA
MASTER-- RISE!
UNTIL YOU CAN PROVE FITTEST, THE ASKANI'SON CAN COMMAND YOUR LEGIONS!
SO THAT'S WHERE IT STANDS, APOCALYPSE...YOUR EARLY BIRTH LEAVES YOU IN A WEAKENED STATE...
...AND I CAN ORDER YOUR OWN DARK RIDERS TO CUT YOU DOWN!
I AM NOT... WEAKENED, CABLE...I AM ARISEN!
AND I AM FULLY PREPARED TO CRUSH ANY AND ALL WHO WOULD CHALLENGE THIS CLAIM!

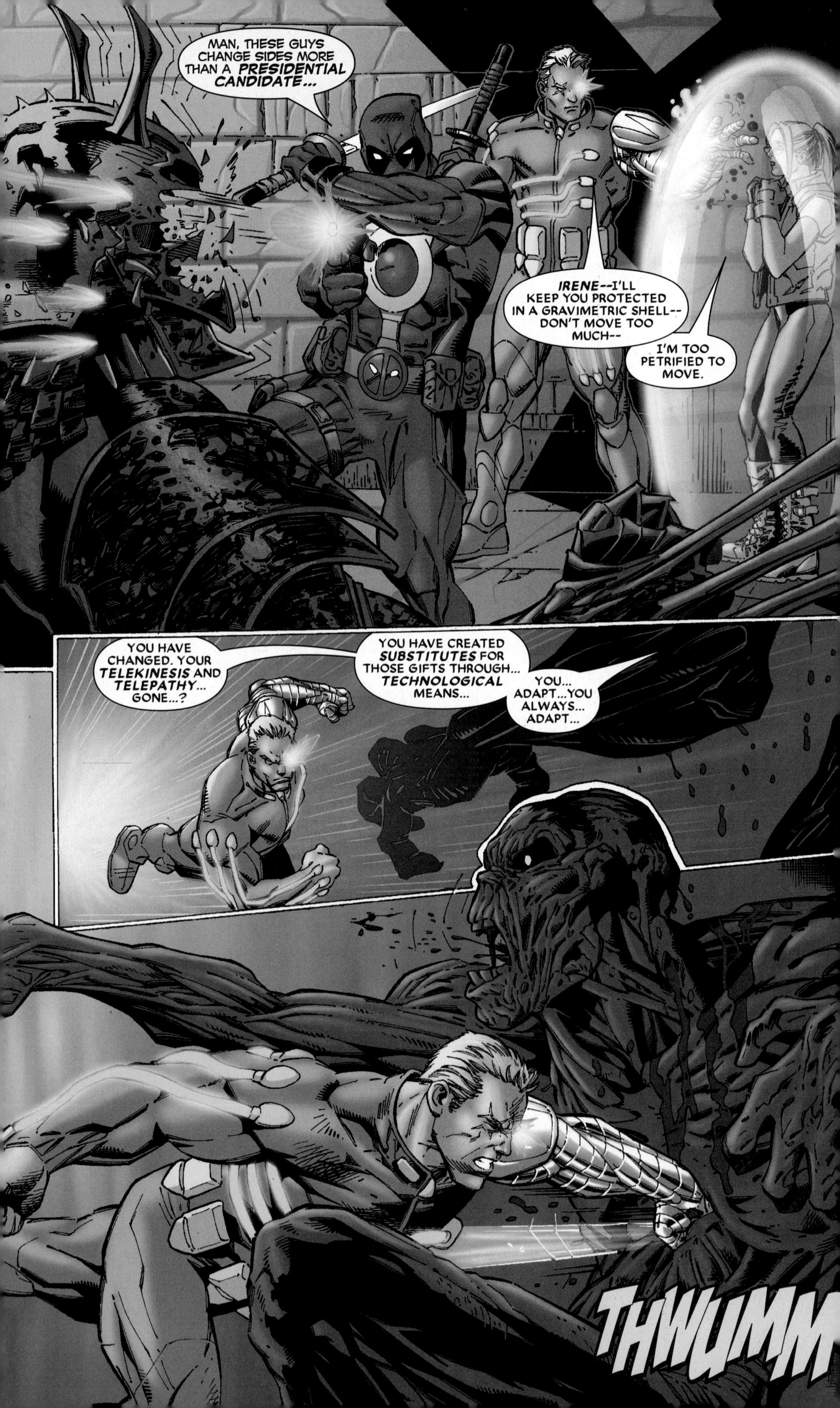
MAN, THESE GUYS CHANGE SIDES MORE THAN A PRESIDENTIAL CANDIDATE...
IRENE--I'LL KEEP YOU PROTECTED IN A GRAVIMETRIC SHELL-- DON'T MOVE TOO MUCH--
I'M TOO PETRIFIED TO MOVE.
YOU HAVE CHANGED. YOUR TELEKINESIS AND TELEPATHY... GONE...?
YOU HAVE CREATED SUBSTITUTES FOR THOSE GIFTS THROUGH... TECHNOLOGICAL MEANS...
YOU... ADAPT...YOU ALWAYS... ADAPT...
THWUMM

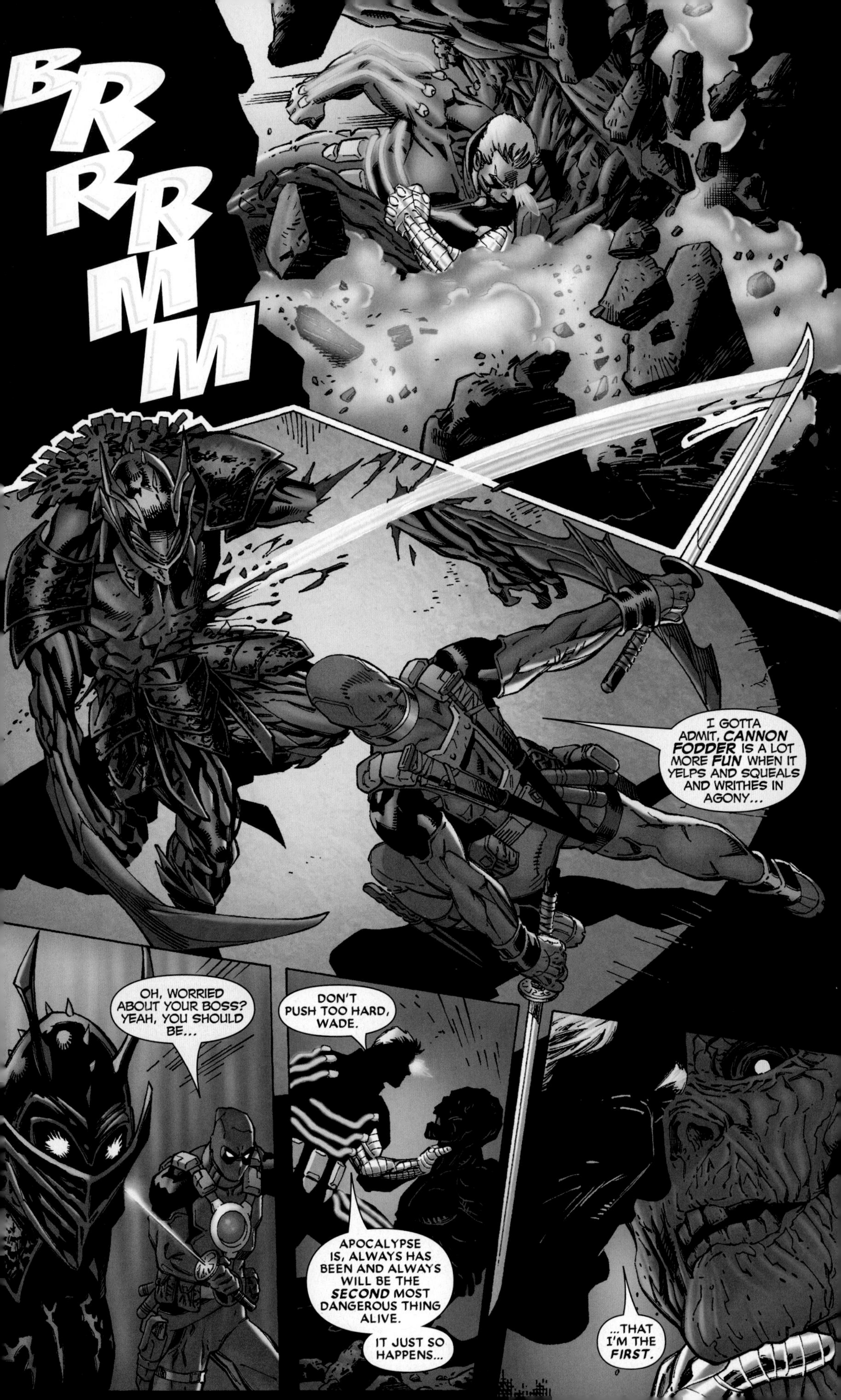
BRRRMM
I GOTTA ADMIT, CANNON FODDER IS A LOT MORE FUN WHEN IT YELPS AND SQUEALS AND WRITHES IN AGONY...
OH, WORRIED ABOUT YOUR BOSS? YEAH, YOU SHOULD BE...
DON'T PUSH TOO HARD, WADE.
APOCALYPSE IS, ALWAYS HAS BEEN AND ALWAYS WILL BE THE SECOND MOST DANGEROUS THING ALIVE.
IT JUST SO HAPPENS...
...THAT I'M THE FIRST.

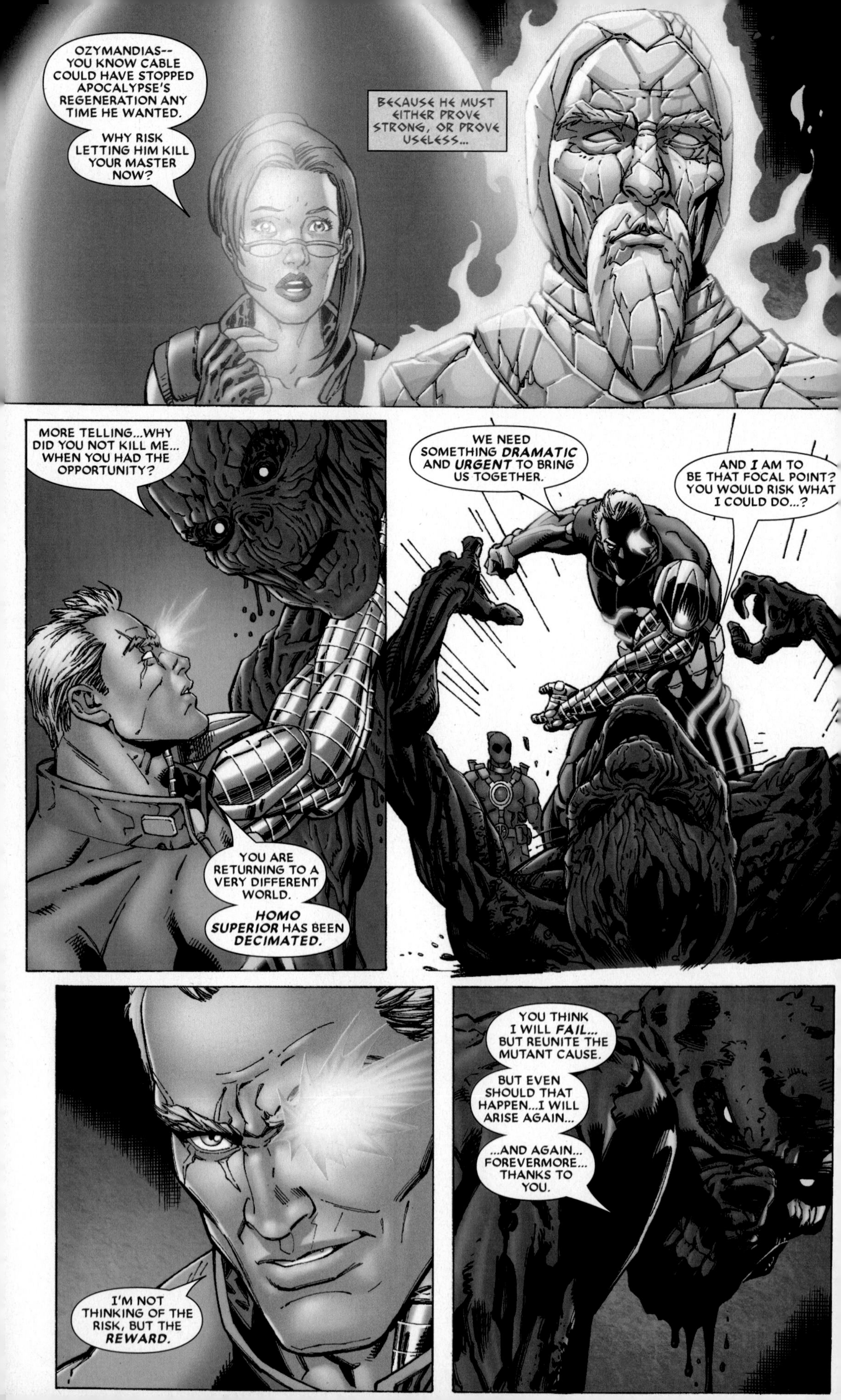
OZYMANDIAS-- YOU KNOW CABLE COULD HAVE STOPPED APOCALYPSE'S REGENERATION ANY TIME HE WANTED.
WHY RISK LETTING HIM KILL YOUR MASTER NOW?
BECAUSE HE MUST EITHER PROVE STRONG, OR PROVE USELESS...
MORE TELLING...WHY DID YOU NOT KILL ME... WHEN YOU HAD THE OPPORTUNITY?
YOU ARE RETURNING TO A VERY DIFFERENT WORLD.
HOMO SUPERIOR HAS BEEN *DECIMATED.*
WE NEED SOMETHING *DRAMATIC* AND *URGENT* TO BRING US TOGETHER.
AND *I* AM TO BE THAT FOCAL POINT? YOU WOULD RISK WHAT I COULD DO...?
I'M NOT THINKING OF THE RISK, BUT THE *REWARD.*
YOU THINK I WILL *FAIL...* BUT REUNITE THE MUTANT CAUSE.
BUT EVEN SHOULD THAT HAPPEN...I WILL ARISE AGAIN...
...AND AGAIN... FOREVERMORE... THANKS TO YOU.

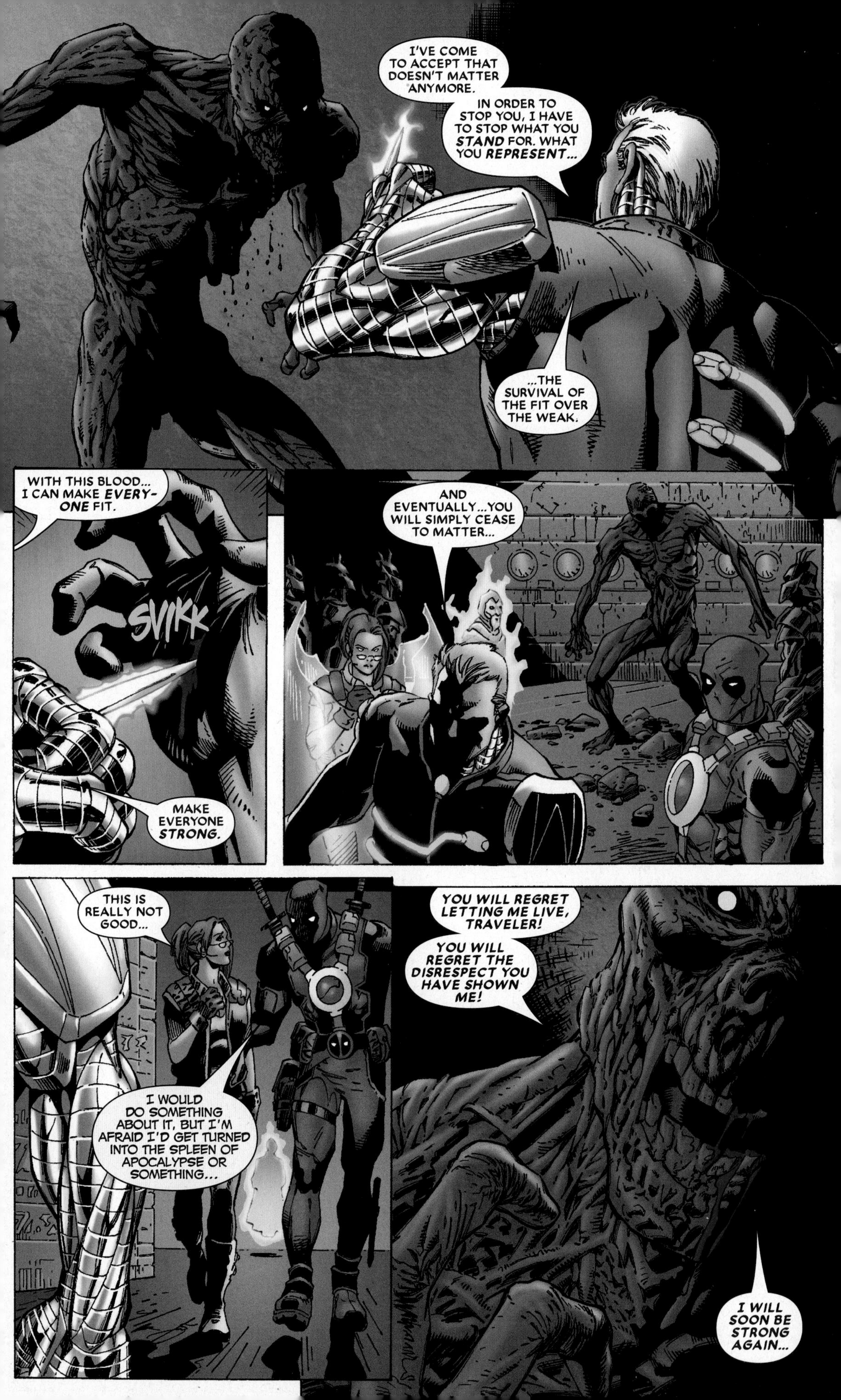
I'VE COME TO ACCEPT THAT DOESN'T MATTER ANYMORE.
IN ORDER TO STOP YOU, I HAVE TO STOP WHAT YOU STAND FOR. WHAT YOU REPRESENT...
...THE SURVIVAL OF THE FIT OVER THE WEAK.
WITH THIS BLOOD... I CAN MAKE EVERY-ONE FIT.
SVIKK
MAKE EVERYONE STRONG.
AND EVENTUALLY...YOU WILL SIMPLY CEASE TO MATTER...
THIS IS REALLY NOT GOOD...
I WOULD DO SOMETHING ABOUT IT, BUT I'M AFRAID I'D GET TURNED INTO THE SPLEEN OF APOCALYPSE OR SOMETHING...
YOU WILL REGRET LETTING ME LIVE, TRAVELER!
YOU WILL REGRET THE DISRESPECT YOU HAVE SHOWN ME!
I WILL SOON BE STRONG AGAIN...

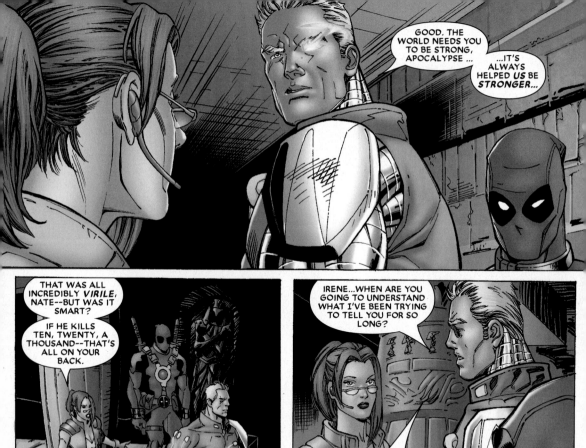

GOOD. THE WORLD NEEDS YOU TO BE STRONG, APOCALYPSE ...

...IT'S ALWAYS HELPED *US* BE STRONGER...

THAT WAS ALL INCREDIBLY *VIRILE*, NATE--BUT WAS IT SMART?

IF HE KILLS TEN, TWENTY, A THOUSAND--THAT'S ALL ON YOUR BACK.

IRENE...WHEN ARE YOU GOING TO UNDERSTAND WHAT I'VE BEEN TRYING TO TELL YOU FOR SO LONG?

I HAVE LIVED AND LOVED AND CRIED AND DIED ACROSS *THOUSANDS* AND *THOUSANDS* OF YEARS GONE BY AND STILL TO COME.

I'VE SEEN APOCALYPSE KILL *BILLIONS*.

AND EVERY SINGLE ONE OF THEM IS ON "MY BACK."

THAT'S WHY I KEEP FACING FORWARD...

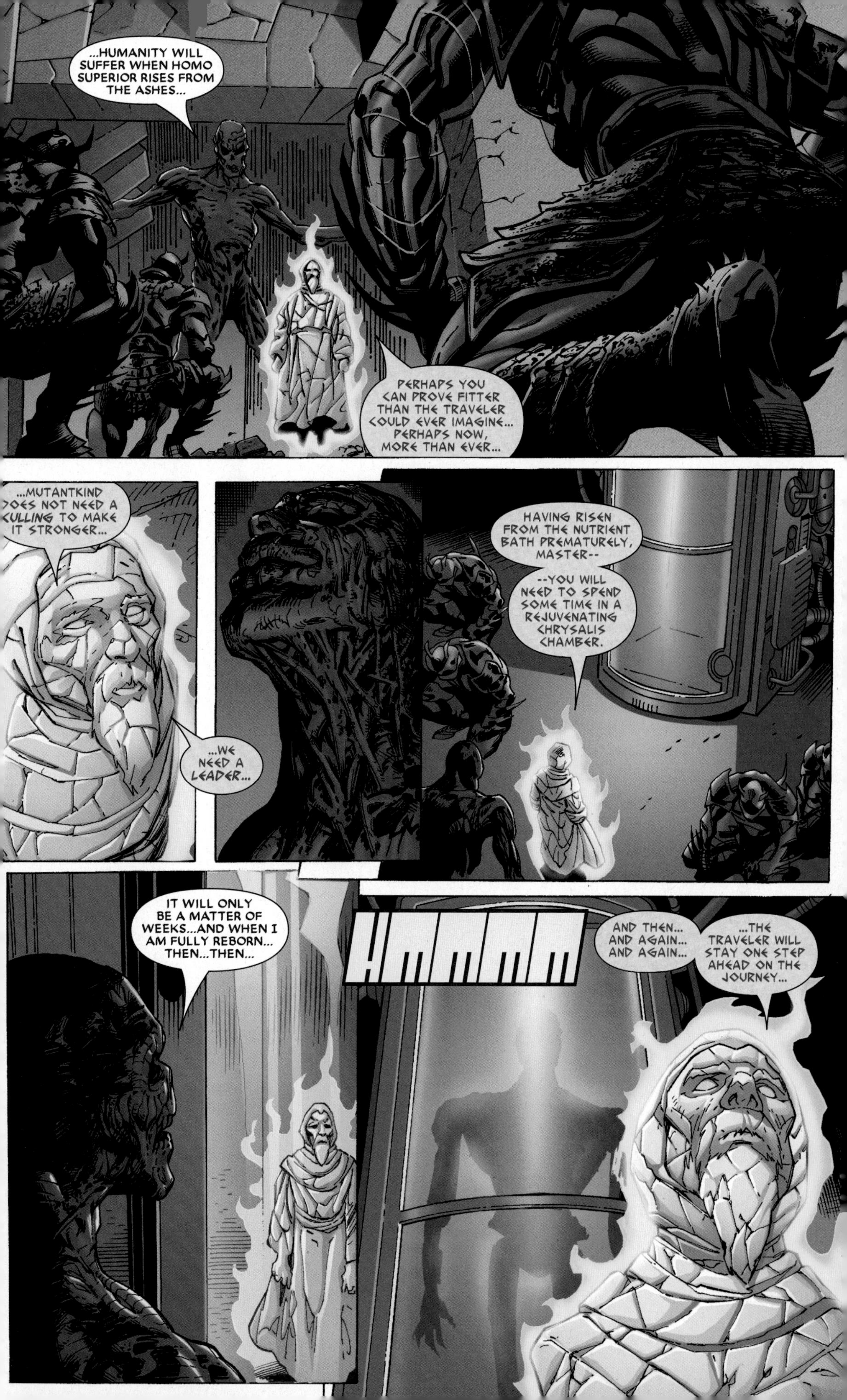
...HUMANITY WILL SUFFER WHEN HOMO SUPERIOR RISES FROM THE ASHES...
PERHAPS YOU CAN PROVE FITTER THAN THE TRAVELER COULD EVER IMAGINE... PERHAPS NOW, MORE THAN EVER...
...MUTANTKIND DOES NOT NEED A CULLING TO MAKE IT STRONGER...
...WE NEED A LEADER...
HAVING RISEN FROM THE NUTRIENT BATH PREMATURELY, MASTER--
--YOU WILL NEED TO SPEND SOME TIME IN A REJUVENATING CHRYSALIS CHAMBER.
IT WILL ONLY BE A MATTER OF WEEKS...AND WHEN I AM FULLY REBORN... THEN...THEN...
HMMMMM
AND THEN... AND AGAIN... AND AGAIN...
...THE TRAVELER WILL STAY ONE STEP AHEAD ON THE JOURNEY...

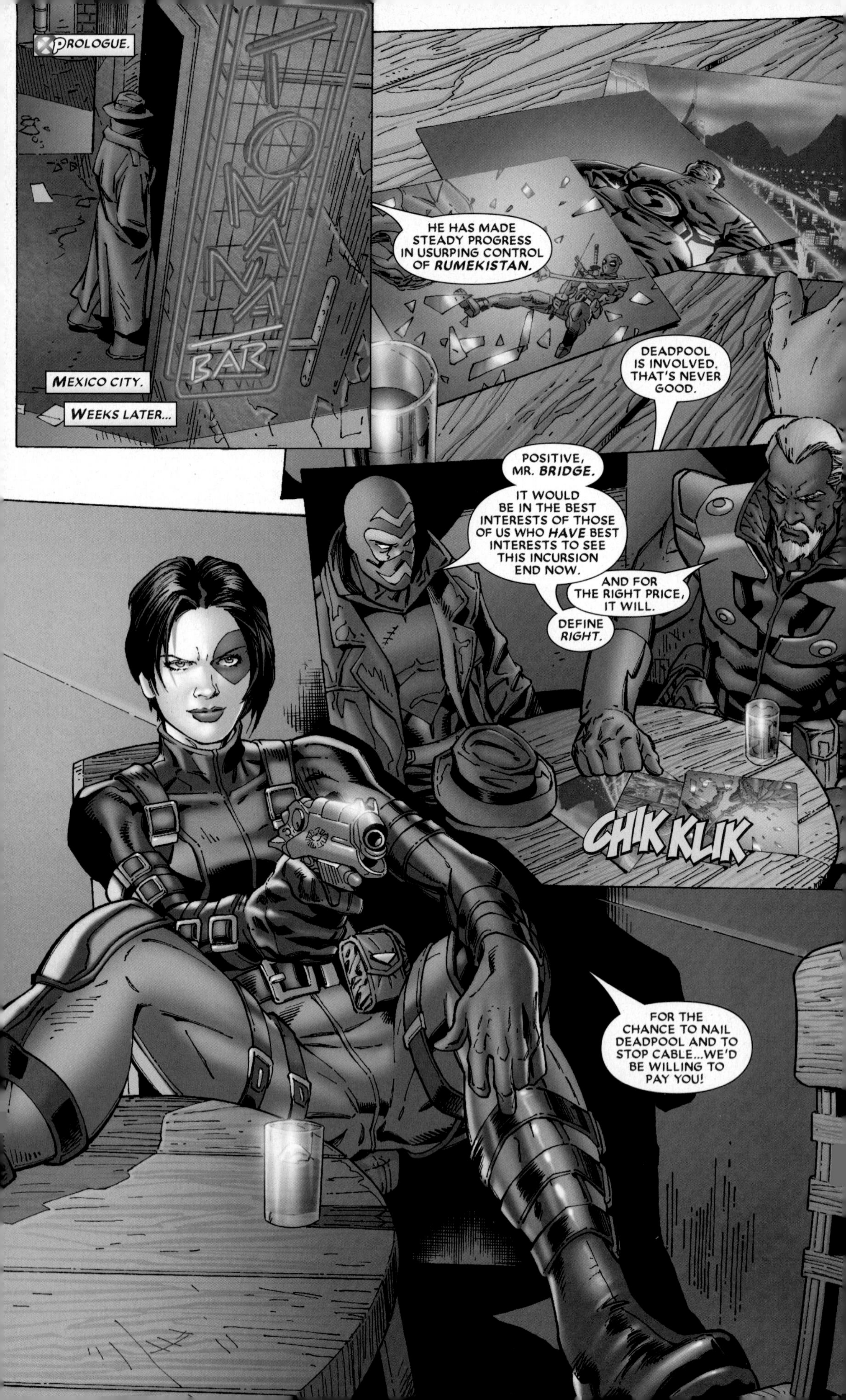
PROLOGUE.
TOMANA
BAR
MEXICO CITY.
WEEKS LATER...
HE HAS MADE STEADY PROGRESS IN USURPING CONTROL OF RUMEKISTAN.
DEADPOOL IS INVOLVED. THAT'S NEVER GOOD.
POSITIVE, MR. BRIDGE.
IT WOULD BE IN THE BEST INTERESTS OF THOSE OF US WHO HAVE BEST INTERESTS TO SEE THIS INCURSION END NOW.
AND FOR THE RIGHT PRICE, IT WILL.
DEFINE RIGHT.
CHIK KLIK
FOR THE CHANCE TO NAIL DEADPOOL AND TO STOP CABLE...WE'D BE WILLING TO PAY YOU!

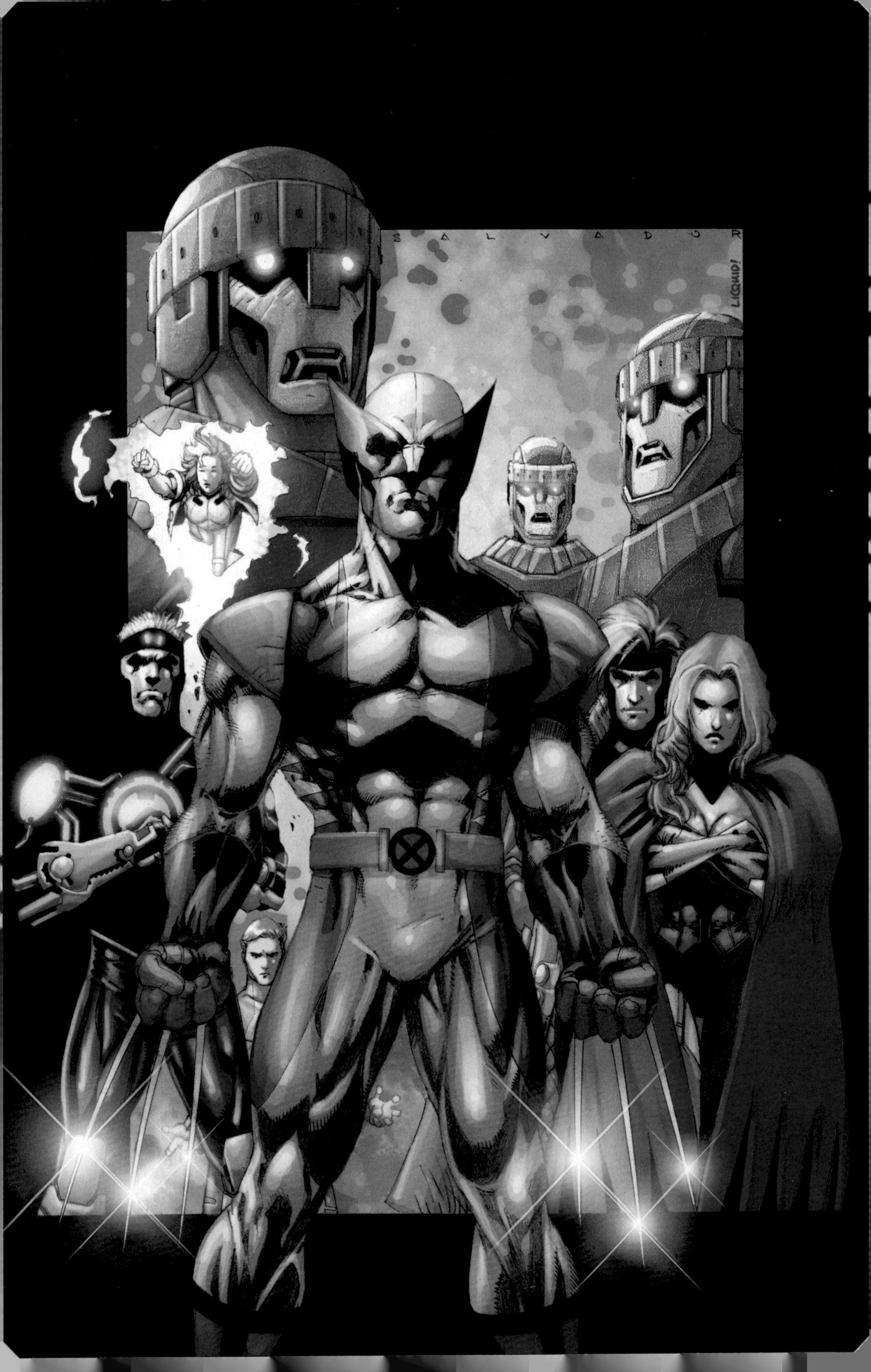
S A L V A D O R
LIQUID!

PREVIOUSLY IN X-MEN

Born with genetic mutations that give them bilities beyond those of normal humans, mutants re the next stage in evolution. As such, they are eared and hated. But a group of mutants known as the X-MEN fight for the peaceful coexistence between mutant and humankind.

That fight just got a lot harder.

MAGNETO'S daughter, THE SCARLET WITCH, had a mental breakdown and changed all of reality. When she returned it back to normal, however, he whispered three words..."No more mutants."

The X-Men soon found themselves in a world here 90% of the mutant population had lost their pecial abilities. Mutantkind has been decimated.

The X-Men now struggle to deal with this crisis. They have lost some of their own ranks to the phenomenon of "M-DAY," and now must deal with more threats from the outside world, like the SAPIEN LEAGUE, an anti-mutant terrorist organization. Two weeks after "M-Day," the Sapien League attacked the Xavier Institute. During the attack, the X-Men are shocked to see five giant Sentinels drop from the sky and land directly on their property.

What the Sentinels want or why they are here has yet to be seen...

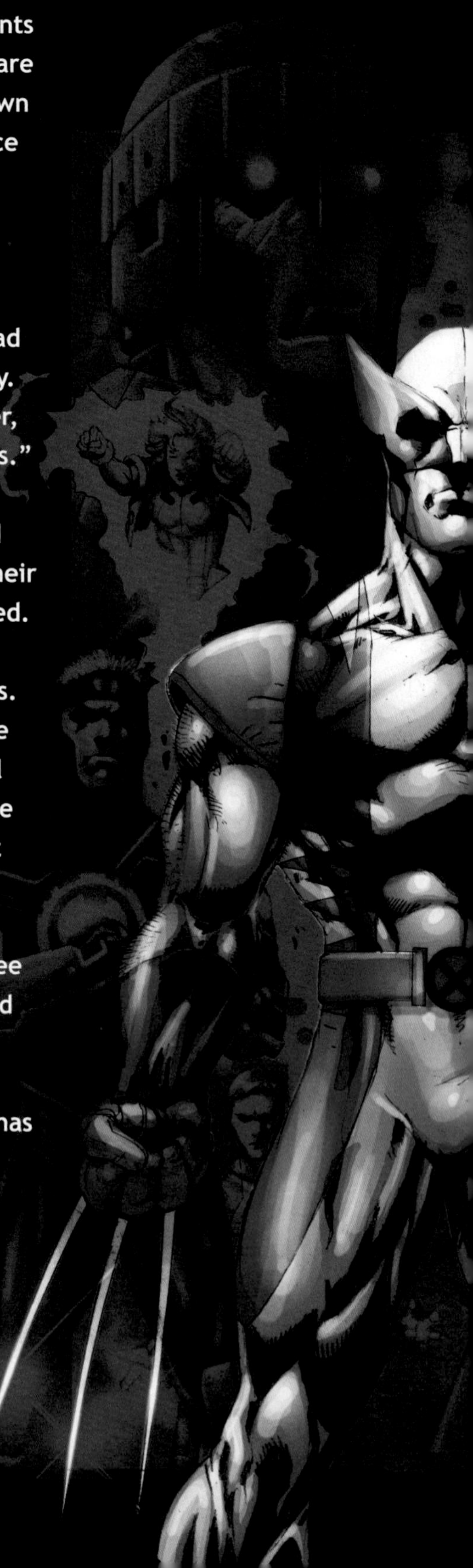

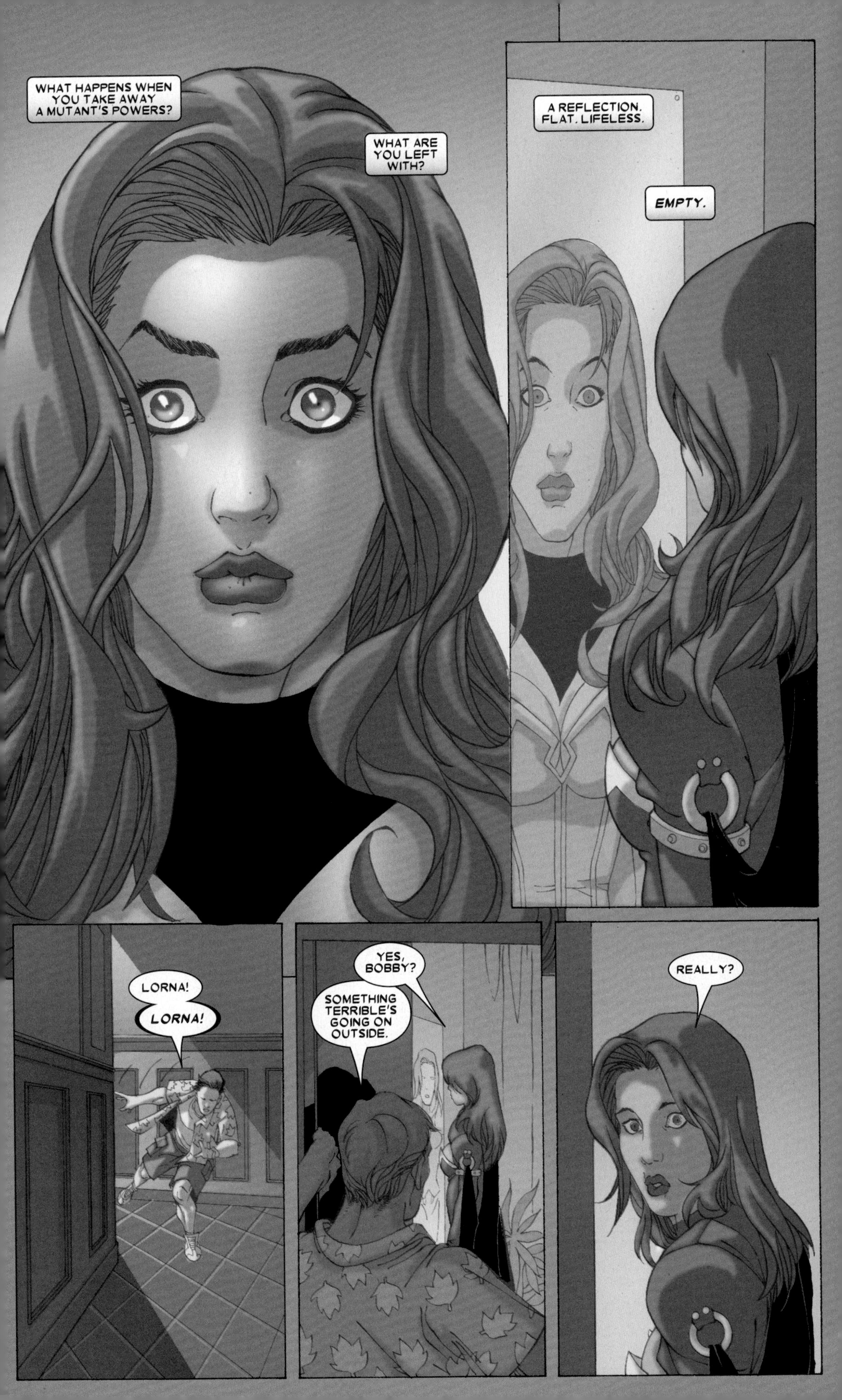
WHAT HAPPENS WHEN YOU TAKE AWAY A MUTANT'S POWERS?
WHAT ARE YOU LEFT WITH?
A REFLECTION. FLAT. LIFELESS.
EMPTY.
LORNA!
LORNA!
YES, BOBBY?
SOMETHING TERRIBLE'S GOING ON OUTSIDE.
REALLY?

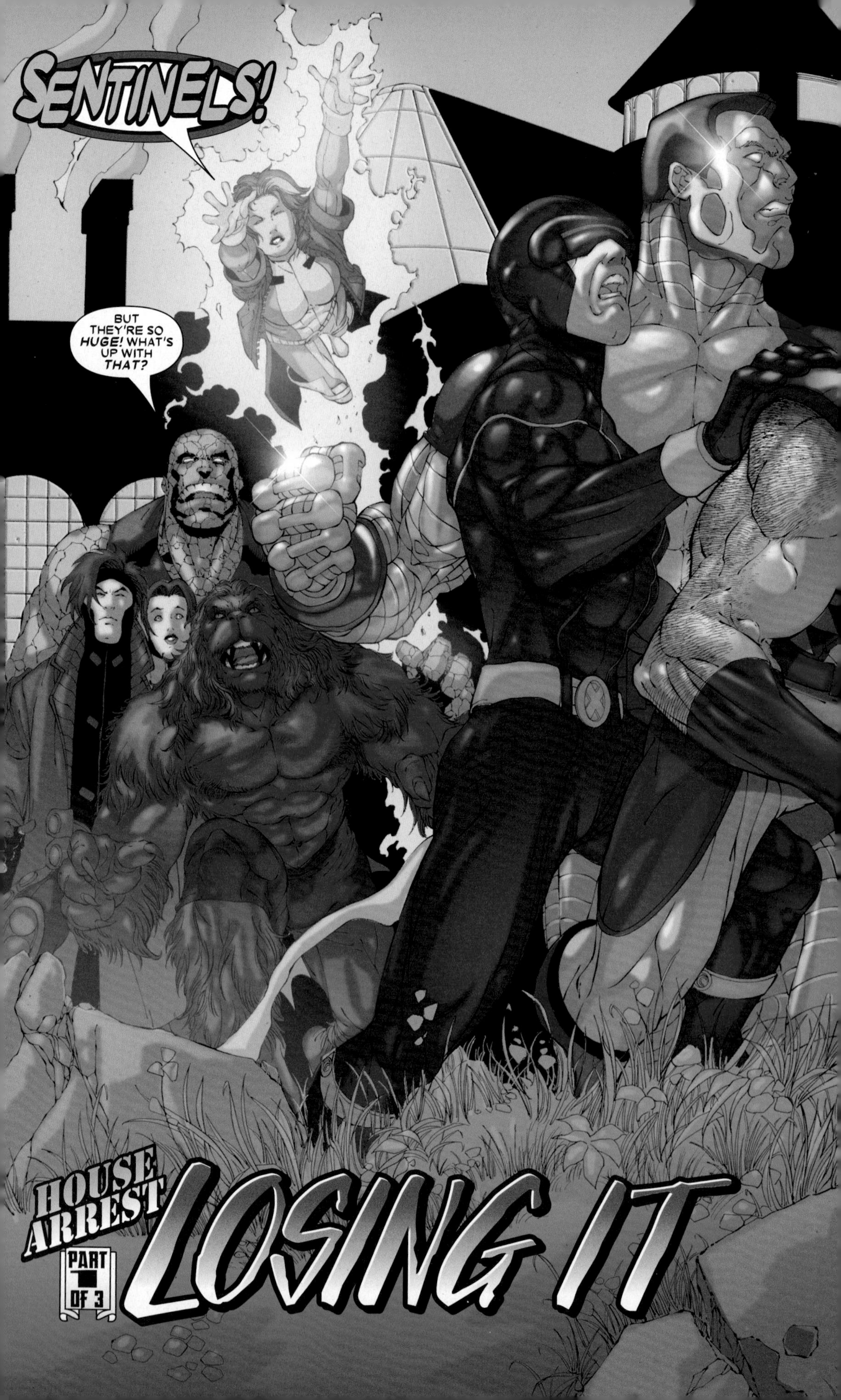
SENTINELS!
BUT THEY'RE SO HUGE! WHAT'S UP WITH THAT?
HOUSE ARREST
PART OF 3
LOSING IT

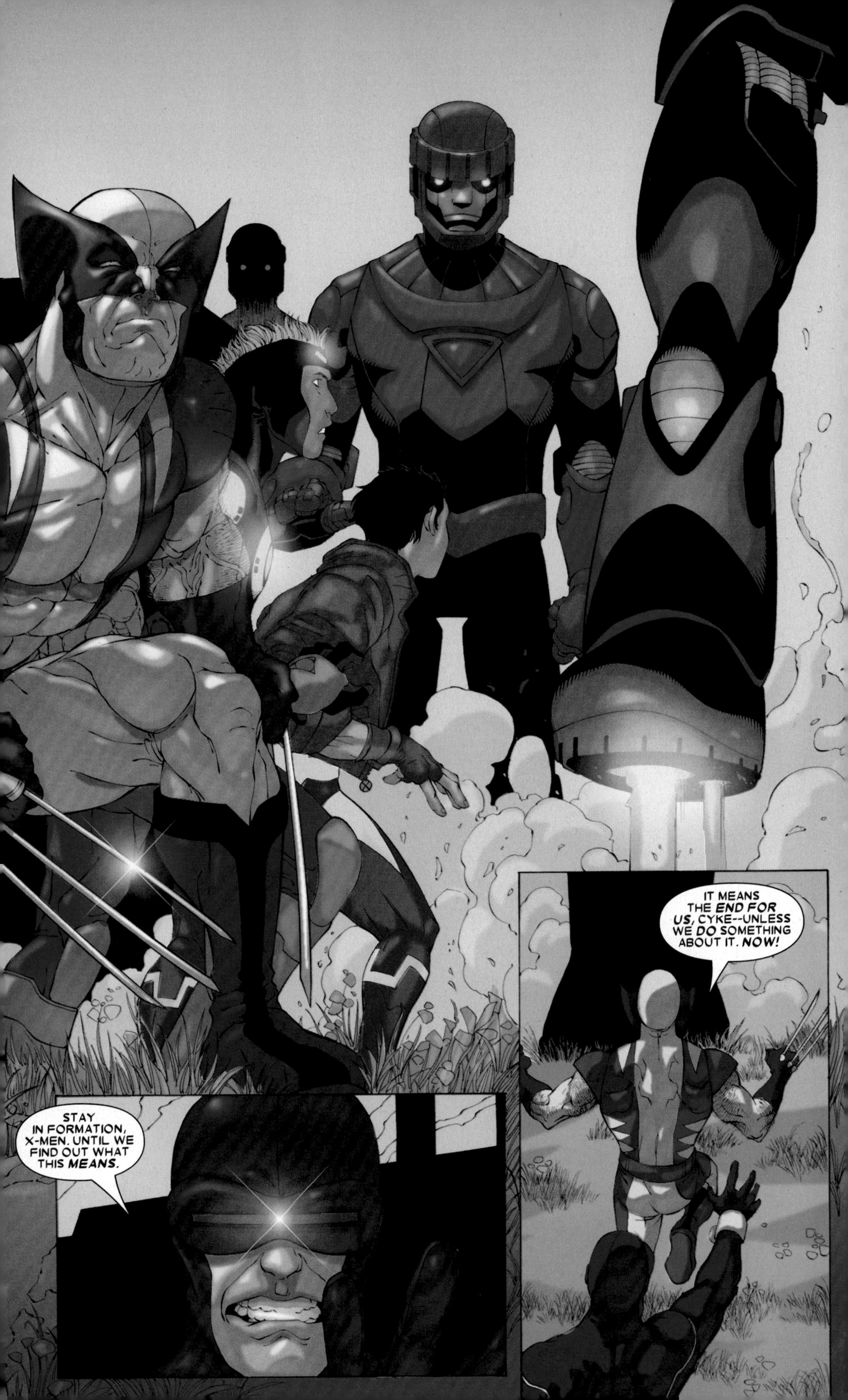
STAY IN FORMATION, X-MEN. UNTIL WE FIND OUT WHAT THIS MEANS.
IT MEANS THE END FOR US, CYKE--UNLESS WE DO SOMETHING ABOUT IT. NOW!

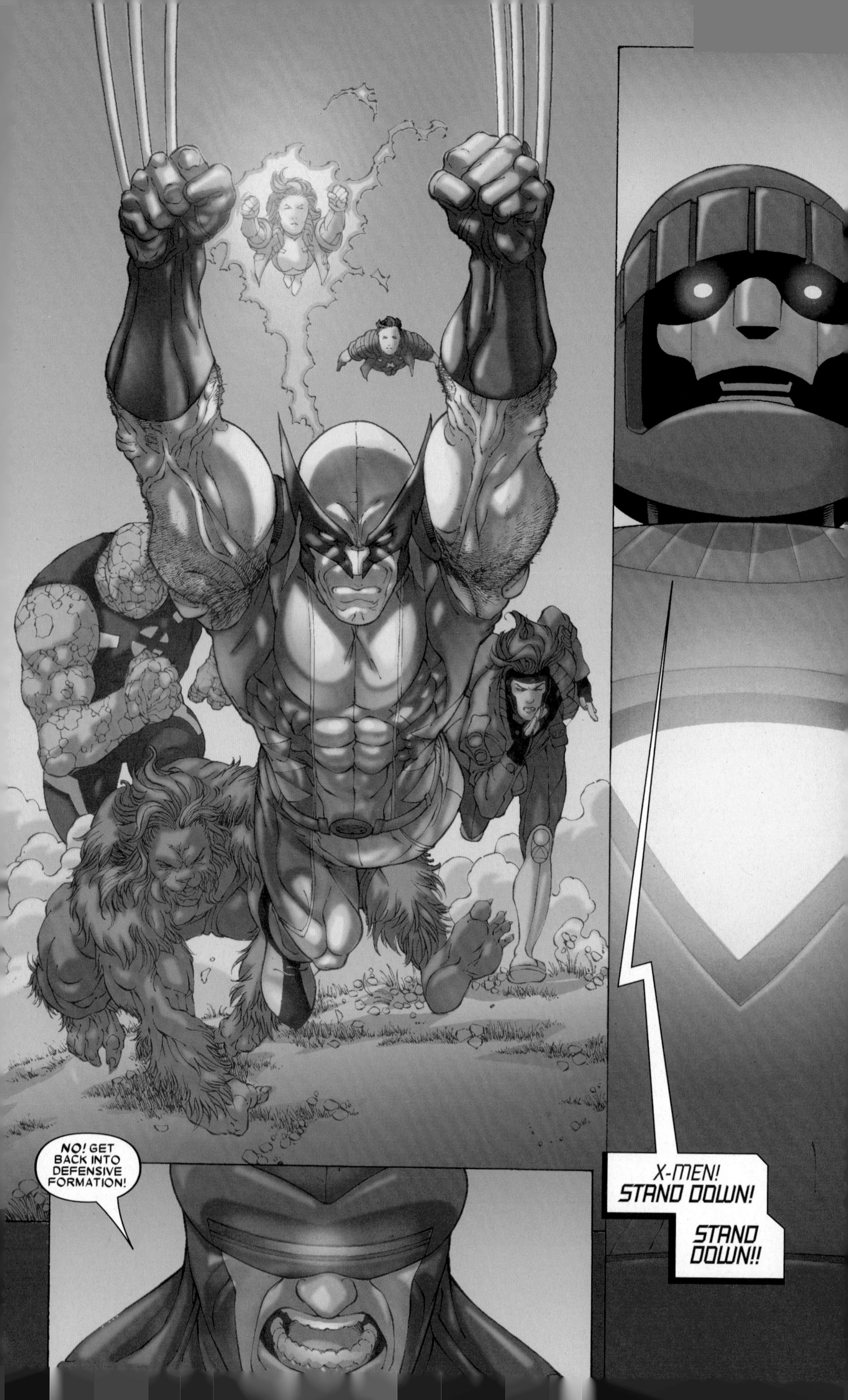
NO! GET BACK INTO DEFENSIVE FORMATION!
X-MEN! STAND DOWN!
STAND DOWN!!

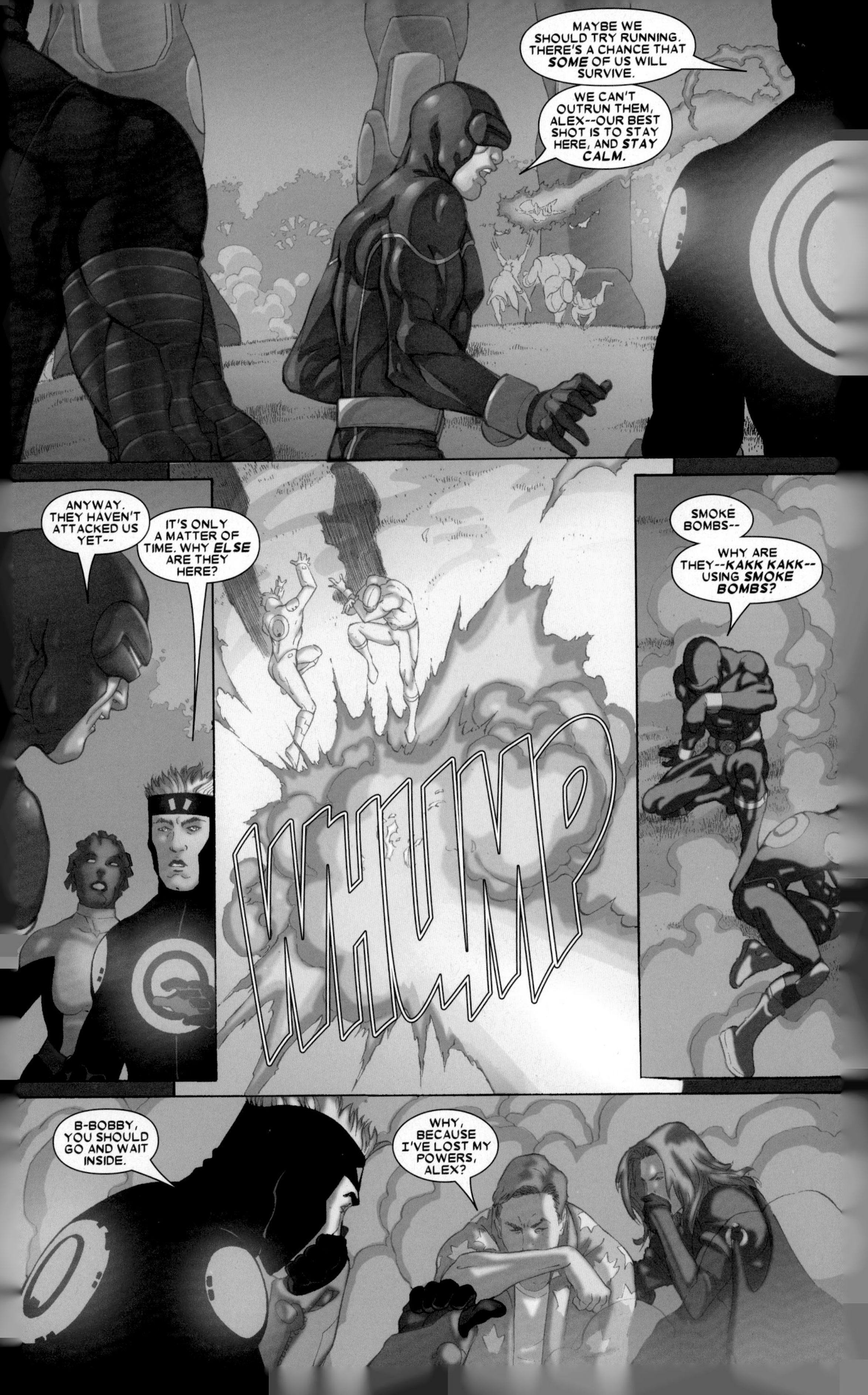
MAYBE WE SHOULD TRY RUNNING. THERE'S A CHANCE THAT SOME OF US WILL SURVIVE.
WE CAN'T OUTRUN THEM, ALEX--OUR BEST SHOT IS TO STAY HERE, AND STAY CALM.
ANYWAY. THEY HAVEN'T ATTACKED US YET--
IT'S ONLY A MATTER OF TIME. WHY ELSE ARE THEY HERE?
WHUMP
SMOKE BOMBS--
WHY ARE THEY--KAKK KAKK--USING SMOKE BOMBS?
B-BOBBY, YOU SHOULD GO AND WAIT INSIDE.
WHY, BECAUSE I'VE LOST MY POWERS, ALEX?

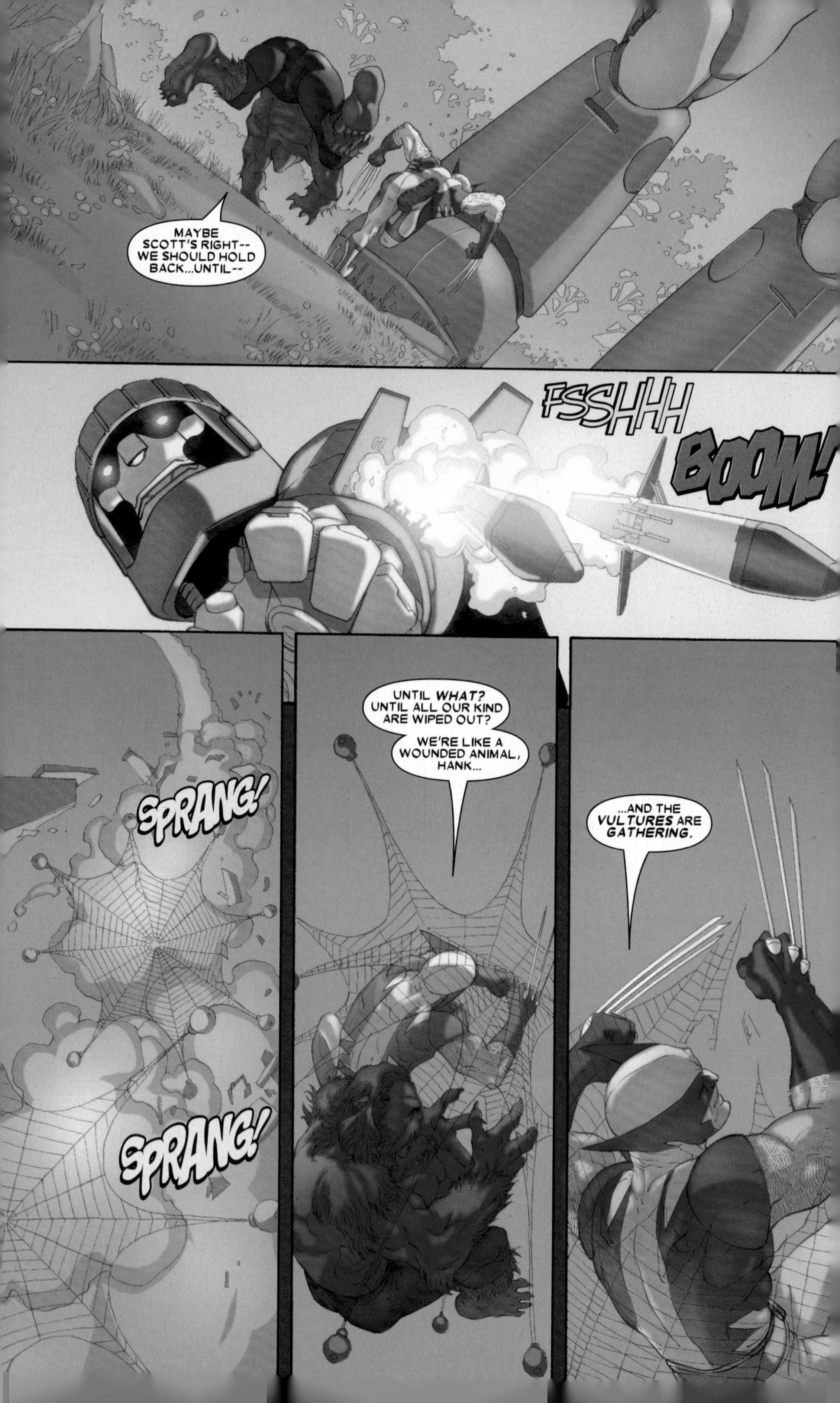
MAYBE SCOTT'S RIGHT-- WE SHOULD HOLD BACK...UNTIL--
FSSHHH
BOOM!
SPRANG!
SPRANG!
UNTIL *WHAT?* UNTIL ALL OUR KIND ARE WIPED OUT?
WE'RE LIKE A WOUNDED ANIMAL, HANK...
...AND THE *VULTURES* ARE *GATHERING.*

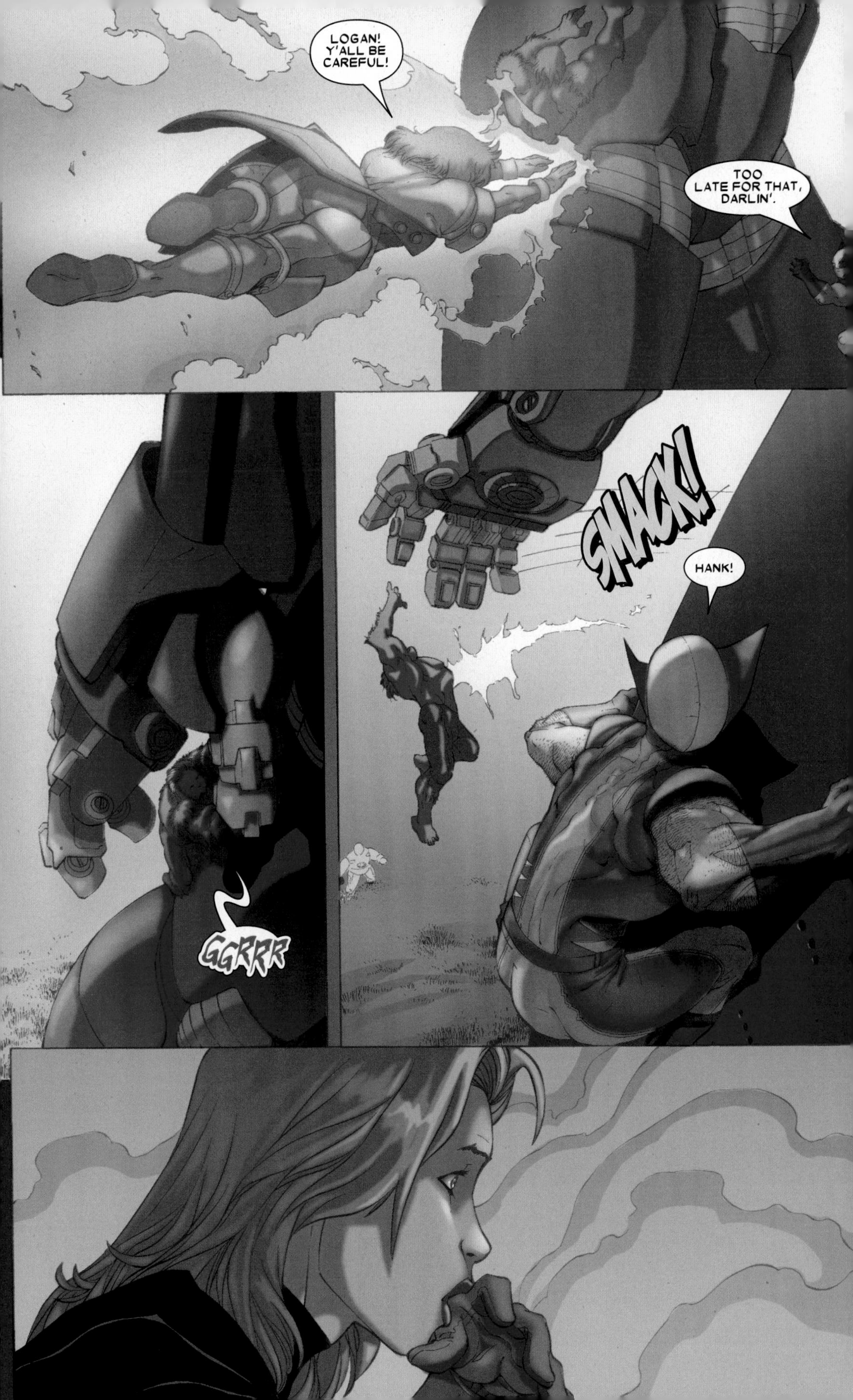
LOGAN! Y'ALL BE CAREFUL!
TOO LATE FOR THAT, DARLIN'.
GGRRR
SMACK!
HANK!

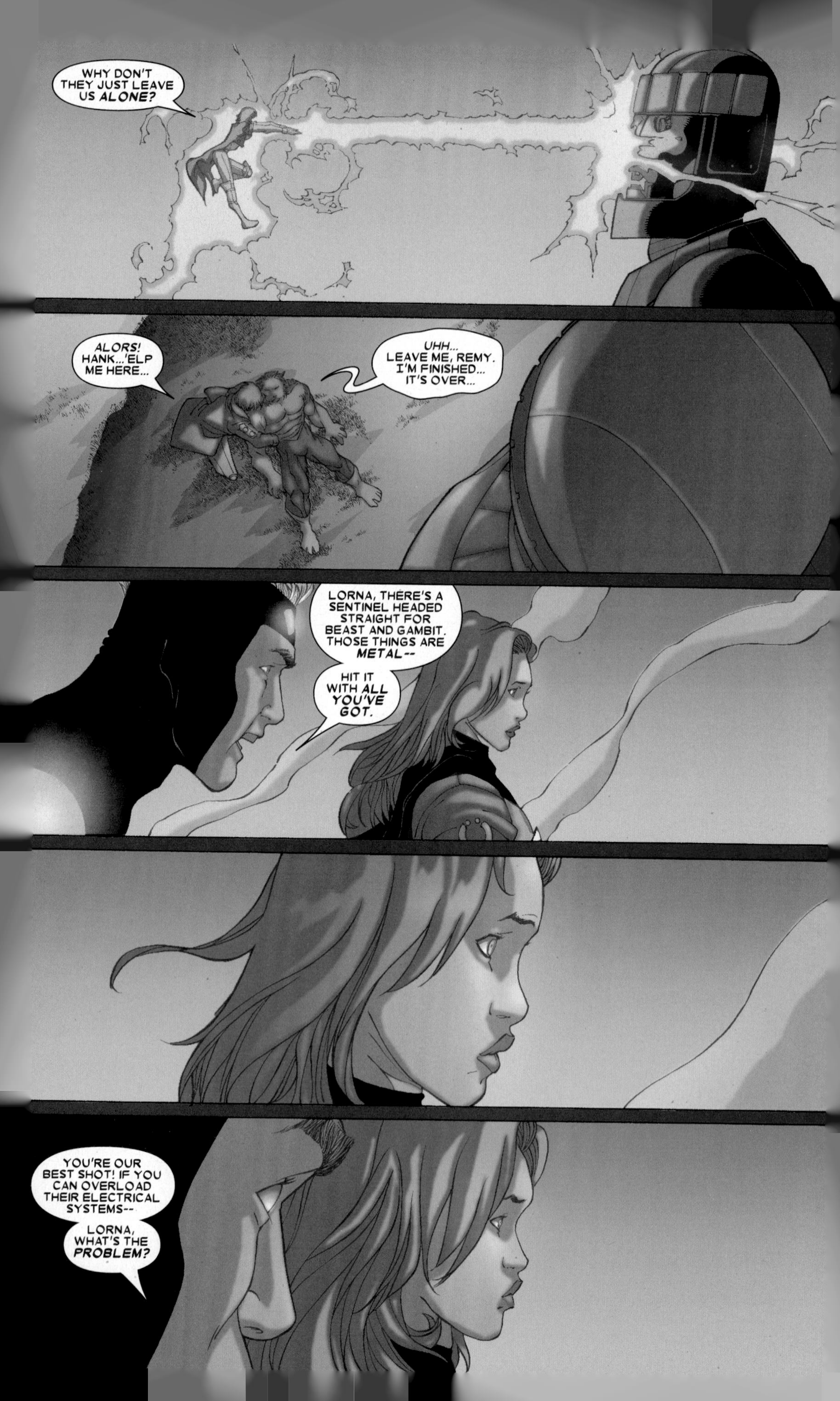
WHY DON'T THEY JUST LEAVE US ALONE?
ALORS! HANK...'ELP ME HERE...
UHH... LEAVE ME, REMY. I'M FINISHED... IT'S OVER...
LORNA, THERE'S A SENTINEL HEADED STRAIGHT FOR BEAST AND GAMBIT. THOSE THINGS ARE METAL--
HIT IT WITH ALL YOU'VE GOT.
YOU'RE OUR BEST SHOT! IF YOU CAN OVERLOAD THEIR ELECTRICAL SYSTEMS--
LORNA, WHAT'S THE PROBLEM?

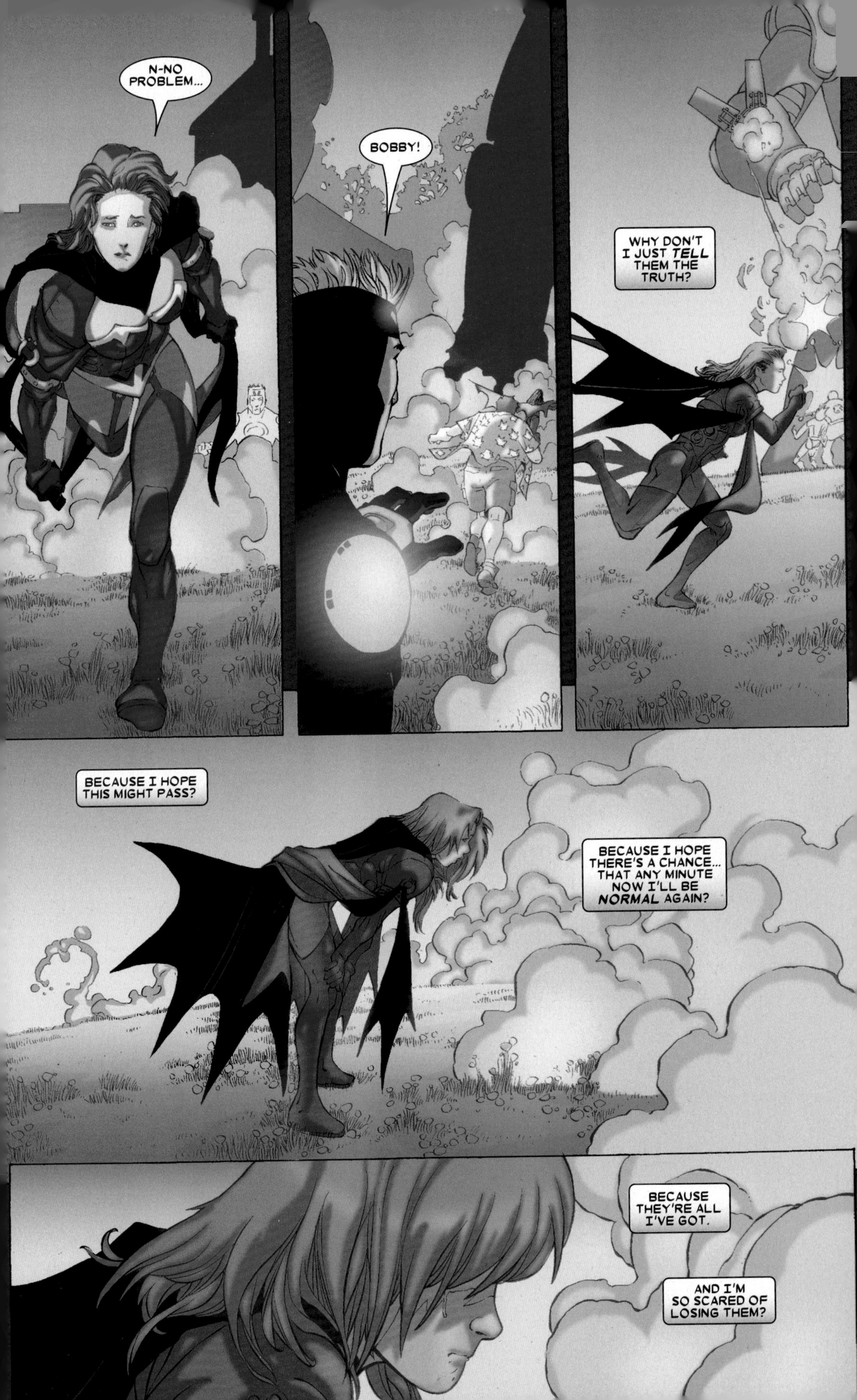

N-NO PROBLEM...
BOBBY!
WHY DON'T I JUST TELL THEM THE TRUTH?
BECAUSE I HOPE THIS MIGHT PASS?
BECAUSE I HOPE THERE'S A CHANCE... THAT ANY MINUTE NOW I'LL BE NORMAL AGAIN?
BECAUSE THEY'RE ALL I'VE GOT.
AND I'M SO SCARED OF LOSING THEM?

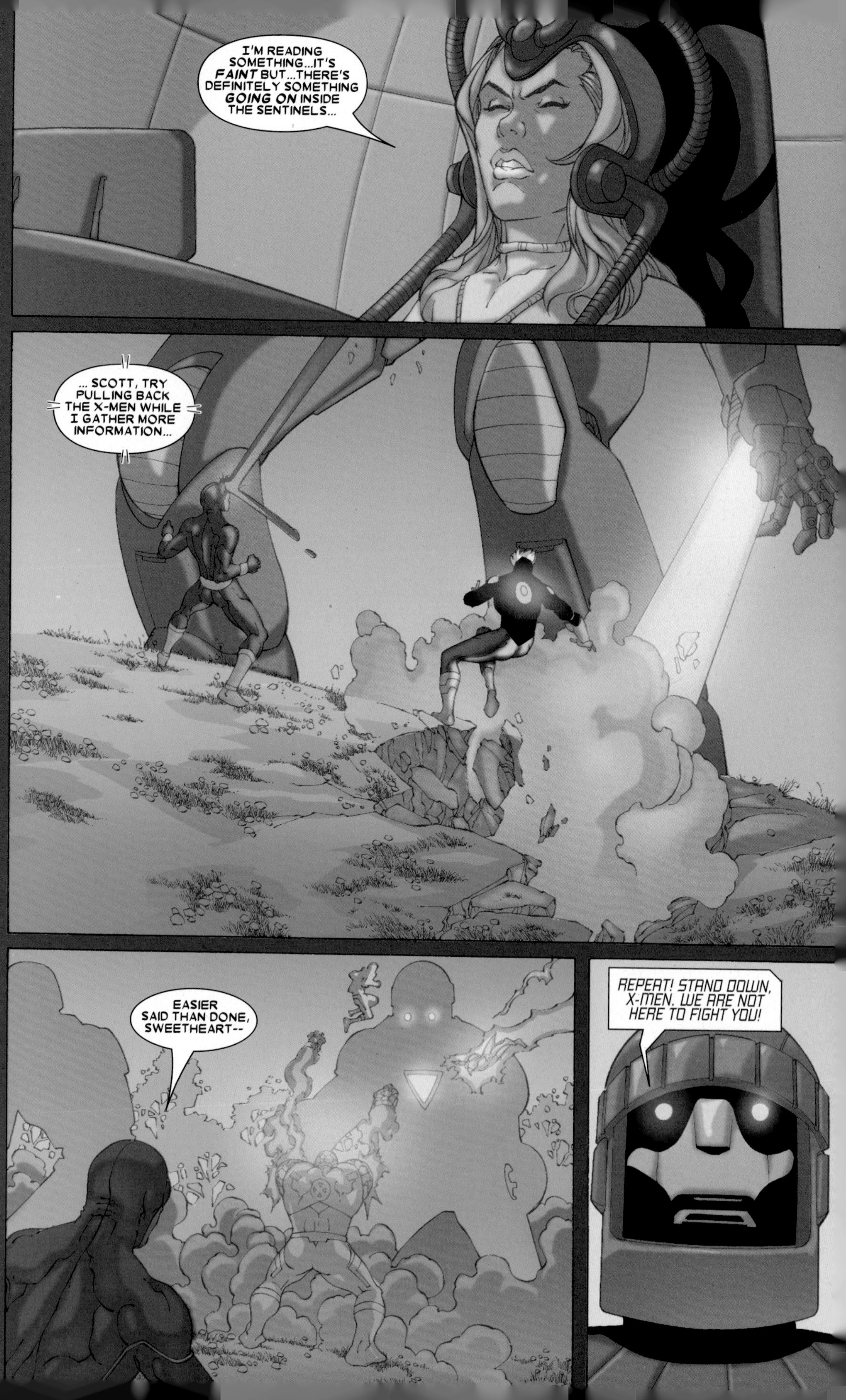
I'M READING SOMETHING...IT'S FAINT BUT...THERE'S DEFINITELY SOMETHING GOING ON INSIDE THE SENTINELS...
... SCOTT, TRY PULLING BACK THE X-MEN WHILE I GATHER MORE INFORMATION...
EASIER SAID THAN DONE, SWEETHEART--
REPEAT! STAND DOWN, X-MEN. WE ARE NOT HERE TO FIGHT YOU!

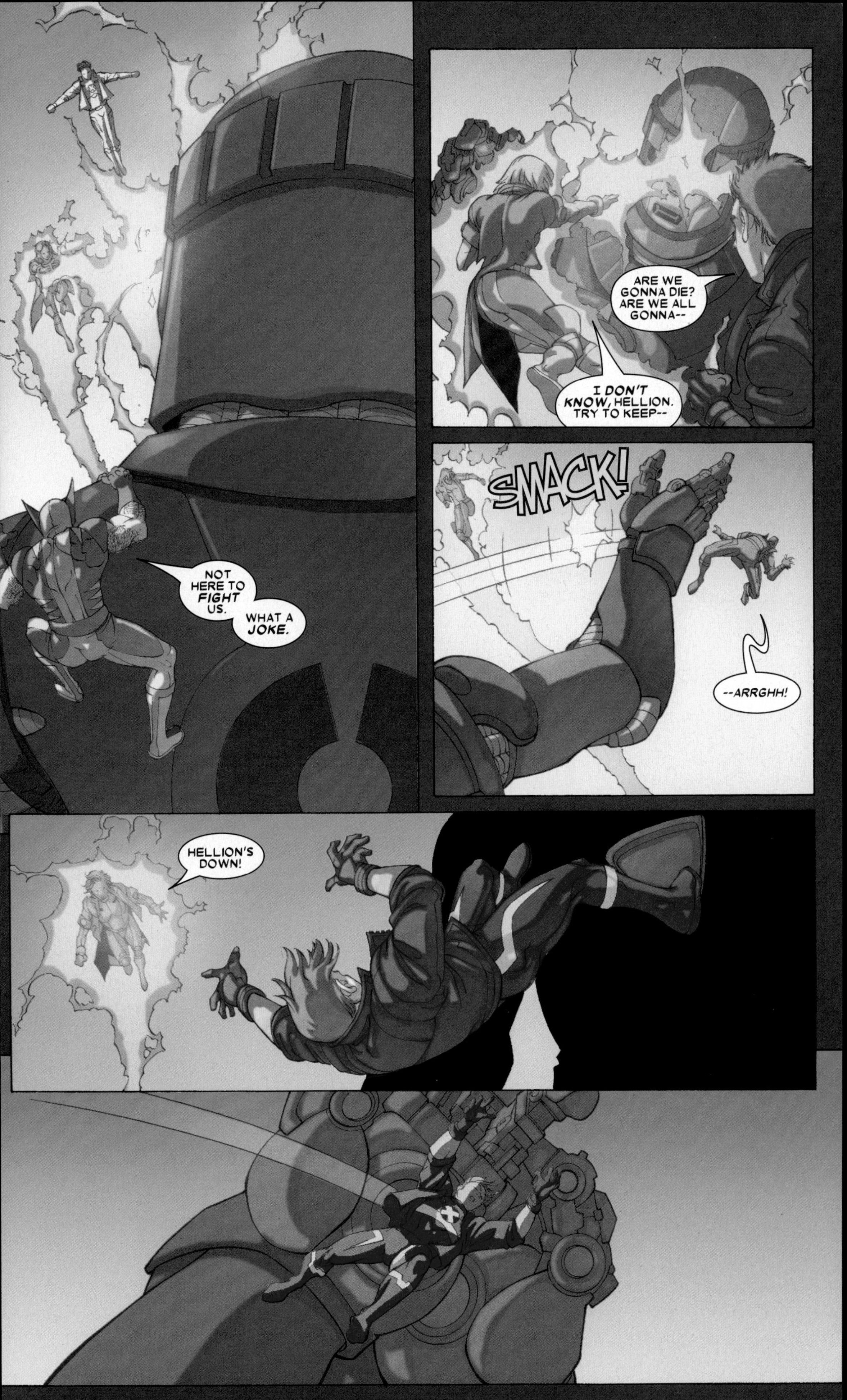
NOT HERE TO FIGHT US.
WHAT A JOKE.
ARE WE GONNA DIE? ARE WE ALL GONNA--
I DON'T KNOW, HELLION. TRY TO KEEP--
SMACK!
--ARRGHH!
HELLION'S DOWN!

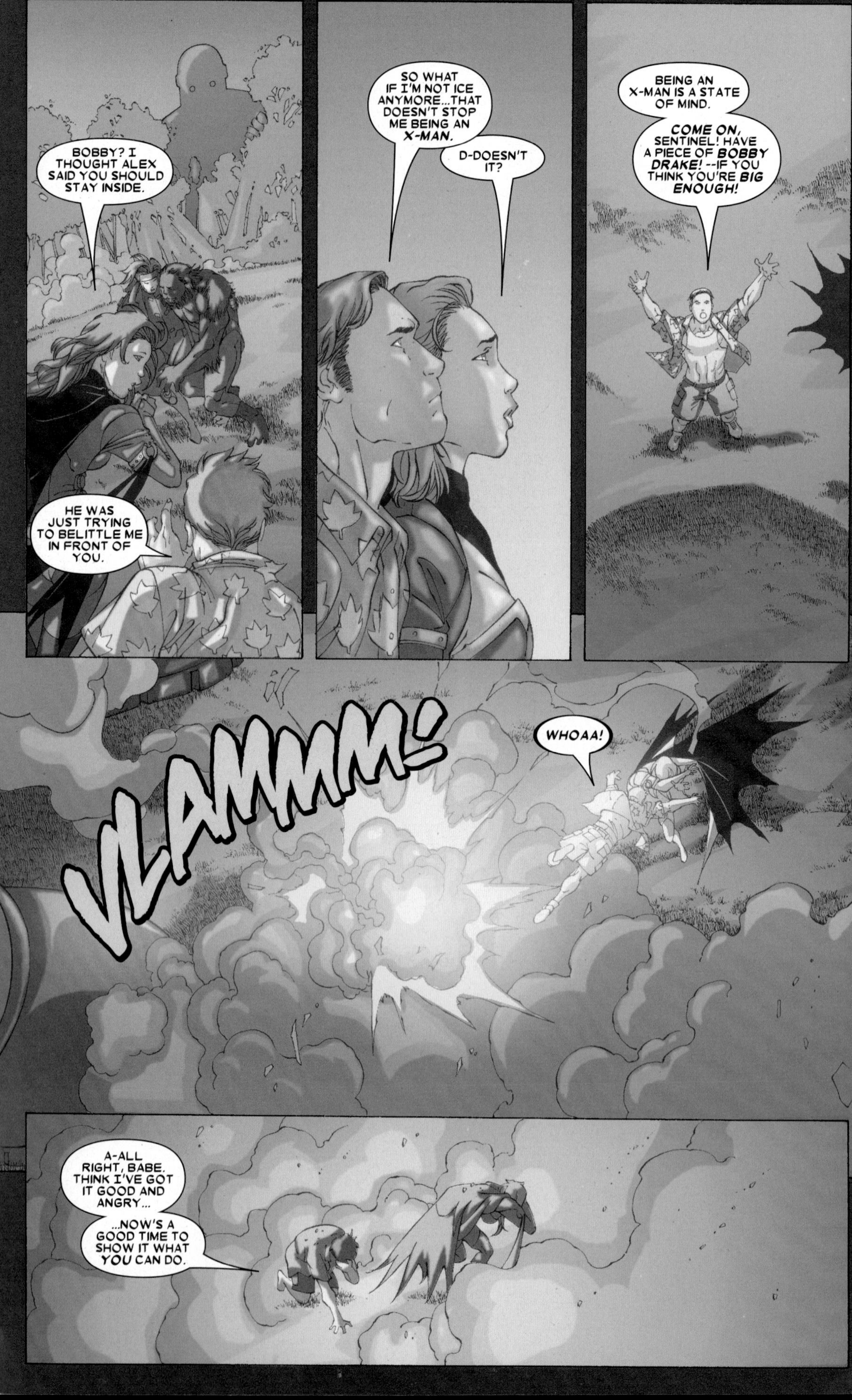
BOBBY? I THOUGHT ALEX SAID YOU SHOULD STAY INSIDE.
HE WAS JUST TRYING TO BELITTLE ME IN FRONT OF YOU.
SO WHAT IF I'M NOT ICE ANYMORE...THAT DOESN'T STOP ME BEING AN X-MAN.
D-DOESN'T IT?
BEING AN X-MAN IS A STATE OF MIND.
COME ON, SENTINEL! HAVE A PIECE OF BOBBY DRAKE! --IF YOU THINK YOU'RE BIG ENOUGH!
VLAMMM!
WHOAA!
A-ALL RIGHT, BABE. THINK I'VE GOT IT GOOD AND ANGRY...
...NOW'S A GOOD TIME TO SHOW IT WHAT YOU CAN DO.

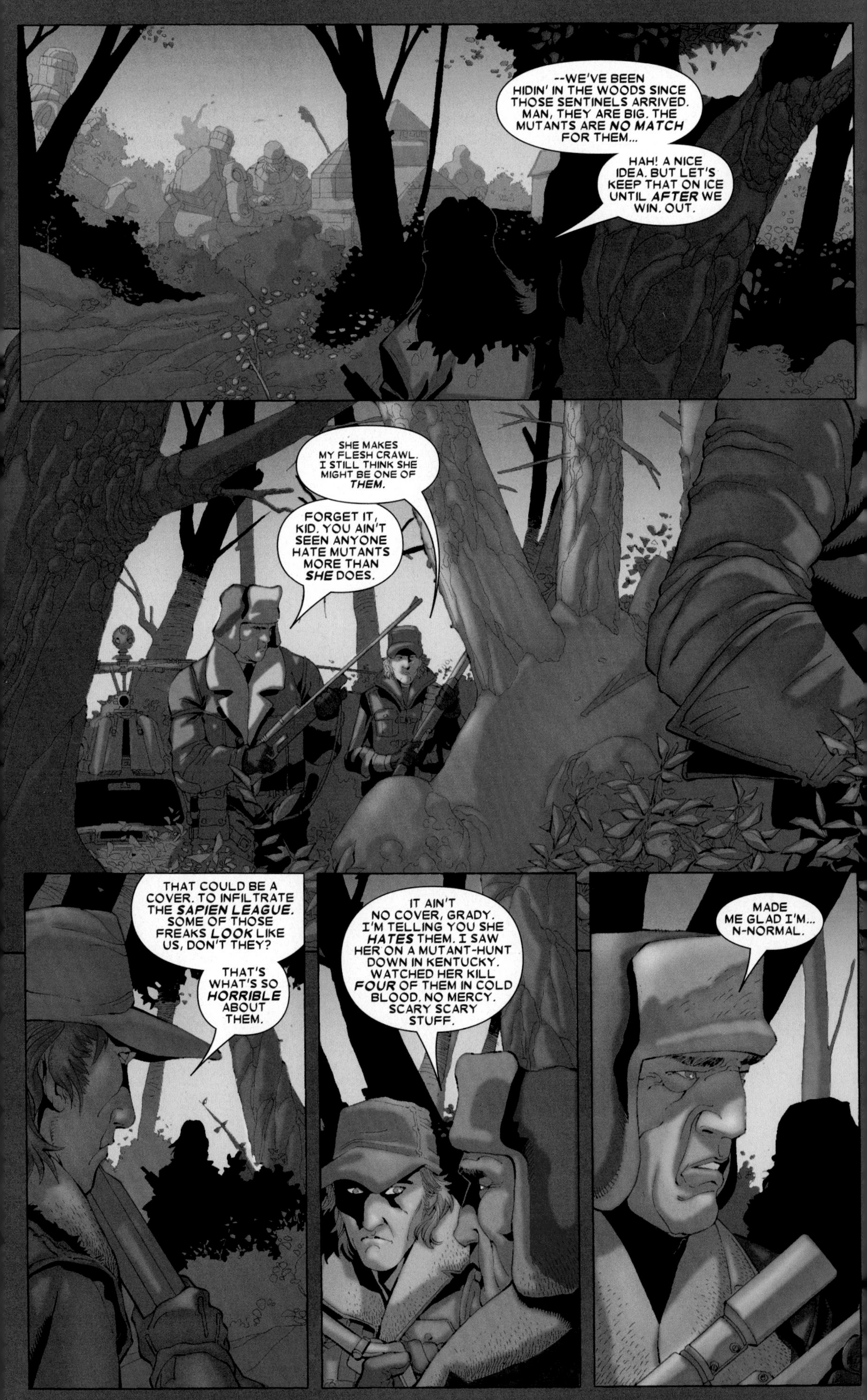
--WE'VE BEEN HIDIN' IN THE WOODS SINCE THOSE SENTINELS ARRIVED. MAN, THEY ARE BIG. THE MUTANTS ARE NO MATCH FOR THEM...
HAH! A NICE IDEA. BUT LET'S KEEP THAT ON ICE UNTIL AFTER WE WIN. OUT.
SHE MAKES MY FLESH CRAWL. I STILL THINK SHE MIGHT BE ONE OF THEM.
FORGET IT, KID. YOU AIN'T SEEN ANYONE HATE MUTANTS MORE THAN SHE DOES.
THAT COULD BE A COVER. TO INFILTRATE THE SAPIEN LEAGUE. SOME OF THOSE FREAKS LOOK LIKE US, DON'T THEY?
THAT'S WHAT'S SO HORRIBLE ABOUT THEM.
IT AIN'T NO COVER, GRADY. I'M TELLING YOU SHE HATES THEM. I SAW HER ON A MUTANT-HUNT DOWN IN KENTUCKY. WATCHED HER KILL FOUR OF THEM IN COLD BLOOD. NO MERCY. SCARY SCARY STUFF.
MADE ME GLAD I'M... N-NORMAL.

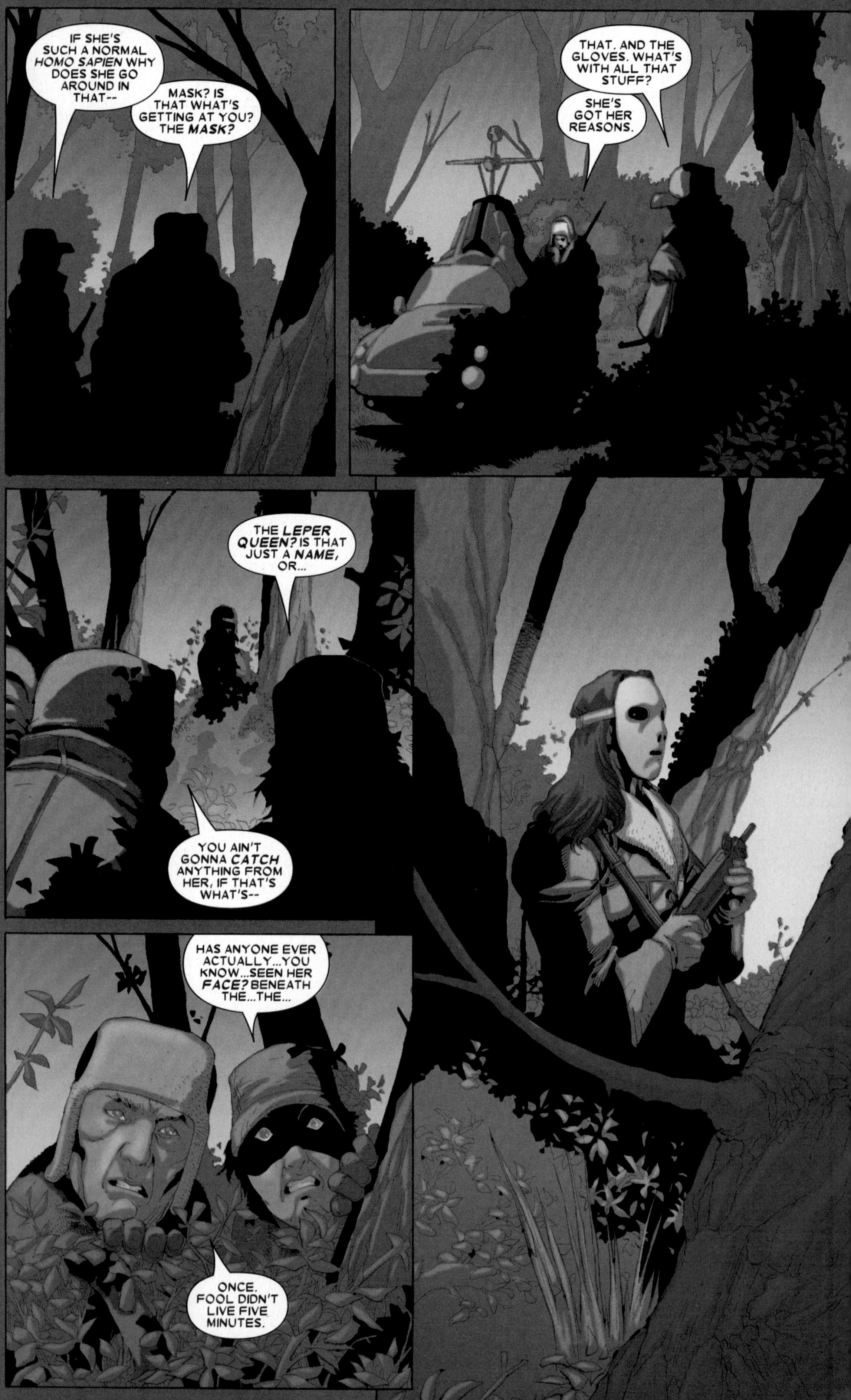
IF SHE'S SUCH A NORMAL HOMO SAPIEN WHY DOES SHE GO AROUND IN THAT--
MASK? IS THAT WHAT'S GETTING AT YOU? THE MASK?
THAT. AND THE GLOVES. WHAT'S WITH ALL THAT STUFF?
SHE'S GOT HER REASONS.
THE LEPER QUEEN? IS THAT JUST A NAME, OR...
YOU AIN'T GONNA CATCH ANYTHING FROM HER, IF THAT'S WHAT'S--
HAS ANYONE EVER ACTUALLY...YOU KNOW...SEEN HER FACE? BENEATH THE...THE...
ONCE. FOOL DIDN'T LIVE FIVE MINUTES.

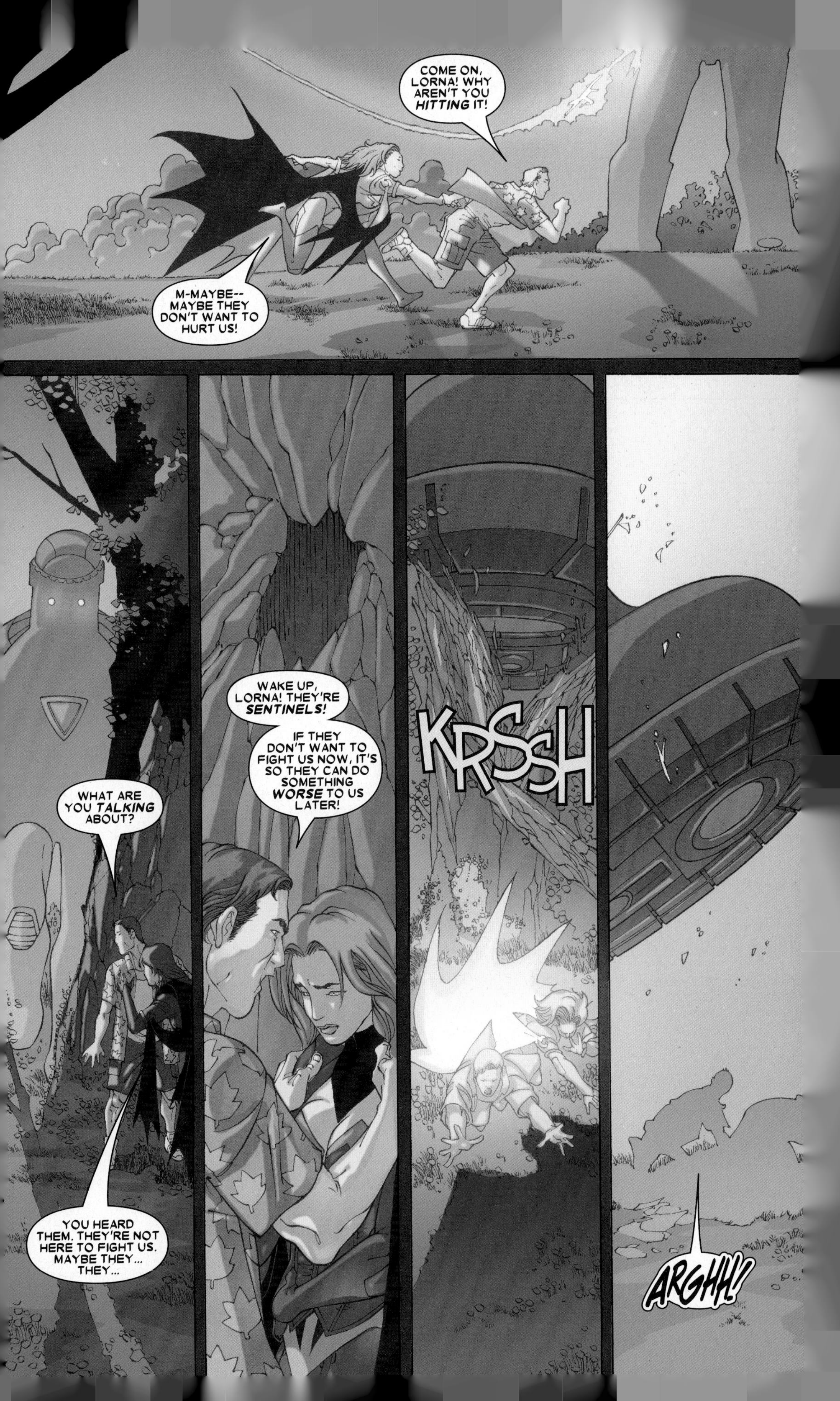
COME ON, LORNA! WHY AREN'T YOU HITTING IT!
M-MAYBE-- MAYBE THEY DON'T WANT TO HURT US!
WHAT ARE YOU TALKING ABOUT?
YOU HEARD THEM. THEY'RE NOT HERE TO FIGHT US. MAYBE THEY... THEY...
WAKE UP, LORNA! THEY'RE SENTINELS!
IF THEY DON'T WANT TO FIGHT US NOW, IT'S SO THEY CAN DO SOMETHING WORSE TO US LATER!
KRSSH
ARGHH!

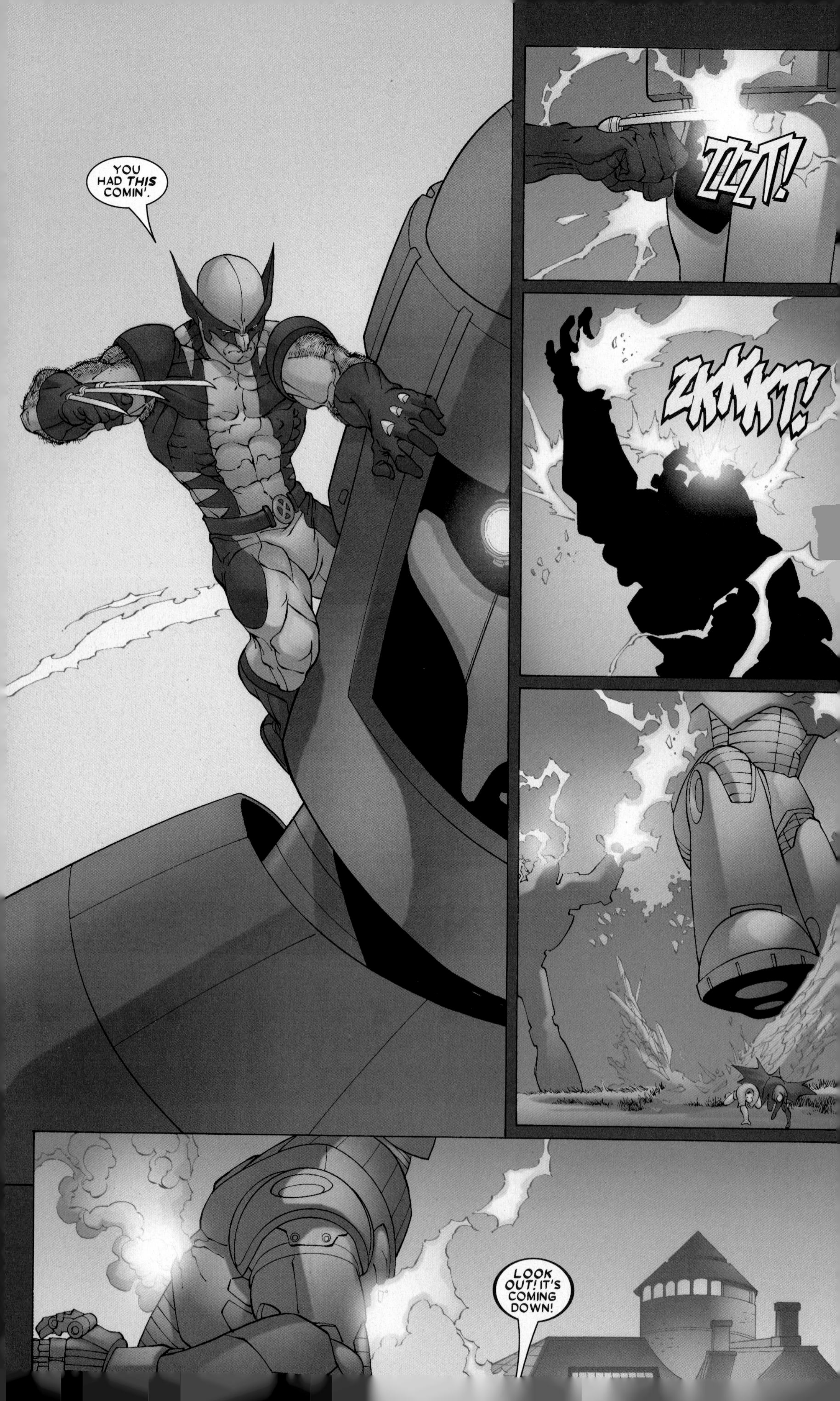

YOU HAD THIS COMIN'.
ZZZAT!
ZKKKT!
LOOK OUT! IT'S COMING DOWN!

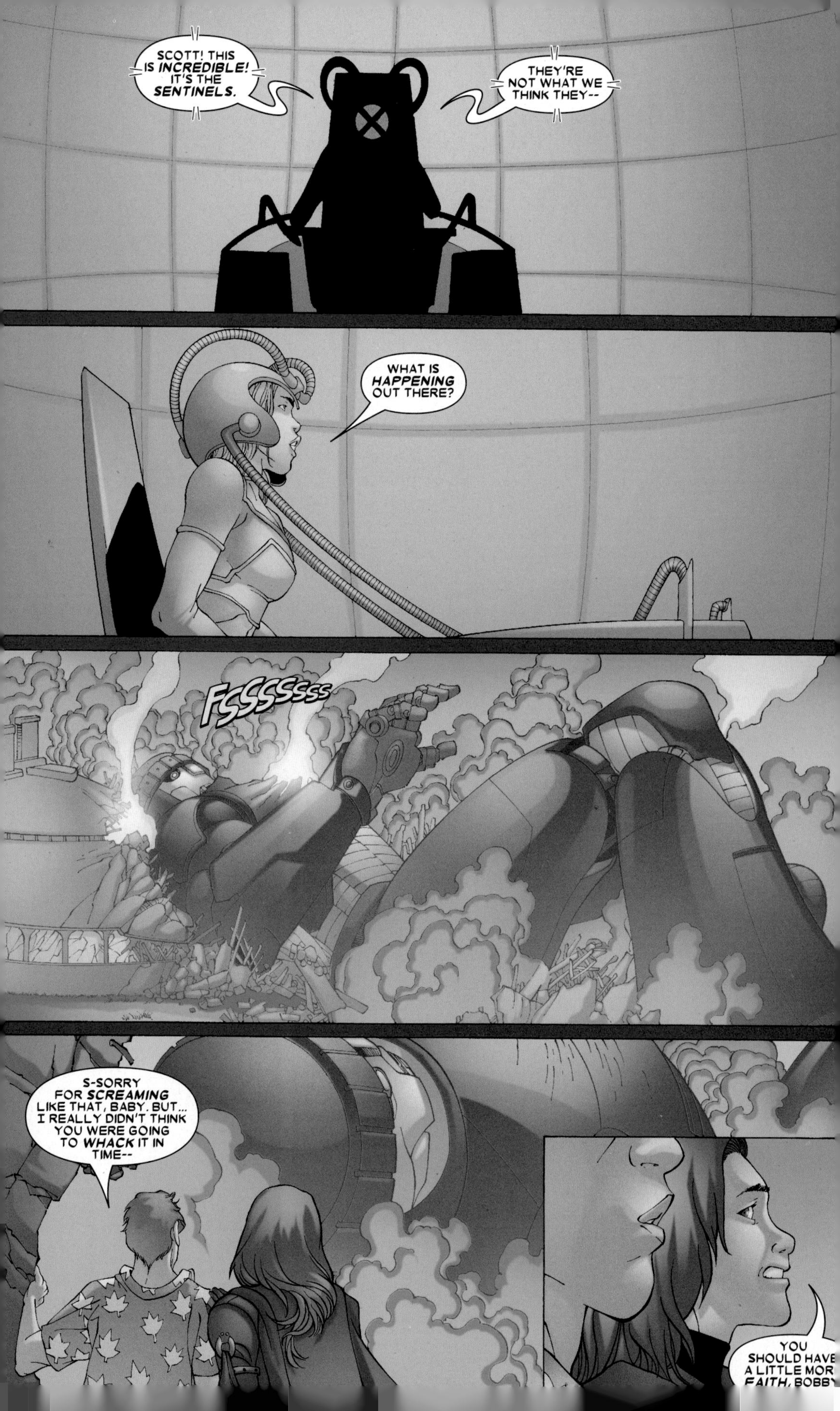

SCOTT! THIS IS INCREDIBLE! IT'S THE SENTINELS.
THEY'RE NOT WHAT WE THINK THEY--
WHAT IS HAPPENING OUT THERE?
FSSSSsss
S-SORRY FOR SCREAMING LIKE THAT, BABY. BUT... I REALLY DIDN'T THINK YOU WERE GOING TO WHACK IT IN TIME--
YOU SHOULD HAVE A LITTLE MOR FAITH, BOBBY

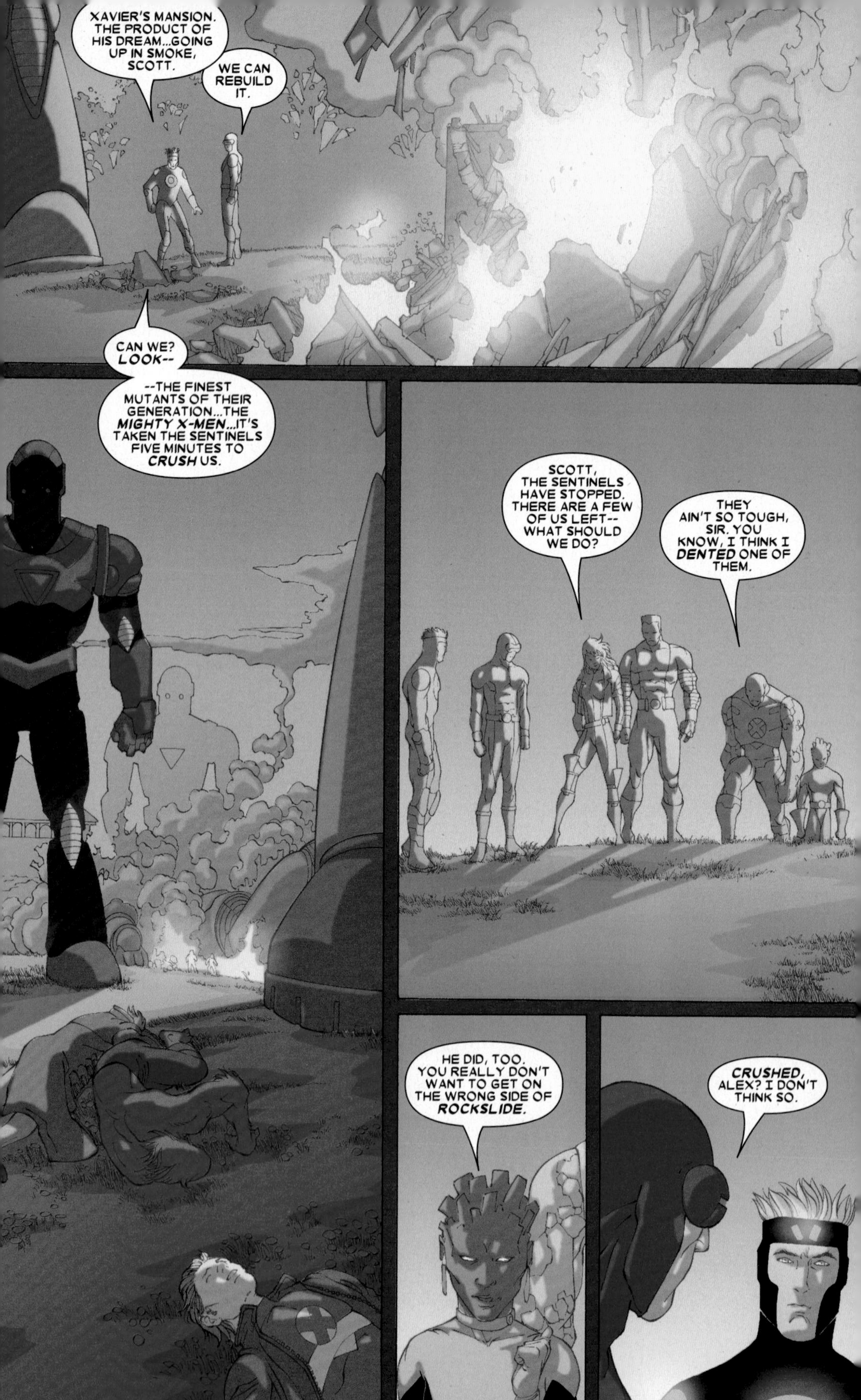

XAVIER'S MANSION. THE PRODUCT OF HIS DREAM...GOING UP IN SMOKE, SCOTT.
WE CAN REBUILD IT.
CAN WE? LOOK--
--THE FINEST MUTANTS OF THEIR GENERATION...THE MIGHTY X-MEN...IT'S TAKEN THE SENTINELS FIVE MINUTES TO CRUSH US.
SCOTT, THE SENTINELS HAVE STOPPED. THERE ARE A FEW OF US LEFT-- WHAT SHOULD WE DO?
THEY AIN'T SO TOUGH, SIR. YOU KNOW, I THINK I DENTED ONE OF THEM.
HE DID, TOO. YOU REALLY DON'T WANT TO GET ON THE WRONG SIDE OF ROCKSLIDE.
CRUSHED, ALEX? I DON'T THINK SO.

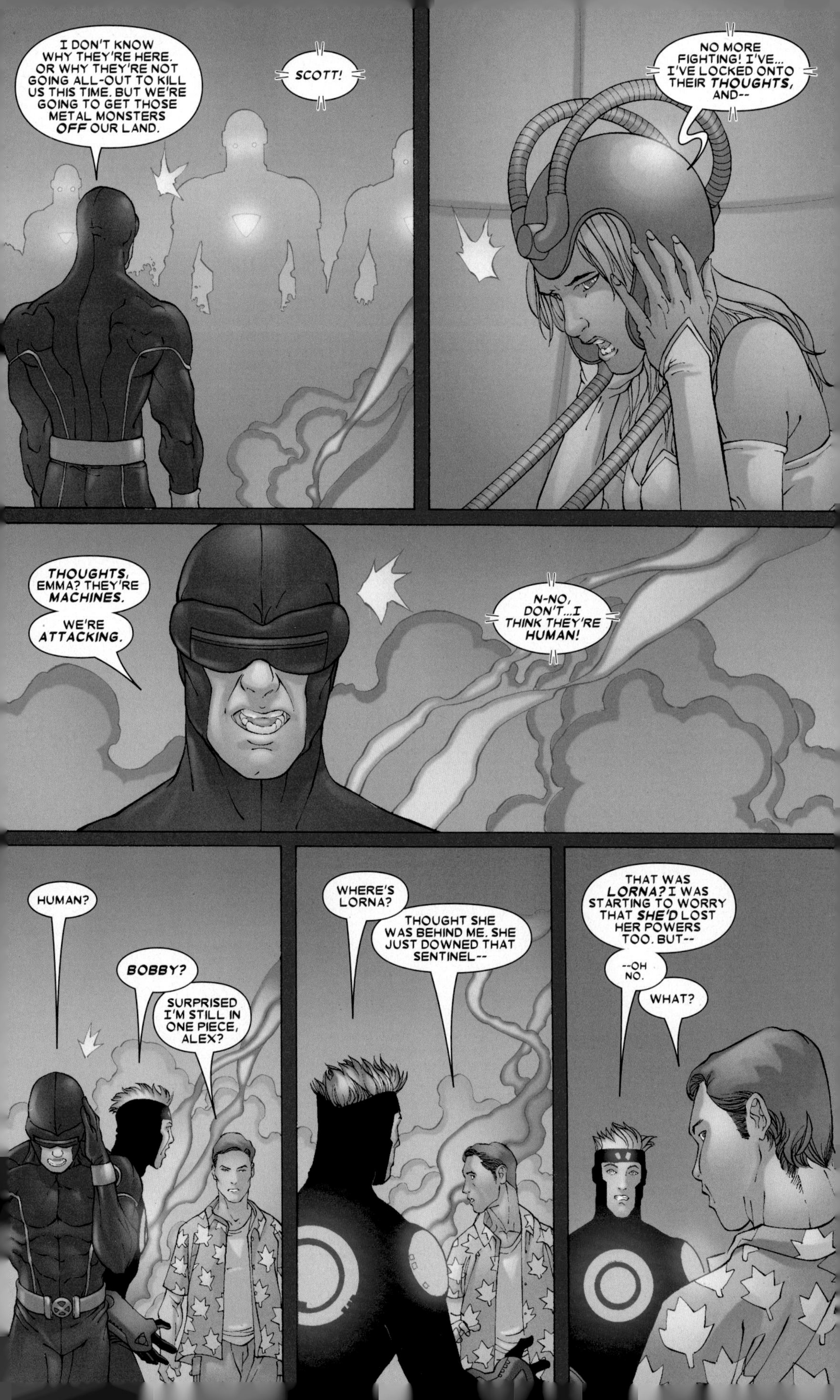
I DON'T KNOW WHY THEY'RE HERE. OR WHY THEY'RE NOT GOING ALL-OUT TO KILL US THIS TIME. BUT WE'RE GOING TO GET THOSE METAL MONSTERS OFF OUR LAND.
SCOTT!
NO MORE FIGHTING! I'VE... I'VE LOCKED ONTO THEIR THOUGHTS, AND--
THOUGHTS, EMMA? THEY'RE MACHINES.
WE'RE ATTACKING.
N-NO, DON'T...I THINK THEY'RE HUMAN!
HUMAN?
BOBBY?
SURPRISED I'M STILL IN ONE PIECE, ALEX?
WHERE'S LORNA?
THOUGHT SHE WAS BEHIND ME. SHE JUST DOWNED THAT SENTINEL--
THAT WAS LORNA? I WAS STARTING TO WORRY THAT SHE'D LOST HER POWERS TOO. BUT--
--OH NO.
WHAT?

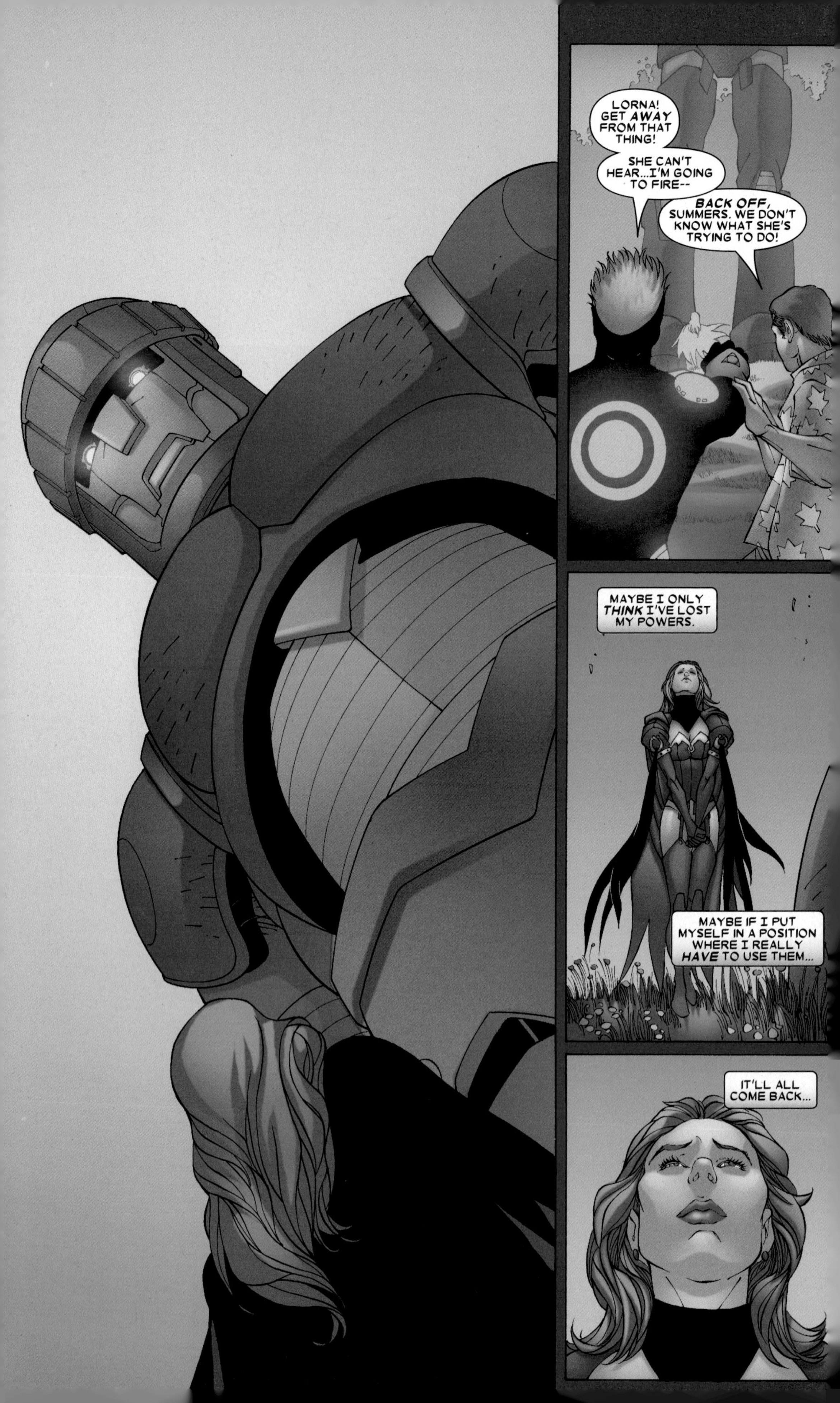

LORNA! GET AWAY FROM THAT THING!
SHE CAN'T HEAR...I'M GOING TO FIRE--
BACK OFF, SUMMERS. WE DON'T KNOW WHAT SHE'S TRYING TO DO!
MAYBE I ONLY THINK I'VE LOST MY POWERS.
MAYBE IF I PUT MYSELF IN A POSITION WHERE I REALLY HAVE TO USE THEM...
IT'LL ALL COME BACK...

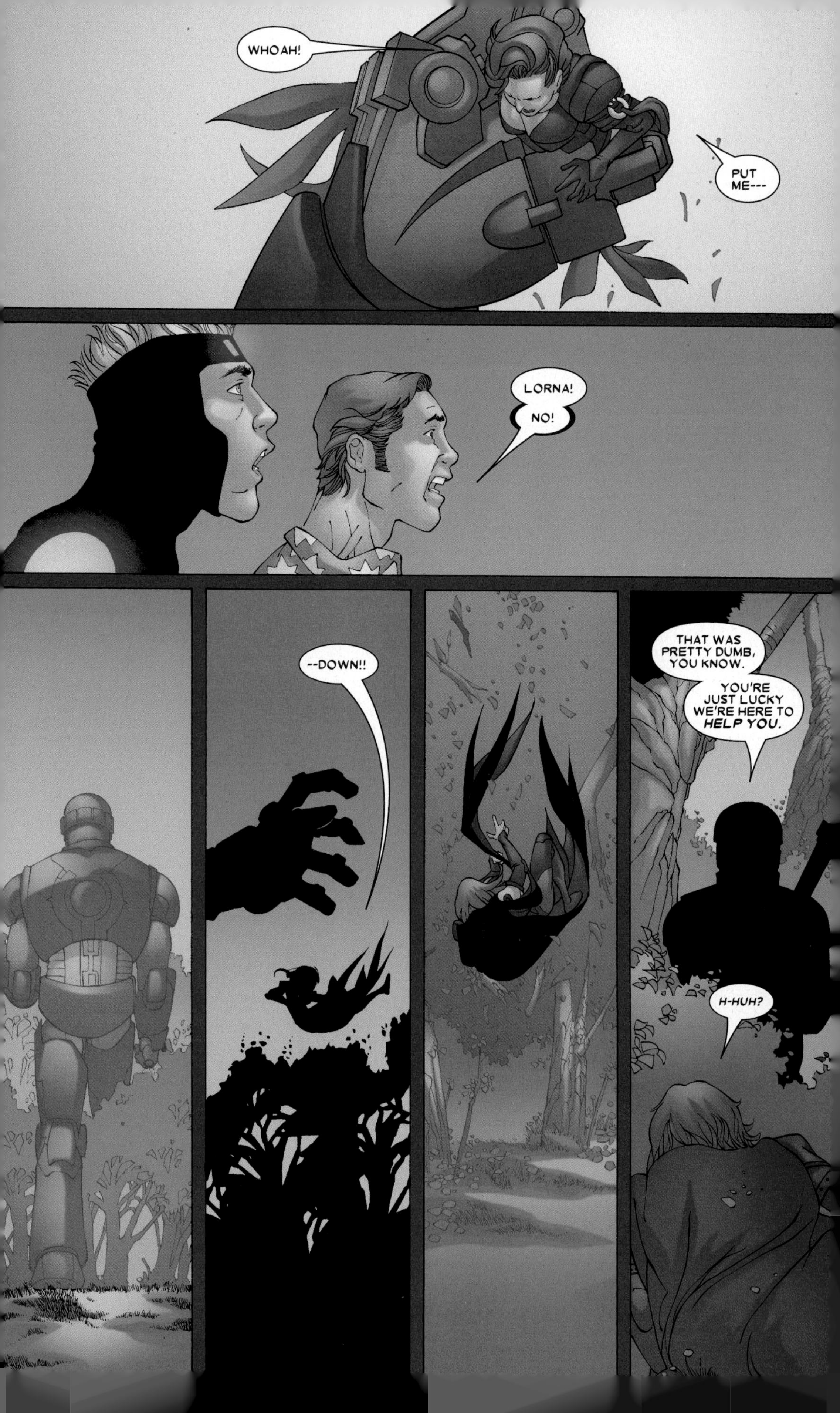
WHOAH!
PUT ME---
LORNA!
NO!
--DOWN!!
THAT WAS PRETTY DUMB, YOU KNOW.
YOU'RE JUST LUCKY WE'RE HERE TO *HELP YOU*.
H-HUH?

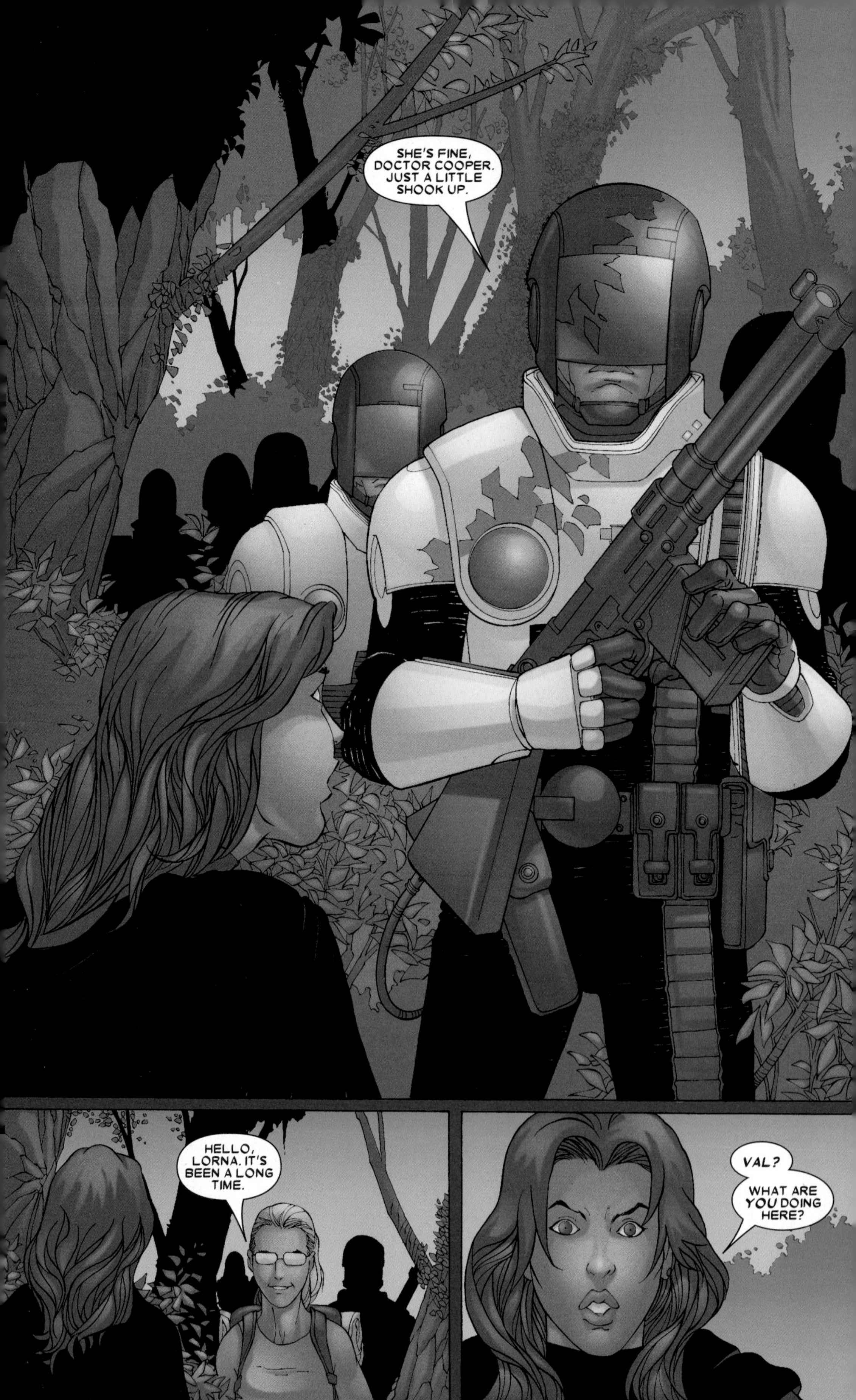
SHE'S FINE, DOCTOR COOPER. JUST A LITTLE SHOOK UP.
HELLO, LORNA. IT'S BEEN A LONG TIME.
VAL?
WHAT ARE YOU DOING HERE?

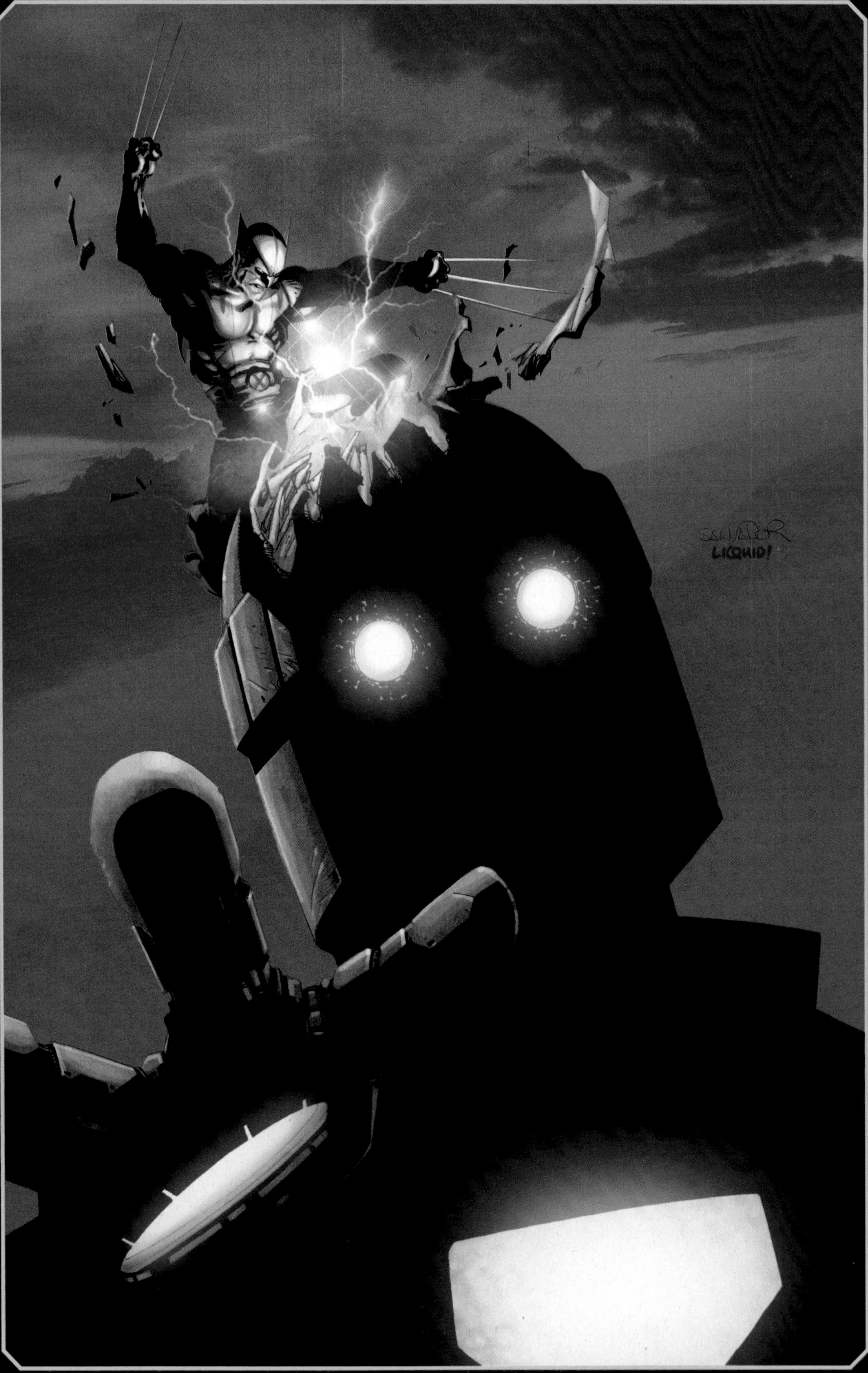
SALVADOR
LIQUID!

X-MEN #178

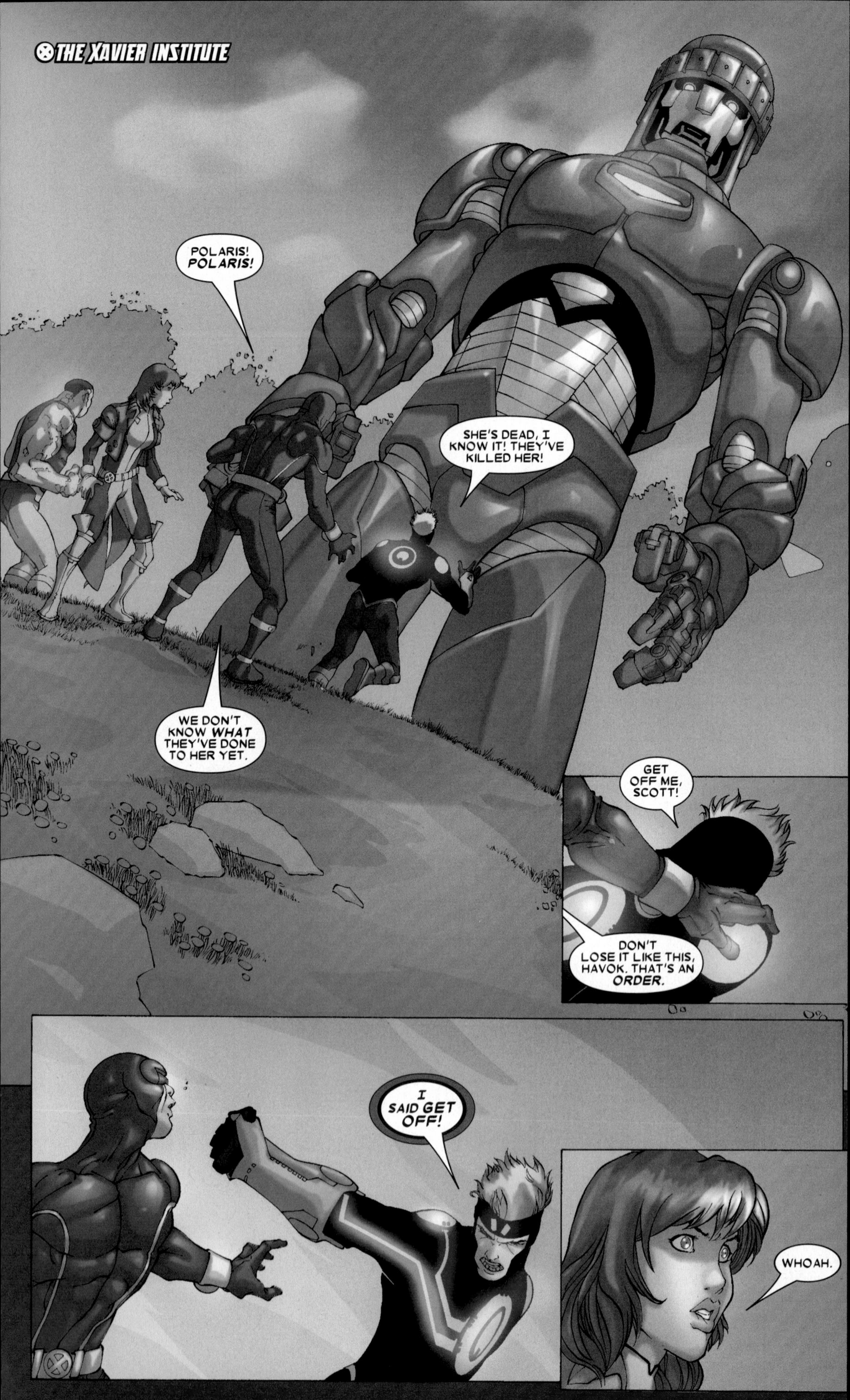
THE XAVIER INSTITUTE
POLARIS! POLARIS!
SHE'S DEAD, I KNOW IT! THEY'VE KILLED HER!
WE DON'T KNOW WHAT THEY'VE DONE TO HER YET.
GET OFF ME, SCOTT!
DON'T LOSE IT LIKE THIS, HAVOK. THAT'S AN ORDER.
I SAID GET OFF!
WHOAH.

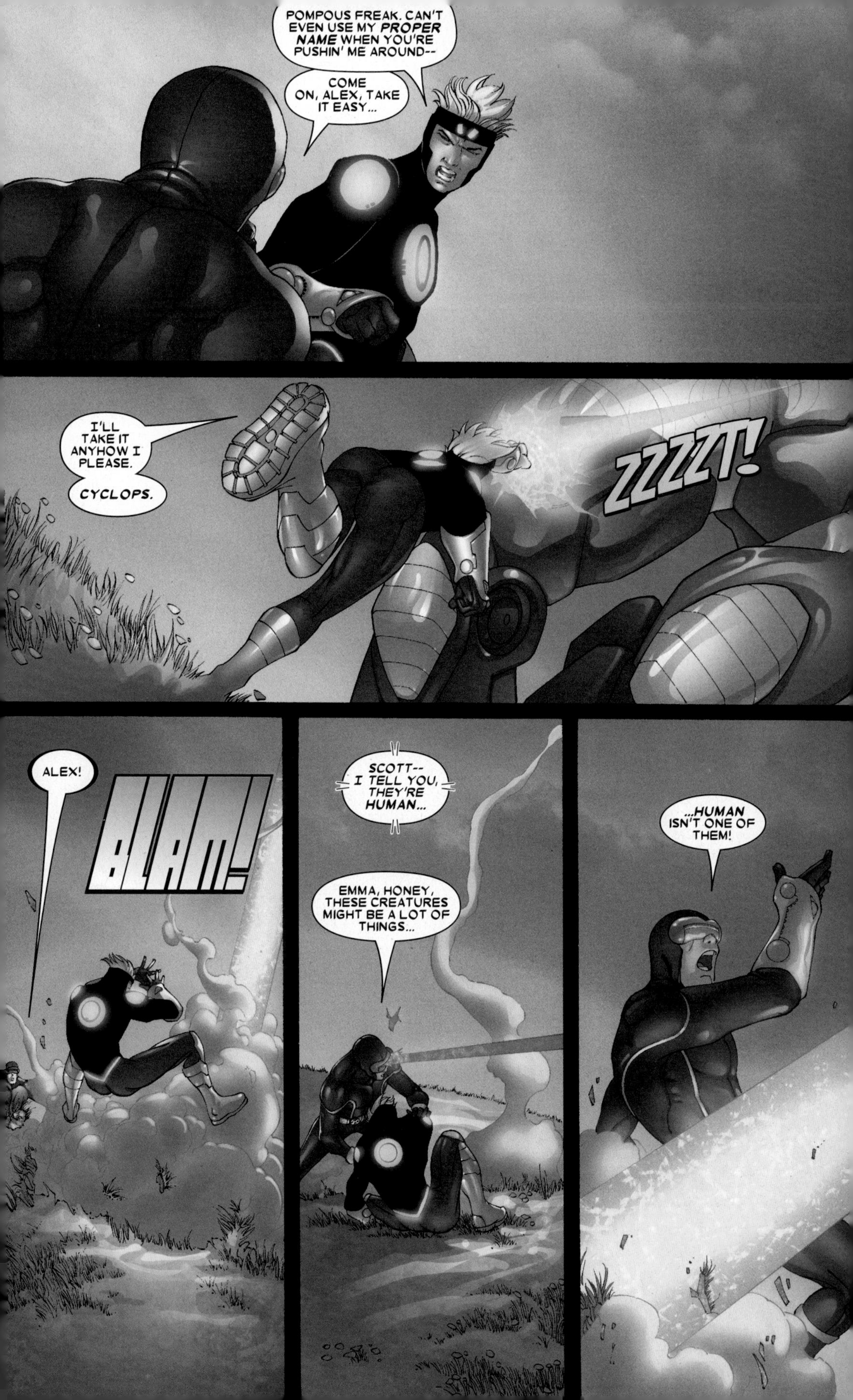

POMPOUS FREAK. CAN'T EVEN USE MY PROPER NAME WHEN YOU'RE PUSHIN' ME AROUND--
COME ON, ALEX, TAKE IT EASY...
I'LL TAKE IT ANYHOW I PLEASE.
CYCLOPS.
ZZZZT!
ALEX!
BLAM!
SCOTT-- I TELL YOU, THEY'RE HUMAN...
EMMA, HONEY, THESE CREATURES MIGHT BE A LOT OF THINGS...
...HUMAN ISN'T ONE OF THEM!

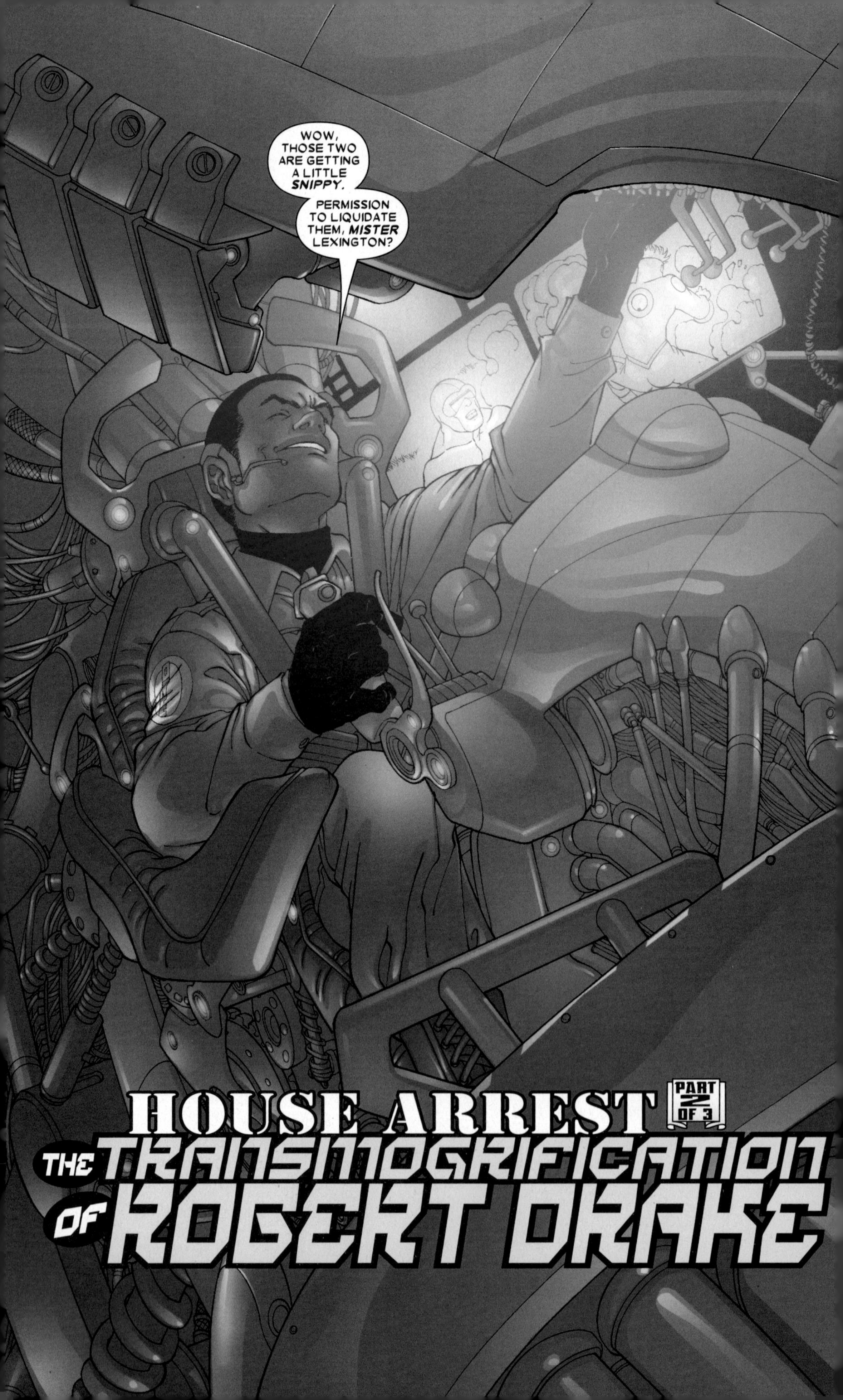

WOW, THOSE TWO ARE GETTING A LITTLE *SNIPPY*.
PERMISSION TO LIQUIDATE THEM, *MISTER* LEXINGTON?
HOUSE ARREST
PART 2 OF 3
THE TRANSMOGRIFICATION OF ROBERT DRAKE

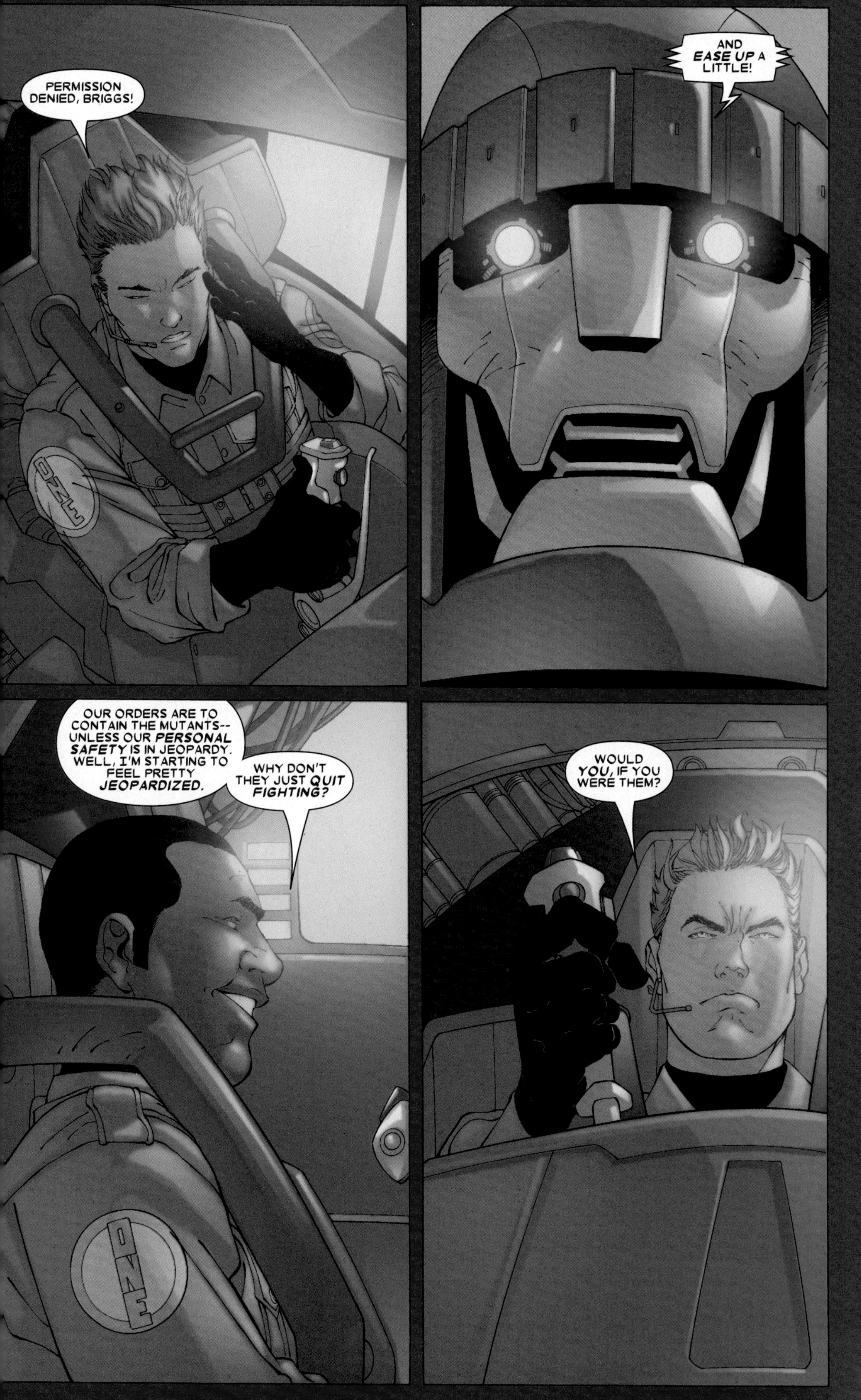

PERMISSION DENIED, BRIGGS!
AND EASE UP A LITTLE!
OUR ORDERS ARE TO CONTAIN THE MUTANTS-- UNLESS OUR PERSONAL SAFETY IS IN JEOPARDY. WELL, I'M STARTING TO FEEL PRETTY JEOPARDIZED.
WHY DON'T THEY JUST QUIT FIGHTING?
WOULD YOU, IF YOU WERE THEM?
ONE
ONE

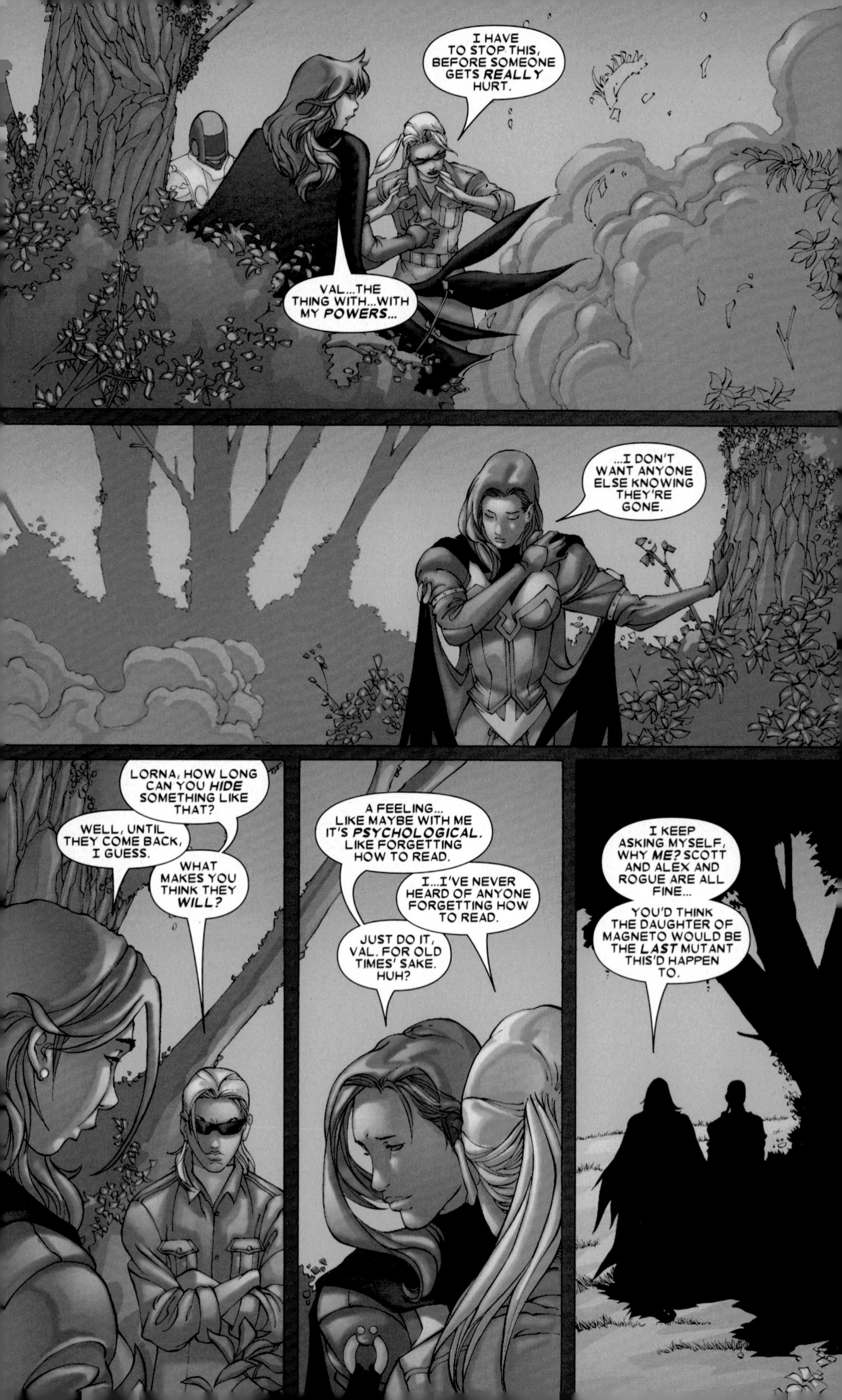
I HAVE TO STOP THIS, BEFORE SOMEONE GETS REALLY HURT.
VAL...THE THING WITH...WITH MY POWERS...
...I DON'T WANT ANYONE ELSE KNOWING THEY'RE GONE.
LORNA, HOW LONG CAN YOU HIDE SOMETHING LIKE THAT?
WELL, UNTIL THEY COME BACK, I GUESS.
WHAT MAKES YOU THINK THEY WILL?
A FEELING... LIKE MAYBE WITH ME IT'S PSYCHOLOGICAL. LIKE FORGETTING HOW TO READ.
I...I'VE NEVER HEARD OF ANYONE FORGETTING HOW TO READ.
JUST DO IT, VAL. FOR OLD TIMES' SAKE. HUH?
I KEEP ASKING MYSELF, WHY ME? SCOTT AND ALEX AND ROGUE ARE ALL FINE...
YOU'D THINK THE DAUGHTER OF MAGNETO WOULD BE THE LAST MUTANT THIS'D HAPPEN TO.

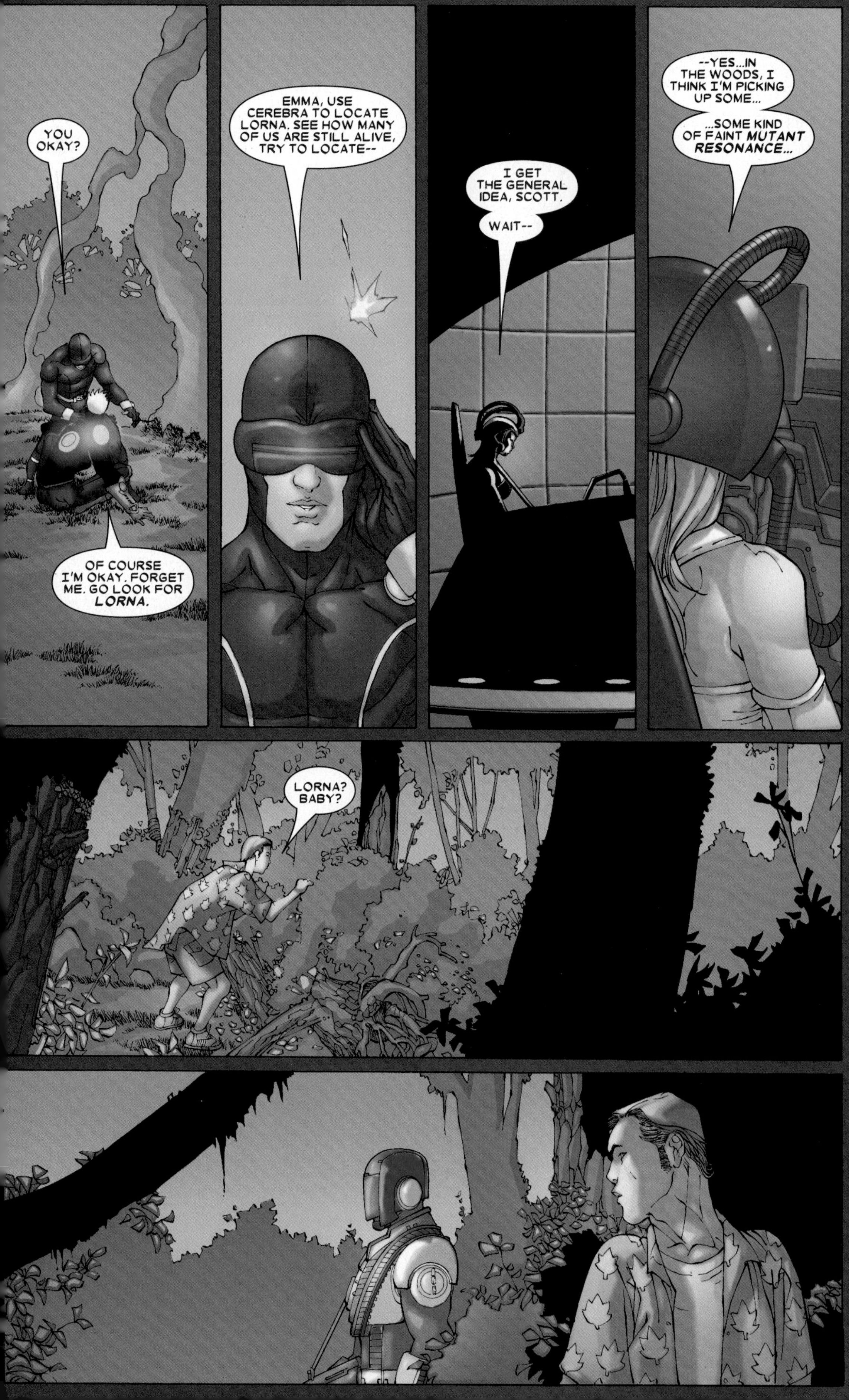
YOU OKAY?
OF COURSE I'M OKAY. FORGET ME. GO LOOK FOR LORNA.
EMMA, USE CEREBRA TO LOCATE LORNA. SEE HOW MANY OF US ARE STILL ALIVE, TRY TO LOCATE--
I GET THE GENERAL IDEA, SCOTT.
WAIT--
--YES...IN THE WOODS, I THINK I'M PICKING UP SOME...
...SOME KIND OF FAINT MUTANT RESONANCE...
LORNA? BABY?

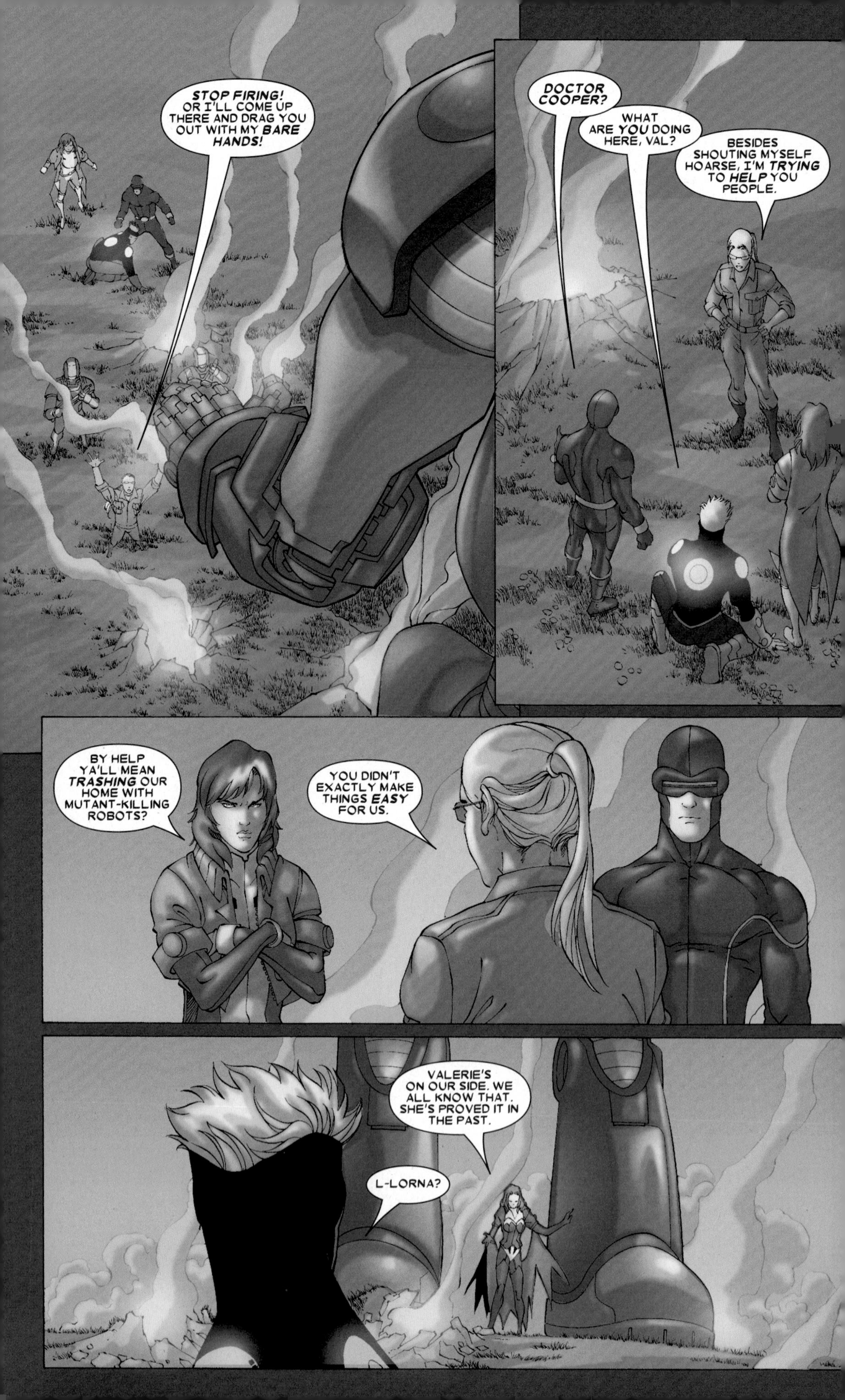
STOP FIRING! OR I'LL COME UP THERE AND DRAG YOU OUT WITH MY BARE HANDS!
DOCTOR COOPER?
WHAT ARE YOU DOING HERE, VAL?
BESIDES SHOUTING MYSELF HOARSE, I'M TRYING TO HELP YOU PEOPLE.
BY HELP YA'LL MEAN TRASHING OUR HOME WITH MUTANT-KILLING ROBOTS?
YOU DIDN'T EXACTLY MAKE THINGS EASY FOR US.
VALERIE'S ON OUR SIDE. WE ALL KNOW THAT. SHE'S PROVED IT IN THE PAST.
L-LORNA?

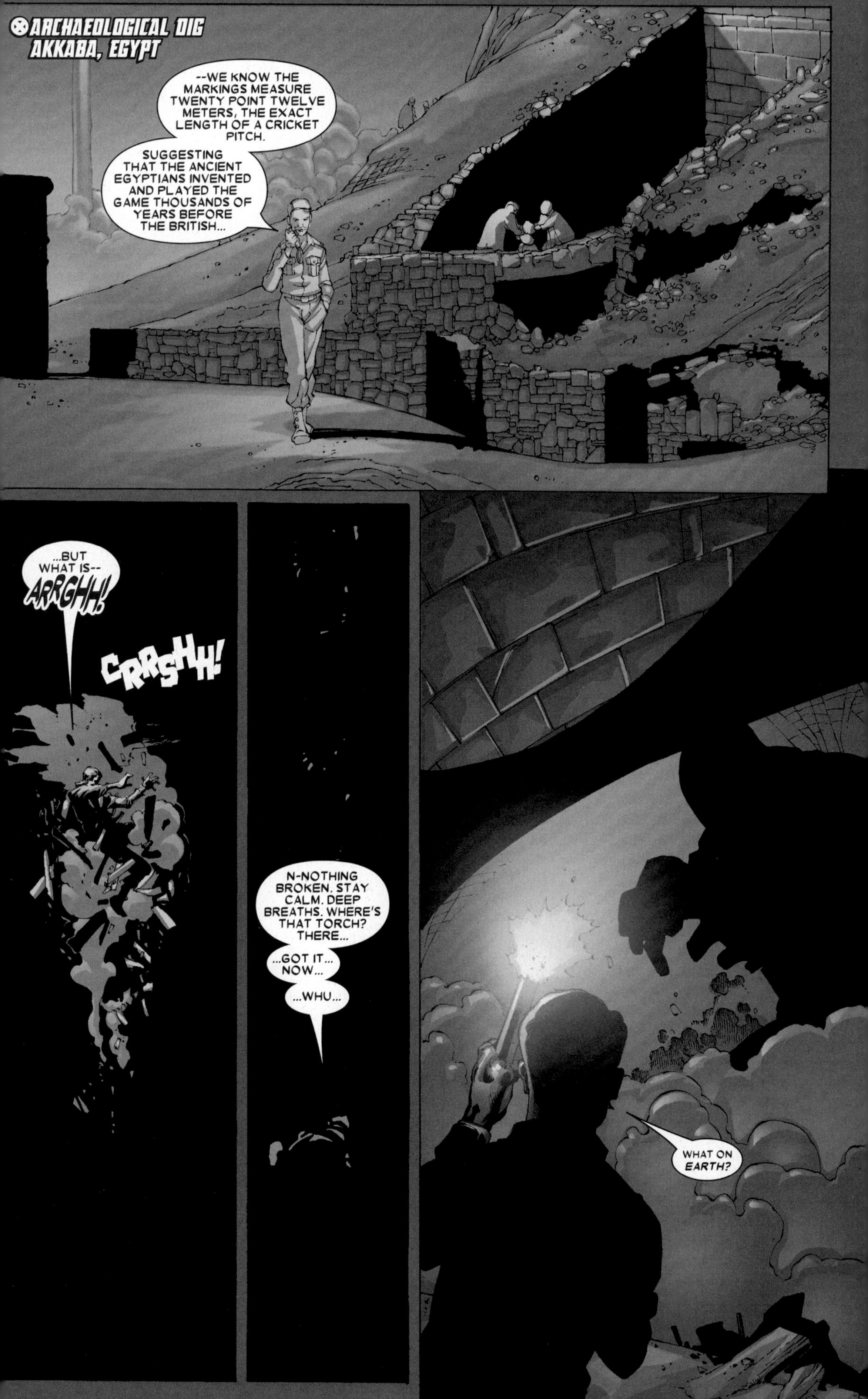
ARCHAEOLOGICAL DIG
AKKABA, EGYPT
--WE KNOW THE MARKINGS MEASURE TWENTY POINT TWELVE METERS, THE EXACT LENGTH OF A CRICKET PITCH.
SUGGESTING THAT THE ANCIENT EGYPTIANS INVENTED AND PLAYED THE GAME THOUSANDS OF YEARS BEFORE THE BRITISH...
...BUT WHAT IS-- ARRGHH!
CRRSHH!
N-NOTHING BROKEN. STAY CALM. DEEP BREATHS. WHERE'S THAT TORCH? THERE...
...GOT IT... NOW...
...WHU...
WHAT ON EARTH?

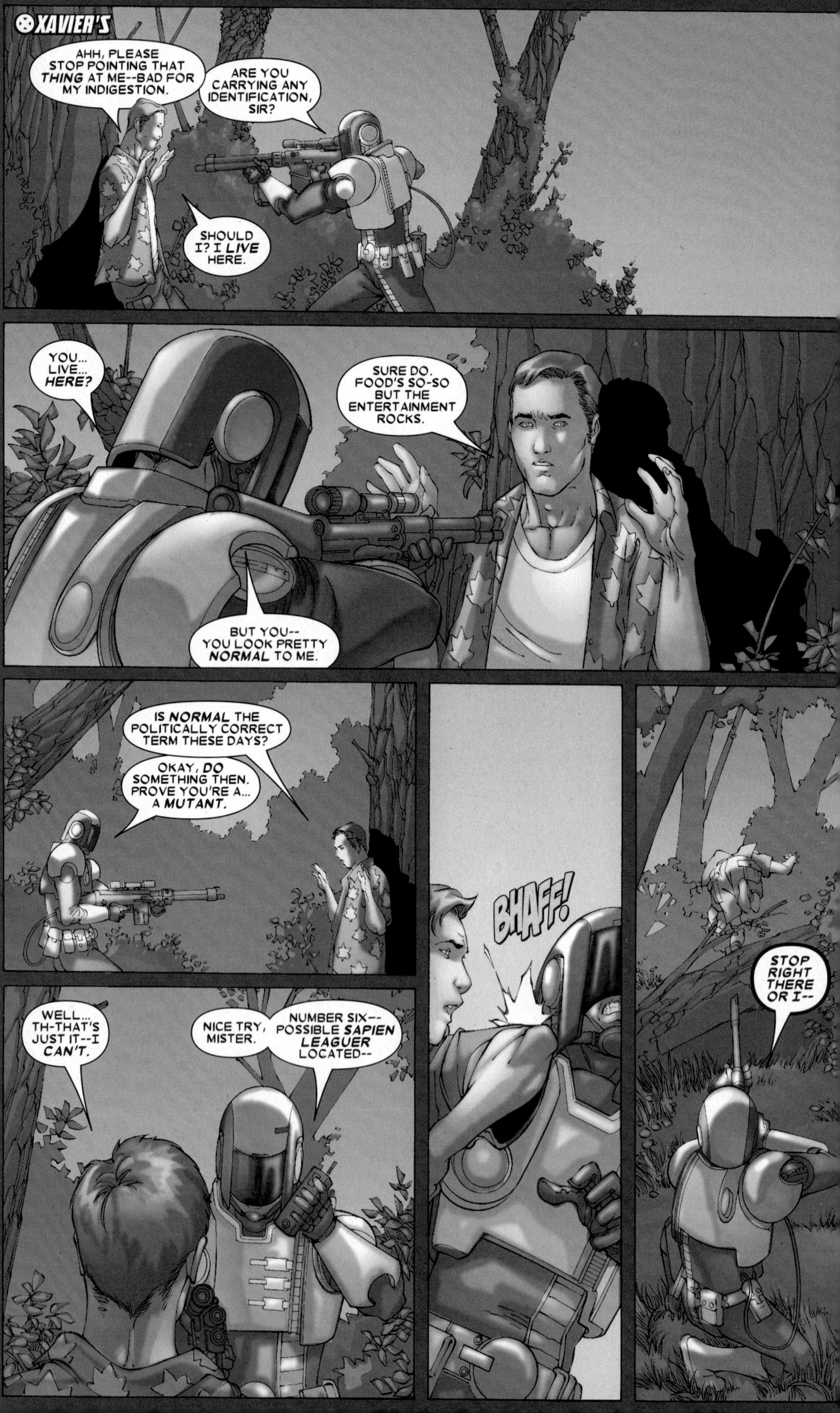
XAVIER'S
AHH, PLEASE STOP POINTING THAT THING AT ME--BAD FOR MY INDIGESTION.
ARE YOU CARRYING ANY IDENTIFICATION, SIR?
SHOULD I? I LIVE HERE.
YOU... LIVE... HERE?
SURE DO. FOOD'S SO-SO BUT THE ENTERTAINMENT ROCKS.
BUT YOU-- YOU LOOK PRETTY NORMAL TO ME.
IS NORMAL THE POLITICALLY CORRECT TERM THESE DAYS?
OKAY, DO SOMETHING THEN. PROVE YOU'RE A... A MUTANT.
WELL... TH-THAT'S JUST IT--I CAN'T.
NICE TRY, MISTER.
NUMBER SIX-- POSSIBLE SAPIEN LEAGUER LOCATED--
BHAFF!
STOP RIGHT THERE OR I--

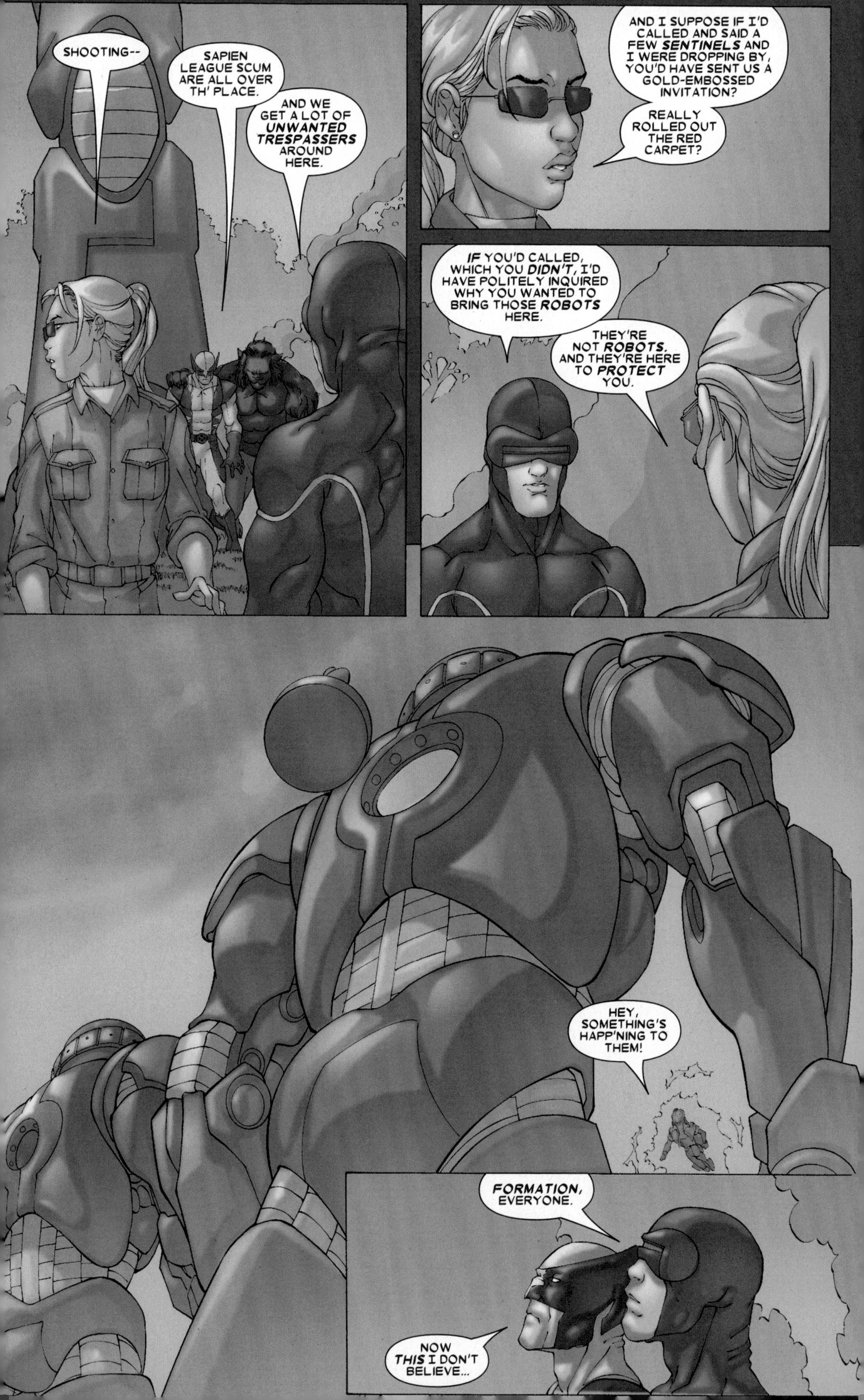

SHOOTING--
SAPIEN LEAGUE SCUM ARE ALL OVER TH' PLACE.
AND WE GET A LOT OF UNWANTED TRESPASSERS AROUND HERE.
AND I SUPPOSE IF I'D CALLED AND SAID A FEW SENTINELS AND I WERE DROPPING BY, YOU'D HAVE SENT US A GOLD-EMBOSSED INVITATION?
REALLY ROLLED OUT THE RED CARPET?
IF YOU'D CALLED, WHICH YOU DIDN'T, I'D HAVE POLITELY INQUIRED WHY YOU WANTED TO BRING THOSE ROBOTS HERE.
THEY'RE NOT ROBOTS. AND THEY'RE HERE TO PROTECT YOU.
HEY, SOMETHING'S HAPP'NING TO THEM!
FORMATION, EVERYONE.
NOW THIS I DON'T BELIEVE...

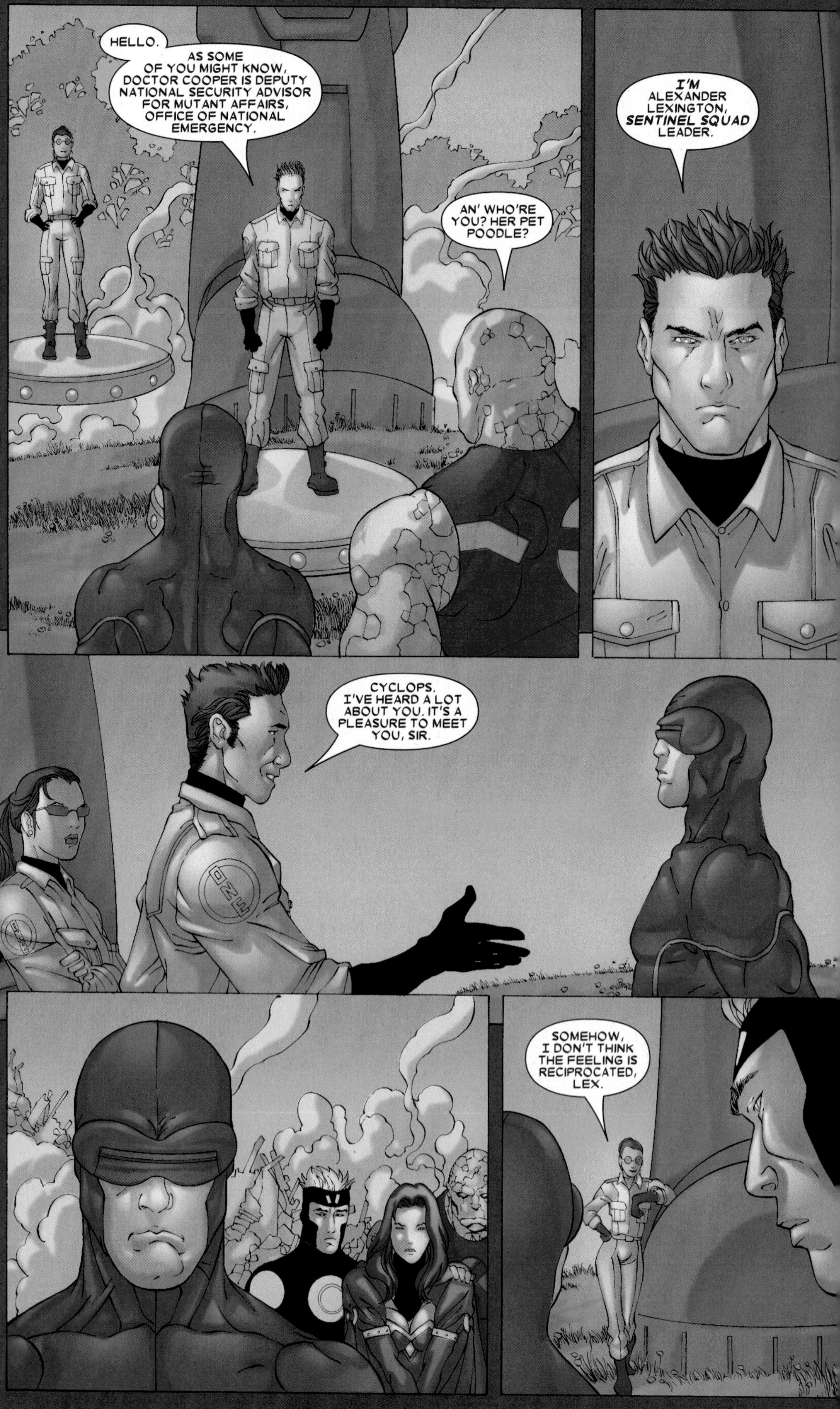
HELLO.
AS SOME OF YOU MIGHT KNOW, DOCTOR COOPER IS DEPUTY NATIONAL SECURITY ADVISOR FOR MUTANT AFFAIRS, OFFICE OF NATIONAL EMERGENCY.
AN' WHO'RE YOU? HER PET POODLE?
I'M ALEXANDER LEXINGTON, SENTINEL SQUAD LEADER.
CYCLOPS. I'VE HEARD A LOT ABOUT YOU. IT'S A PLEASURE TO MEET YOU, SIR.
SOMEHOW, I DON'T THINK THE FEELING IS RECIPROCATED, LEX.

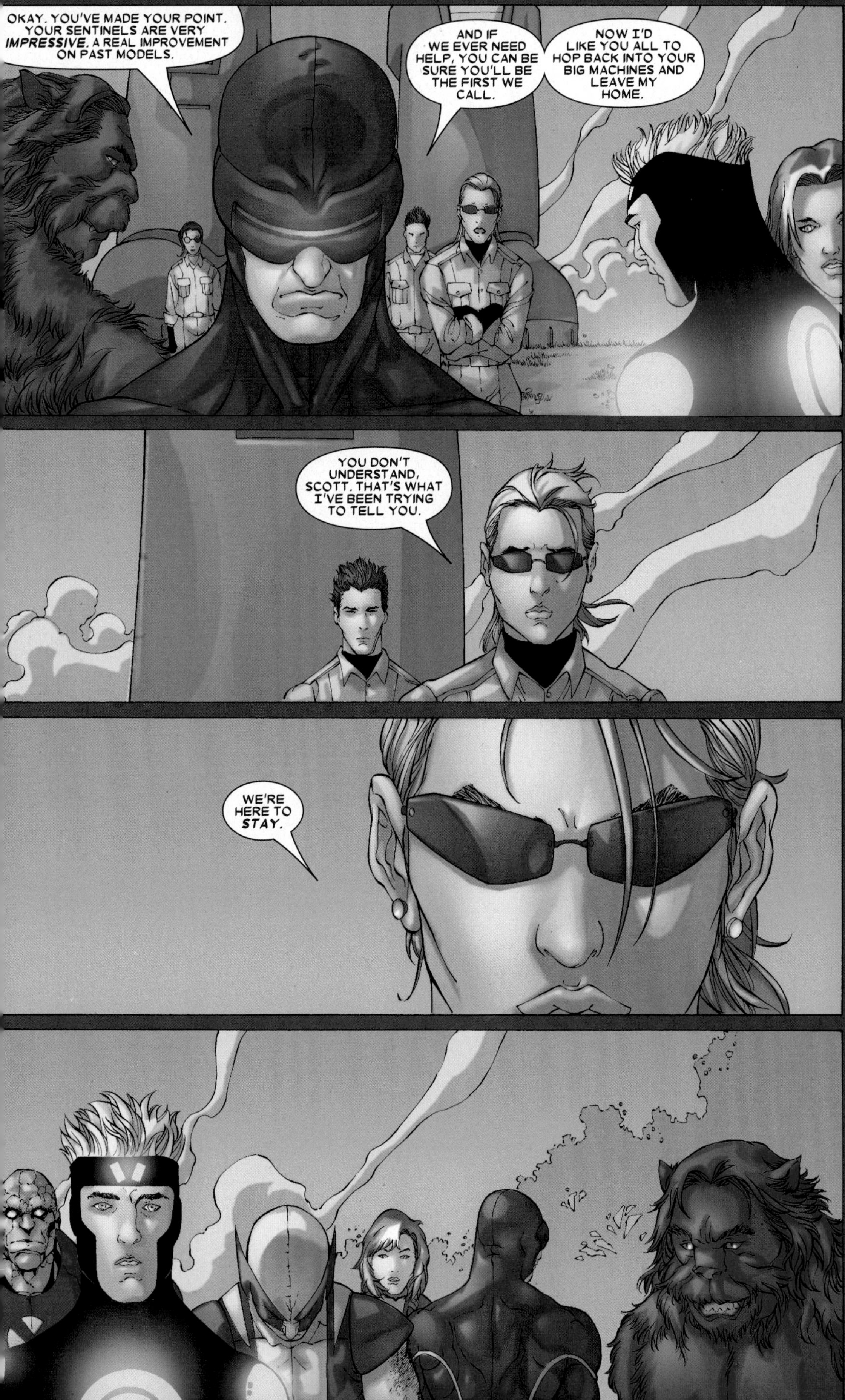
OKAY. YOU'VE MADE YOUR POINT. YOUR SENTINELS ARE VERY *IMPRESSIVE*. A REAL IMPROVEMENT ON PAST MODELS.
AND IF WE EVER NEED HELP, YOU CAN BE SURE YOU'LL BE THE FIRST WE CALL.
NOW I'D LIKE YOU ALL TO HOP BACK INTO YOUR BIG MACHINES AND LEAVE MY HOME.
YOU DON'T UNDERSTAND, SCOTT. THAT'S WHAT I'VE BEEN TRYING TO TELL YOU.
WE'RE HERE TO *STAY*.

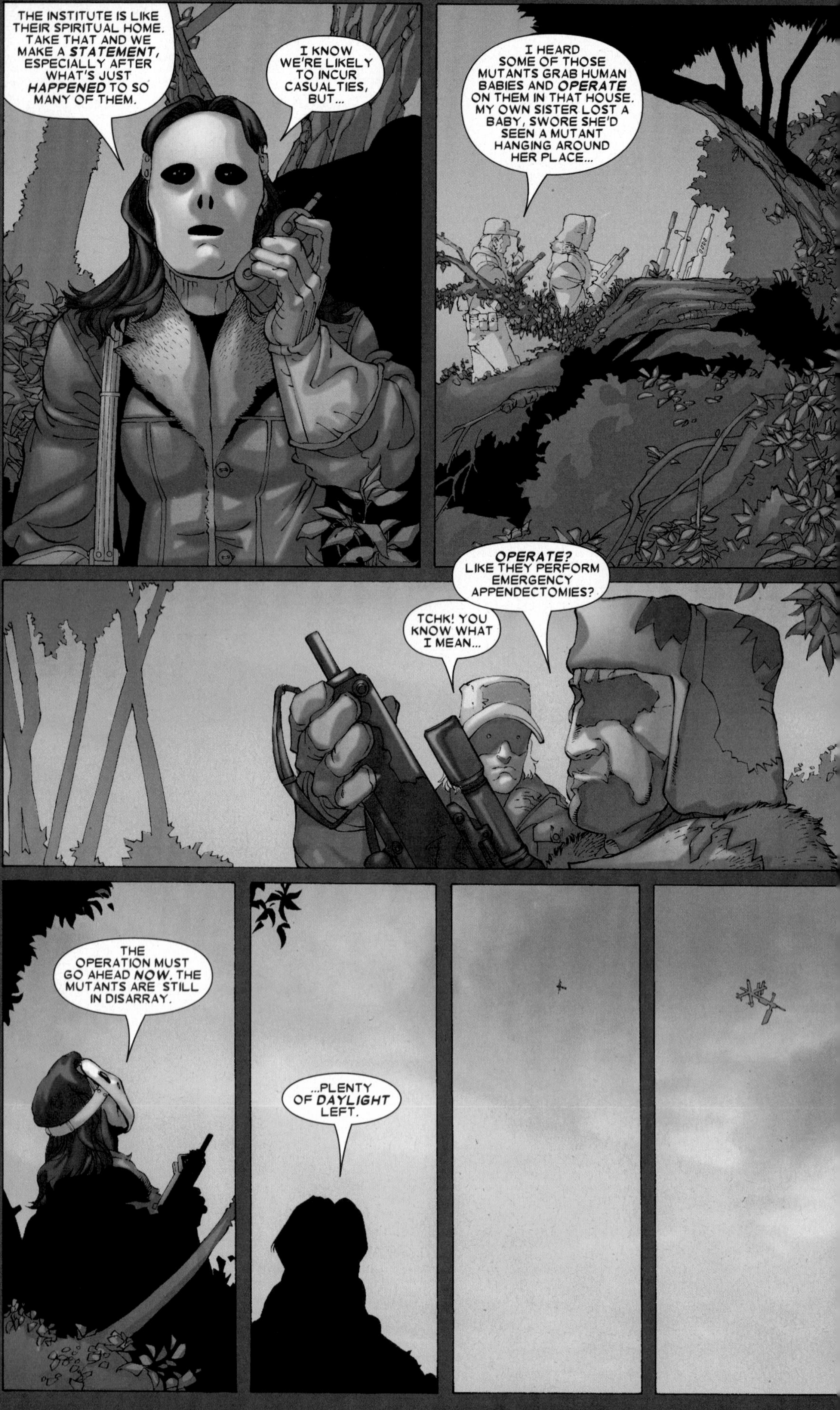

THE INSTITUTE IS LIKE THEIR SPIRITUAL HOME. TAKE THAT AND WE MAKE A STATEMENT, ESPECIALLY AFTER WHAT'S JUST HAPPENED TO SO MANY OF THEM.
I KNOW WE'RE LIKELY TO INCUR CASUALTIES, BUT...
I HEARD SOME OF THOSE MUTANTS GRAB HUMAN BABIES AND OPERATE ON THEM IN THAT HOUSE. MY OWN SISTER LOST A BABY, SWORE SHE'D SEEN A MUTANT HANGING AROUND HER PLACE...
OPERATE? LIKE THEY PERFORM EMERGENCY APPENDECTOMIES?
TCHK! YOU KNOW WHAT I MEAN...
THE OPERATION MUST GO AHEAD NOW. THE MUTANTS ARE STILL IN DISARRAY.
...PLENTY OF DAYLIGHT LEFT.

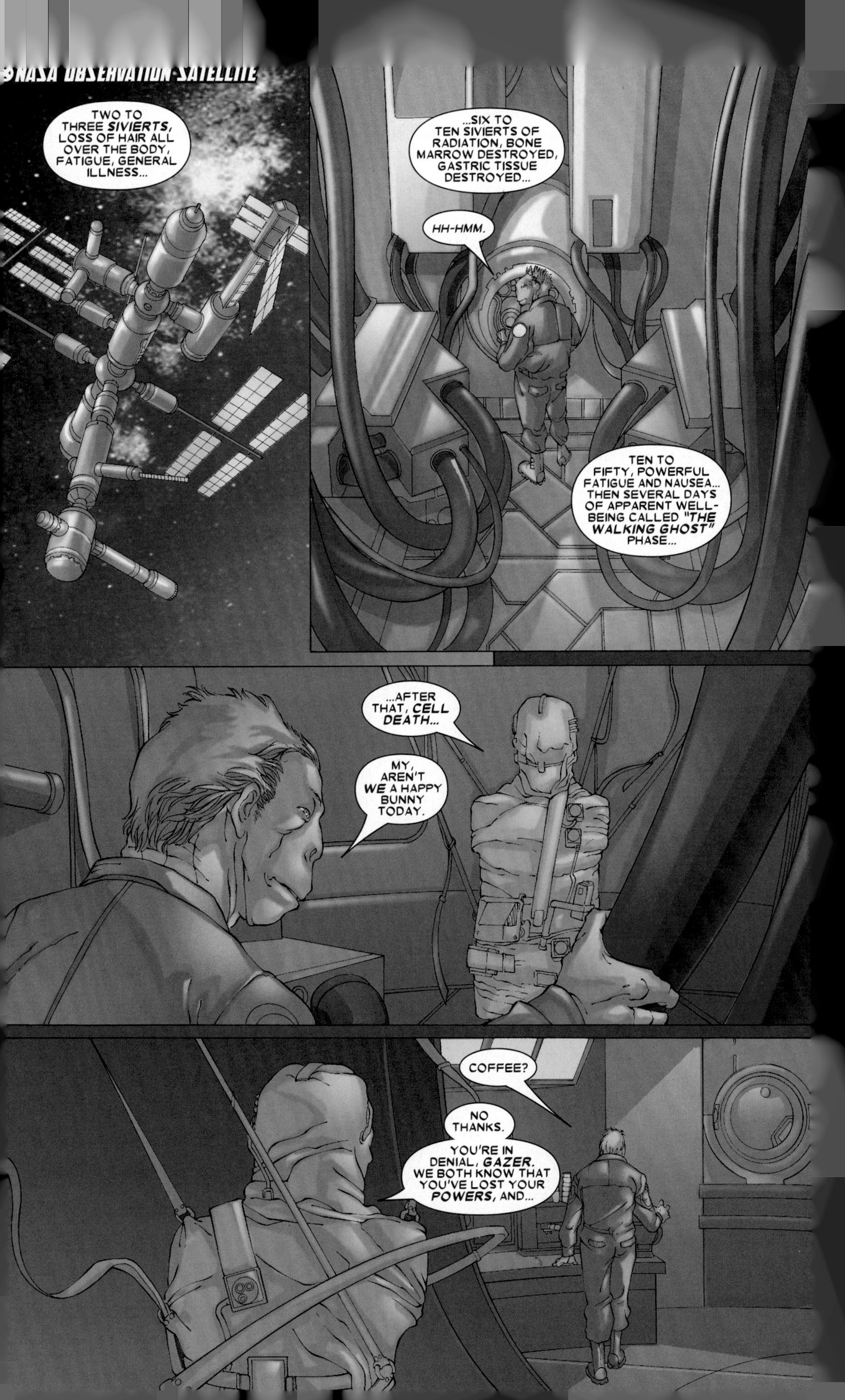
NASA OBSERVATION SATELLITE
TWO TO THREE SIVIERTS, LOSS OF HAIR ALL OVER THE BODY, FATIGUE, GENERAL ILLNESS...
...SIX TO TEN SIVIERTS OF RADIATION, BONE MARROW DESTROYED, GASTRIC TISSUE DESTROYED...
HH-HMM.
TEN TO FIFTY, POWERFUL FATIGUE AND NAUSEA... THEN SEVERAL DAYS OF APPARENT WELL-BEING CALLED "THE WALKING GHOST" PHASE...
...AFTER THAT, CELL DEATH...
MY, AREN'T WE A HAPPY BUNNY TODAY.
COFFEE?
NO THANKS.
YOU'RE IN DENIAL, GAZER. WE BOTH KNOW THAT YOU'VE LOST YOUR POWERS, AND...

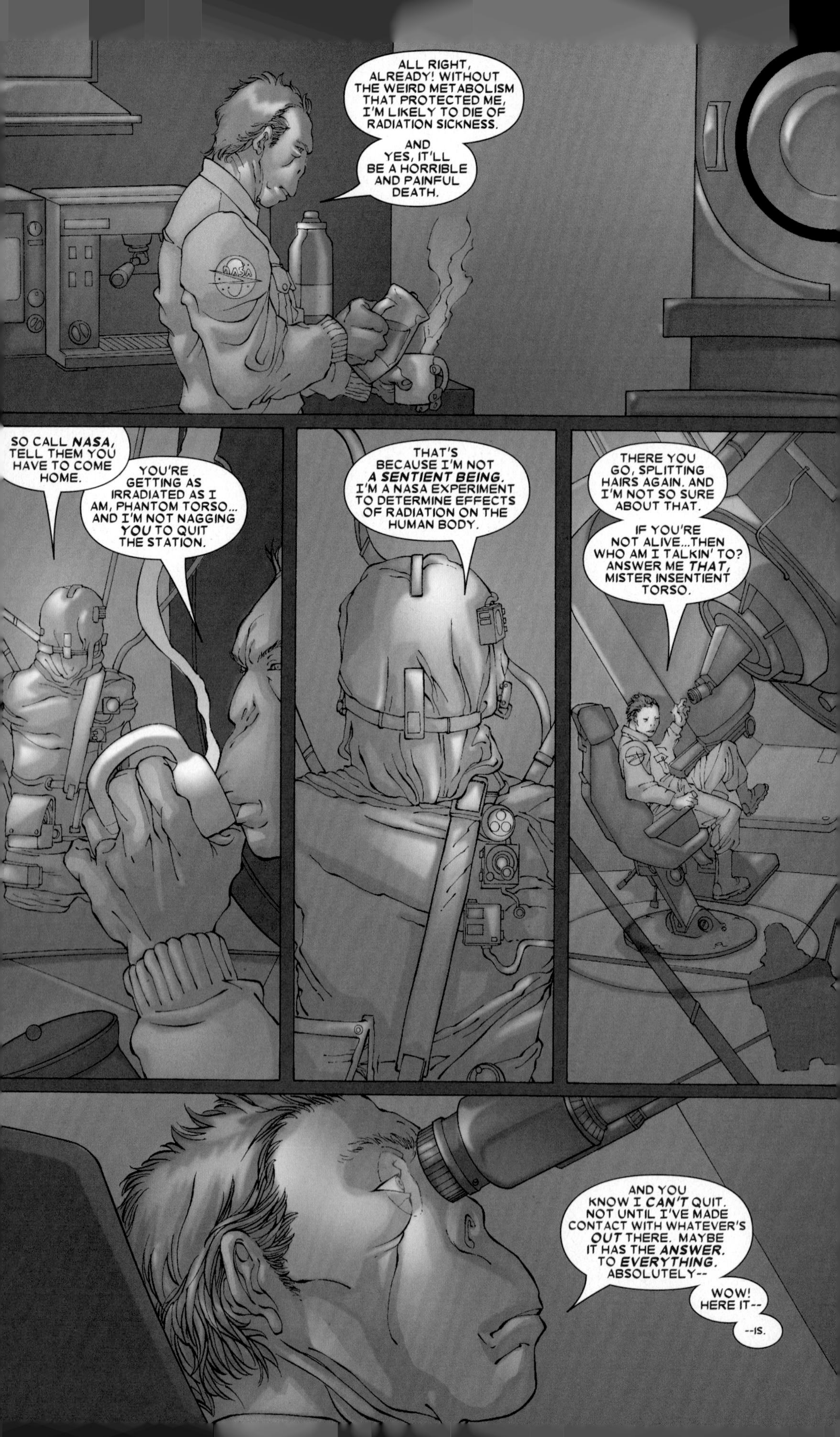
ALL RIGHT, ALREADY! WITHOUT THE WEIRD METABOLISM THAT PROTECTED ME, I'M LIKELY TO DIE OF RADIATION SICKNESS.
AND YES, IT'LL BE A HORRIBLE AND PAINFUL DEATH.
SO CALL NASA, TELL THEM YOU HAVE TO COME HOME.
YOU'RE GETTING AS IRRADIATED AS I AM, PHANTOM TORSO... AND I'M NOT NAGGING YOU TO QUIT THE STATION.
THAT'S BECAUSE I'M NOT A SENTIENT BEING. I'M A NASA EXPERIMENT TO DETERMINE EFFECTS OF RADIATION ON THE HUMAN BODY.
THERE YOU GO, SPLITTING HAIRS AGAIN. AND I'M NOT SO SURE ABOUT THAT.
IF YOU'RE NOT ALIVE...THEN WHO AM I TALKIN' TO? ANSWER ME THAT, MISTER INSENTIENT TORSO.
AND YOU KNOW I CAN'T QUIT. NOT UNTIL I'VE MADE CONTACT WITH WHATEVER'S OUT THERE. MAYBE IT HAS THE ANSWER. TO EVERYTHING. ABSOLUTELY--
WOW! HERE IT--
--IS.

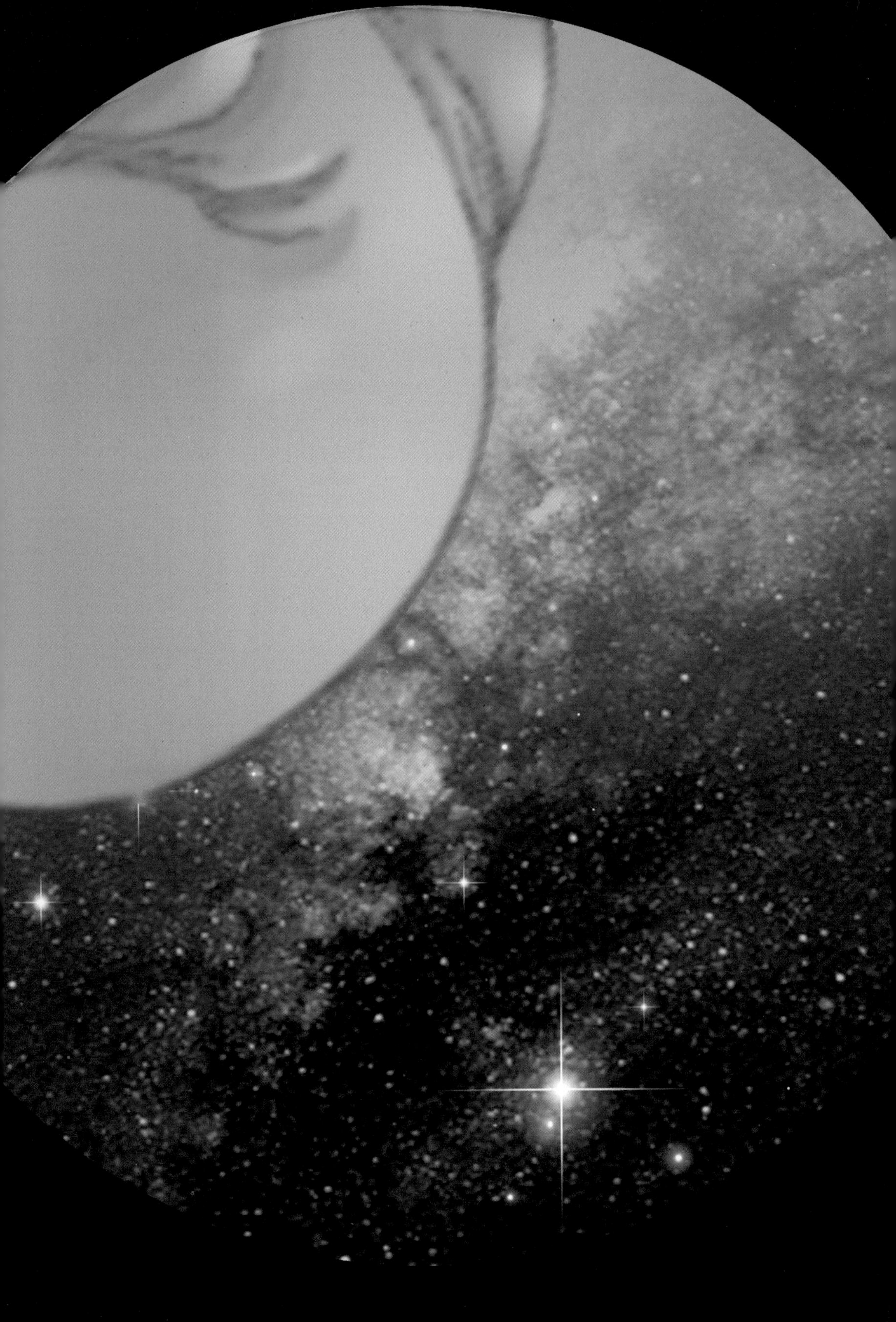

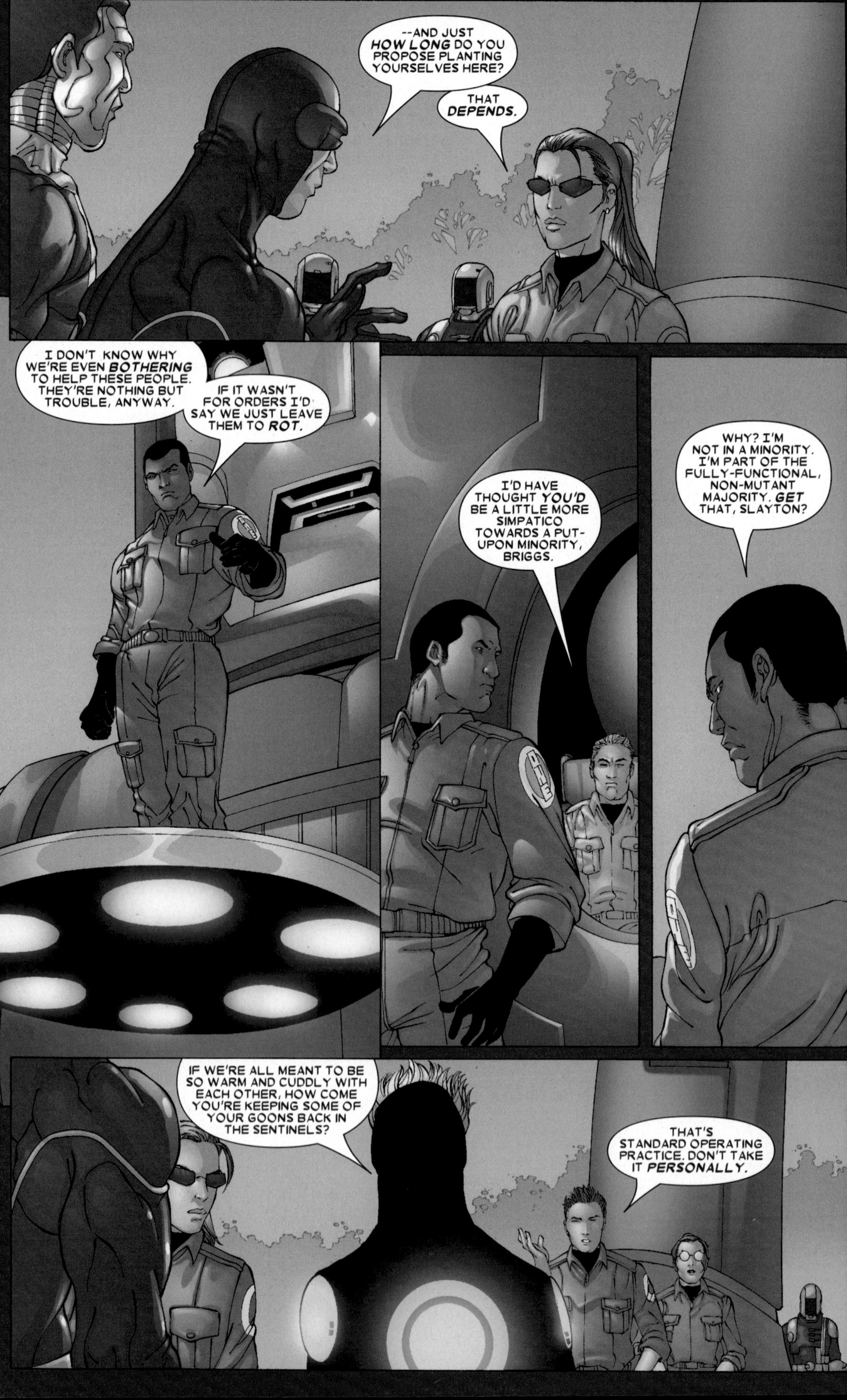
--AND JUST HOW LONG DO YOU PROPOSE PLANTING YOURSELVES HERE?
THAT DEPENDS.
I DON'T KNOW WHY WE'RE EVEN BOTHERING TO HELP THESE PEOPLE. THEY'RE NOTHING BUT TROUBLE, ANYWAY.
IF IT WASN'T FOR ORDERS I'D SAY WE JUST LEAVE THEM TO ROT.
I'D HAVE THOUGHT YOU'D BE A LITTLE MORE SIMPATICO TOWARDS A PUT-UPON MINORITY, BRIGGS.
WHY? I'M NOT IN A MINORITY. I'M PART OF THE FULLY-FUNCTIONAL, NON-MUTANT MAJORITY. GET THAT, SLAYTON?
IF WE'RE ALL MEANT TO BE SO WARM AND CUDDLY WITH EACH OTHER, HOW COME YOU'RE KEEPING SOME OF YOUR GOONS BACK IN THE SENTINELS?
THAT'S STANDARD OPERATING PRACTICE. DON'T TAKE IT PERSONALLY.

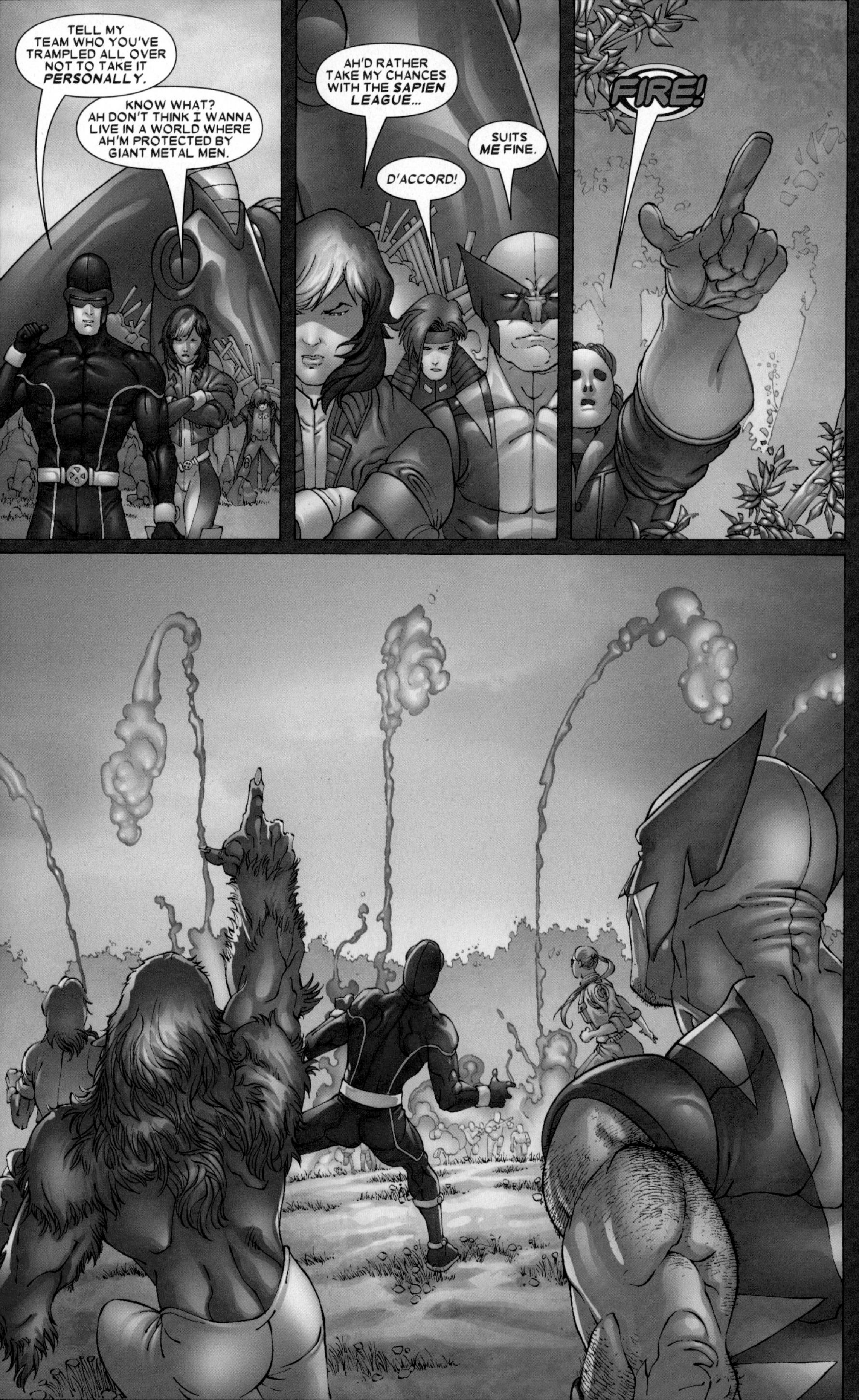
TELL MY TEAM WHO YOU'VE TRAMPLED ALL OVER NOT TO TAKE IT PERSONALLY.
KNOW WHAT? AH DON'T THINK I WANNA LIVE IN A WORLD WHERE AH'M PROTECTED BY GIANT METAL MEN.
AH'D RATHER TAKE MY CHANCES WITH THE SAPIEN LEAGUE...
D'ACCORD!
SUITS ME FINE.
FIRE!

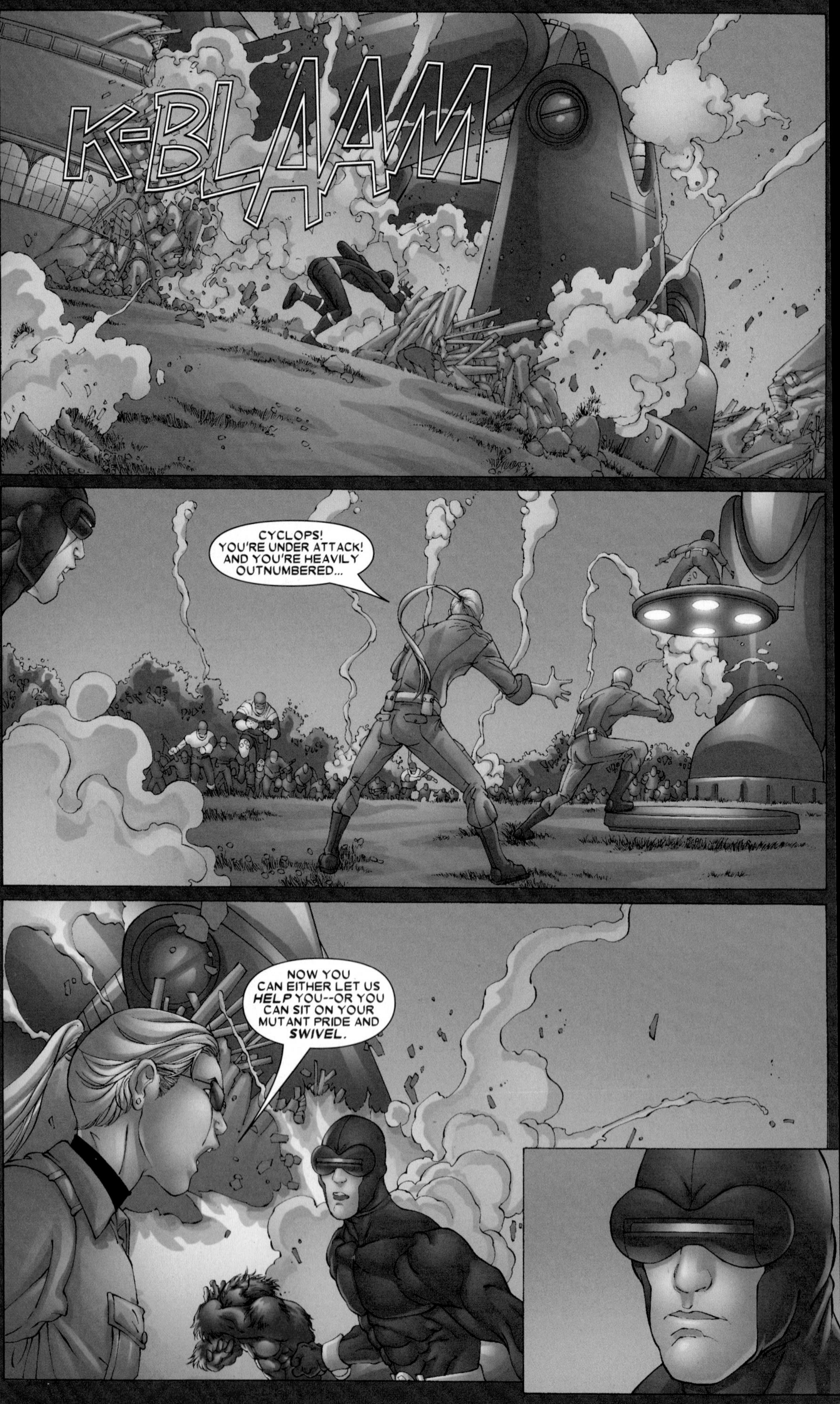
K-BLAAM
CYCLOPS! YOU'RE UNDER ATTACK! AND YOU'RE HEAVILY OUTNUMBERED...
NOW YOU CAN EITHER LET US HELP YOU--OR YOU CAN SIT ON YOUR MUTANT PRIDE AND SWIVEL.

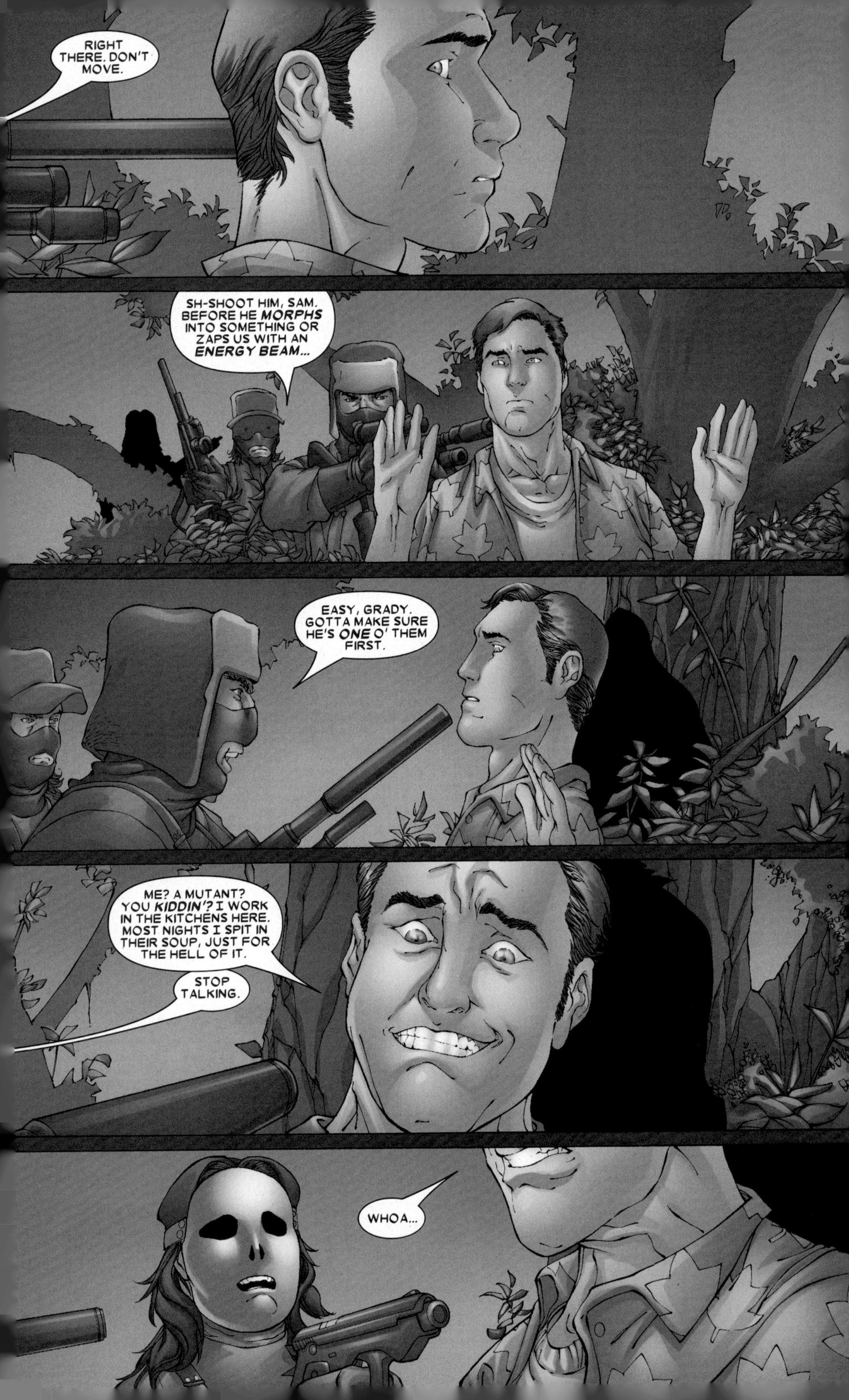
RIGHT THERE. DON'T MOVE.
SH-SHOOT HIM, SAM. BEFORE HE MORPHS INTO SOMETHING OR ZAPS US WITH AN ENERGY BEAM...
EASY, GRADY. GOTTA MAKE SURE HE'S ONE O' THEM FIRST.
ME? A MUTANT? YOU KIDDIN'? I WORK IN THE KITCHENS HERE. MOST NIGHTS I SPIT IN THEIR SOUP, JUST FOR THE HELL OF IT.
STOP TALKING.
WHOA...

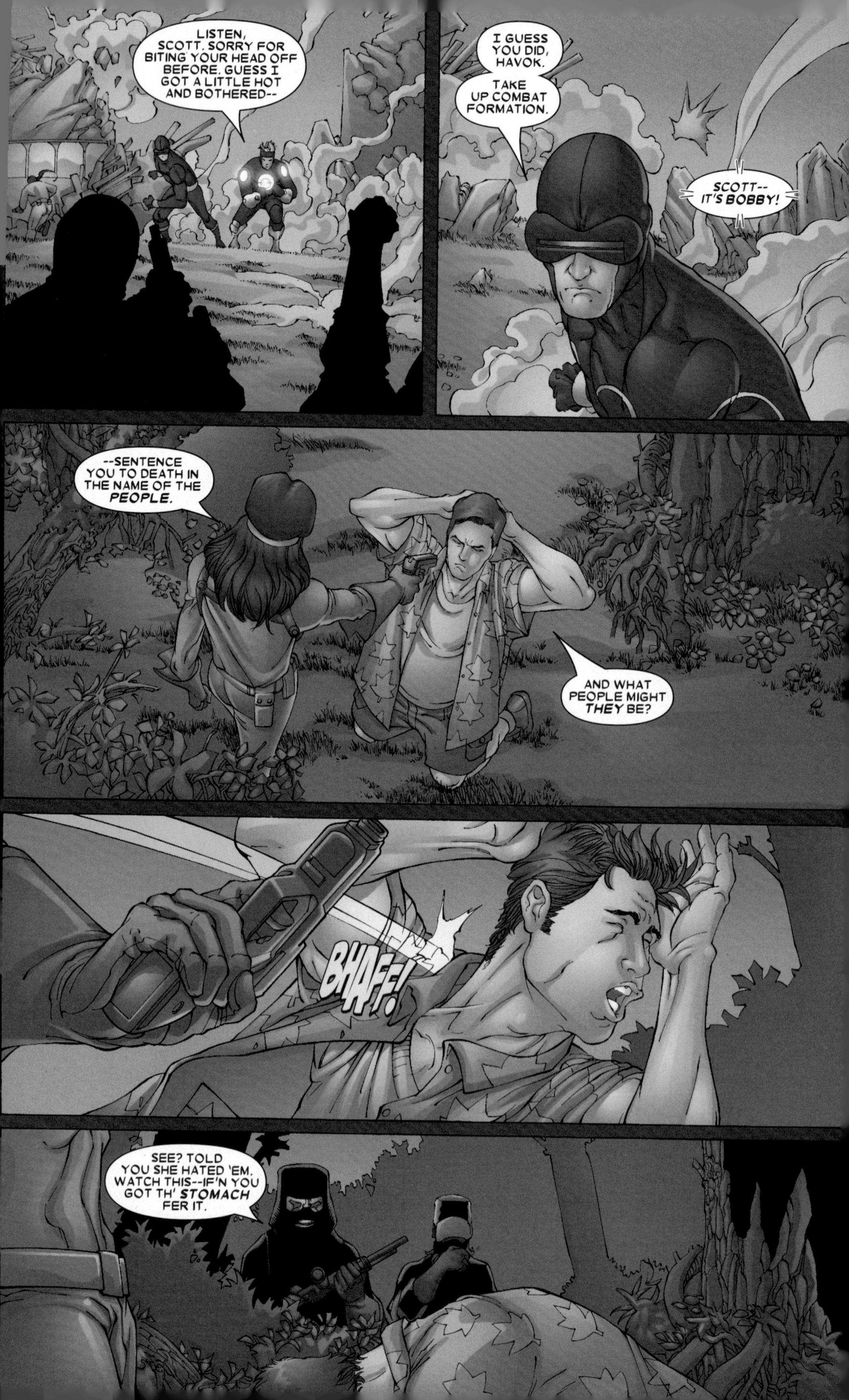
LISTEN, SCOTT. SORRY FOR BITING YOUR HEAD OFF BEFORE. GUESS I GOT A LITTLE HOT AND BOTHERED--
I GUESS YOU DID, HAVOK.
TAKE UP COMBAT FORMATION.
SCOTT-- IT'S BOBBY!
--SENTENCE YOU TO DEATH IN THE NAME OF THE PEOPLE.
AND WHAT PEOPLE MIGHT THEY BE?
BHAFF!
SEE? TOLD YOU SHE HATED 'EM. WATCH THIS--IF'N YOU GOT TH' STOMACH FER IT.

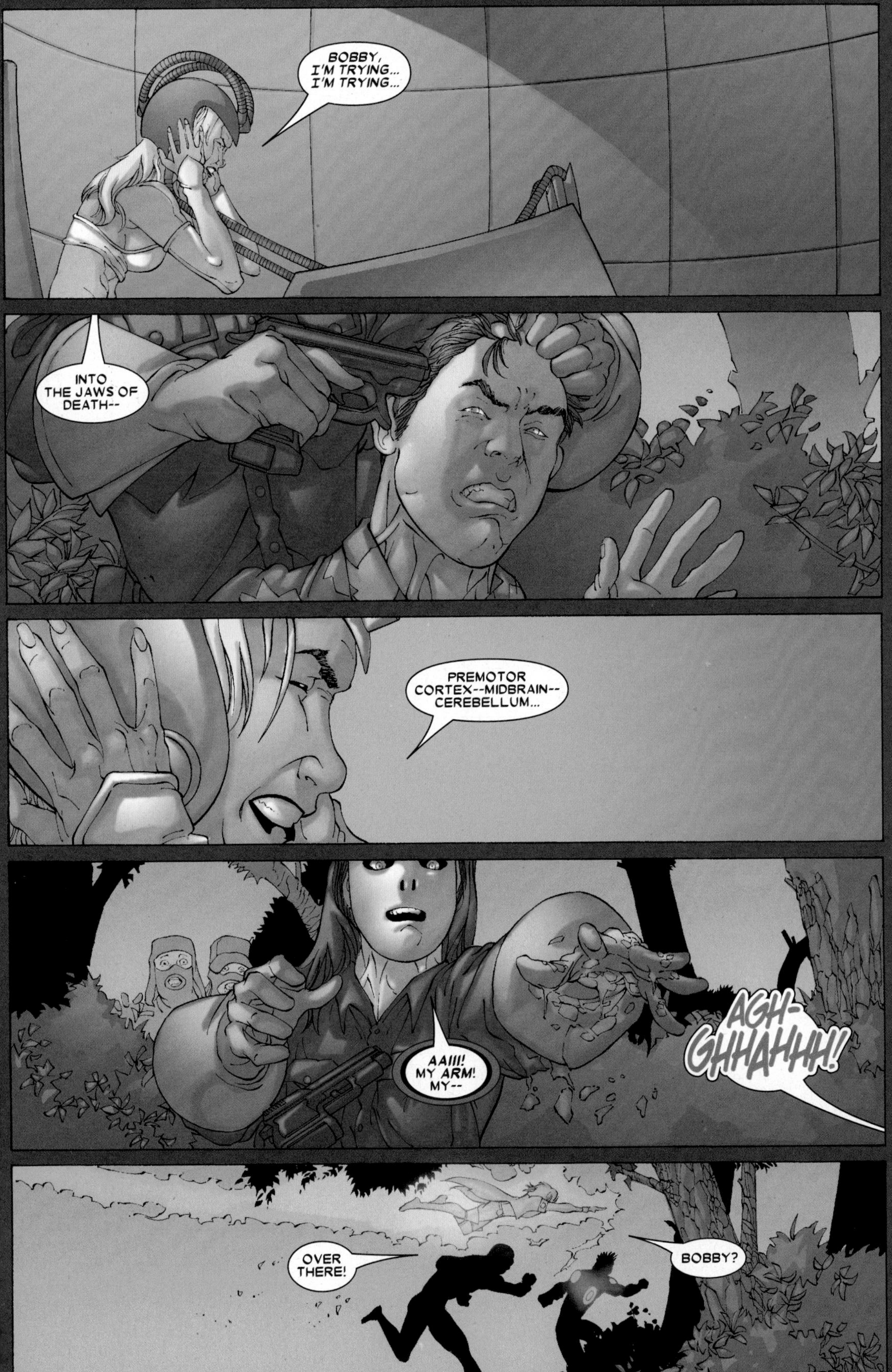
BOBBY, I'M TRYING... I'M TRYING...
INTO THE JAWS OF DEATH--
PREMOTOR CORTEX--MIDBRAIN--CEREBELLUM...
AAIII! MY ARM! MY--
AGH-GHHAHHH!
OVER THERE!
BOBBY?

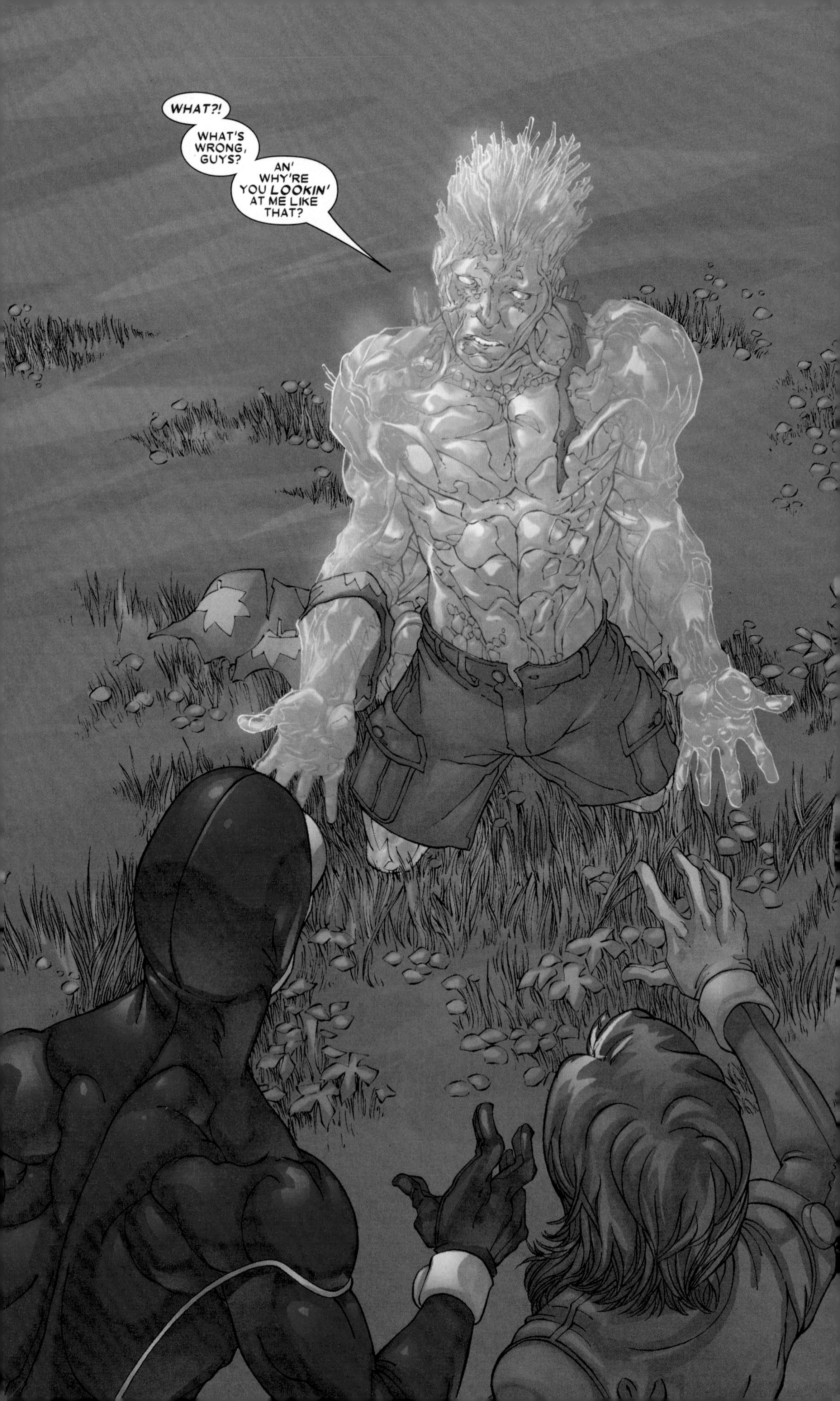
WHAT?!
WHAT'S WRONG, GUYS?
AN' WHY'RE YOU LOOKIN' AT ME LIKE THAT?

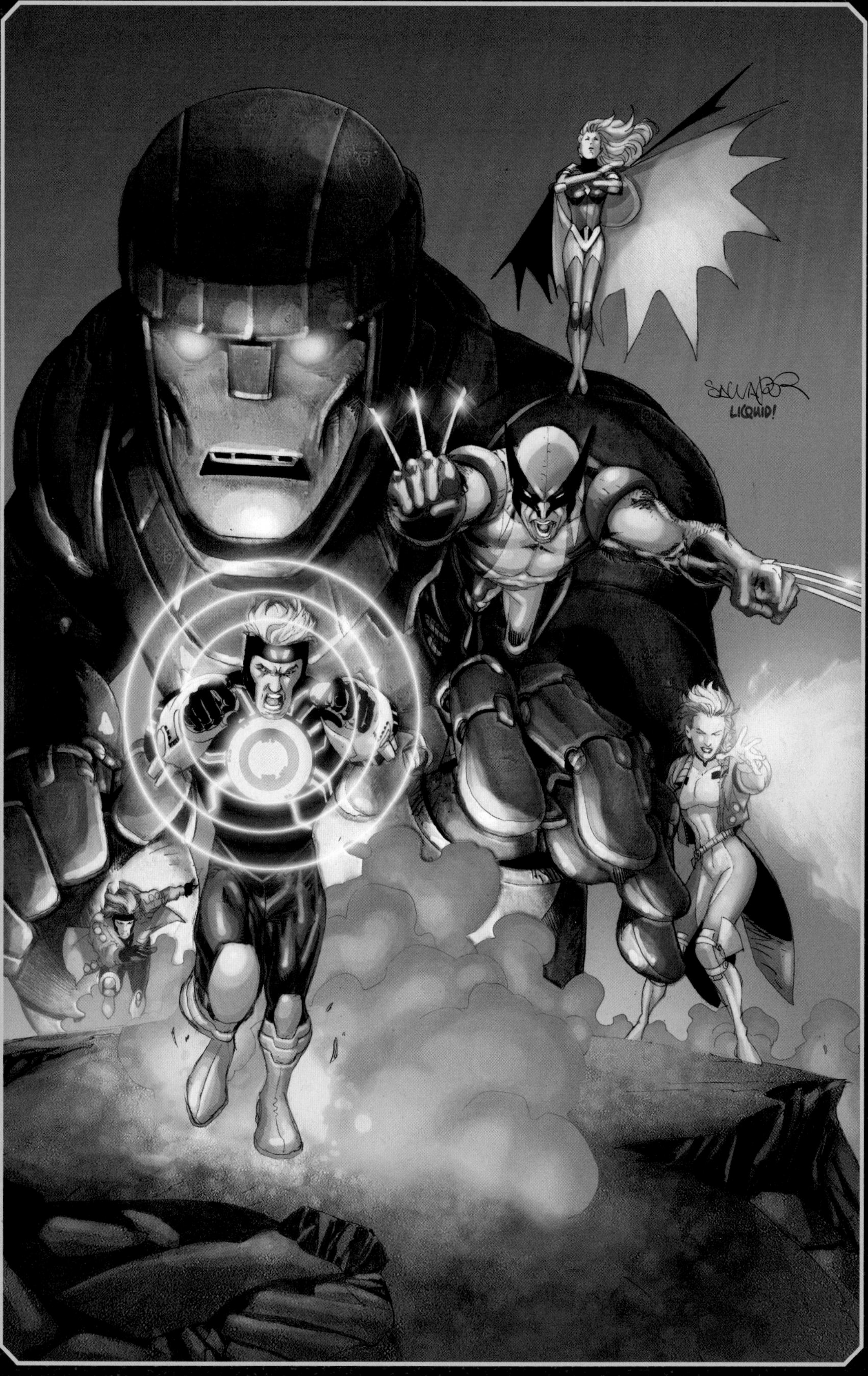
LICQUID!

X-MEN #179

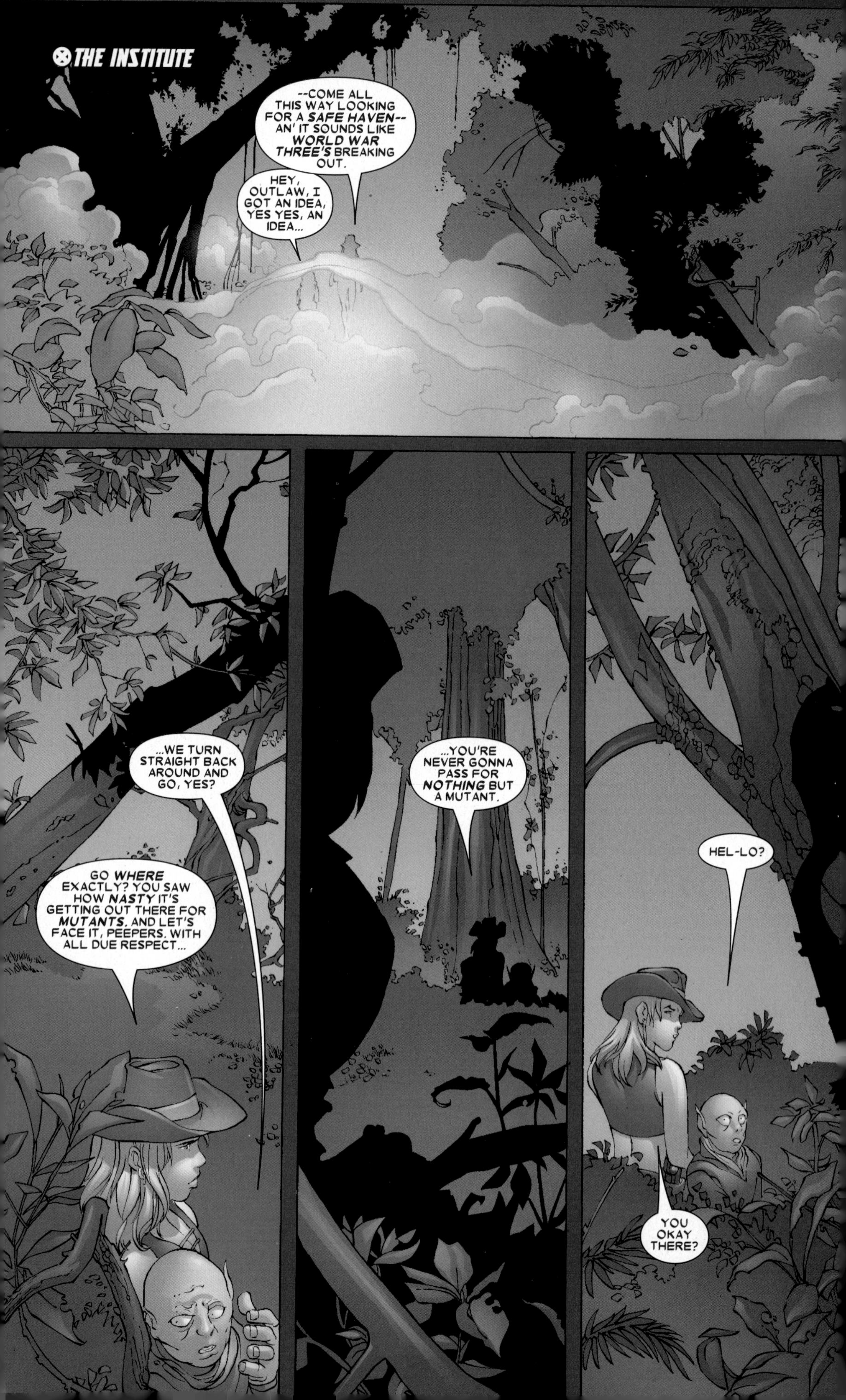
THE INSTITUTE
--COME ALL THIS WAY LOOKING FOR A SAFE HAVEN-- AN' IT SOUNDS LIKE WORLD WAR THREE'S BREAKING OUT.
HEY, OUTLAW, I GOT AN IDEA, YES YES, AN IDEA...
...WE TURN STRAIGHT BACK AROUND AND GO, YES?
GO WHERE EXACTLY? YOU SAW HOW NASTY IT'S GETTING OUT THERE FOR MUTANTS. AND LET'S FACE IT, PEEPERS. WITH ALL DUE RESPECT...
...YOU'RE NEVER GONNA PASS FOR NOTHING BUT A MUTANT.
HEL-LO?
YOU OKAY THERE?

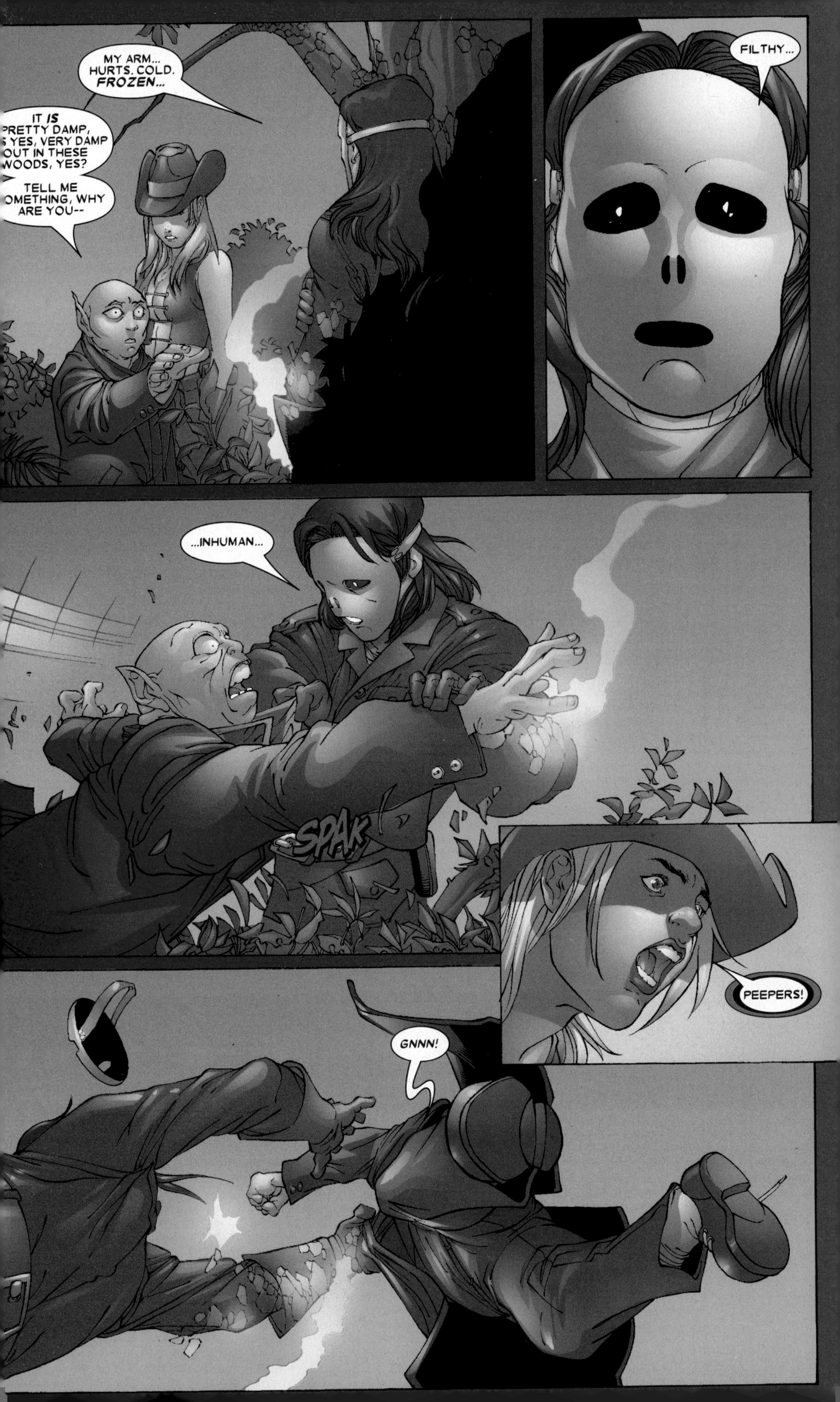
MY ARM... HURTS. COLD. FROZEN...
IT IS PRETTY DAMP, YES, VERY DAMP OUT IN THESE WOODS, YES?
TELL ME OMETHING, WHY ARE YOU--
FILTHY...
...INHUMAN...
SPAK
PEEPERS!
GNNN!

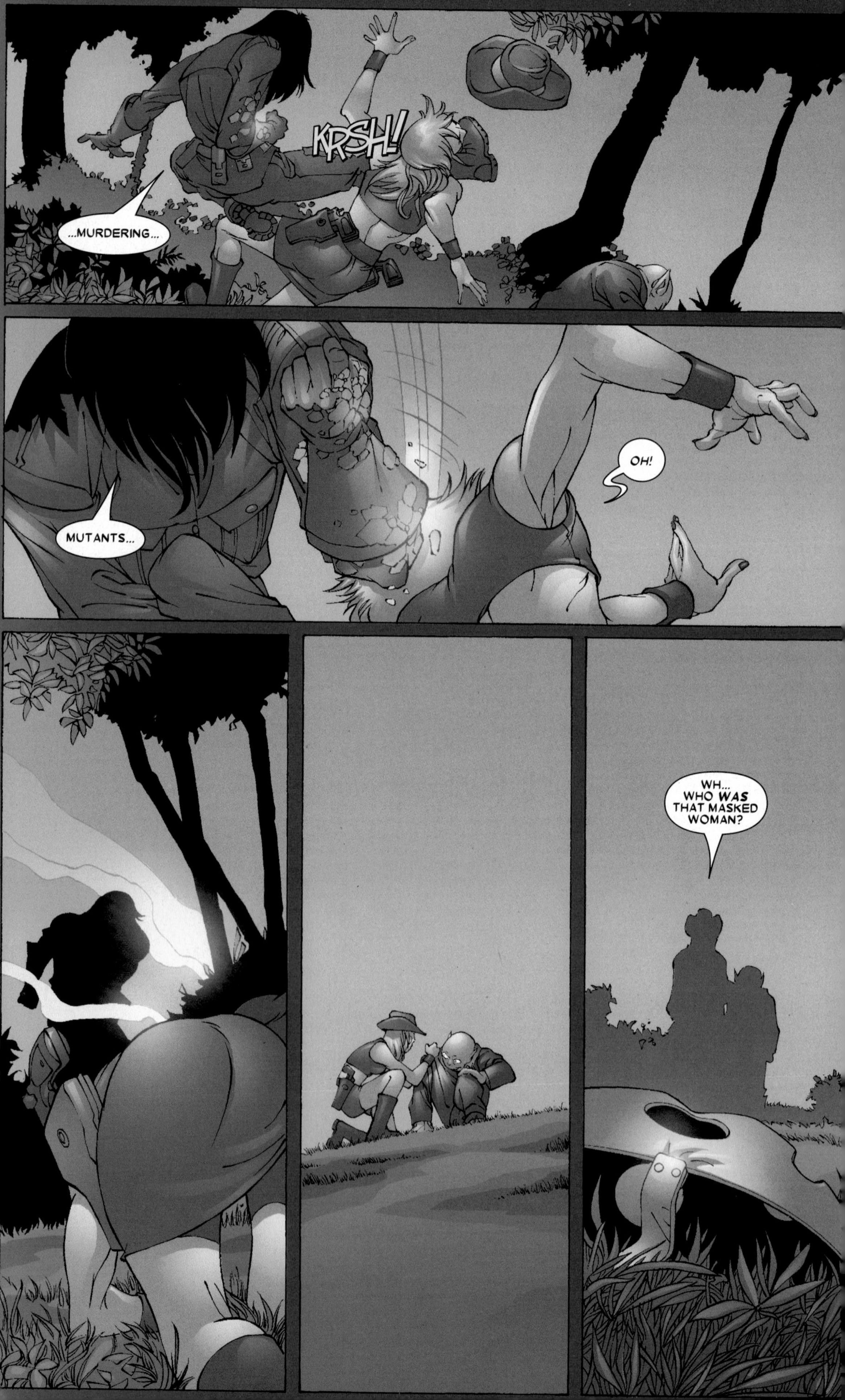
KRSH!!
...MURDERING...
MUTANTS...
OH!
WH... WHO WAS THAT MASKED WOMAN?

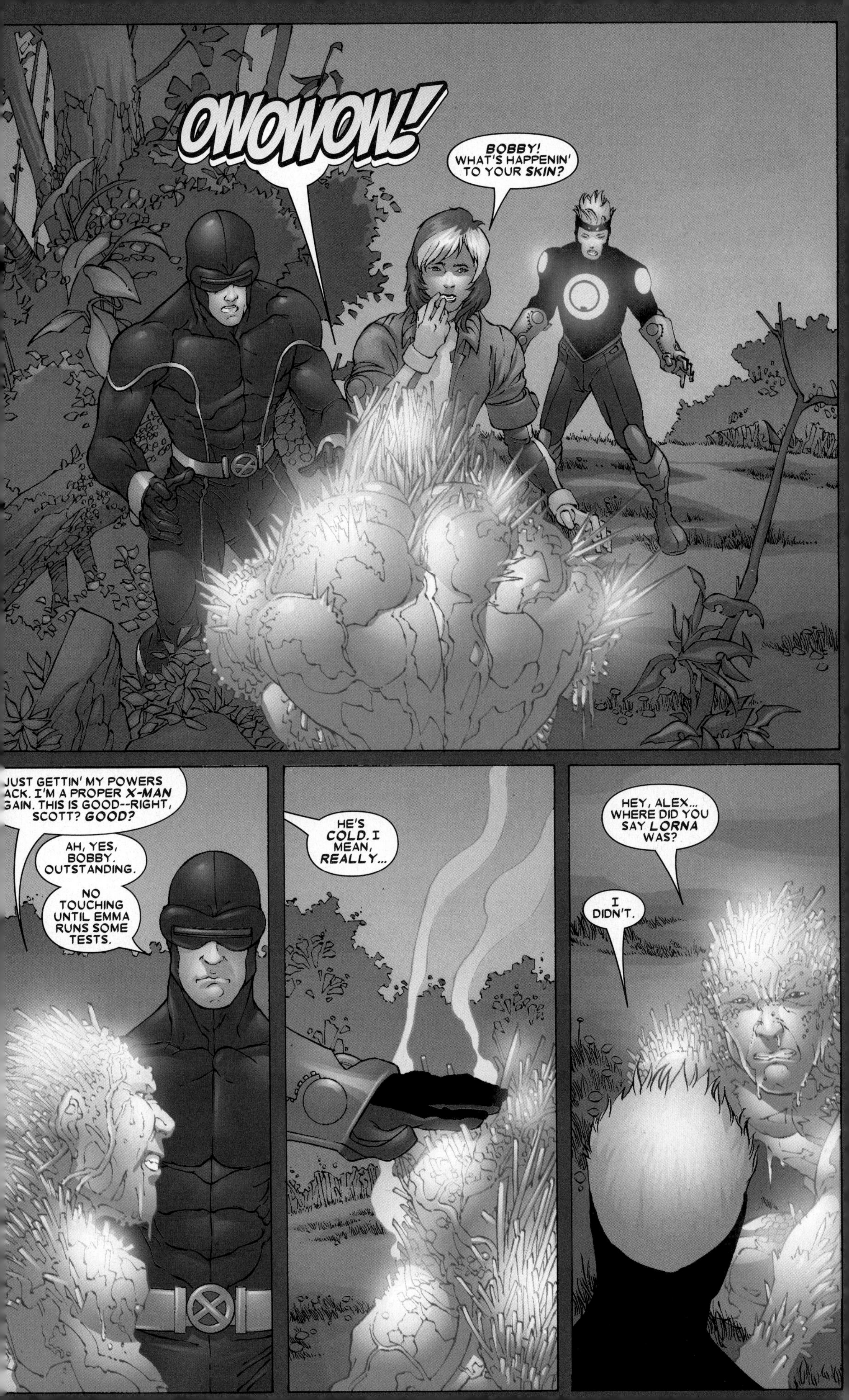
OWOWOW!
BOBBY! WHAT'S HAPPENIN' TO YOUR SKIN?
JUST GETTIN' MY POWERS ACK. I'M A PROPER X-MAN GAIN. THIS IS GOOD--RIGHT, SCOTT? GOOD?
AH, YES, BOBBY. OUTSTANDING.
NO TOUCHING UNTIL EMMA RUNS SOME TESTS.
HE'S COLD. I MEAN, REALLY...
HEY, ALEX... WHERE DID YOU SAY LORNA WAS?
I DIDN'T.

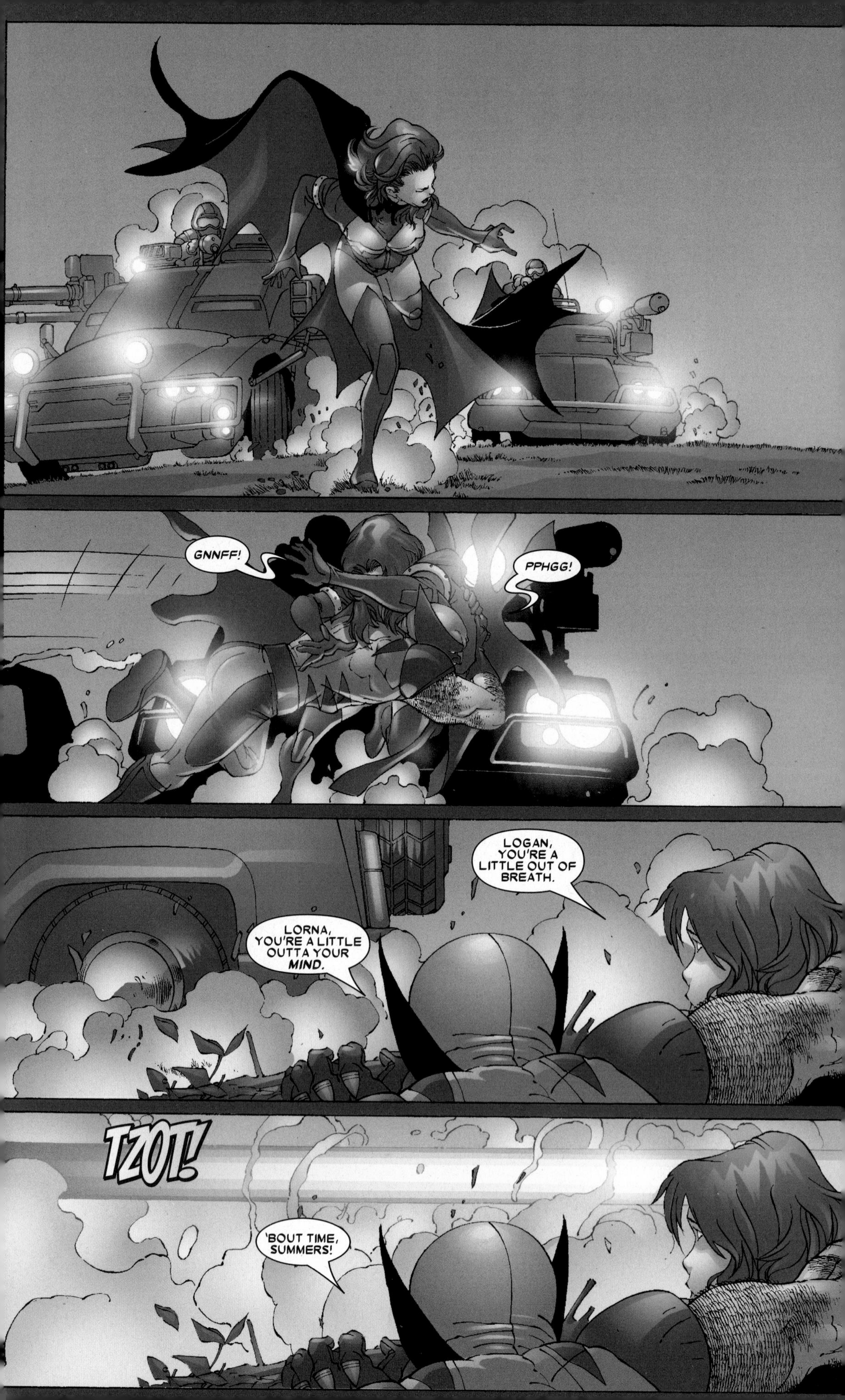
GNNFF!
PPHGG!
LOGAN, YOU'RE A LITTLE OUT OF BREATH.
LORNA, YOU'RE A LITTLE OUTTA YOUR MIND.
TZOT!
'BOUT TIME, SUMMERS!

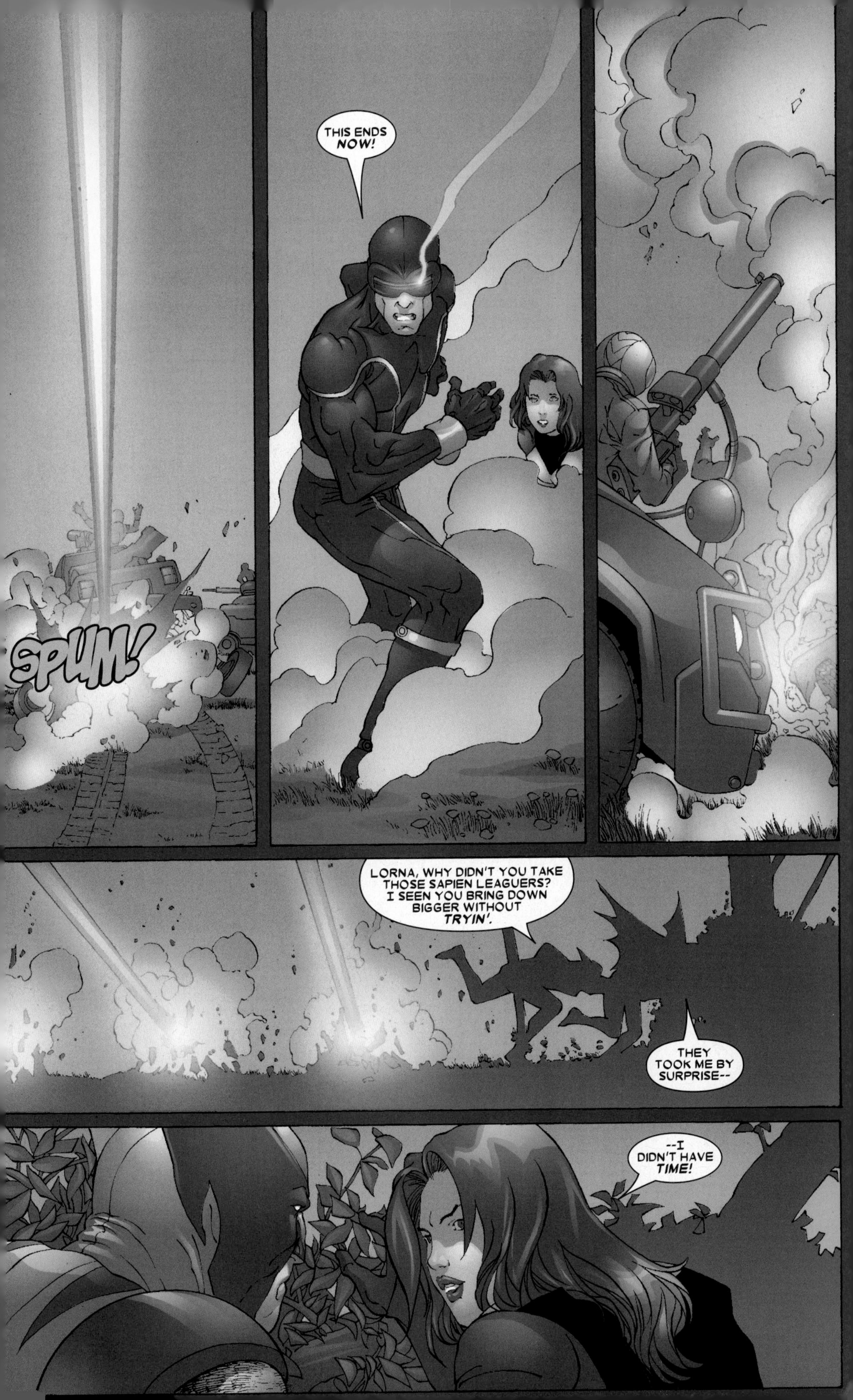
SPUM!
THIS ENDS NOW!
LORNA, WHY DIDN'T YOU TAKE THOSE SAPIEN LEAGUERS? I SEEN YOU BRING DOWN BIGGER WITHOUT TRYIN'.
THEY TOOK ME BY SURPRISE--
--I DIDN'T HAVE TIME!

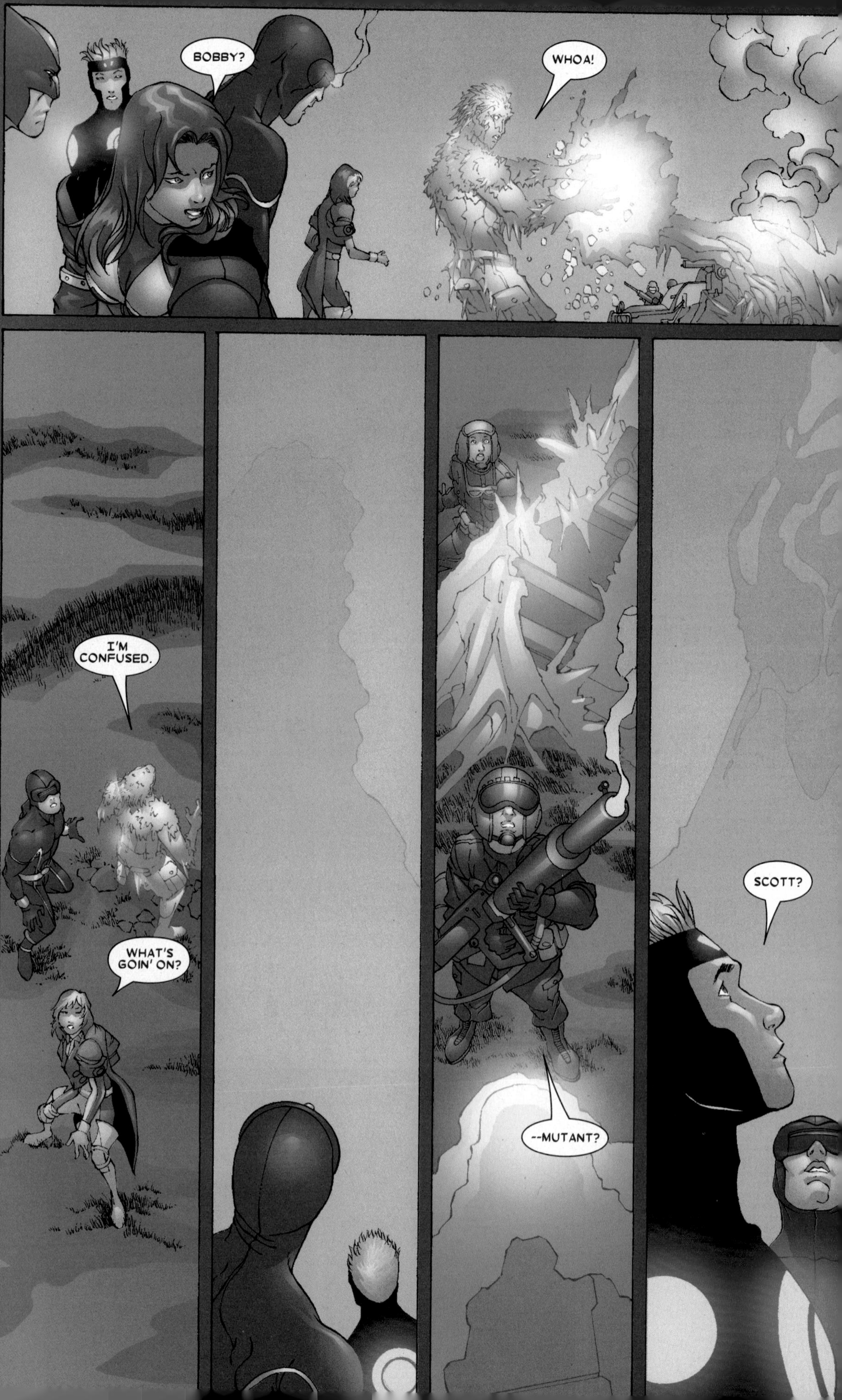
BOBBY?
WHOA!
I'M CONFUSED.
WHAT'S GOIN' ON?
--MUTANT?
SCOTT?

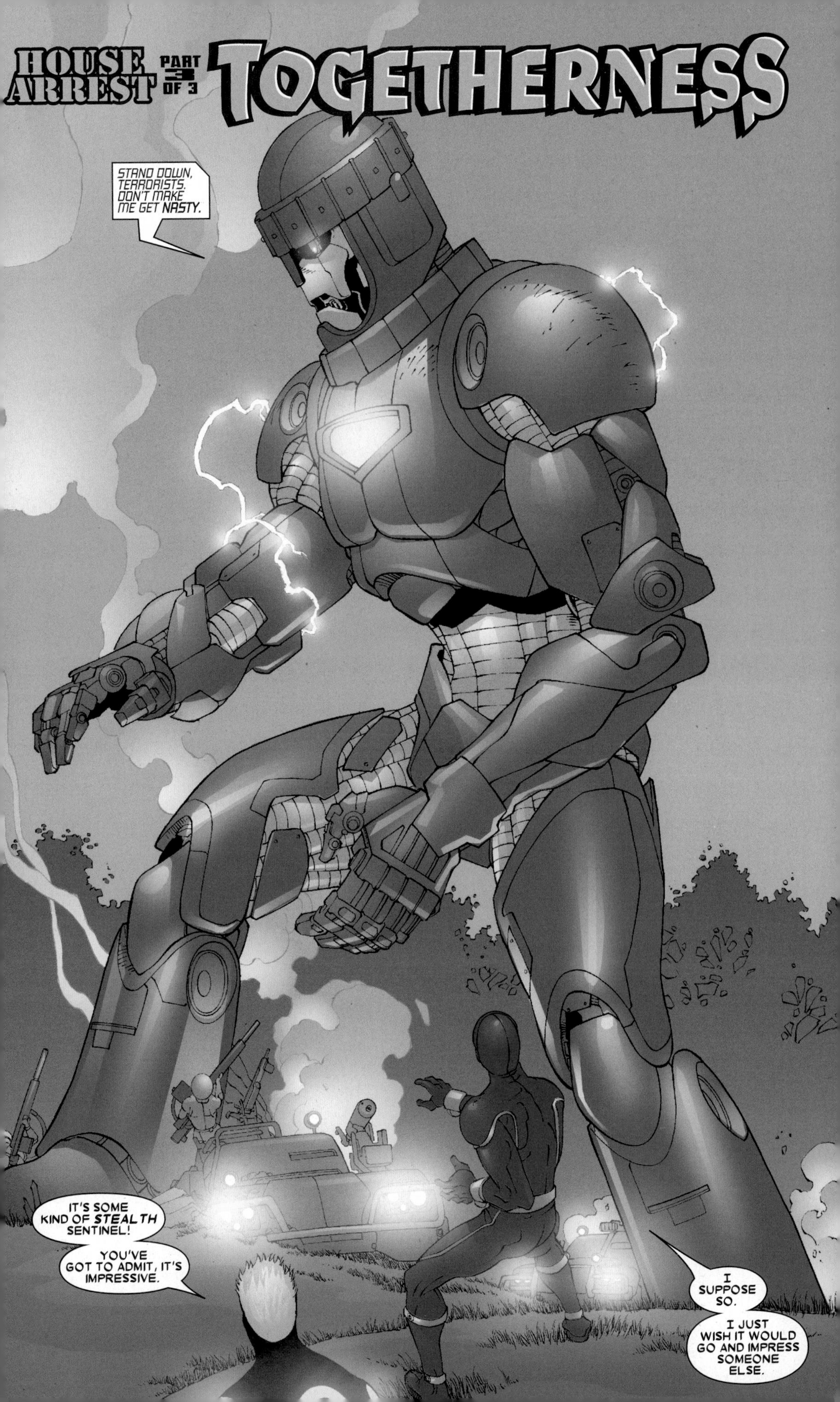
HOUSE ARREST PART 3 OF 3
TOGETHERNESS
STAND DOWN, TERRORISTS. DON'T MAKE ME GET NASTY.
IT'S SOME KIND OF STEALTH SENTINEL!
YOU'VE GOT TO ADMIT, IT'S IMPRESSIVE.
I SUPPOSE SO.
I JUST WISH IT WOULD GO AND IMPRESS SOMEONE ELSE.

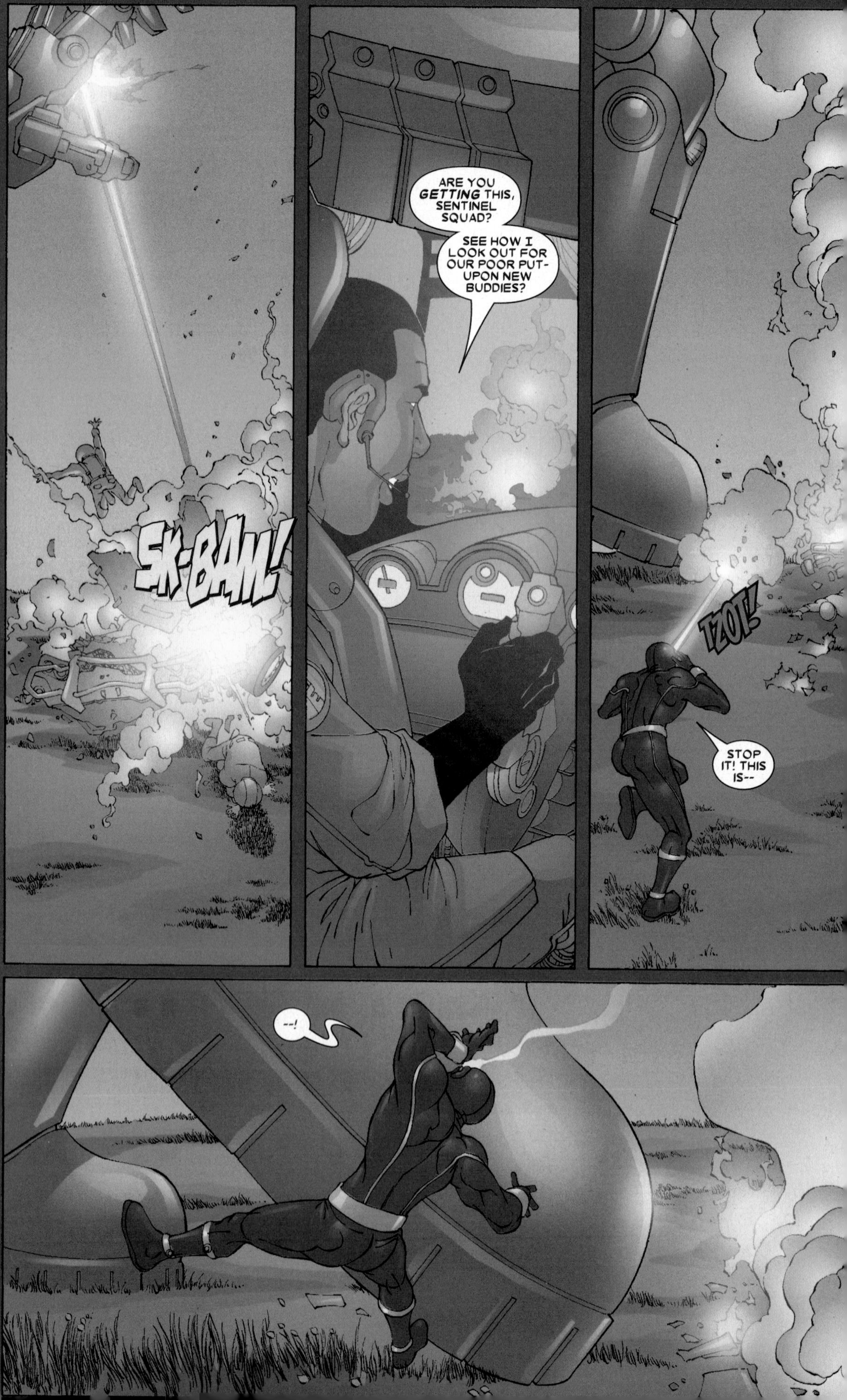
SK-BAM!
ARE YOU GETTING THIS, SENTINEL SQUAD?
SEE HOW I LOOK OUT FOR OUR POOR PUT-UPON NEW BUDDIES?
TZOT!
STOP IT! THIS IS--
--!

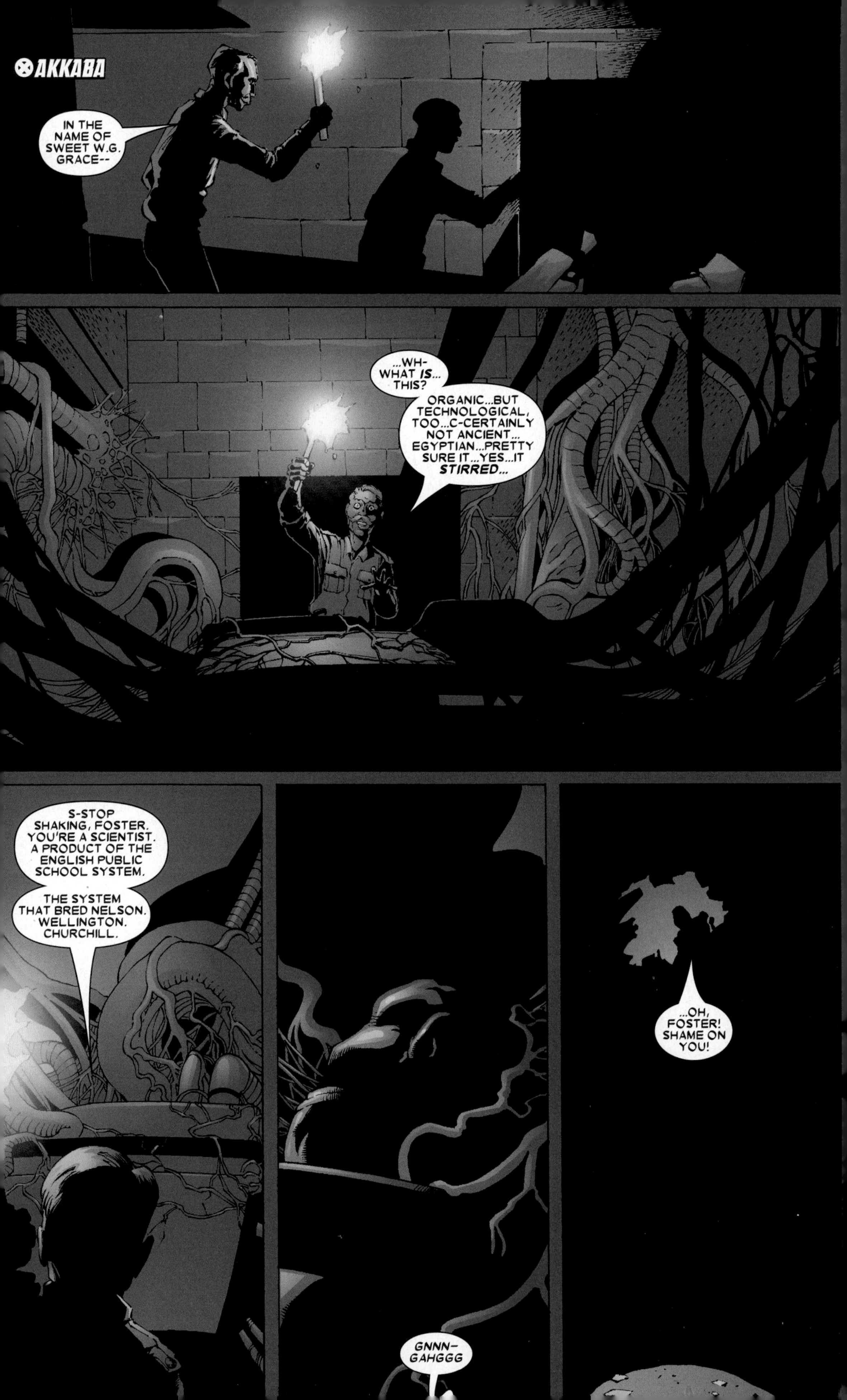
AKKABA
IN THE NAME OF SWEET W.G. GRACE--
...WH- WHAT IS... THIS?
ORGANIC...BUT TECHNOLOGICAL, TOO...C-CERTAINLY NOT ANCIENT... EGYPTIAN...PRETTY SURE IT...YES...IT STIRRED...
S-STOP SHAKING, FOSTER. YOU'RE A SCIENTIST. A PRODUCT OF THE ENGLISH PUBLIC SCHOOL SYSTEM.
THE SYSTEM THAT BRED NELSON. WELLINGTON. CHURCHILL.
GNNN-GAHGGG
...OH, FOSTER! SHAME ON YOU!

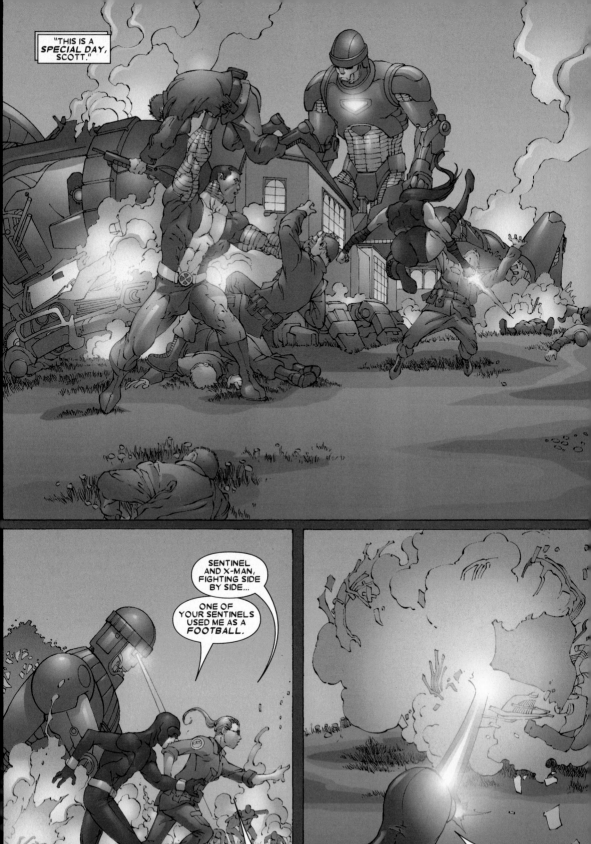

"THIS IS A **SPECIAL DAY**, SCOTT."

SENTINEL AND X-MAN, FIGHTING SIDE BY SIDE...

ONE OF YOUR SENTINELS USED ME AS A **FOOTBALL**.

AN ACCIDENT.

I THINK HE TRIED TO **KILL** ME.

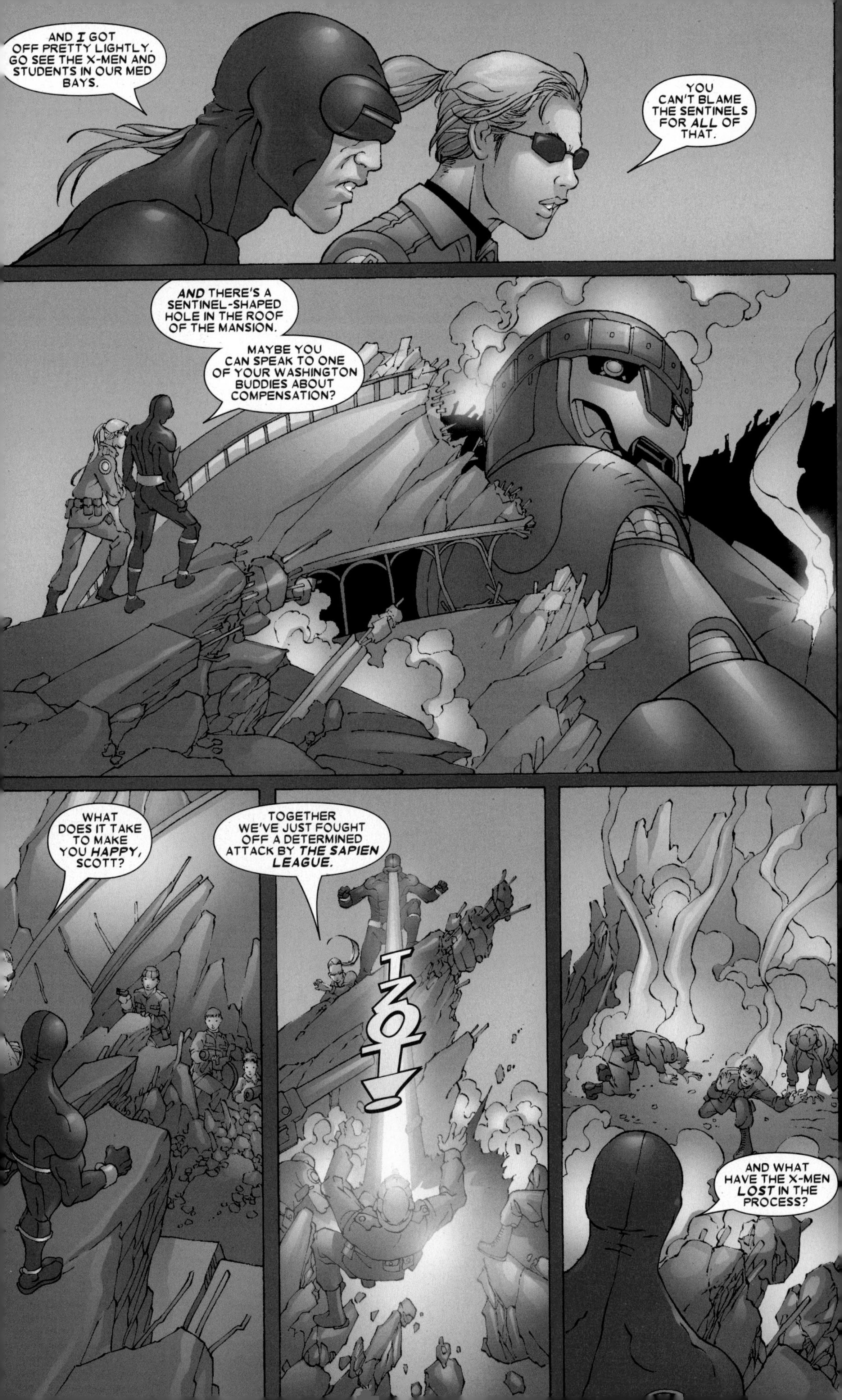
AND *I* GOT OFF PRETTY LIGHTLY. GO SEE THE X-MEN AND STUDENTS IN OUR MED BAYS.
YOU CAN'T BLAME THE SENTINELS FOR *ALL* OF THAT.
AND THERE'S A SENTINEL-SHAPED HOLE IN THE ROOF OF THE MANSION.
MAYBE YOU CAN SPEAK TO ONE OF YOUR WASHINGTON BUDDIES ABOUT COMPENSATION?
WHAT DOES IT TAKE TO MAKE YOU *HAPPY,* SCOTT?
TOGETHER WE'VE JUST FOUGHT OFF A DETERMINED ATTACK BY *THE SAPIEN LEAGUE.*
TZOT!
AND WHAT HAVE THE X-MEN *LOST* IN THE PROCESS?

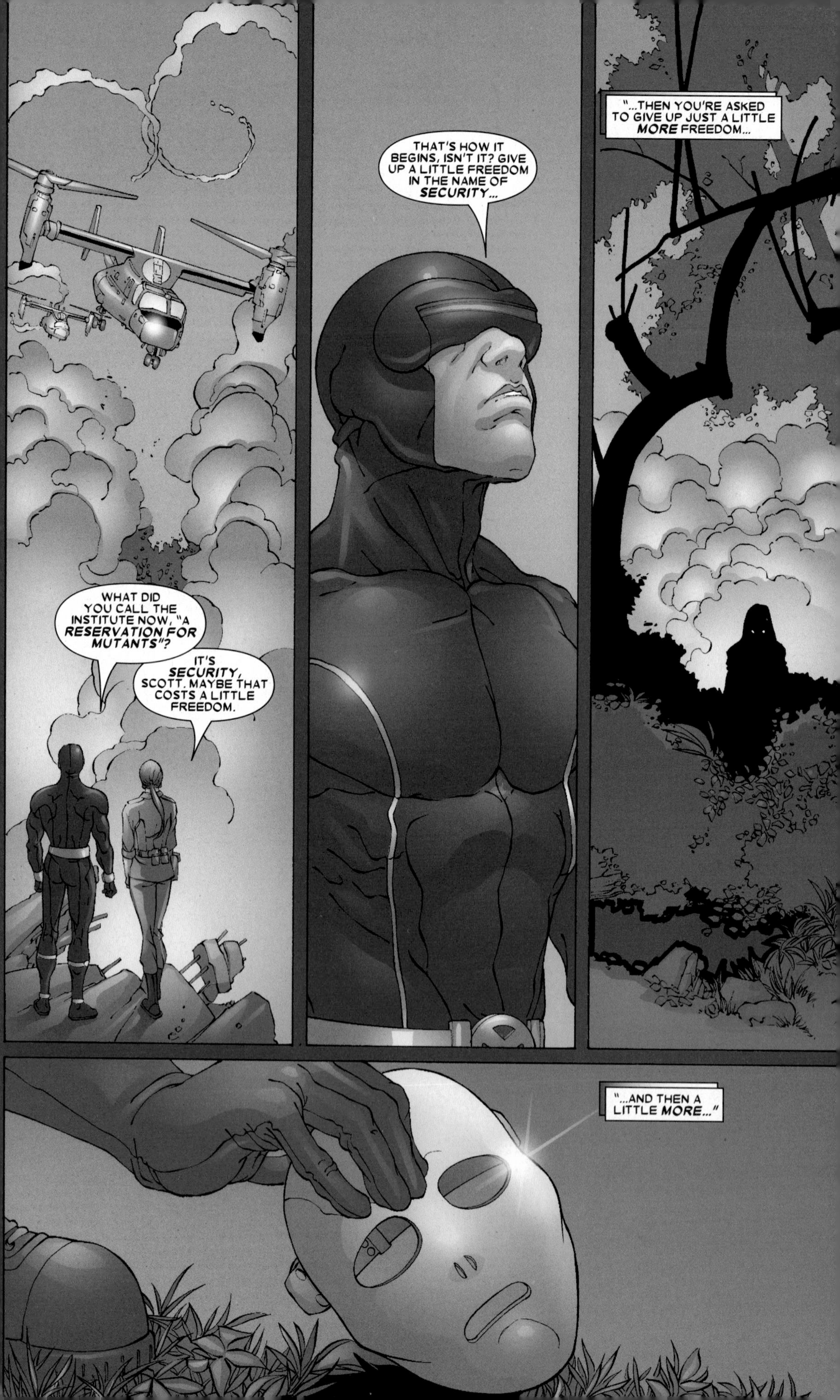
WHAT DID YOU CALL THE INSTITUTE NOW, "A RESERVATION FOR MUTANTS"?
IT'S SECURITY, SCOTT. MAYBE THAT COSTS A LITTLE FREEDOM.
THAT'S HOW IT BEGINS, ISN'T IT? GIVE UP A LITTLE FREEDOM IN THE NAME OF SECURITY...
"...THEN YOU'RE ASKED TO GIVE UP JUST A LITTLE MORE FREEDOM...
"...AND THEN A LITTLE MORE..."

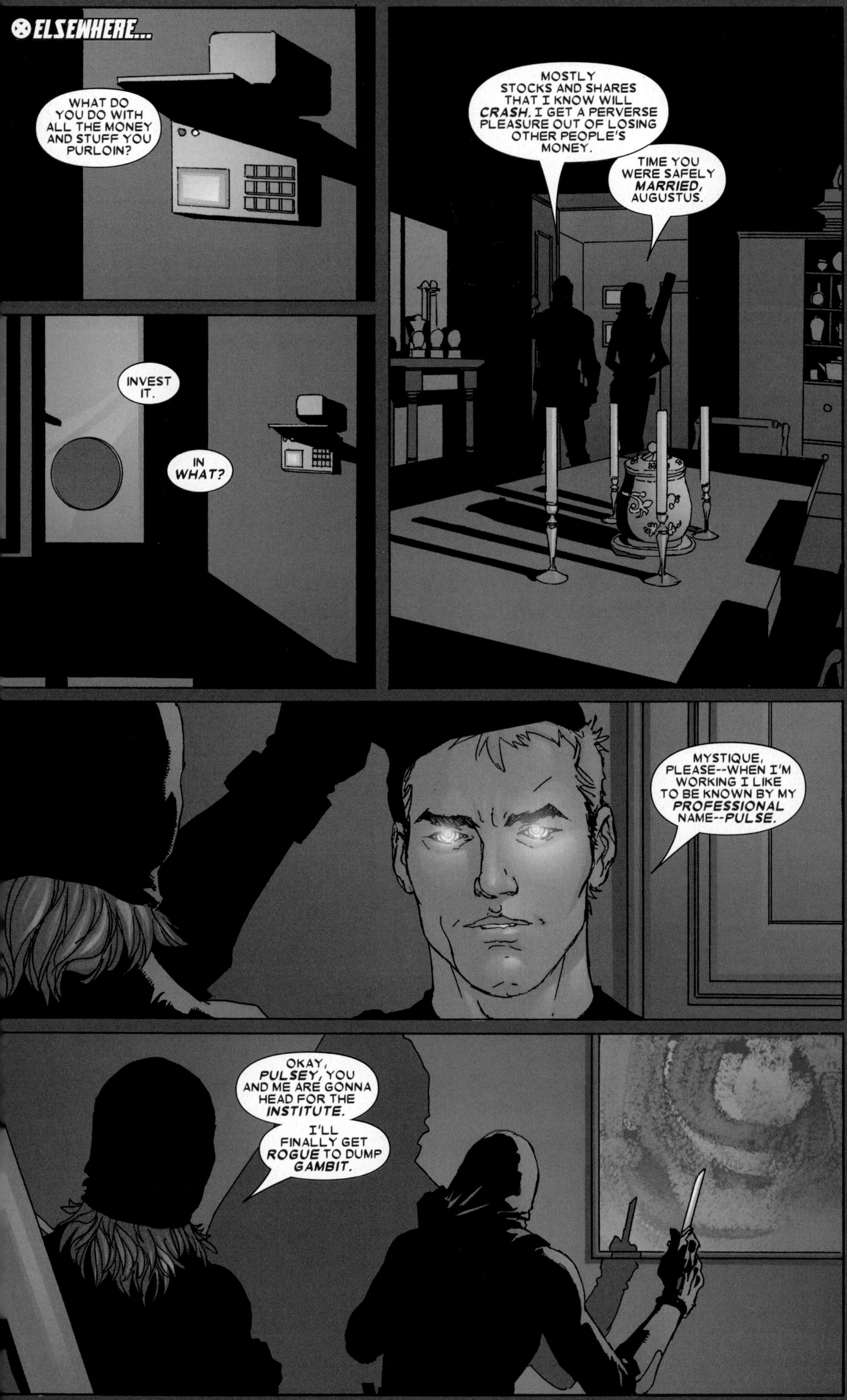
ELSEWHERE...
WHAT DO YOU DO WITH ALL THE MONEY AND STUFF YOU PURLOIN?
INVEST IT.
IN WHAT?
MOSTLY STOCKS AND SHARES THAT I KNOW WILL CRASH. I GET A PERVERSE PLEASURE OUT OF LOSING OTHER PEOPLE'S MONEY.
TIME YOU WERE SAFELY MARRIED, AUGUSTUS.
MYSTIQUE, PLEASE--WHEN I'M WORKING I LIKE TO BE KNOWN BY MY PROFESSIONAL NAME--PULSE.
OKAY, PULSEY, YOU AND ME ARE GONNA HEAD FOR THE INSTITUTE.
I'LL FINALLY GET ROGUE TO DUMP GAMBIT.

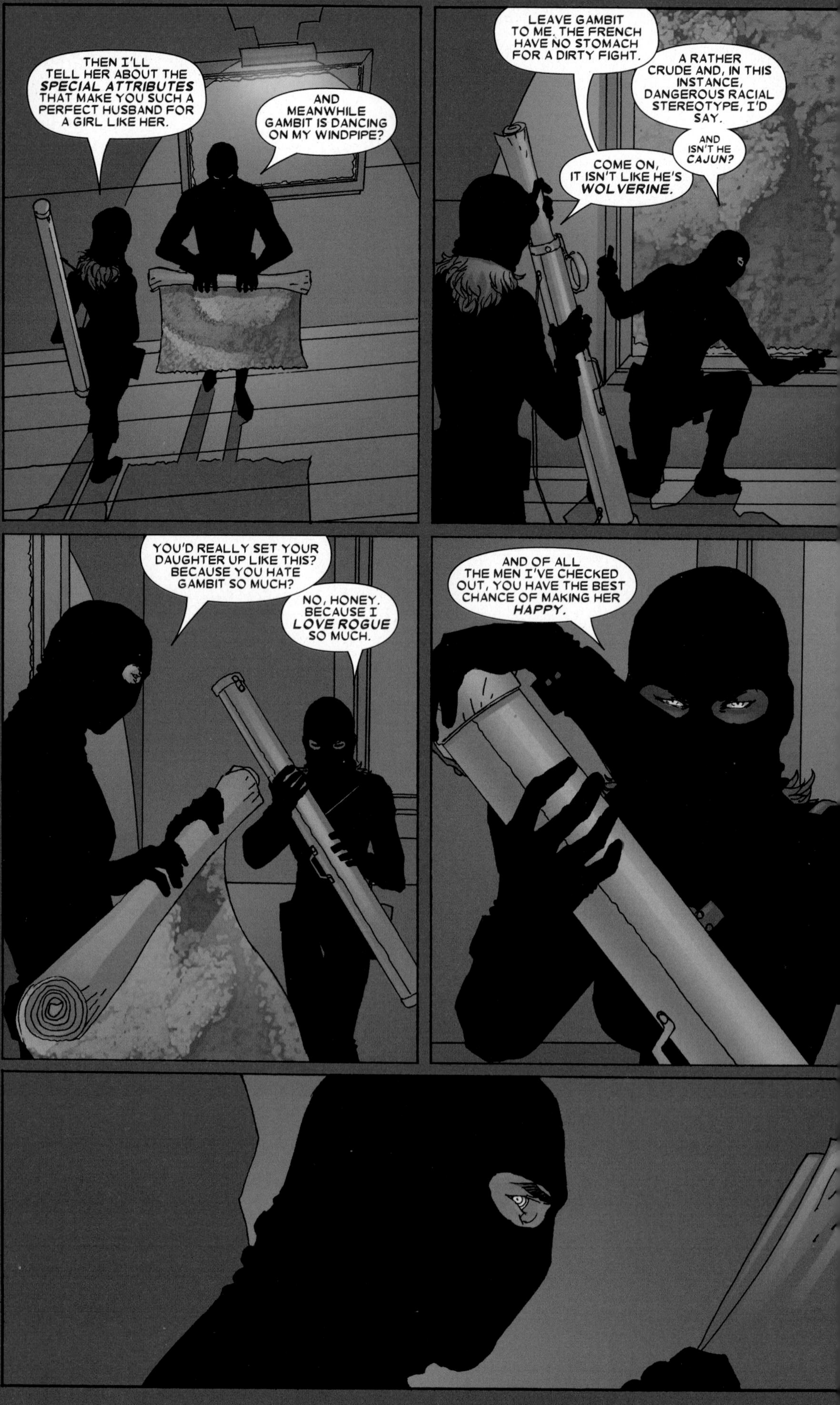
THEN I'LL TELL HER ABOUT THE SPECIAL ATTRIBUTES THAT MAKE YOU SUCH A PERFECT HUSBAND FOR A GIRL LIKE HER.
AND MEANWHILE GAMBIT IS DANCING ON MY WINDPIPE?
LEAVE GAMBIT TO ME. THE FRENCH HAVE NO STOMACH FOR A DIRTY FIGHT.
A RATHER CRUDE AND, IN THIS INSTANCE, DANGEROUS RACIAL STEREOTYPE, I'D SAY.
AND ISN'T HE CAJUN?
COME ON, IT ISN'T LIKE HE'S WOLVERINE.
YOU'D REALLY SET YOUR DAUGHTER UP LIKE THIS? BECAUSE YOU HATE GAMBIT SO MUCH?
NO, HONEY. BECAUSE I LOVE ROGUE SO MUCH.
AND OF ALL THE MEN I'VE CHECKED OUT, YOU HAVE THE BEST CHANCE OF MAKING HER HAPPY.

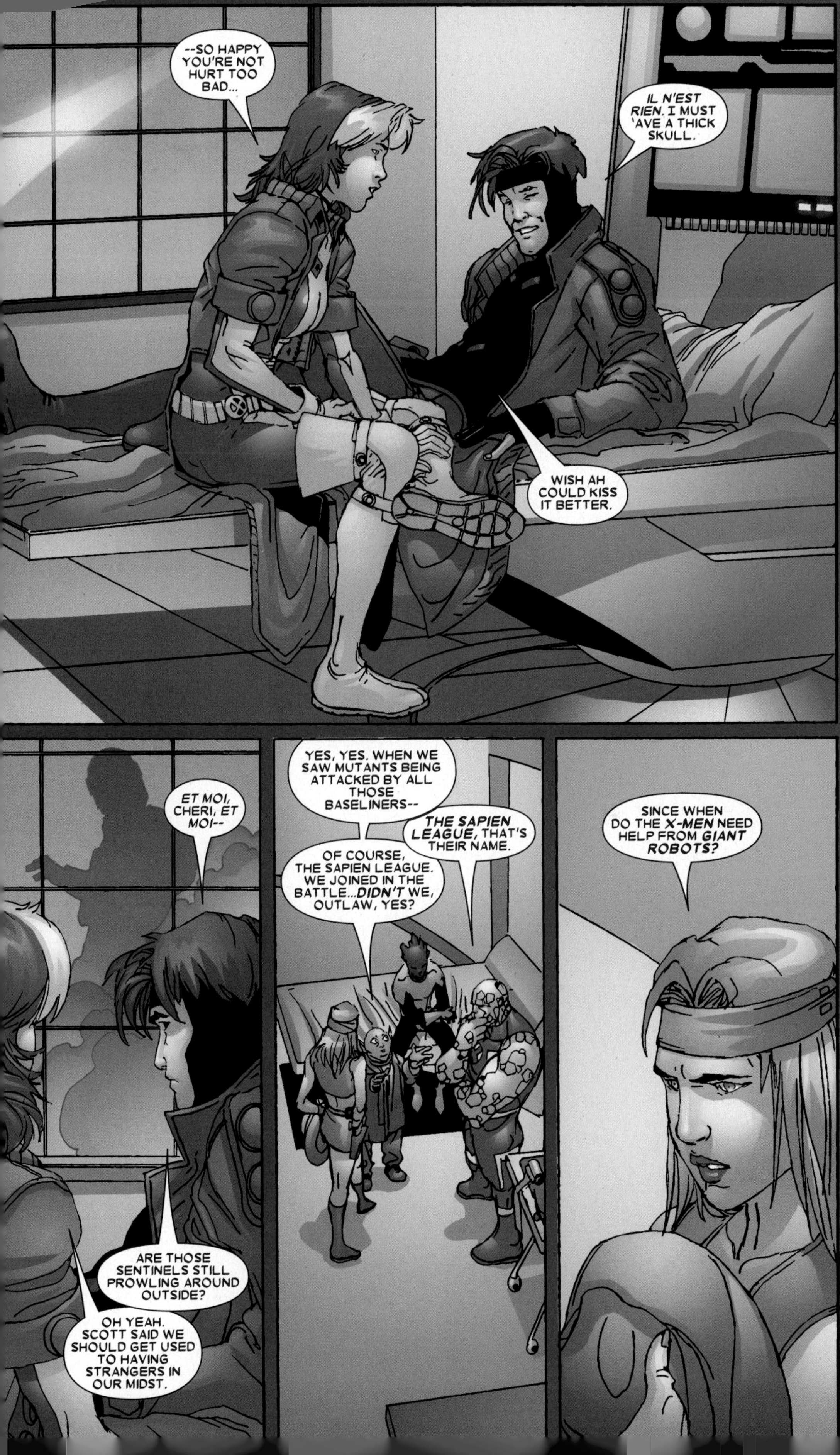
--SO HAPPY YOU'RE NOT HURT TOO BAD...
IL N'EST RIEN. I MUST 'AVE A THICK SKULL.
WISH AH COULD KISS IT BETTER.
ET MOI, CHERI, ET MOI--
ARE THOSE SENTINELS STILL PROWLING AROUND OUTSIDE?
OH YEAH. SCOTT SAID WE SHOULD GET USED TO HAVING STRANGERS IN OUR MIDST.
YES, YES. WHEN WE SAW MUTANTS BEING ATTACKED BY ALL THOSE BASELINERS--
THE SAPIEN LEAGUE, THAT'S THEIR NAME.
OF COURSE, THE SAPIEN LEAGUE. WE JOINED IN THE BATTLE...DIDN'T WE, OUTLAW, YES?
SINCE WHEN DO THE X-MEN NEED HELP FROM GIANT ROBOTS?

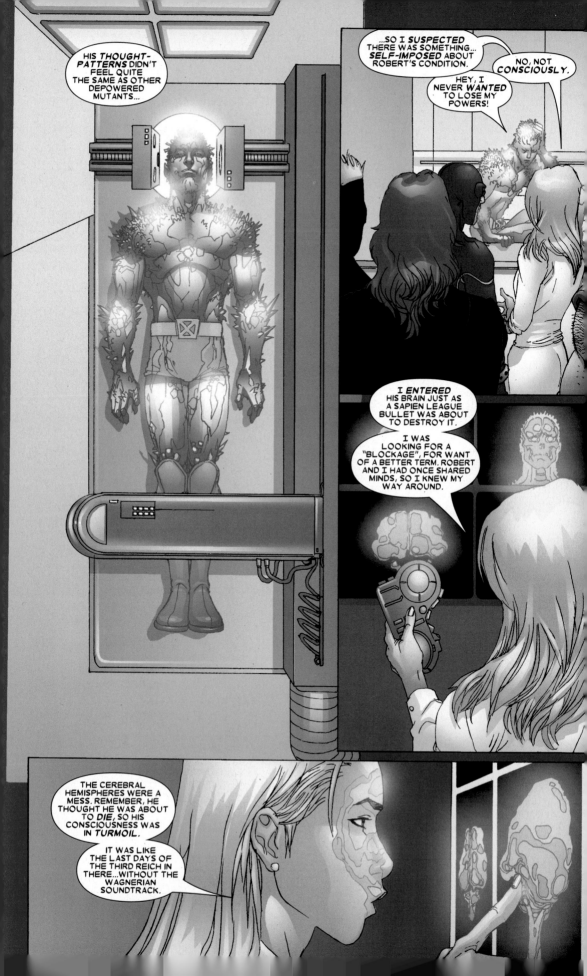

HIS *THOUGHT-PATTERNS* DIDN'T FEEL QUITE THE SAME AS OTHER DEPOWERED MUTANTS...

...SO I *SUSPECTED* THERE WAS SOMETHING... *SELF-IMPOSED* ABOUT ROBERT'S CONDITION.

NO, NOT *CONSCIOUSLY.*

HEY, I NEVER *WANTED* TO LOSE MY POWERS!

I *ENTERED* HIS BRAIN JUST AS A SAPIEN LEAGUE BULLET WAS ABOUT TO DESTROY IT.

I WAS LOOKING FOR A "BLOCKAGE", FOR WANT OF A BETTER TERM. ROBERT AND I HAD ONCE SHARED MINDS, SO I KNEW MY WAY AROUND.

THE CEREBRAL HEMISPHERES WERE A MESS. REMEMBER, HE THOUGHT HE WAS ABOUT TO *DIE*, SO HIS CONSCIOUSNESS WAS IN *TURMOIL.*

IT WAS LIKE THE LAST DAYS OF THE THIRD REICH IN THERE...WITHOUT THE WAGNERIAN SOUNDTRACK.

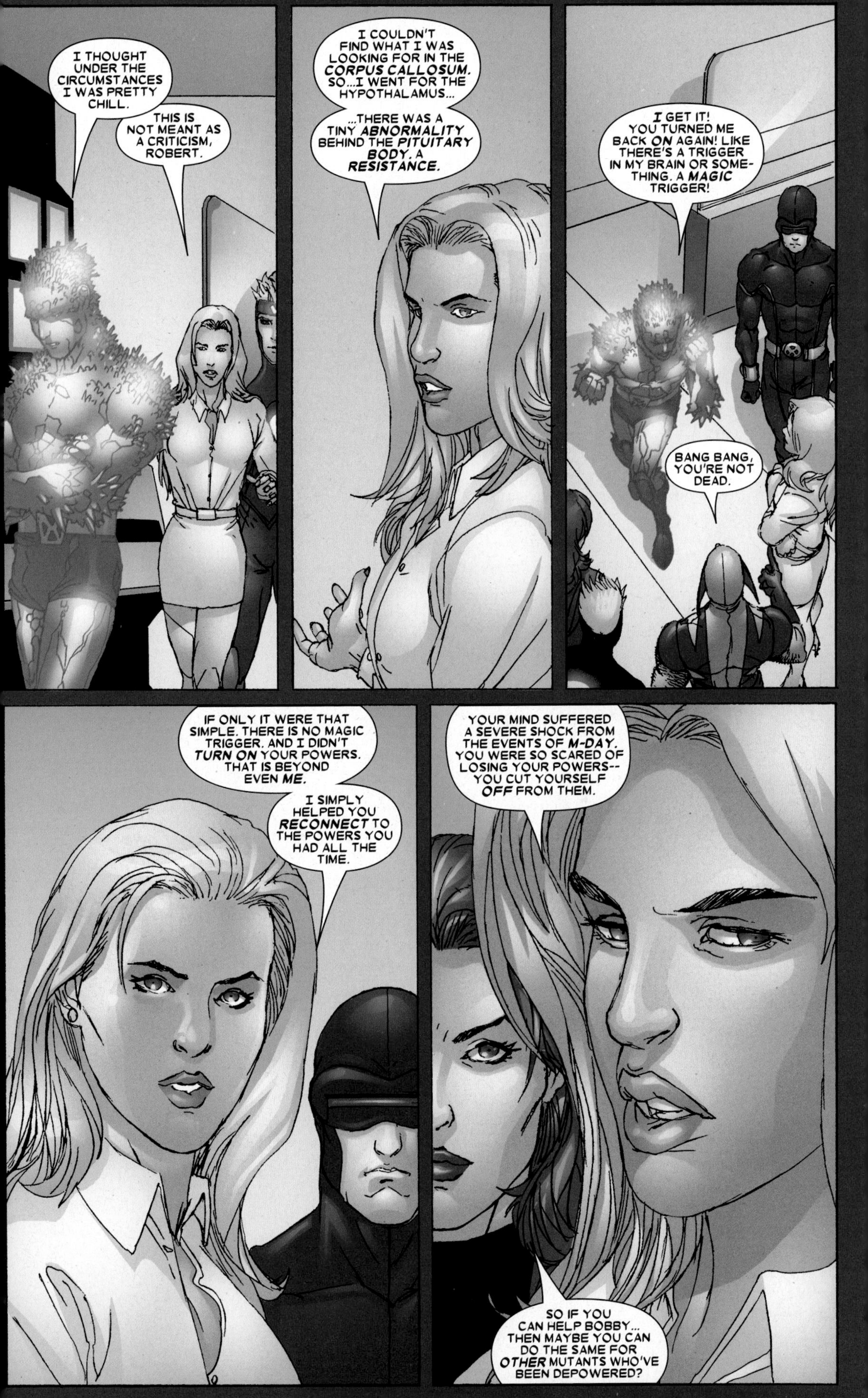
I THOUGHT UNDER THE CIRCUMSTANCES I WAS PRETTY CHILL.
THIS IS NOT MEANT AS A CRITICISM, ROBERT.
I COULDN'T FIND WHAT I WAS LOOKING FOR IN THE CORPUS CALLOSUM. SO...I WENT FOR THE HYPOTHALAMUS...
...THERE WAS A TINY ABNORMALITY BEHIND THE PITUITARY BODY. A RESISTANCE.
I GET IT! YOU TURNED ME BACK ON AGAIN! LIKE THERE'S A TRIGGER IN MY BRAIN OR SOME-THING. A MAGIC TRIGGER!
BANG BANG, YOU'RE NOT DEAD.
IF ONLY IT WERE THAT SIMPLE. THERE IS NO MAGIC TRIGGER. AND I DIDN'T TURN ON YOUR POWERS. THAT IS BEYOND EVEN ME.
I SIMPLY HELPED YOU RECONNECT TO THE POWERS YOU HAD ALL THE TIME.
YOUR MIND SUFFERED A SEVERE SHOCK FROM THE EVENTS OF M-DAY. YOU WERE SO SCARED OF LOSING YOUR POWERS-- YOU CUT YOURSELF OFF FROM THEM.
SO IF YOU CAN HELP BOBBY... THEN MAYBE YOU CAN DO THE SAME FOR OTHER MUTANTS WHO'VE BEEN DEPOWERED?

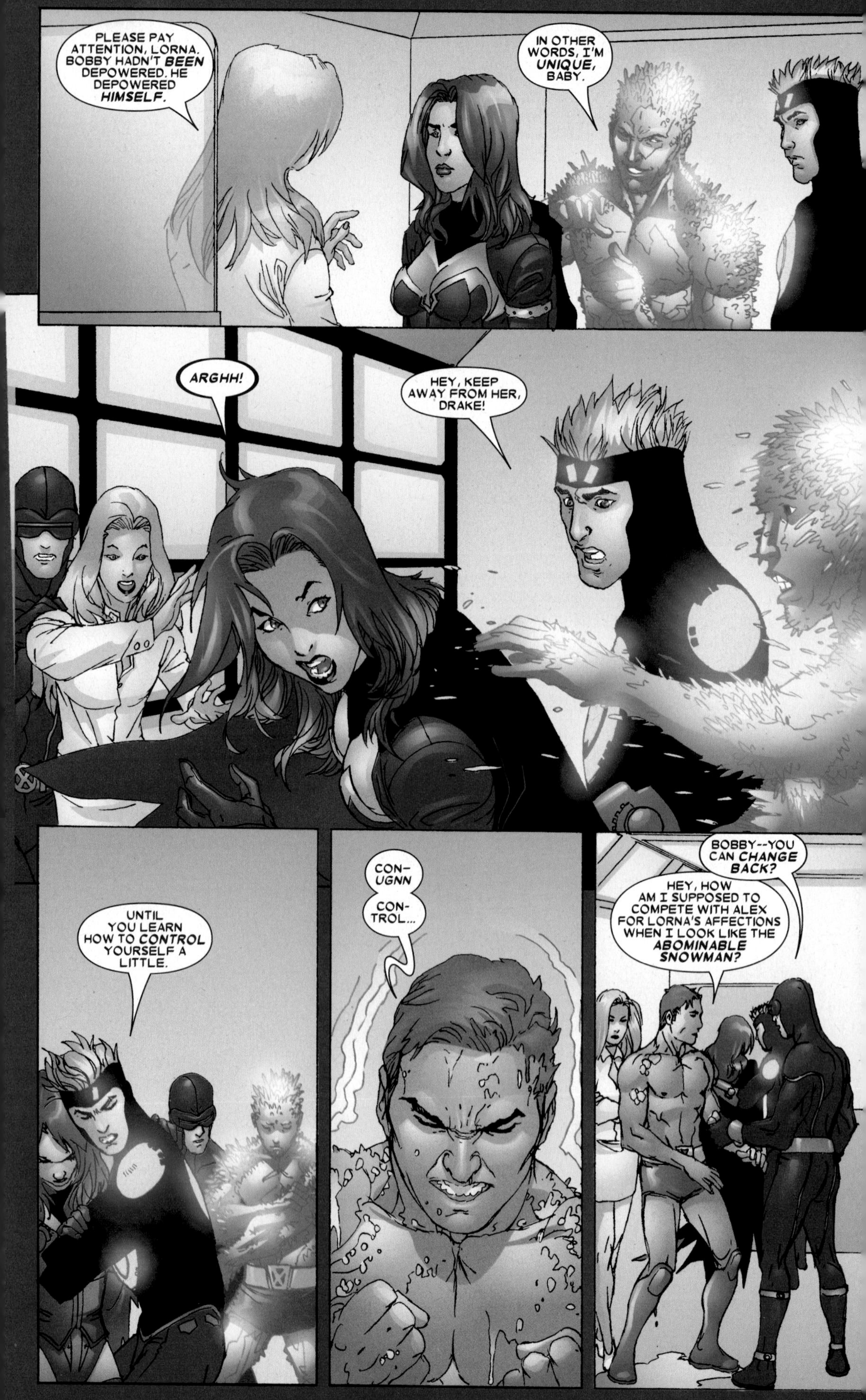
PLEASE PAY ATTENTION, LORNA. BOBBY HADN'T *BEEN* DEPOWERED. HE DEPOWERED *HIMSELF*.
IN OTHER WORDS, I'M *UNIQUE*, BABY.
ARGHH!
HEY, KEEP AWAY FROM HER, DRAKE!
UNTIL YOU LEARN HOW TO *CONTROL* YOURSELF A LITTLE.
CON-UGNN
CON-TROL...
BOBBY--YOU CAN *CHANGE BACK?*
HEY, HOW AM I SUPPOSED TO COMPETE WITH ALEX FOR LORNA'S AFFECTIONS WHEN I LOOK LIKE THE *ABOMINABLE SNOWMAN?*

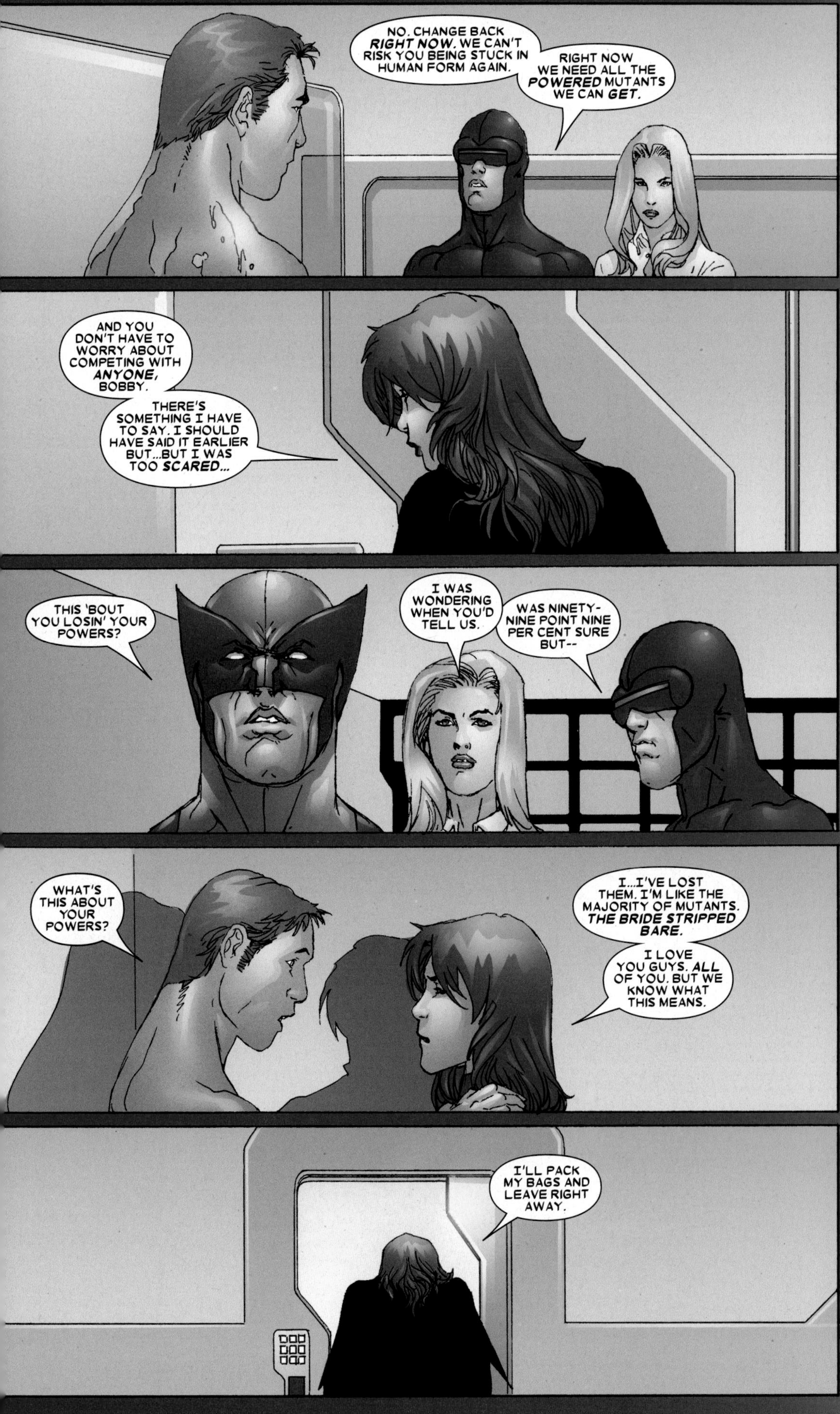
NO. CHANGE BACK RIGHT NOW. WE CAN'T RISK YOU BEING STUCK IN HUMAN FORM AGAIN.
RIGHT NOW WE NEED ALL THE POWERED MUTANTS WE CAN GET.
AND YOU DON'T HAVE TO WORRY ABOUT COMPETING WITH ANYONE, BOBBY.
THERE'S SOMETHING I HAVE TO SAY. I SHOULD HAVE SAID IT EARLIER BUT...BUT I WAS TOO SCARED...
THIS 'BOUT YOU LOSIN' YOUR POWERS?
I WAS WONDERING WHEN YOU'D TELL US.
WAS NINETY-NINE POINT NINE PER CENT SURE BUT--
WHAT'S THIS ABOUT YOUR POWERS?
I...I'VE LOST THEM. I'M LIKE THE MAJORITY OF MUTANTS. THE BRIDE STRIPPED BARE.
I LOVE YOU GUYS. ALL OF YOU. BUT WE KNOW WHAT THIS MEANS.
I'LL PACK MY BAGS AND LEAVE RIGHT AWAY.

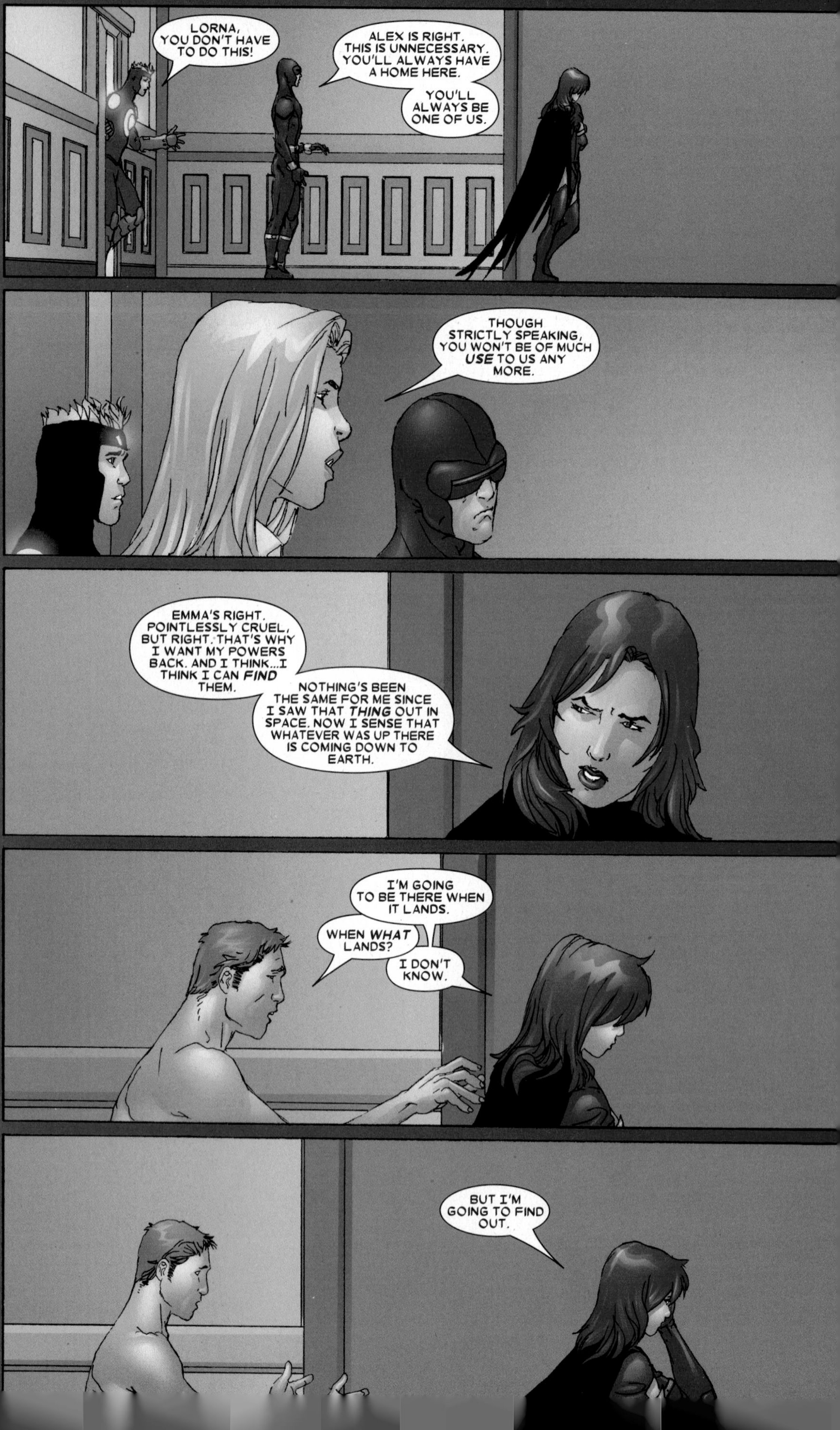

LORNA, YOU DON'T HAVE TO DO THIS!
ALEX IS RIGHT. THIS IS UNNECESSARY. YOU'LL ALWAYS HAVE A HOME HERE.
YOU'LL ALWAYS BE ONE OF US.
THOUGH STRICTLY SPEAKING, YOU WON'T BE OF MUCH *USE* TO US ANY MORE.
EMMA'S RIGHT. POINTLESSLY CRUEL, BUT RIGHT. THAT'S WHY I WANT MY POWERS BACK. AND I THINK...I THINK I CAN *FIND* THEM.
NOTHING'S BEEN THE SAME FOR ME SINCE I SAW THAT *THING* OUT IN SPACE. NOW I SENSE THAT WHATEVER WAS UP THERE IS COMING DOWN TO EARTH.
I'M GOING TO BE THERE WHEN IT LANDS.
WHEN *WHAT* LANDS?
I DON'T KNOW.
BUT I'M GOING TO FIND OUT.

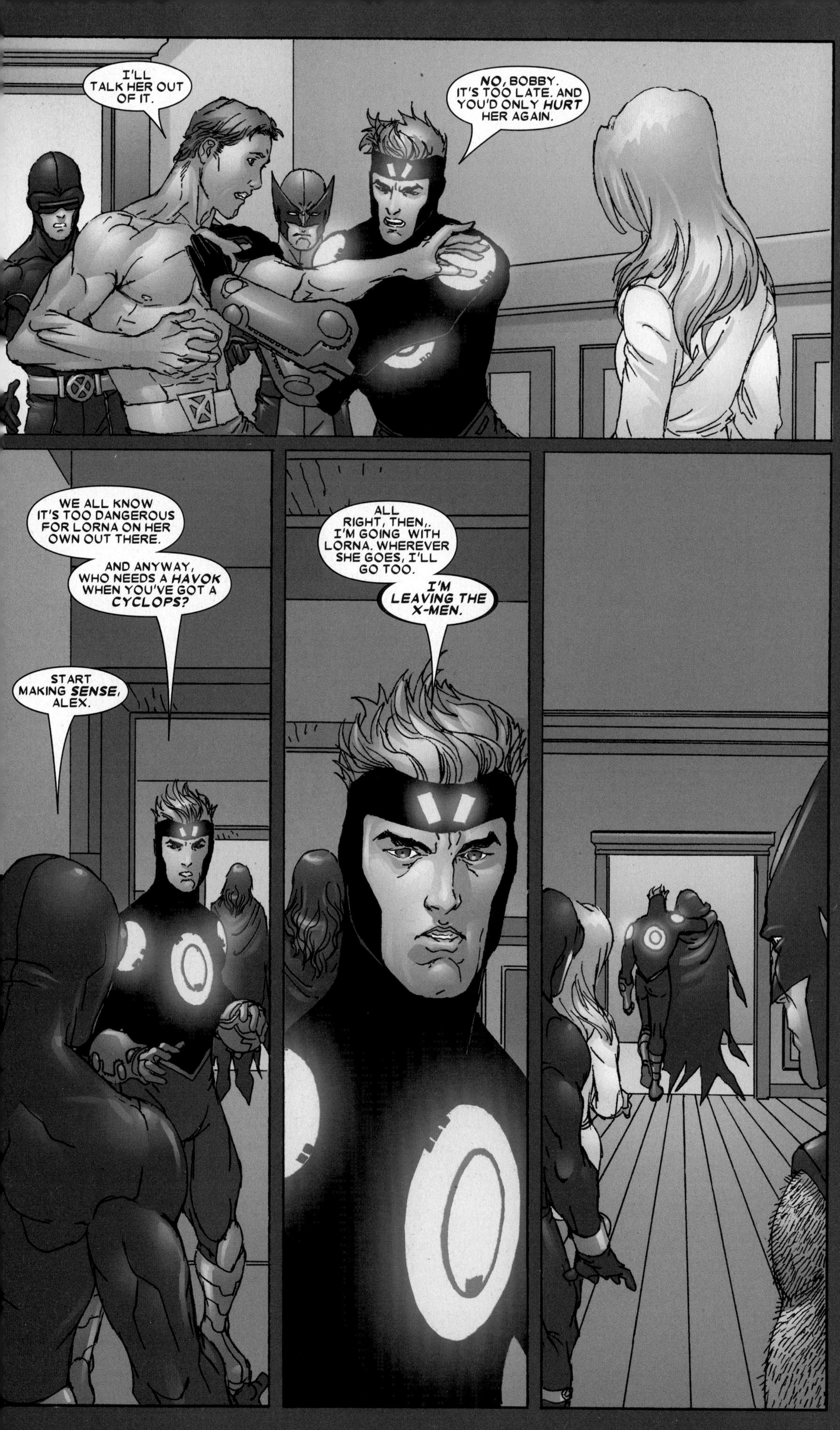
I'LL TALK HER OUT OF IT.
NO, BOBBY. IT'S TOO LATE. AND YOU'D ONLY HURT HER AGAIN.
WE ALL KNOW IT'S TOO DANGEROUS FOR LORNA ON HER OWN OUT THERE.
AND ANYWAY, WHO NEEDS A HAVOK WHEN YOU'VE GOT A CYCLOPS?
START MAKING SENSE, ALEX.
ALL RIGHT, THEN,. I'M GOING WITH LORNA. WHEREVER SHE GOES, I'LL GO TOO.
I'M LEAVING THE X-MEN.

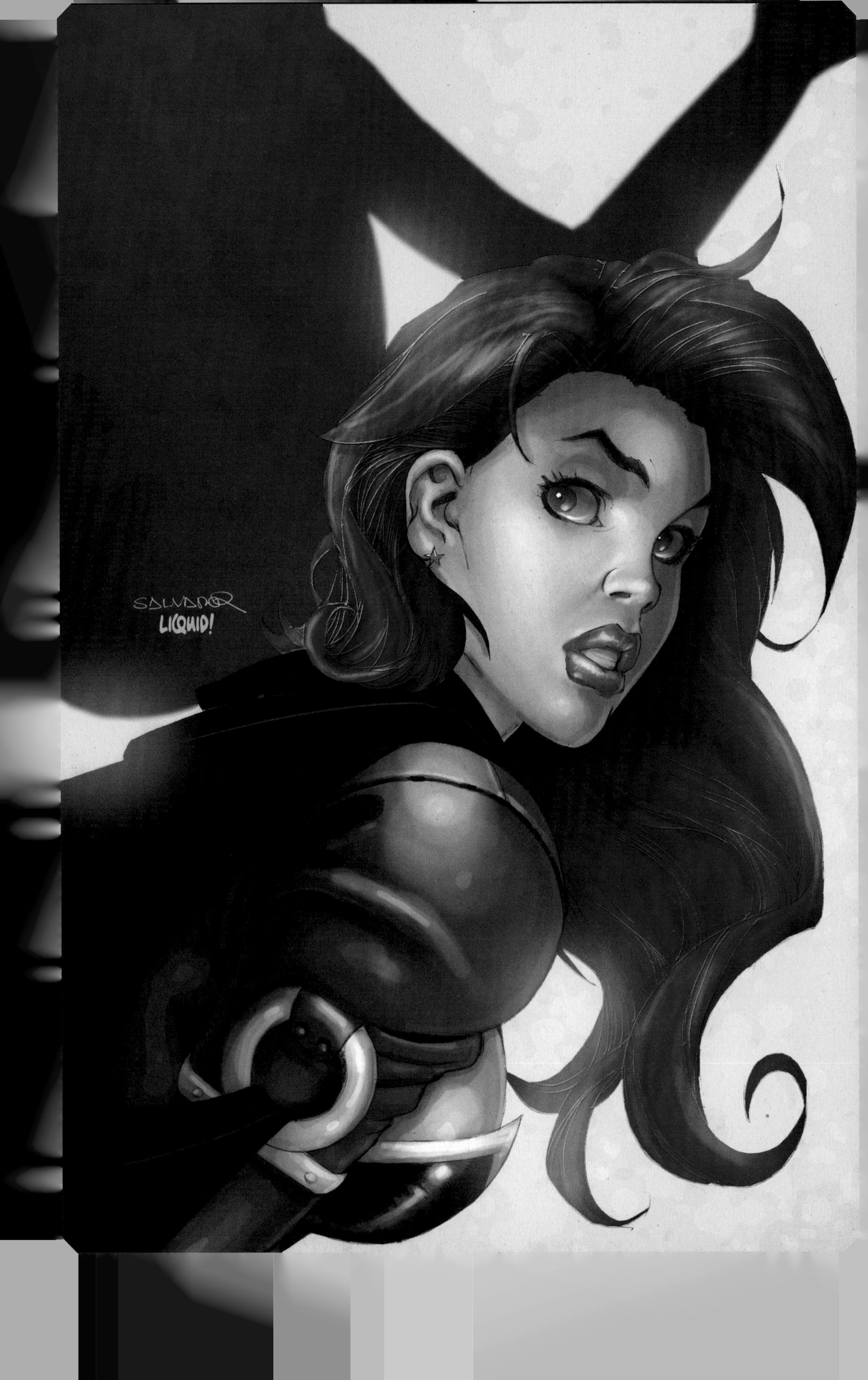
SALVADOR
LICQUID!

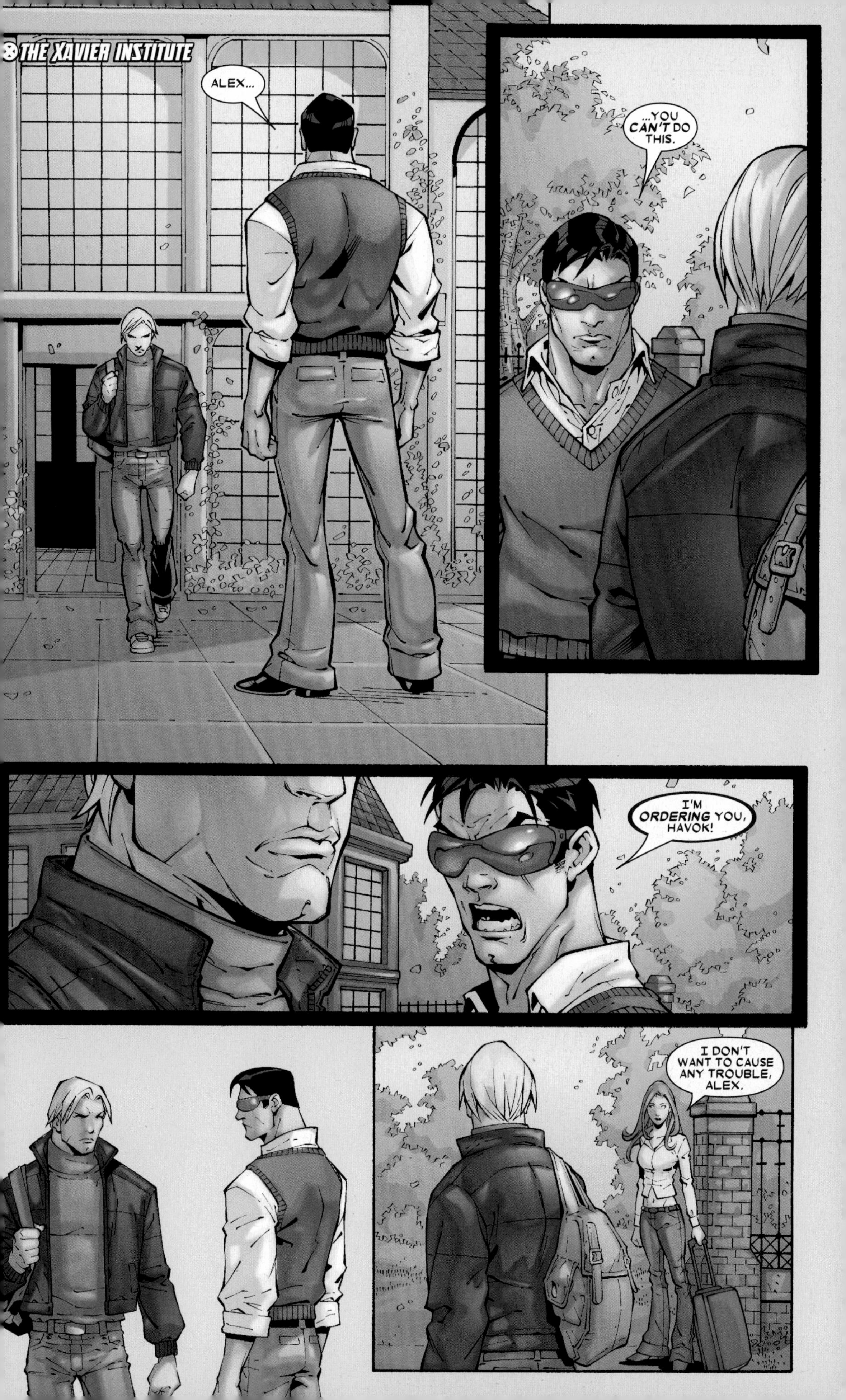
THE XAVIER INSTITUTE
ALEX...
...YOU CAN'T DO THIS.
I'M ORDERING YOU, HAVOK!
I DON'T WANT TO CAUSE ANY TROUBLE, ALEX.

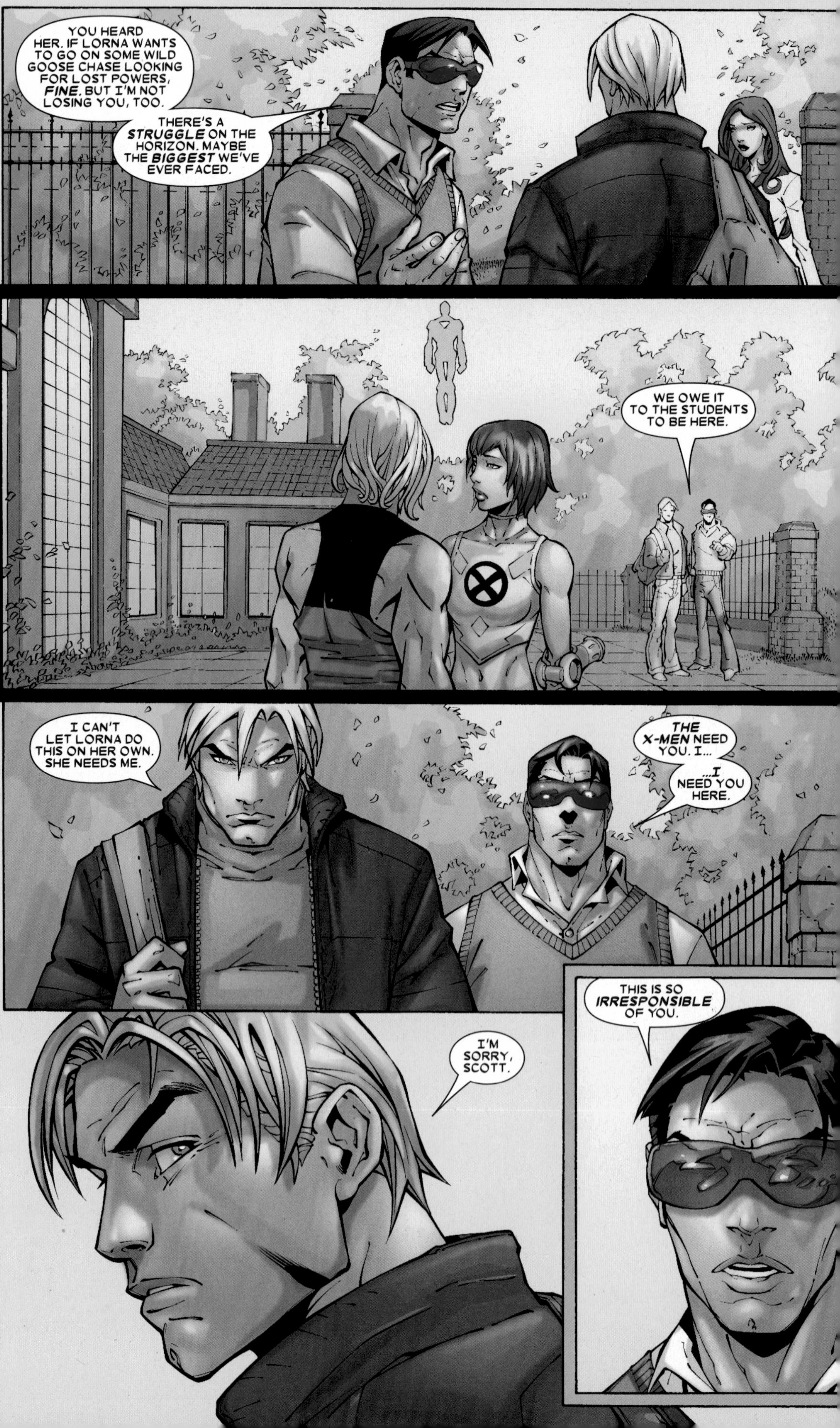
YOU HEARD HER. IF LORNA WANTS TO GO ON SOME WILD GOOSE CHASE LOOKING FOR LOST POWERS, FINE. BUT I'M NOT LOSING YOU, TOO.
THERE'S A STRUGGLE ON THE HORIZON. MAYBE THE BIGGEST WE'VE EVER FACED.
WE OWE IT TO THE STUDENTS TO BE HERE.
I CAN'T LET LORNA DO THIS ON HER OWN. SHE NEEDS ME.
THE X-MEN NEED YOU. I...
...I NEED YOU HERE.
I'M SORRY, SCOTT.
THIS IS SO IRRESPONSIBLE OF YOU.

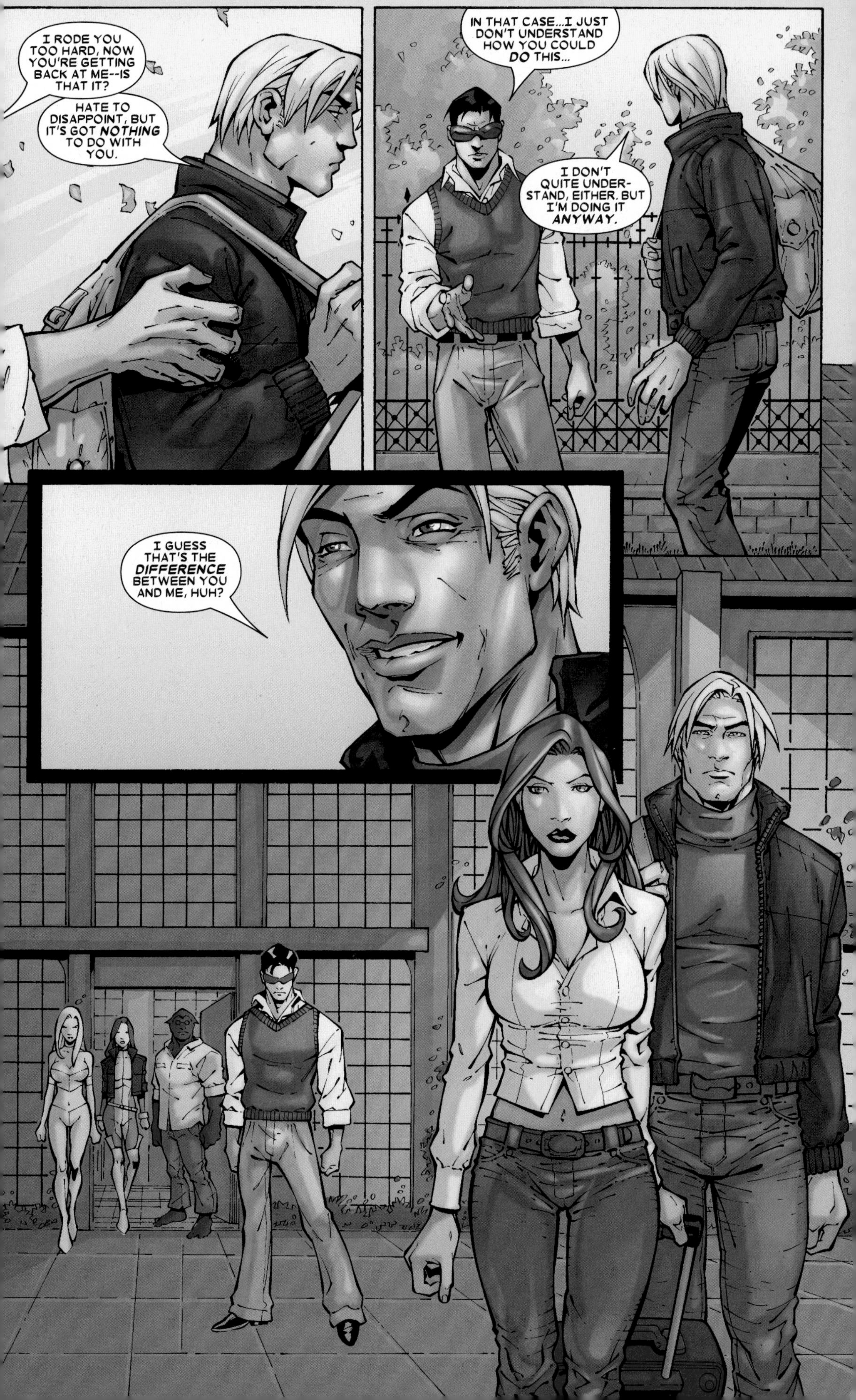
I RODE YOU TOO HARD, NOW YOU'RE GETTING BACK AT ME--IS THAT IT?
HATE TO DISAPPOINT, BUT IT'S GOT NOTHING TO DO WITH YOU.
IN THAT CASE...I JUST DON'T UNDERSTAND HOW YOU COULD DO THIS...
I DON'T QUITE UNDER-STAND, EITHER. BUT I'M DOING IT ANYWAY.
I GUESS THAT'S THE DIFFERENCE BETWEEN YOU AND ME, HUH?

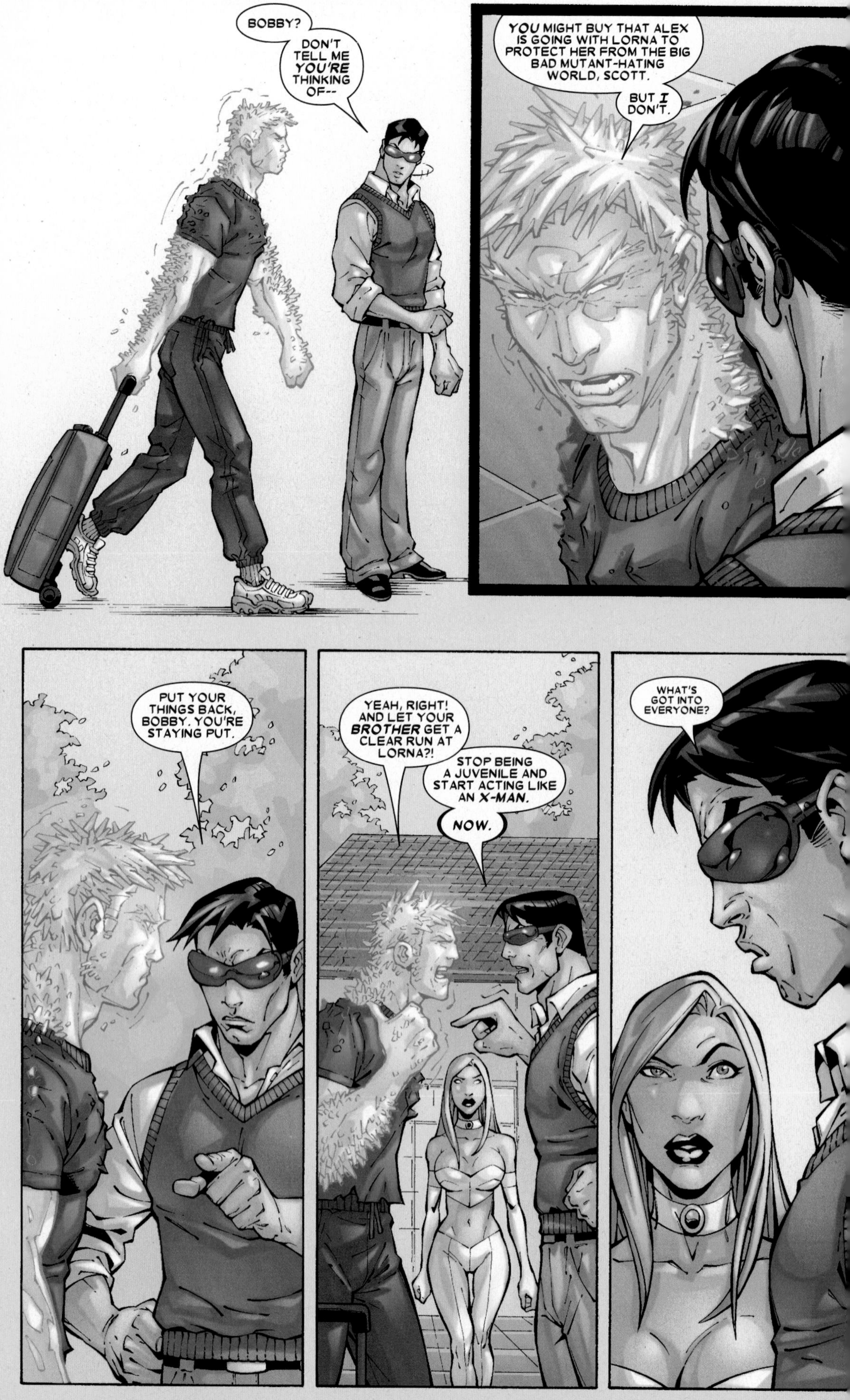
BOBBY?
DON'T TELL ME YOU'RE THINKING OF--
YOU MIGHT BUY THAT ALEX IS GOING WITH LORNA TO PROTECT HER FROM THE BIG BAD MUTANT-HATING WORLD, SCOTT.
BUT I DON'T.
PUT YOUR THINGS BACK, BOBBY. YOU'RE STAYING PUT.
YEAH, RIGHT! AND LET YOUR BROTHER GET A CLEAR RUN AT LORNA?!
STOP BEING A JUVENILE AND START ACTING LIKE AN X-MAN.
NOW.
WHAT'S GOT INTO EVERYONE?

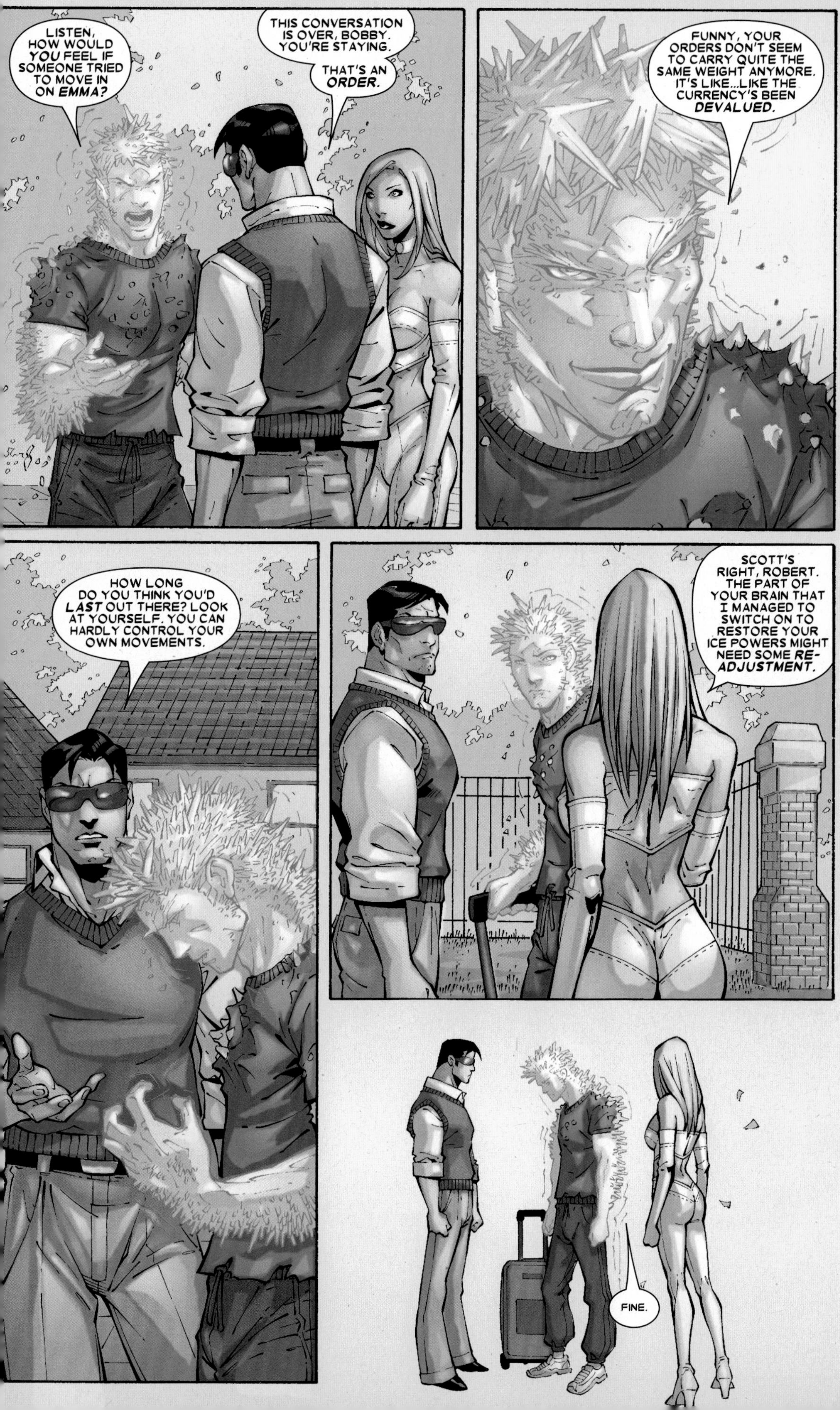
LISTEN, HOW WOULD YOU FEEL IF SOMEONE TRIED TO MOVE IN ON EMMA?
THIS CONVERSATION IS OVER, BOBBY. YOU'RE STAYING.
THAT'S AN ORDER.
FUNNY, YOUR ORDERS DON'T SEEM TO CARRY QUITE THE SAME WEIGHT ANYMORE. IT'S LIKE...LIKE THE CURRENCY'S BEEN DEVALUED.
HOW LONG DO YOU THINK YOU'D LAST OUT THERE? LOOK AT YOURSELF. YOU CAN HARDLY CONTROL YOUR OWN MOVEMENTS.
SCOTT'S RIGHT, ROBERT. THE PART OF YOUR BRAIN THAT I MANAGED TO SWITCH ON TO RESTORE YOUR ICE POWERS MIGHT NEED SOME RE-ADJUSTMENT.
FINE.

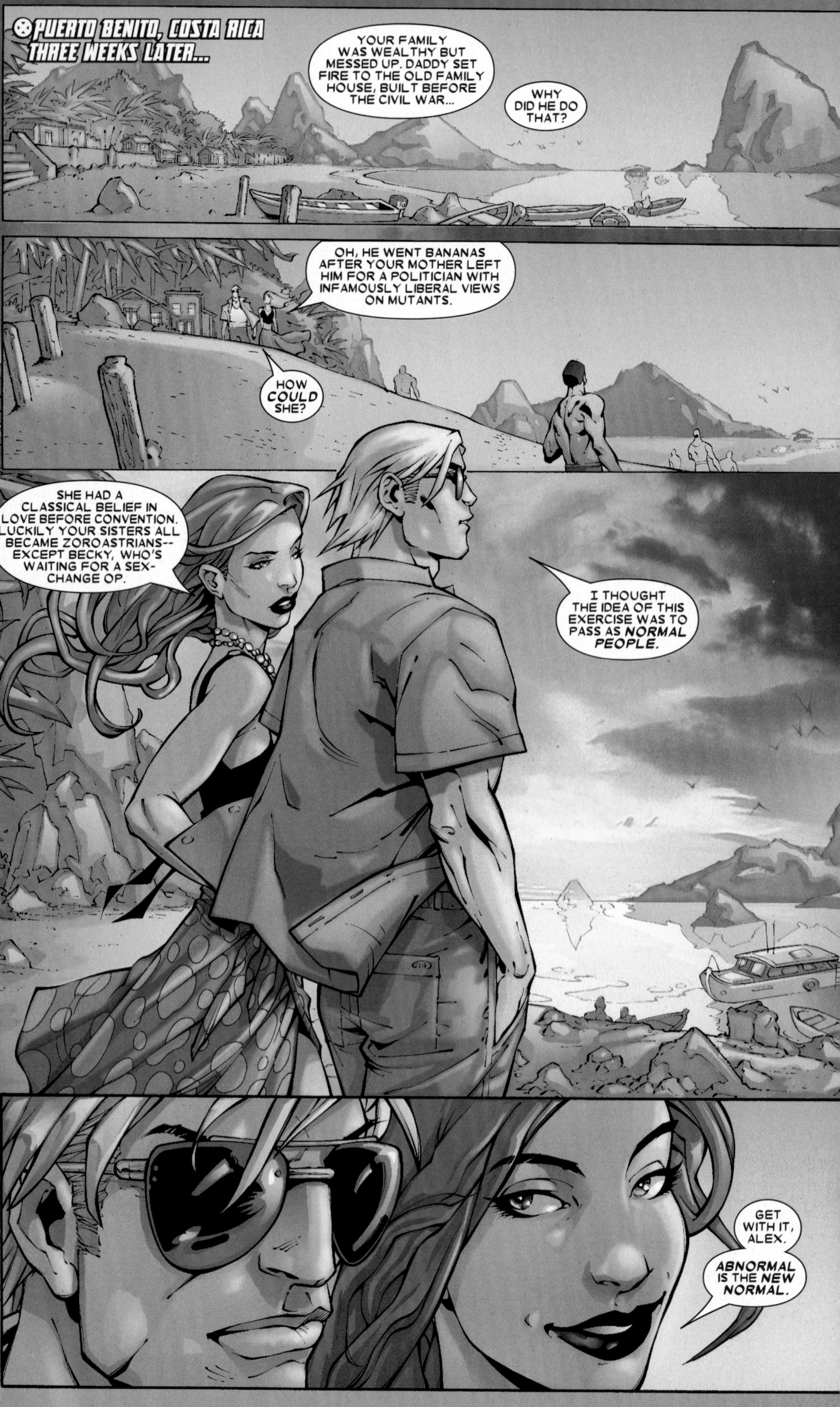
PUERTO BENITO, COSTA RICA
THREE WEEKS LATER...
YOUR FAMILY WAS WEALTHY BUT MESSED UP. DADDY SET FIRE TO THE OLD FAMILY HOUSE, BUILT BEFORE THE CIVIL WAR...
WHY DID HE DO THAT?
OH, HE WENT BANANAS AFTER YOUR MOTHER LEFT HIM FOR A POLITICIAN WITH INFAMOUSLY LIBERAL VIEWS ON MUTANTS.
HOW COULD SHE?
SHE HAD A CLASSICAL BELIEF IN LOVE BEFORE CONVENTION. LUCKILY YOUR SISTERS ALL BECAME ZOROASTRIANS-- EXCEPT BECKY, WHO'S WAITING FOR A SEX-CHANGE OP.
I THOUGHT THE IDEA OF THIS EXERCISE WAS TO PASS AS NORMAL PEOPLE.
GET WITH IT, ALEX.
ABNORMAL IS THE NEW NORMAL.

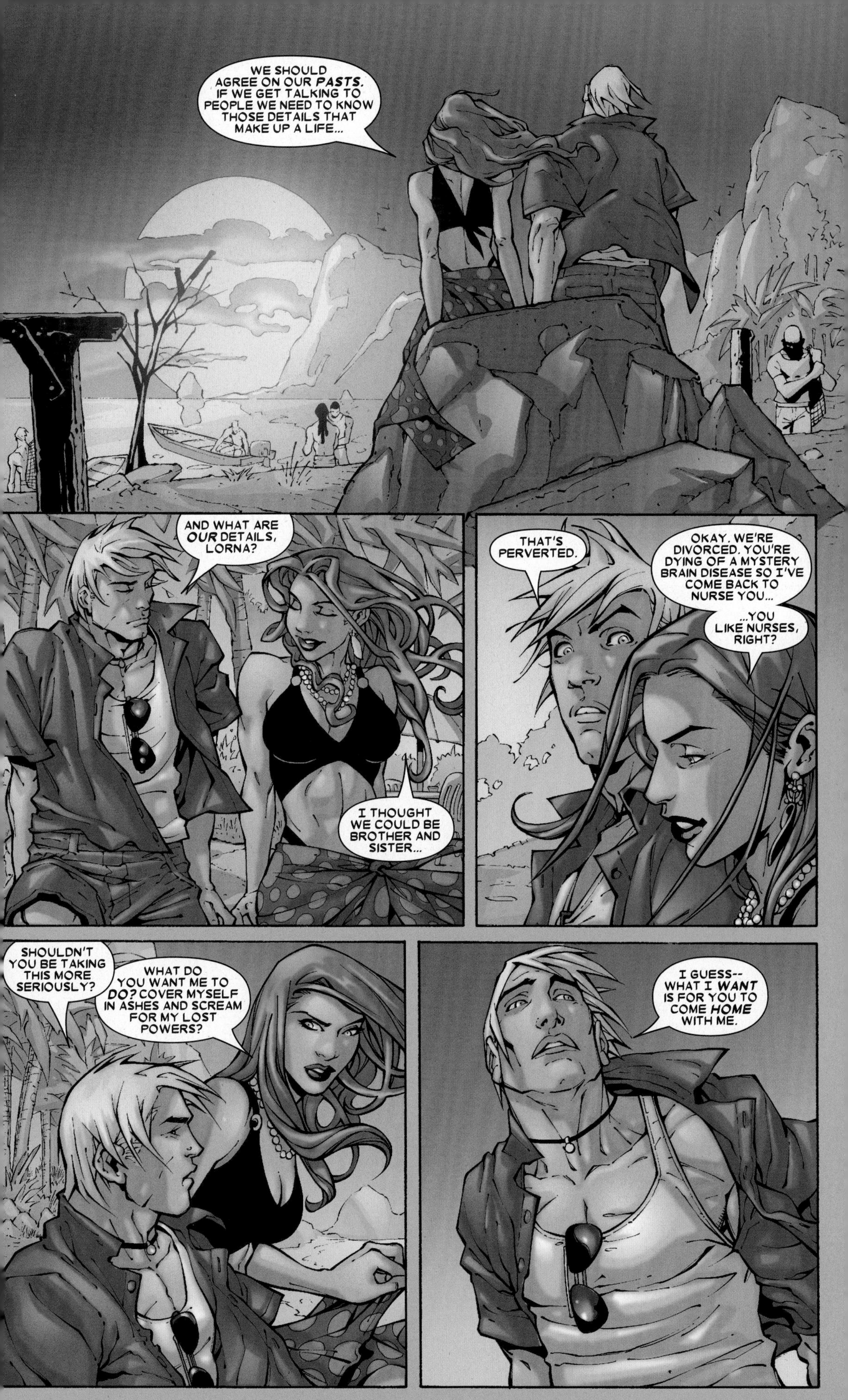

WE SHOULD AGREE ON OUR PASTS. IF WE GET TALKING TO PEOPLE WE NEED TO KNOW THOSE DETAILS THAT MAKE UP A LIFE...
AND WHAT ARE OUR DETAILS, LORNA?
I THOUGHT WE COULD BE BROTHER AND SISTER...
THAT'S PERVERTED.
OKAY. WE'RE DIVORCED. YOU'RE DYING OF A MYSTERY BRAIN DISEASE SO I'VE COME BACK TO NURSE YOU...
...YOU LIKE NURSES, RIGHT?
SHOULDN'T YOU BE TAKING THIS MORE SERIOUSLY?
WHAT DO YOU WANT ME TO DO? COVER MYSELF IN ASHES AND SCREAM FOR MY LOST POWERS?
I GUESS-- WHAT I WANT IS FOR YOU TO COME HOME WITH ME.

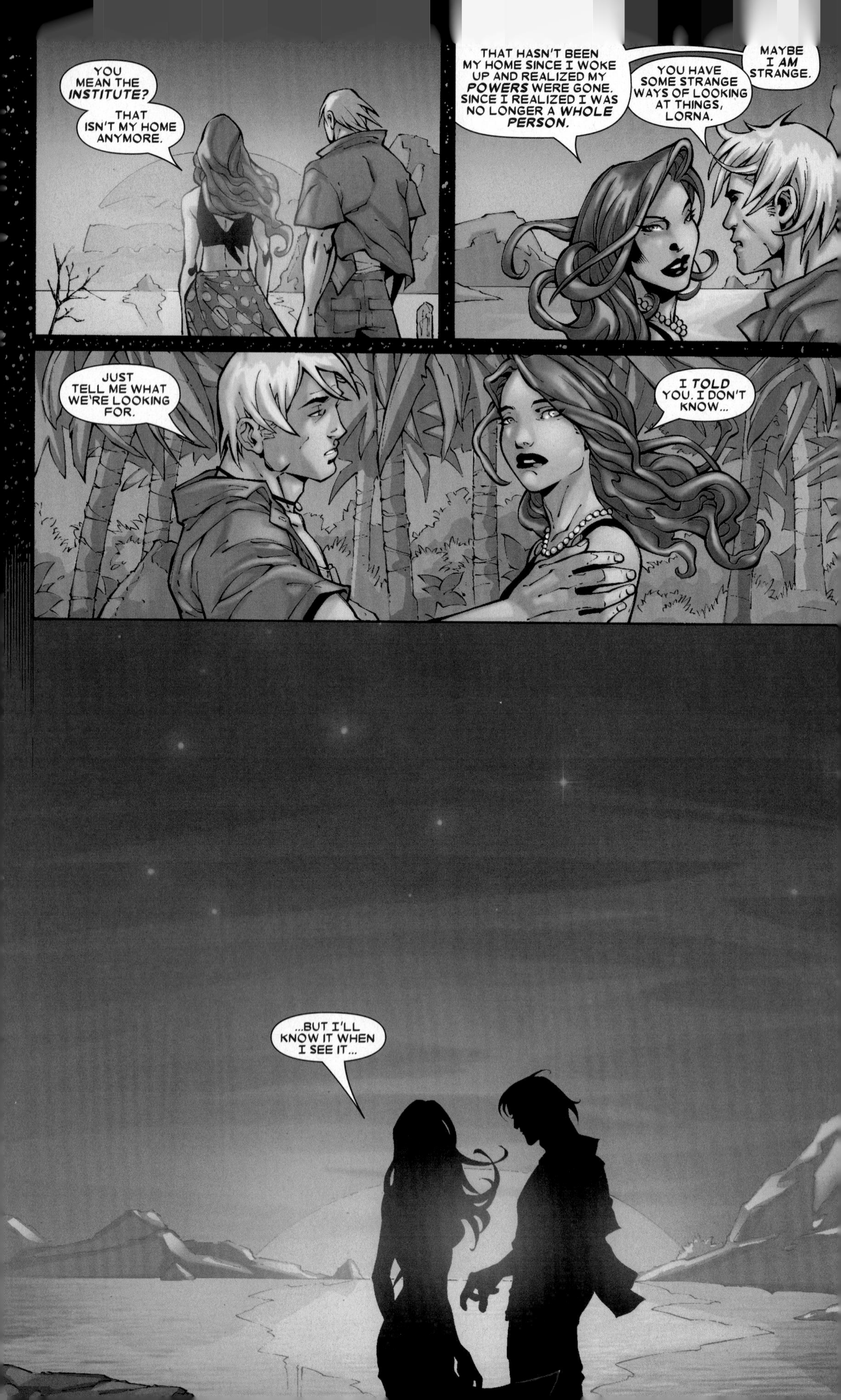

YOU MEAN THE INSTITUTE?
THAT ISN'T MY HOME ANYMORE.
THAT HASN'T BEEN MY HOME SINCE I WOKE UP AND REALIZED MY POWERS WERE GONE. SINCE I REALIZED I WAS NO LONGER A WHOLE PERSON.
YOU HAVE SOME STRANGE WAYS OF LOOKING AT THINGS, LORNA.
MAYBE I AM STRANGE.
JUST TELL ME WHAT WE'RE LOOKING FOR.
I TOLD YOU. I DON'T KNOW...
...BUT I'LL KNOW IT WHEN I SEE IT...

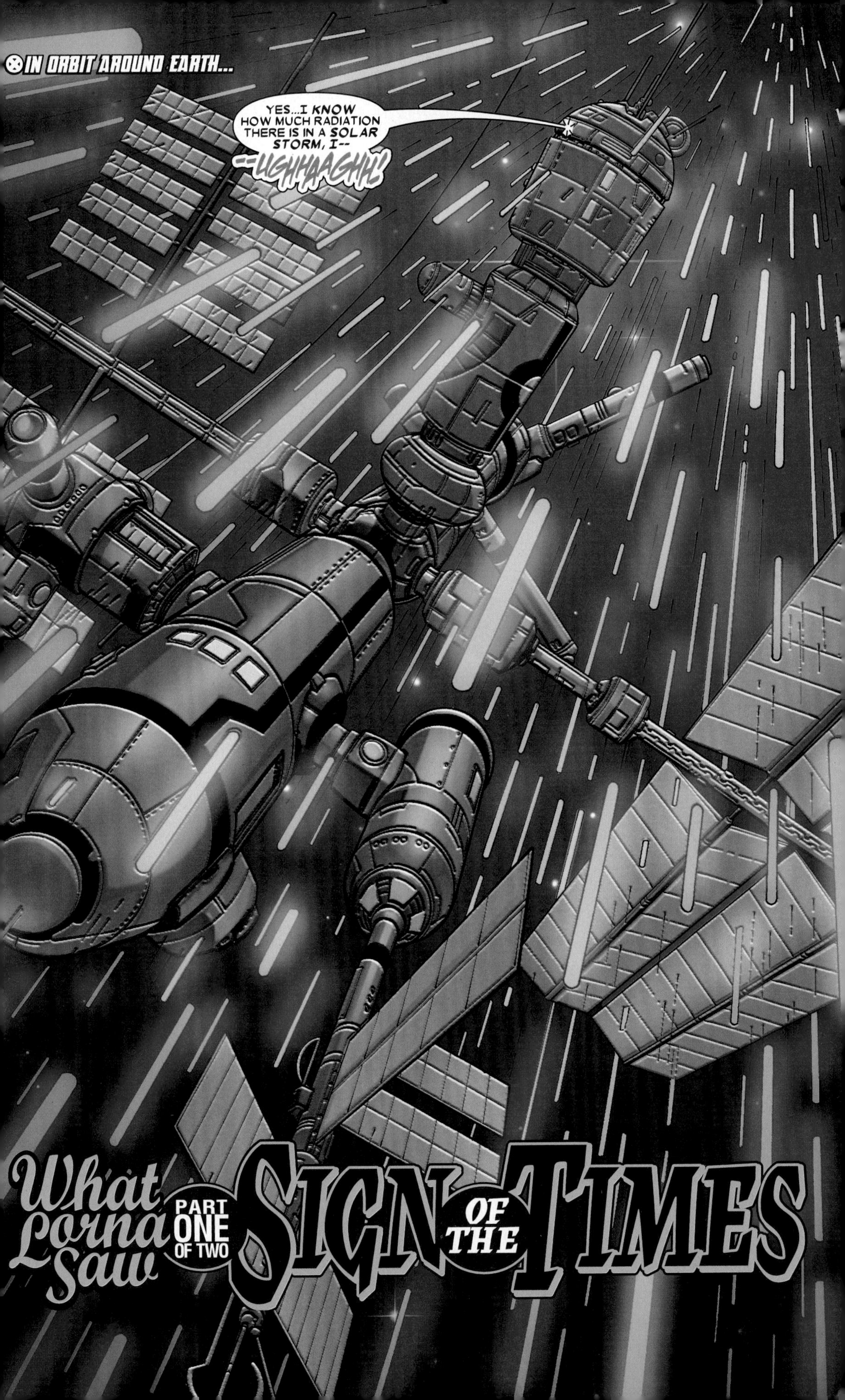
IN ORBIT AROUND EARTH...
YES...I KNOW HOW MUCH RADIATION THERE IS IN A SOLAR STORM, I--
--UGHHAAGHH!
What Lorna Saw
PART ONE OF TWO
SIGN OF THE TIMES

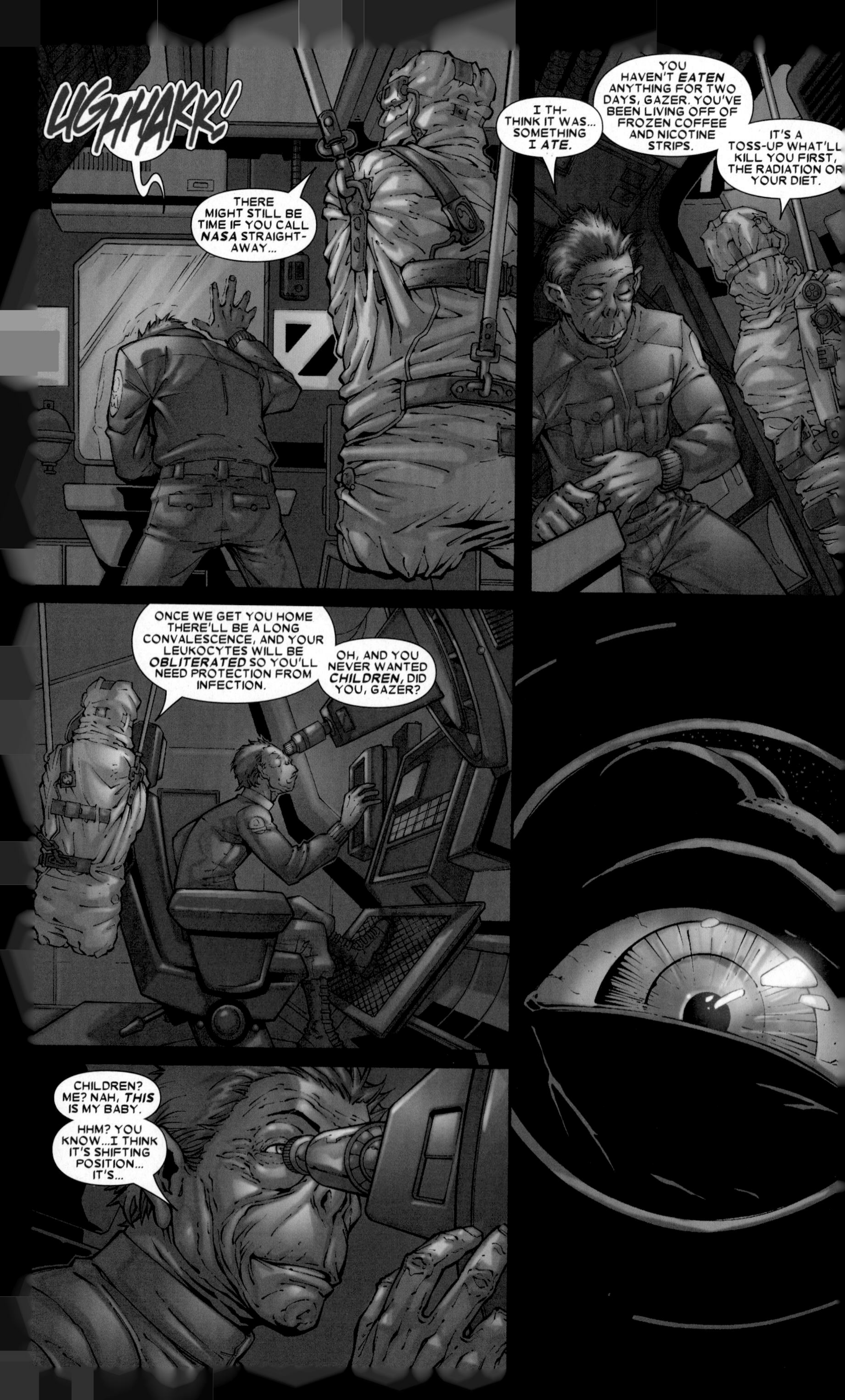
UGHHAKK!
THERE MIGHT STILL BE TIME IF YOU CALL NASA STRAIGHT-AWAY...
I TH-THINK IT WAS... SOMETHING I ATE.
YOU HAVEN'T EATEN ANYTHING FOR TWO DAYS, GAZER. YOU'VE BEEN LIVING OFF OF FROZEN COFFEE AND NICOTINE STRIPS.
IT'S A TOSS-UP WHAT'LL KILL YOU FIRST, THE RADIATION OR YOUR DIET.
ONCE WE GET YOU HOME THERE'LL BE A LONG CONVALESCENCE, AND YOUR LEUKOCYTES WILL BE OBLITERATED SO YOU'LL NEED PROTECTION FROM INFECTION.
OH, AND YOU NEVER WANTED CHILDREN, DID YOU, GAZER?
CHILDREN? ME? NAH, THIS IS MY BABY.
HHM? YOU KNOW...I THINK IT'S SHIFTING POSITION... IT'S...

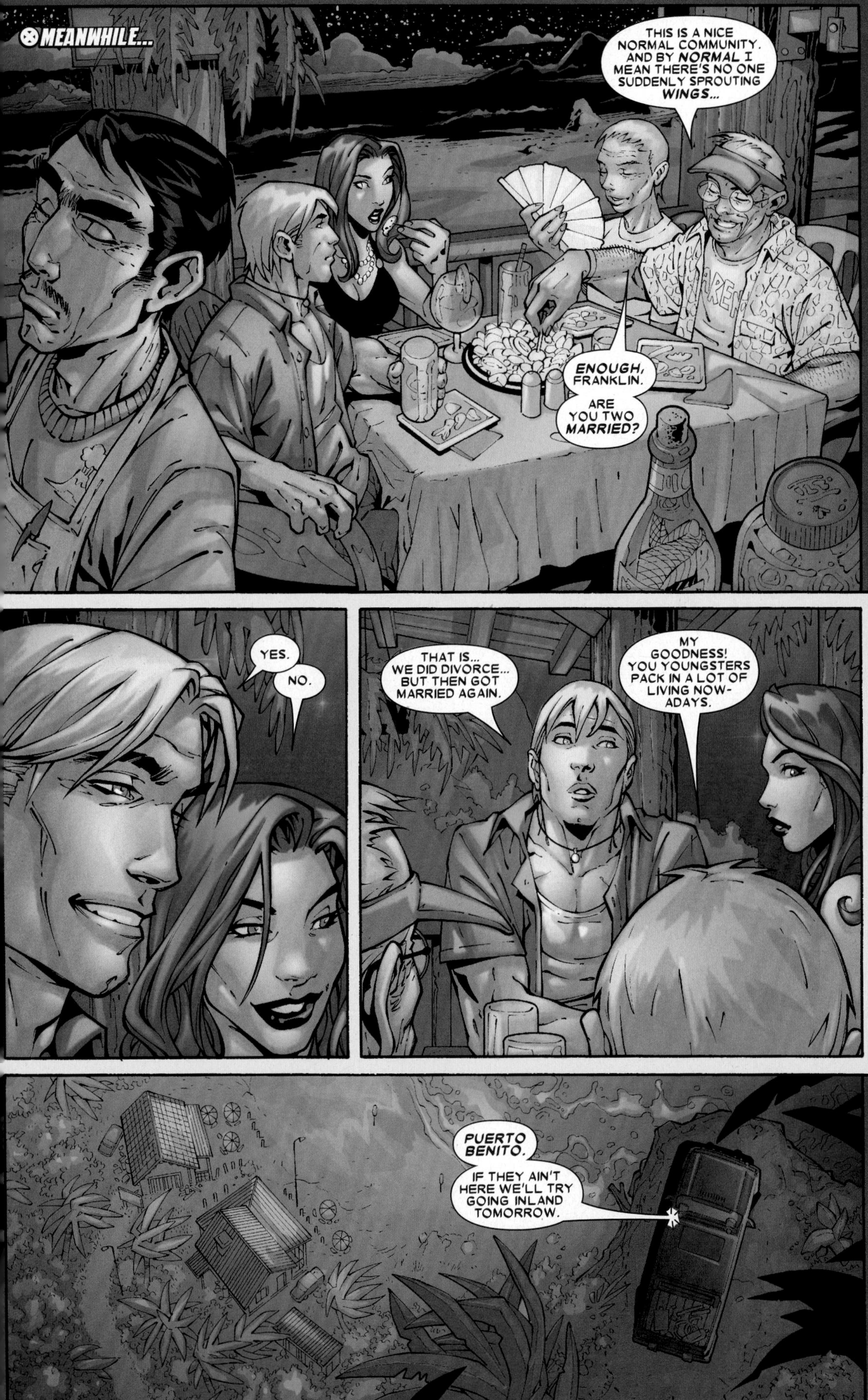
MEANWHILE...
THIS IS A NICE NORMAL COMMUNITY. AND BY NORMAL I MEAN THERE'S NO ONE SUDDENLY SPROUTING WINGS...
ENOUGH, FRANKLIN.
ARE YOU TWO MARRIED?
YES.
NO.
THAT IS... WE DID DIVORCE... BUT THEN GOT MARRIED AGAIN.
MY GOODNESS! YOU YOUNGSTERS PACK IN A LOT OF LIVING NOW-ADAYS.
PUERTO BENITO.
IF THEY AIN'T HERE WE'LL TRY GOING INLAND TOMORROW.

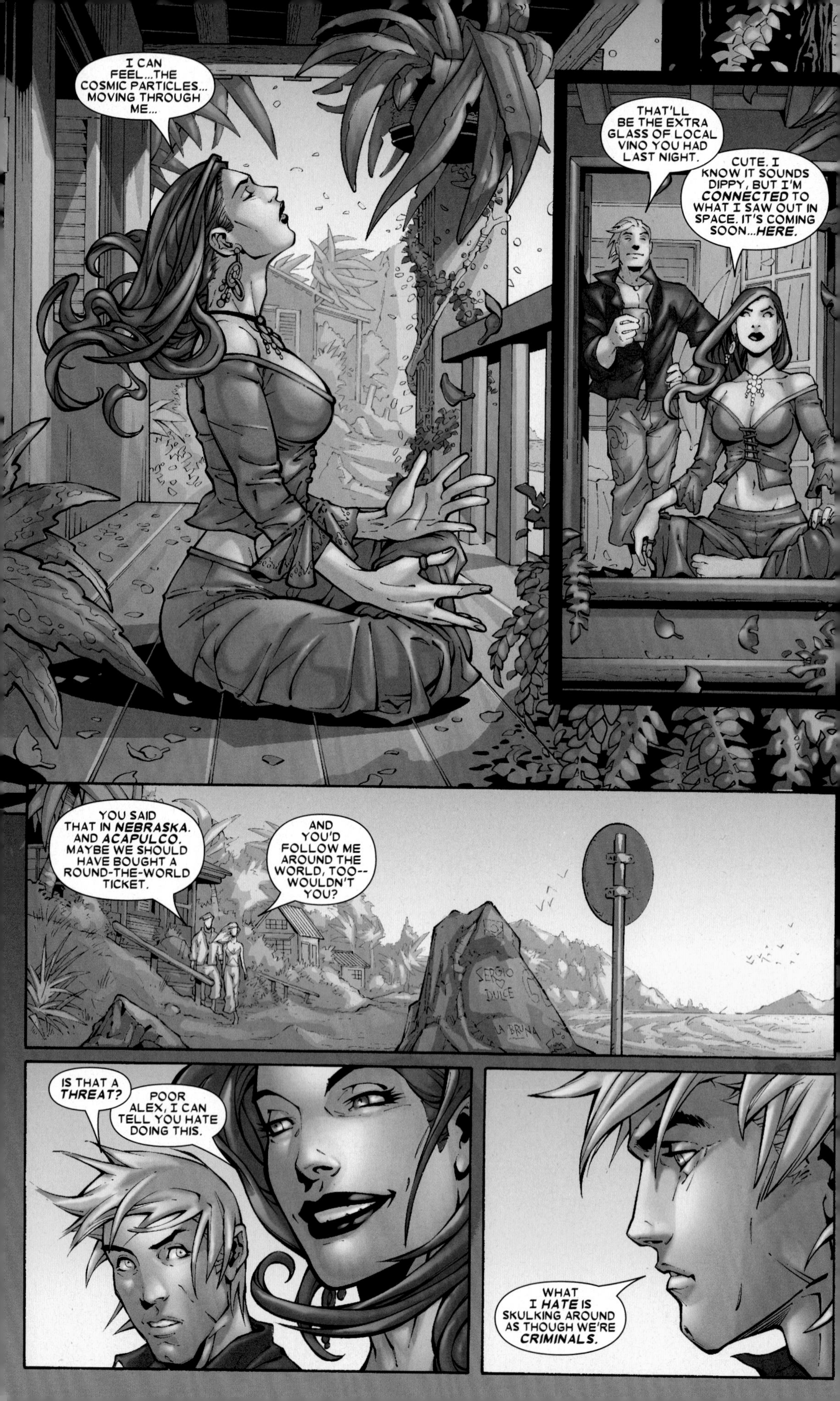

I CAN FEEL...THE COSMIC PARTICLES... MOVING THROUGH ME...
THAT'LL BE THE EXTRA GLASS OF LOCAL VINO YOU HAD LAST NIGHT.
CUTE. I KNOW IT SOUNDS DIPPY, BUT I'M **CONNECTED** TO WHAT I SAW OUT IN SPACE. IT'S COMING SOON...**HERE.**
YOU SAID THAT IN **NEBRASKA**. AND **ACAPULCO**. MAYBE WE SHOULD HAVE BOUGHT A ROUND-THE-WORLD TICKET.
AND YOU'D FOLLOW ME AROUND THE WORLD, TOO--WOULDN'T YOU?
SERGIO DULCE
LA BRUNA
IS THAT A **THREAT**?
POOR ALEX, I CAN TELL YOU HATE DOING THIS.
WHAT I **HATE** IS SKULKING AROUND AS THOUGH WE'RE **CRIMINALS.**

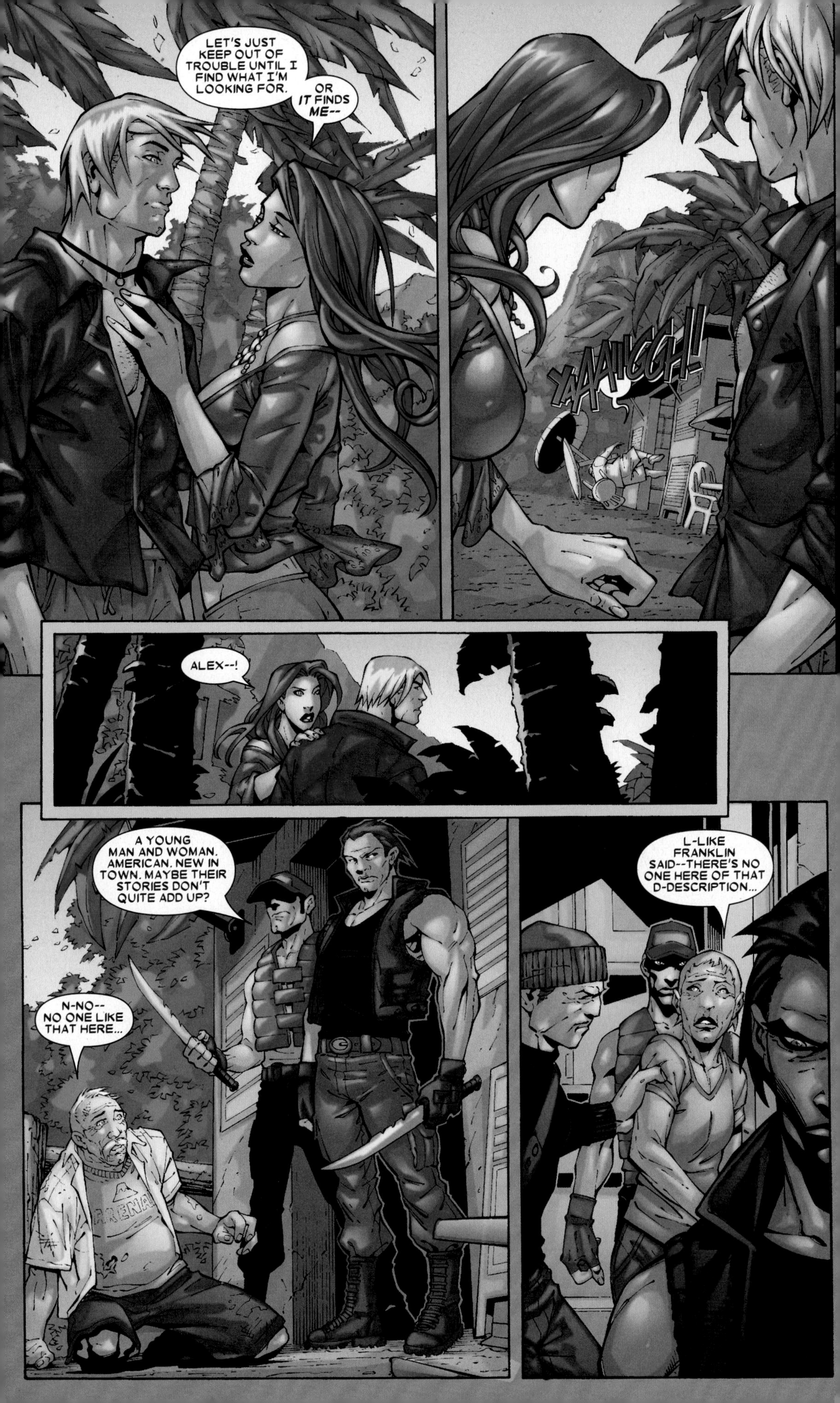
LET'S JUST KEEP OUT OF TROUBLE UNTIL I FIND WHAT I'M LOOKING FOR.
OR *IT* FINDS *ME*--
YAAAIGGH!!
ALEX--!
A YOUNG MAN AND WOMAN. AMERICAN. NEW IN TOWN. MAYBE THEIR STORIES DON'T QUITE ADD UP?
N-NO-- NO ONE LIKE THAT HERE...
L-LIKE FRANKLIN SAID--THERE'S NO ONE HERE OF THAT D-DESCRIPTION...

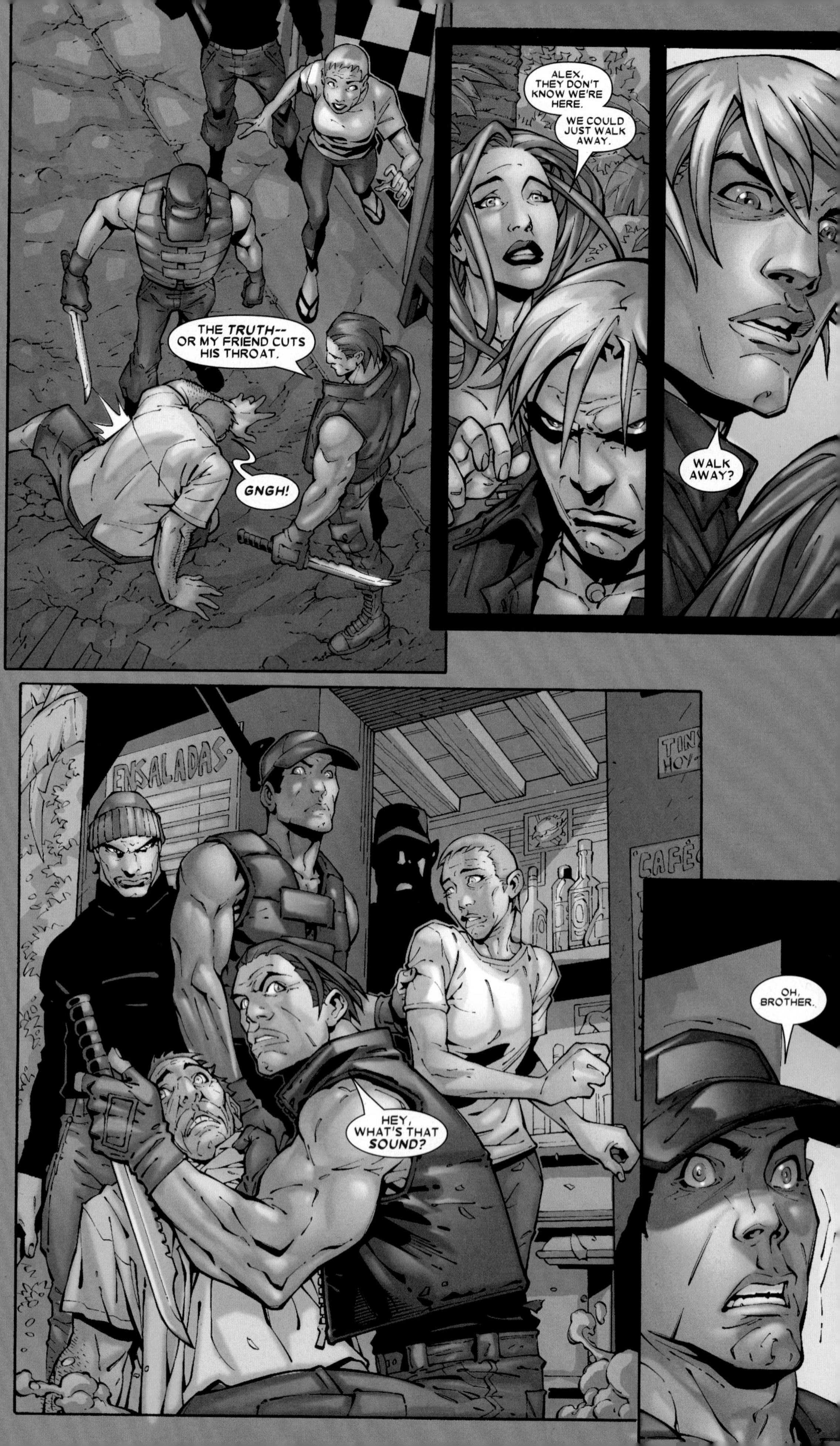
THE TRUTH--
OR MY FRIEND CUTS HIS THROAT.
GNGH!
ALEX, THEY DON'T KNOW WE'RE HERE.
WE COULD JUST WALK AWAY.
WALK AWAY?
ENSALADAS
CAFÉ
HEY, WHAT'S THAT SOUND?
OH, BROTHER.

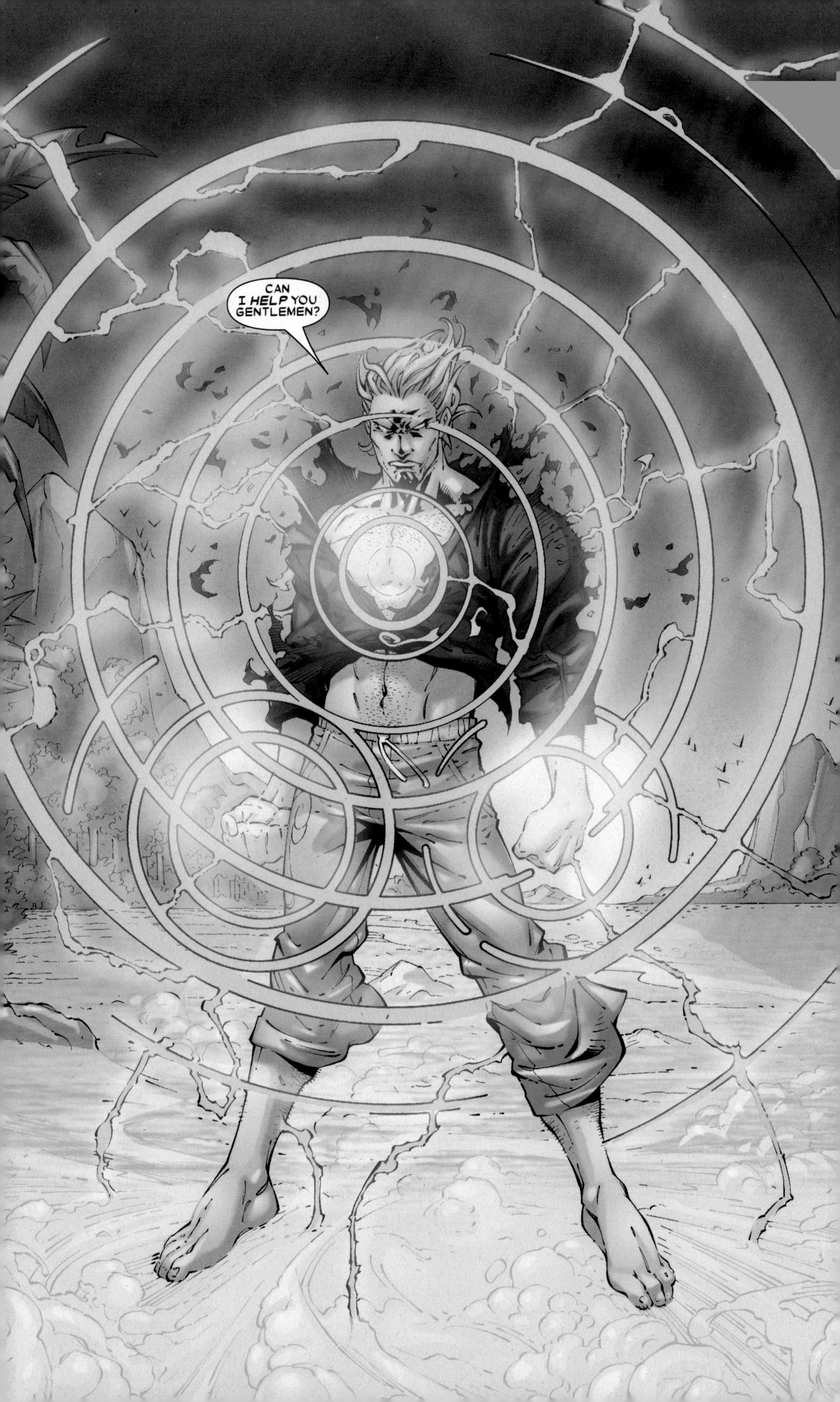
CAN I HELP YOU GENTLEMEN?

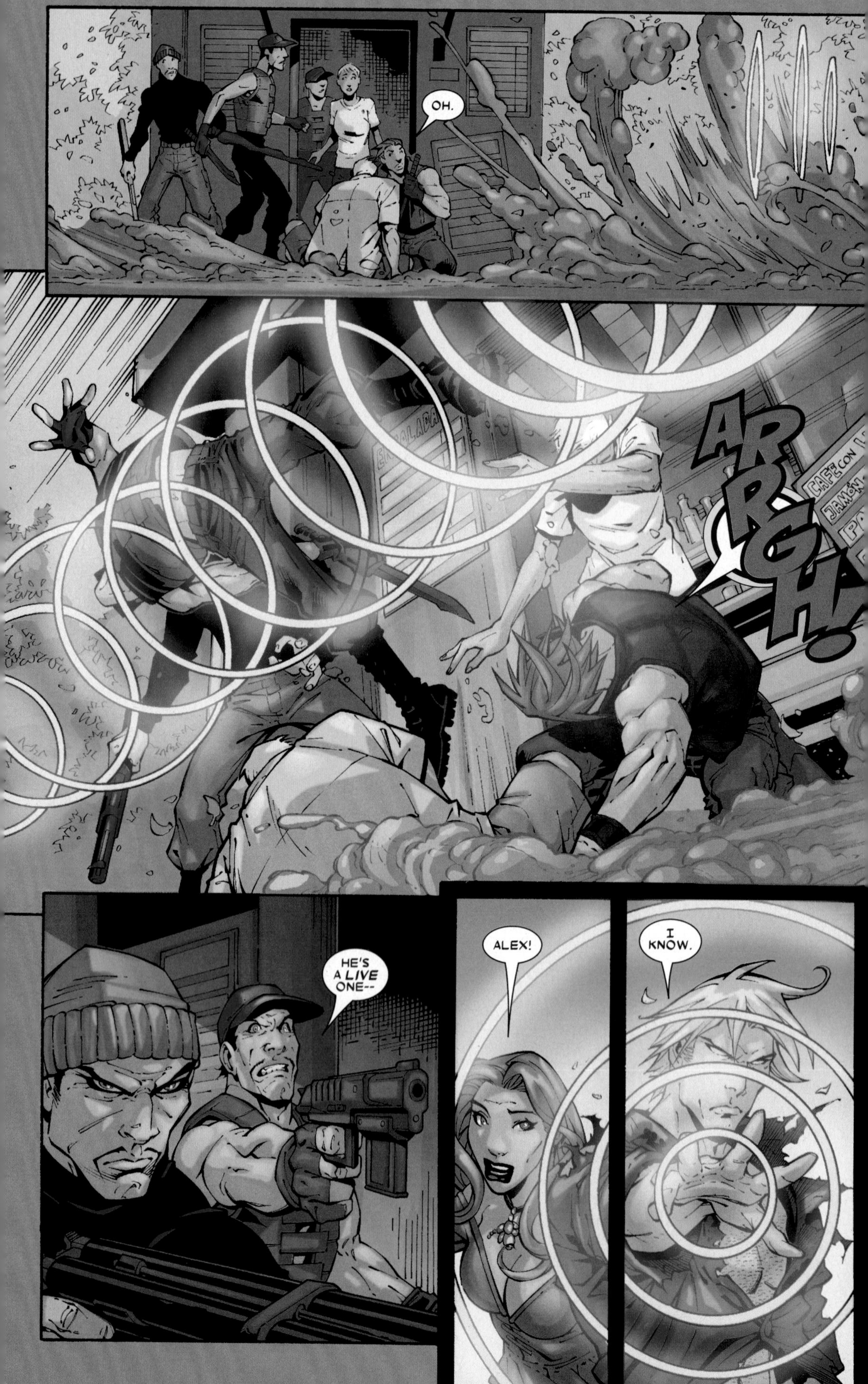
OH.
ARRGH!
HE'S A *LIVE* ONE--
ALEX!
I KNOW.

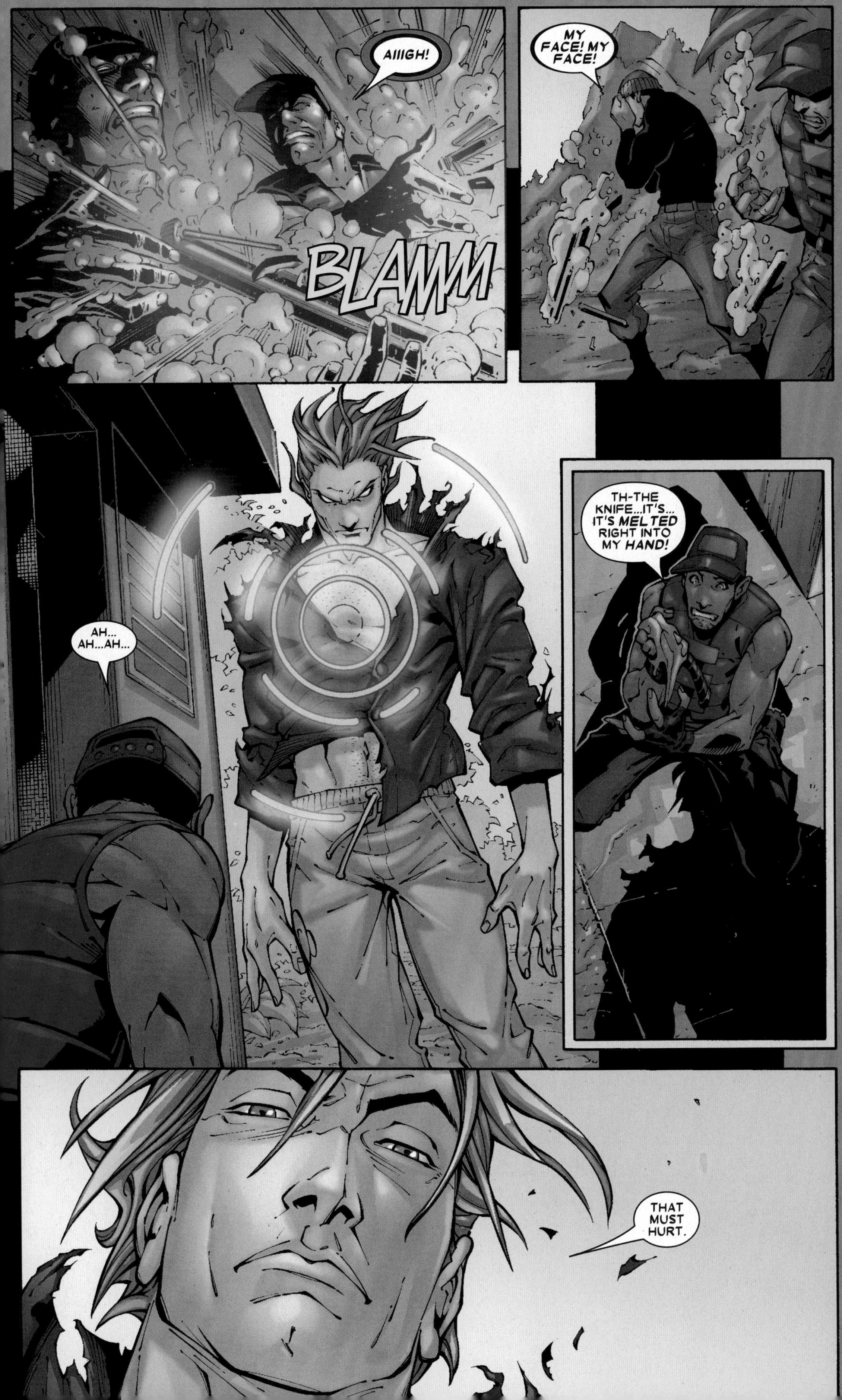
AIIIGH!
BLAMM
MY FACE! MY FACE!
AH... AH...AH...
TH-THE KNIFE...IT'S... IT'S MELTED RIGHT INTO MY HAND!
THAT MUST HURT.

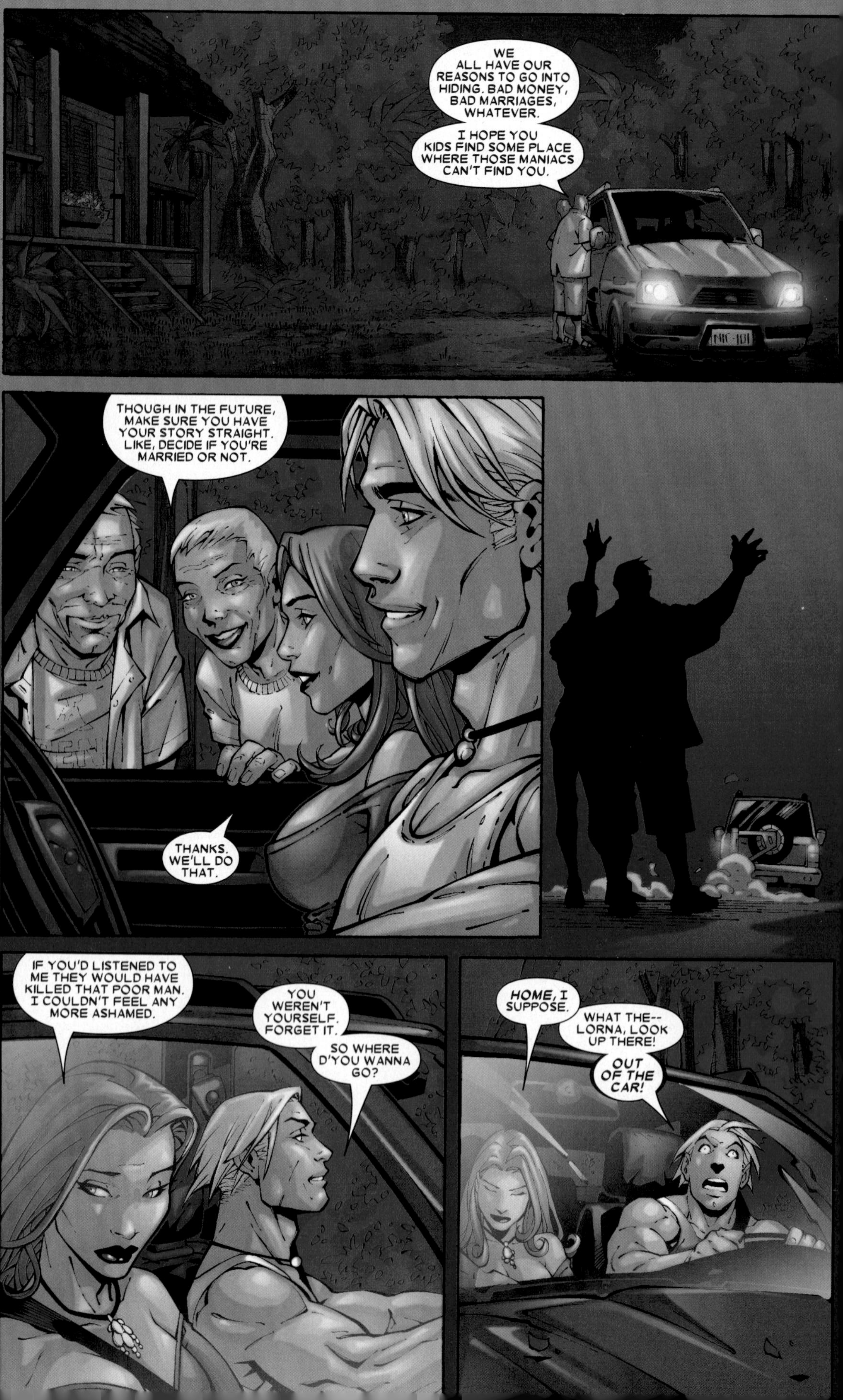
WE ALL HAVE OUR REASONS TO GO INTO HIDING. BAD MONEY, BAD MARRIAGES, WHATEVER.
I HOPE YOU KIDS FIND SOME PLACE WHERE THOSE MANIACS CAN'T FIND YOU.
THOUGH IN THE FUTURE, MAKE SURE YOU HAVE YOUR STORY STRAIGHT. LIKE, DECIDE IF YOU'RE MARRIED OR NOT.
THANKS. WE'LL DO THAT.
IF YOU'D LISTENED TO ME THEY WOULD HAVE KILLED THAT POOR MAN. I COULDN'T FEEL ANY MORE ASHAMED.
YOU WEREN'T YOURSELF. FORGET IT.
SO WHERE D'YOU WANNA GO?
HOME, I SUPPOSE.
WHAT THE-- LORNA, LOOK UP THERE!
OUT OF THE CAR!

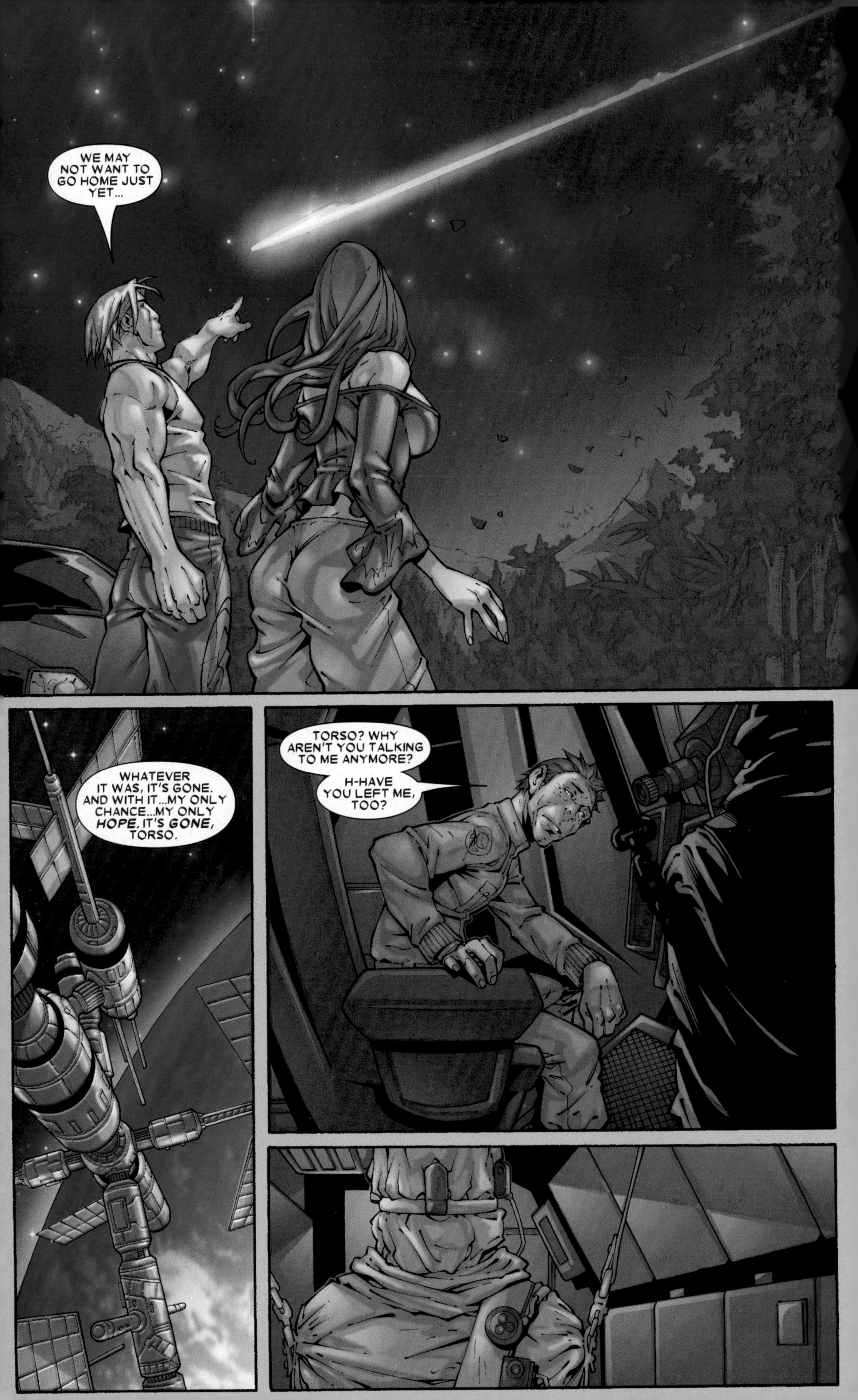
WE MAY NOT WANT TO GO HOME JUST YET...
WHATEVER IT WAS, IT'S GONE. AND WITH IT...MY ONLY CHANCE...MY ONLY *HOPE*. IT'S *GONE*, TORSO.
TORSO? WHY AREN'T YOU TALKING TO ME ANYMORE?
H-HAVE YOU LEFT ME, TOO?

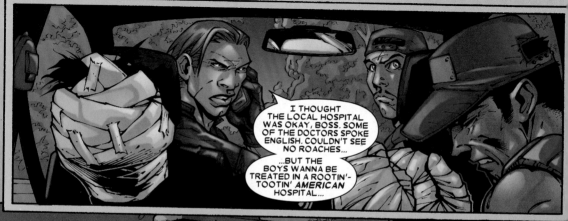

I THOUGHT THE LOCAL HOSPITAL WAS OKAY, BOSS. SOME OF THE DOCTORS SPOKE ENGLISH. COULDN'T SEE NO ROACHES...

...BUT THE BOYS WANNA BE TREATED IN A ROOTIN'-TOOTIN' *AMERICAN* HOSPITAL...

WHATEVER THE OTHERS DO, YOU MUST NOT LOSE THE *MUTANTS*, STAY WITH THEM...

...I'LL BE THERE AS QUICKLY AS I CAN.

Lucie Page
DIED AGED TWO
MY DARLING
DAUGHTER
KILLED BY MUTANTS

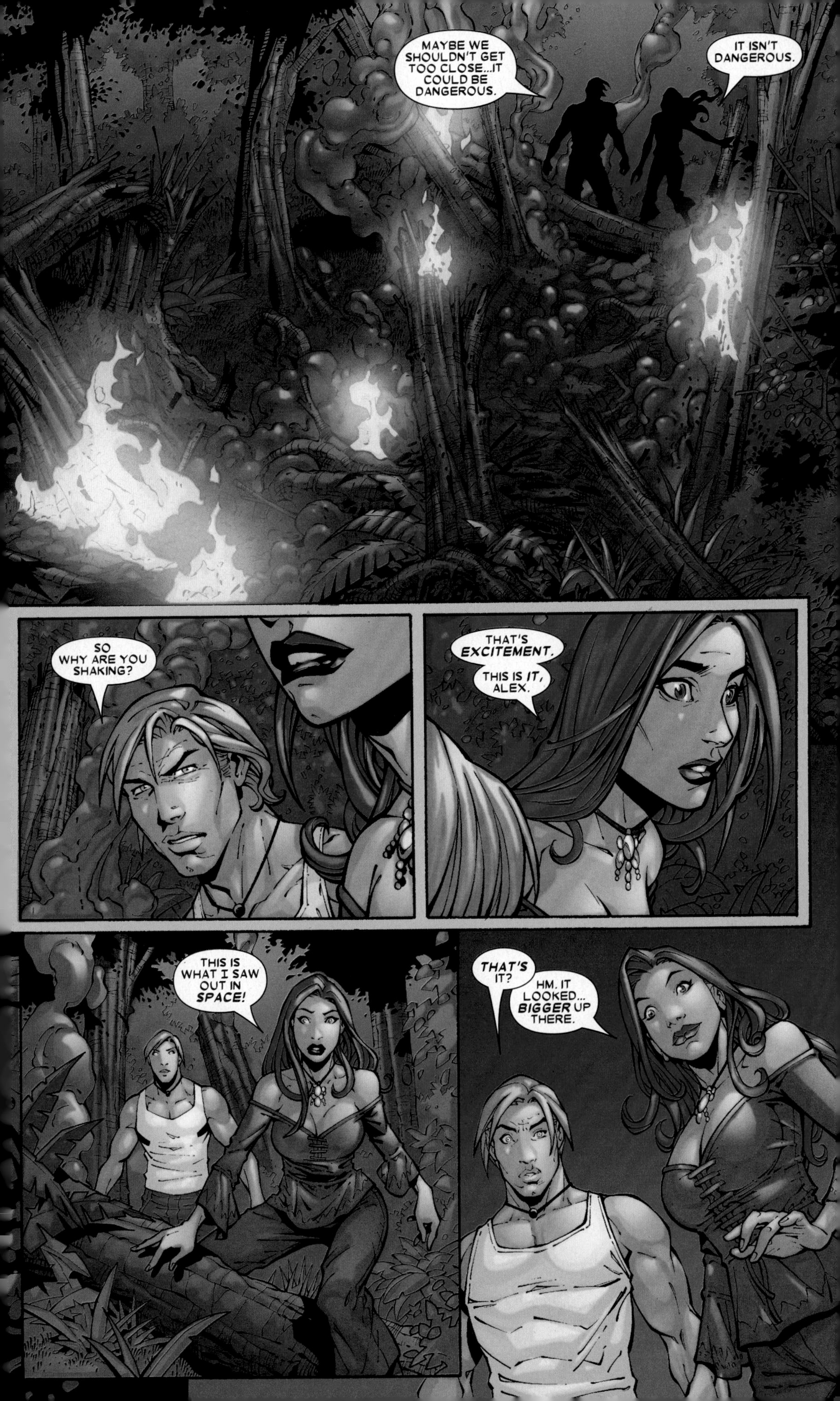
MAYBE WE SHOULDN'T GET TOO CLOSE...IT COULD BE DANGEROUS.
IT ISN'T DANGEROUS.
SO WHY ARE YOU SHAKING?
THAT'S *EXCITEMENT.*
THIS IS *IT,* ALEX.
THIS IS WHAT I SAW OUT IN *SPACE!*
THAT'S IT?
HM. IT LOOKED... *BIGGER* UP THERE.

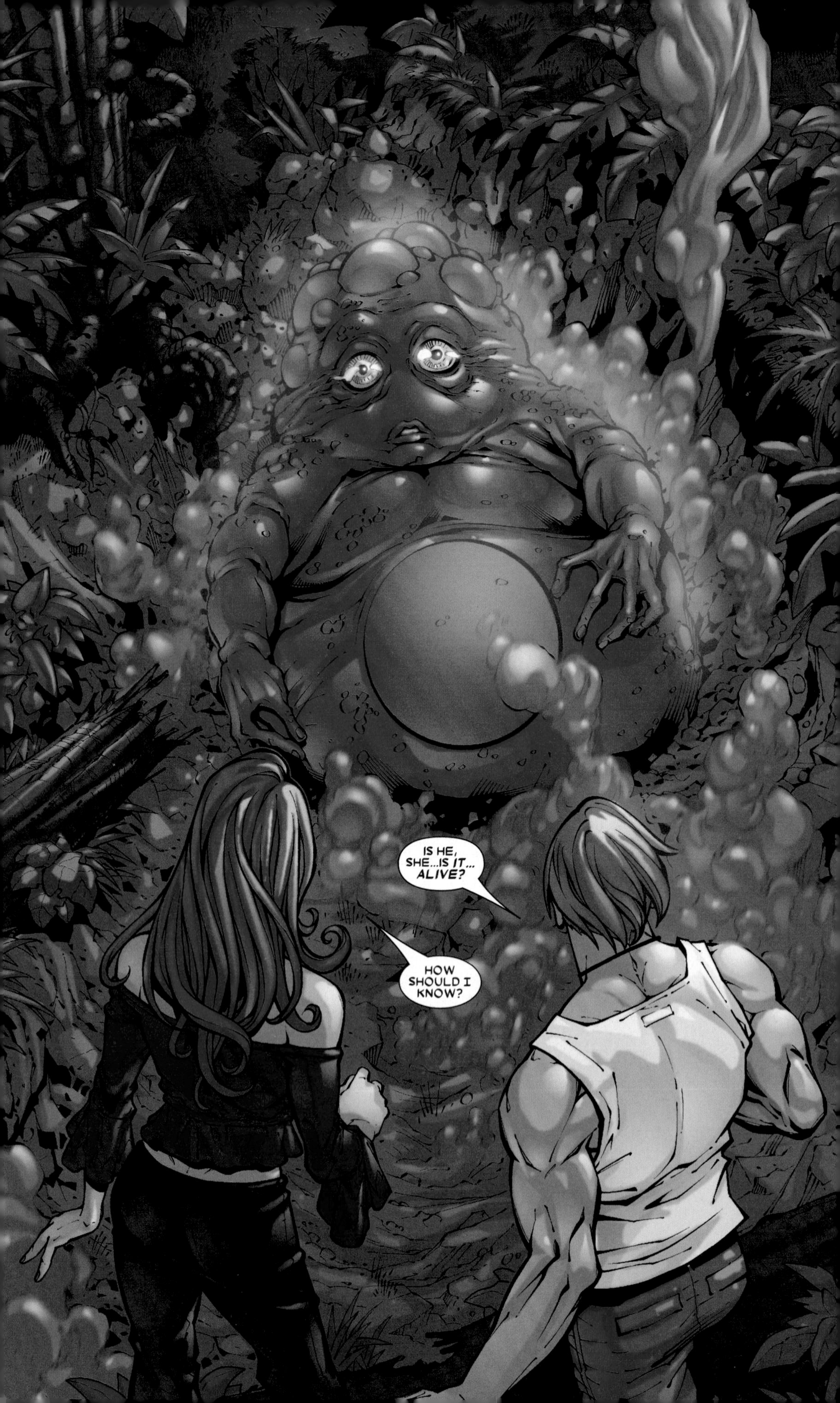
IS HE, SHE...IS *IT*... *ALIVE?*
HOW SHOULD I KNOW?

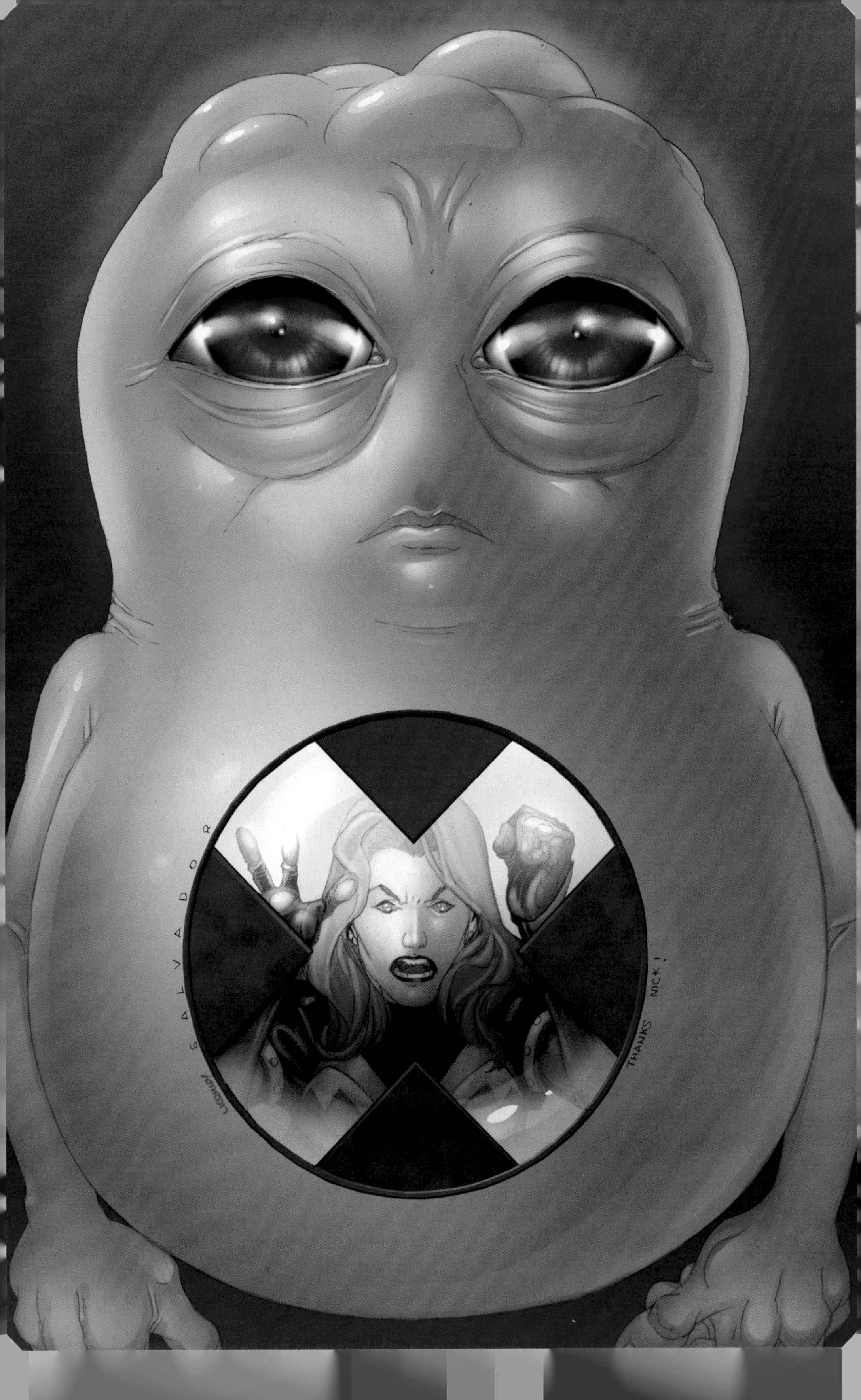
SALVADOR
THANKS NICK!

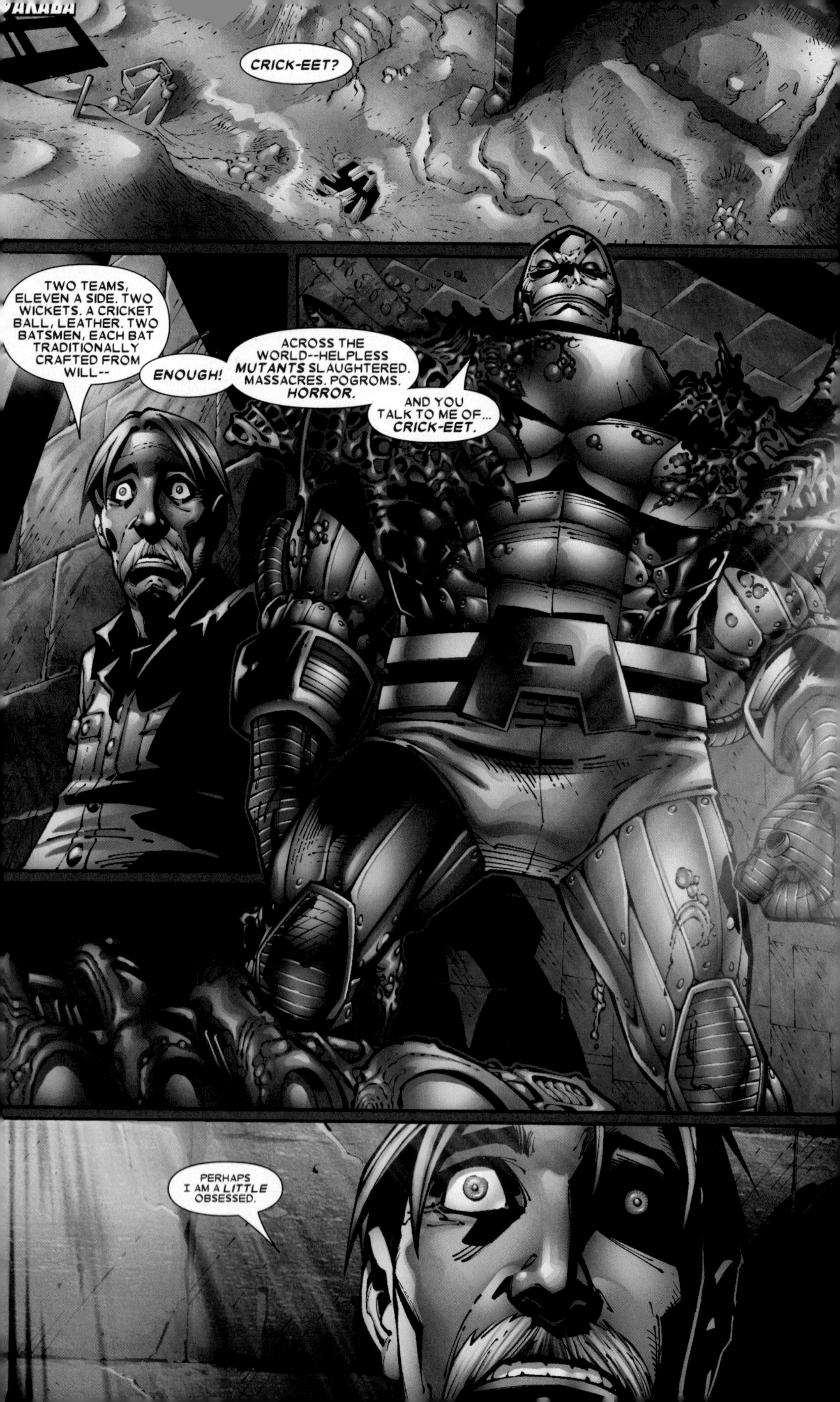
CRICK-EET?
TWO TEAMS, ELEVEN A SIDE. TWO WICKETS. A CRICKET BALL, LEATHER. TWO BATSMEN, EACH BAT TRADITIONALLY CRAFTED FROM WILL--
ENOUGH!
ACROSS THE WORLD--HELPLESS MUTANTS SLAUGHTERED. MASSACRES. POGROMS. HORROR.
AND YOU TALK TO ME OF... CRICK-EET.
PERHAPS I AM A LITTLE OBSESSED.

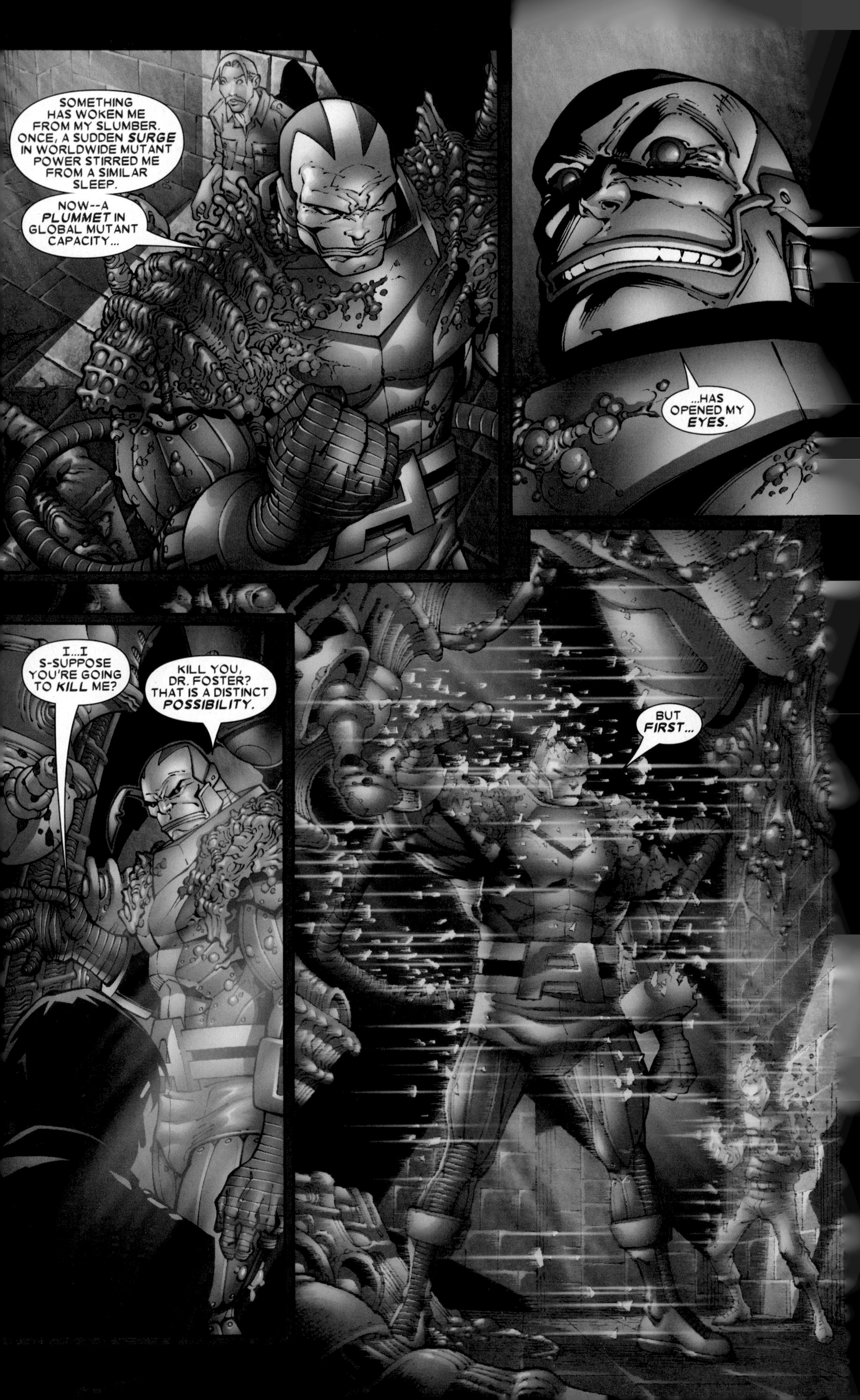
SOMETHING HAS WOKEN ME FROM MY SLUMBER. ONCE, A SUDDEN SURGE IN WORLDWIDE MUTANT POWER STIRRED ME FROM A SIMILAR SLEEP.
NOW--A PLUMMET IN GLOBAL MUTANT CAPACITY...
...HAS OPENED MY EYES.
I...I S-SUPPOSE YOU'RE GOING TO KILL ME?
KILL YOU, DR. FOSTER? THAT IS A DISTINCT POSSIBILITY.
BUT FIRST...

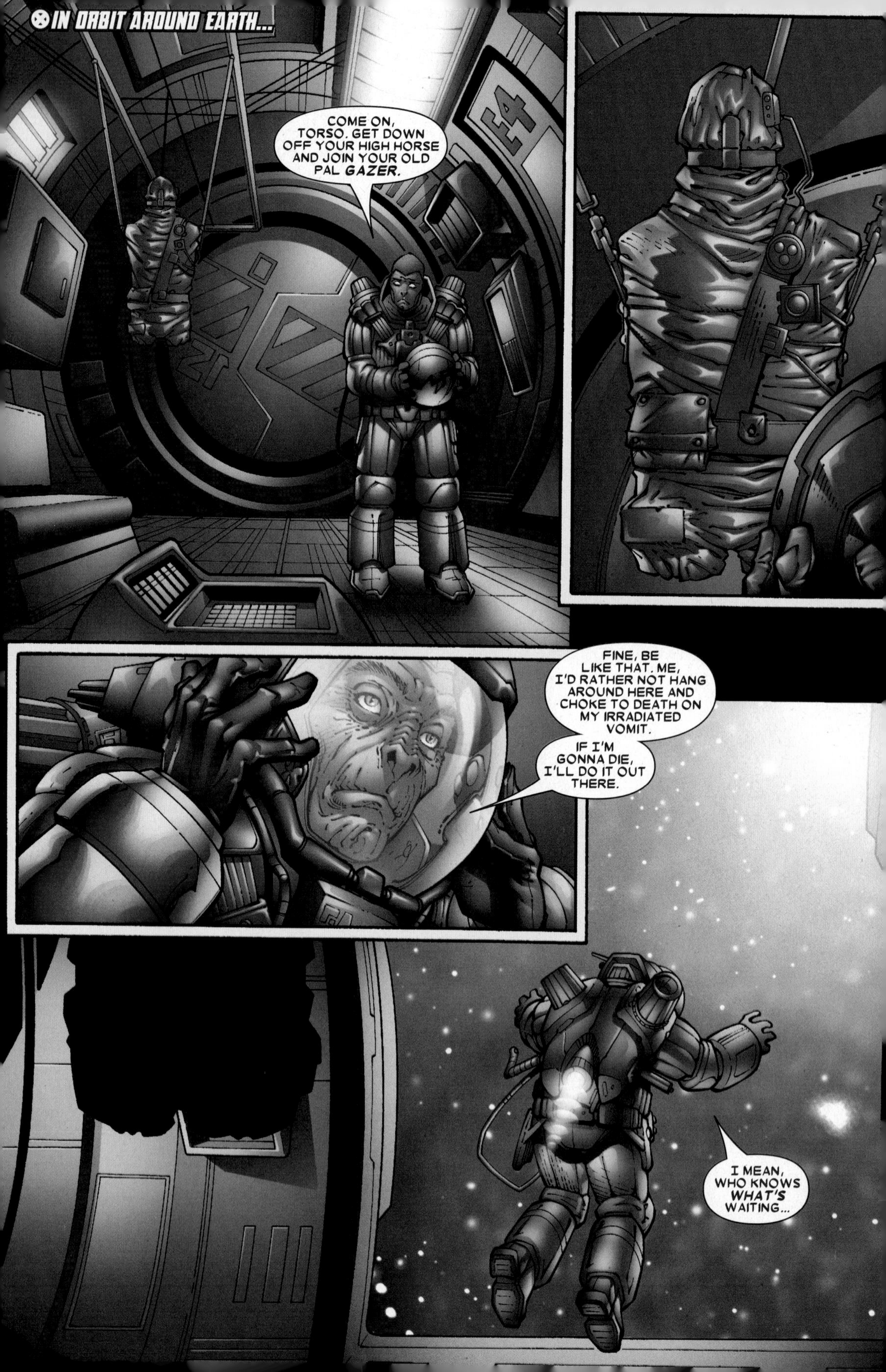
IN ORBIT AROUND EARTH...
COME ON, TORSO. GET DOWN OFF YOUR HIGH HORSE AND JOIN YOUR OLD PAL GAZER.
FINE, BE LIKE THAT. ME, I'D RATHER NOT HANG AROUND HERE AND CHOKE TO DEATH ON MY IRRADIATED VOMIT.
IF I'M GONNA DIE, I'LL DO IT OUT THERE.
I MEAN, WHO KNOWS WHAT'S WAITING...

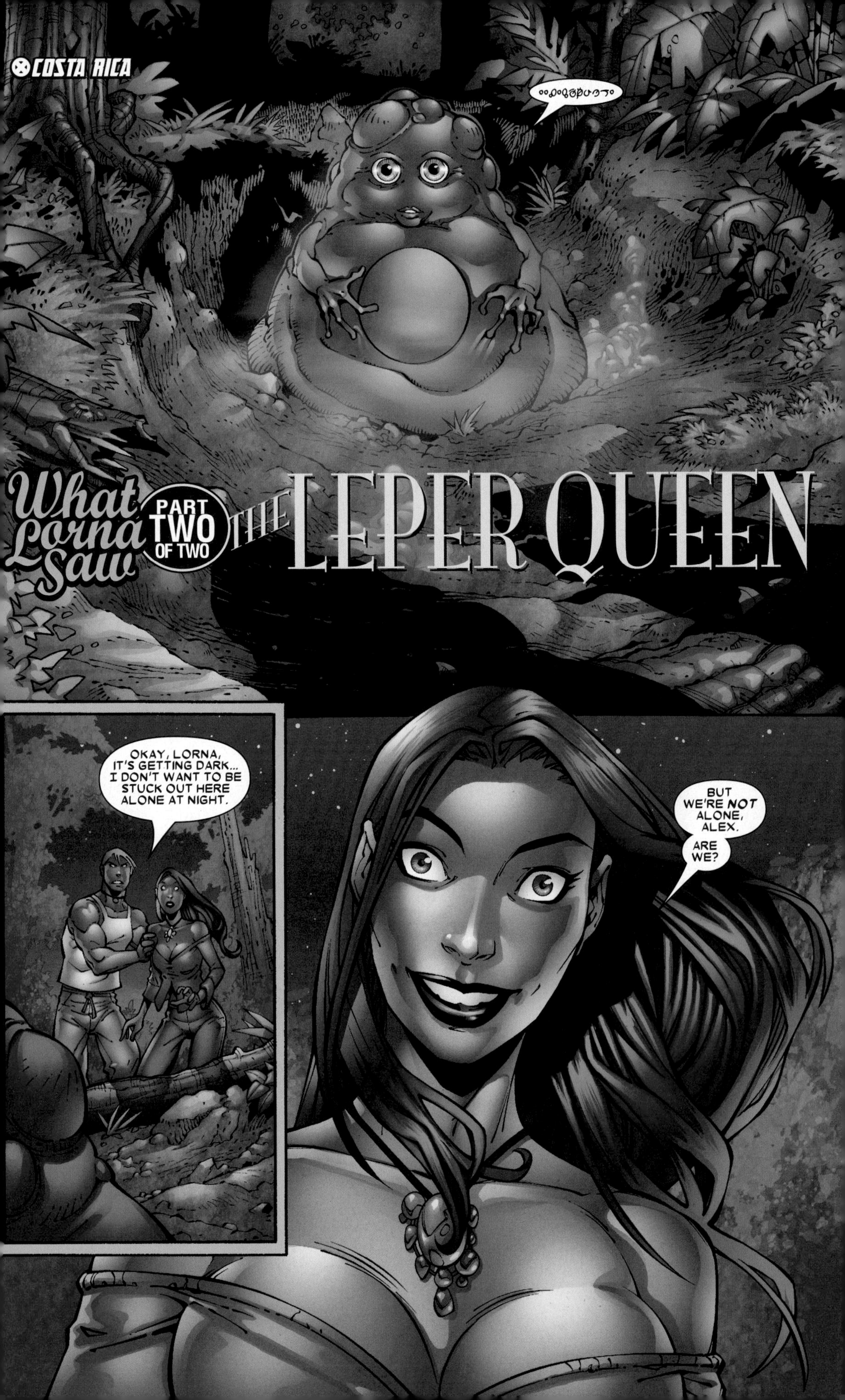
COSTA RICA
What Lorna Saw
PART TWO OF TWO
THE LEPER QUEEN
OKAY, LORNA, IT'S GETTING DARK... I DON'T WANT TO BE STUCK OUT HERE ALONE AT NIGHT.
BUT WE'RE NOT ALONE, ALEX.
ARE WE?

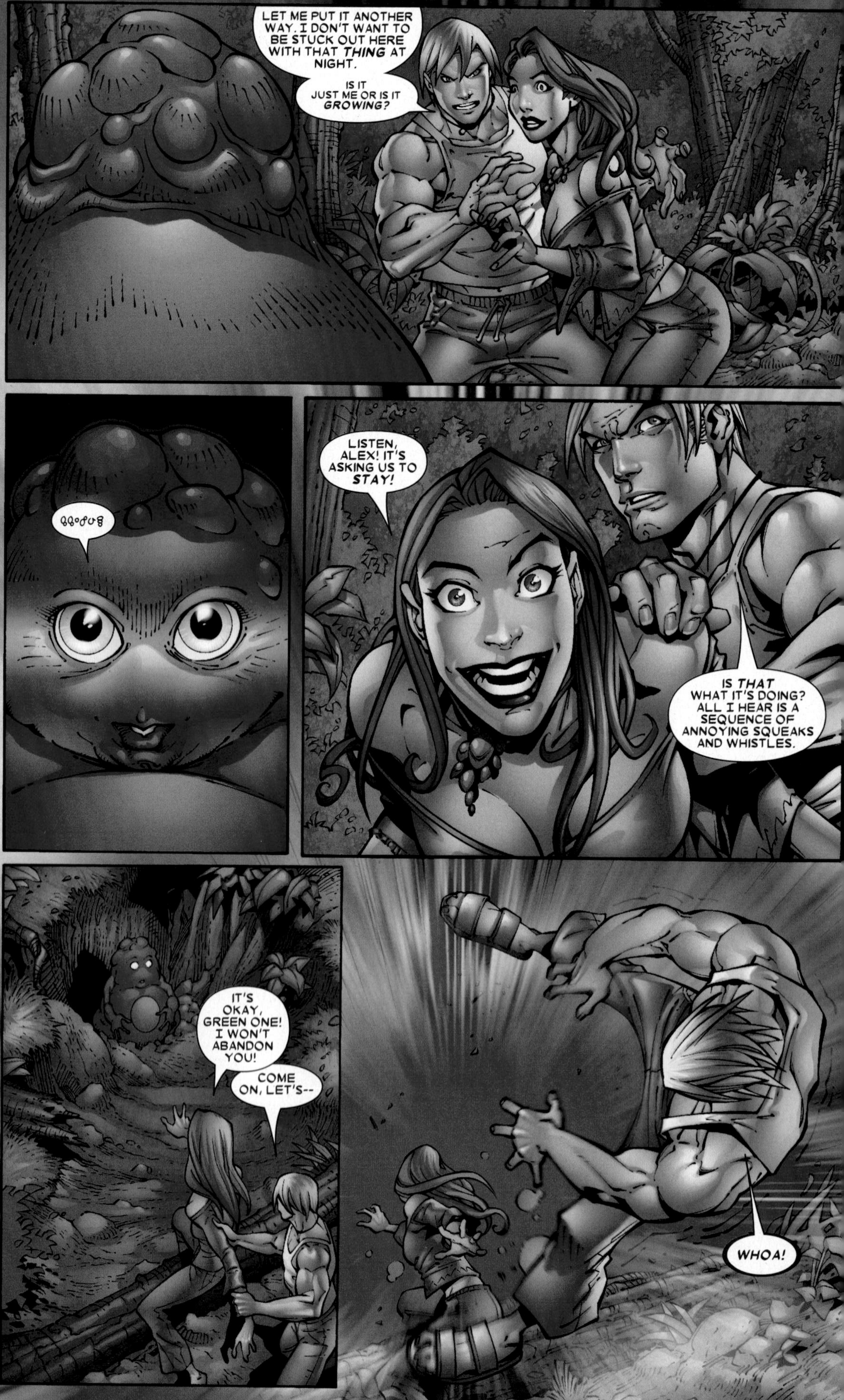
LET ME PUT IT ANOTHER WAY. I DON'T WANT TO BE STUCK OUT HERE WITH THAT THING AT NIGHT.
IS IT JUST ME OR IS IT GROWING?
LISTEN, ALEX! IT'S ASKING US TO STAY!
IS THAT WHAT IT'S DOING? ALL I HEAR IS A SEQUENCE OF ANNOYING SQUEAKS AND WHISTLES.
IT'S OKAY, GREEN ONE! I WON'T ABANDON YOU!
COME ON, LET'S--
WHOA!

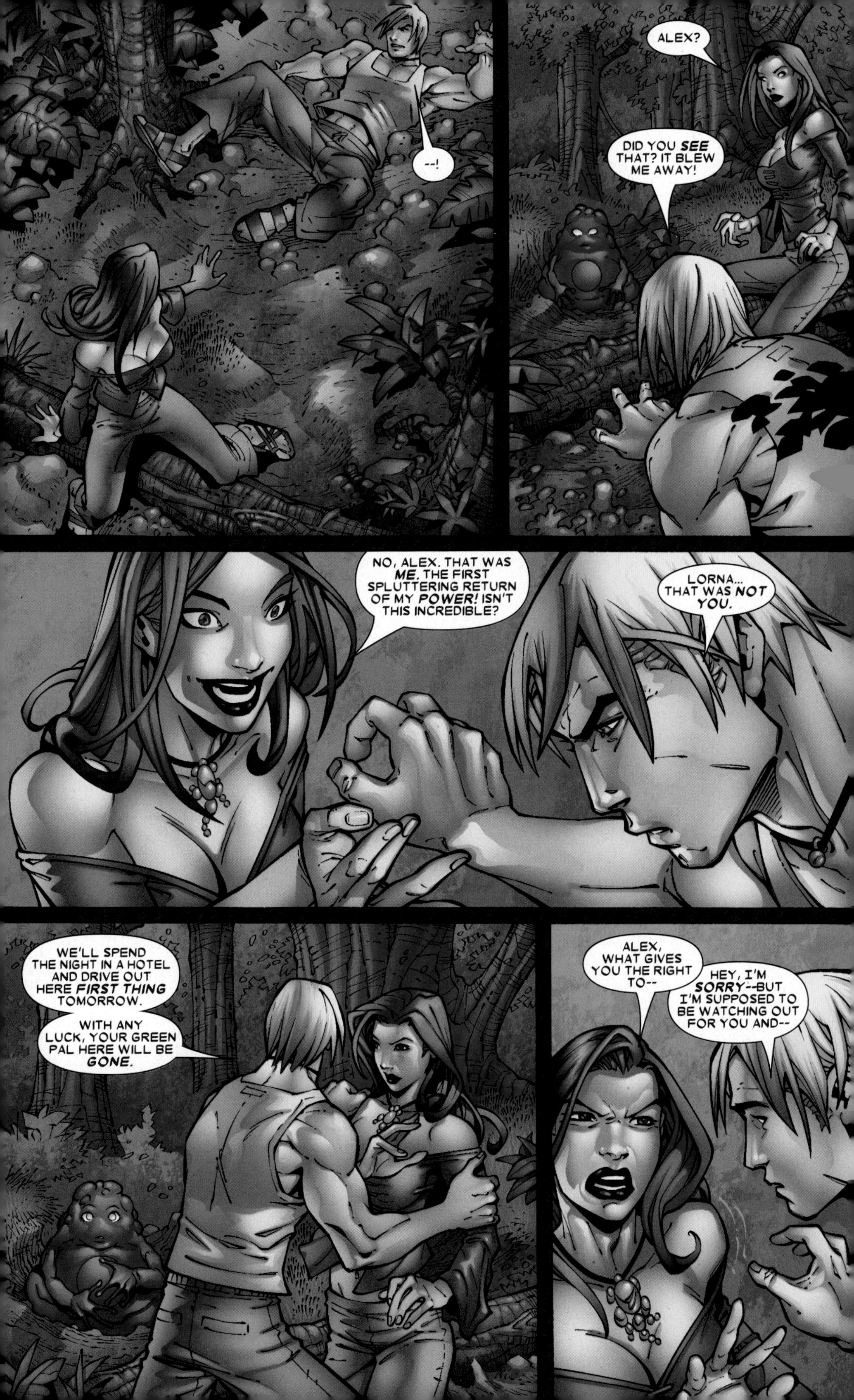
--!
ALEX?
DID YOU **SEE** THAT? IT BLEW ME AWAY!
NO, ALEX. THAT WAS ***ME.*** THE FIRST SPLUTTERING RETURN OF MY ***POWER!*** ISN'T THIS INCREDIBLE?
LORNA... THAT WAS **NOT YOU.**
WE'LL SPEND THE NIGHT IN A HOTEL AND DRIVE OUT HERE ***FIRST THING*** TOMORROW.
WITH ANY LUCK, YOUR GREEN PAL HERE WILL BE ***GONE.***
ALEX, WHAT GIVES YOU THE RIGHT TO--
HEY, I'M ***SORRY***--BUT I'M SUPPOSED TO BE WATCHING OUT FOR YOU AND--

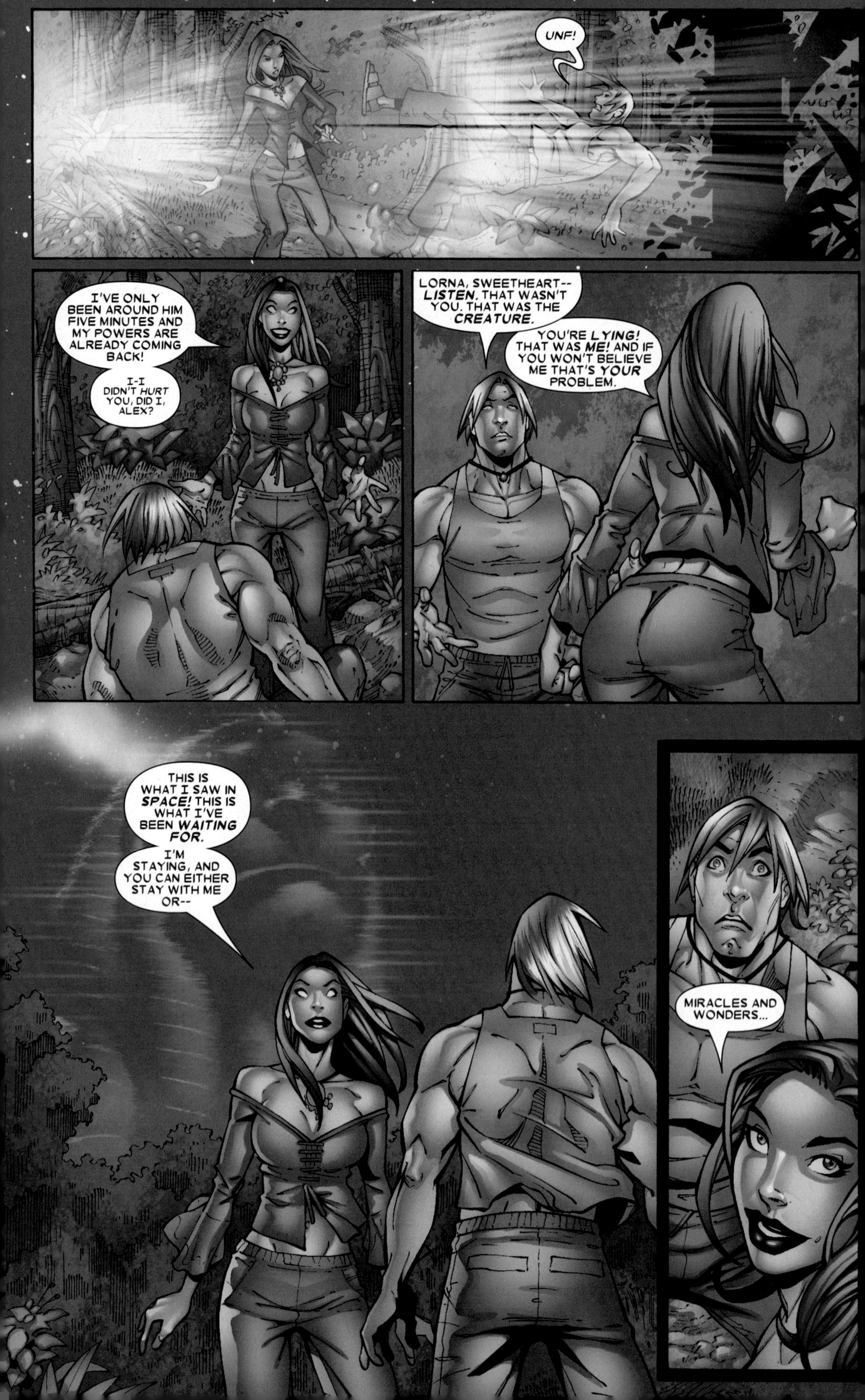
UNF!
I'VE ONLY BEEN AROUND HIM FIVE MINUTES AND MY POWERS ARE ALREADY COMING BACK!
I-I DIDN'T HURT YOU, DID I, ALEX?
LORNA, SWEETHEART-- LISTEN. THAT WASN'T YOU. THAT WAS THE CREATURE.
YOU'RE LYING! THAT WAS ME! AND IF YOU WON'T BELIEVE ME THAT'S YOUR PROBLEM.
THIS IS WHAT I SAW IN SPACE! THIS IS WHAT I'VE BEEN WAITING FOR.
I'M STAYING, AND YOU CAN EITHER STAY WITH ME OR--
MIRACLES AND WONDERS...

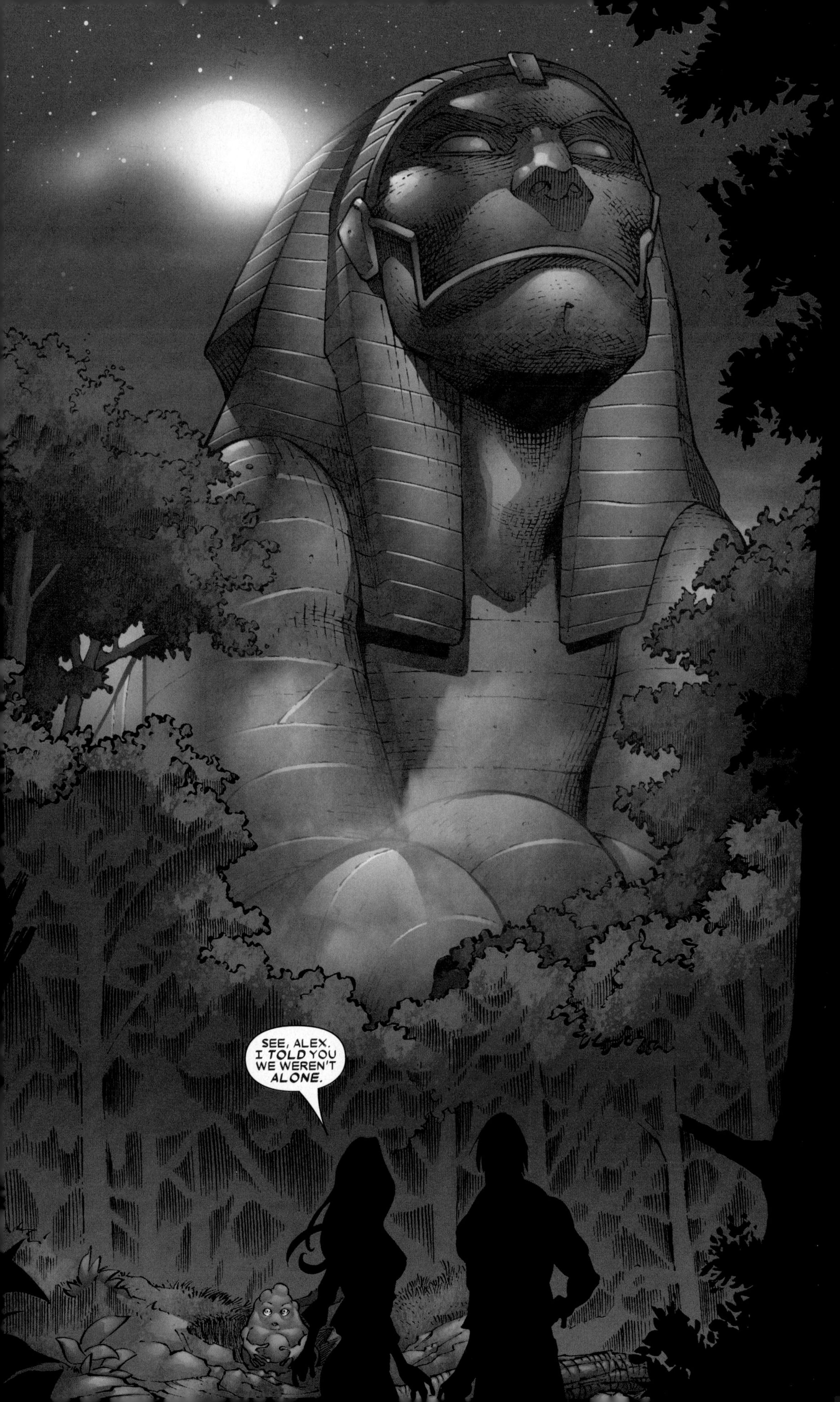
SEE, ALEX. I TOLD YOU WE WEREN'T ALONE.

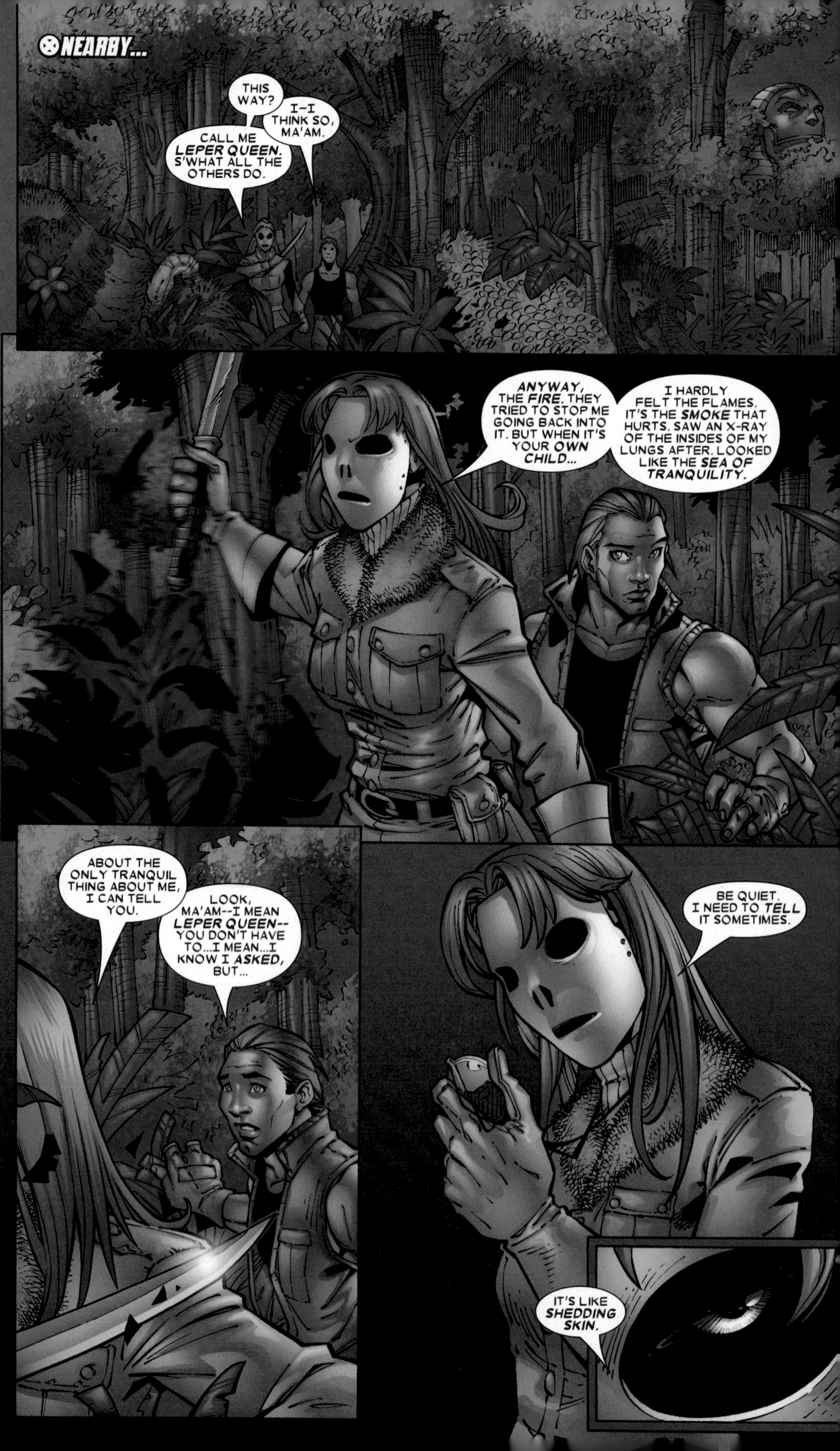

NEARBY...
THIS WAY?
I-I THINK SO, MA'AM.
CALL ME LEPER QUEEN. S'WHAT ALL THE OTHERS DO.
ANYWAY, THE FIRE. THEY TRIED TO STOP ME GOING BACK INTO IT. BUT WHEN IT'S YOUR OWN CHILD...
I HARDLY FELT THE FLAMES. IT'S THE SMOKE THAT HURTS. SAW AN X-RAY OF THE INSIDES OF MY LUNGS AFTER. LOOKED LIKE THE SEA OF TRANQUILITY.
ABOUT THE ONLY TRANQUIL THING ABOUT ME, I CAN TELL YOU.
LOOK, MA'AM--I MEAN LEPER QUEEN--YOU DON'T HAVE TO...I MEAN...I KNOW I ASKED, BUT...
BE QUIET. I NEED TO TELL IT SOMETIMES.
IT'S LIKE SHEDDING SKIN.

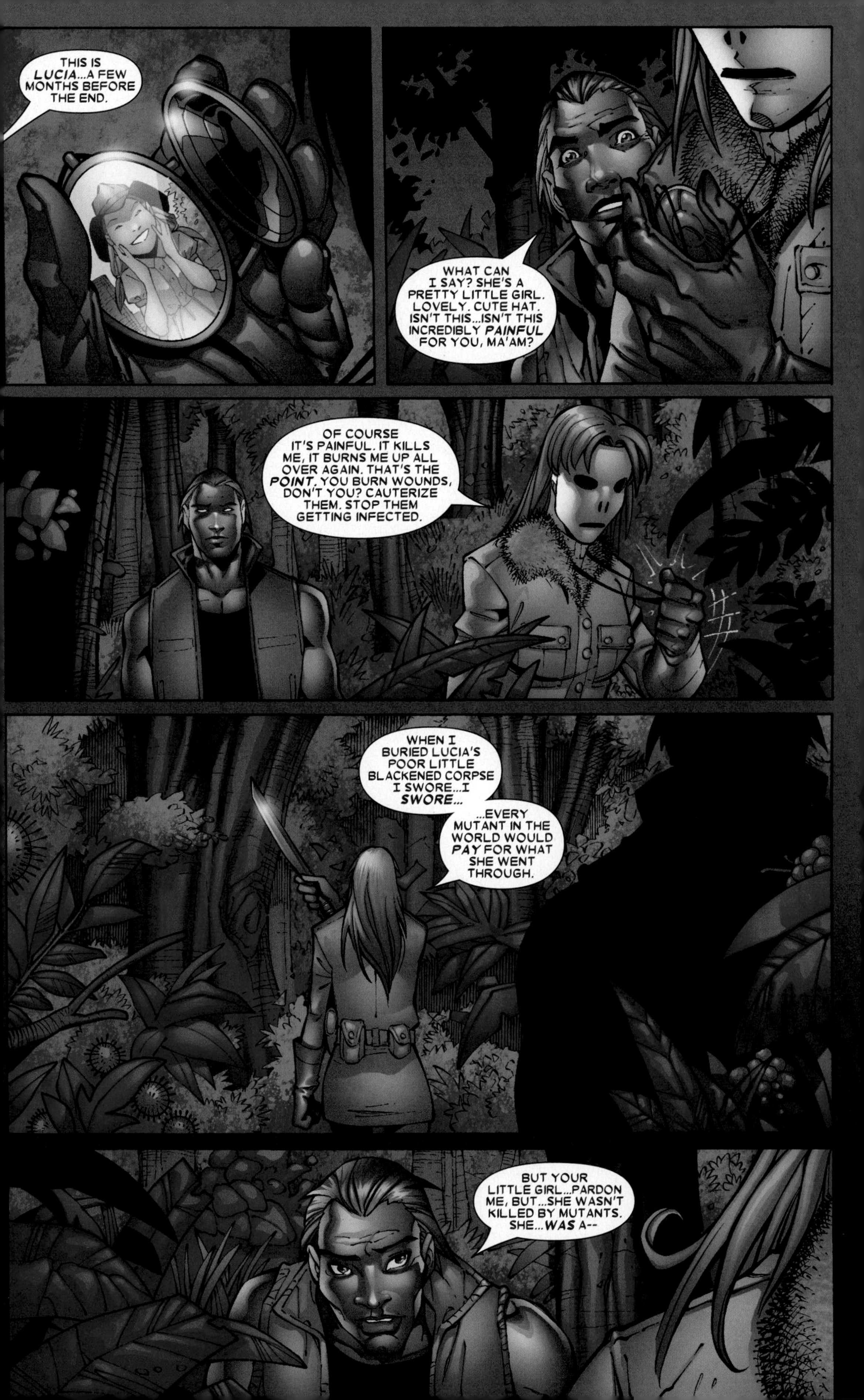
THIS IS LUCIA...A FEW MONTHS BEFORE THE END.
WHAT CAN I SAY? SHE'S A PRETTY LITTLE GIRL. LOVELY. CUTE HAT. ISN'T THIS...ISN'T THIS INCREDIBLY PAINFUL FOR YOU, MA'AM?
OF COURSE IT'S PAINFUL. IT KILLS ME, IT BURNS ME UP ALL OVER AGAIN. THAT'S THE POINT. YOU BURN WOUNDS, DON'T YOU? CAUTERIZE THEM. STOP THEM GETTING INFECTED.
WHEN I BURIED LUCIA'S POOR LITTLE BLACKENED CORPSE I SWORE...I SWORE...
...EVERY MUTANT IN THE WORLD WOULD PAY FOR WHAT SHE WENT THROUGH.
BUT YOUR LITTLE GIRL...PARDON ME, BUT...SHE WASN'T KILLED BY MUTANTS. SHE...WAS A--

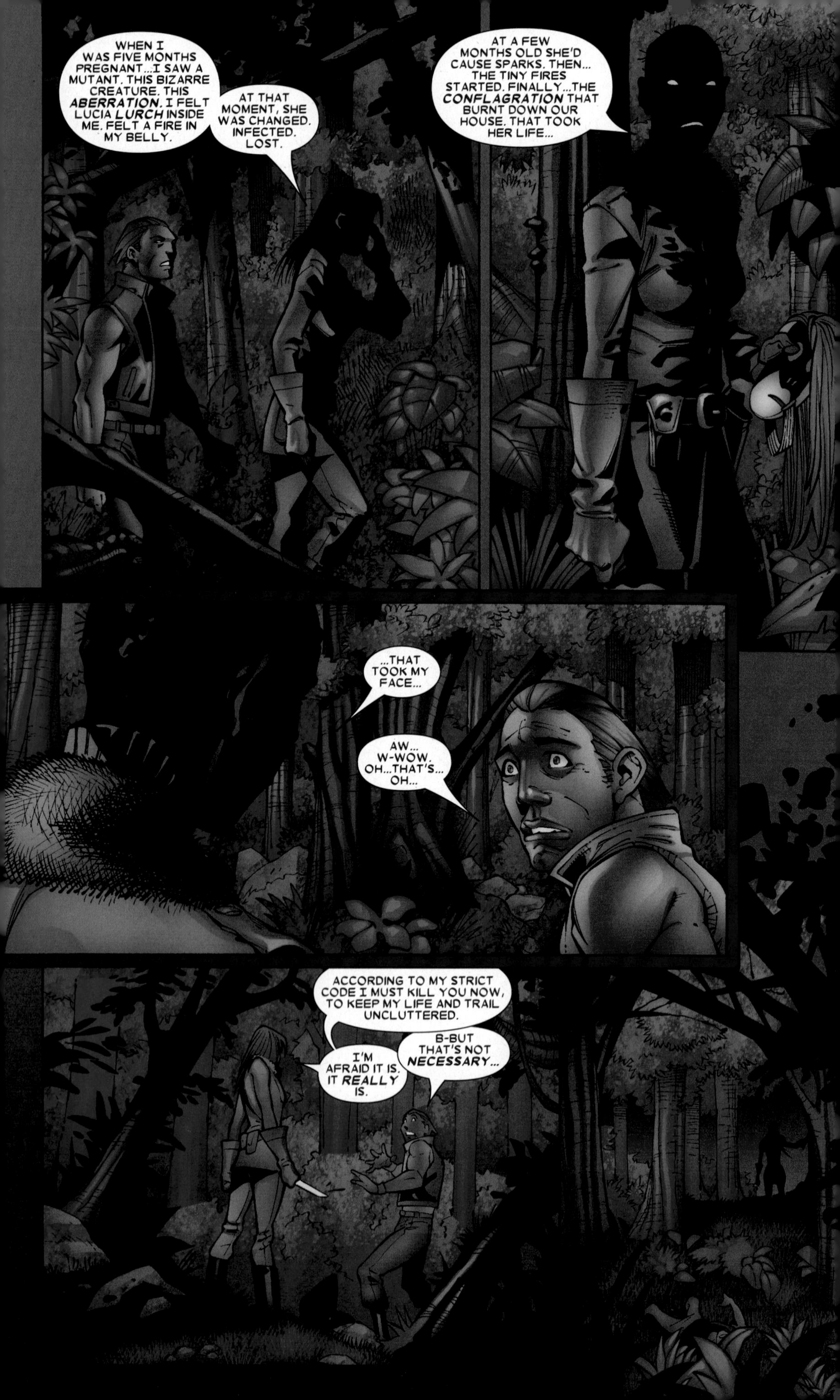
WHEN I WAS FIVE MONTHS PREGNANT...I SAW A MUTANT. THIS BIZARRE CREATURE. THIS ABERRATION. I FELT LUCIA LURCH INSIDE ME. FELT A FIRE IN MY BELLY.
AT THAT MOMENT, SHE WAS CHANGED. INFECTED. LOST.
AT A FEW MONTHS OLD SHE'D CAUSE SPARKS. THEN... THE TINY FIRES STARTED. FINALLY...THE CONFLAGRATION THAT BURNT DOWN OUR HOUSE. THAT TOOK HER LIFE...
...THAT TOOK MY FACE...
AW... W-WOW. OH...THAT'S... OH...
ACCORDING TO MY STRICT CODE I MUST KILL YOU NOW, TO KEEP MY LIFE AND TRAIL UNCLUTTERED.
B-BUT THAT'S NOT NECESSARY...
I'M AFRAID IT IS. IT REALLY IS.

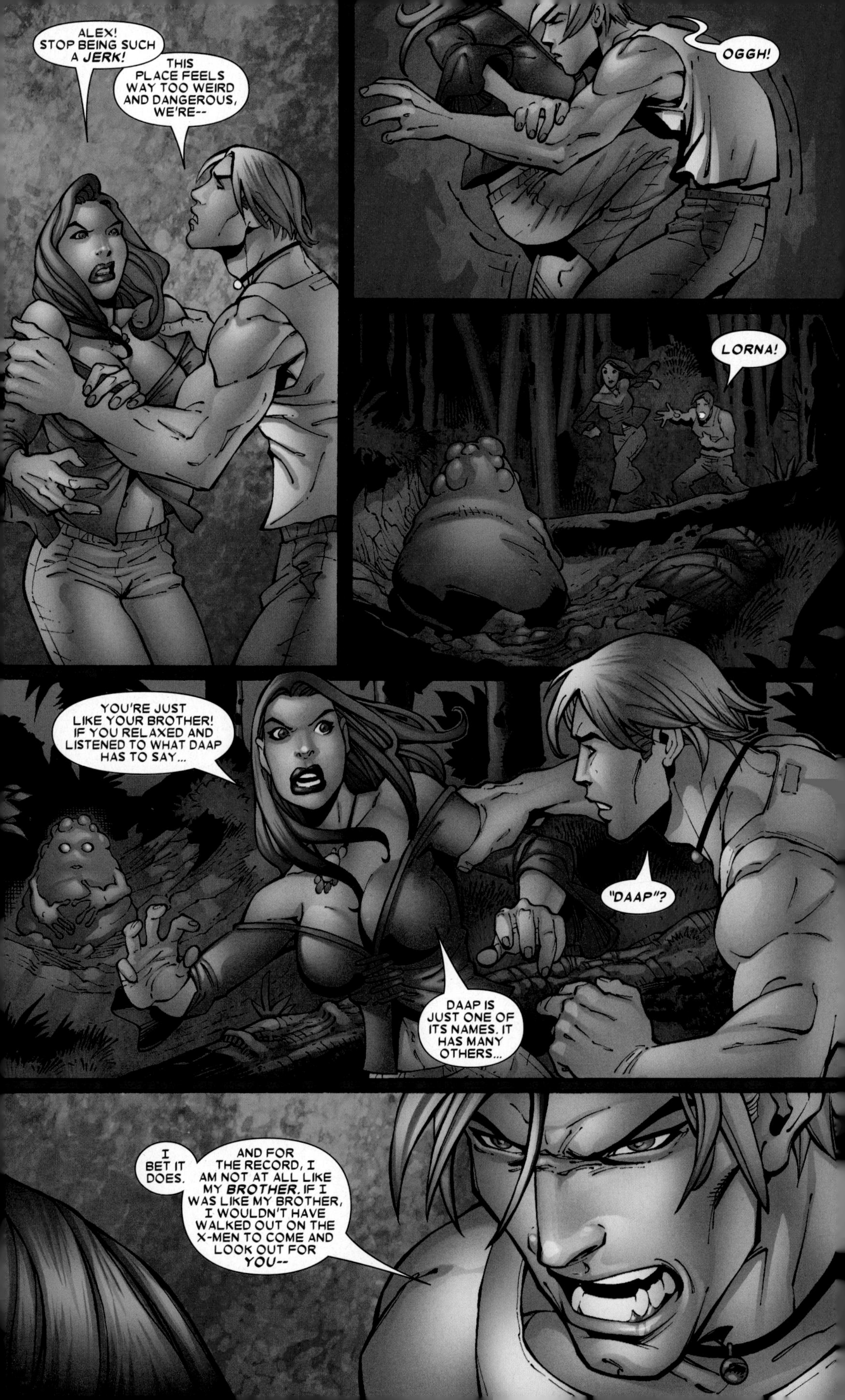
ALEX! STOP BEING SUCH A JERK!
THIS PLACE FEELS WAY TOO WEIRD AND DANGEROUS, WE'RE--
OGGH!
LORNA!
YOU'RE JUST LIKE YOUR BROTHER! IF YOU RELAXED AND LISTENED TO WHAT DAAP HAS TO SAY...
"DAAP"?
DAAP IS JUST ONE OF ITS NAMES. IT HAS MANY OTHERS...
I BET IT DOES.
AND FOR THE RECORD, I AM NOT AT ALL LIKE MY BROTHER. IF I WAS LIKE MY BROTHER, I WOULDN'T HAVE WALKED OUT ON THE X-MEN TO COME AND LOOK OUT FOR YOU--

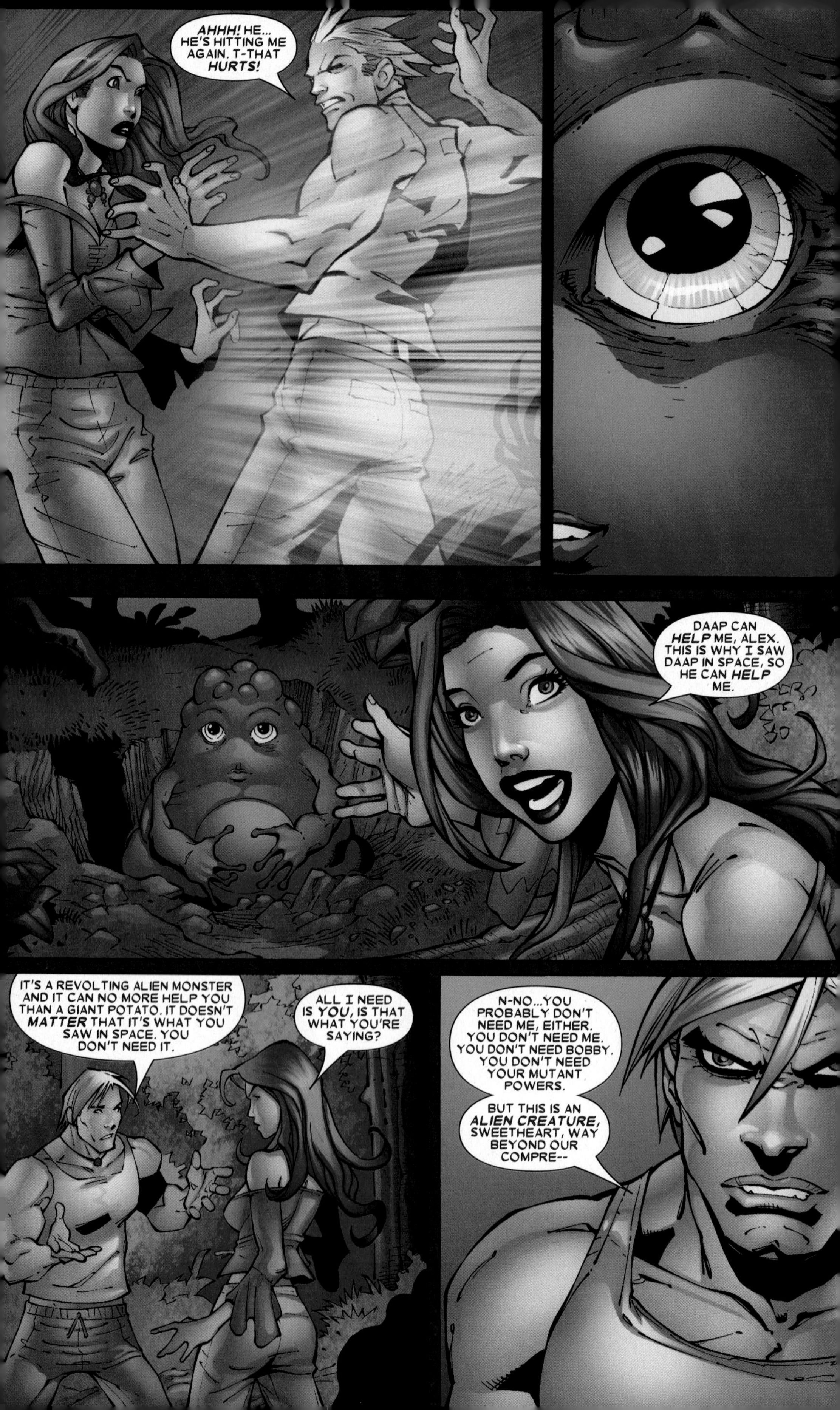
AHHH! HE... HE'S HITTING ME AGAIN. T-THAT HURTS!
DAAP CAN HELP ME, ALEX. THIS IS WHY I SAW DAAP IN SPACE, SO HE CAN HELP ME.
IT'S A REVOLTING ALIEN MONSTER AND IT CAN NO MORE HELP YOU THAN A GIANT POTATO. IT DOESN'T MATTER THAT IT'S WHAT YOU SAW IN SPACE. YOU DON'T NEED IT.
ALL I NEED IS YOU, IS THAT WHAT YOU'RE SAYING?
N-NO...YOU PROBABLY DON'T NEED ME, EITHER. YOU DON'T NEED ME. YOU DON'T NEED BOBBY. YOU DON'T NEED YOUR MUTANT POWERS.
BUT THIS IS AN ALIEN CREATURE, SWEETHEART, WAY BEYOND OUR COMPRE--

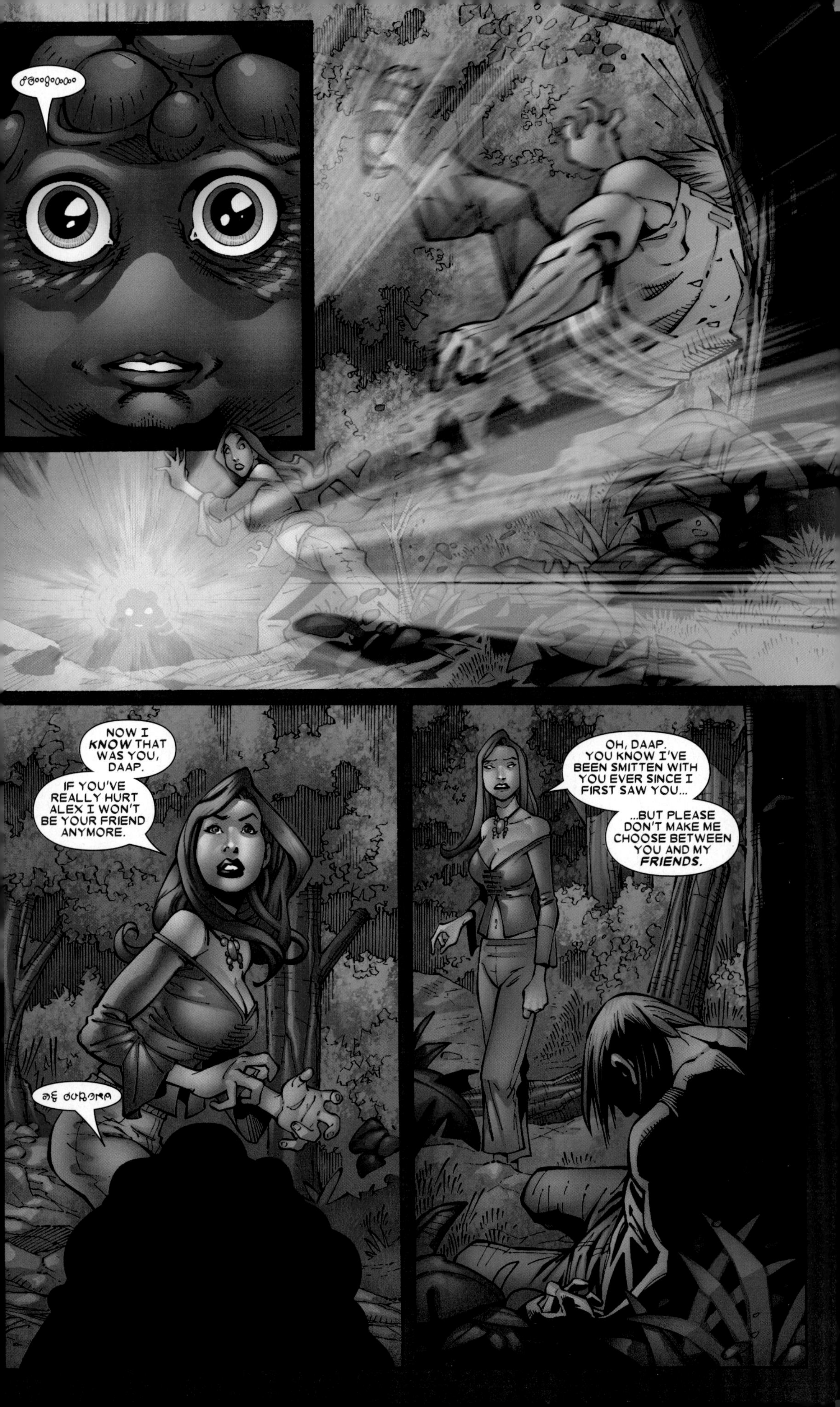
NOW I KNOW THAT WAS YOU, DAAP.
IF YOU'VE REALLY HURT ALEX I WON'T BE YOUR FRIEND ANYMORE.
OH, DAAP. YOU KNOW I'VE BEEN SMITTEN WITH YOU EVER SINCE I FIRST SAW YOU...
...BUT PLEASE DON'T MAKE ME CHOOSE BETWEEN YOU AND MY FRIENDS.

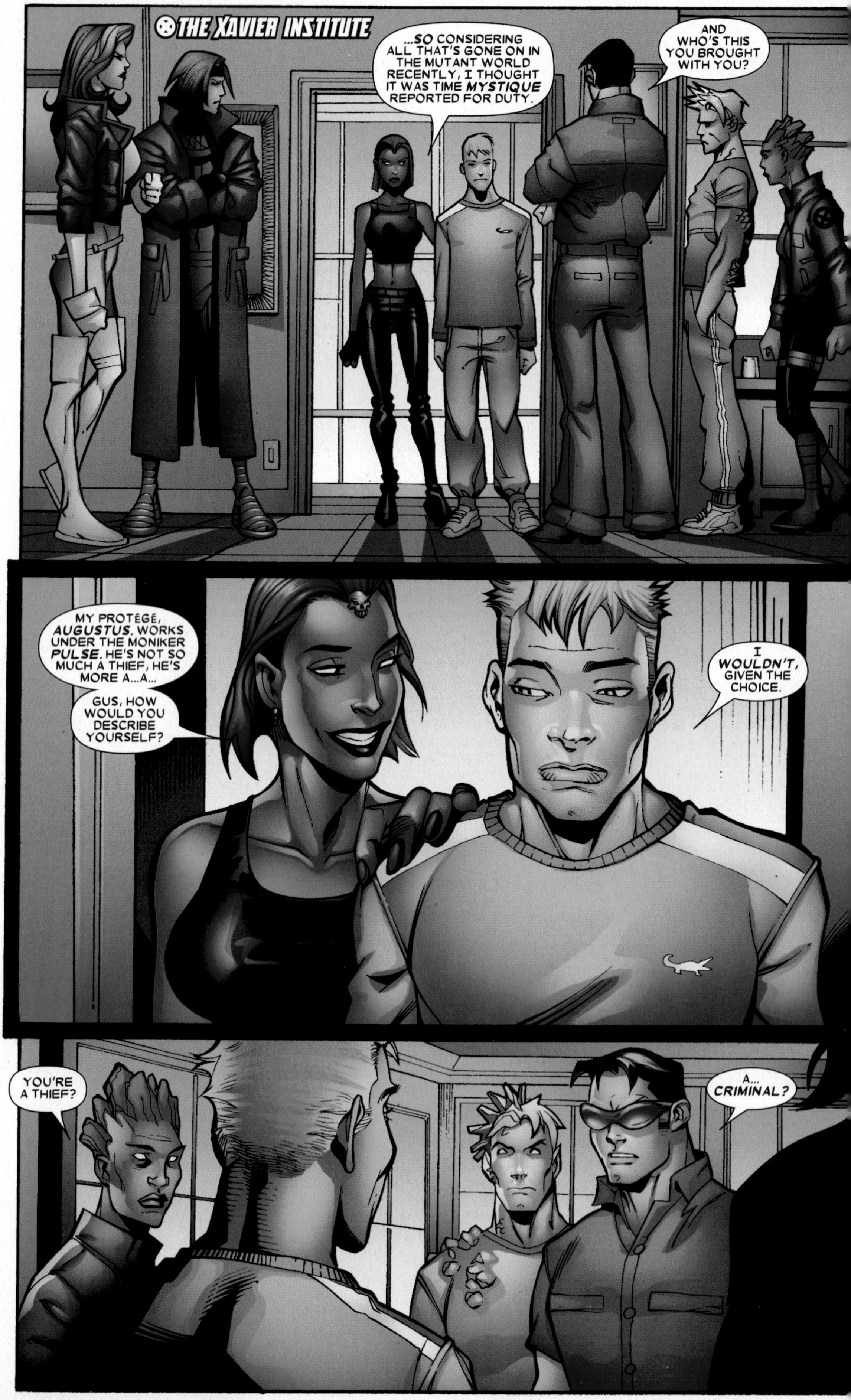
THE XAVIER INSTITUTE
...SO CONSIDERING ALL THAT'S GONE ON IN THE MUTANT WORLD RECENTLY, I THOUGHT IT WAS TIME MYSTIQUE REPORTED FOR DUTY.
AND WHO'S THIS YOU BROUGHT WITH YOU?
MY PROTÉGÉ, AUGUSTUS. WORKS UNDER THE MONIKER PULSE. HE'S NOT SO MUCH A THIEF, HE'S MORE A...A...
GUS, HOW WOULD YOU DESCRIBE YOURSELF?
I WOULDN'T, GIVEN THE CHOICE.
YOU'RE A THIEF?
A... CRIMINAL?

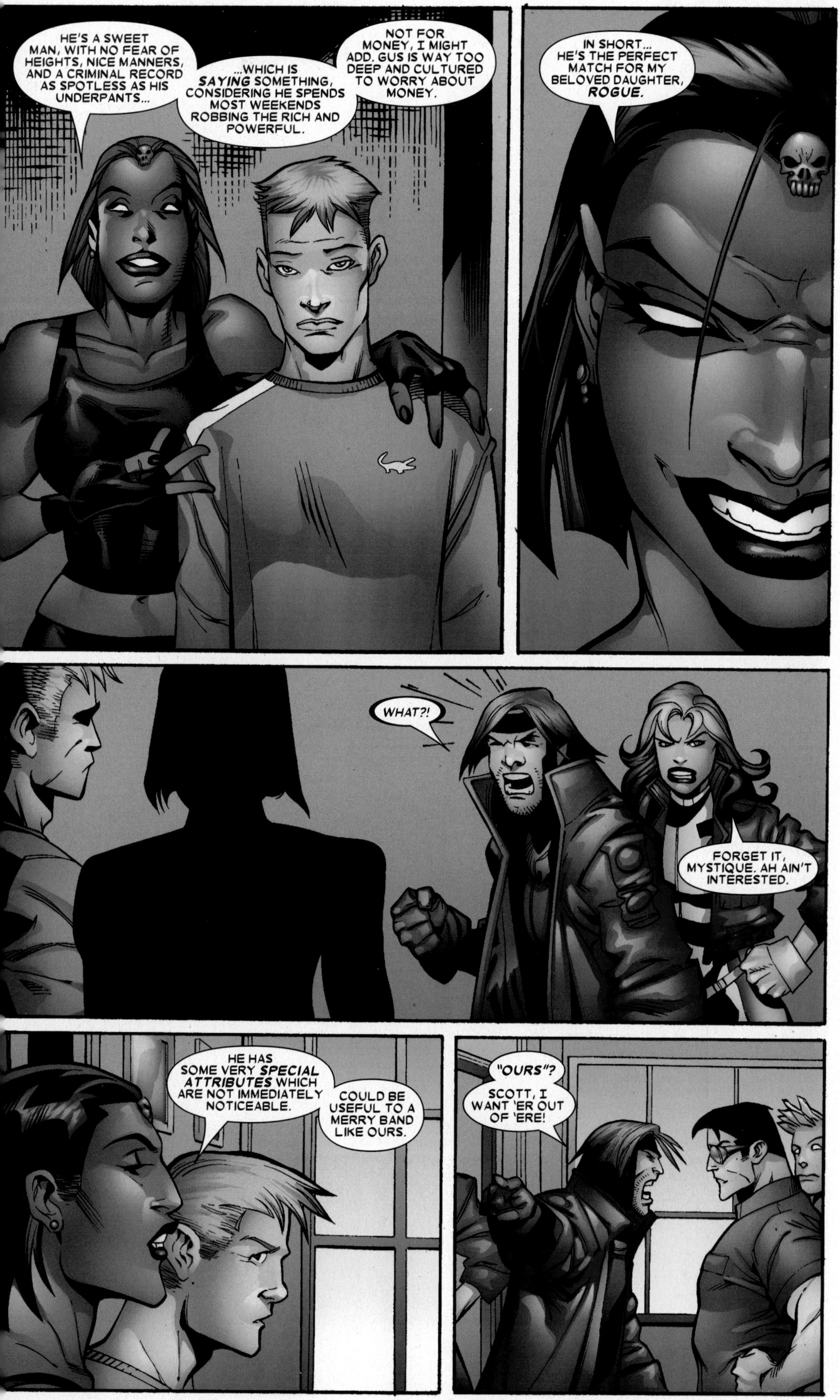
HE'S A SWEET MAN, WITH NO FEAR OF HEIGHTS, NICE MANNERS, AND A CRIMINAL RECORD AS SPOTLESS AS HIS UNDERPANTS...
...WHICH IS SAYING SOMETHING, CONSIDERING HE SPENDS MOST WEEKENDS ROBBING THE RICH AND POWERFUL.
NOT FOR MONEY, I MIGHT ADD. GUS IS WAY TOO DEEP AND CULTURED TO WORRY ABOUT MONEY.
IN SHORT... HE'S THE PERFECT MATCH FOR MY BELOVED DAUGHTER, ROGUE.
WHAT?!
FORGET IT, MYSTIQUE. AH AIN'T INTERESTED.
HE HAS SOME VERY SPECIAL ATTRIBUTES WHICH ARE NOT IMMEDIATELY NOTICEABLE.
COULD BE USEFUL TO A MERRY BAND LIKE OURS.
"OURS"?
SCOTT, I WANT 'ER OUT OF 'ERE!

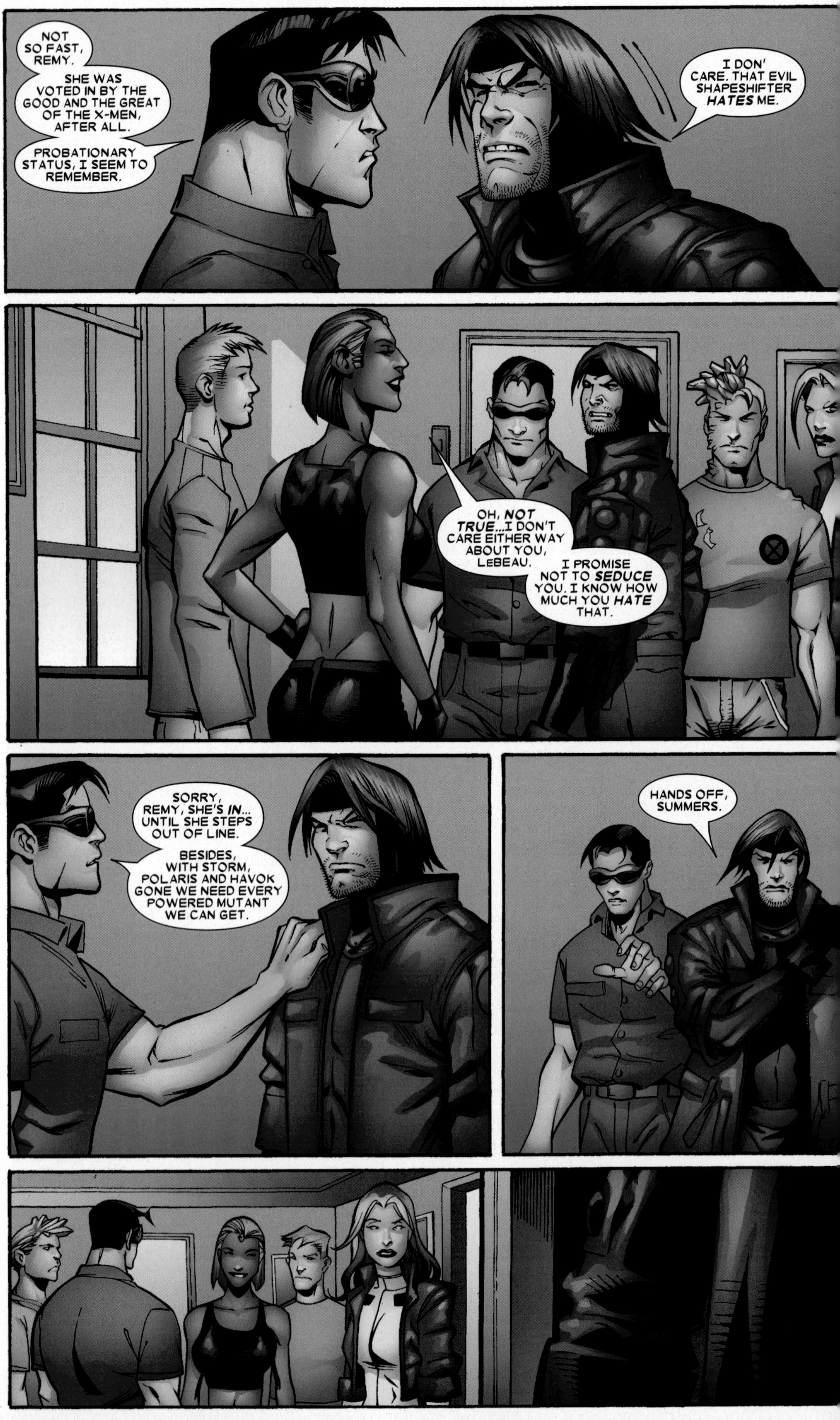

NOT SO FAST, REMY.
SHE WAS VOTED IN BY THE GOOD AND THE GREAT OF THE X-MEN, AFTER ALL.
PROBATIONARY STATUS, I SEEM TO REMEMBER.
I DON' CARE. THAT EVIL SHAPESHIFTER HATES ME.
OH, NOT TRUE...I DON'T CARE EITHER WAY ABOUT YOU, LEBEAU.
I PROMISE NOT TO SEDUCE YOU. I KNOW HOW MUCH YOU HATE THAT.
SORRY, REMY, SHE'S IN... UNTIL SHE STEPS OUT OF LINE.
BESIDES, WITH STORM, POLARIS AND HAVOK GONE WE NEED EVERY POWERED MUTANT WE CAN GET.
HANDS OFF, SUMMERS.

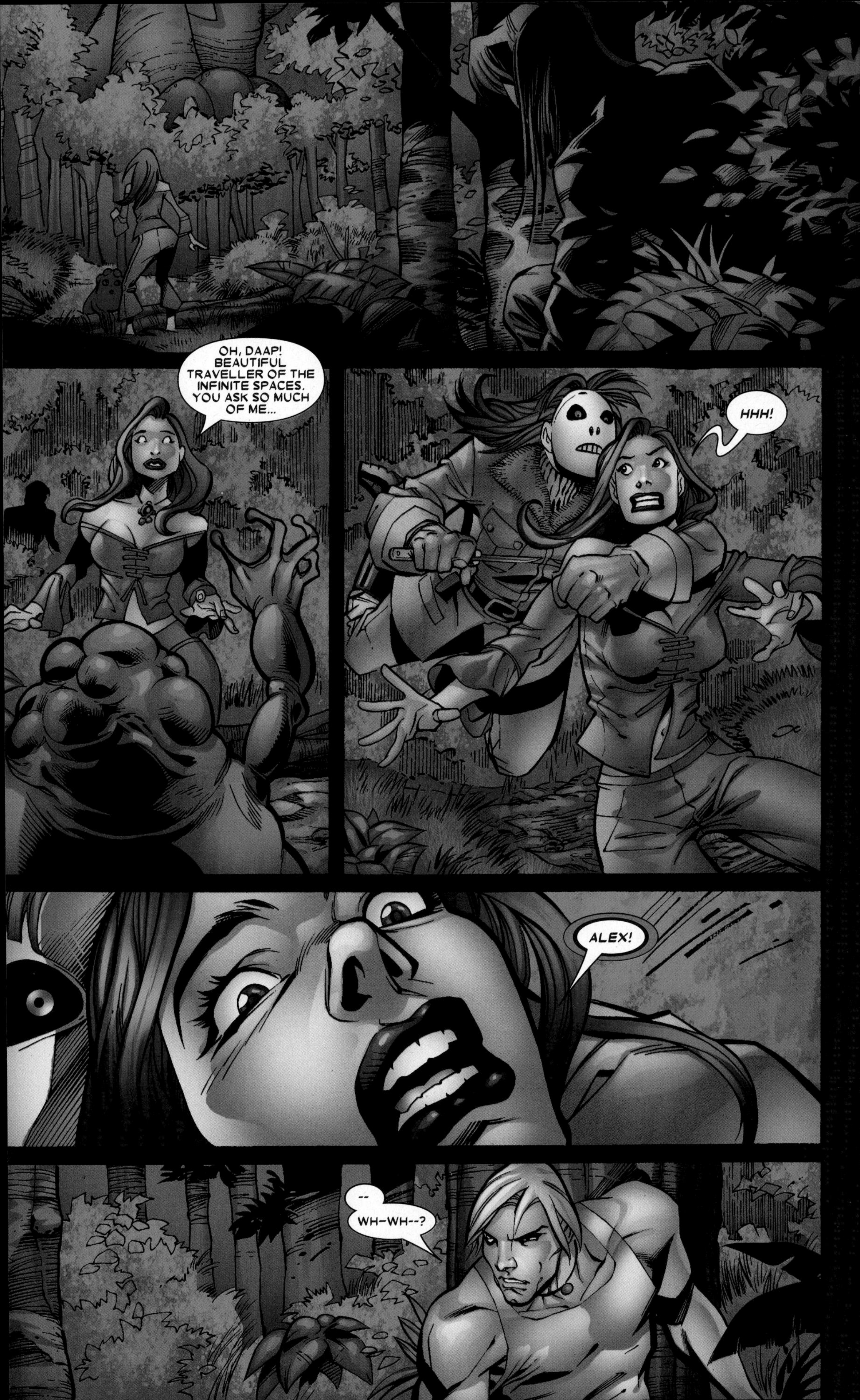
OH, DAAP! BEAUTIFUL TRAVELLER OF THE INFINITE SPACES. YOU ASK SO MUCH OF ME...
HHH!
ALEX!
--
WH-WH--?

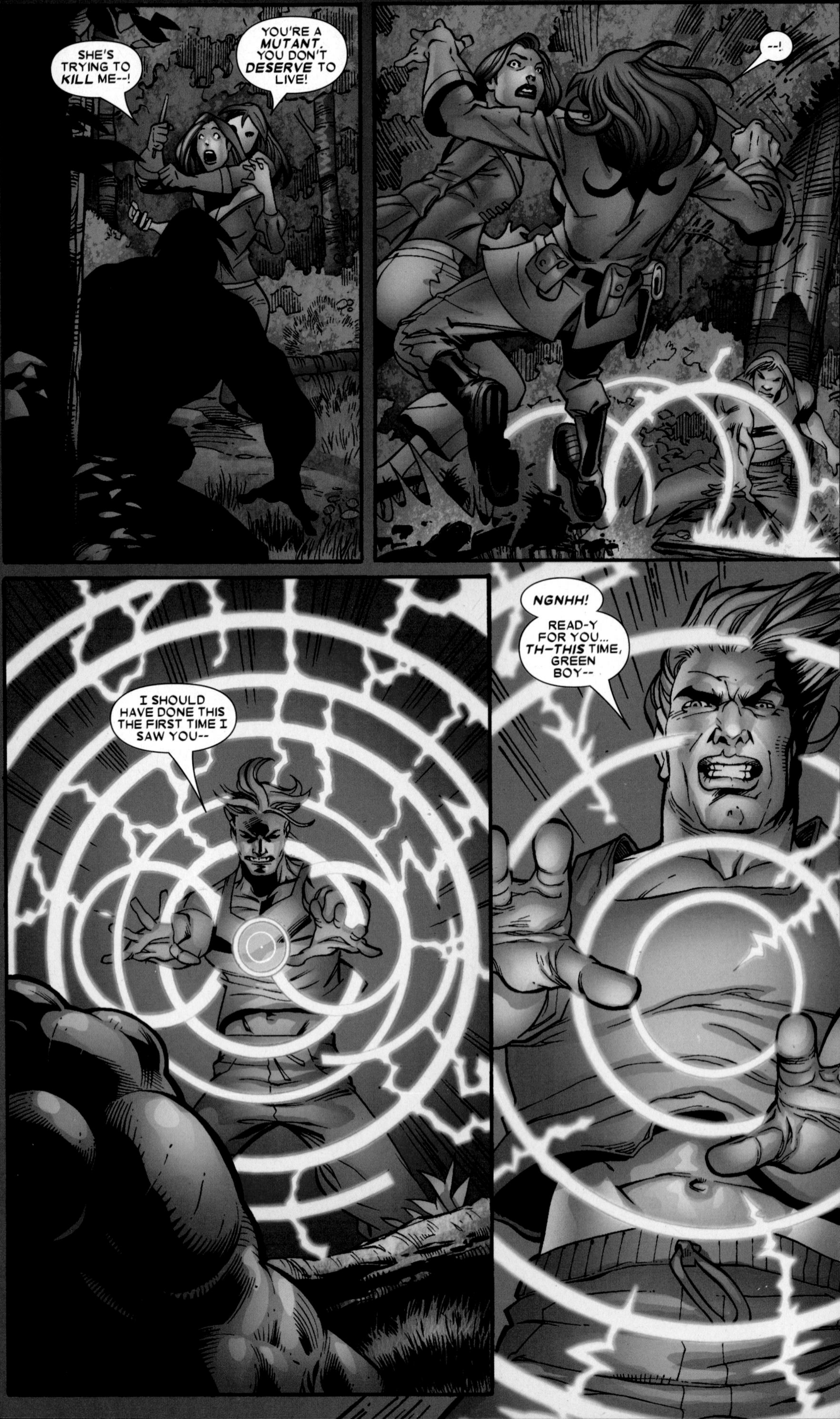
SHE'S TRYING TO KILL ME--!
YOU'RE A MUTANT. YOU DON'T DESERVE TO LIVE!
--!
I SHOULD HAVE DONE THIS THE FIRST TIME I SAW YOU--
NGNHH!
READ-Y FOR YOU... TH-THIS TIME, GREEN BOY--

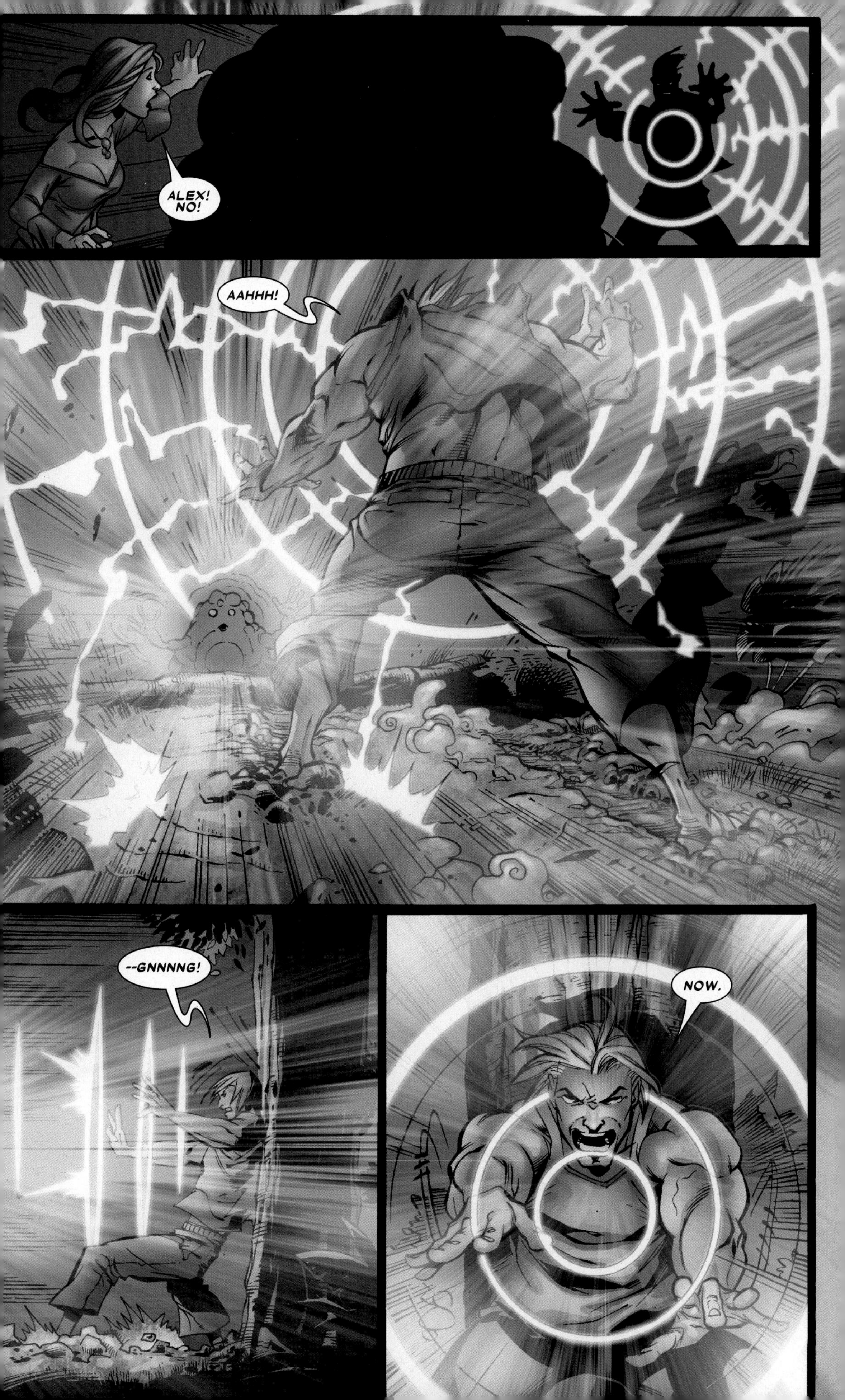
ALEX! NO!
AAHHH!
--GNNNNG!
NOW.

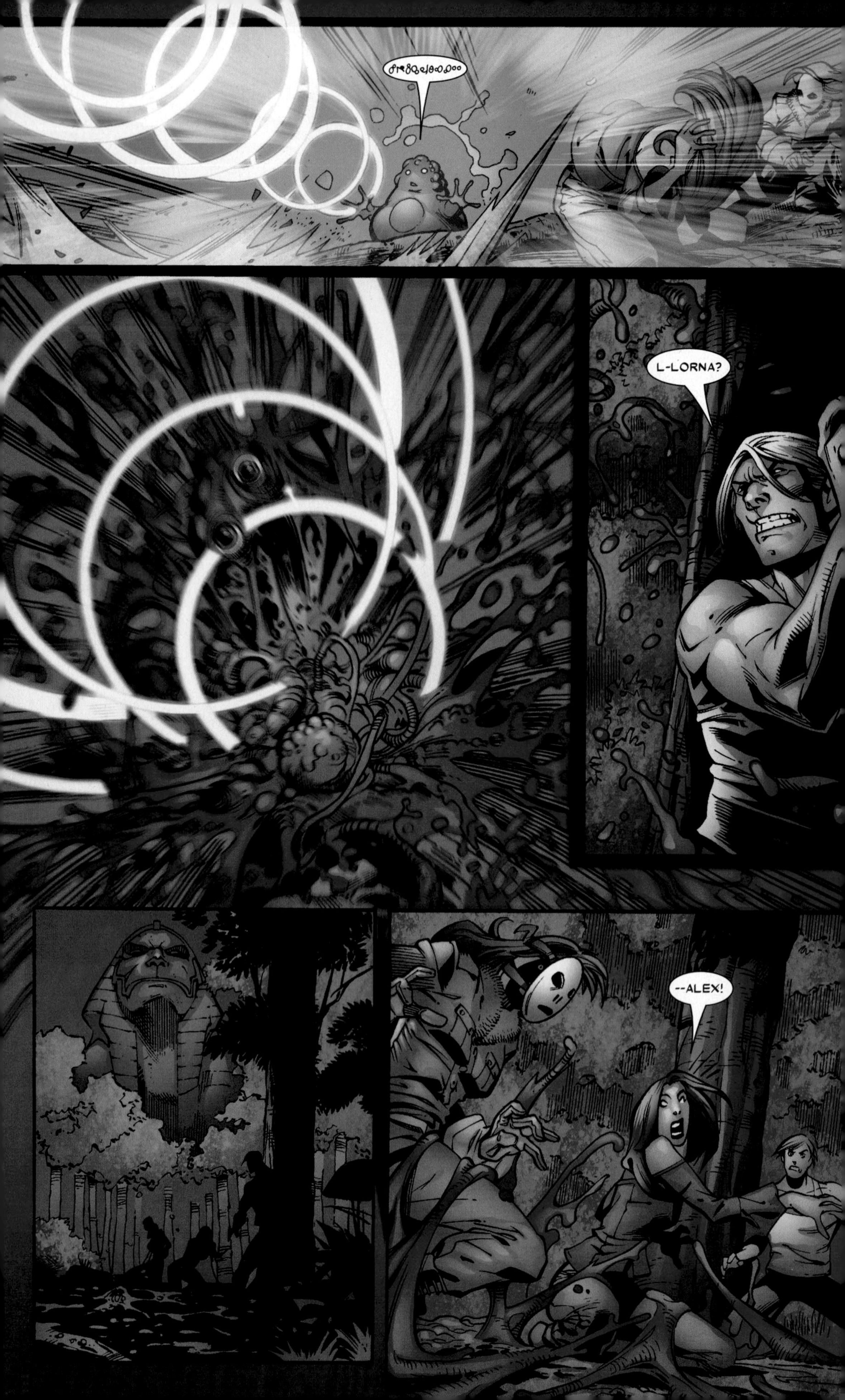
L-LORNA?
--ALEX!

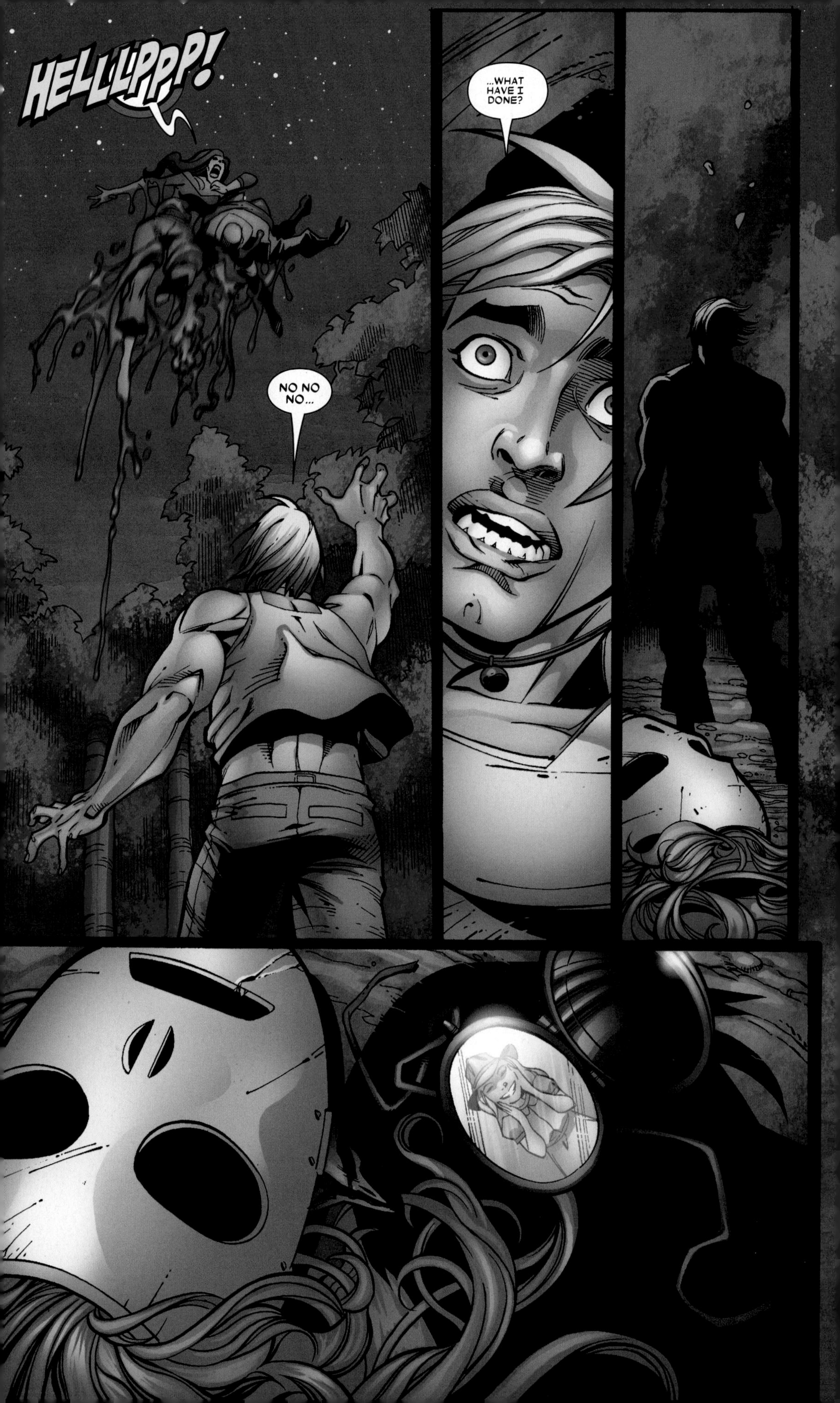
HELLLLPPP!
NO NO NO...
...WHAT HAVE I DONE?

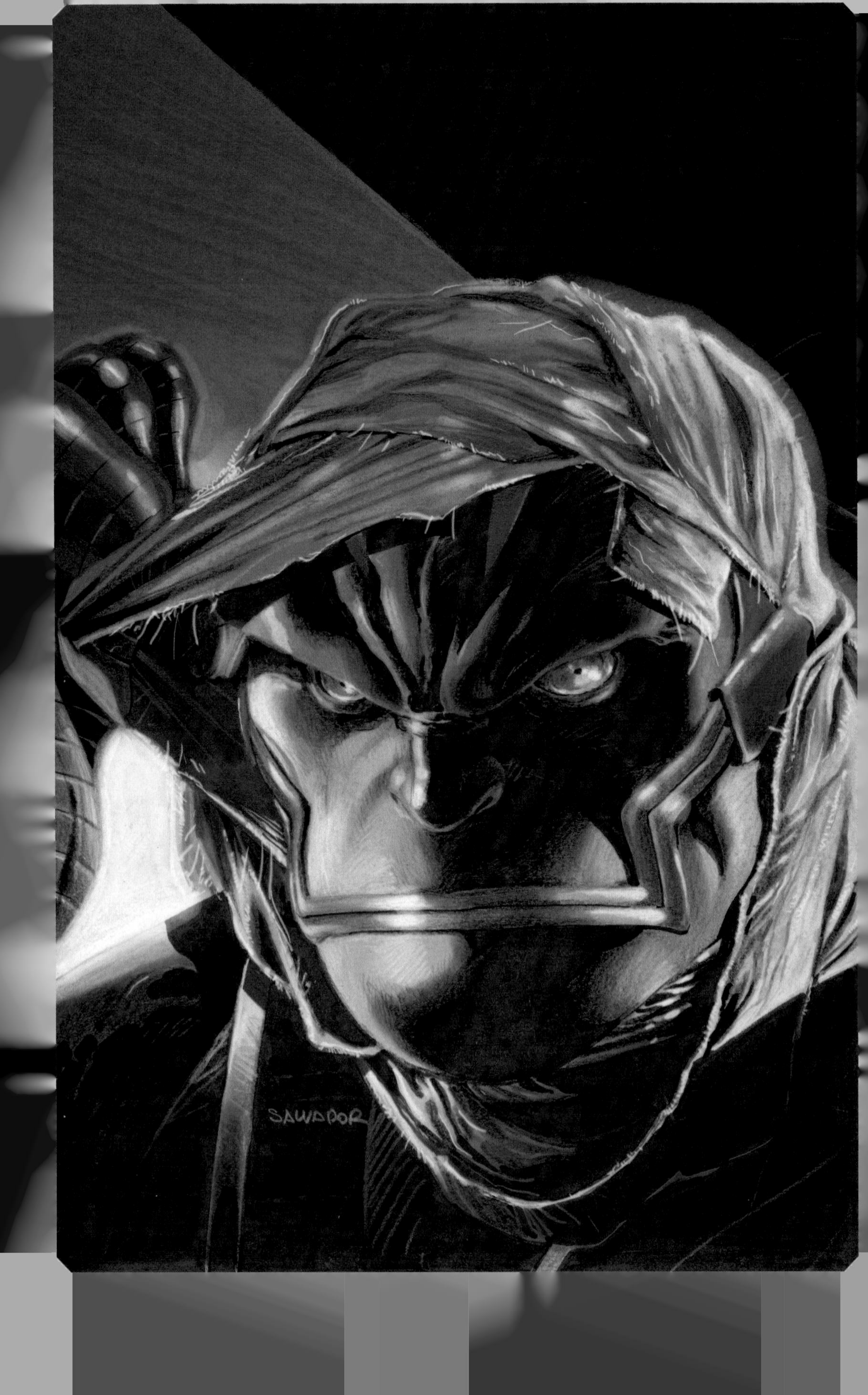
SALVADOR

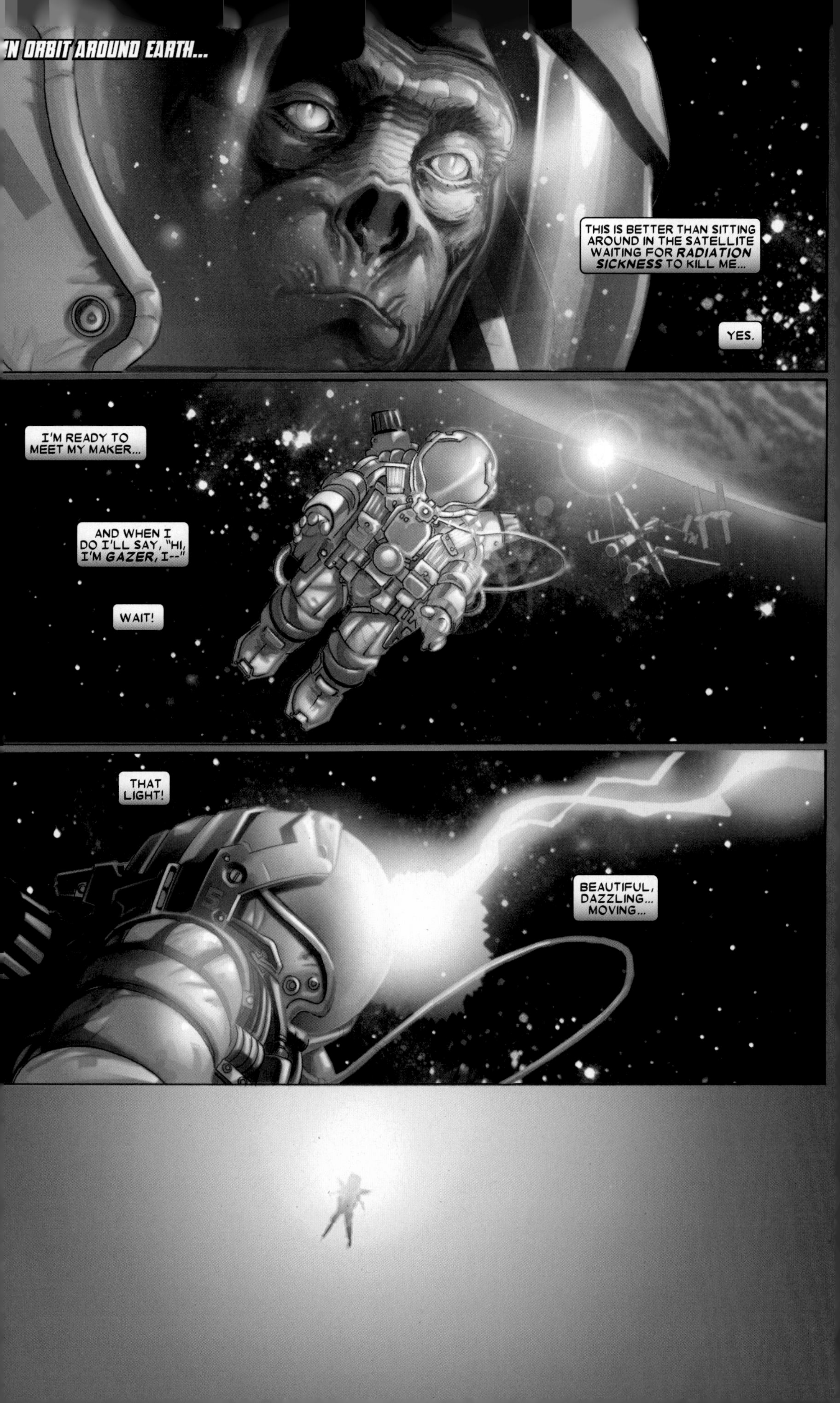

'N ORBIT AROUND EARTH...
THIS IS BETTER THAN SITTING AROUND IN THE SATELLITE WAITING FOR RADIATION SICKNESS TO KILL ME...
YES.
I'M READY TO MEET MY MAKER...
AND WHEN I DO I'LL SAY, "HI, I'M GAZER, I--"
WAIT!
THAT LIGHT!
BEAUTIFUL, DAZZLING... MOVING...

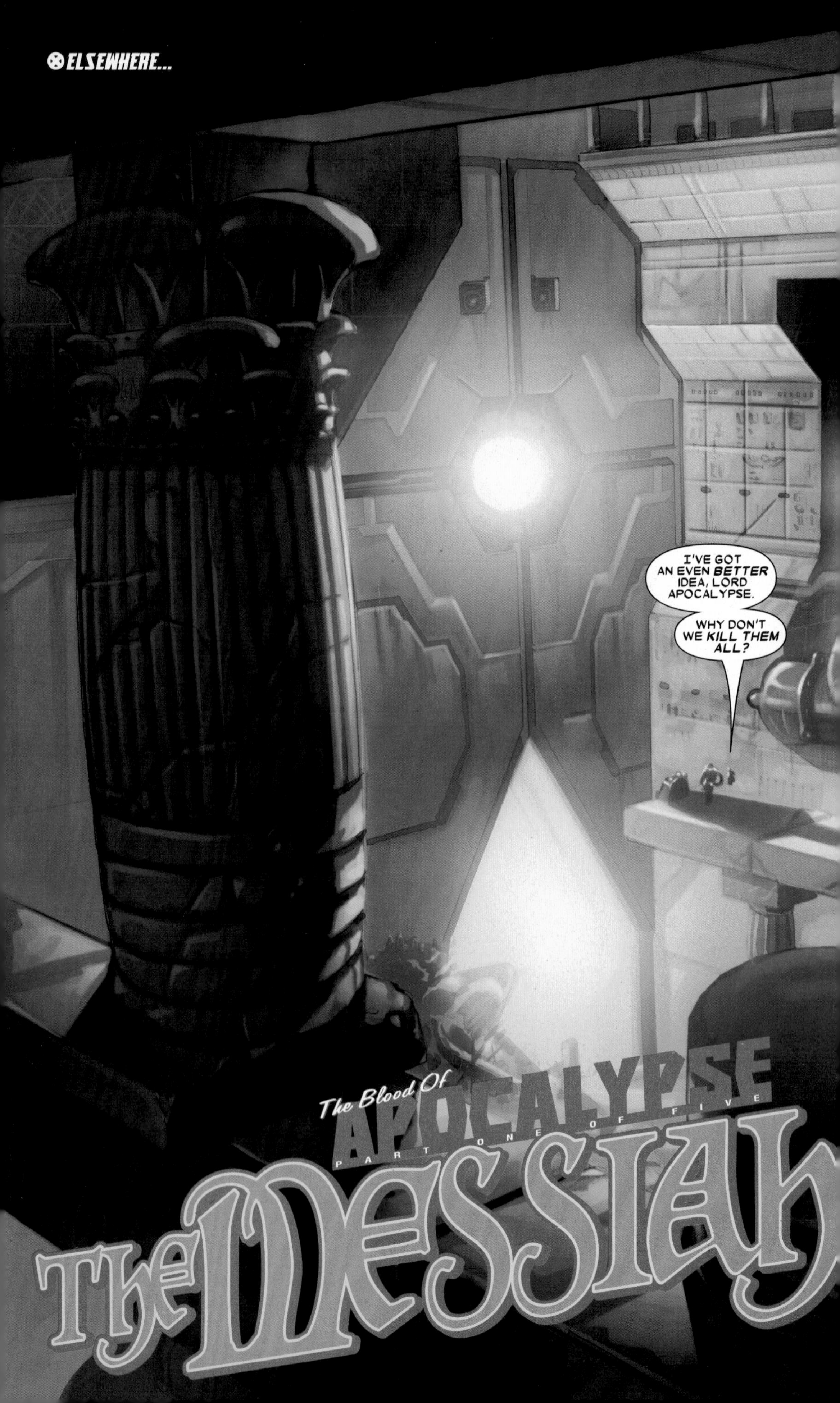
ELSEWHERE...
I'VE GOT AN EVEN BETTER IDEA, LORD APOCALYPSE.
WHY DON'T WE KILL THEM ALL?
The Blood Of
APOCALYPSE
PART ONE OF FIVE
THE MESSIAH

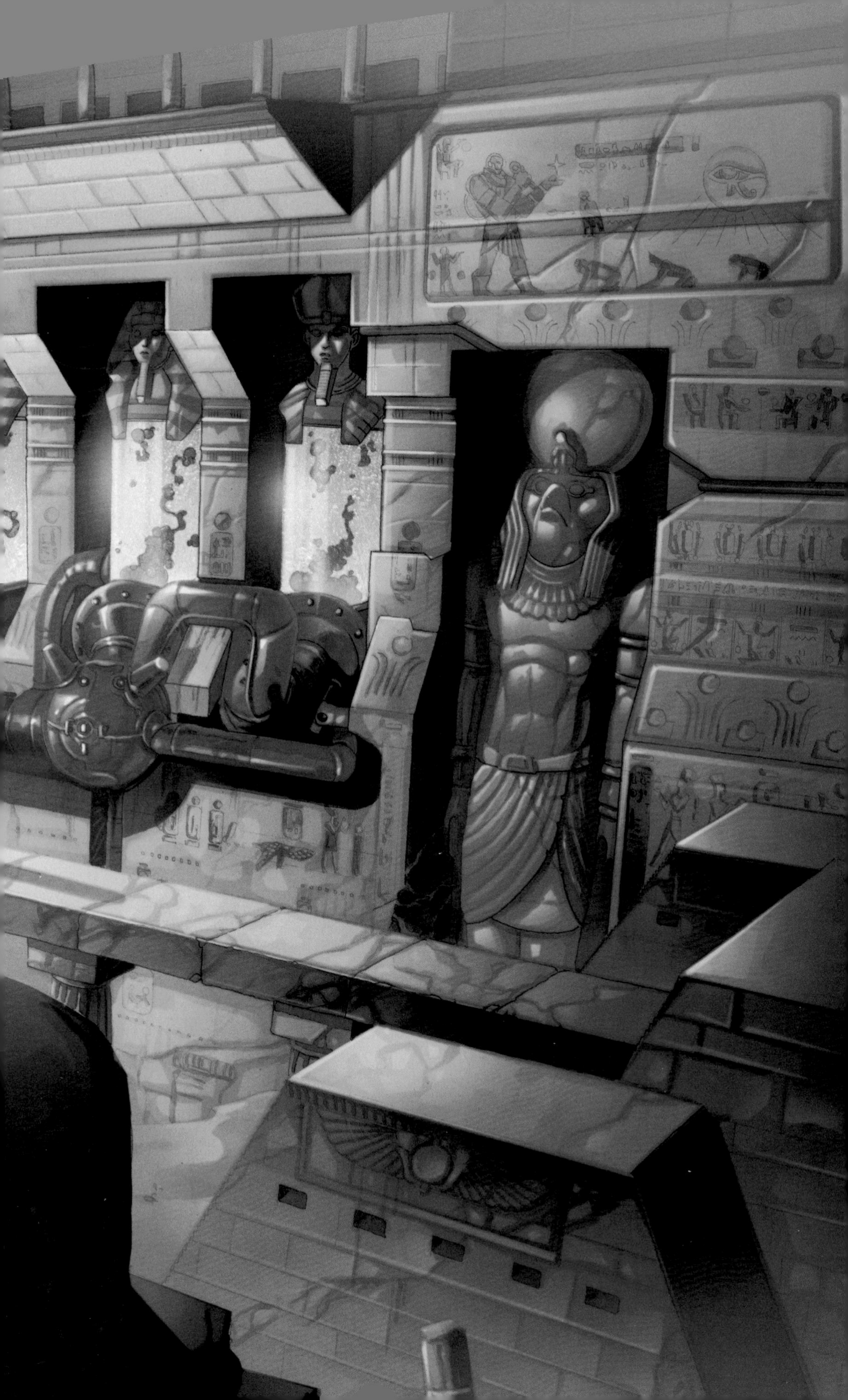

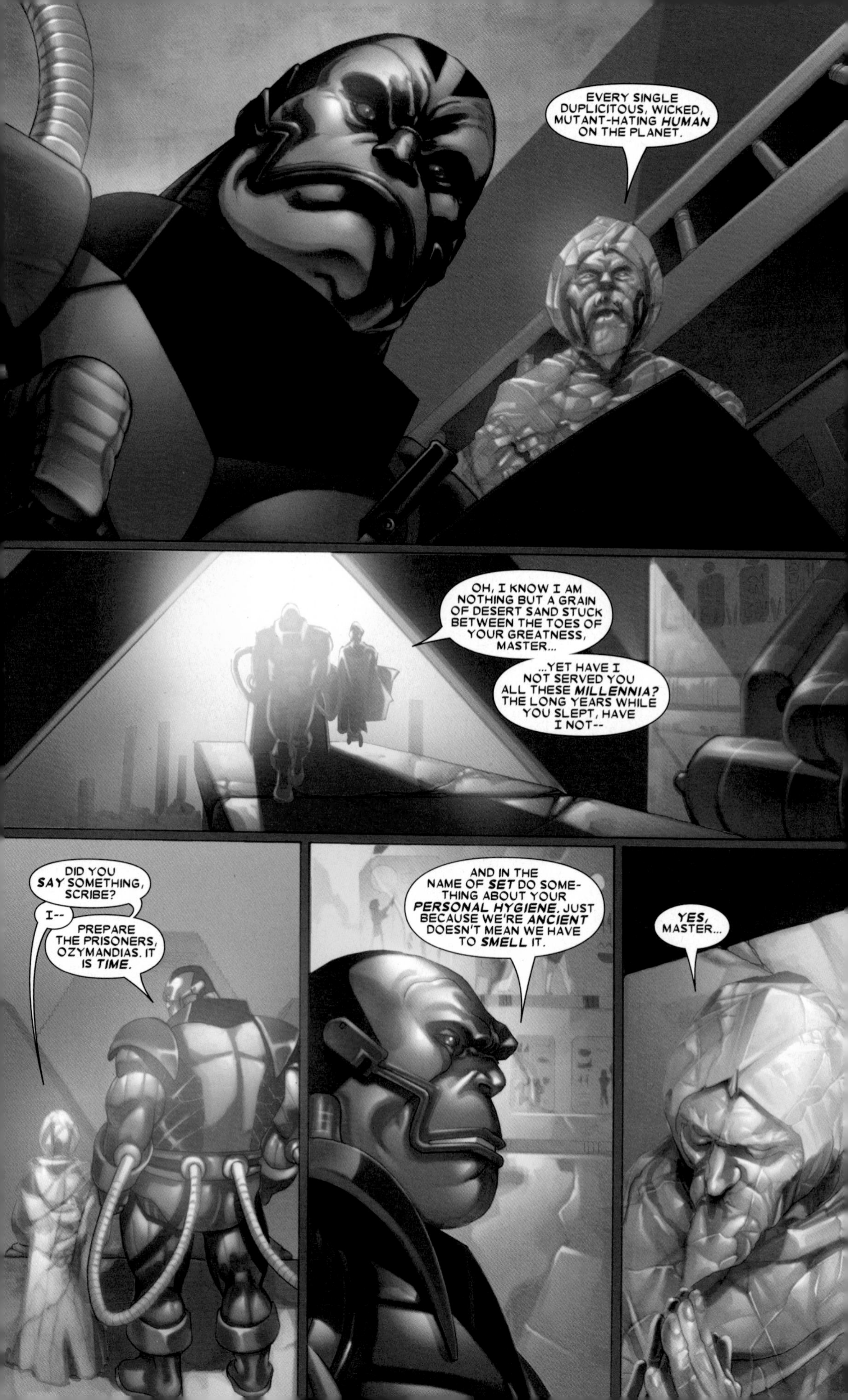
EVERY SINGLE DUPLICITOUS, WICKED, MUTANT-HATING HUMAN ON THE PLANET.
OH, I KNOW I AM NOTHING BUT A GRAIN OF DESERT SAND STUCK BETWEEN THE TOES OF YOUR GREATNESS, MASTER...
...YET HAVE I NOT SERVED YOU ALL THESE MILLENNIA? THE LONG YEARS WHILE YOU SLEPT, HAVE I NOT--
DID YOU SAY SOMETHING, SCRIBE?
I--
PREPARE THE PRISONERS, OZYMANDIAS. IT IS TIME.
AND IN THE NAME OF SET DO SOMETHING ABOUT YOUR PERSONAL HYGIENE. JUST BECAUSE WE'RE ANCIENT DOESN'T MEAN WE HAVE TO SMELL IT.
YES, MASTER...

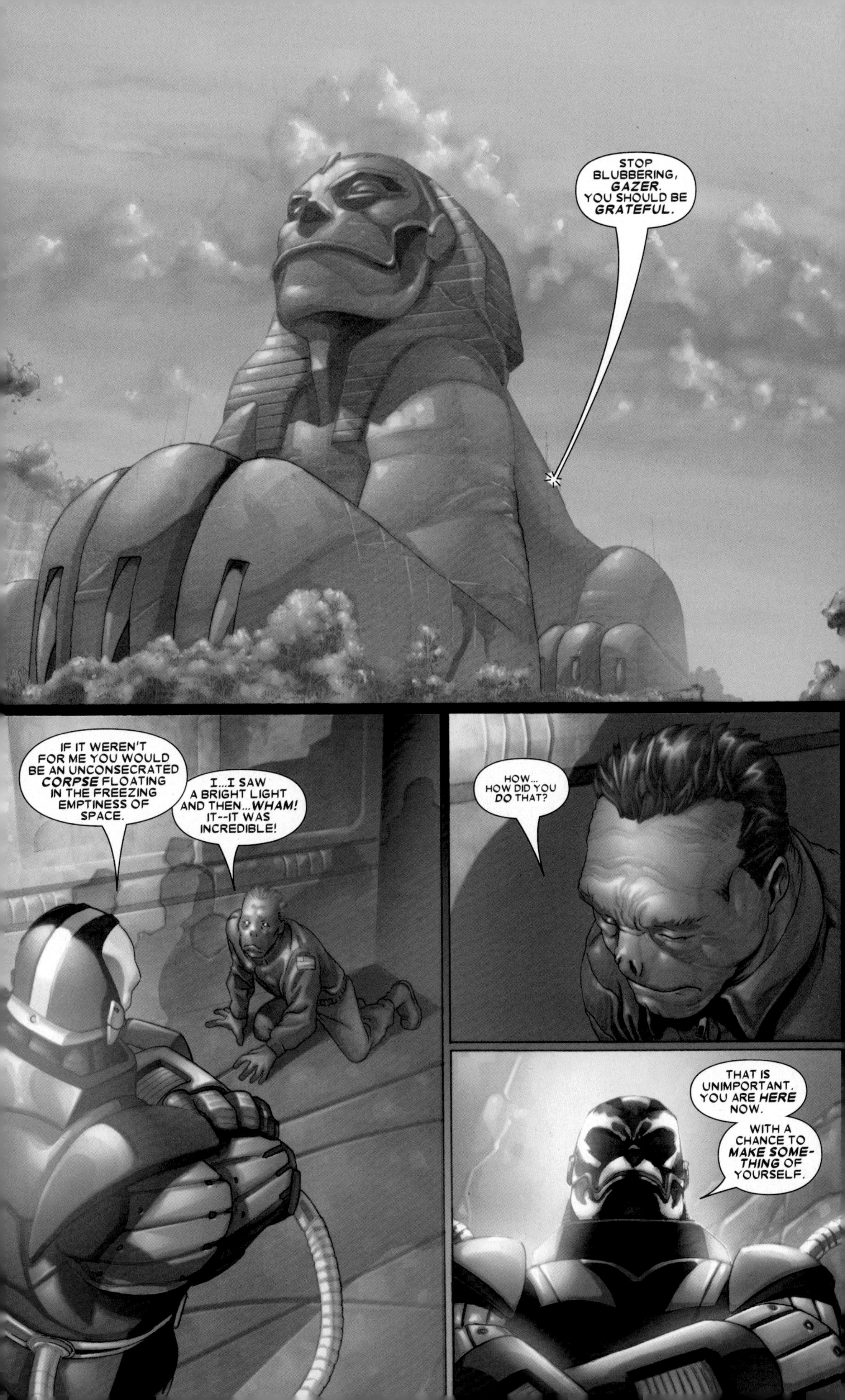
STOP BLUBBERING, GAZER. YOU SHOULD BE GRATEFUL.
IF IT WEREN'T FOR ME YOU WOULD BE AN UNCONSECRATED CORPSE FLOATING IN THE FREEZING EMPTINESS OF SPACE.
I...I SAW A BRIGHT LIGHT AND THEN...WHAM! IT--IT WAS INCREDIBLE!
HOW... HOW DID YOU DO THAT?
THAT IS UNIMPORTANT. YOU ARE HERE NOW.
WITH A CHANCE TO MAKE SOME-THING OF YOURSELF.

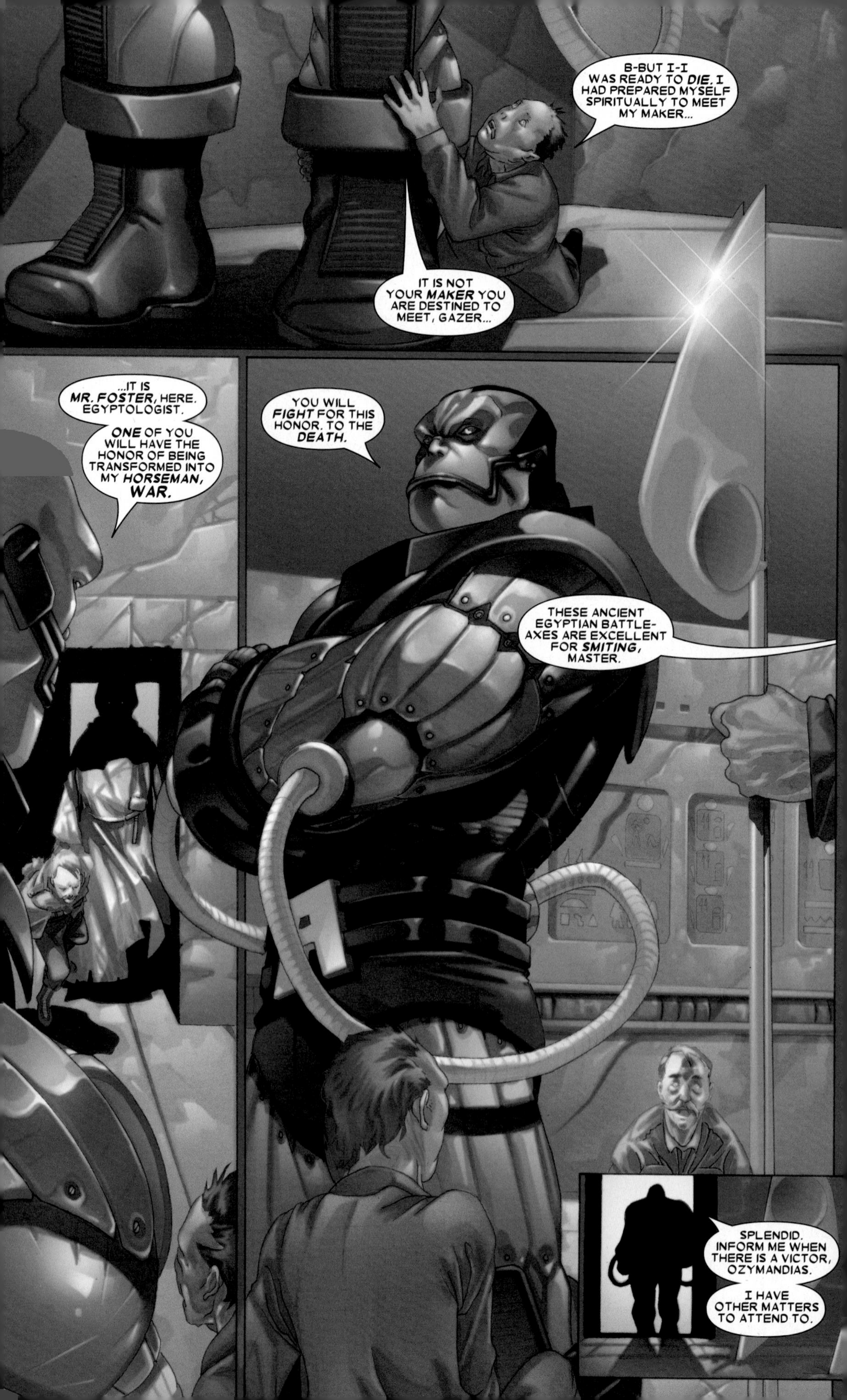
B-BUT I-I WAS READY TO DIE. I HAD PREPARED MYSELF SPIRITUALLY TO MEET MY MAKER...
IT IS NOT YOUR MAKER YOU ARE DESTINED TO MEET, GAZER...
...IT IS MR. FOSTER, HERE. EGYPTOLOGIST.
ONE OF YOU WILL HAVE THE HONOR OF BEING TRANSFORMED INTO MY HORSEMAN, WAR.
YOU WILL FIGHT FOR THIS HONOR. TO THE DEATH.
THESE ANCIENT EGYPTIAN BATTLE-AXES ARE EXCELLENT FOR SMITING, MASTER.
SPLENDID. INFORM ME WHEN THERE IS A VICTOR, OZYMANDIAS.
I HAVE OTHER MATTERS TO ATTEND TO.

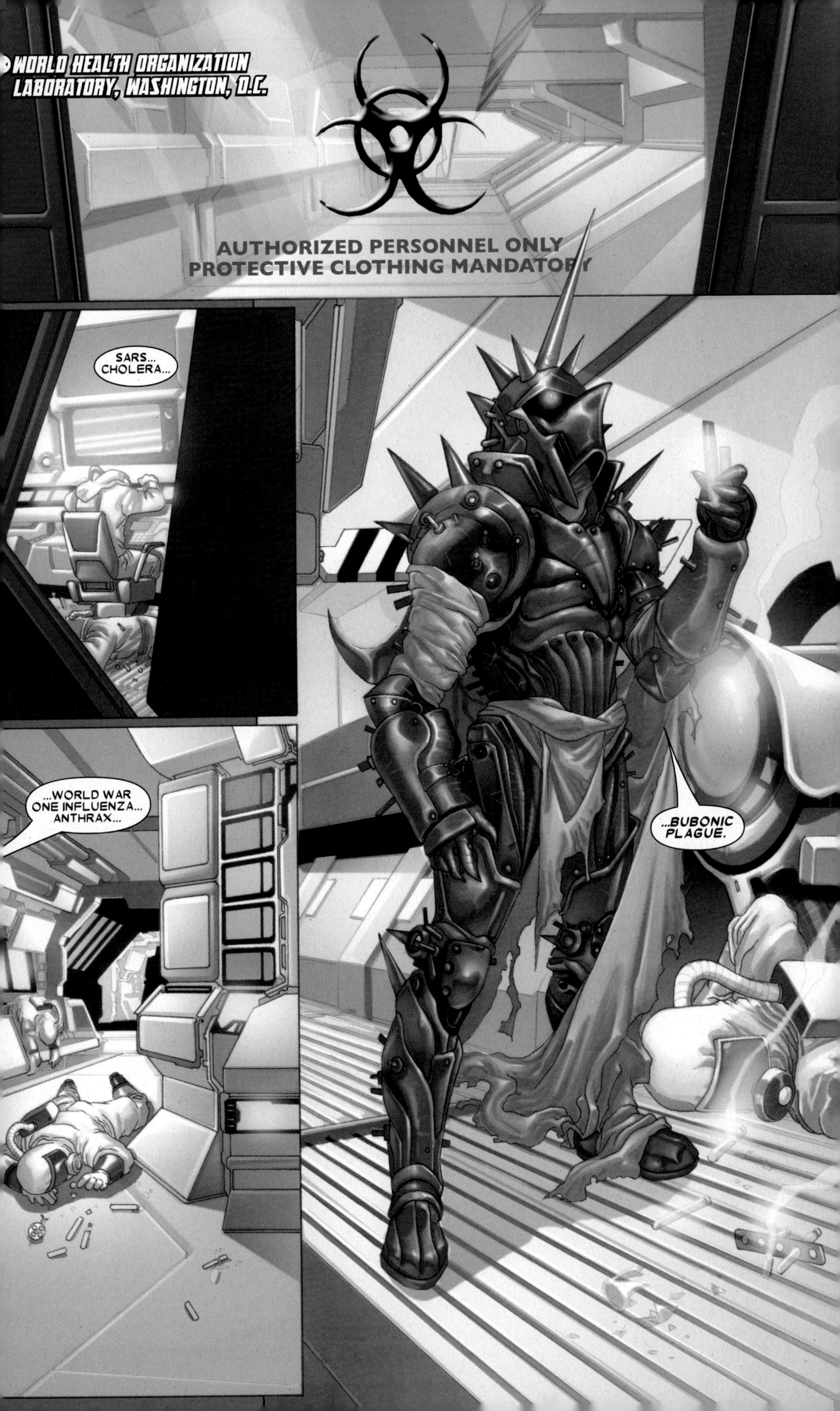
WORLD HEALTH ORGANIZATION LABORATORY, WASHINGTON, D.C.
AUTHORIZED PERSONNEL ONLY
PROTECTIVE CLOTHING MANDATORY
SARS... CHOLERA...
...WORLD WAR ONE INFLUENZA... ANTHRAX...
...BUBONIC PLAGUE.

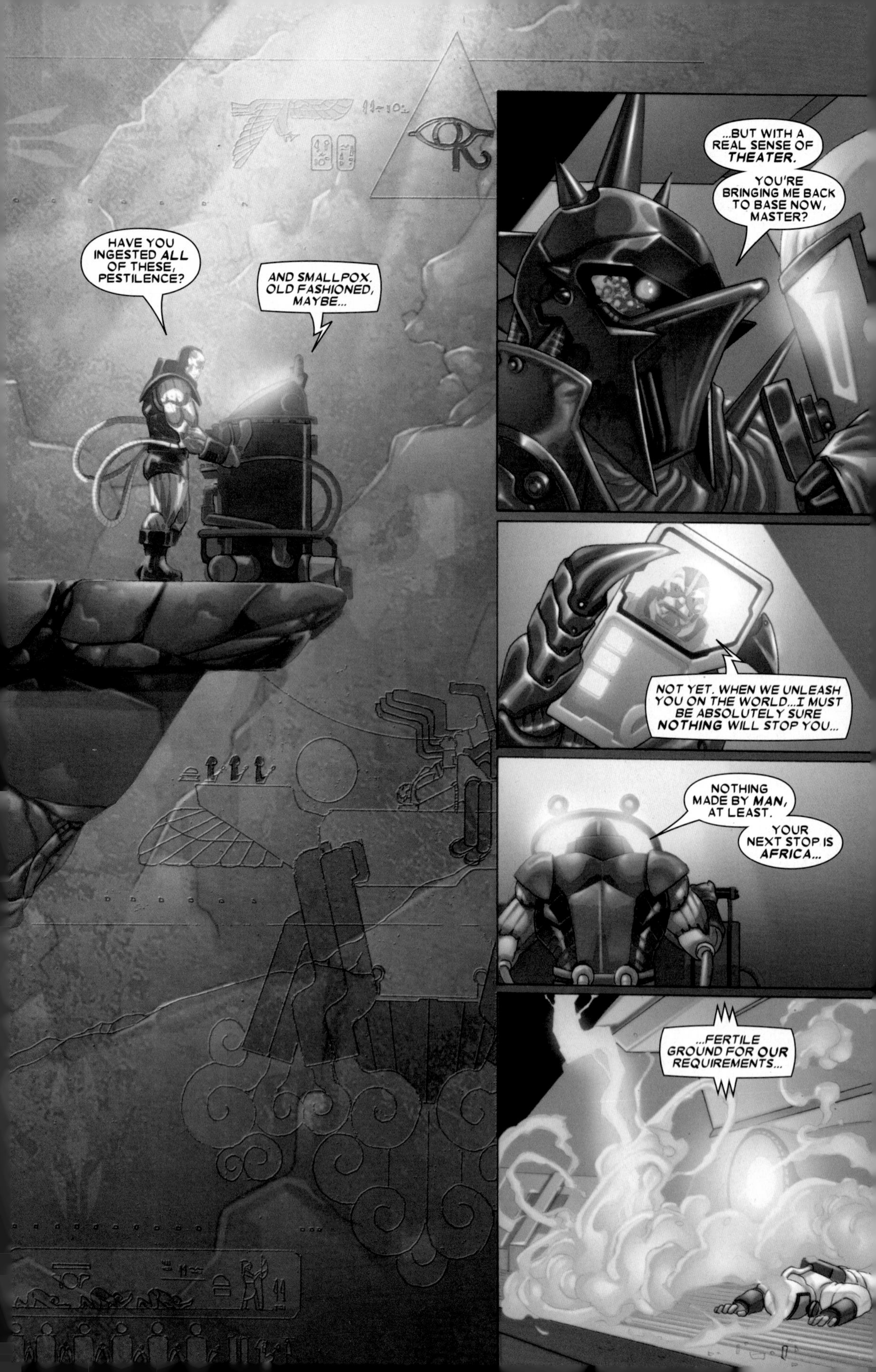
HAVE YOU INGESTED ALL OF THESE, PESTILENCE?
AND SMALLPOX. OLD FASHIONED, MAYBE...
...BUT WITH A REAL SENSE OF THEATER.
YOU'RE BRINGING ME BACK TO BASE NOW, MASTER?
NOT YET. WHEN WE UNLEASH YOU ON THE WORLD...I MUST BE ABSOLUTELY SURE NOTHING WILL STOP YOU...
NOTHING MADE BY MAN, AT LEAST.
YOUR NEXT STOP IS AFRICA...
...FERTILE GROUND FOR OUR REQUIREMENTS...

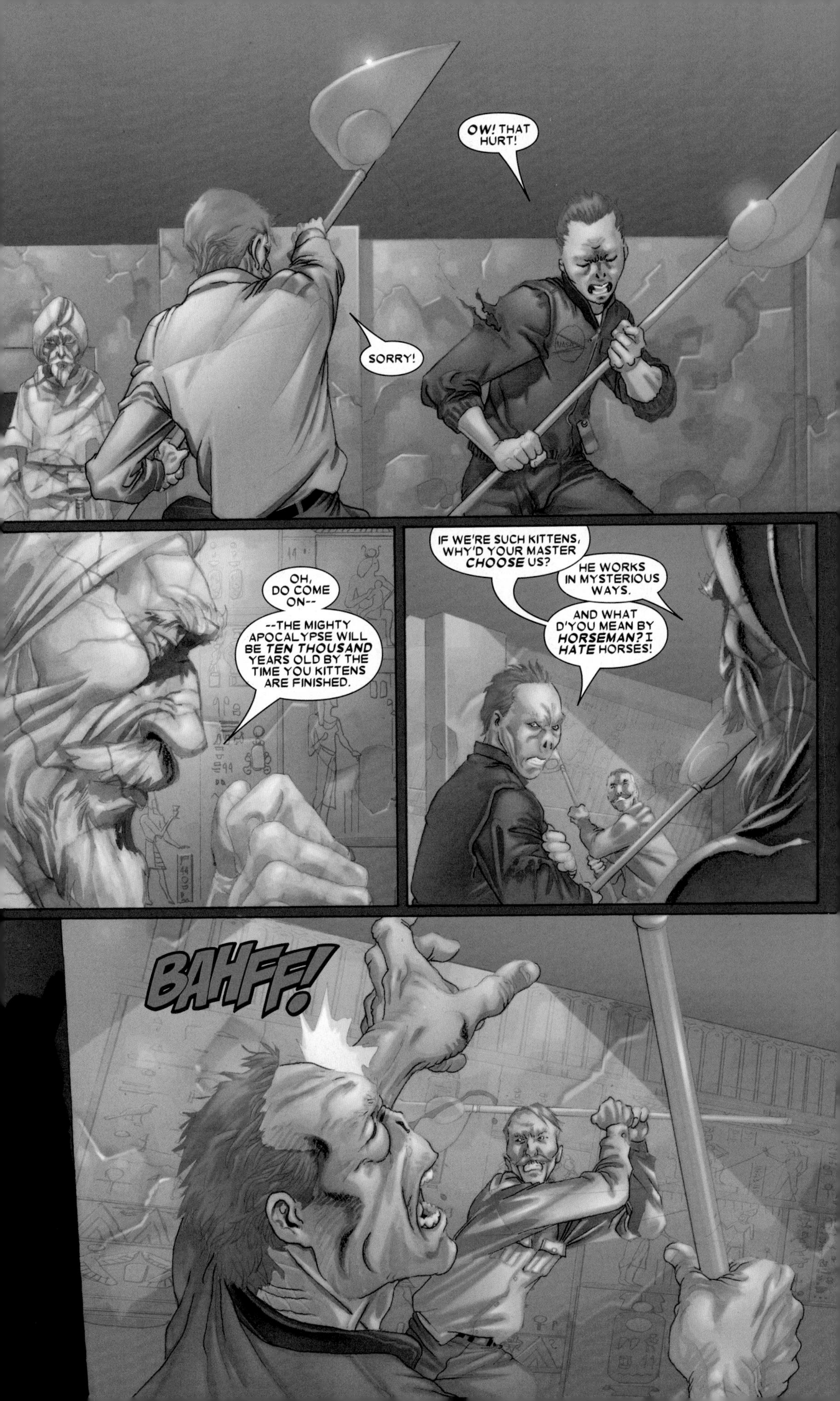
OW! THAT HURT!
SORRY!
OH, DO COME ON--
--THE MIGHTY APOCALYPSE WILL BE TEN THOUSAND YEARS OLD BY THE TIME YOU KITTENS ARE FINISHED.
IF WE'RE SUCH KITTENS, WHY'D YOUR MASTER CHOOSE US?
HE WORKS IN MYSTERIOUS WAYS.
AND WHAT D'YOU MEAN BY HORSEMAN? I HATE HORSES!
BAHFF!

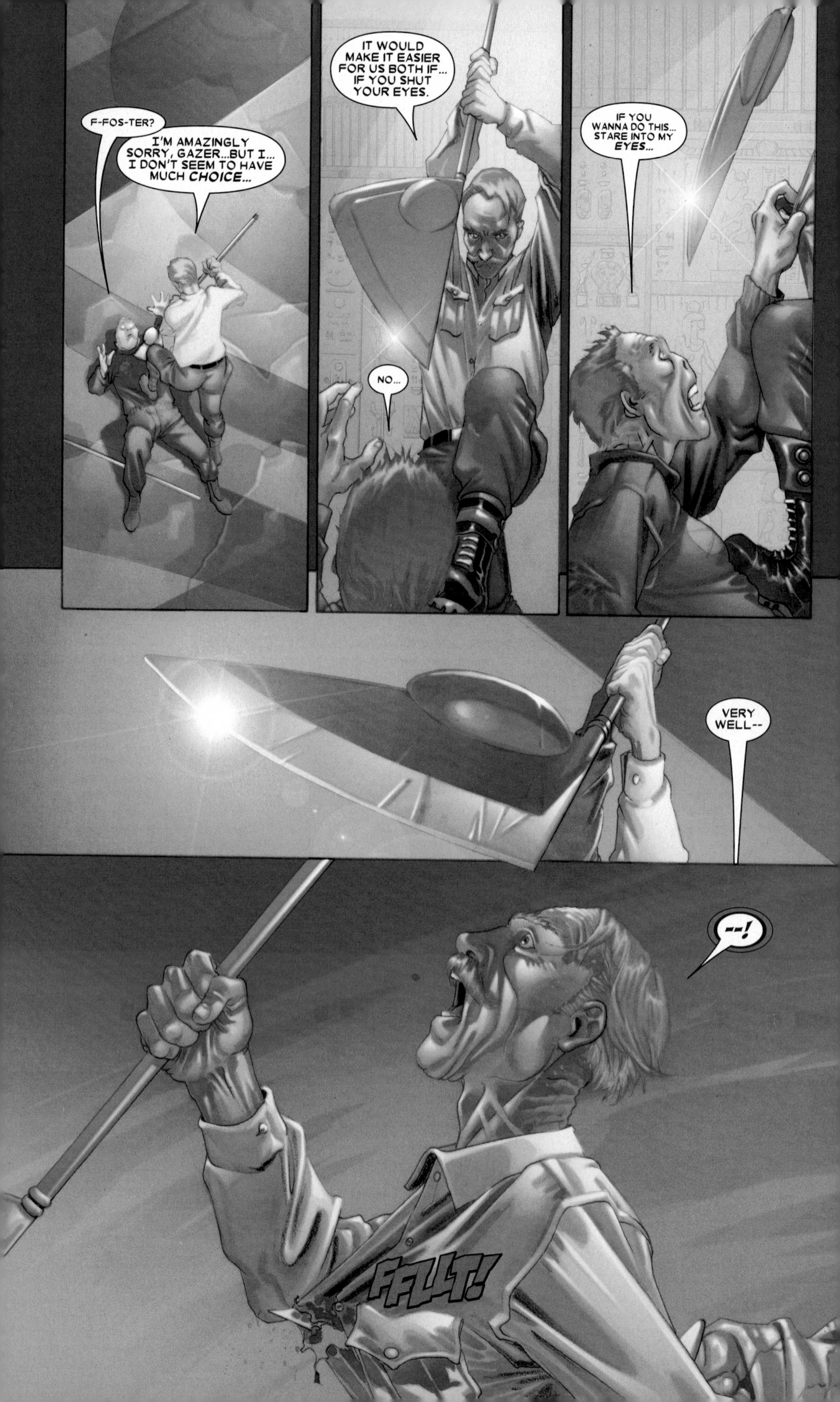
F-FOS-TER?
I'M AMAZINGLY SORRY, GAZER...BUT I... I DON'T SEEM TO HAVE MUCH CHOICE...
IT WOULD MAKE IT EASIER FOR US BOTH IF... IF YOU SHUT YOUR EYES.
NO...
IF YOU WANNA DO THIS... STARE INTO MY EYES...
VERY WELL--
--!
FFLLT!

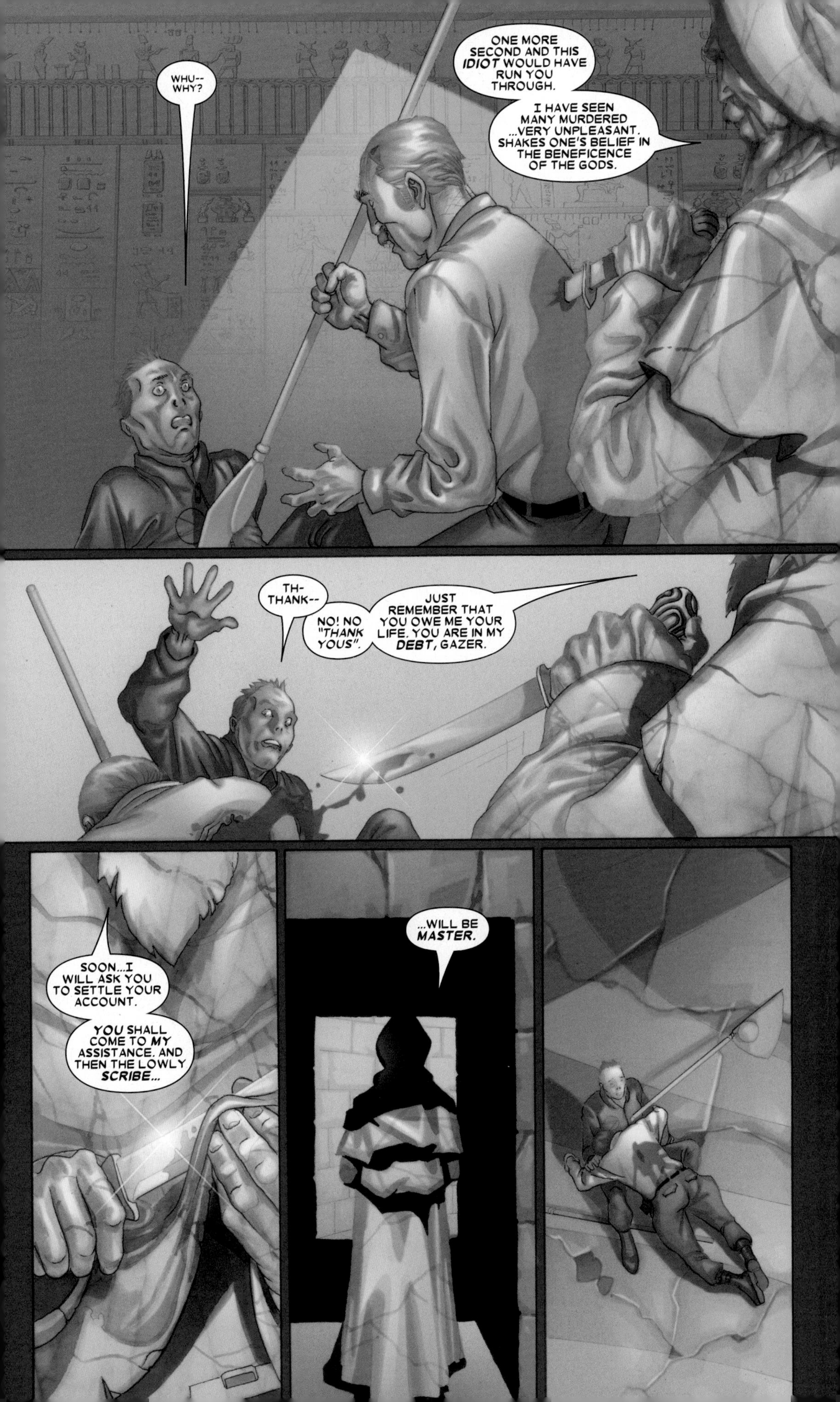
WHU-- WHY?
ONE MORE SECOND AND THIS IDIOT WOULD HAVE RUN YOU THROUGH.
I HAVE SEEN MANY MURDERED ...VERY UNPLEASANT. SHAKES ONE'S BELIEF IN THE BENEFICENCE OF THE GODS.
TH- THANK--
NO! NO "THANK YOUS".
JUST REMEMBER THAT YOU OWE ME YOUR LIFE. YOU ARE IN MY DEBT, GAZER.
SOON...I WILL ASK YOU TO SETTLE YOUR ACCOUNT.
YOU SHALL COME TO MY ASSISTANCE. AND THEN THE LOWLY SCRIBE...
...WILL BE MASTER.

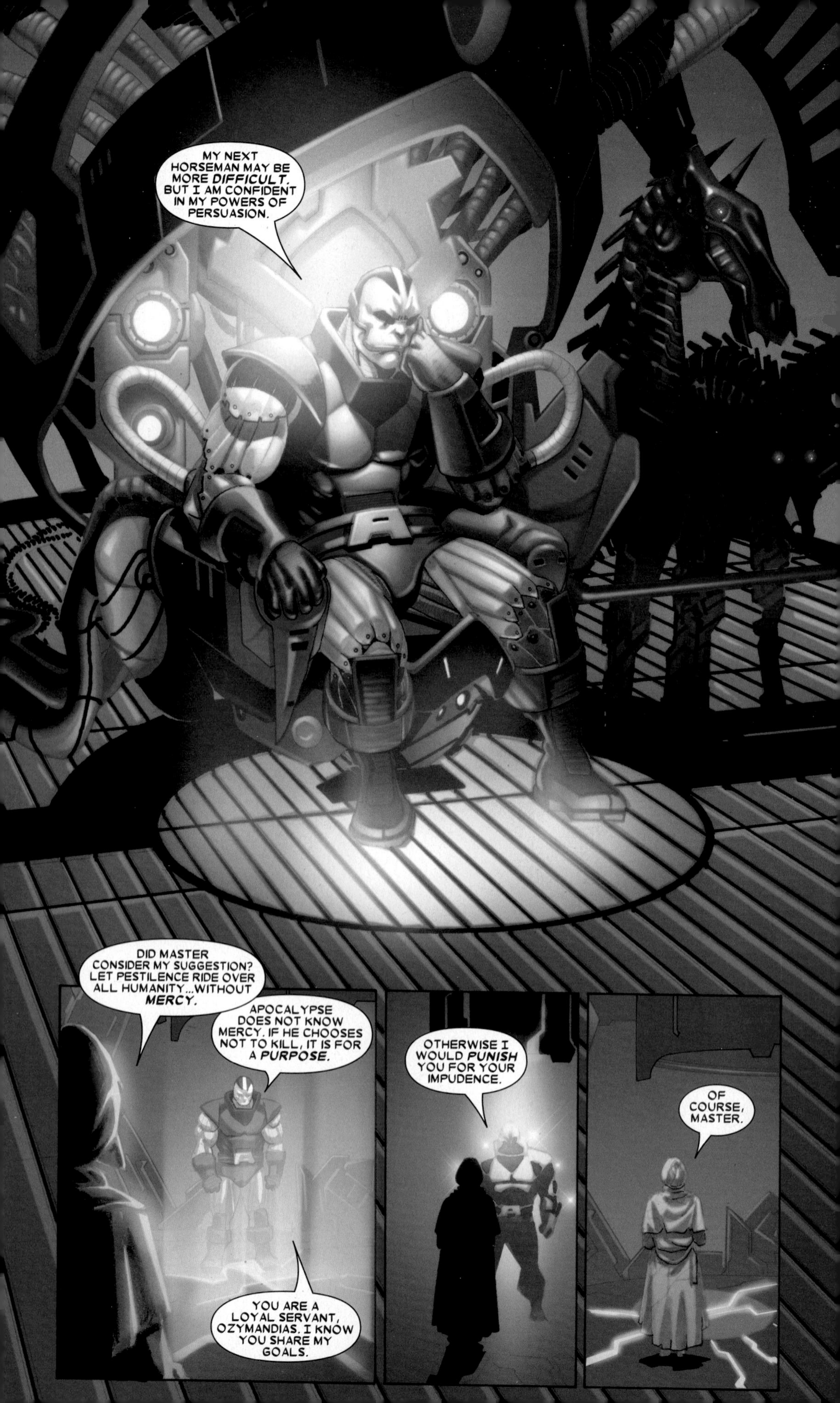
MY NEXT HORSEMAN MAY BE MORE DIFFICULT. BUT I AM CONFIDENT IN MY POWERS OF PERSUASION.
DID MASTER CONSIDER MY SUGGESTION? LET PESTILENCE RIDE OVER ALL HUMANITY...WITHOUT MERCY.
APOCALYPSE DOES NOT KNOW MERCY. IF HE CHOOSES NOT TO KILL, IT IS FOR A PURPOSE.
YOU ARE A LOYAL SERVANT, OZYMANDIAS. I KNOW YOU SHARE MY GOALS.
OTHERWISE I WOULD PUNISH YOU FOR YOUR IMPUDENCE.
OF COURSE, MASTER.

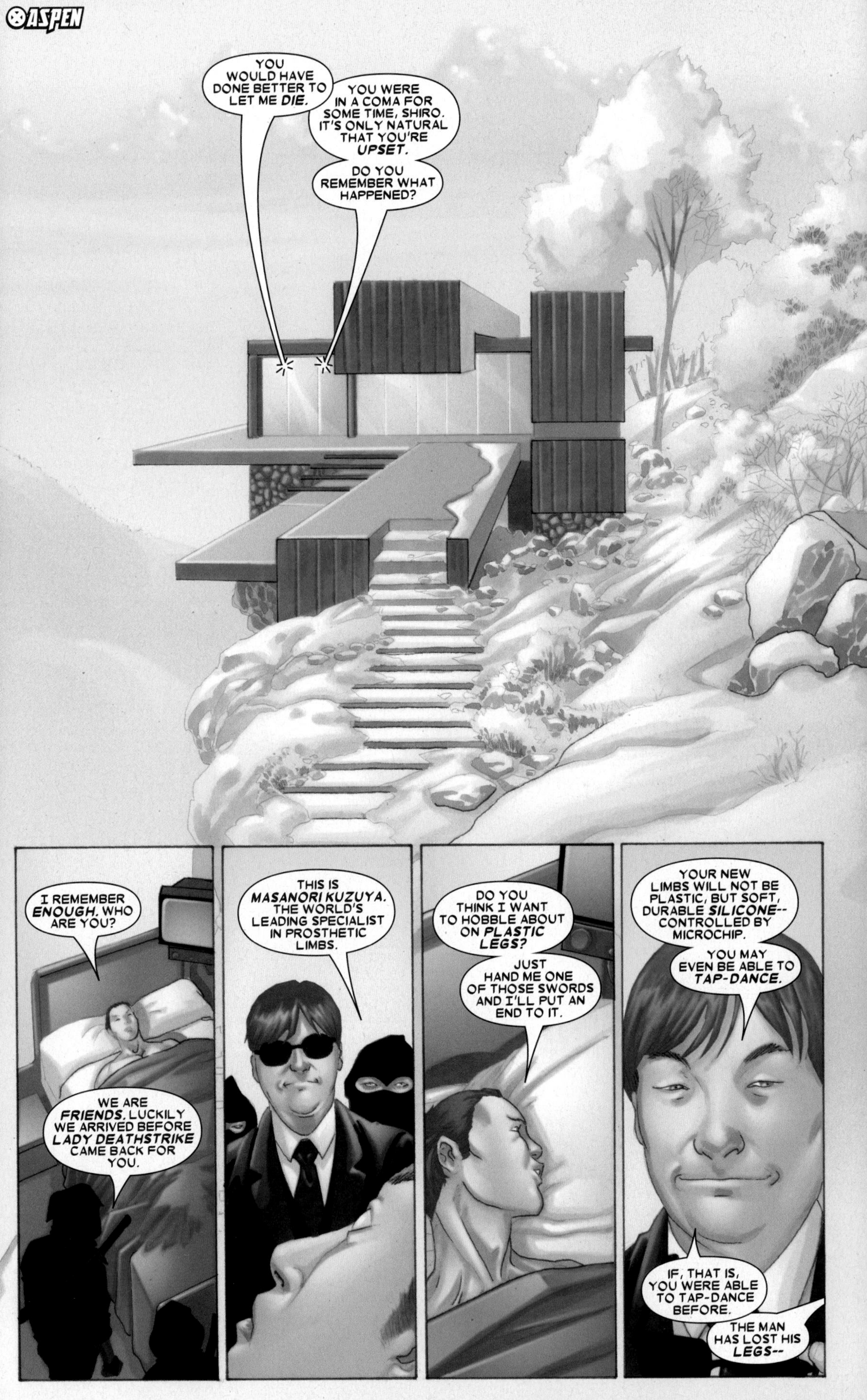
ASPEN
YOU WOULD HAVE DONE BETTER TO LET ME *DIE.*
YOU WERE IN A COMA FOR SOME TIME, SHIRO. IT'S ONLY NATURAL THAT YOU'RE *UPSET.*
DO YOU REMEMBER WHAT HAPPENED?
I REMEMBER *ENOUGH.* WHO ARE YOU?
WE ARE *FRIENDS.* LUCKILY WE ARRIVED BEFORE *LADY DEATHSTRIKE* CAME BACK FOR YOU.
THIS IS *MASANORI KUZUYA.* THE WORLD'S LEADING SPECIALIST IN PROSTHETIC LIMBS.
DO YOU THINK I WANT TO HOBBLE ABOUT ON *PLASTIC LEGS?*
JUST HAND ME ONE OF THOSE SWORDS AND I'LL PUT AN END TO IT.
YOUR NEW LIMBS WILL NOT BE PLASTIC, BUT SOFT, DURABLE *SILICONE*--CONTROLLED BY MICROCHIP.
YOU MAY EVEN BE ABLE TO *TAP-DANCE.*
IF, THAT IS, YOU WERE ABLE TO TAP-DANCE BEFORE.
THE MAN HAS LOST HIS *LEGS*--

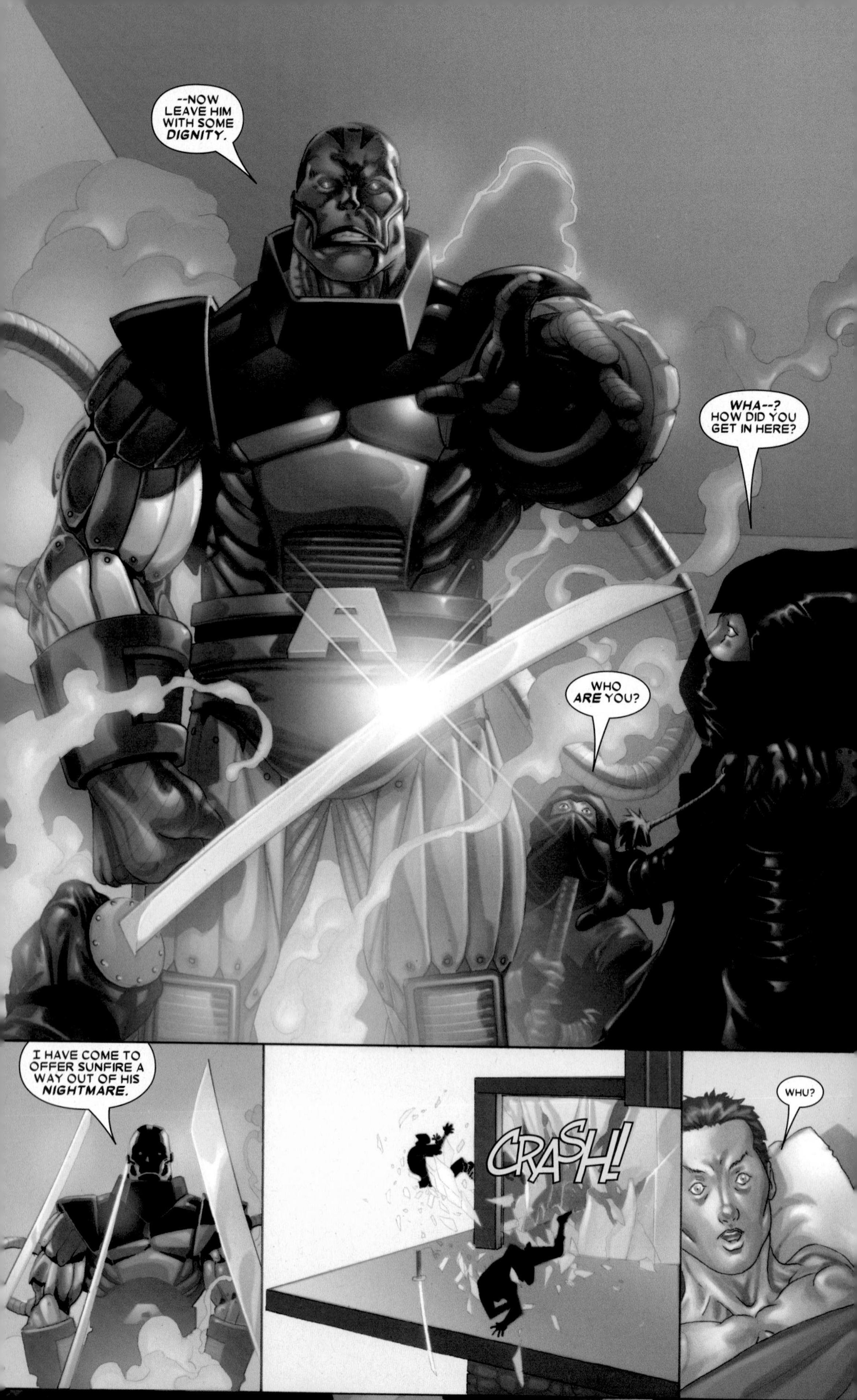

--NOW LEAVE HIM WITH SOME DIGNITY.
WHA--? HOW DID YOU GET IN HERE?
WHO ARE YOU?
I HAVE COME TO OFFER SUNFIRE A WAY OUT OF HIS NIGHTMARE.
CRASH!
WHU?

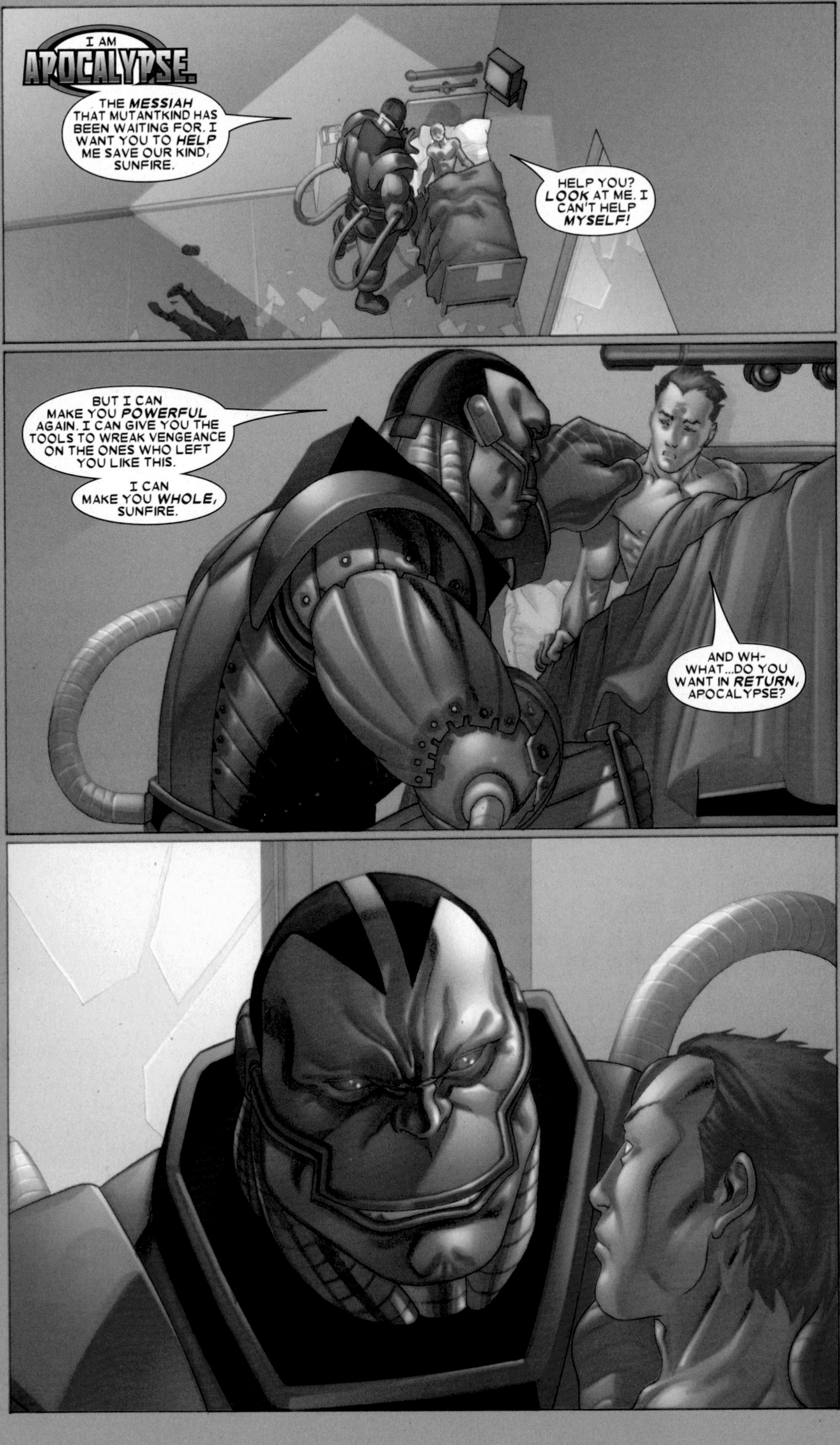
I AM APOCALYPSE.
THE MESSIAH THAT MUTANTKIND HAS BEEN WAITING FOR. I WANT YOU TO HELP ME SAVE OUR KIND, SUNFIRE.
HELP YOU? LOOK AT ME. I CAN'T HELP MYSELF!
BUT I CAN MAKE YOU POWERFUL AGAIN. I CAN GIVE YOU THE TOOLS TO WREAK VENGEANCE ON THE ONES WHO LEFT YOU LIKE THIS.
I CAN MAKE YOU WHOLE, SUNFIRE.
AND WH-WHAT...DO YOU WANT IN RETURN, APOCALYPSE?

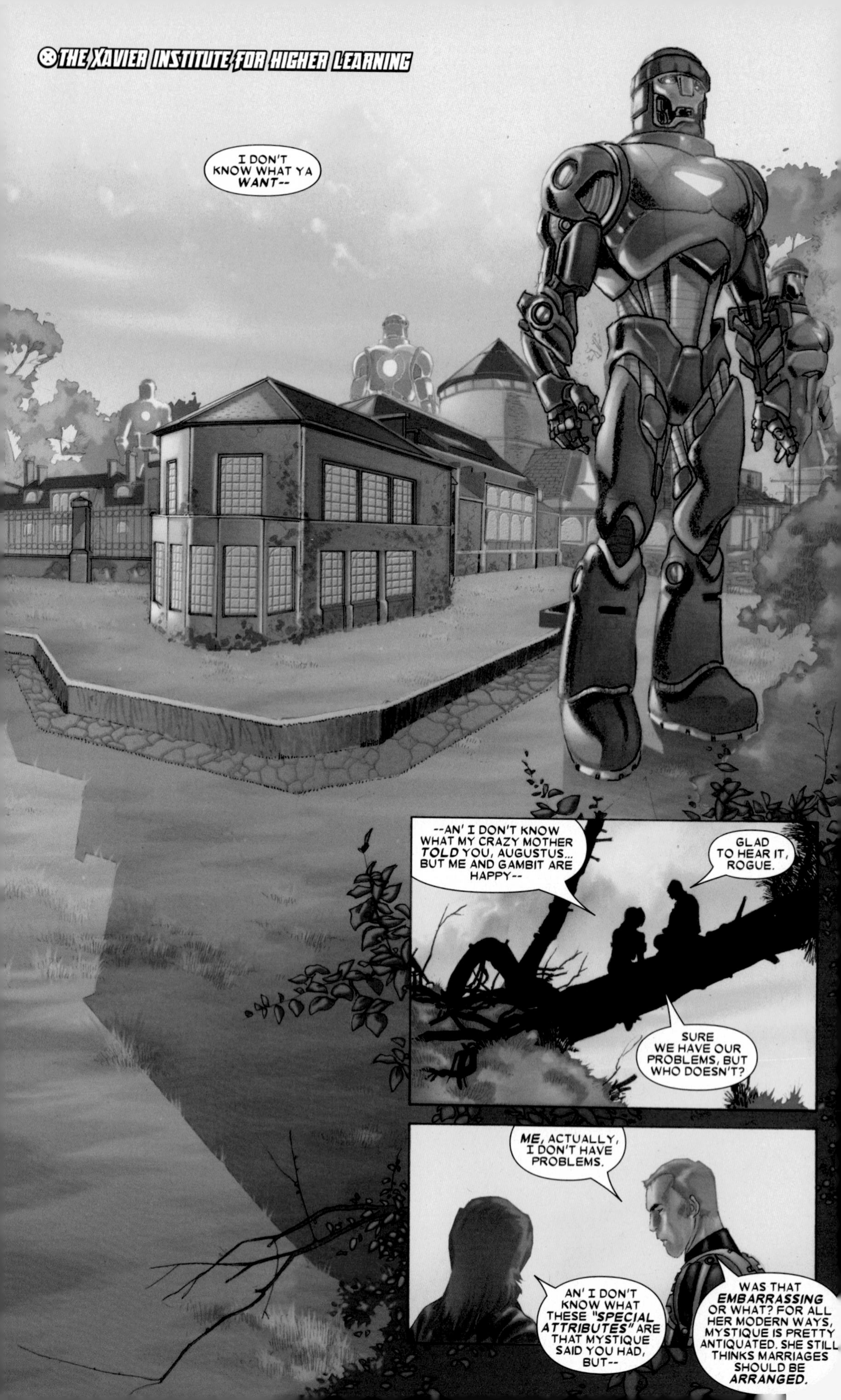

THE XAVIER INSTITUTE FOR HIGHER LEARNING
I DON'T KNOW WHAT YA WANT--
--AN' I DON'T KNOW WHAT MY CRAZY MOTHER TOLD YOU, AUGUSTUS... BUT ME AND GAMBIT ARE HAPPY--
GLAD TO HEAR IT, ROGUE.
SURE WE HAVE OUR PROBLEMS, BUT WHO DOESN'T?
ME, ACTUALLY, I DON'T HAVE PROBLEMS.
AN' I DON'T KNOW WHAT THESE "SPECIAL ATTRIBUTES" ARE THAT MYSTIQUE SAID YOU HAD, BUT--
WAS THAT EMBARRASSING OR WHAT? FOR ALL HER MODERN WAYS, MYSTIQUE IS PRETTY ANTIQUATED. SHE STILL THINKS MARRIAGES SHOULD BE ARRANGED.

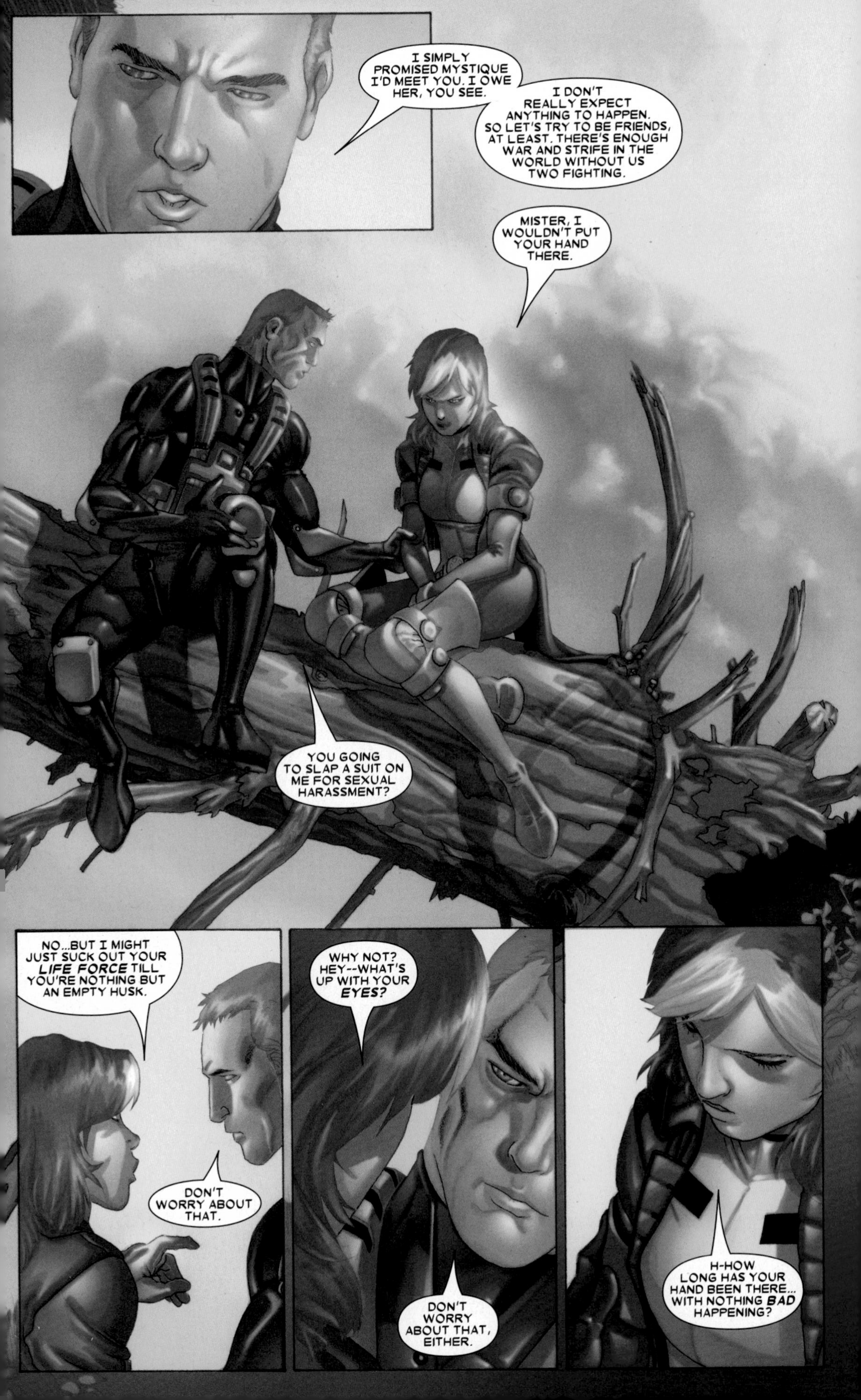
I SIMPLY PROMISED MYSTIQUE I'D MEET YOU. I OWE HER, YOU SEE.
I DON'T REALLY EXPECT ANYTHING TO HAPPEN. SO LET'S TRY TO BE FRIENDS, AT LEAST. THERE'S ENOUGH WAR AND STRIFE IN THE WORLD WITHOUT US TWO FIGHTING.
MISTER, I WOULDN'T PUT YOUR HAND THERE.
YOU GOING TO SLAP A SUIT ON ME FOR SEXUAL HARASSMENT?
NO...BUT I MIGHT JUST SUCK OUT YOUR *LIFE FORCE* TILL YOU'RE NOTHING BUT AN EMPTY HUSK.
DON'T WORRY ABOUT THAT.
WHY NOT? HEY--WHAT'S UP WITH YOUR *EYES?*
DON'T WORRY ABOUT THAT, EITHER.
H-HOW LONG HAS YOUR HAND BEEN THERE... WITH NOTHING *BAD* HAPPENING?

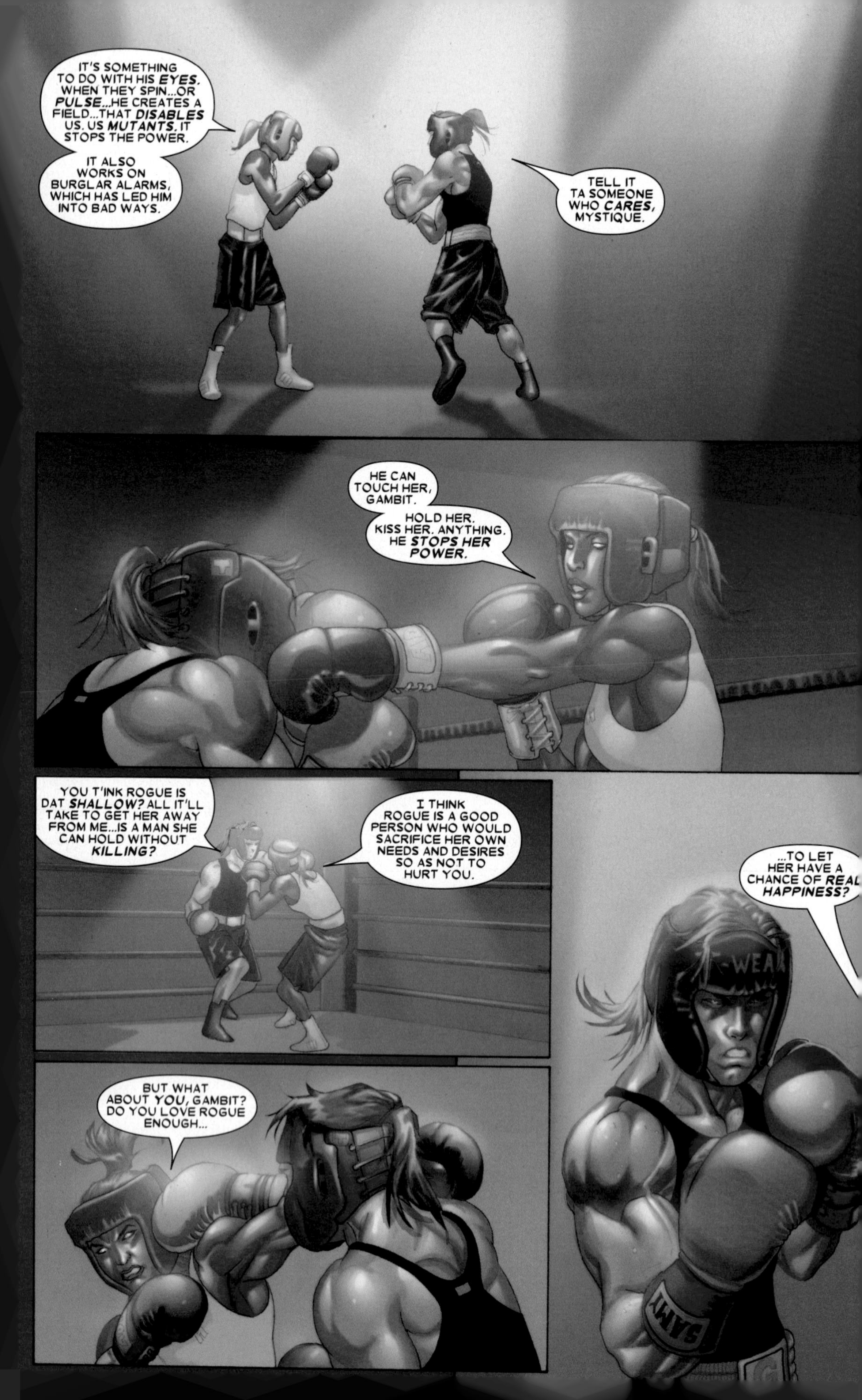

IT'S SOMETHING TO DO WITH HIS EYES. WHEN THEY SPIN...OR PULSE...HE CREATES A FIELD...THAT DISABLES US. US MUTANTS. IT STOPS THE POWER.
IT ALSO WORKS ON BURGLAR ALARMS, WHICH HAS LED HIM INTO BAD WAYS.
TELL IT TA SOMEONE WHO CARES, MYSTIQUE.
HE CAN TOUCH HER, GAMBIT.
HOLD HER. KISS HER. ANYTHING. HE STOPS HER POWER.
YOU T'INK ROGUE IS DAT SHALLOW? ALL IT'LL TAKE TO GET HER AWAY FROM ME...IS A MAN SHE CAN HOLD WITHOUT KILLING?
I THINK ROGUE IS A GOOD PERSON WHO WOULD SACRIFICE HER OWN NEEDS AND DESIRES SO AS NOT TO HURT YOU.
BUT WHAT ABOUT YOU, GAMBIT? DO YOU LOVE ROGUE ENOUGH...
...TO LET HER HAVE A CHANCE OF REAL HAPPINESS?

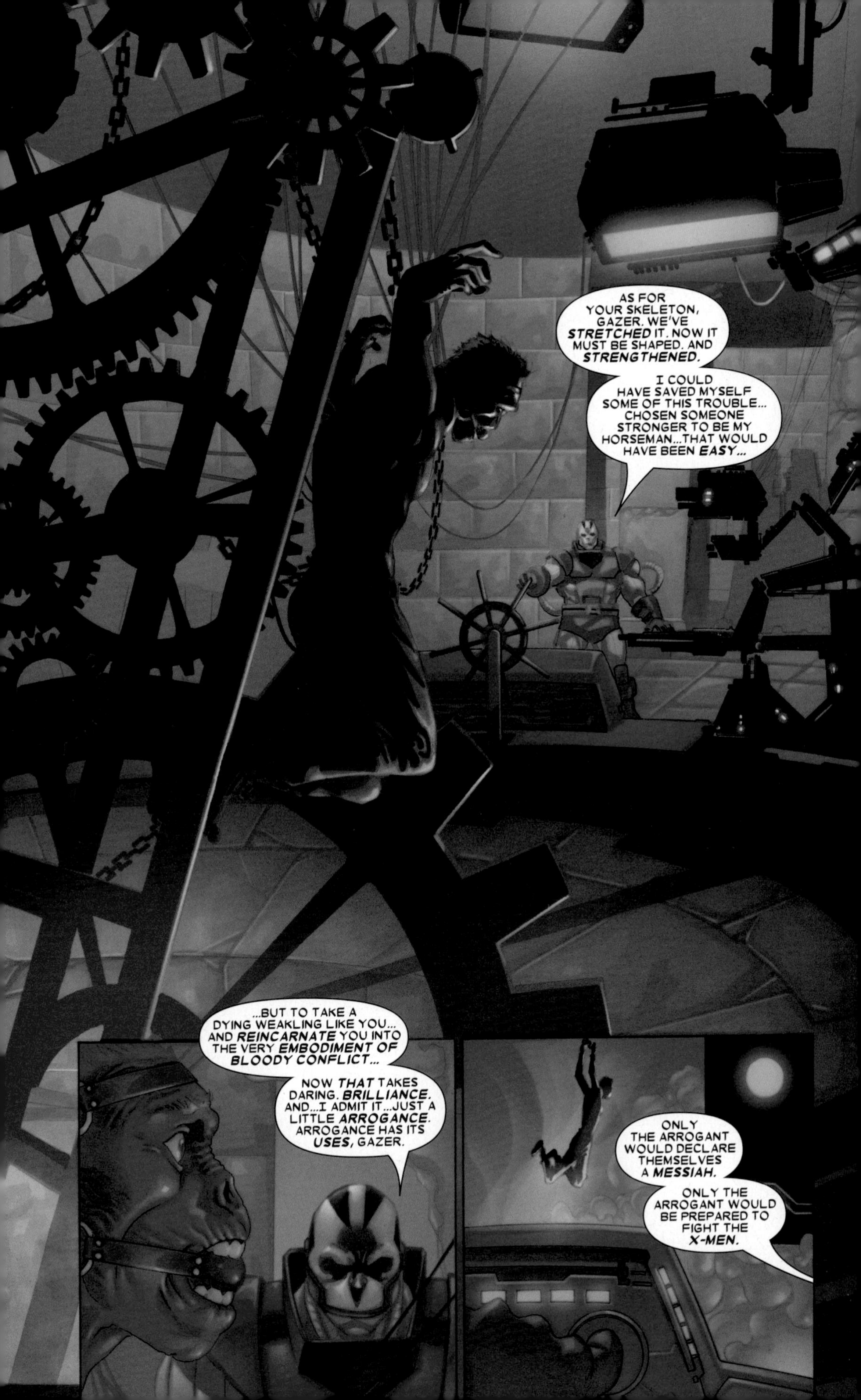
AS FOR YOUR SKELETON, GAZER. WE'VE STRETCHED IT. NOW IT MUST BE SHAPED. AND STRENGTHENED.
I COULD HAVE SAVED MYSELF SOME OF THIS TROUBLE... CHOSEN SOMEONE STRONGER TO BE MY HORSEMAN...THAT WOULD HAVE BEEN EASY...
...BUT TO TAKE A DYING WEAKLING LIKE YOU... AND REINCARNATE YOU INTO THE VERY EMBODIMENT OF BLOODY CONFLICT...
NOW THAT TAKES DARING. BRILLIANCE. AND...I ADMIT IT...JUST A LITTLE ARROGANCE. ARROGANCE HAS ITS USES, GAZER.
ONLY THE ARROGANT WOULD DECLARE THEMSELVES A MESSIAH.
ONLY THE ARROGANT WOULD BE PREPARED TO FIGHT THE X-MEN.

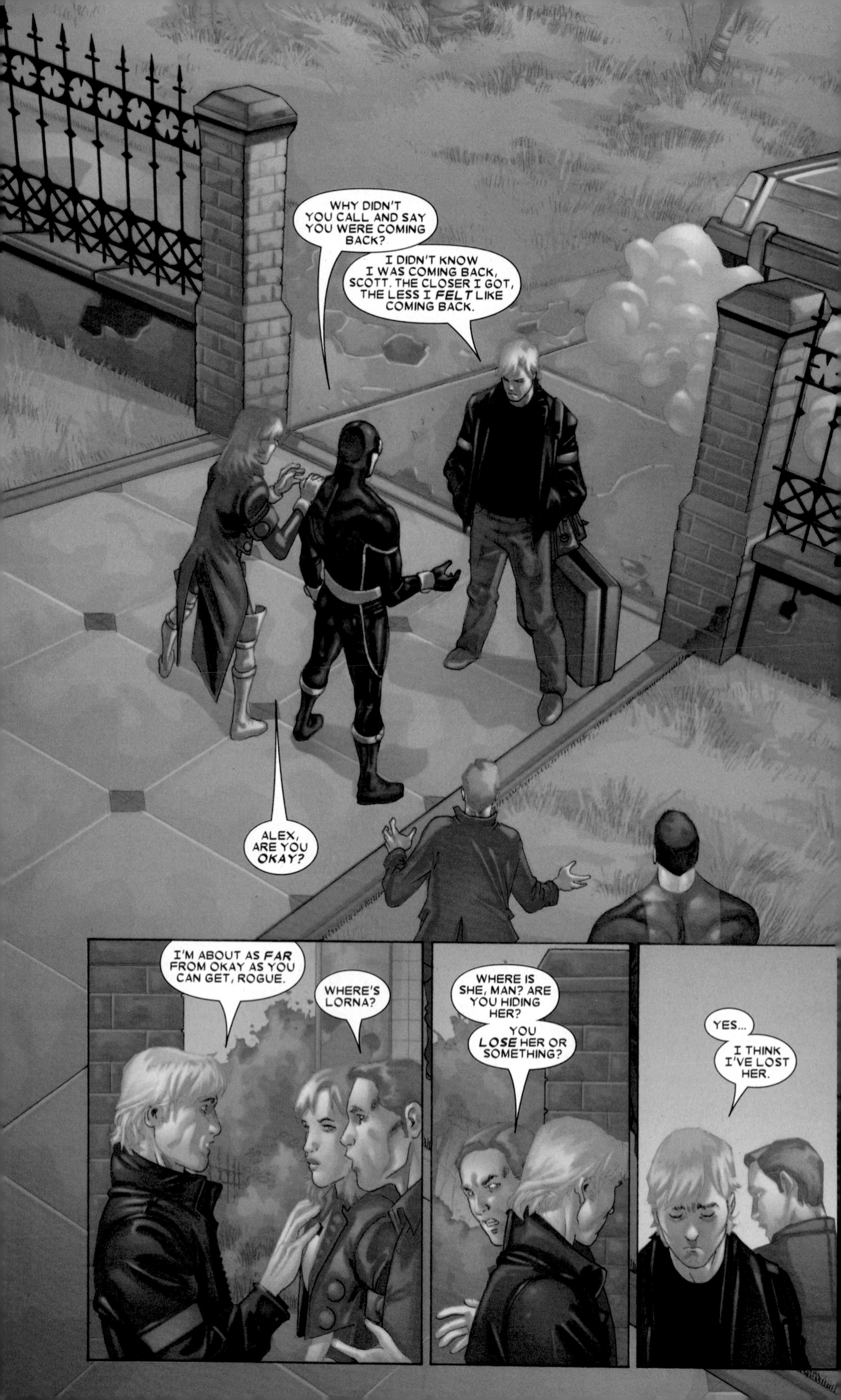
WHY DIDN'T YOU CALL AND SAY YOU WERE COMING BACK?
I DIDN'T KNOW I WAS COMING BACK, SCOTT. THE CLOSER I GOT, THE LESS I FELT LIKE COMING BACK.
ALEX, ARE YOU OKAY?
I'M ABOUT AS FAR FROM OKAY AS YOU CAN GET, ROGUE.
WHERE'S LORNA?
WHERE IS SHE, MAN? ARE YOU HIDING HER?
YOU LOSE HER OR SOMETHING?
YES...
I THINK I'VE LOST HER.

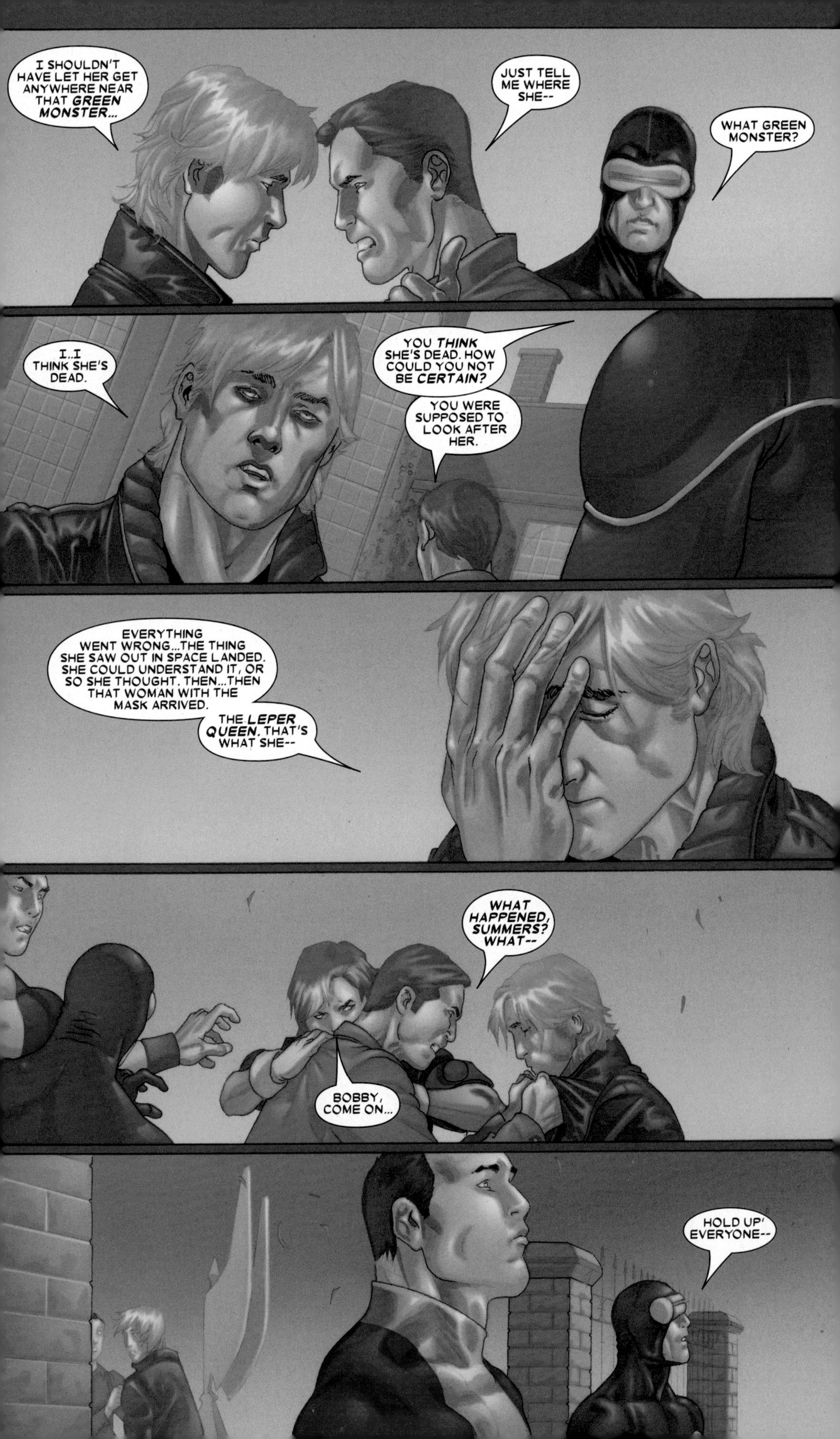

I SHOULDN'T HAVE LET HER GET ANYWHERE NEAR THAT GREEN MONSTER...
JUST TELL ME WHERE SHE--
WHAT GREEN MONSTER?
I..I THINK SHE'S DEAD.
YOU THINK SHE'S DEAD. HOW COULD YOU NOT BE CERTAIN?
YOU WERE SUPPOSED TO LOOK AFTER HER.
EVERYTHING WENT WRONG...THE THING SHE SAW OUT IN SPACE LANDED. SHE COULD UNDERSTAND IT, OR SO SHE THOUGHT. THEN...THEN THAT WOMAN WITH THE MASK ARRIVED.
THE LEPER QUEEN. THAT'S WHAT SHE--
WHAT HAPPENED, SUMMERS? WHAT--
BOBBY, COME ON...
HOLD UP' EVERYONE--

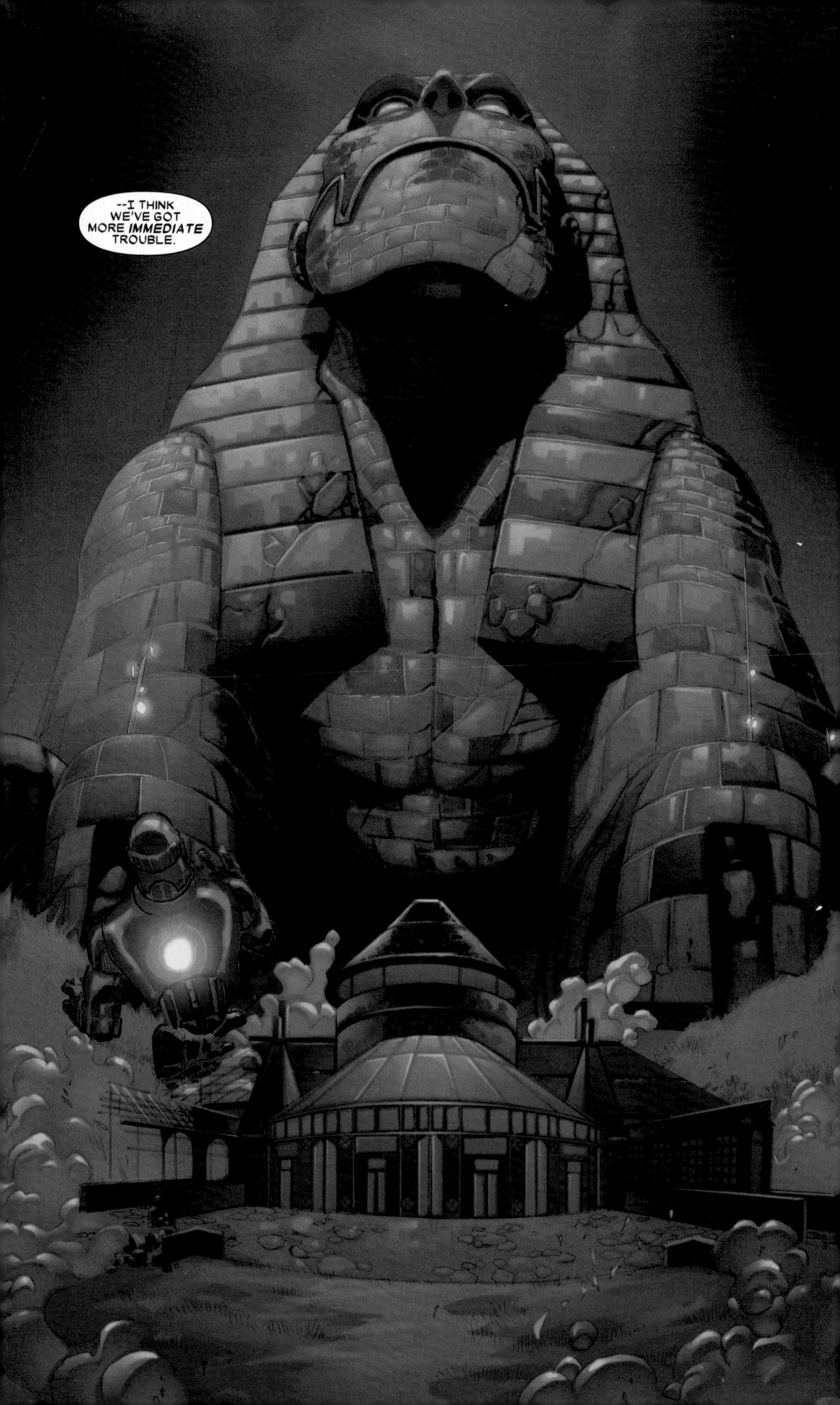
--I THINK WE'VE GOT MORE *IMMEDIATE* TROUBLE.

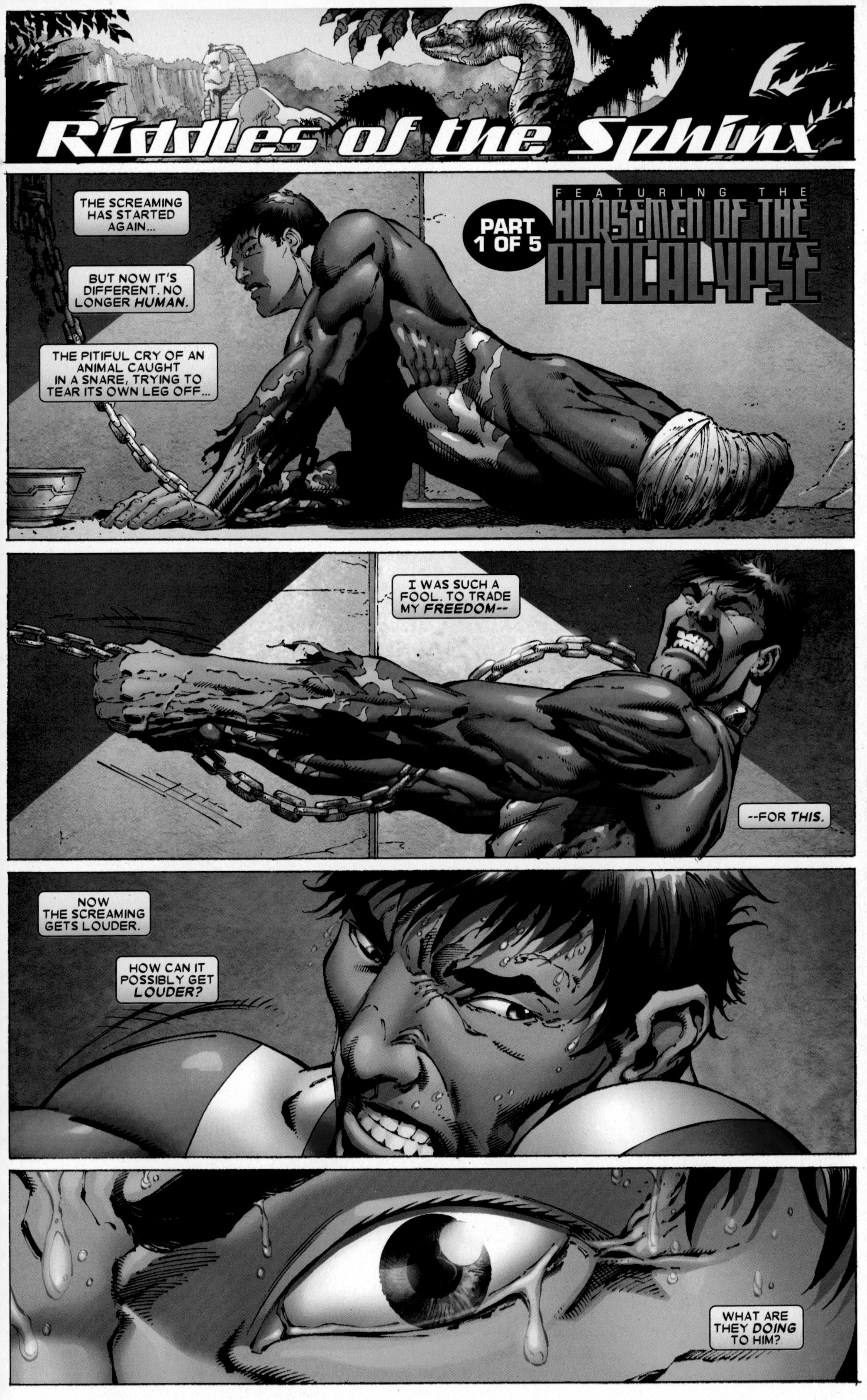
Riddles of the Sphinx
THE SCREAMING HAS STARTED AGAIN...
FEATURING THE
PART 1 OF 5
HORSEMEN OF THE APOCALYPSE
BUT NOW IT'S DIFFERENT. NO LONGER HUMAN.
THE PITIFUL CRY OF AN ANIMAL CAUGHT IN A SNARE, TRYING TO TEAR ITS OWN LEG OFF...
I WAS SUCH A FOOL. TO TRADE MY FREEDOM--
--FOR THIS.
NOW THE SCREAMING GETS LOUDER.
HOW CAN IT POSSIBLY GET LOUDER?
WHAT ARE THEY DOING TO HIM?

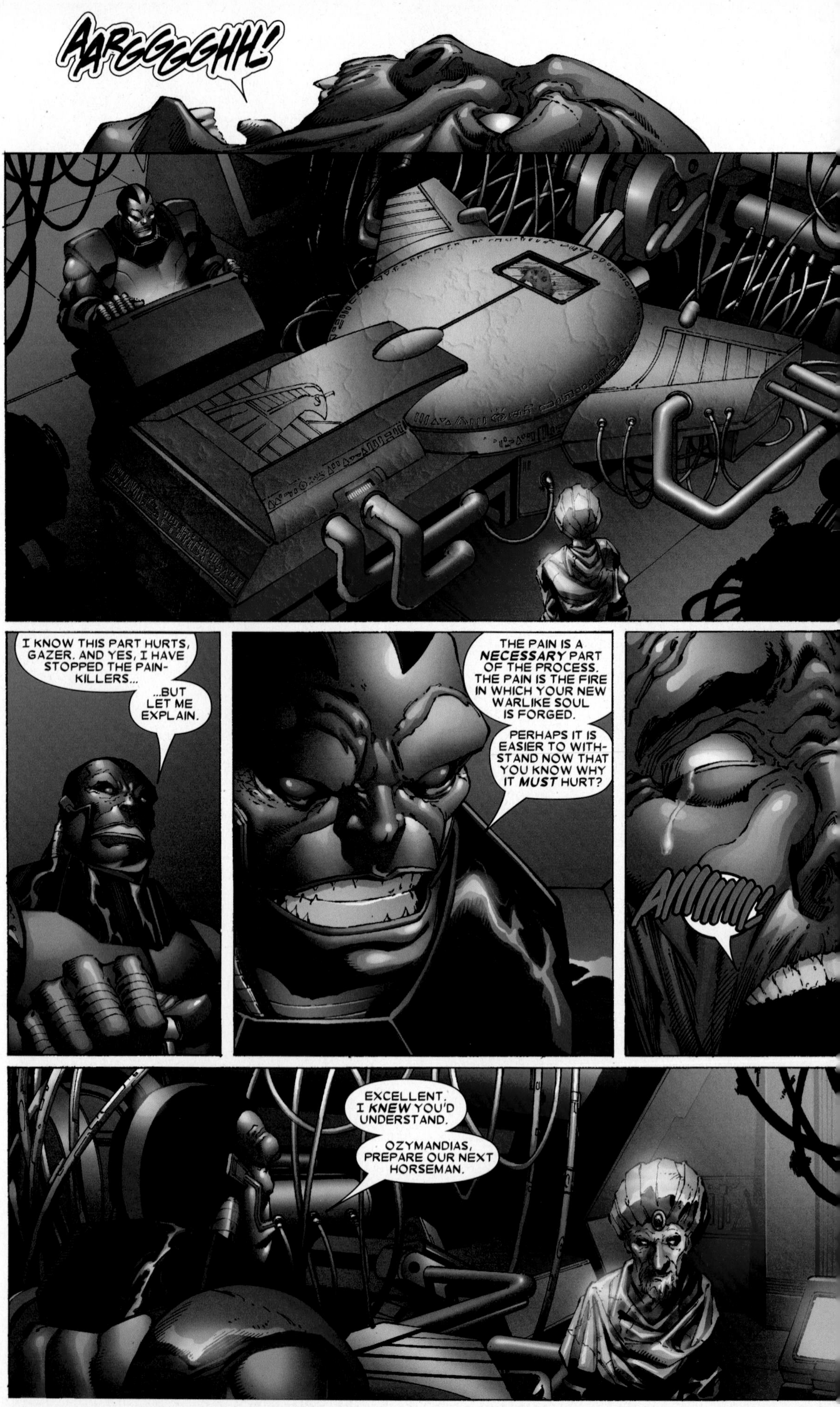
AARGGGGHH!
I KNOW THIS PART HURTS, GAZER. AND YES, I HAVE STOPPED THE PAIN-KILLERS...
...BUT LET ME EXPLAIN.
THE PAIN IS A NECESSARY PART OF THE PROCESS. THE PAIN IS THE FIRE IN WHICH YOUR NEW WARLIKE SOUL IS FORGED.
PERHAPS IT IS EASIER TO WITH-STAND NOW THAT YOU KNOW WHY IT MUST HURT?
EXCELLENT. I KNEW YOU'D UNDERSTAND.
OZYMANDIAS, PREPARE OUR NEXT HORSEMAN.

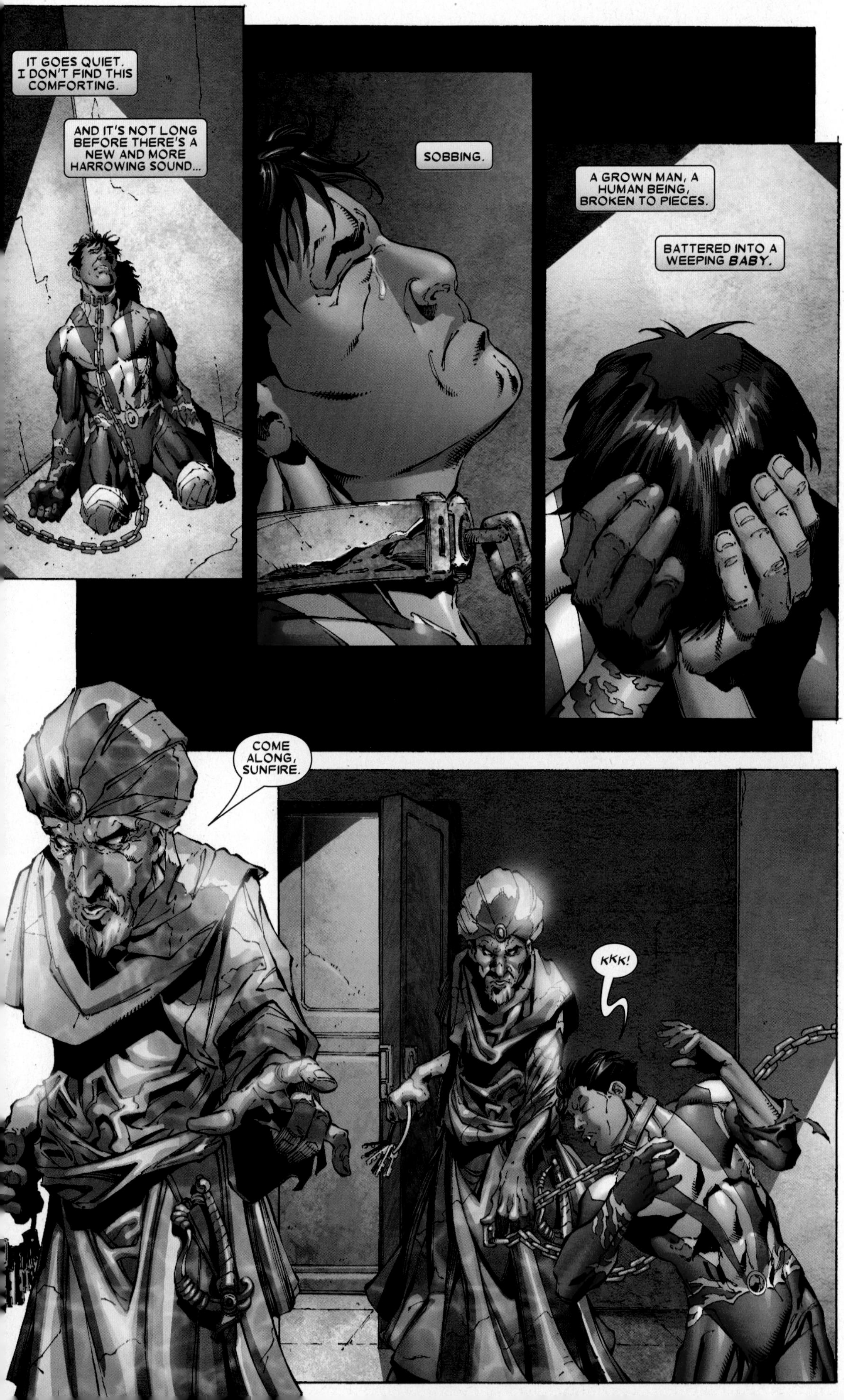
IT GOES QUIET. I DON'T FIND THIS COMFORTING.
AND IT'S NOT LONG BEFORE THERE'S A NEW AND MORE HARROWING SOUND...
SOBBING.
A GROWN MAN, A HUMAN BEING, BROKEN TO PIECES.
BATTERED INTO A WEEPING BABY.
COME ALONG, SUNFIRE.
KKK!

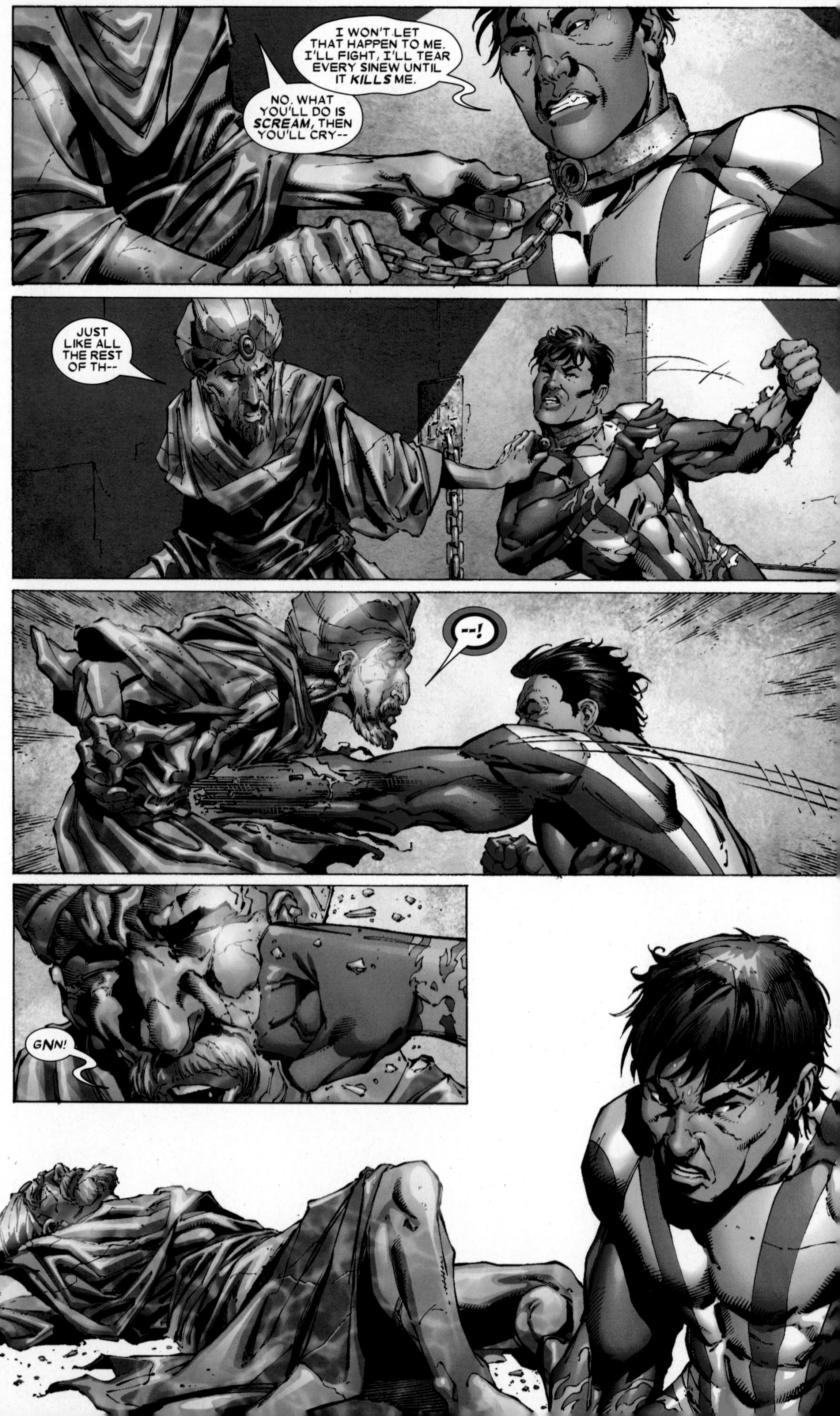
I WON'T LET THAT HAPPEN TO ME. I'LL FIGHT, I'LL TEAR EVERY SINEW UNTIL IT KILLS ME.
NO. WHAT YOU'LL DO IS SCREAM, THEN YOU'LL CRY--
JUST LIKE ALL THE REST OF TH--
--!
GNN!

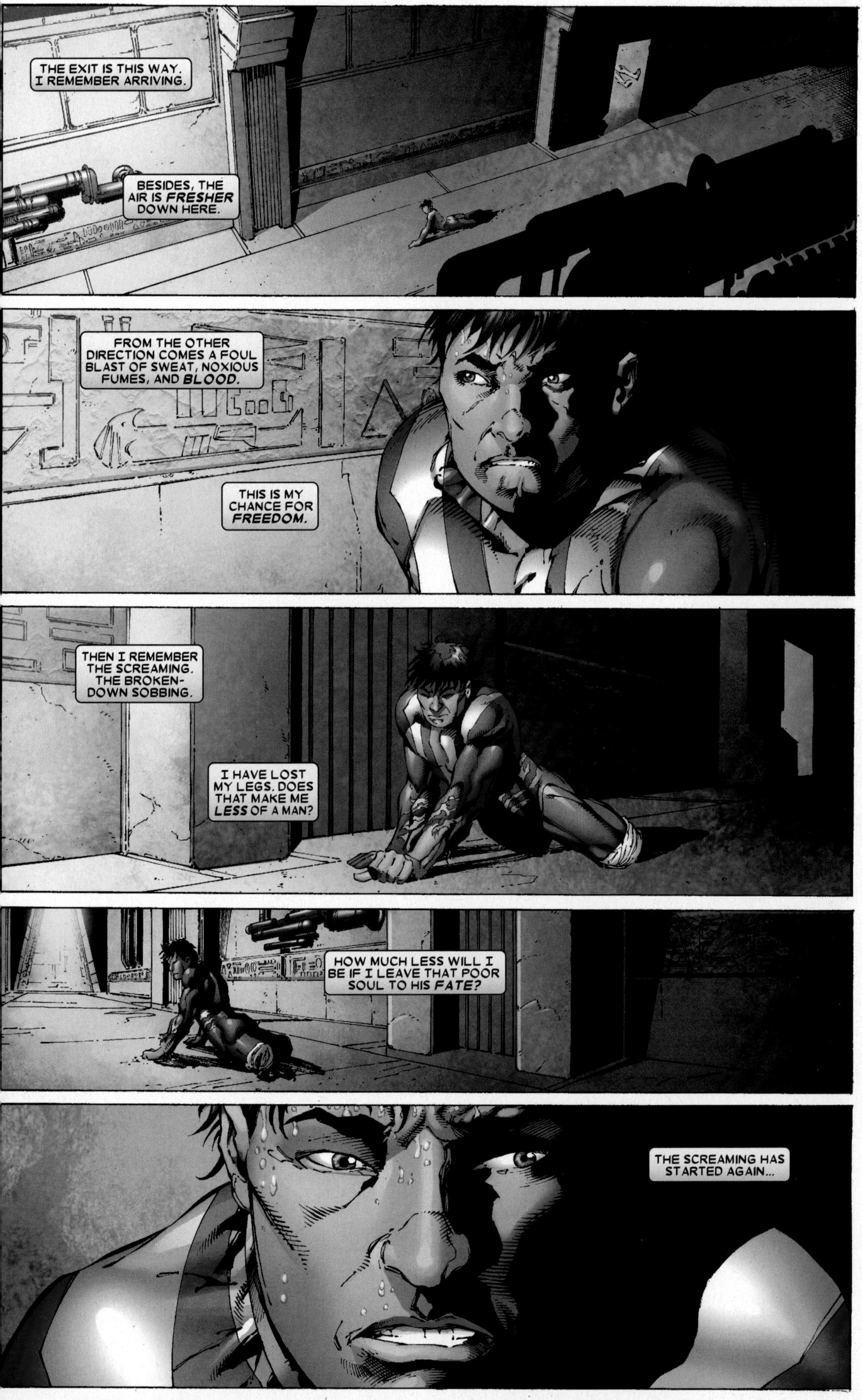
THE EXIT IS THIS WAY. I REMEMBER ARRIVING.
BESIDES, THE AIR IS FRESHER DOWN HERE.
FROM THE OTHER DIRECTION COMES A FOUL BLAST OF SWEAT, NOXIOUS FUMES, AND BLOOD.
THIS IS MY CHANCE FOR FREEDOM.
THEN I REMEMBER THE SCREAMING. THE BROKEN-DOWN SOBBING.
I HAVE LOST MY LEGS. DOES THAT MAKE ME LESS OF A MAN?
HOW MUCH LESS WILL I BE IF I LEAVE THAT POOR SOUL TO HIS FATE?
THE SCREAMING HAS STARTED AGAIN...

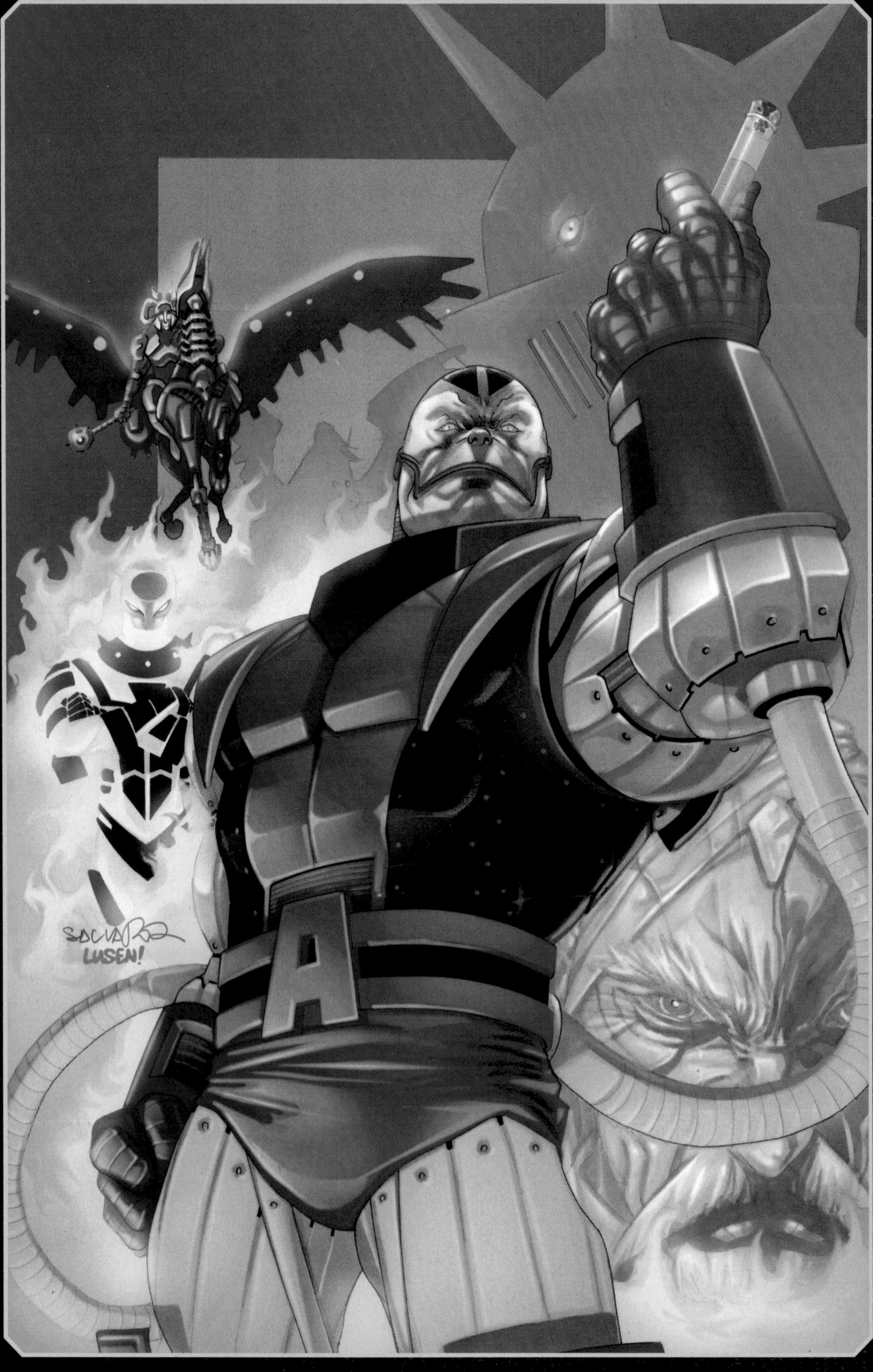

X-MEN #183

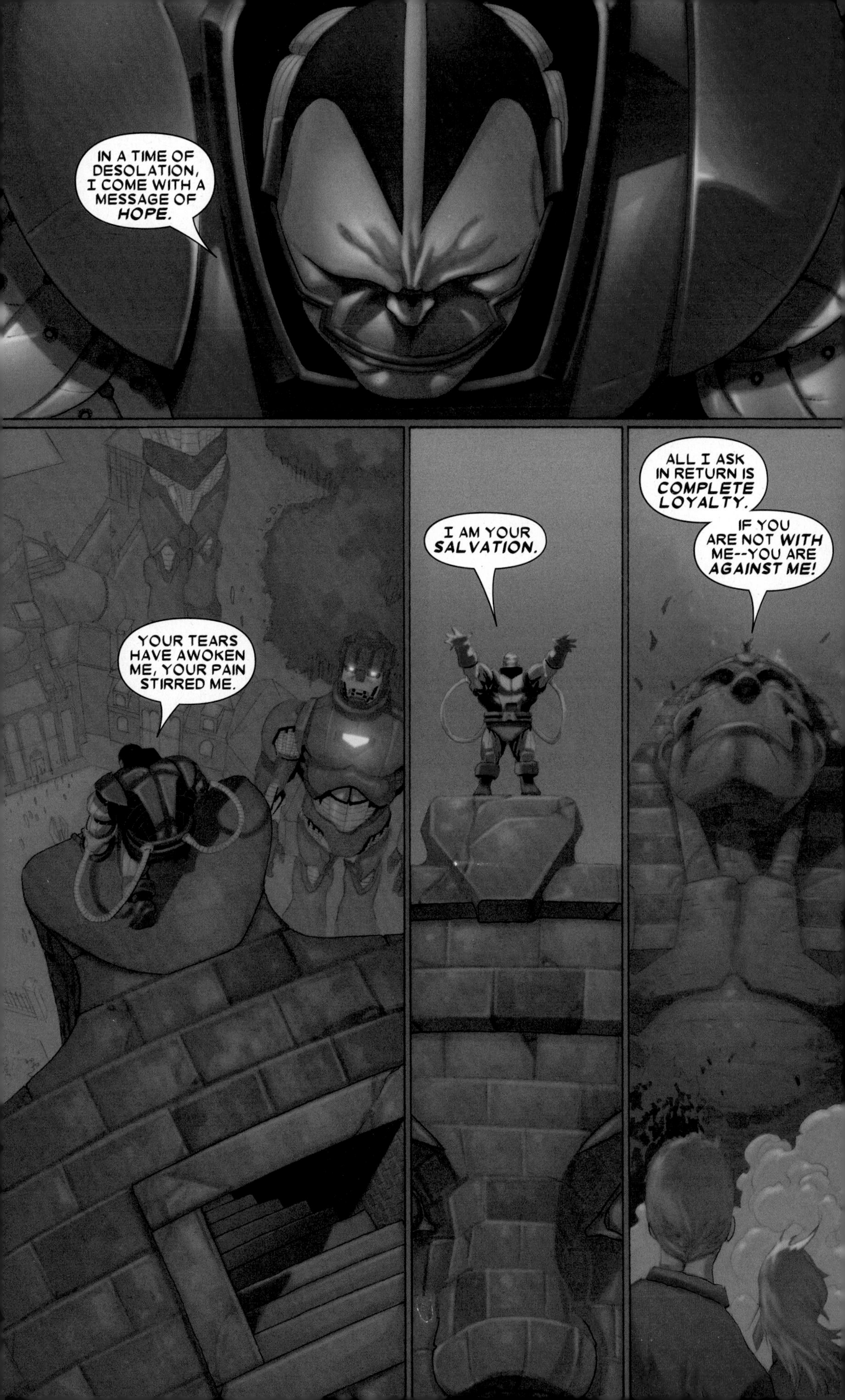
IN A TIME OF DESOLATION, I COME WITH A MESSAGE OF *HOPE.*
YOUR TEARS HAVE AWOKEN ME, YOUR PAIN STIRRED ME.
I AM YOUR *SALVATION.*
ALL I ASK IN RETURN IS *COMPLETE LOYALTY.*
IF YOU ARE NOT *WITH* ME--YOU ARE *AGAINST ME!*

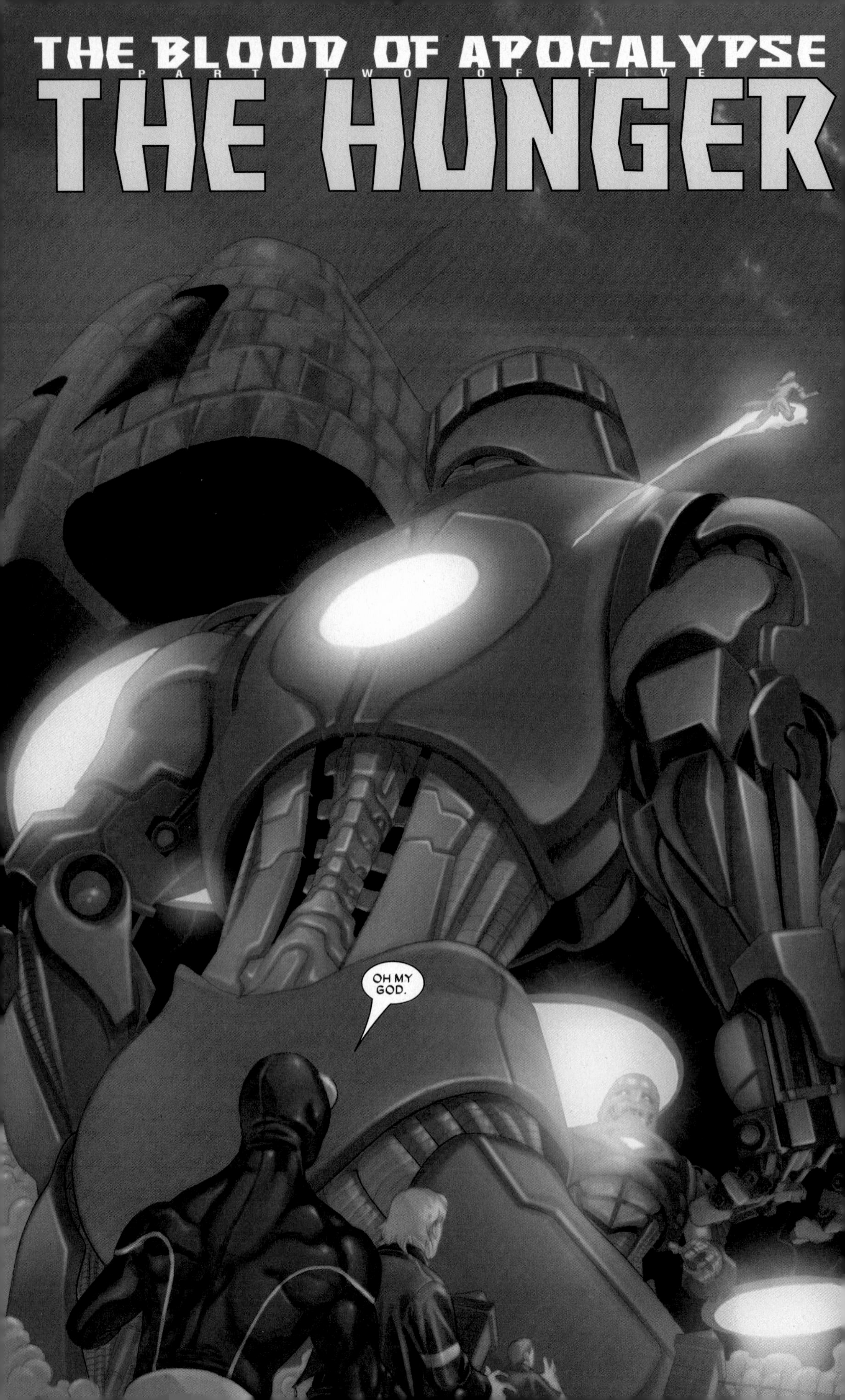
THE BLOOD OF APOCALYPSE
PART TWO OF FIVE
THE HUNGER
OH MY GOD.

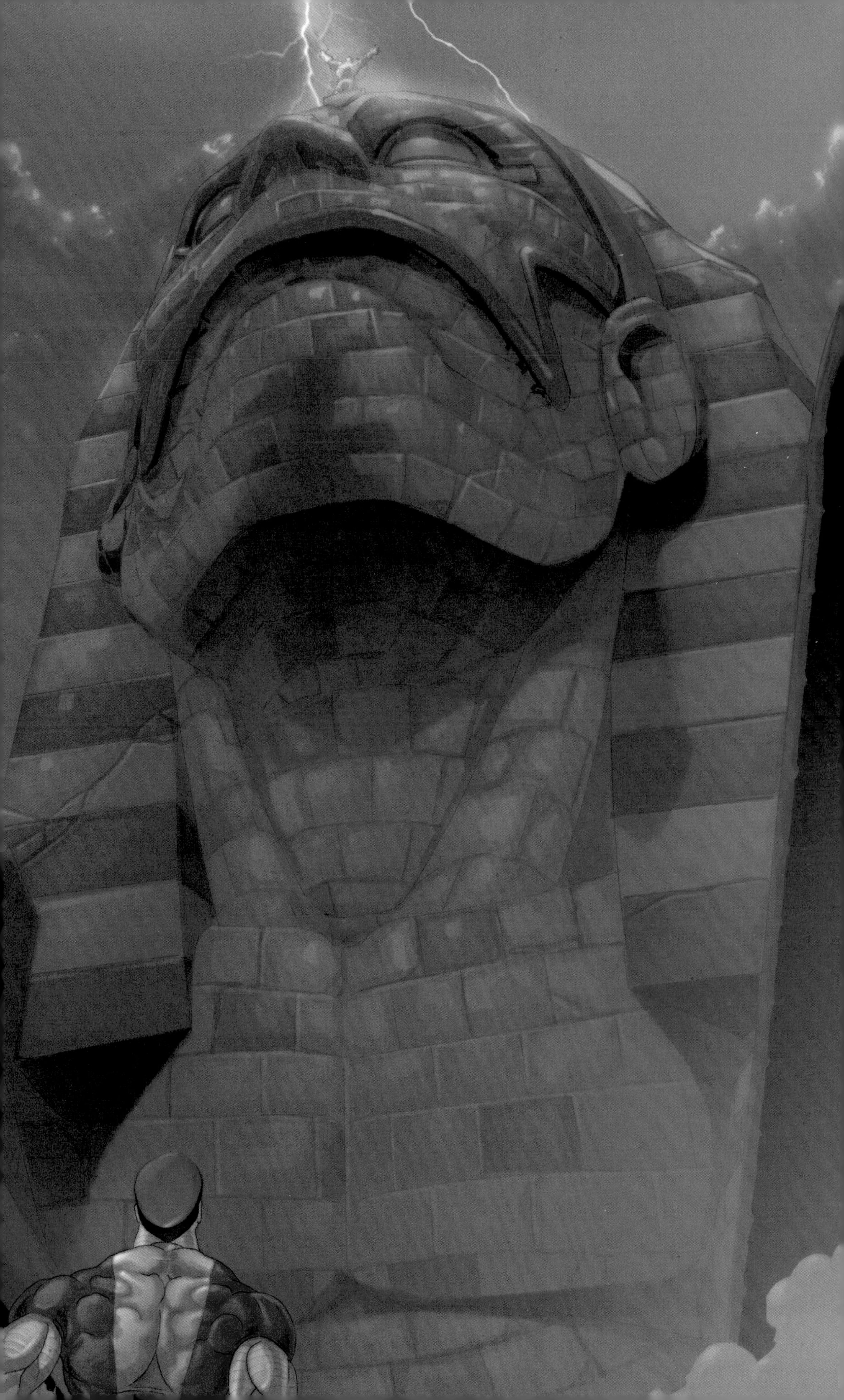

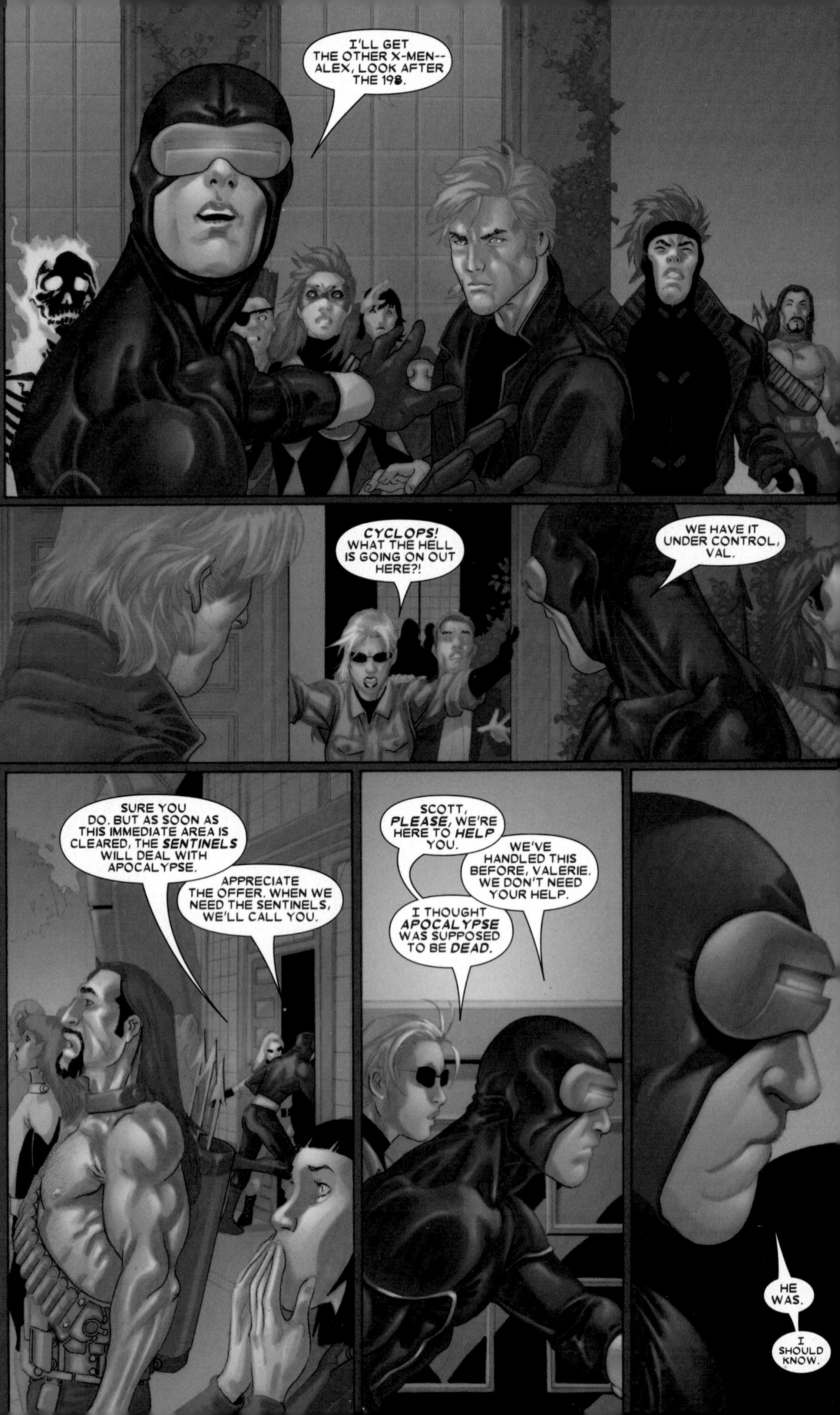
I'LL GET THE OTHER X-MEN-- ALEX, LOOK AFTER THE 198.
CYCLOPS! WHAT THE HELL IS GOING ON OUT HERE?!
WE HAVE IT UNDER CONTROL, VAL.
SURE YOU DO. BUT AS SOON AS THIS IMMEDIATE AREA IS CLEARED, THE SENTINELS WILL DEAL WITH APOCALYPSE.
APPRECIATE THE OFFER. WHEN WE NEED THE SENTINELS, WE'LL CALL YOU.
SCOTT, PLEASE, WE'RE HERE TO HELP YOU.
WE'VE HANDLED THIS BEFORE, VALERIE. WE DON'T NEED YOUR HELP.
I THOUGHT APOCALYPSE WAS SUPPOSED TO BE DEAD.
HE WAS.
I SHOULD KNOW.

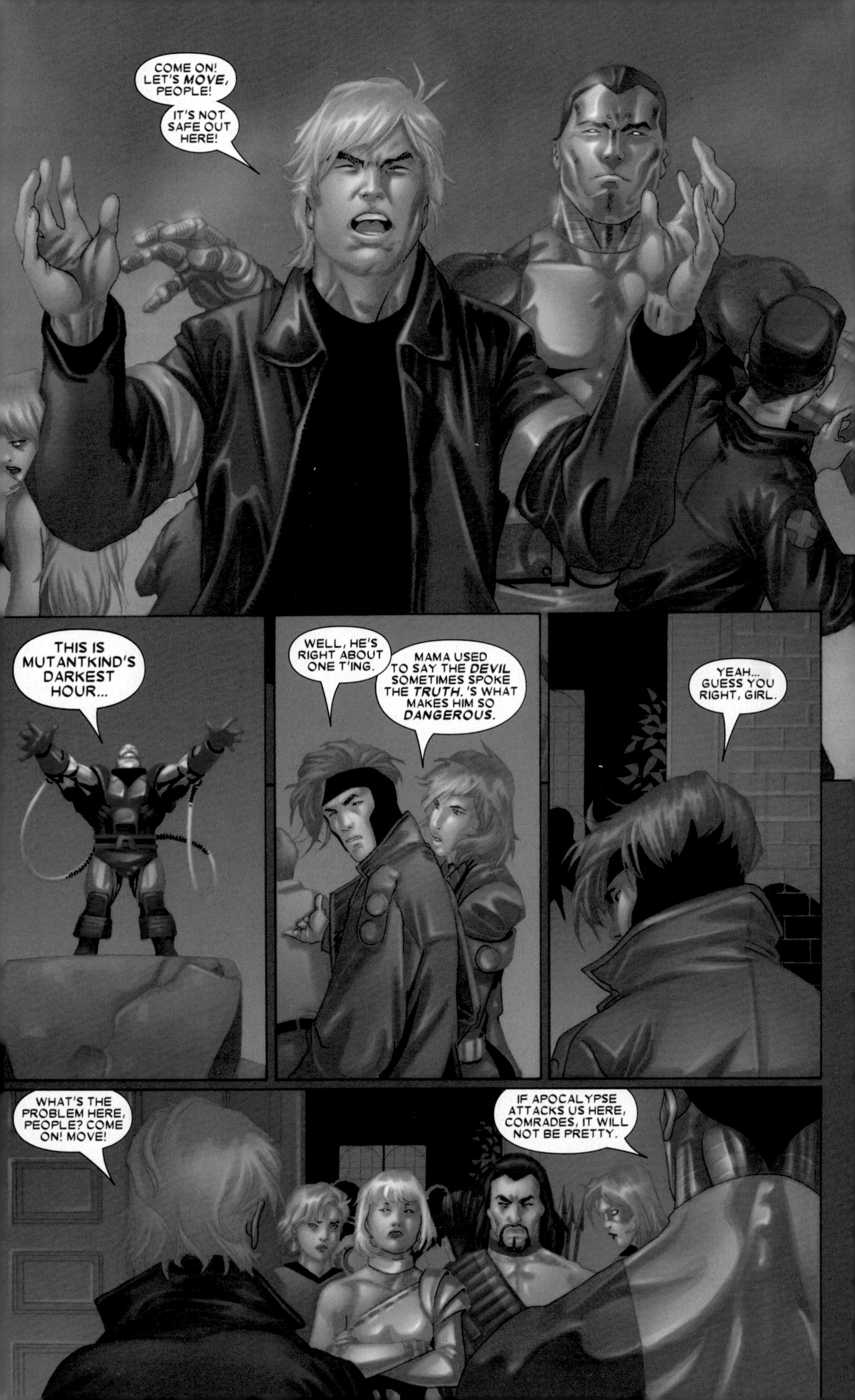
COME ON! LET'S MOVE, PEOPLE!
IT'S NOT SAFE OUT HERE!
THIS IS MUTANTKIND'S DARKEST HOUR...
WELL, HE'S RIGHT ABOUT ONE T'ING.
MAMA USED TO SAY THE DEVIL SOMETIMES SPOKE THE TRUTH. 'S WHAT MAKES HIM SO DANGEROUS.
YEAH... GUESS YOU RIGHT, GIRL.
WHAT'S THE PROBLEM HERE, PEOPLE? COME ON! MOVE!
IF APOCALYPSE ATTACKS US HERE, COMRADES, IT WILL NOT BE PRETTY.

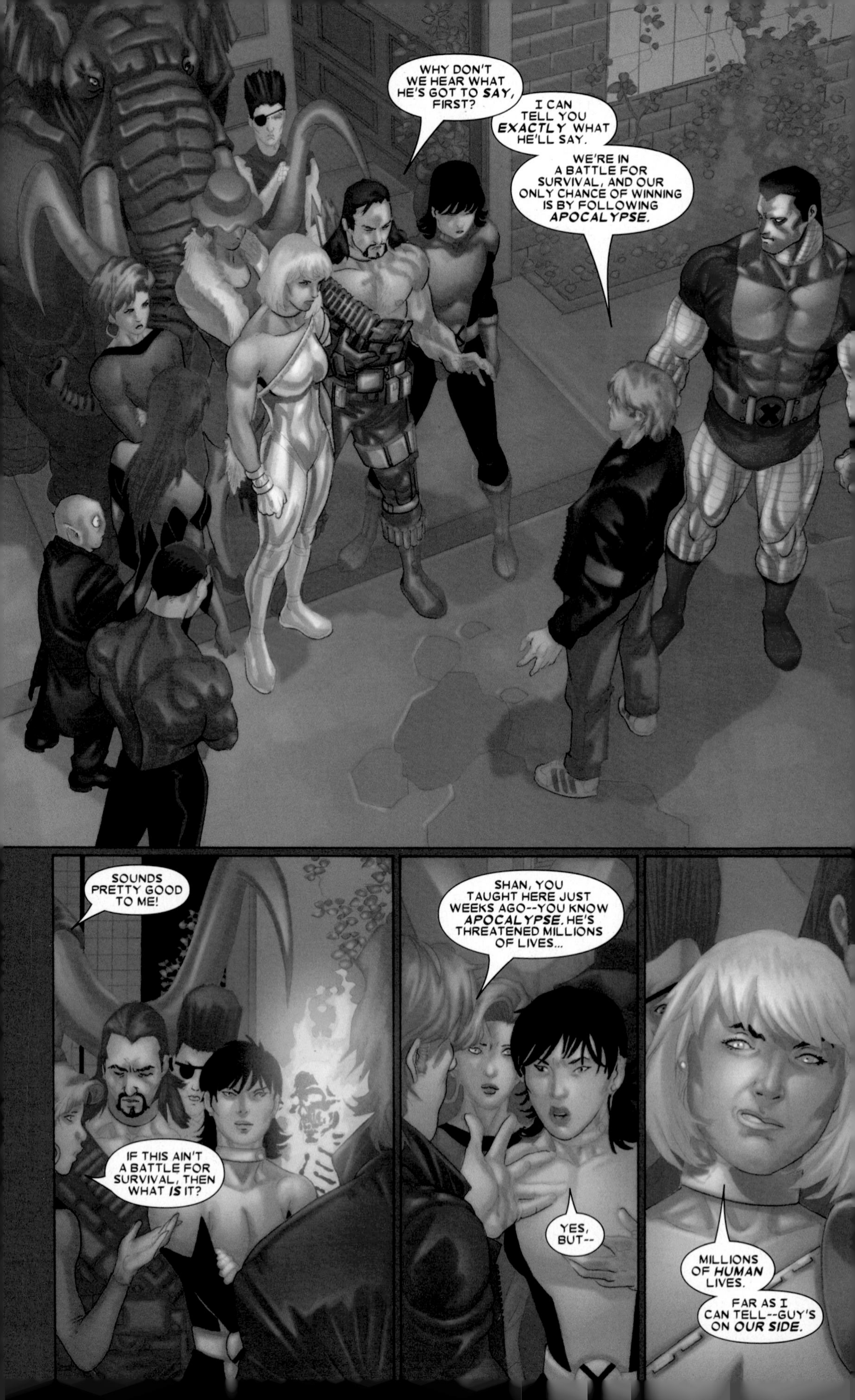
WHY DON'T WE HEAR WHAT HE'S GOT TO SAY, FIRST?
I CAN TELL YOU EXACTLY WHAT HE'LL SAY.
WE'RE IN A BATTLE FOR SURVIVAL, AND OUR ONLY CHANCE OF WINNING IS BY FOLLOWING APOCALYPSE.
SOUNDS PRETTY GOOD TO ME!
IF THIS AIN'T A BATTLE FOR SURVIVAL, THEN WHAT IS IT?
SHAN, YOU TAUGHT HERE JUST WEEKS AGO--YOU KNOW APOCALYPSE. HE'S THREATENED MILLIONS OF LIVES...
YES, BUT--
MILLIONS OF HUMAN LIVES.
FAR AS I CAN TELL--GUY'S ON OUR SIDE.

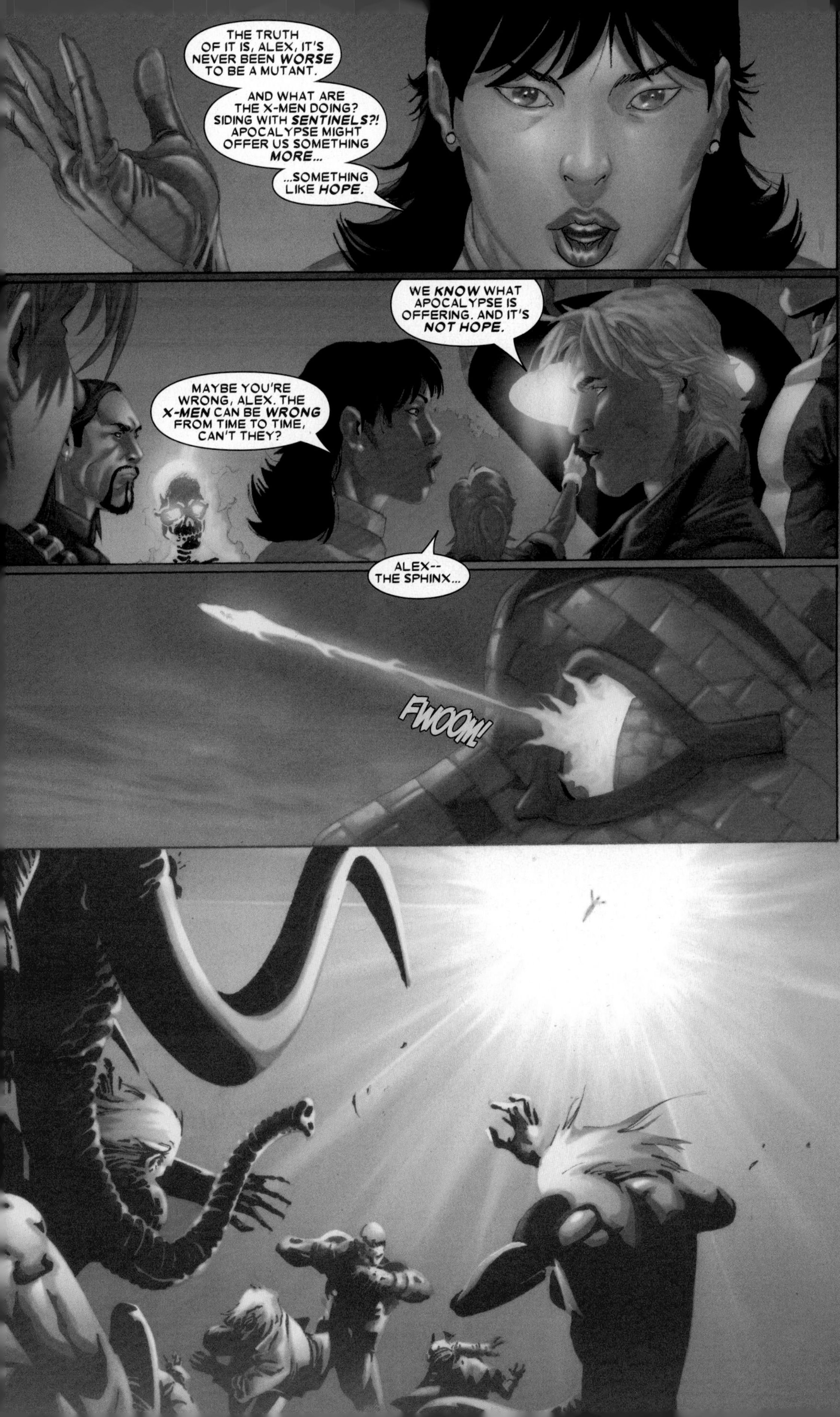
THE TRUTH OF IT IS, ALEX, IT'S NEVER BEEN WORSE TO BE A MUTANT.
AND WHAT ARE THE X-MEN DOING? SIDING WITH SENTINELS?! APOCALYPSE MIGHT OFFER US SOMETHING MORE...
...SOMETHING LIKE HOPE.
WE KNOW WHAT APOCALYPSE IS OFFERING. AND IT'S NOT HOPE.
MAYBE YOU'RE WRONG, ALEX. THE X-MEN CAN BE WRONG FROM TIME TO TIME, CAN'T THEY?
ALEX-- THE SPHINX...
FWOOM!

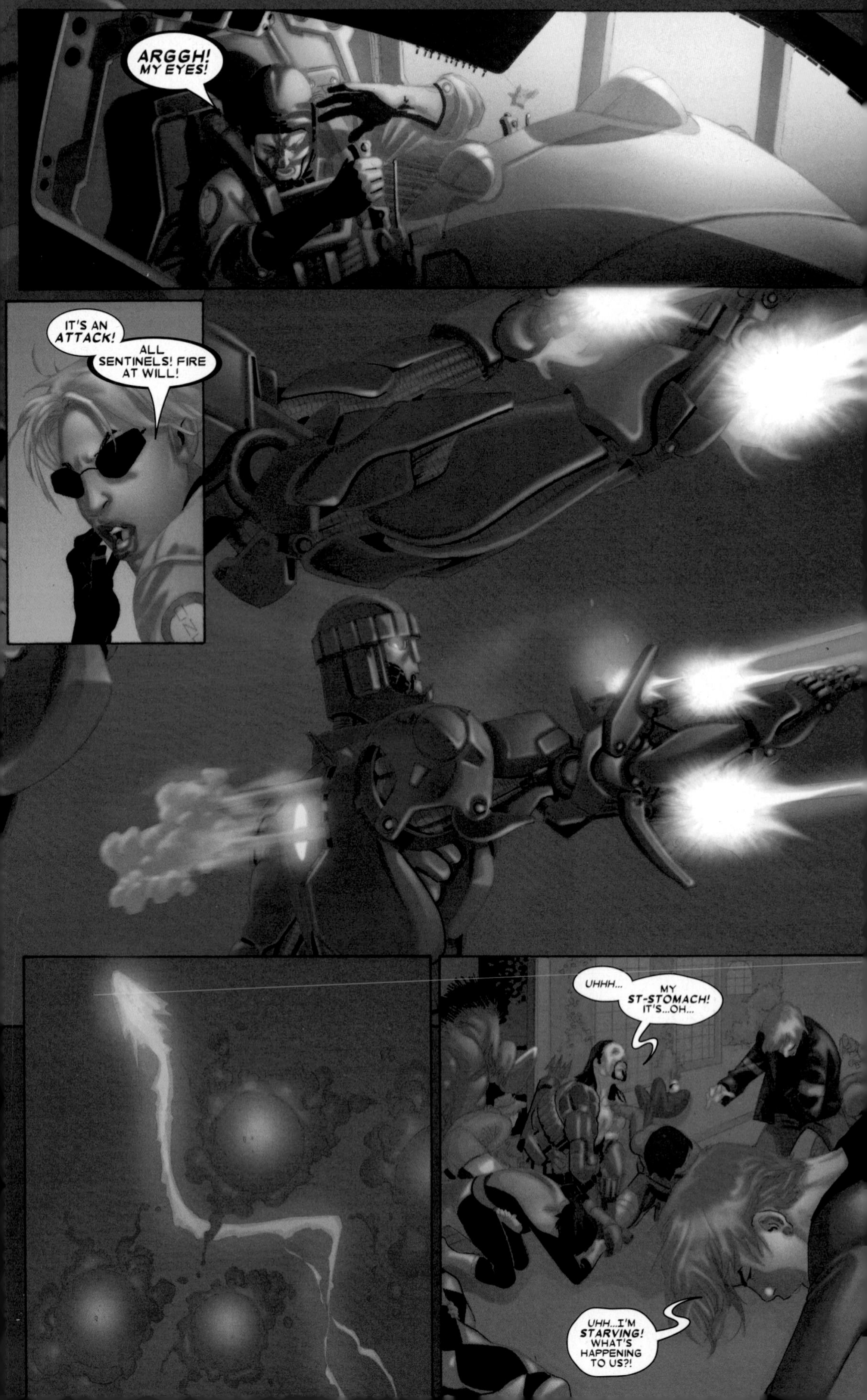
ARGGH! MY EYES!
IT'S AN ATTACK!
ALL SENTINELS! FIRE AT WILL!
UHHH...
MY ST-STOMACH! IT'S...OH...
UHH...I'M STARVING! WHAT'S HAPPENING TO US?!

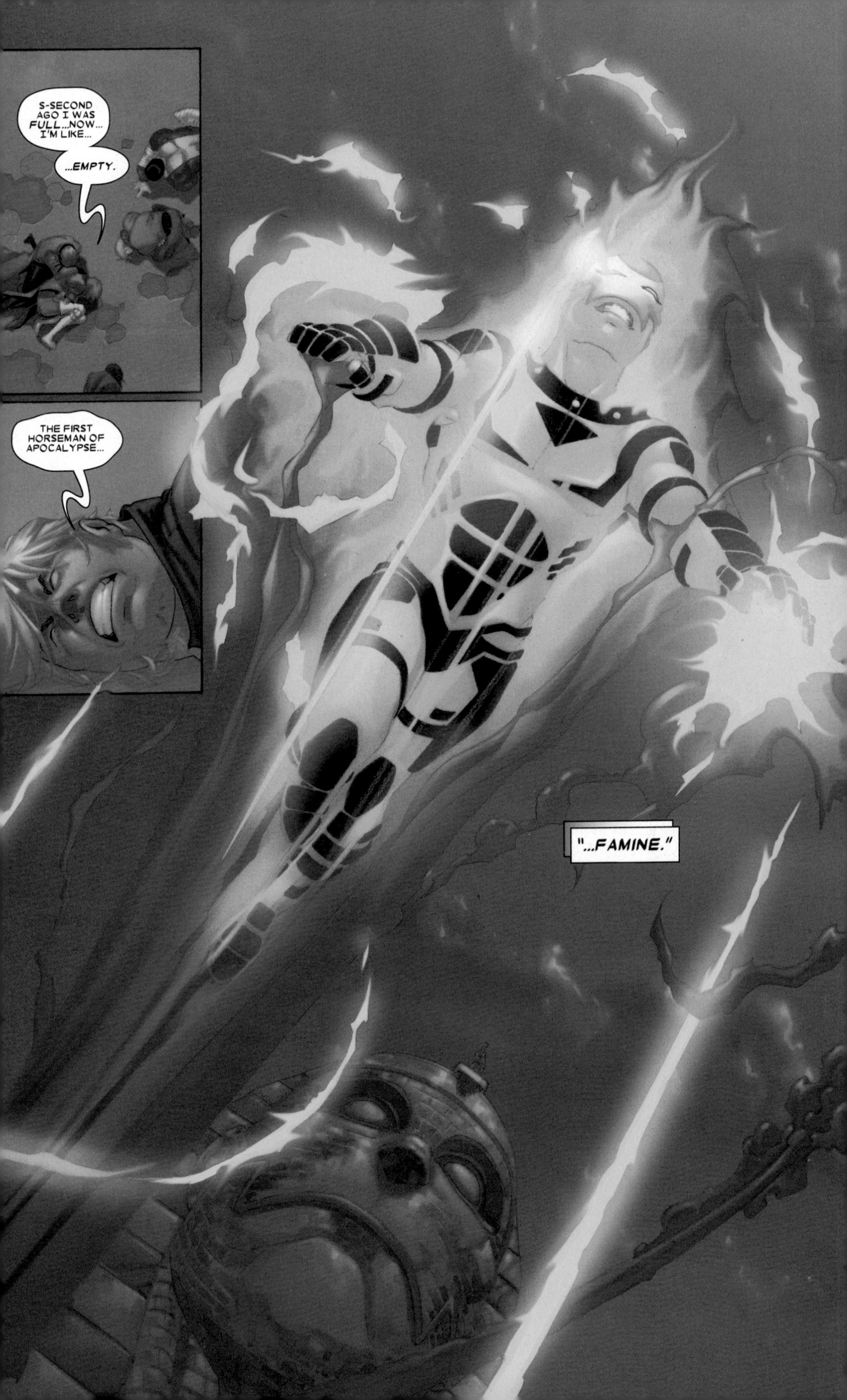
S-SECOND AGO I WAS FULL...NOW... I'M LIKE...
...EMPTY.
THE FIRST HORSEMAN OF APOCALYPSE...
"...FAMINE."

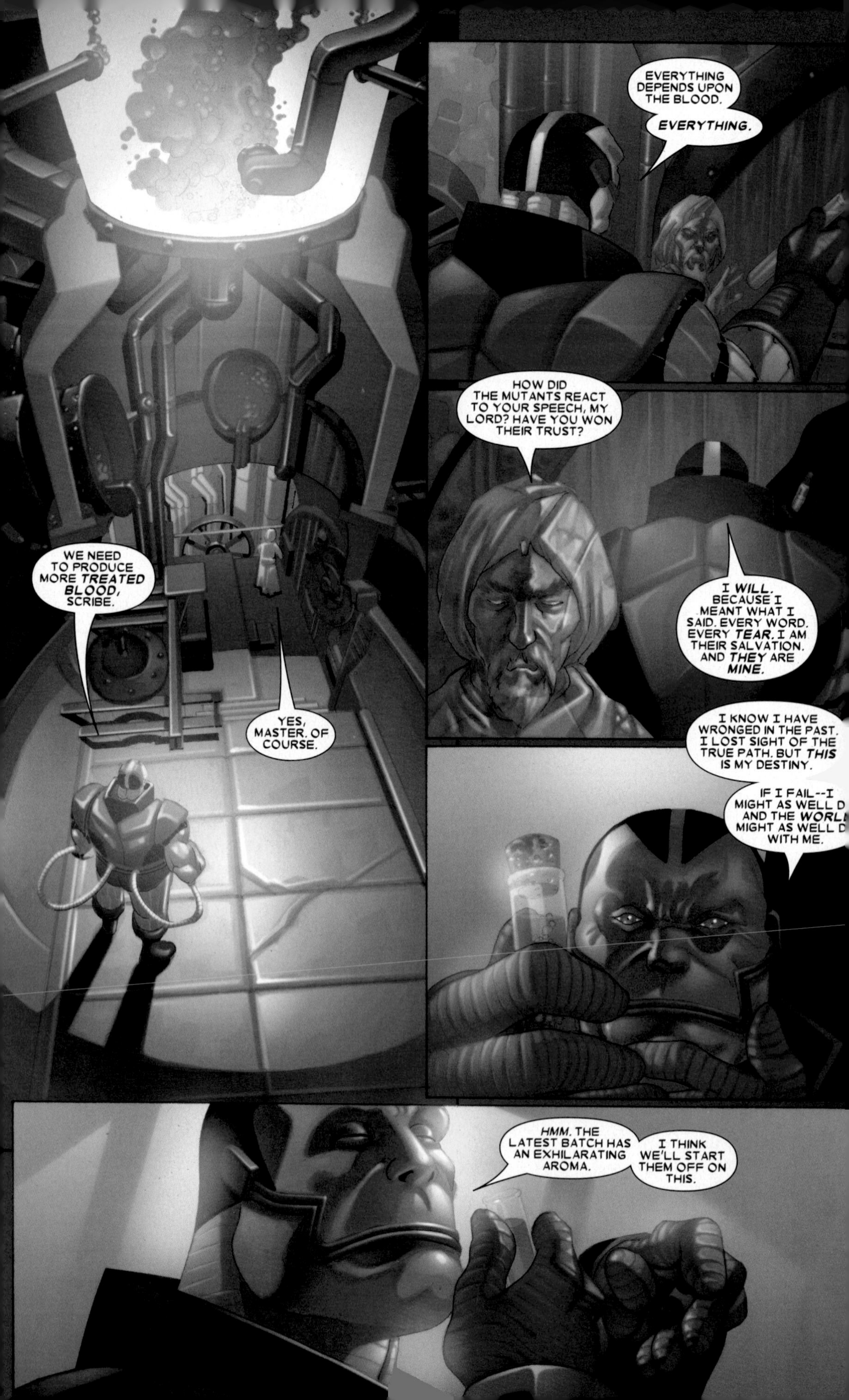

WE NEED TO PRODUCE MORE TREATED BLOOD, SCRIBE.
YES, MASTER. OF COURSE.
EVERYTHING DEPENDS UPON THE BLOOD.
EVERYTHING.
HOW DID THE MUTANTS REACT TO YOUR SPEECH, MY LORD? HAVE YOU WON THEIR TRUST?
I WILL. BECAUSE I MEANT WHAT I SAID. EVERY WORD. EVERY TEAR. I AM THEIR SALVATION. AND THEY ARE MINE.
I KNOW I HAVE WRONGED IN THE PAST. I LOST SIGHT OF THE TRUE PATH. BUT THIS IS MY DESTINY.
HMM. THE LATEST BATCH HAS AN EXHILARATING AROMA.
I THINK WE'LL START THEM OFF ON THIS.

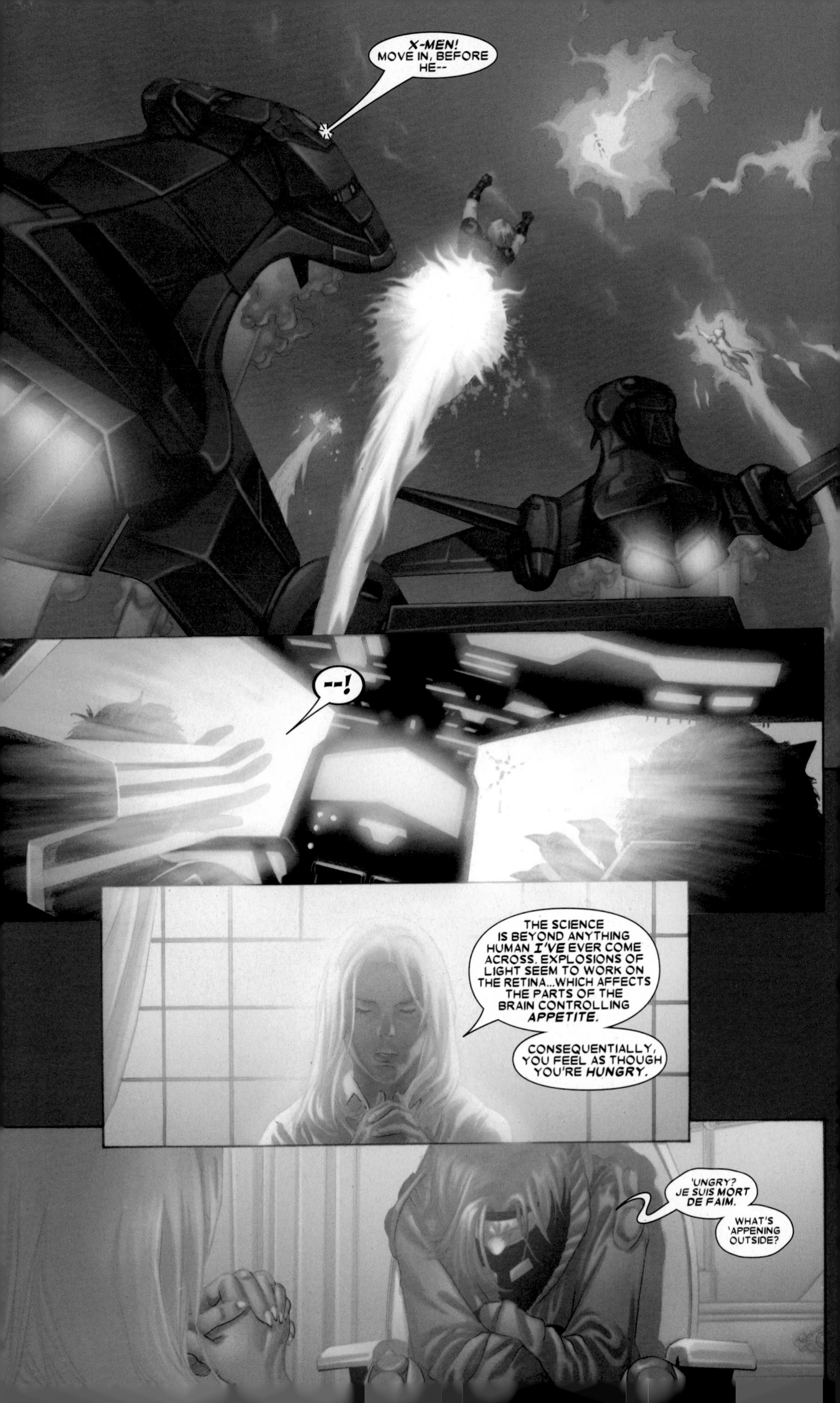
X-MEN! MOVE IN, BEFORE HE--
--!
THE SCIENCE IS BEYOND ANYTHING HUMAN I'VE EVER COME ACROSS. EXPLOSIONS OF LIGHT SEEM TO WORK ON THE RETINA...WHICH AFFECTS THE PARTS OF THE BRAIN CONTROLLING APPETITE.
CONSEQUENTIALLY, YOU FEEL AS THOUGH YOU'RE HUNGRY.
'UNGRY? JE SUIS MORT DE FAIM.
WHAT'S 'APPENING OUTSIDE?

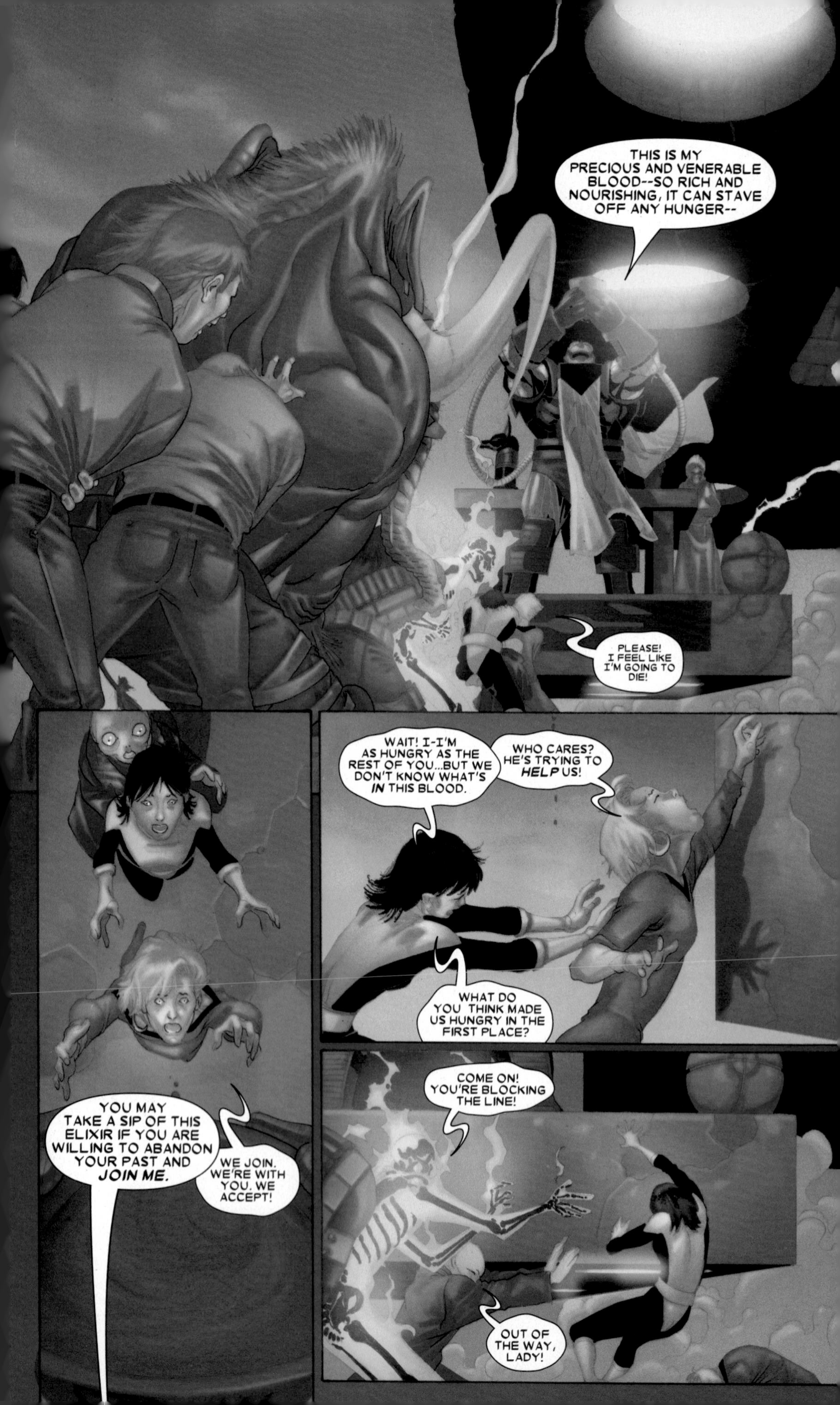
THIS IS MY PRECIOUS AND VENERABLE BLOOD--SO RICH AND NOURISHING, IT CAN STAVE OFF ANY HUNGER--
PLEASE! I FEEL LIKE I'M GOING TO DIE!
YOU MAY TAKE A SIP OF THIS ELIXIR IF YOU ARE WILLING TO ABANDON YOUR PAST AND JOIN ME.
WE JOIN. WE'RE WITH YOU. WE ACCEPT!
WAIT! I-I'M AS HUNGRY AS THE REST OF YOU...BUT WE DON'T KNOW WHAT'S IN THIS BLOOD.
WHO CARES? HE'S TRYING TO HELP US!
WHAT DO YOU THINK MADE US HUNGRY IN THE FIRST PLACE?
COME ON! YOU'RE BLOCKING THE LINE!
OUT OF THE WAY, LADY!

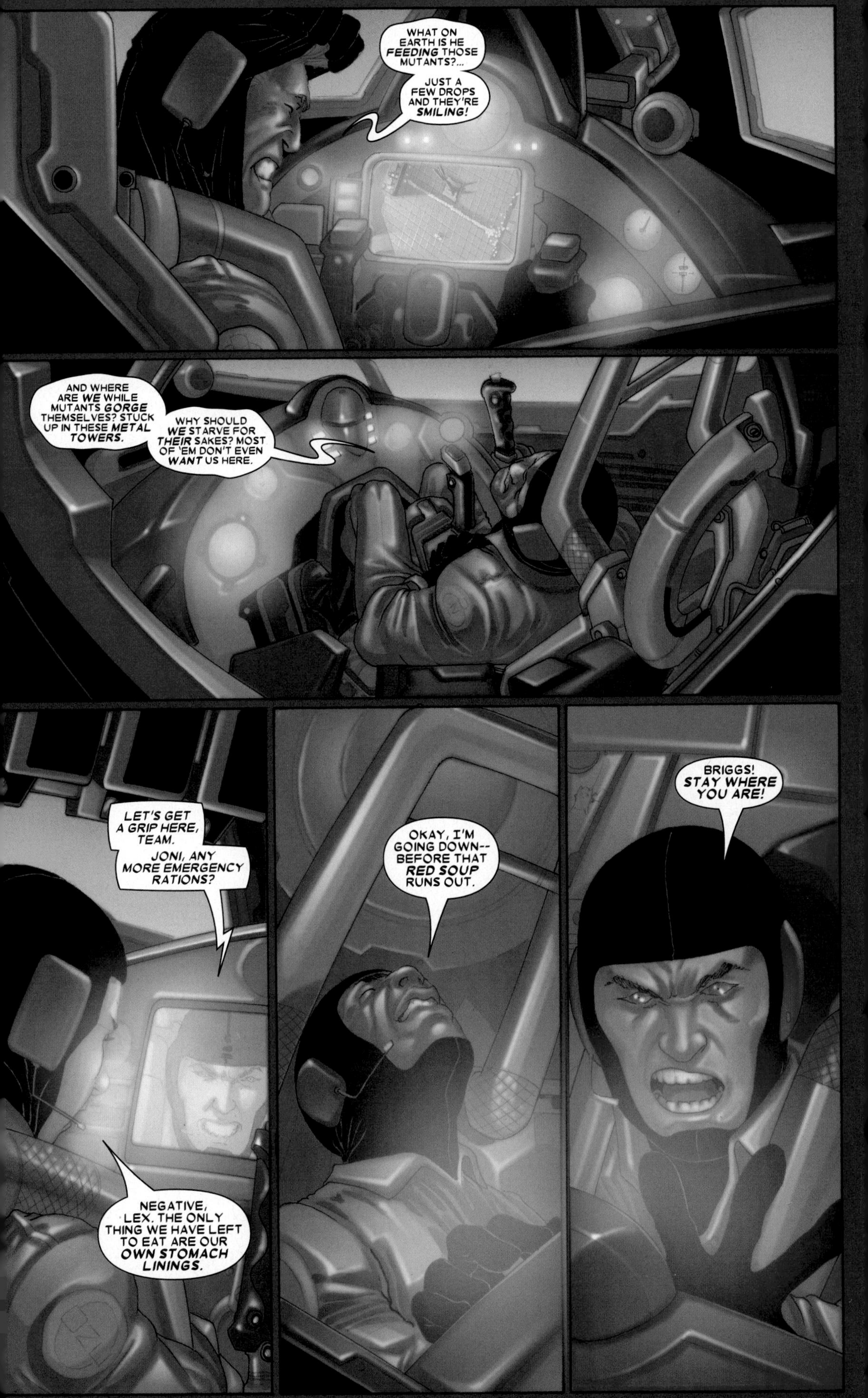
WHAT ON EARTH IS HE FEEDING THOSE MUTANTS?...
JUST A FEW DROPS AND THEY'RE SMILING!
AND WHERE ARE WE WHILE MUTANTS GORGE THEMSELVES? STUCK UP IN THESE METAL TOWERS.
WHY SHOULD WE STARVE FOR THEIR SAKES? MOST OF 'EM DON'T EVEN WANT US HERE.
LET'S GET A GRIP HERE, TEAM.
JONI, ANY MORE EMERGENCY RATIONS?
NEGATIVE, LEX. THE ONLY THING WE HAVE LEFT TO EAT ARE OUR OWN STOMACH LININGS.
OKAY, I'M GOING DOWN-- BEFORE THAT RED SOUP RUNS OUT.
BRIGGS! STAY WHERE YOU ARE!

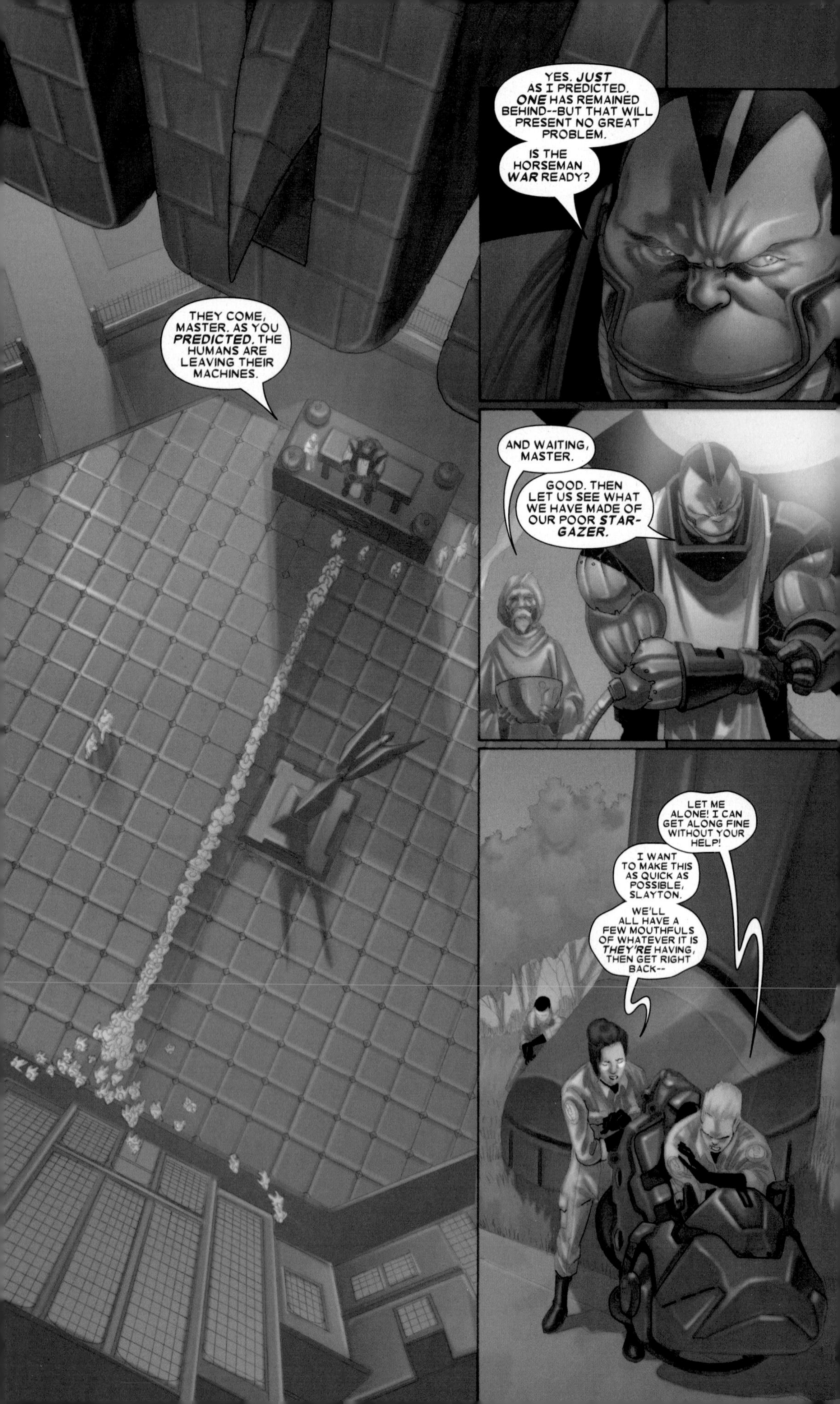
THEY COME, MASTER. AS YOU PREDICTED. THE HUMANS ARE LEAVING THEIR MACHINES.
YES. JUST AS I PREDICTED. ONE HAS REMAINED BEHIND--BUT THAT WILL PRESENT NO GREAT PROBLEM.
IS THE HORSEMAN WAR READY?
AND WAITING, MASTER.
GOOD. THEN LET US SEE WHAT WE HAVE MADE OF OUR POOR STAR-GAZER.
LET ME ALONE! I CAN GET ALONG FINE WITHOUT YOUR HELP!
I WANT TO MAKE THIS AS QUICK AS POSSIBLE, SLAYTON.
WE'LL ALL HAVE A FEW MOUTHFULS OF WHATEVER IT IS THEY'RE HAVING, THEN GET RIGHT BACK--

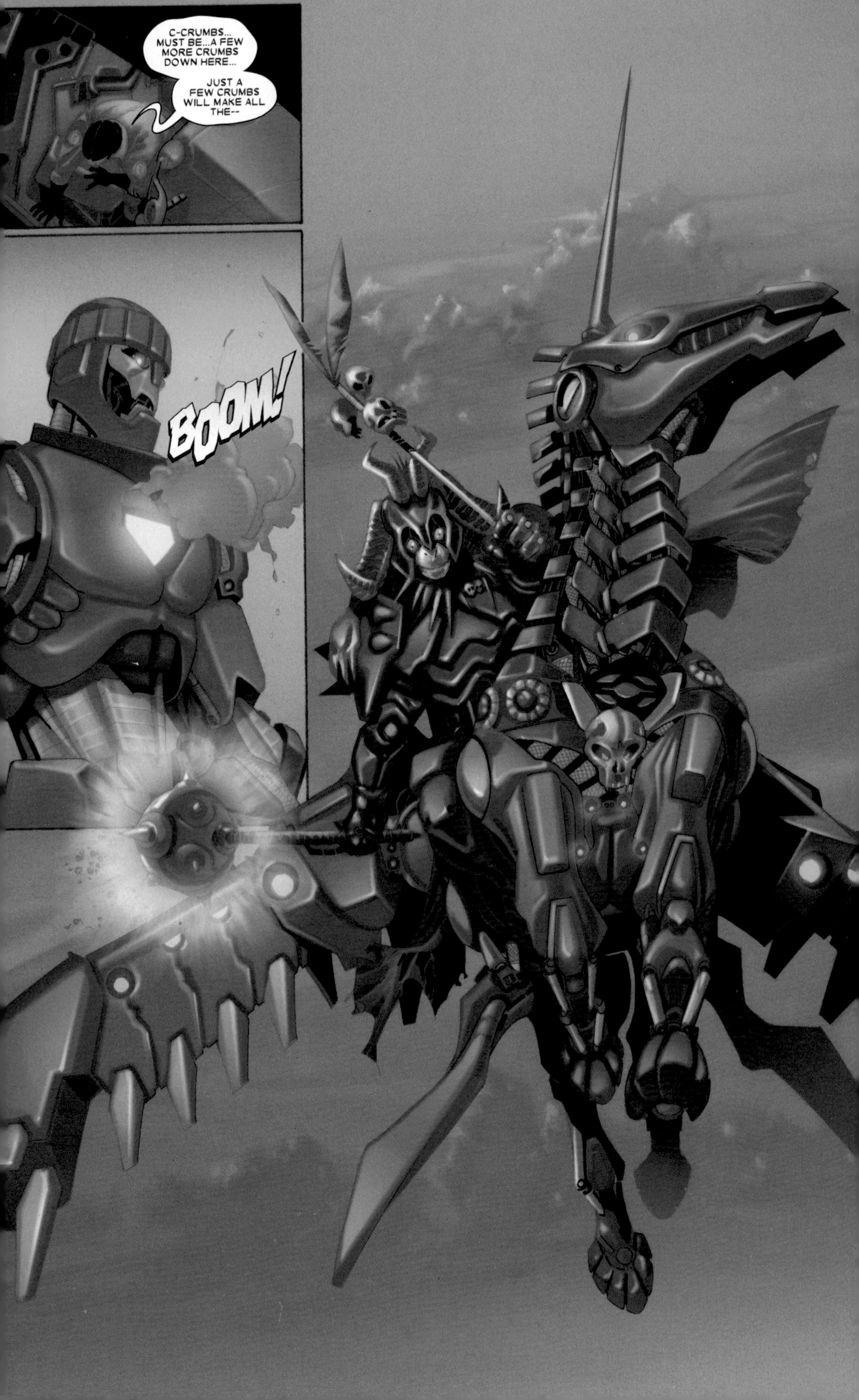
C-CRUMBS... MUST BE...A FEW MORE CRUMBS DOWN HERE...
JUST A FEW CRUMBS WILL MAKE ALL THE--
BOOM!

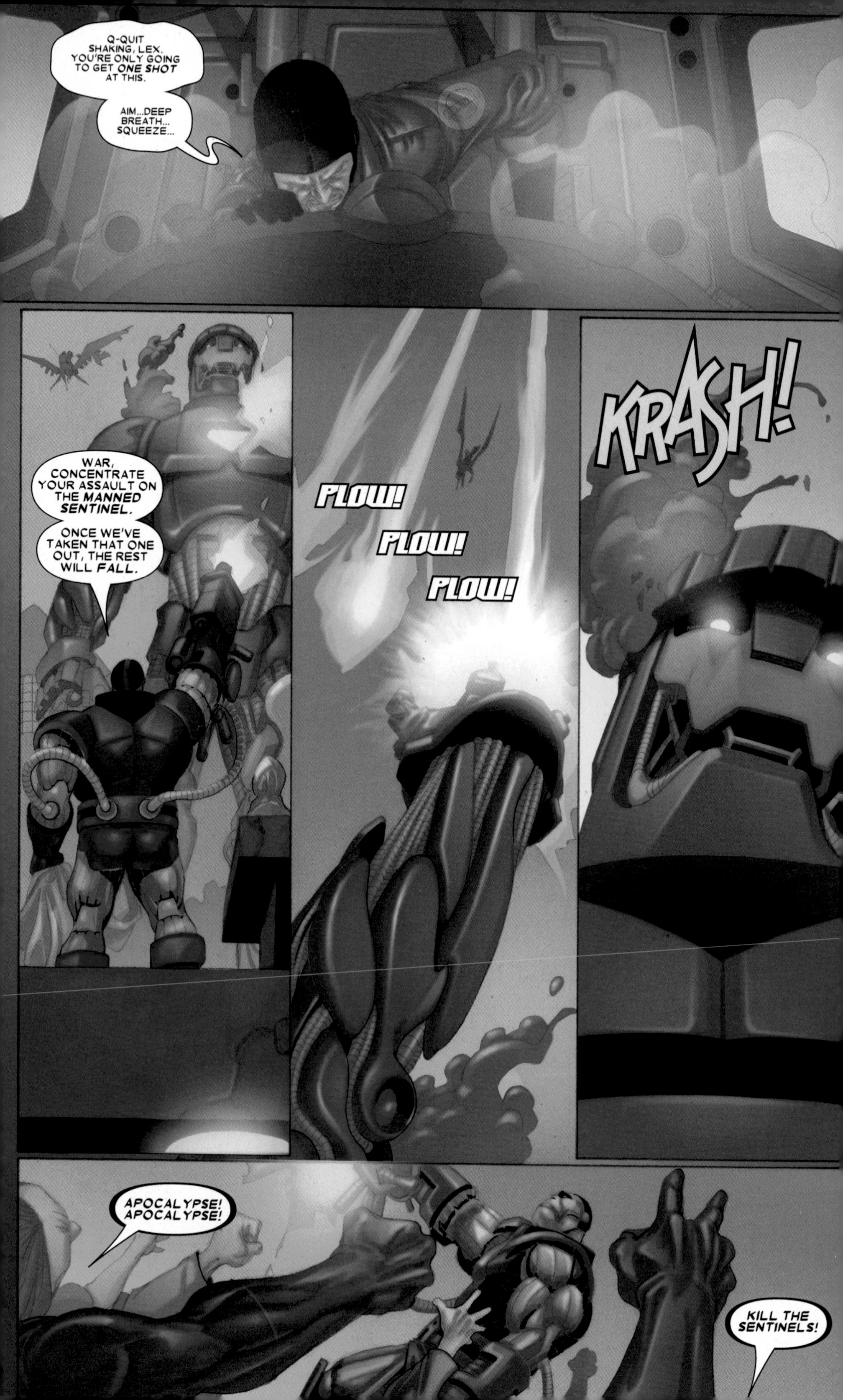

Q-QUIT SHAKING, LEX. YOU'RE ONLY GOING TO GET ONE SHOT AT THIS.
AIM...DEEP BREATH... SQUEEZE...
WAR, CONCENTRATE YOUR ASSAULT ON THE MANNED SENTINEL.
ONCE WE'VE TAKEN THAT ONE OUT, THE REST WILL FALL.
PLOW!
PLOW!
PLOW!
KRASH!
APOCALYPSE! APOCALYPSE!
KILL THE SENTINELS!

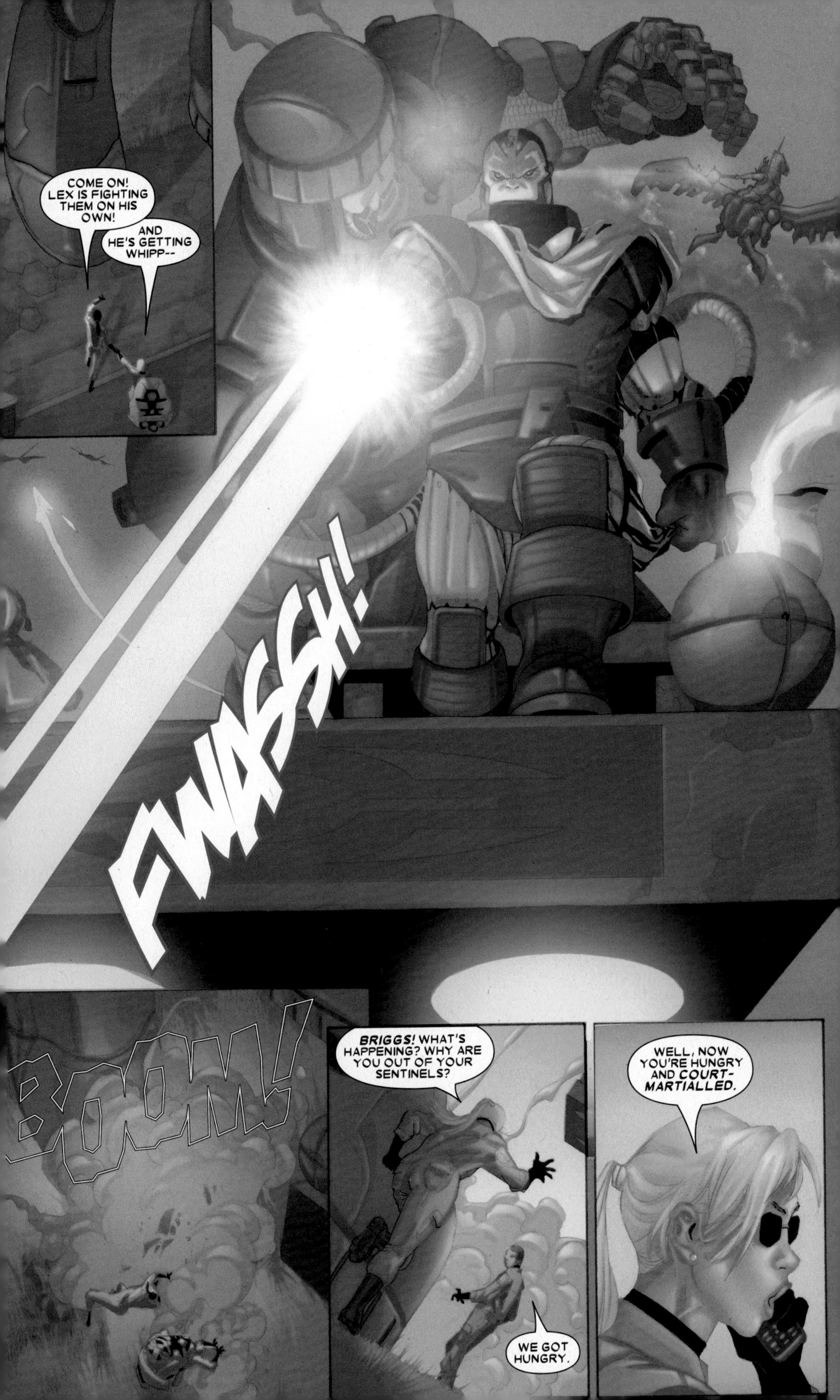

COME ON! LEX IS FIGHTING THEM ON HIS OWN!
AND HE'S GETTING WHIPP--
FWASSH!
BOOOM!
BRIGGS! WHAT'S HAPPENING? WHY ARE YOU OUT OF YOUR SENTINELS?
WE GOT HUNGRY.
WELL, NOW YOU'RE HUNGRY AND COURT-MARTIALLED.

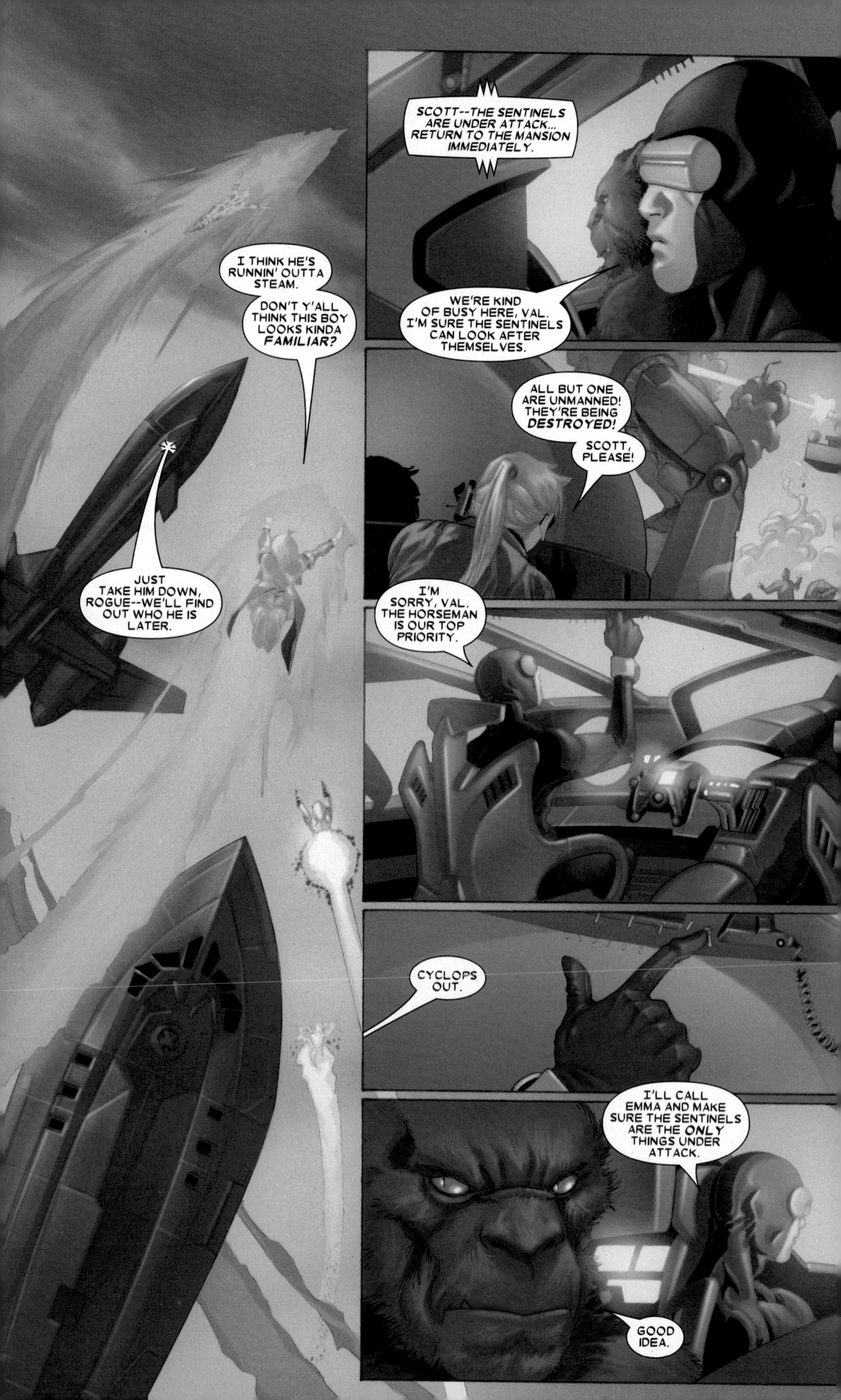

SCOTT--THE SENTINELS ARE UNDER ATTACK... RETURN TO THE MANSION IMMEDIATELY.
WE'RE KIND OF BUSY HERE, VAL. I'M SURE THE SENTINELS CAN LOOK AFTER THEMSELVES.
I THINK HE'S RUNNIN' OUTTA STEAM.
DON'T Y'ALL THINK THIS BOY LOOKS KINDA FAMILIAR?
JUST TAKE HIM DOWN, ROGUE--WE'LL FIND OUT WHO HE IS LATER.
ALL BUT ONE ARE UNMANNED! THEY'RE BEING DESTROYED!
SCOTT, PLEASE!
I'M SORRY, VAL. THE HORSEMAN IS OUR TOP PRIORITY.
CYCLOPS OUT.
I'LL CALL EMMA AND MAKE SURE THE SENTINELS ARE THE ONLY THINGS UNDER ATTACK.
GOOD IDEA.

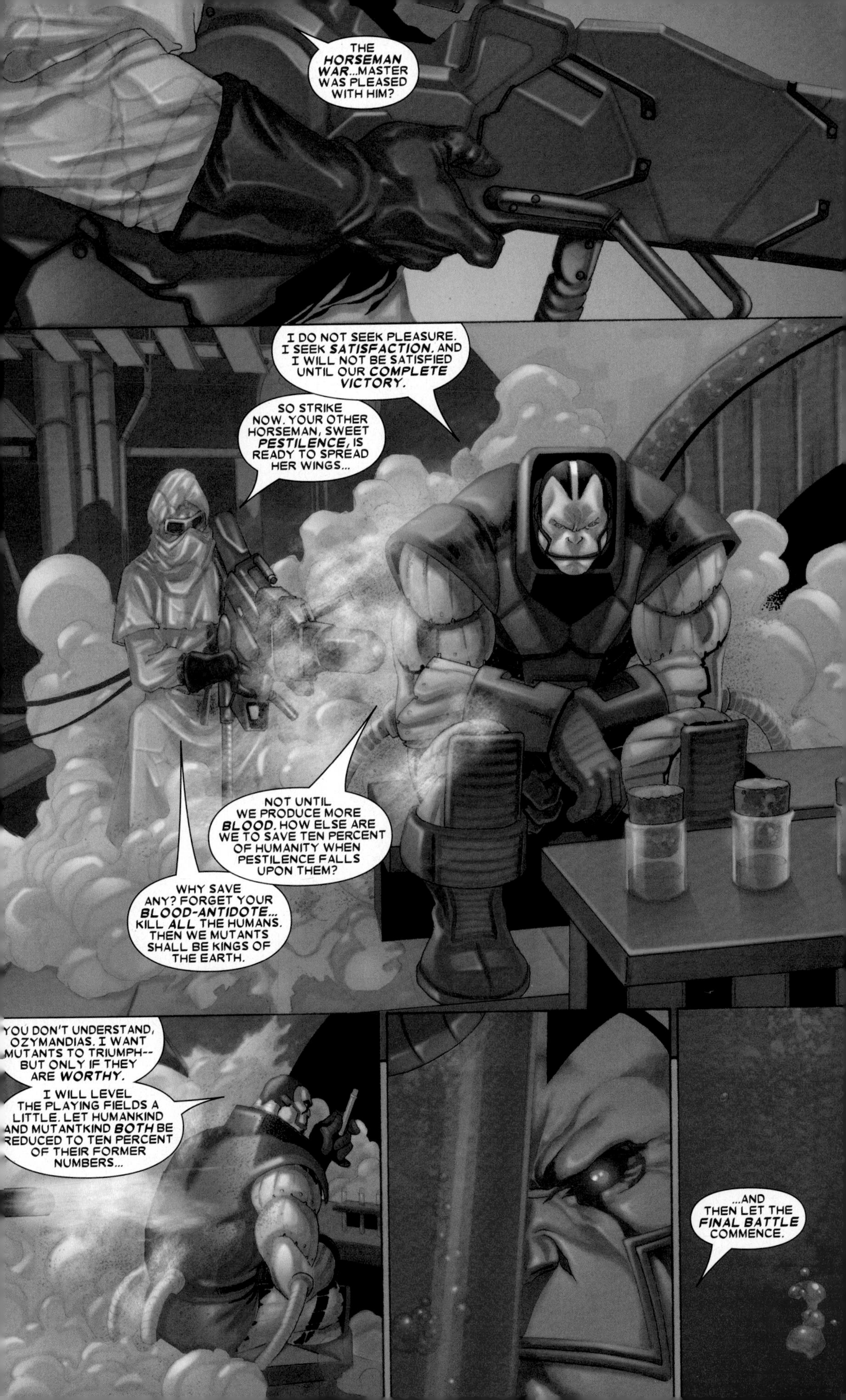
THE HORSEMAN WAR...MASTER WAS PLEASED WITH HIM?
I DO NOT SEEK PLEASURE. I SEEK SATISFACTION. AND I WILL NOT BE SATISFIED UNTIL OUR COMPLETE VICTORY.
SO STRIKE NOW. YOUR OTHER HORSEMAN, SWEET PESTILENCE, IS READY TO SPREAD HER WINGS...
NOT UNTIL WE PRODUCE MORE BLOOD. HOW ELSE ARE WE TO SAVE TEN PERCENT OF HUMANITY WHEN PESTILENCE FALLS UPON THEM?
WHY SAVE ANY? FORGET YOUR BLOOD-ANTIDOTE... KILL ALL THE HUMANS. THEN WE MUTANTS SHALL BE KINGS OF THE EARTH.
YOU DON'T UNDERSTAND, OZYMANDIAS. I WANT MUTANTS TO TRIUMPH-- BUT ONLY IF THEY ARE WORTHY.
I WILL LEVEL THE PLAYING FIELDS A LITTLE. LET HUMANKIND AND MUTANTKIND BOTH BE REDUCED TO TEN PERCENT OF THEIR FORMER NUMBERS...
...AND THEN LET THE FINAL BATTLE COMMENCE.

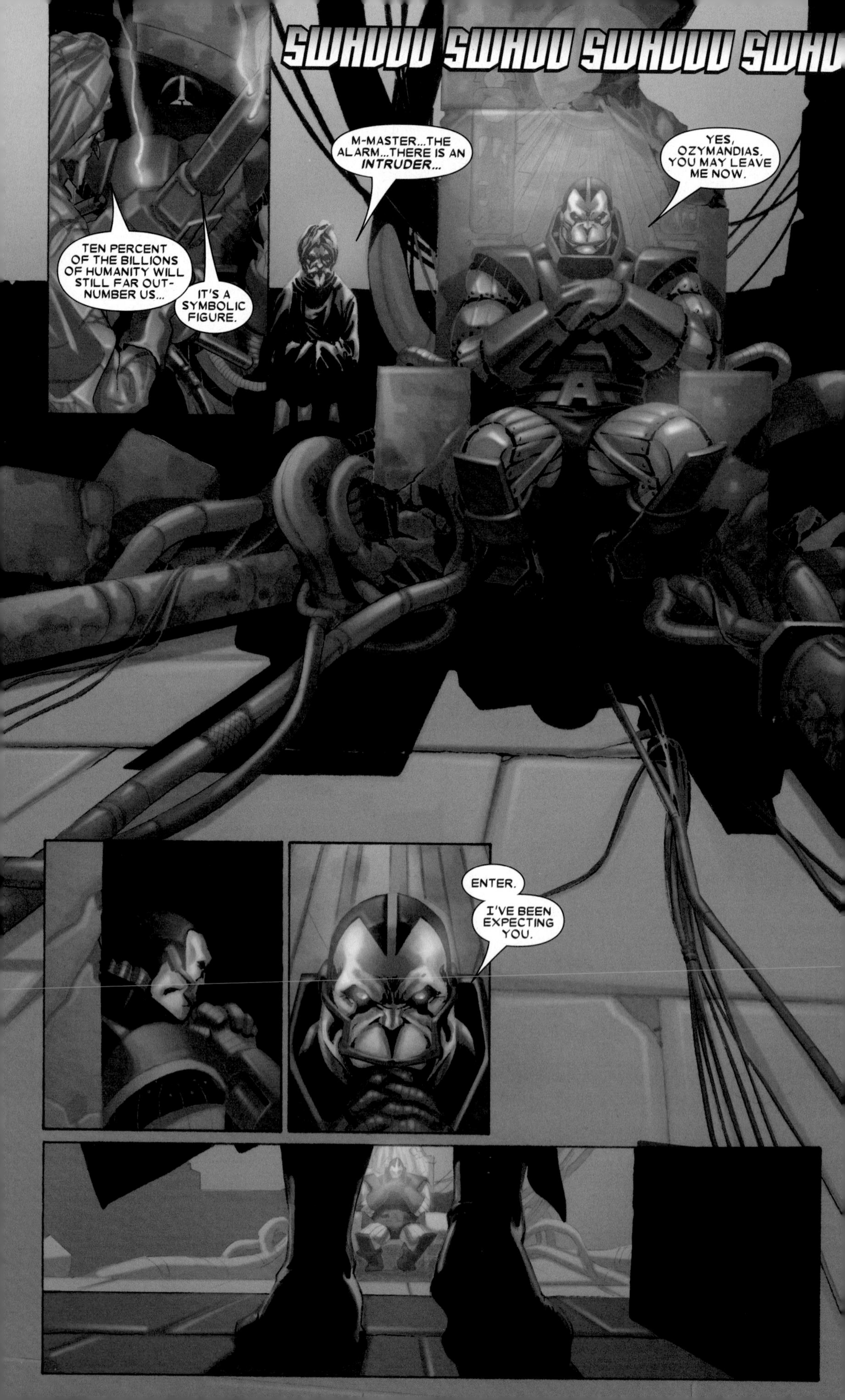
SWHUUU SWHUU SWHUUU SWHU
TEN PERCENT OF THE BILLIONS OF HUMANITY WILL STILL FAR OUT-NUMBER US...
IT'S A SYMBOLIC FIGURE.
M-MASTER...THE ALARM...THERE IS AN INTRUDER...
YES, OZYMANDIAS. YOU MAY LEAVE ME NOW.
ENTER.
I'VE BEEN EXPECTING YOU.

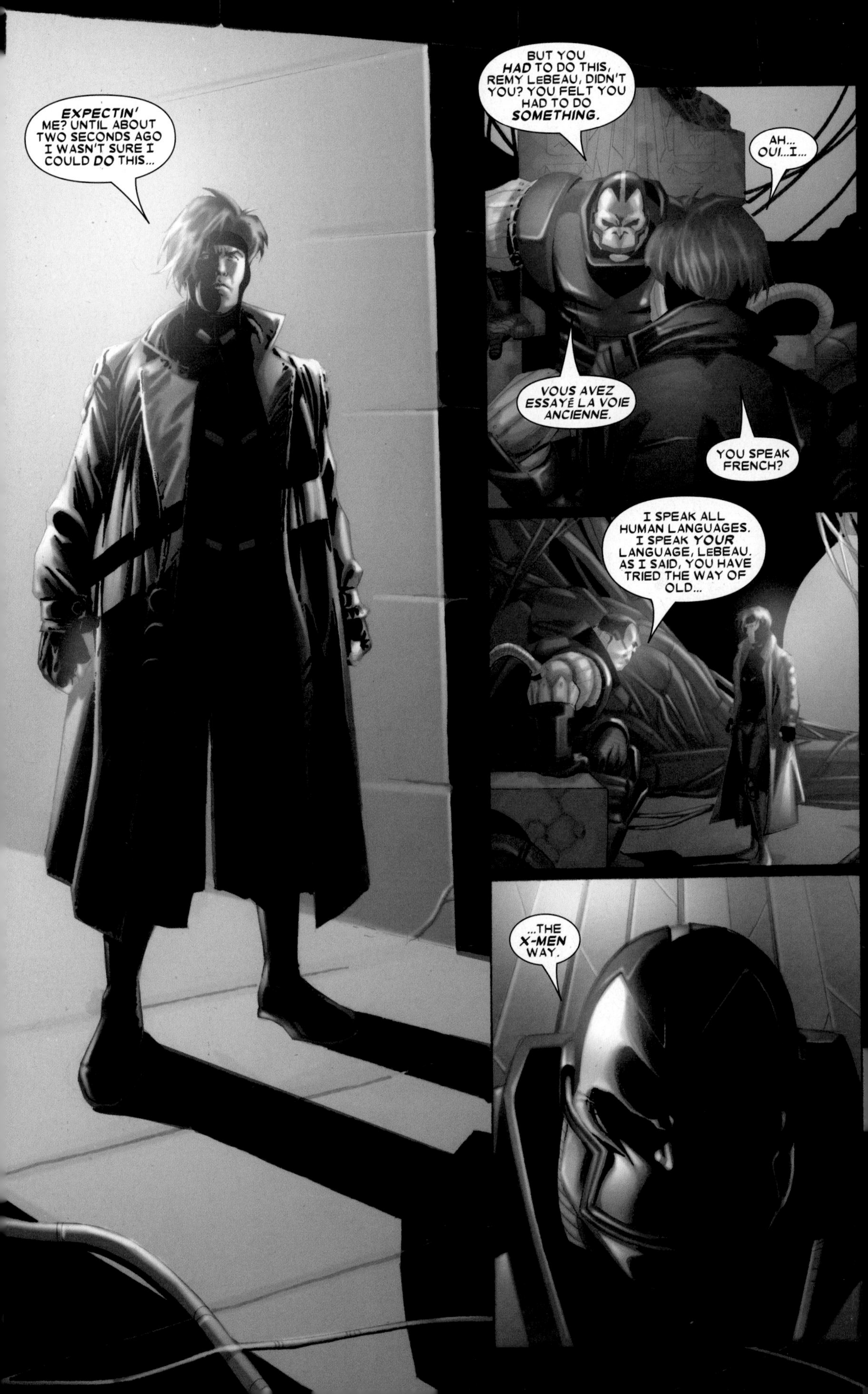

EXPECTIN' ME? UNTIL ABOUT TWO SECONDS AGO I WASN'T SURE I COULD DO THIS...
BUT YOU HAD TO DO THIS, REMY LeBEAU, DIDN'T YOU? YOU FELT YOU HAD TO DO SOMETHING.
AH... OUI...I...
VOUS AVEZ ESSAYÉ LA VOIE ANCIENNE.
YOU SPEAK FRENCH?
I SPEAK ALL HUMAN LANGUAGES. I SPEAK YOUR LANGUAGE, LeBEAU. AS I SAID, YOU HAVE TRIED THE WAY OF OLD...
...THE X-MEN WAY.

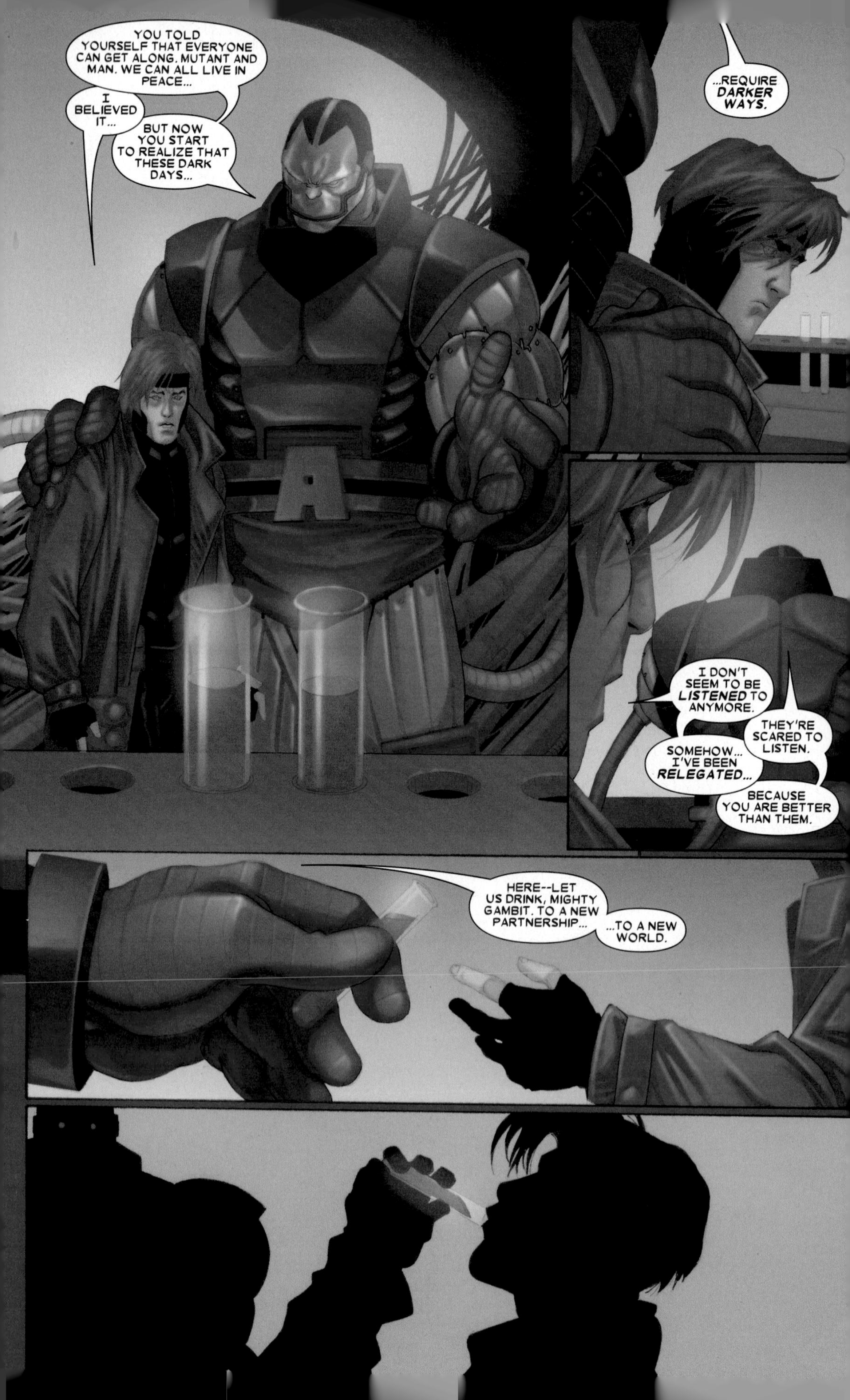
YOU TOLD YOURSELF THAT EVERYONE CAN GET ALONG, MUTANT AND MAN. WE CAN ALL LIVE IN PEACE...
I BELIEVED IT...
BUT NOW YOU START TO REALIZE THAT THESE DARK DAYS...
...REQUIRE DARKER WAYS.
I DON'T SEEM TO BE LISTENED TO ANYMORE.
SOMEHOW... I'VE BEEN RELEGATED...
THEY'RE SCARED TO LISTEN.
BECAUSE YOU ARE BETTER THAN THEM.
HERE--LET US DRINK, MIGHTY GAMBIT. TO A NEW PARTNERSHIP...
...TO A NEW WORLD.

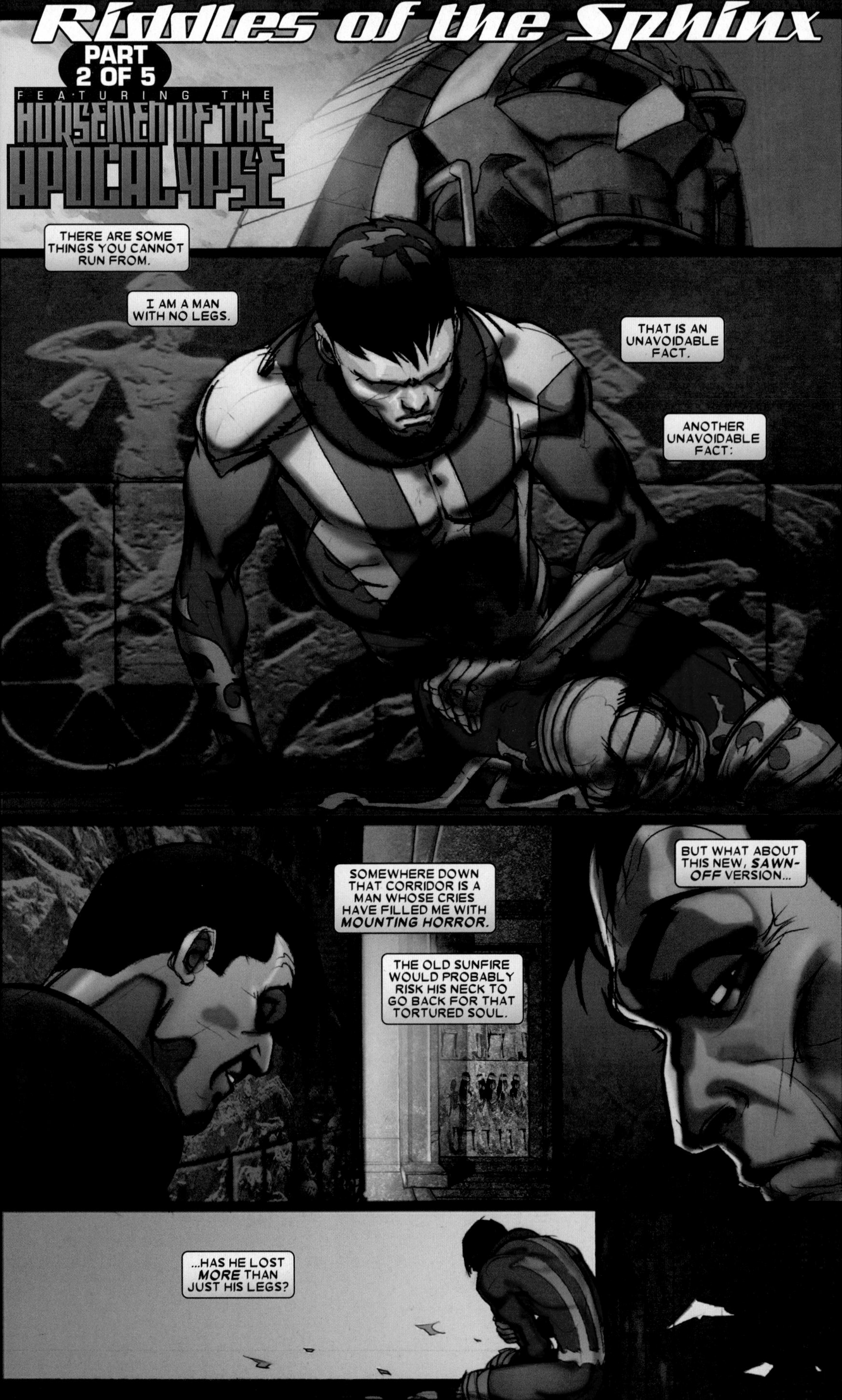

Riddles of the Sphinx
PART 2 OF 5
FEATURING THE
HORSEMEN OF THE APOCALYPSE
THERE ARE SOME THINGS YOU CANNOT RUN FROM.
I AM A MAN WITH NO LEGS.
THAT IS AN UNAVOIDABLE FACT.
ANOTHER UNAVOIDABLE FACT:
SOMEWHERE DOWN THAT CORRIDOR IS A MAN WHOSE CRIES HAVE FILLED ME WITH MOUNTING HORROR.
THE OLD SUNFIRE WOULD PROBABLY RISK HIS NECK TO GO BACK FOR THAT TORTURED SOUL.
BUT WHAT ABOUT THIS NEW, SAWN-OFF VERSION...
...HAS HE LOST MORE THAN JUST HIS LEGS?

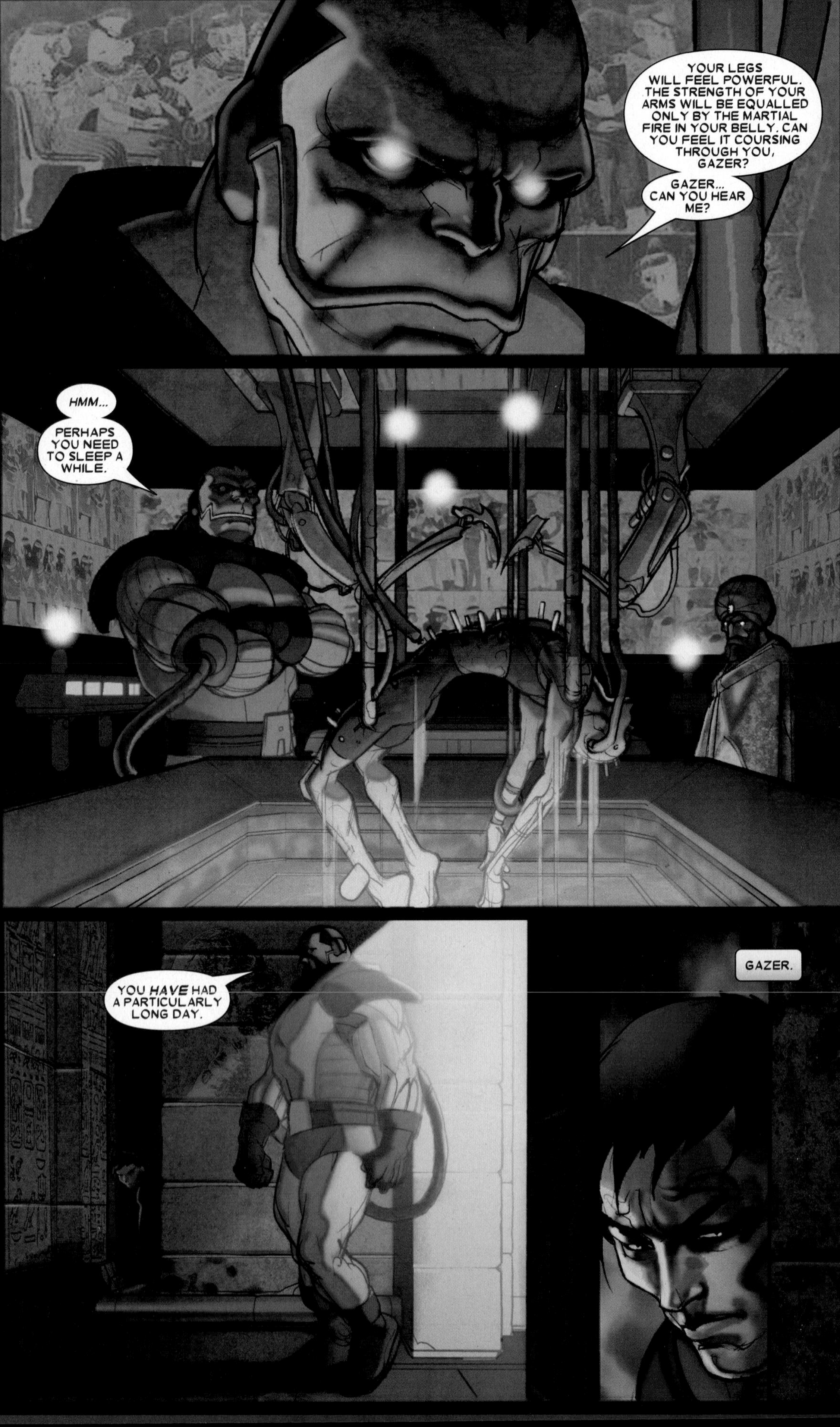
YOUR LEGS WILL FEEL POWERFUL. THE STRENGTH OF YOUR ARMS WILL BE EQUALLED ONLY BY THE MARTIAL FIRE IN YOUR BELLY. CAN YOU FEEL IT COURSING THROUGH YOU, GAZER?
GAZER... CAN YOU HEAR ME?
HMM...
PERHAPS YOU NEED TO SLEEP A WHILE.
YOU HAVE HAD A PARTICULARLY LONG DAY.
GAZER.

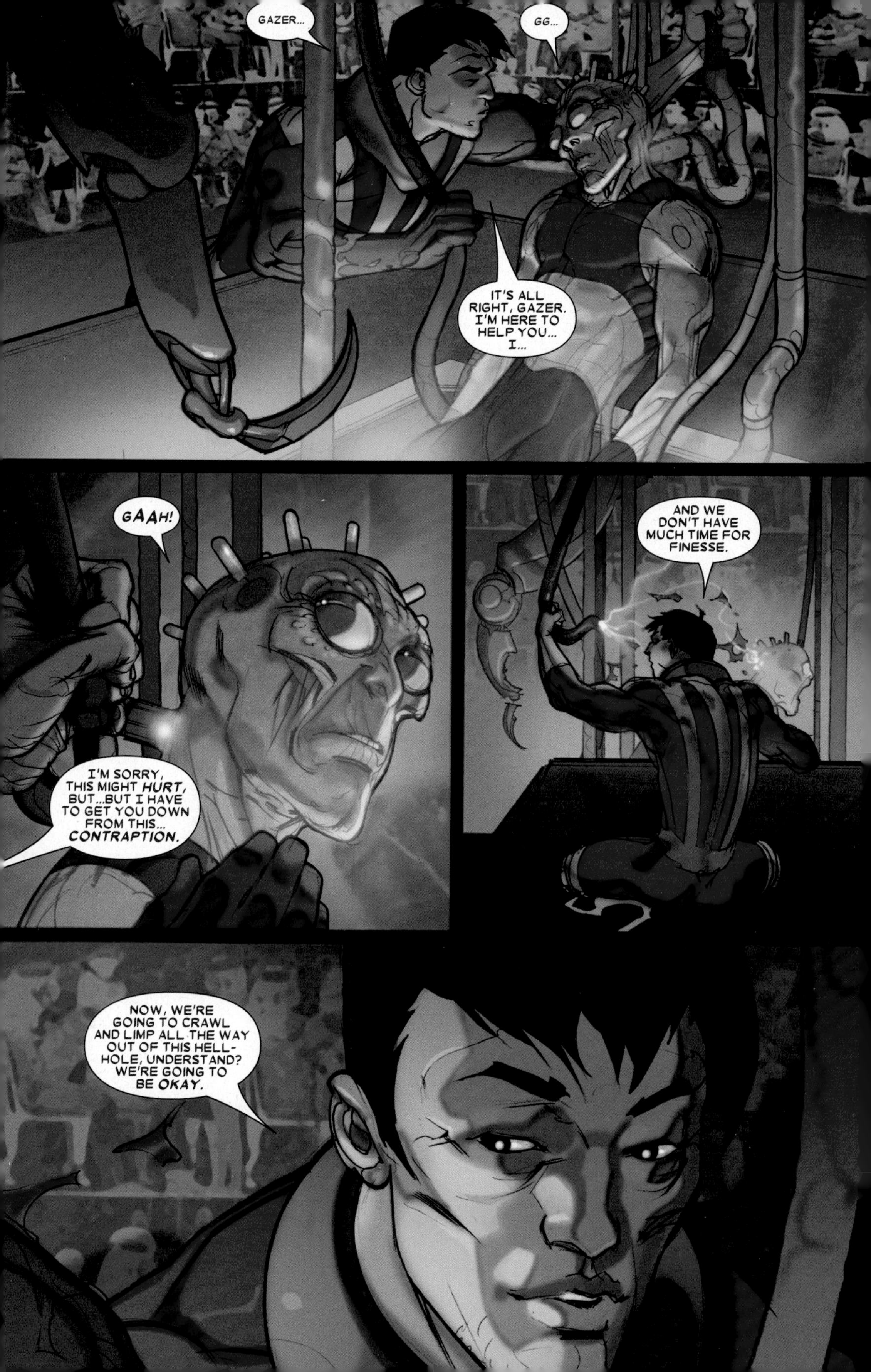
GAZER...
GG...
IT'S ALL RIGHT, GAZER. I'M HERE TO HELP YOU... I...
GAAH!
I'M SORRY, THIS MIGHT *HURT*, BUT...BUT I HAVE TO GET YOU DOWN FROM THIS... ***CONTRAPTION***.
AND WE DON'T HAVE MUCH TIME FOR FINESSE.
NOW, WE'RE GOING TO CRAWL AND LIMP ALL THE WAY OUT OF THIS HELL-HOLE, UNDERSTAND? WE'RE GOING TO BE *OKAY*.

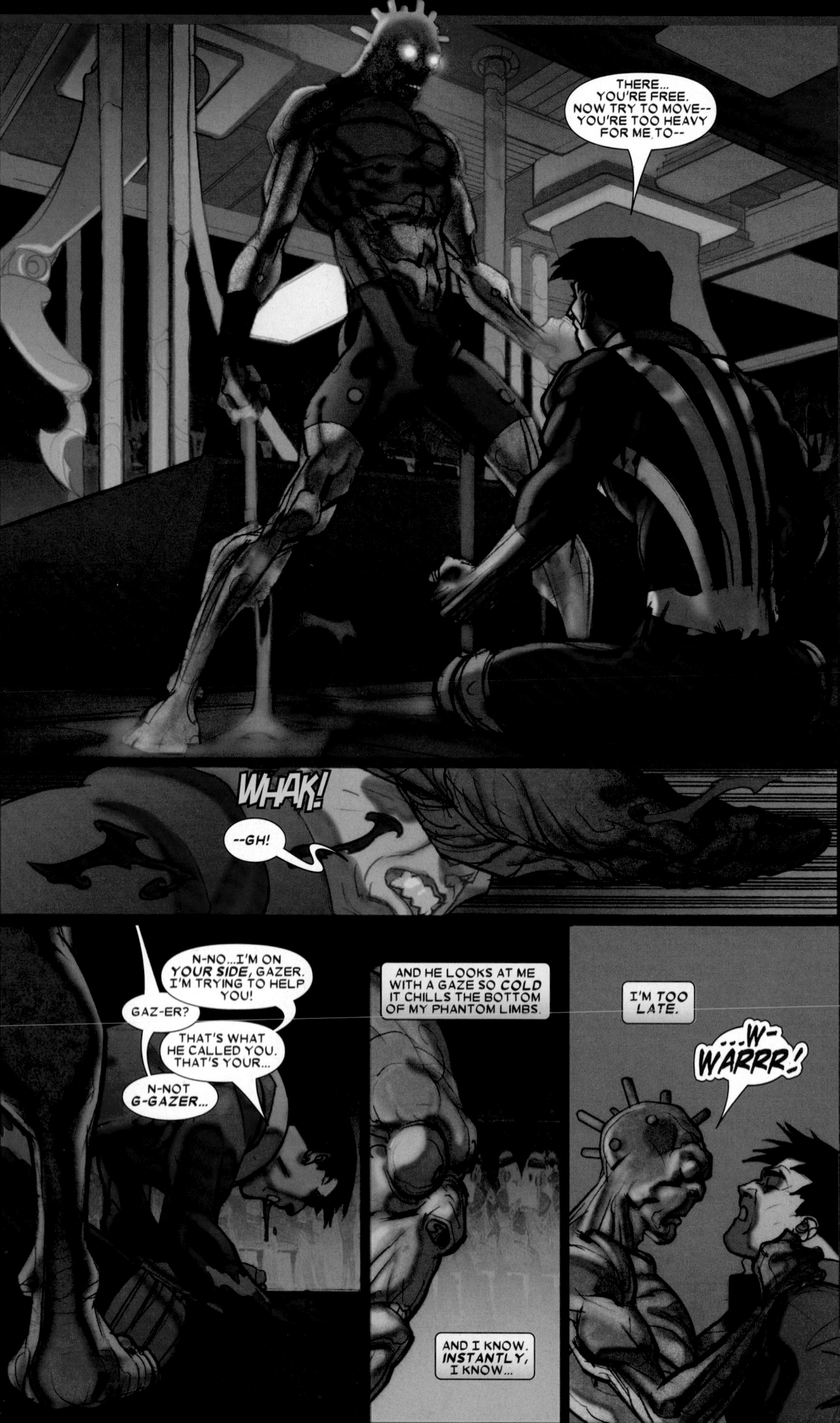
THERE... YOU'RE FREE. NOW TRY TO MOVE-- YOU'RE TOO HEAVY FOR ME TO--
WHAK!
--GH!
N-NO...I'M ON YOUR SIDE, GAZER. I'M TRYING TO HELP YOU!
GAZ-ER?
THAT'S WHAT HE CALLED YOU. THAT'S YOUR...
N-NOT G-GAZER...
AND HE LOOKS AT ME WITH A GAZE SO COLD IT CHILLS THE BOTTOM OF MY PHANTOM LIMBS.
AND I KNOW. INSTANTLY, I KNOW...
I'M TOO LATE.
...W-WARRR!

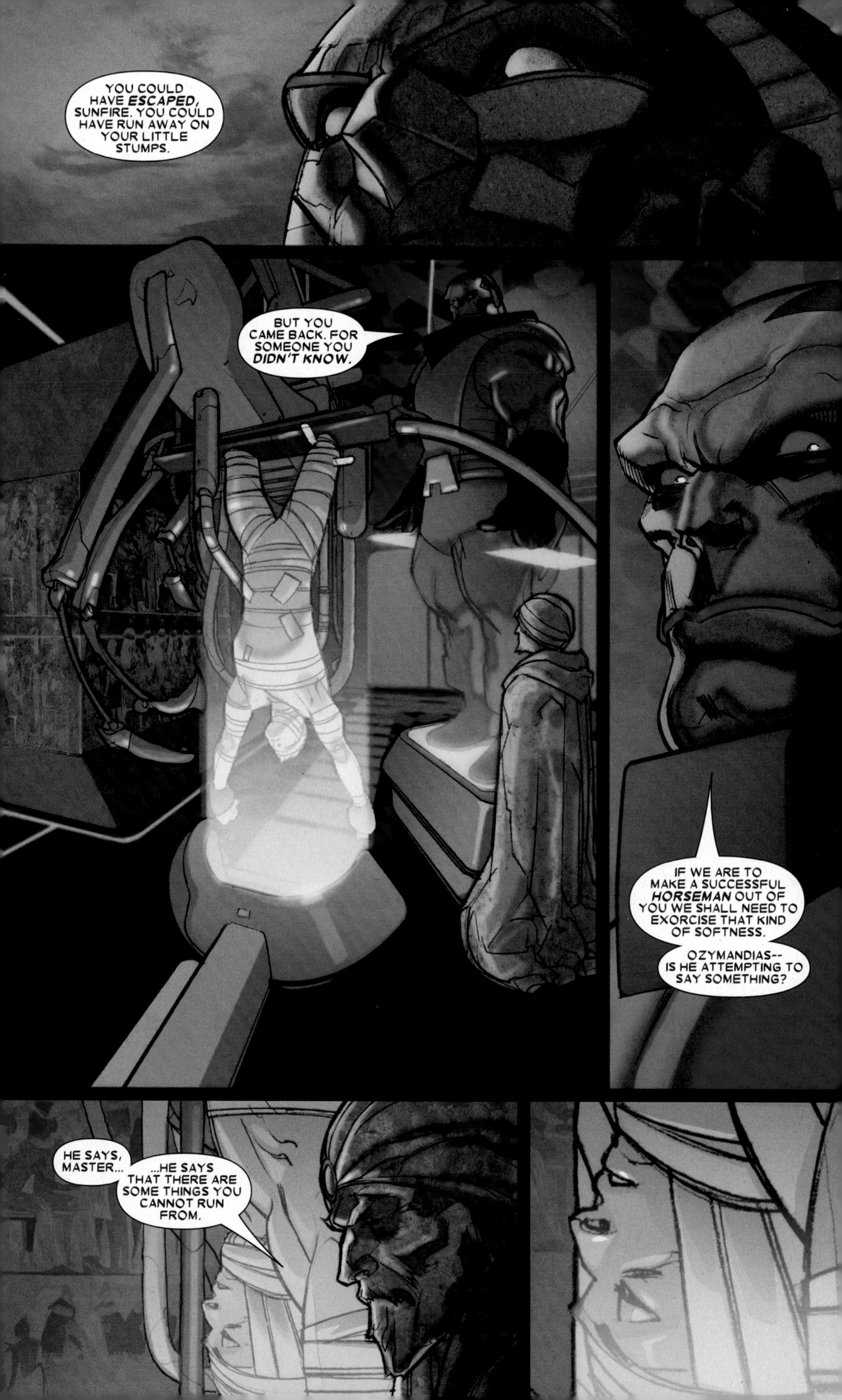
YOU COULD HAVE ESCAPED, SUNFIRE. YOU COULD HAVE RUN AWAY ON YOUR LITTLE STUMPS.
BUT YOU CAME BACK. FOR SOMEONE YOU DIDN'T KNOW.
IF WE ARE TO MAKE A SUCCESSFUL HORSEMAN OUT OF YOU WE SHALL NEED TO EXORCISE THAT KIND OF SOFTNESS.
OZYMANDIAS-- IS HE ATTEMPTING TO SAY SOMETHING?
HE SAYS, MASTER...
...HE SAYS THAT THERE ARE SOME THINGS YOU CANNOT RUN FROM.

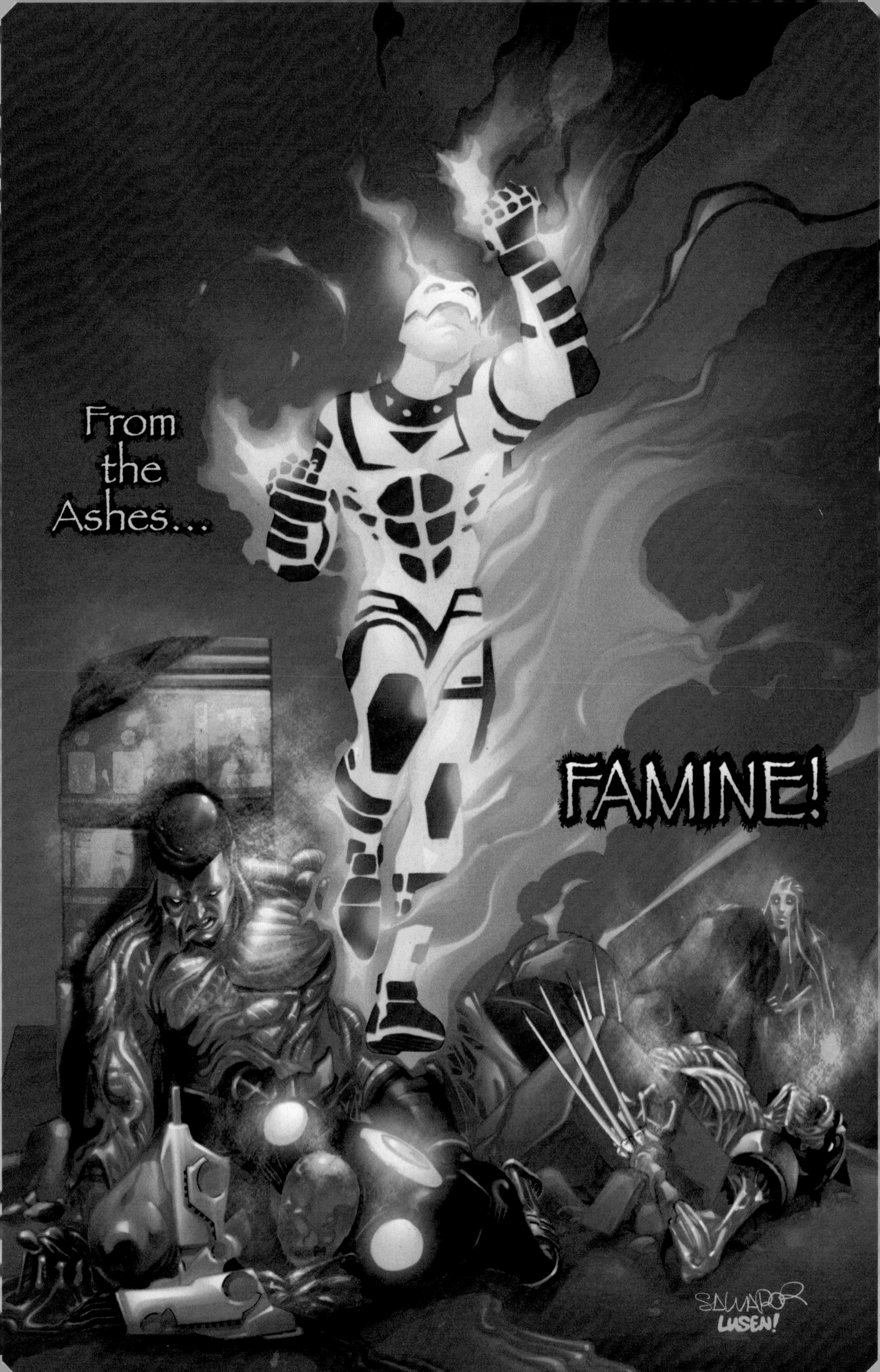
From the Ashes...
FAMINE!
SALVADOR LUSEN!

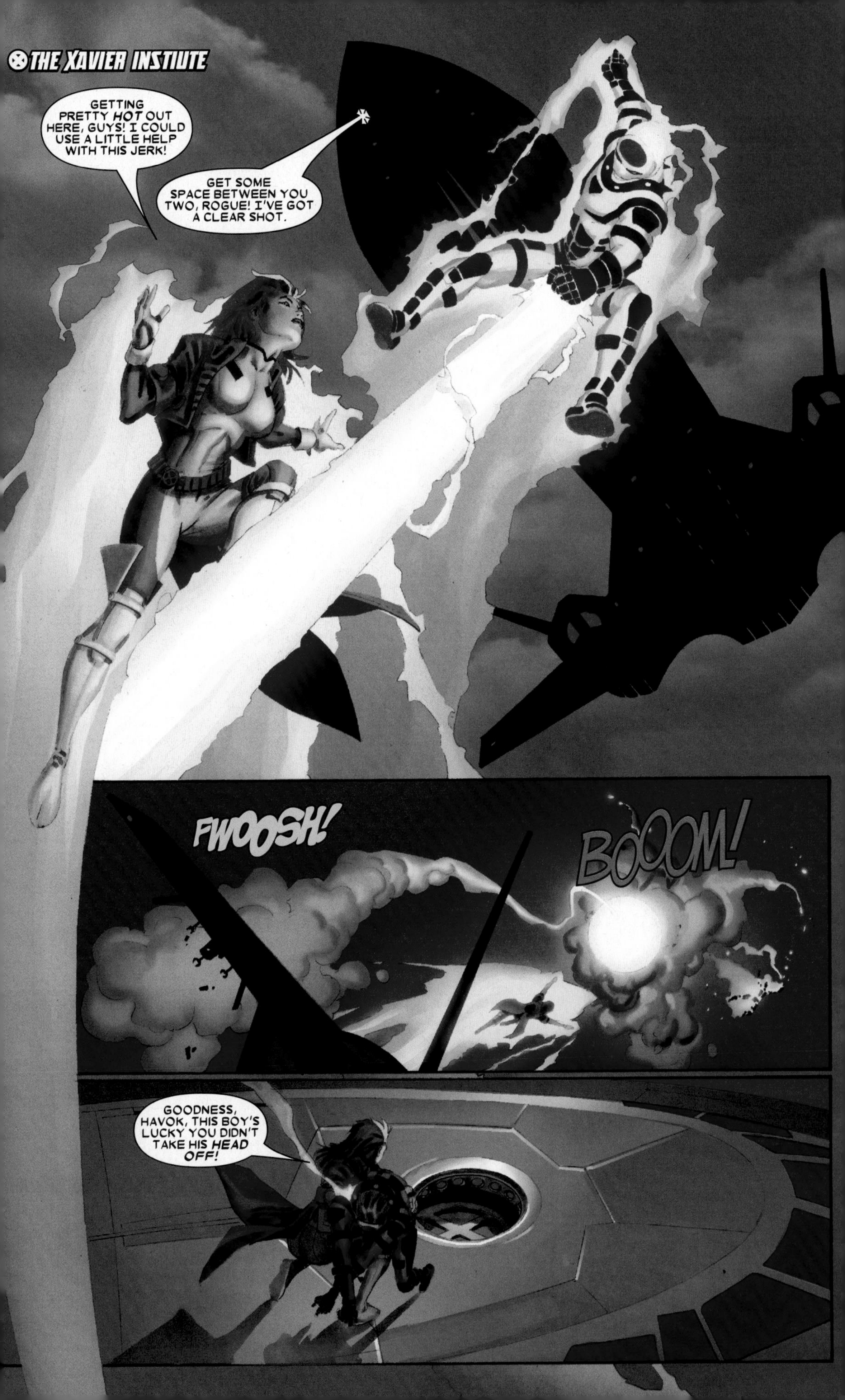
THE XAVIER INSTITUTE
GETTING PRETTY HOT OUT HERE, GUYS! I COULD USE A LITTLE HELP WITH THIS JERK!
GET SOME SPACE BETWEEN YOU TWO, ROGUE! I'VE GOT A CLEAR SHOT.
FWOOSH!
BOOOM!
GOODNESS, HAVOK, THIS BOY'S LUCKY YOU DIDN'T TAKE HIS HEAD OFF!

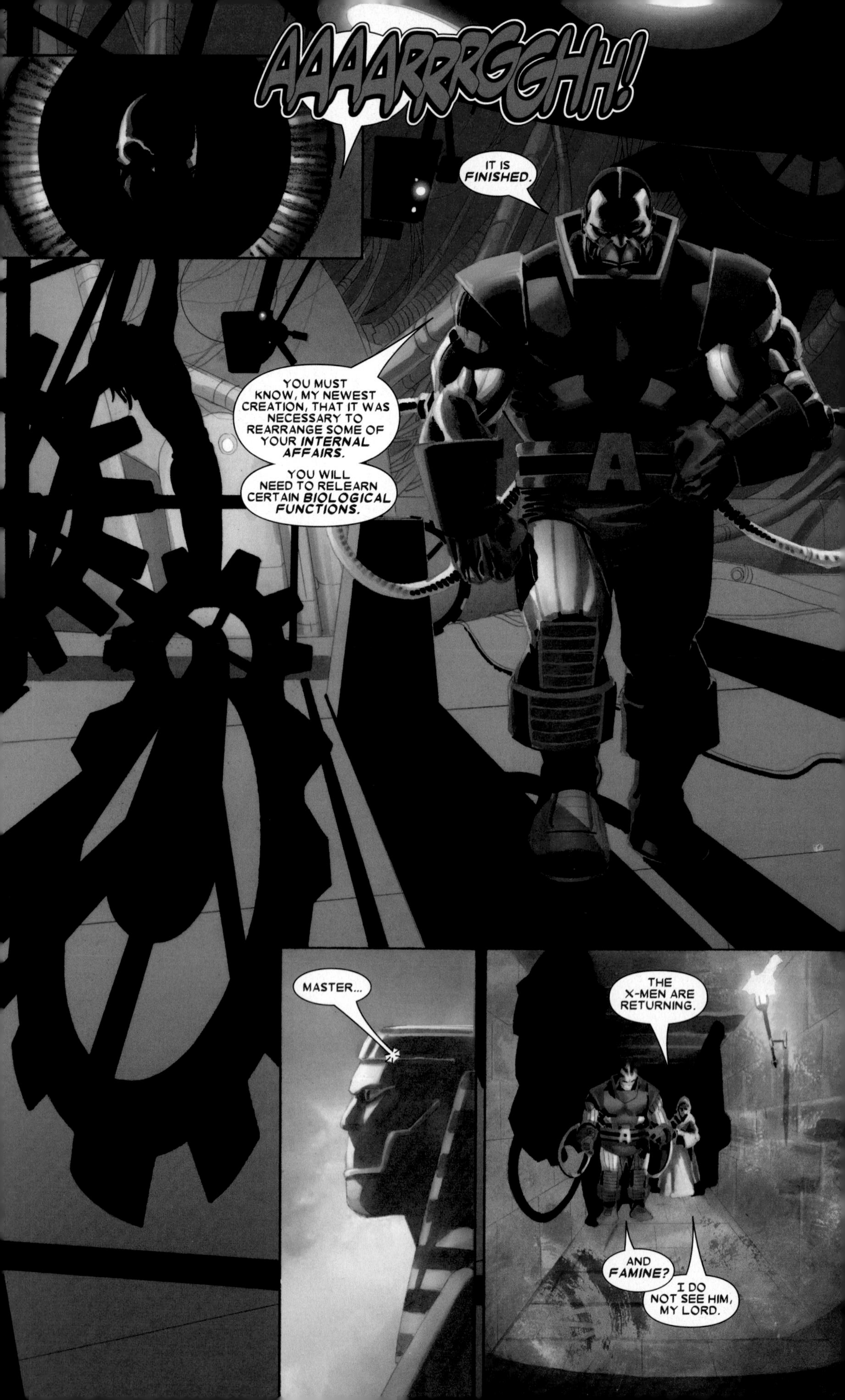
AAAARRRGGHH!
IT IS FINISHED.
YOU MUST KNOW, MY NEWEST CREATION, THAT IT WAS NECESSARY TO REARRANGE SOME OF YOUR INTERNAL AFFAIRS.
YOU WILL NEED TO RELEARN CERTAIN BIOLOGICAL FUNCTIONS.
MASTER...
THE X-MEN ARE RETURNING.
AND FAMINE?
I DO NOT SEE HIM, MY LORD.

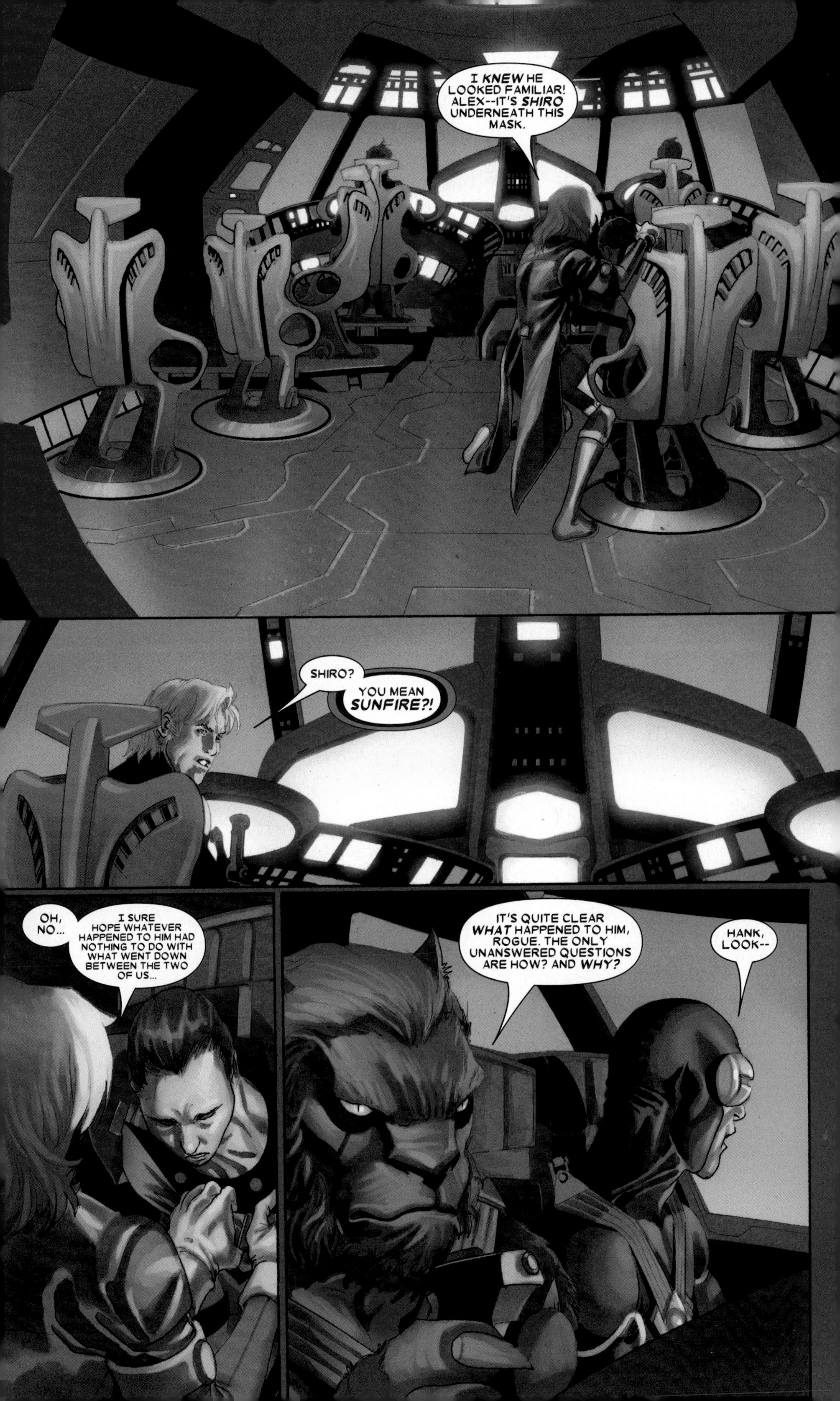
I KNEW HE LOOKED FAMILIAR! ALEX--IT'S SHIRO UNDERNEATH THIS MASK.
SHIRO?
YOU MEAN SUNFIRE?!
OH, NO...
I SURE HOPE WHATEVER HAPPENED TO HIM HAD NOTHING TO DO WITH WHAT WENT DOWN BETWEEN THE TWO OF US...
IT'S QUITE CLEAR WHAT HAPPENED TO HIM, ROGUE. THE ONLY UNANSWERED QUESTIONS ARE HOW? AND WHY?
HANK, LOOK--

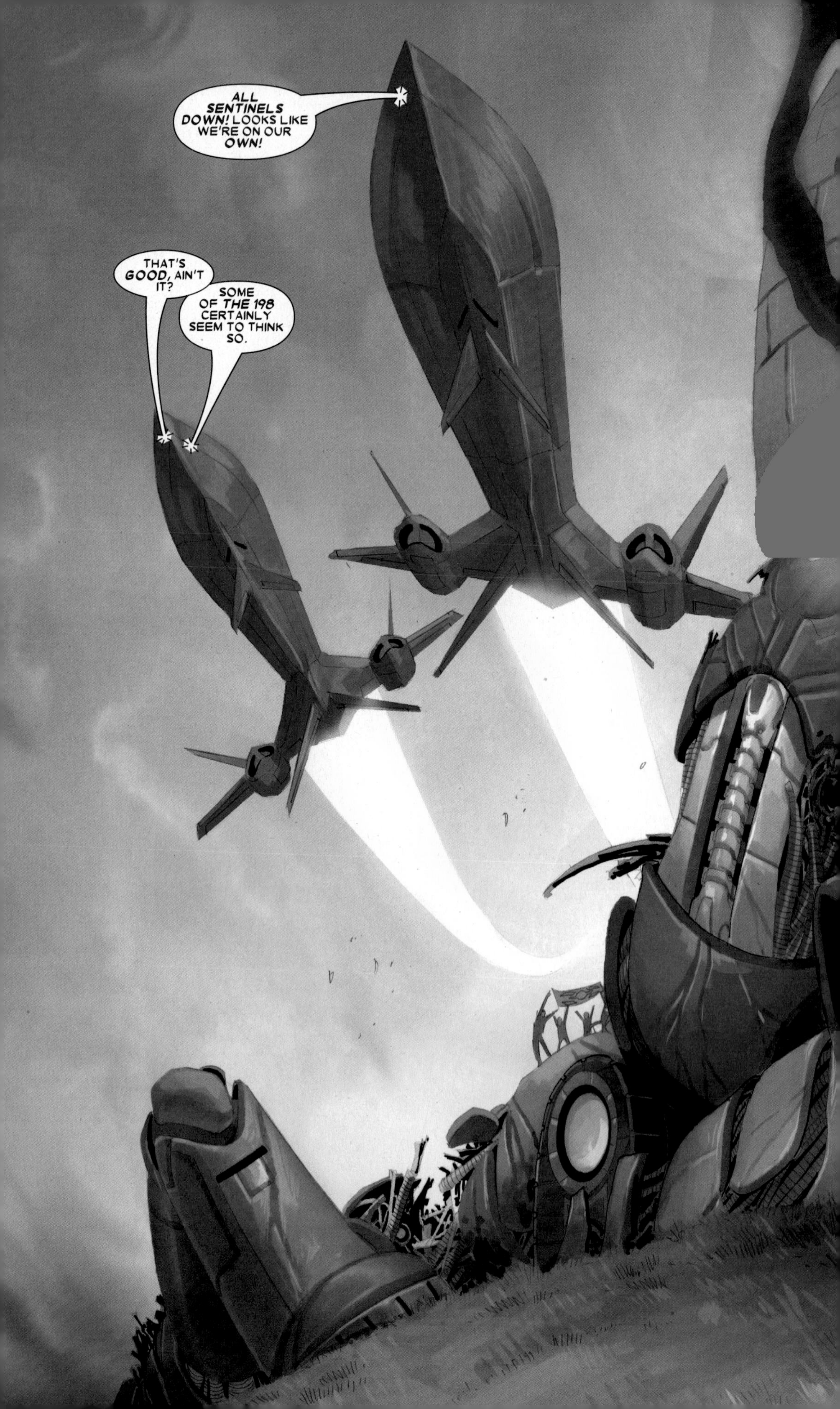
ALL SENTINELS DOWN! LOOKS LIKE WE'RE ON OUR OWN!
THAT'S GOOD, AIN'T IT?
SOME OF THE 198 CERTAINLY SEEM TO THINK SO.

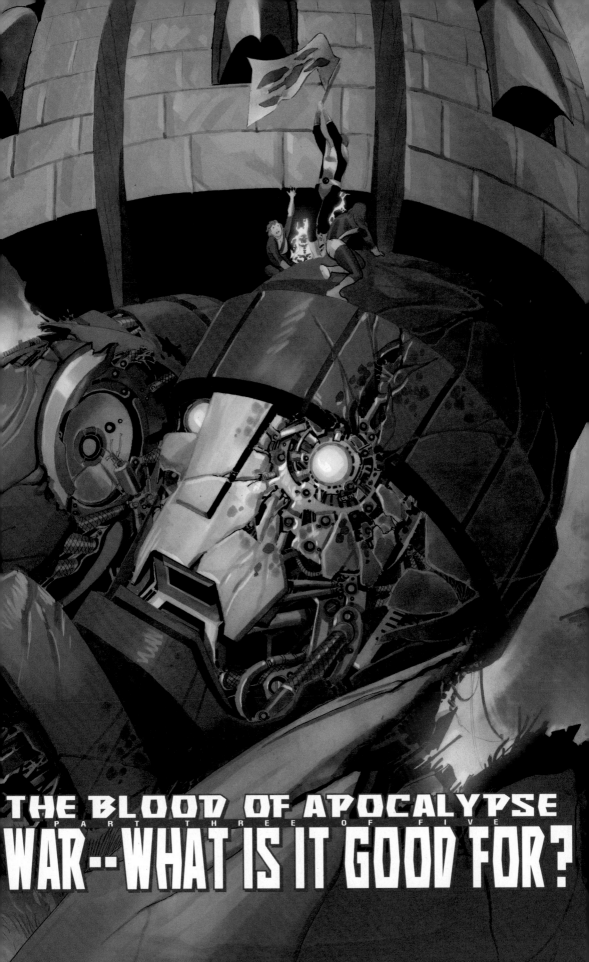

THE BLOOD OF APOCALYPSE
PART THREE OF FIVE
WAR--WHAT IS IT GOOD FOR?

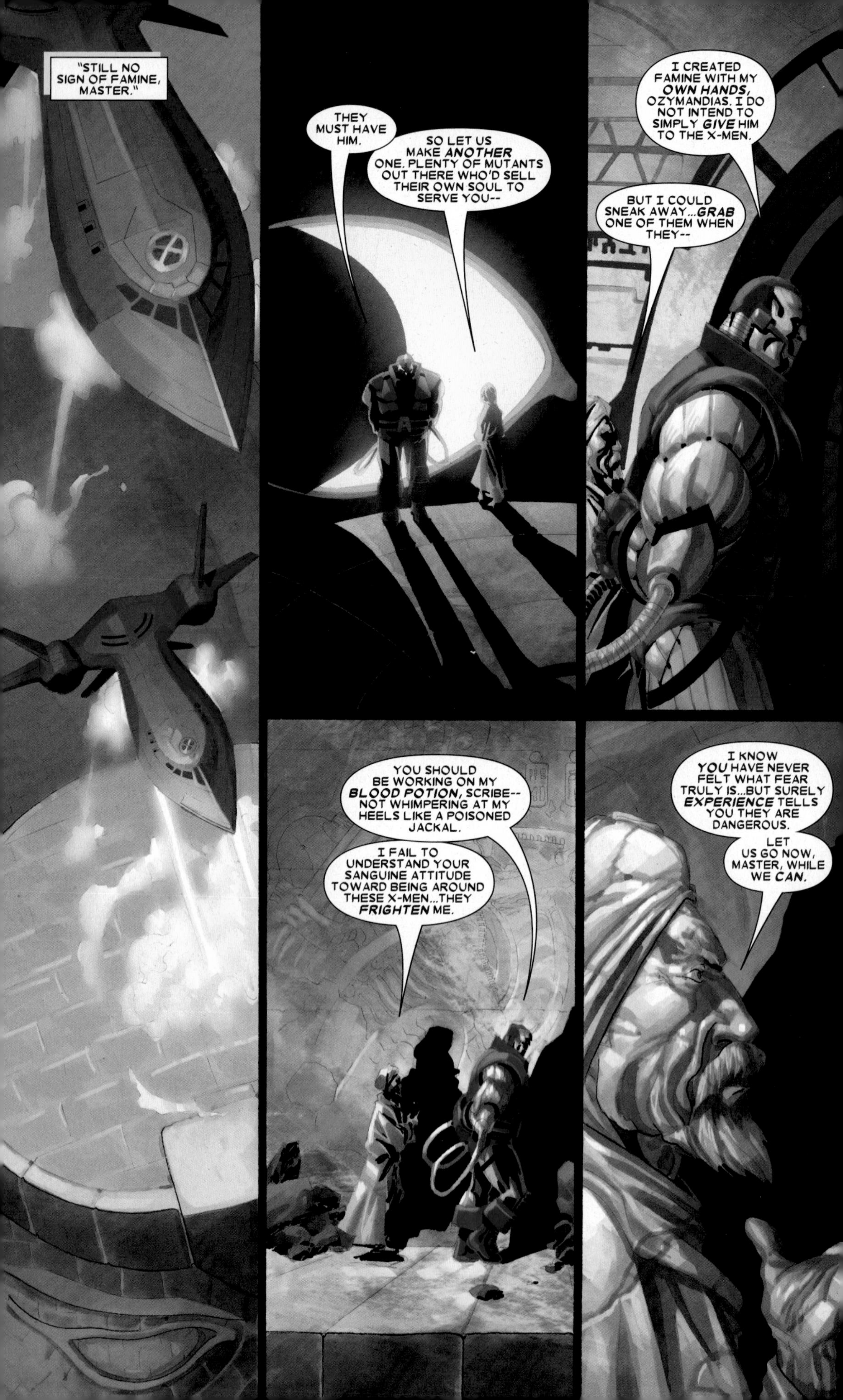
"STILL NO SIGN OF FAMINE, MASTER."
THEY MUST HAVE HIM.
SO LET US MAKE ANOTHER ONE. PLENTY OF MUTANTS OUT THERE WHO'D SELL THEIR OWN SOUL TO SERVE YOU--
I CREATED FAMINE WITH MY OWN HANDS, OZYMANDIAS. I DO NOT INTEND TO SIMPLY GIVE HIM TO THE X-MEN.
BUT I COULD SNEAK AWAY...GRAB ONE OF THEM WHEN THEY--
YOU SHOULD BE WORKING ON MY BLOOD POTION, SCRIBE--NOT WHIMPERING AT MY HEELS LIKE A POISONED JACKAL.
I FAIL TO UNDERSTAND YOUR SANGUINE ATTITUDE TOWARD BEING AROUND THESE X-MEN...THEY FRIGHTEN ME.
I KNOW YOU HAVE NEVER FELT WHAT FEAR TRULY IS...BUT SURELY EXPERIENCE TELLS YOU THEY ARE DANGEROUS.
LET US GO NOW, MASTER, WHILE WE CAN.

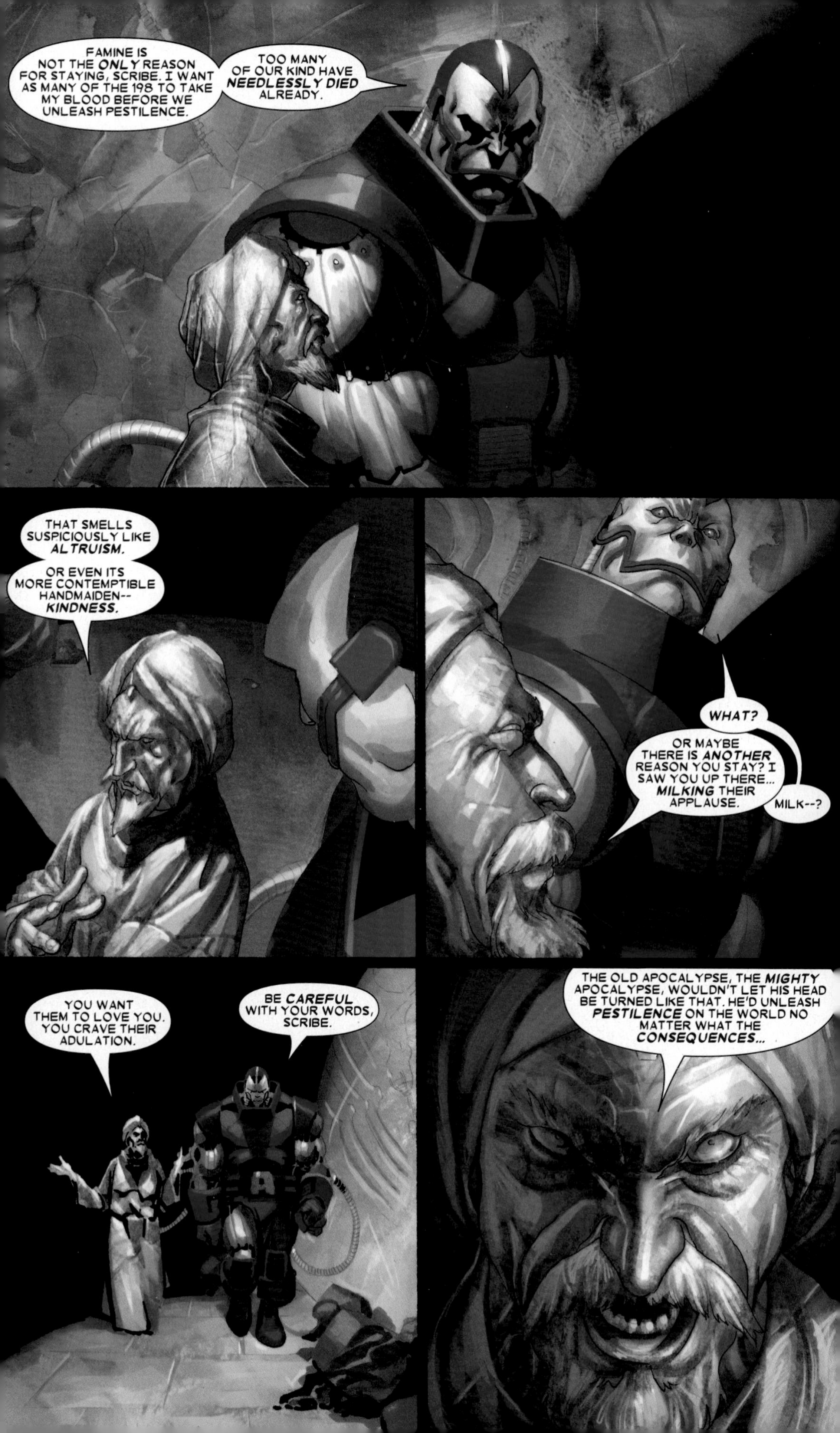
FAMINE IS NOT THE ONLY REASON FOR STAYING, SCRIBE. I WANT AS MANY OF THE 198 TO TAKE MY BLOOD BEFORE WE UNLEASH PESTILENCE.
TOO MANY OF OUR KIND HAVE NEEDLESSLY DIED ALREADY.
THAT SMELLS SUSPICIOUSLY LIKE ALTRUISM.
OR EVEN ITS MORE CONTEMPTIBLE HANDMAIDEN-- KINDNESS.
WHAT?
OR MAYBE THERE IS ANOTHER REASON YOU STAY? I SAW YOU UP THERE... MILKING THEIR APPLAUSE.
MILK--?
YOU WANT THEM TO LOVE YOU. YOU CRAVE THEIR ADULATION.
BE CAREFUL WITH YOUR WORDS, SCRIBE.
THE OLD APOCALYPSE, THE MIGHTY APOCALYPSE, WOULDN'T LET HIS HEAD BE TURNED LIKE THAT. HE'D UNLEASH PESTILENCE ON THE WORLD NO MATTER WHAT THE CONSEQUENCES...

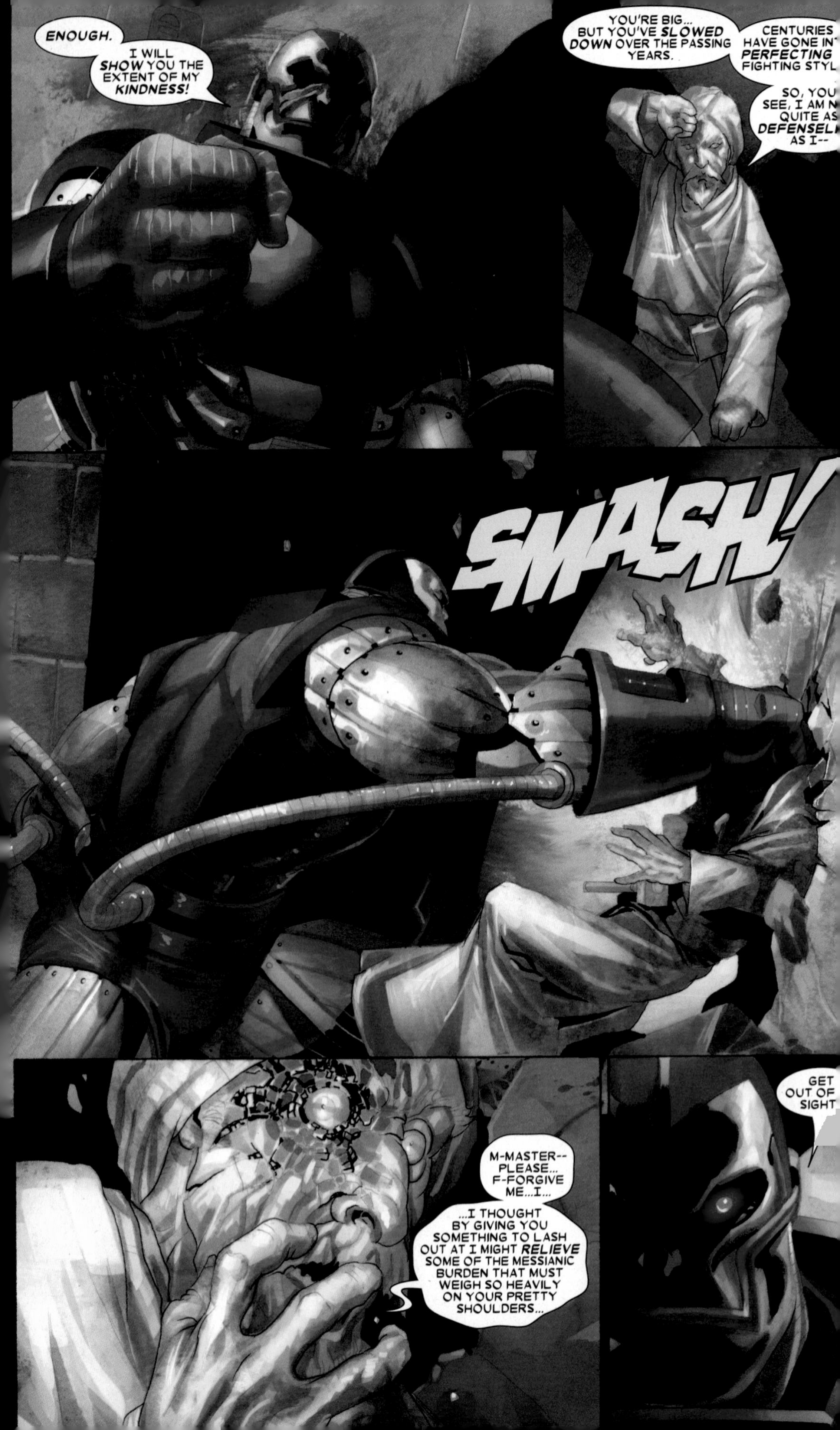
ENOUGH.
I WILL SHOW YOU THE EXTENT OF MY KINDNESS!
YOU'RE BIG... BUT YOU'VE SLOWED DOWN OVER THE PASSING YEARS.
CENTURIES HAVE GONE IN PERFECTING FIGHTING STYL
SO, YOU SEE, I AM N QUITE AS DEFENSEL AS I--
SMASH!
M-MASTER-- PLEASE... F-FORGIVE ME...I...
...I THOUGHT BY GIVING YOU SOMETHING TO LASH OUT AT I MIGHT RELIEVE SOME OF THE MESSIANIC BURDEN THAT MUST WEIGH SO HEAVILY ON YOUR PRETTY SHOULDERS...
GET OUT OF SIGHT

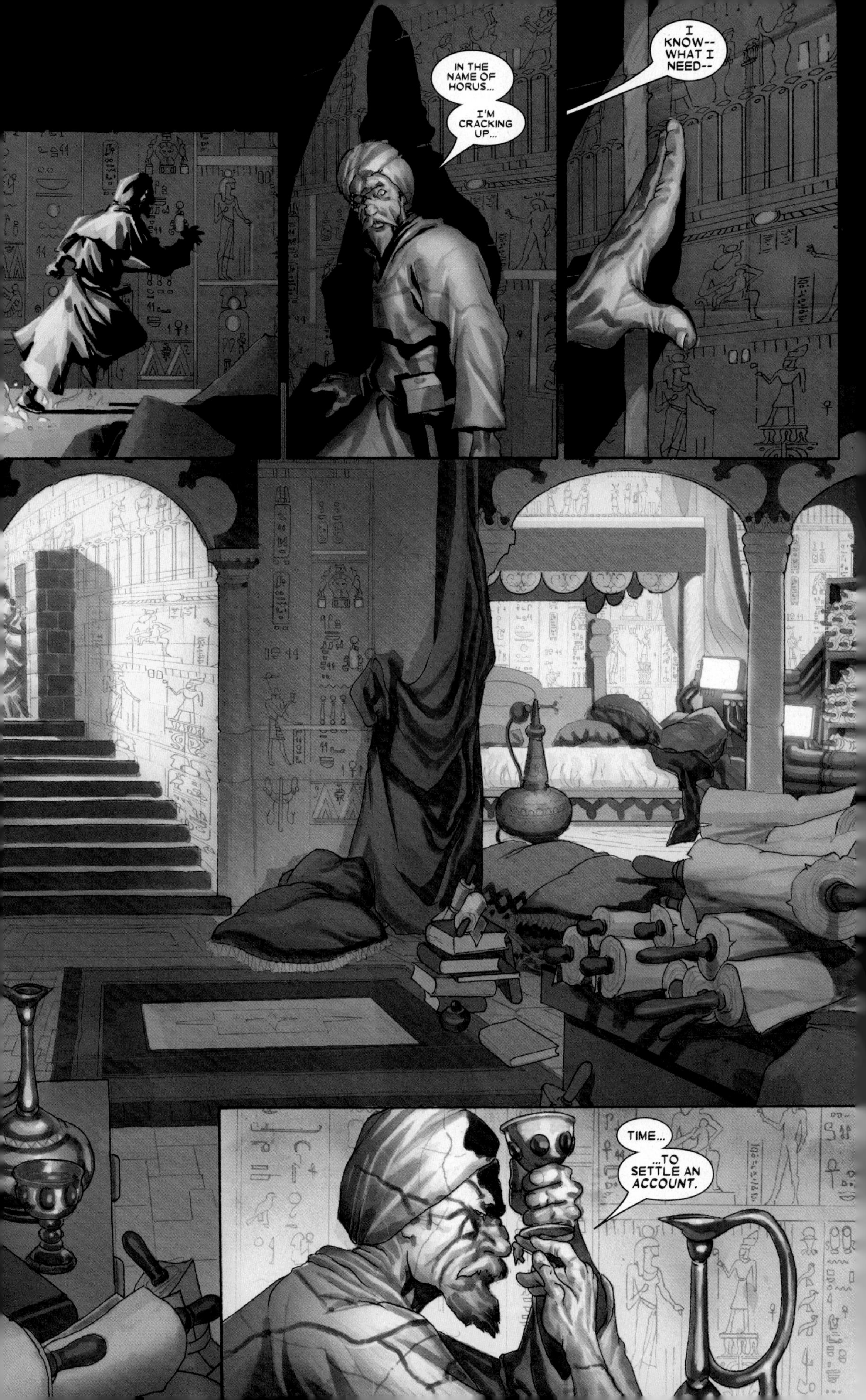
IN THE NAME OF HORUS...
I'M CRACKING UP...
I KNOW-- WHAT I NEED--
TIME...
...TO SETTLE AN ACCOUNT.

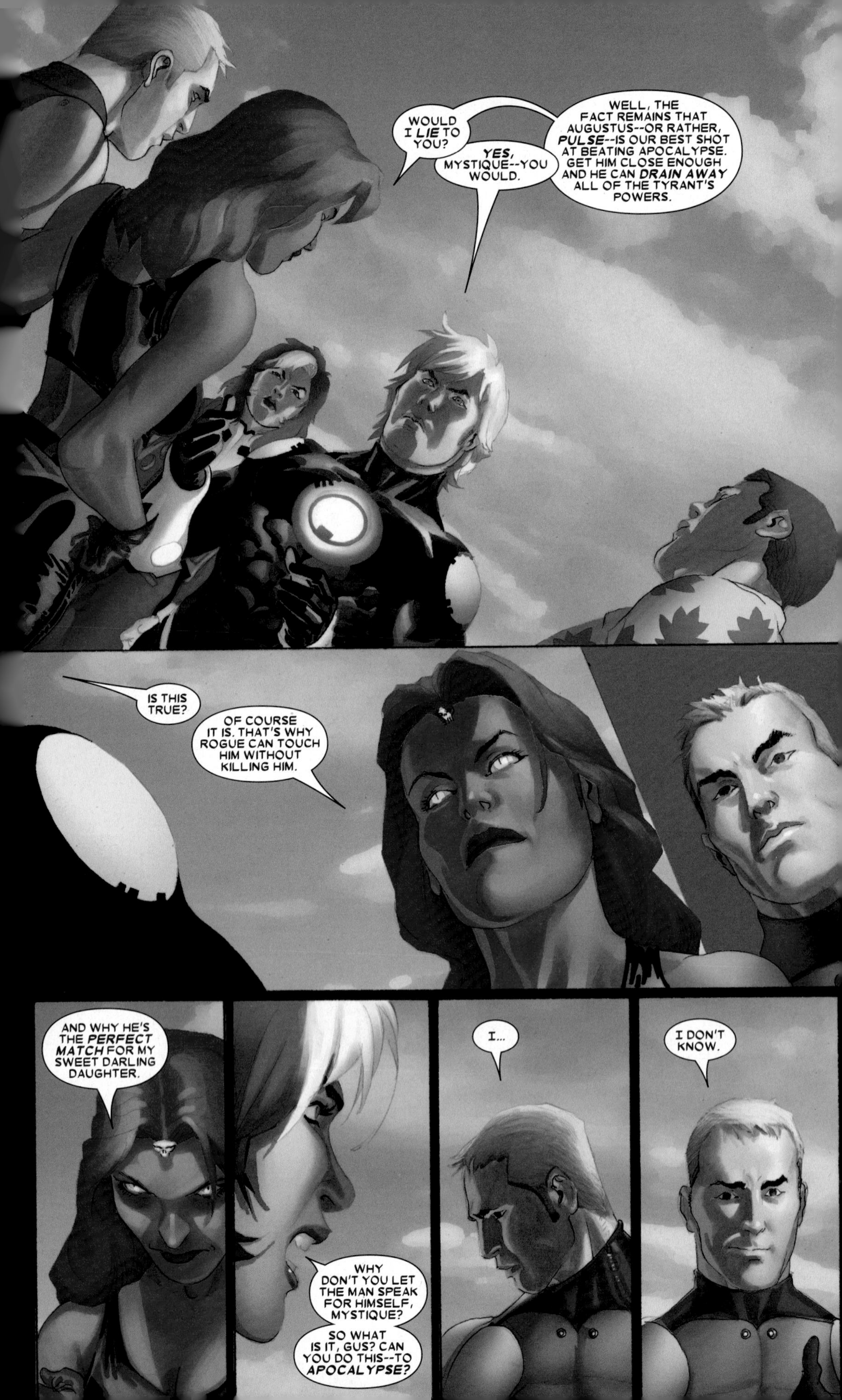

WOULD I *LIE* TO YOU?
YES, MYSTIQUE--YOU WOULD.
WELL, THE FACT REMAINS THAT AUGUSTUS--OR RATHER, *PULSE*--IS OUR BEST SHOT AT BEATING APOCALYPSE. GET HIM CLOSE ENOUGH AND HE CAN *DRAIN AWAY* ALL OF THE TYRANT'S POWERS.
IS THIS TRUE?
OF COURSE IT IS. THAT'S WHY ROGUE CAN TOUCH HIM WITHOUT KILLING HIM.
AND WHY HE'S THE *PERFECT MATCH* FOR MY SWEET DARLING DAUGHTER.
WHY DON'T YOU LET THE MAN SPEAK FOR HIMSELF, MYSTIQUE?
SO WHAT IS IT, GUS? CAN YOU DO THIS--TO *APOCALYPSE?*
I...
I DON'T KNOW.

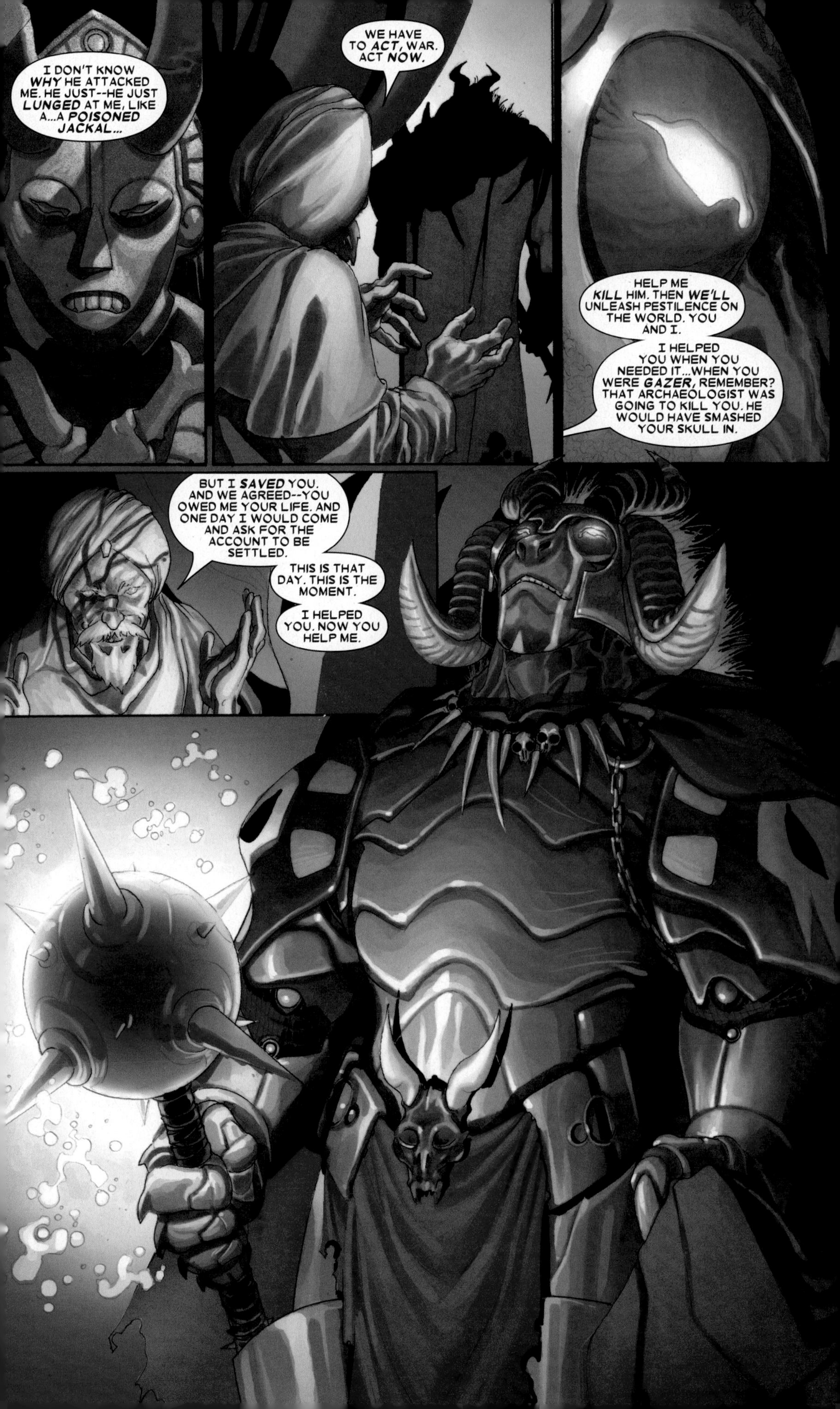

I DON'T KNOW **WHY** HE ATTACKED ME. HE JUST--HE JUST **LUNGED** AT ME, LIKE A...A **POISONED JACKAL**...
WE HAVE TO **ACT**, WAR. ACT **NOW**.
HELP ME **KILL** HIM. THEN **WE'LL** UNLEASH PESTILENCE ON THE WORLD. YOU AND I.
I HELPED YOU WHEN YOU NEEDED IT...WHEN YOU WERE **GAZER**, REMEMBER? THAT ARCHAEOLOGIST WAS GOING TO KILL YOU. HE WOULD HAVE SMASHED YOUR SKULL IN.
BUT I **SAVED** YOU. AND WE AGREED--YOU OWED ME YOUR LIFE. AND ONE DAY I WOULD COME AND ASK FOR THE ACCOUNT TO BE SETTLED.
THIS IS THAT DAY. THIS IS THE MOMENT.
I HELPED YOU. NOW YOU HELP ME.

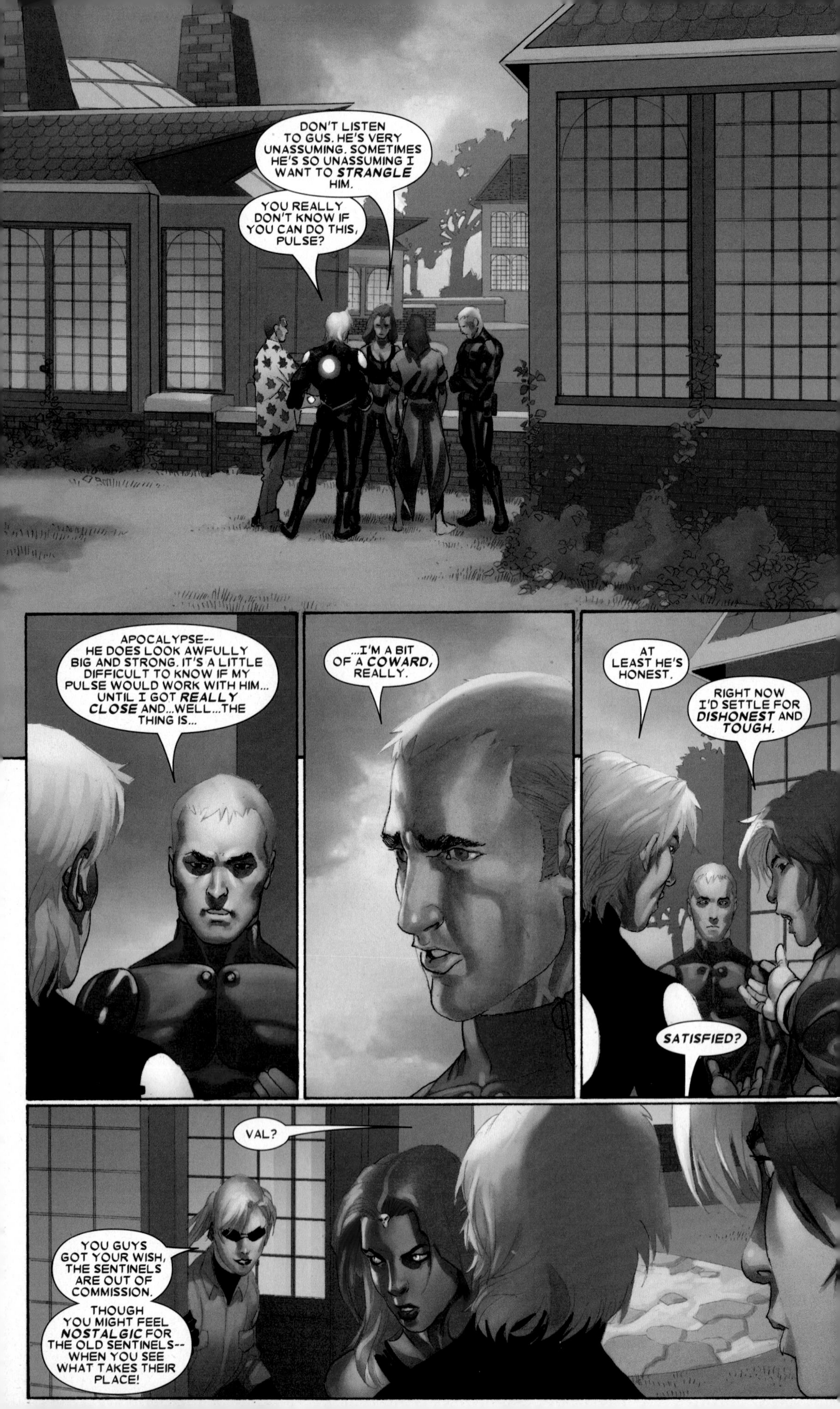
DON'T LISTEN TO GUS. HE'S VERY UNASSUMING. SOMETIMES HE'S SO UNASSUMING I WANT TO STRANGLE HIM.
YOU REALLY DON'T KNOW IF YOU CAN DO THIS, PULSE?
APOCALYPSE-- HE DOES LOOK AWFULLY BIG AND STRONG. IT'S A LITTLE DIFFICULT TO KNOW IF MY PULSE WOULD WORK WITH HIM... UNTIL I GOT REALLY CLOSE AND...WELL...THE THING IS...
...I'M A BIT OF A COWARD, REALLY.
AT LEAST HE'S HONEST.
RIGHT NOW I'D SETTLE FOR DISHONEST AND TOUGH.
SATISFIED?
VAL?
YOU GUYS GOT YOUR WISH, THE SENTINELS ARE OUT OF COMMISSION.
THOUGH YOU MIGHT FEEL NOSTALGIC FOR THE OLD SENTINELS-- WHEN YOU SEE WHAT TAKES THEIR PLACE!

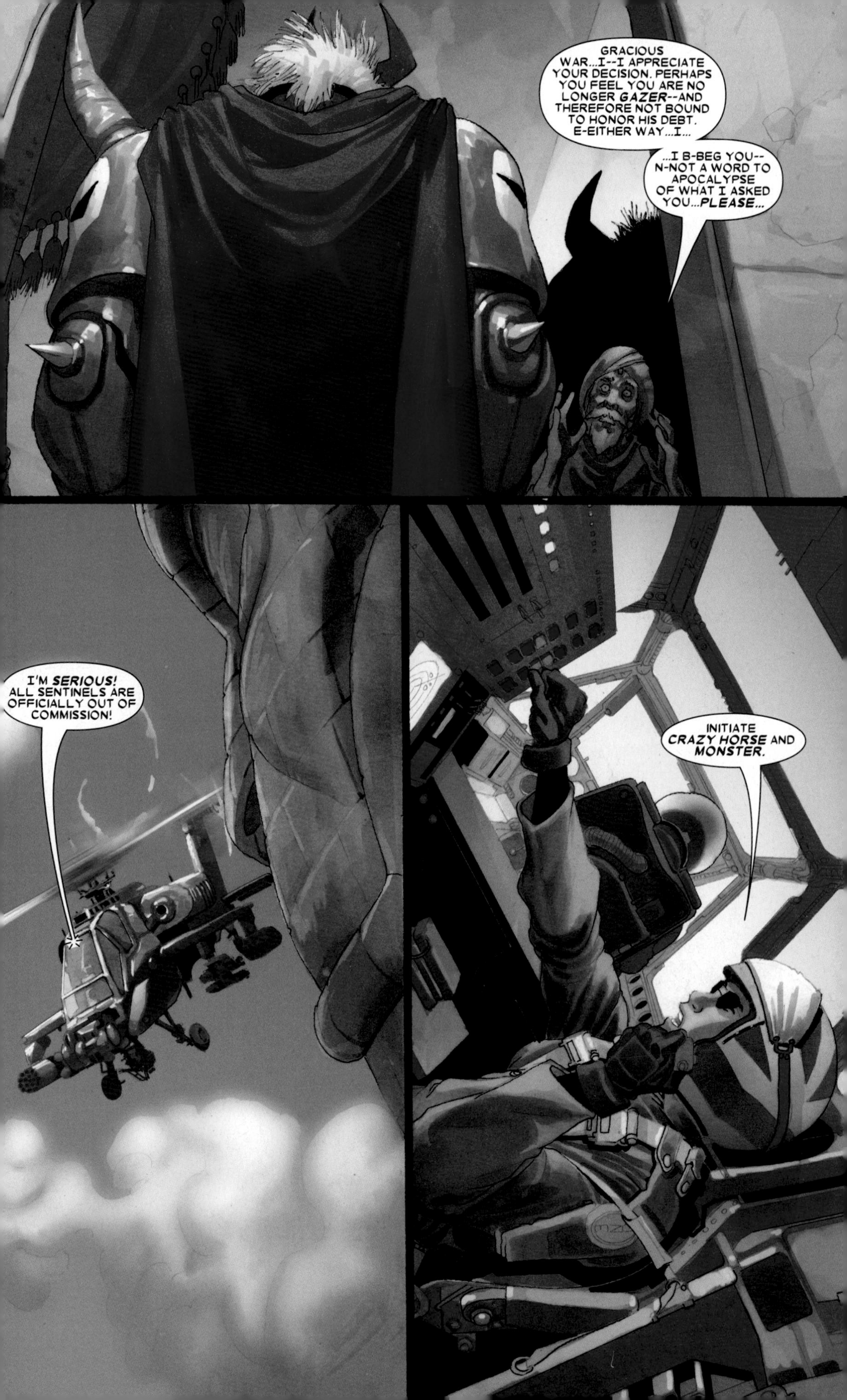
GRACIOUS WAR...I--I APPRECIATE YOUR DECISION. PERHAPS YOU FEEL YOU ARE NO LONGER GAZER--AND THEREFORE NOT BOUND TO HONOR HIS DEBT. E-EITHER WAY...I...
...I B-BEG YOU-- N-NOT A WORD TO APOCALYPSE OF WHAT I ASKED YOU...PLEASE...
I'M SERIOUS! ALL SENTINELS ARE OFFICIALLY OUT OF COMMISSION!
INITIATE CRAZY HORSE AND MONSTER.

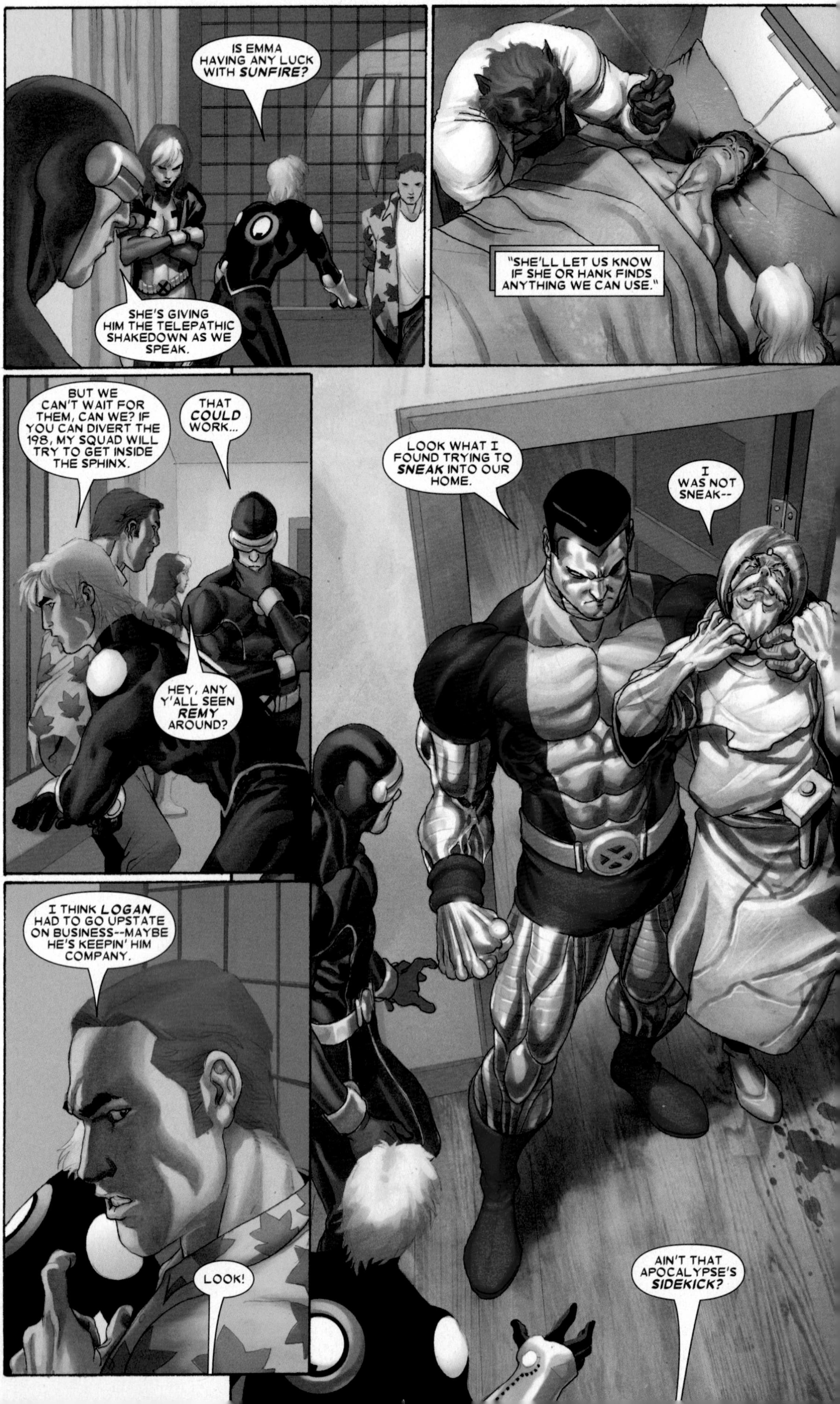
IS EMMA HAVING ANY LUCK WITH SUNFIRE?
SHE'S GIVING HIM THE TELEPATHIC SHAKEDOWN AS WE SPEAK.
"SHE'LL LET US KNOW IF SHE OR HANK FINDS ANYTHING WE CAN USE."
BUT WE CAN'T WAIT FOR THEM, CAN WE? IF YOU CAN DIVERT THE 198, MY SQUAD WILL TRY TO GET INSIDE THE SPHINX.
THAT COULD WORK...
HEY, ANY Y'ALL SEEN REMY AROUND?
I THINK LOGAN HAD TO GO UPSTATE ON BUSINESS--MAYBE HE'S KEEPIN' HIM COMPANY.
LOOK!
LOOK WHAT I FOUND TRYING TO SNEAK INTO OUR HOME.
I WAS NOT SNEAK--
AIN'T THAT APOCALYPSE'S SIDEKICK?

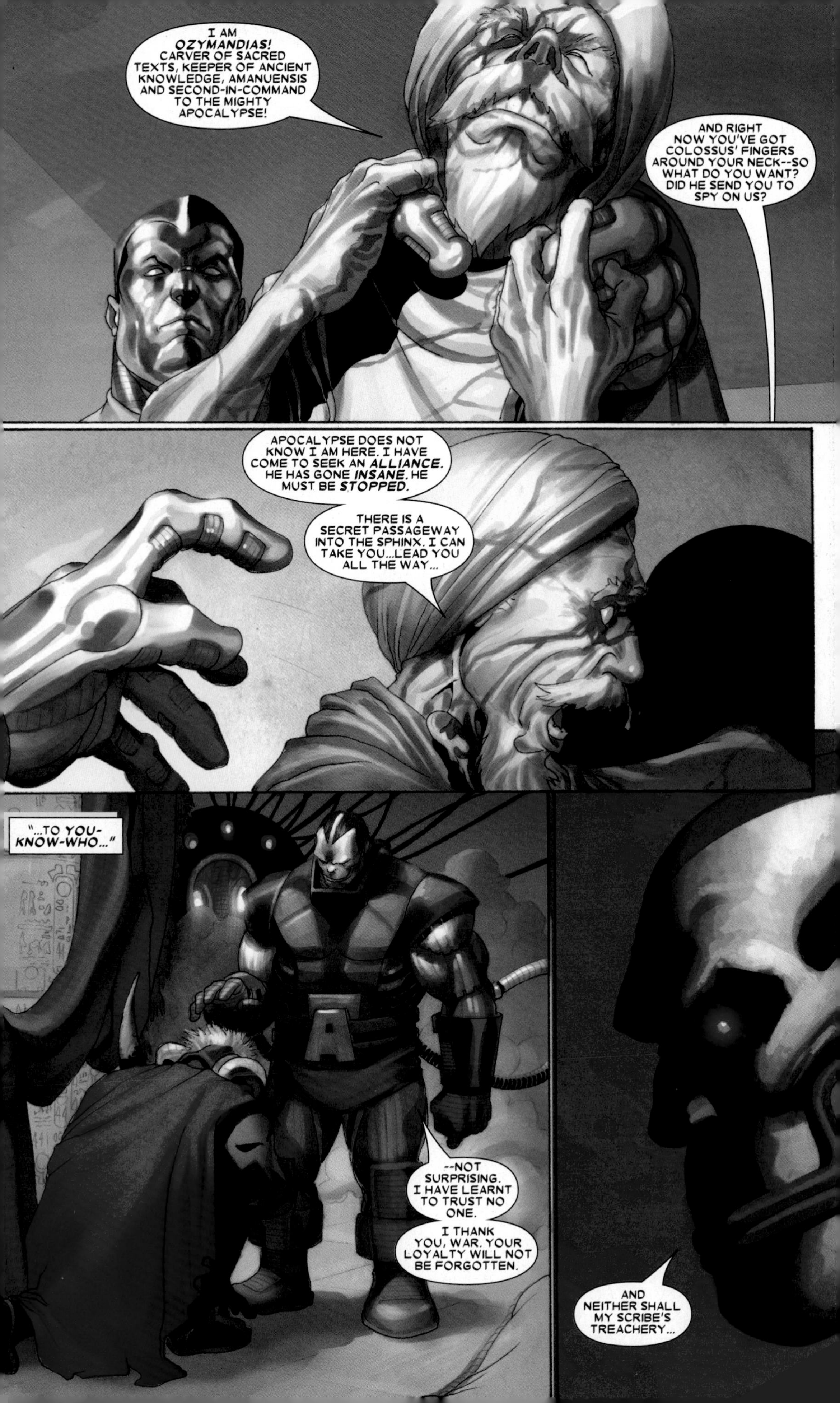

I AM OZYMANDIAS! CARVER OF SACRED TEXTS, KEEPER OF ANCIENT KNOWLEDGE, AMANUENSIS AND SECOND-IN-COMMAND TO THE MIGHTY APOCALYPSE!
AND RIGHT NOW YOU'VE GOT COLOSSUS' FINGERS AROUND YOUR NECK--SO WHAT DO YOU WANT? DID HE SEND YOU TO SPY ON US?
APOCALYPSE DOES NOT KNOW I AM HERE. I HAVE COME TO SEEK AN ALLIANCE. HE HAS GONE INSANE. HE MUST BE STOPPED.
THERE IS A SECRET PASSAGEWAY INTO THE SPHINX. I CAN TAKE YOU...LEAD YOU ALL THE WAY...
"...TO YOU-KNOW-WHO..."
--NOT SURPRISING. I HAVE LEARNT TO TRUST NO ONE.
I THANK YOU, WAR. YOUR LOYALTY WILL NOT BE FORGOTTEN.
AND NEITHER SHALL MY SCRIBE'S TREACHERY...

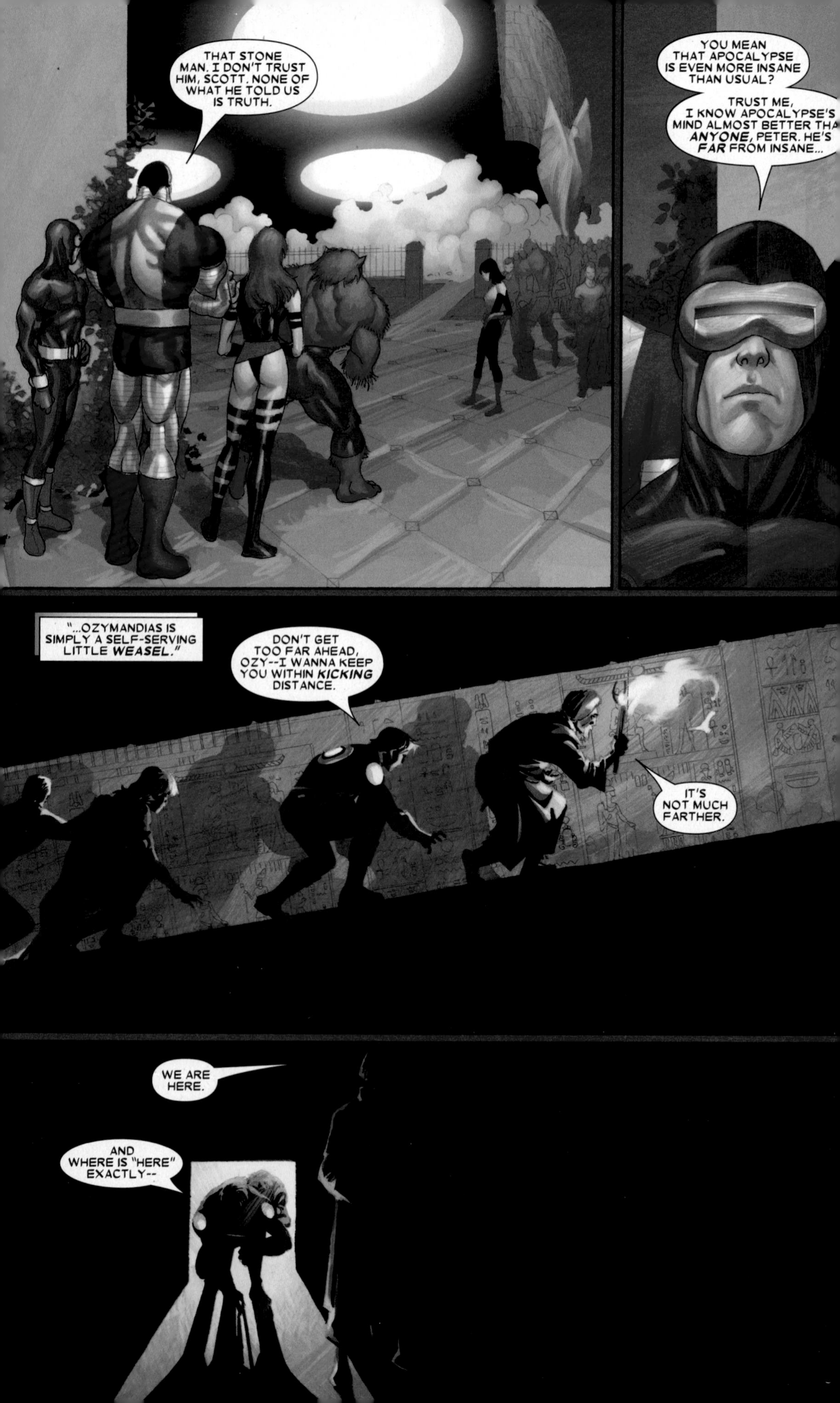
THAT STONE MAN. I DON'T TRUST HIM, SCOTT. NONE OF WHAT HE TOLD US IS TRUTH.
YOU MEAN THAT APOCALYPSE IS EVEN MORE INSANE THAN USUAL?
TRUST ME, I KNOW APOCALYPSE'S MIND ALMOST BETTER THA ANYONE, PETER. HE'S FAR FROM INSANE...
"...OZYMANDIAS IS SIMPLY A SELF-SERVING LITTLE WEASEL."
DON'T GET TOO FAR AHEAD, OZY--I WANNA KEEP YOU WITHIN KICKING DISTANCE.
IT'S NOT MUCH FARTHER.
WE ARE HERE.
AND WHERE IS "HERE" EXACTLY--

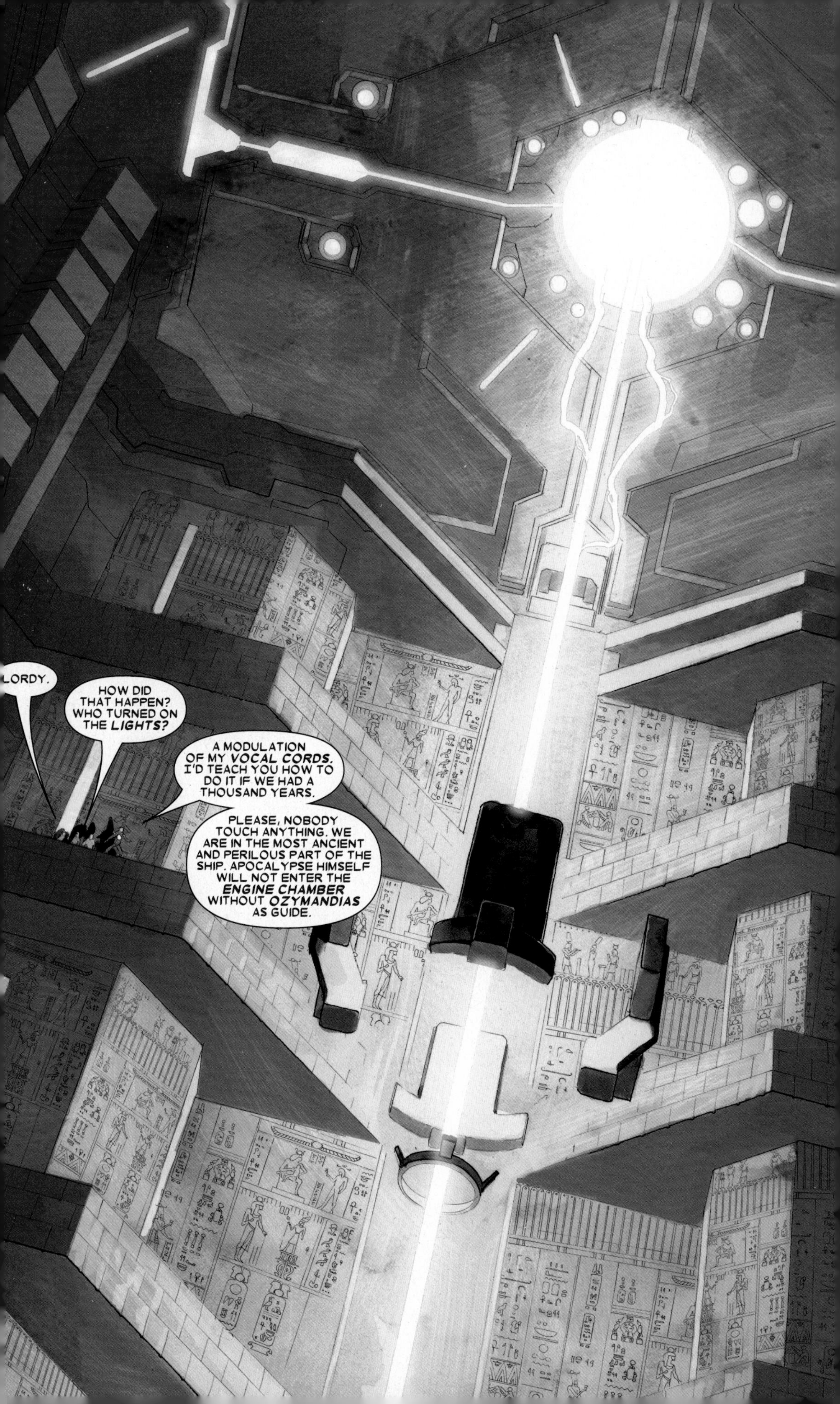

LORDY.
HOW DID THAT HAPPEN? WHO TURNED ON THE LIGHTS?
A MODULATION OF MY VOCAL CORDS. I'D TEACH YOU HOW TO DO IT IF WE HAD A THOUSAND YEARS.
PLEASE, NOBODY TOUCH ANYTHING. WE ARE IN THE MOST ANCIENT AND PERILOUS PART OF THE SHIP. APOCALYPSE HIMSELF WILL NOT ENTER THE ENGINE CHAMBER WITHOUT OZYMANDIAS AS GUIDE.

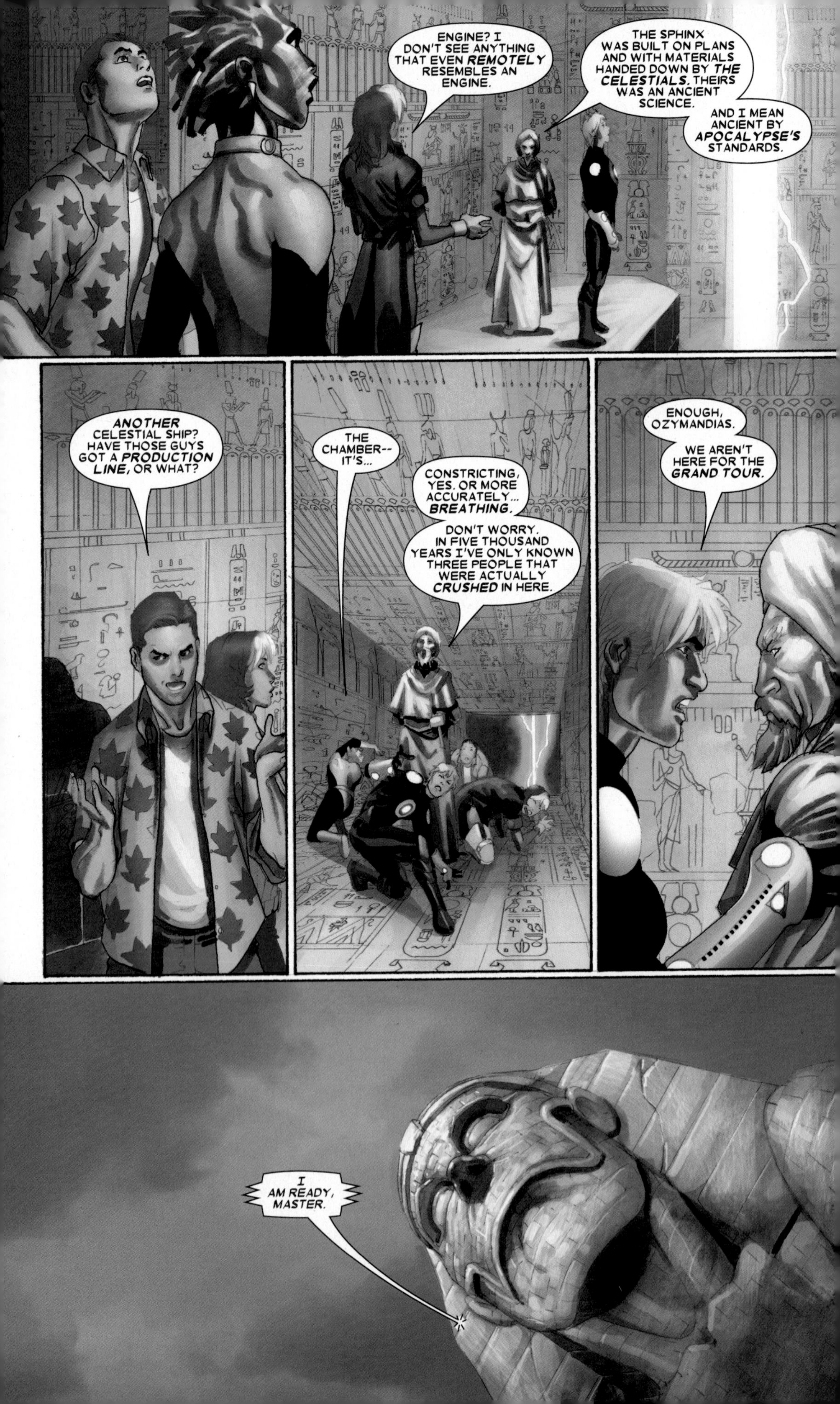
ENGINE? I DON'T SEE ANYTHING THAT EVEN REMOTELY RESEMBLES AN ENGINE.
THE SPHINX WAS BUILT ON PLANS AND WITH MATERIALS HANDED DOWN BY THE CELESTIALS. THEIRS WAS AN ANCIENT SCIENCE.
AND I MEAN ANCIENT BY APOCALYPSE'S STANDARDS.
ANOTHER CELESTIAL SHIP? HAVE THOSE GUYS GOT A PRODUCTION LINE, OR WHAT?
THE CHAMBER-- IT'S...
CONSTRICTING, YES. OR MORE ACCURATELY... BREATHING.
DON'T WORRY. IN FIVE THOUSAND YEARS I'VE ONLY KNOWN THREE PEOPLE THAT WERE ACTUALLY CRUSHED IN HERE.
ENOUGH, OZYMANDIAS.
WE AREN'T HERE FOR THE GRAND TOUR.
I AM READY, MASTER.

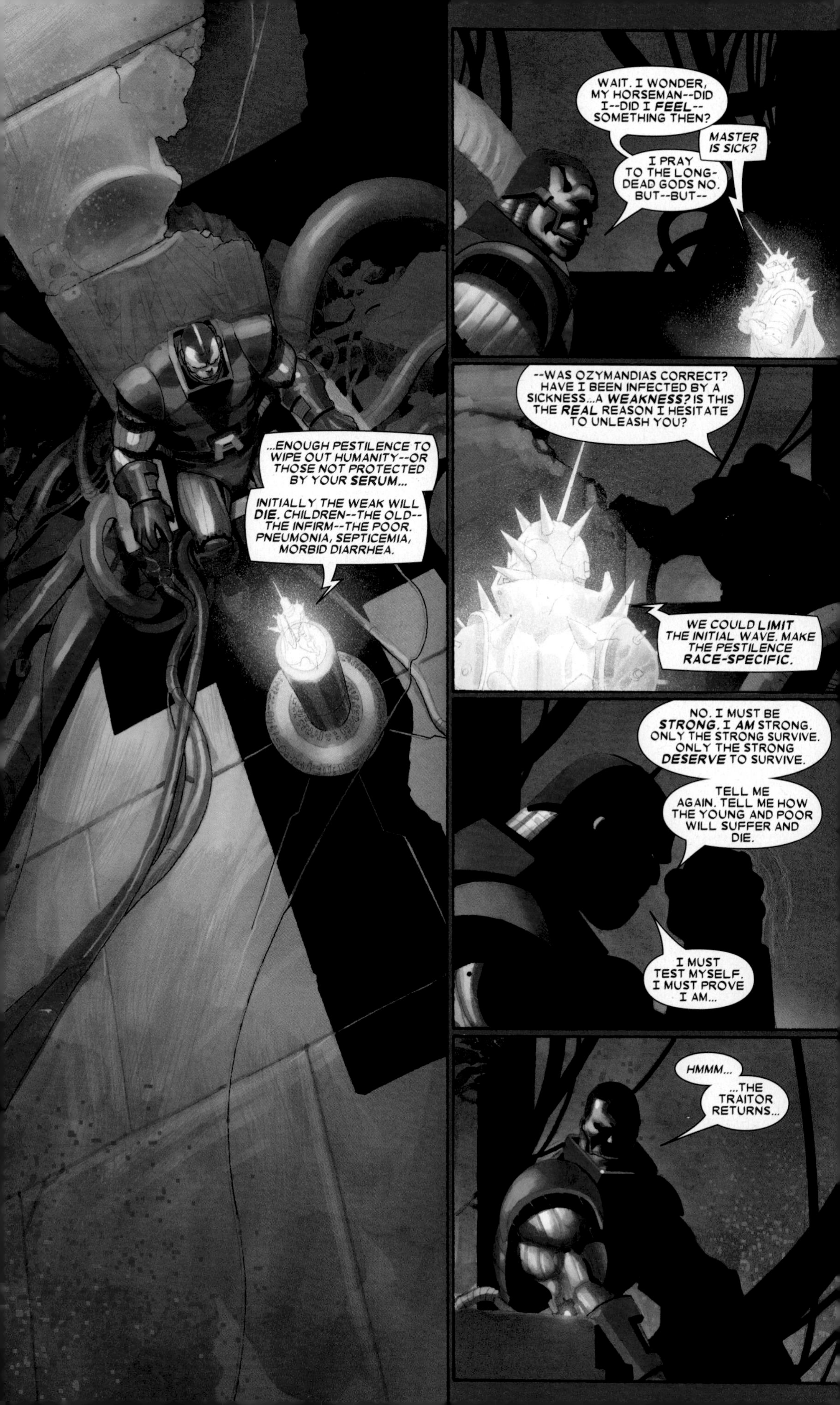
...ENOUGH PESTILENCE TO WIPE OUT HUMANITY--OR THOSE NOT PROTECTED BY YOUR SERUM...
INITIALLY THE WEAK WILL DIE. CHILDREN--THE OLD--THE INFIRM--THE POOR. PNEUMONIA, SEPTICEMIA, MORBID DIARRHEA.
WAIT. I WONDER, MY HORSEMAN--DID I--DID I FEEL--SOMETHING THEN?
MASTER IS SICK?
I PRAY TO THE LONG-DEAD GODS NO. BUT--BUT--
--WAS OZYMANDIAS CORRECT? HAVE I BEEN INFECTED BY A SICKNESS...A WEAKNESS? IS THIS THE REAL REASON I HESITATE TO UNLEASH YOU?
WE COULD LIMIT THE INITIAL WAVE. MAKE THE PESTILENCE RACE-SPECIFIC.
NO. I MUST BE STRONG. I AM STRONG. ONLY THE STRONG SURVIVE. ONLY THE STRONG DESERVE TO SURVIVE.
TELL ME AGAIN. TELL ME HOW THE YOUNG AND POOR WILL SUFFER AND DIE.
I MUST TEST MYSELF. I MUST PROVE I AM...
HMMM...
...THE TRAITOR RETURNS...

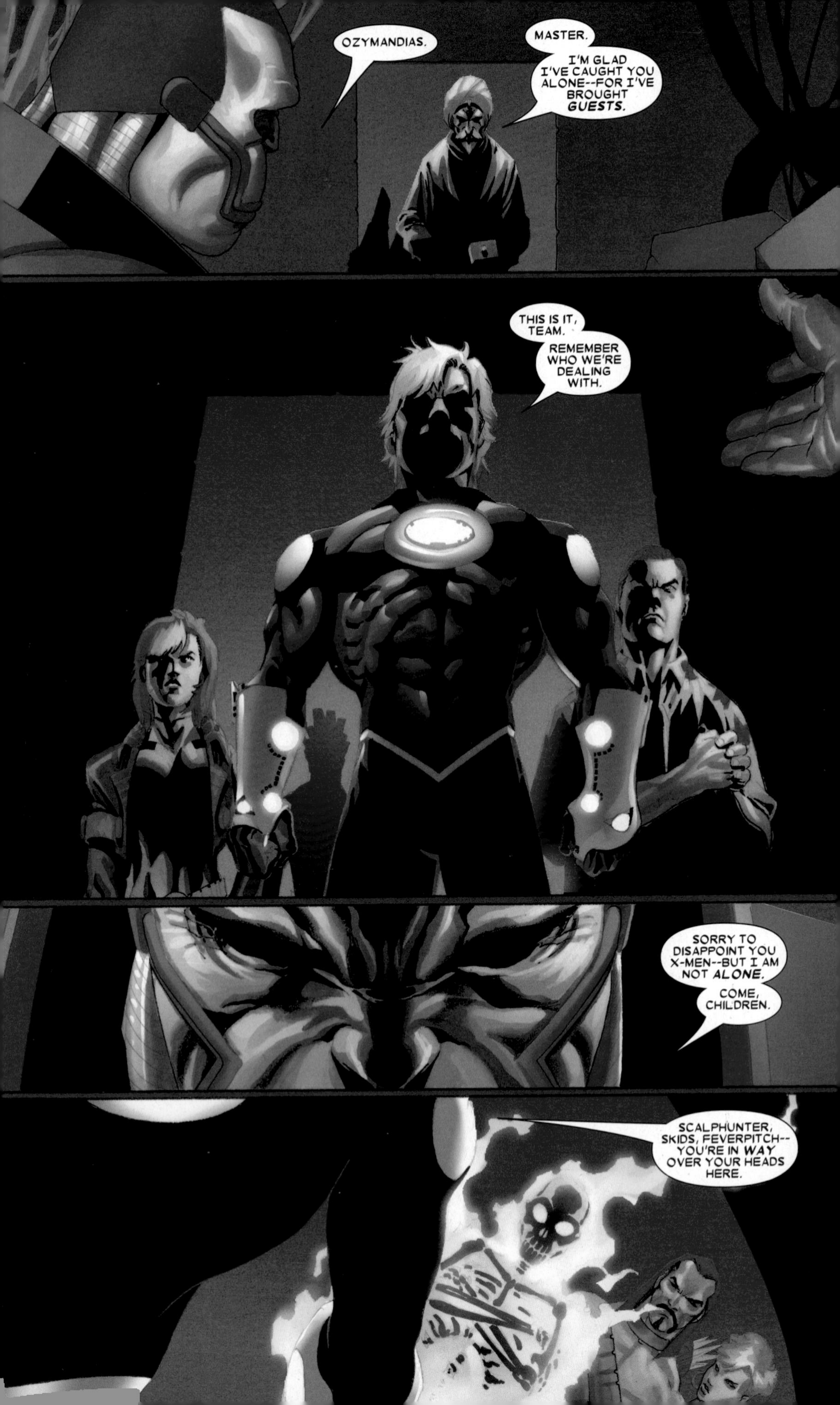

OZYMANDIAS.
MASTER.
I'M GLAD I'VE CAUGHT YOU ALONE--FOR I'VE BROUGHT GUESTS.
THIS IS IT, TEAM.
REMEMBER WHO WE'RE DEALING WITH.
SORRY TO DISAPPOINT YOU X-MEN--BUT I AM NOT ALONE.
COME, CHILDREN.
SCALPHUNTER, SKIDS, FEVERPITCH-- YOU'RE IN WAY OVER YOUR HEADS HERE.

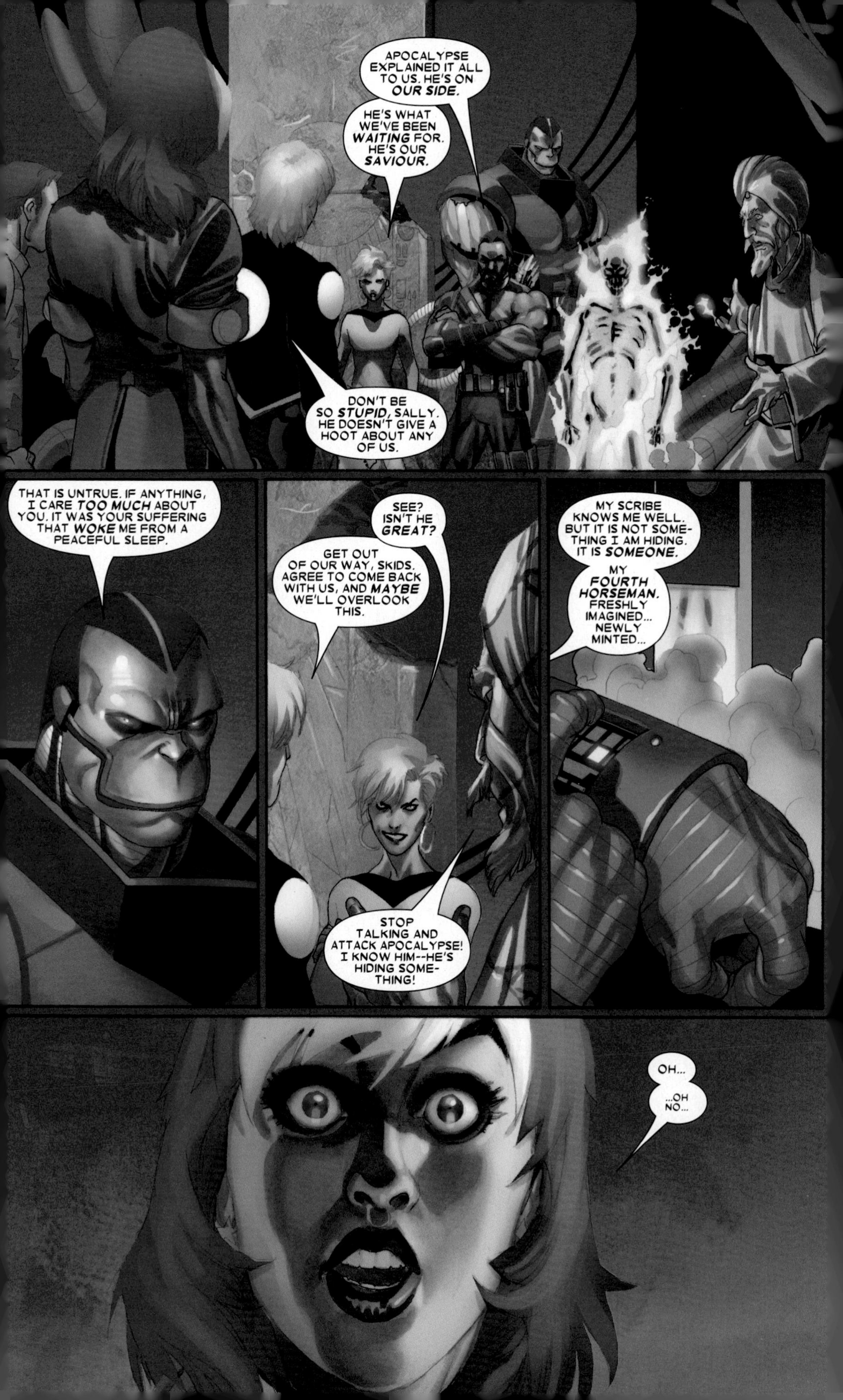

APOCALYPSE EXPLAINED IT ALL TO US. HE'S ON OUR SIDE.
HE'S WHAT WE'VE BEEN WAITING FOR. HE'S OUR SAVIOUR.
DON'T BE SO STUPID, SALLY. HE DOESN'T GIVE A HOOT ABOUT ANY OF US.
THAT IS UNTRUE. IF ANYTHING, I CARE TOO MUCH ABOUT YOU. IT WAS YOUR SUFFERING THAT WOKE ME FROM A PEACEFUL SLEEP.
SEE? ISN'T HE GREAT?
GET OUT OF OUR WAY, SKIDS. AGREE TO COME BACK WITH US, AND MAYBE WE'LL OVERLOOK THIS.
STOP TALKING AND ATTACK APOCALYPSE! I KNOW HIM--HE'S HIDING SOME-THING!
MY SCRIBE KNOWS ME WELL. BUT IT IS NOT SOME-THING I AM HIDING. IT IS SOMEONE.
MY FOURTH HORSEMAN. FRESHLY IMAGINED... NEWLY MINTED...
OH...
...OH NO...

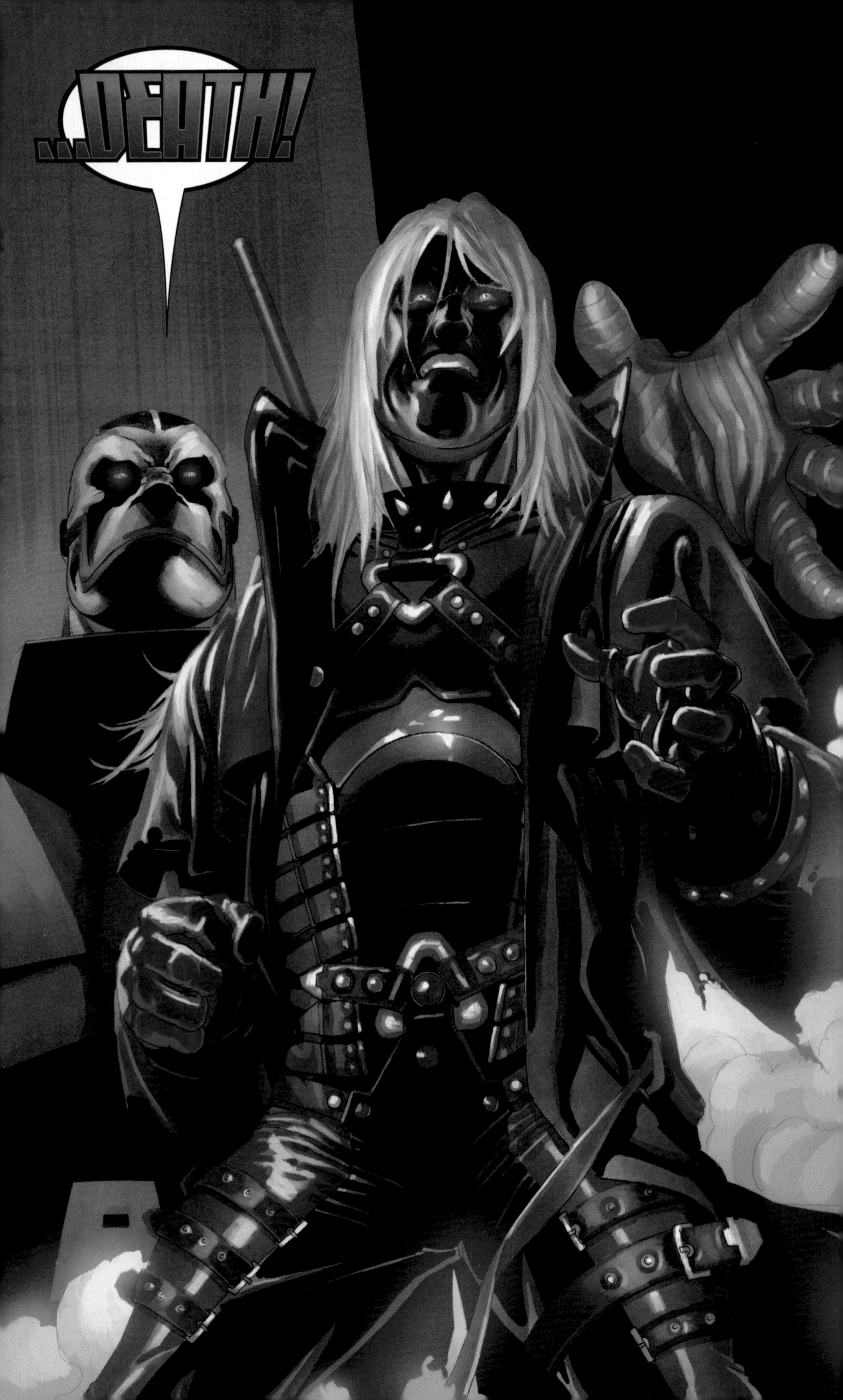
...DEATH!

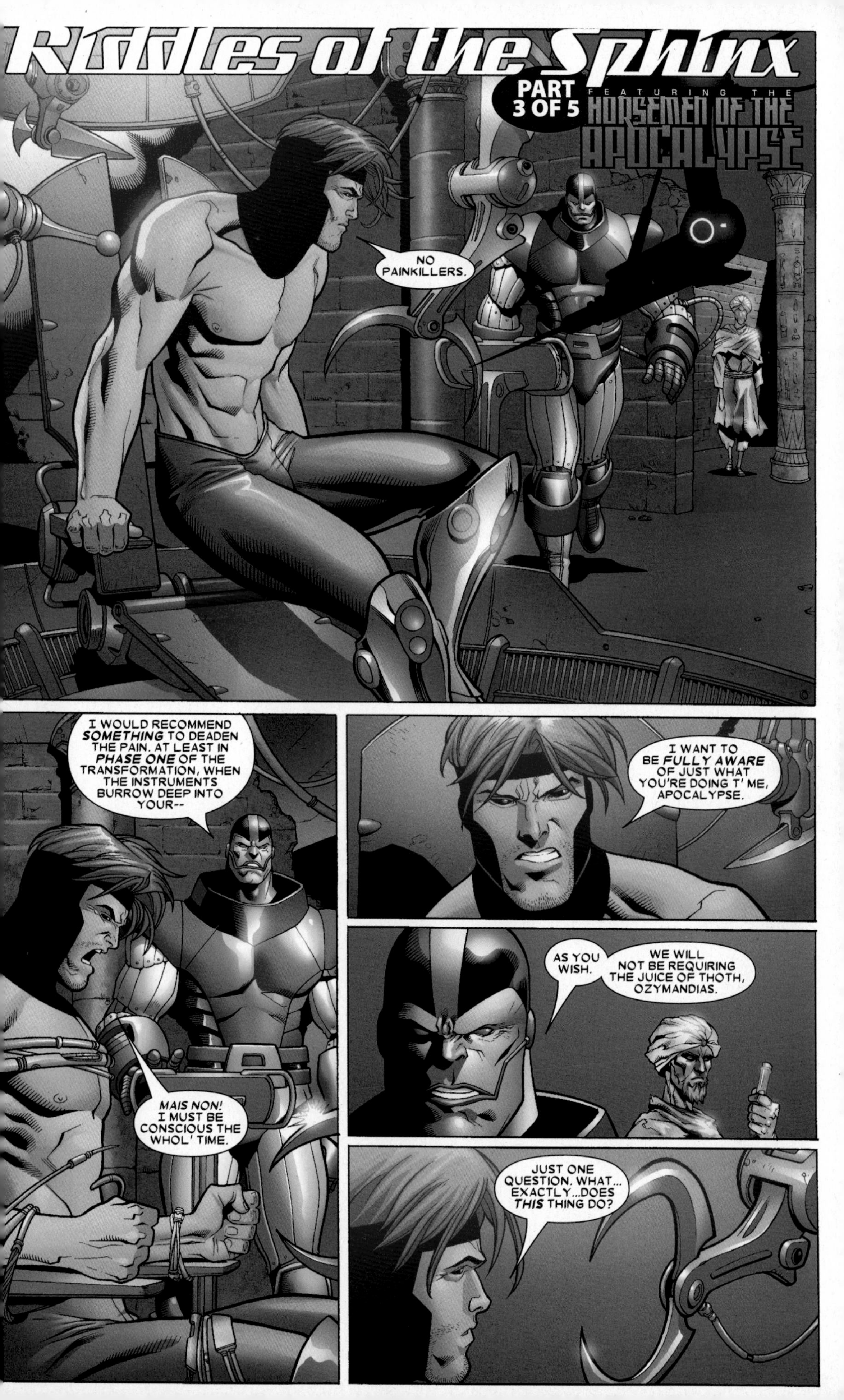
Riddles of the Sphinx
PART 3 OF 5
FEATURING THE HORSEMEN OF THE APOCALYPSE
NO PAINKILLERS.
I WOULD RECOMMEND SOMETHING TO DEADEN THE PAIN. AT LEAST IN PHASE ONE OF THE TRANSFORMATION, WHEN THE INSTRUMENTS BURROW DEEP INTO YOUR--
MAIS NON! I MUST BE CONSCIOUS THE WHOL' TIME.
I WANT TO BE FULLY AWARE OF JUST WHAT YOU'RE DOING T' ME, APOCALYPSE.
AS YOU WISH.
WE WILL NOT BE REQUIRING THE JUICE OF THOTH, OZYMANDIAS.
JUST ONE QUESTION. WHAT... EXACTLY...DOES THIS THING DO?

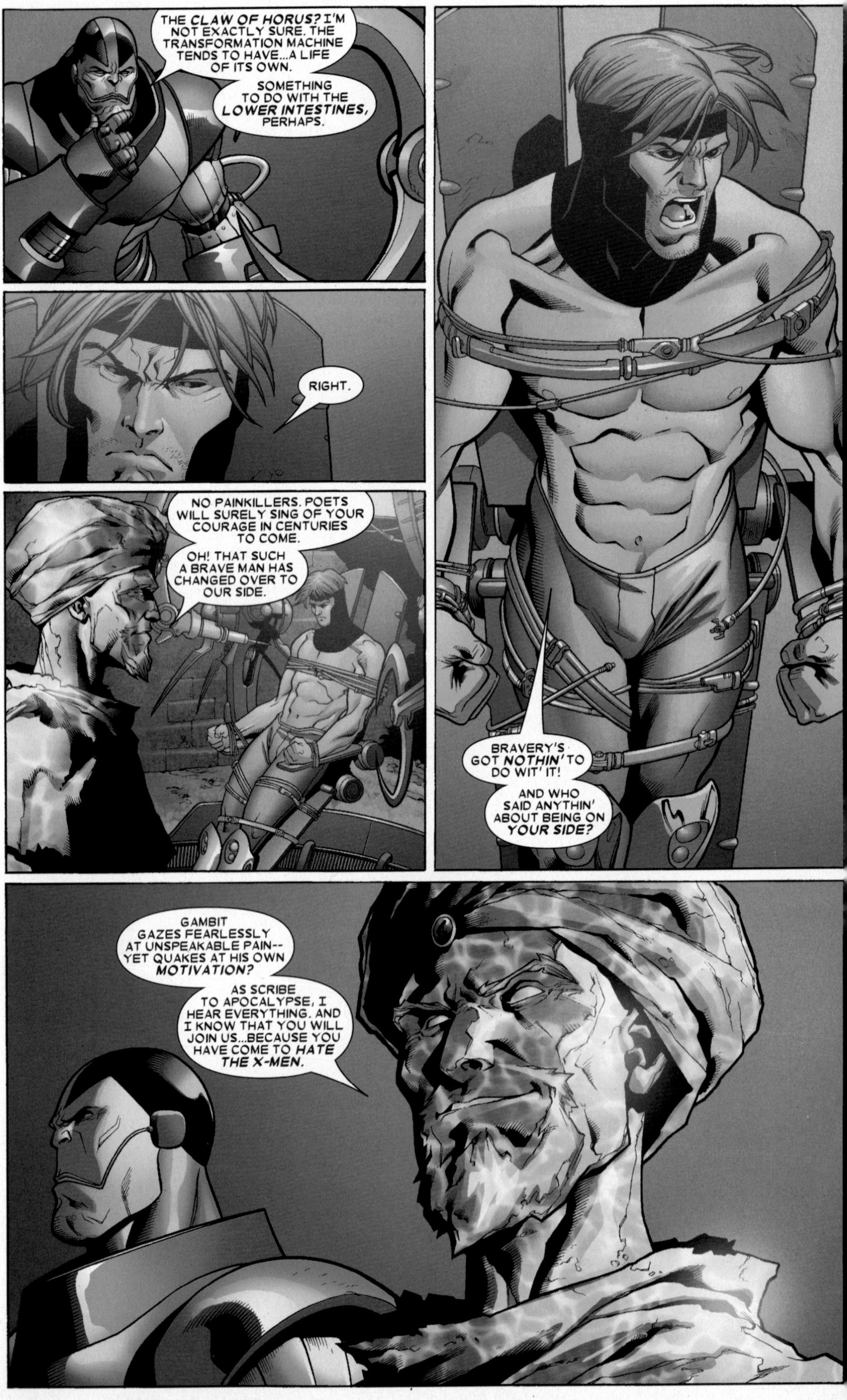
THE CLAW OF HORUS? I'M NOT EXACTLY SURE. THE TRANSFORMATION MACHINE TENDS TO HAVE...A LIFE OF ITS OWN.
SOMETHING TO DO WITH THE LOWER INTESTINES, PERHAPS.
RIGHT.
NO PAINKILLERS. POETS WILL SURELY SING OF YOUR COURAGE IN CENTURIES TO COME.
OH! THAT SUCH A BRAVE MAN HAS CHANGED OVER TO OUR SIDE.
BRAVERY'S GOT NOTHIN' TO DO WIT' IT!
AND WHO SAID ANYTHIN' ABOUT BEING ON YOUR SIDE?
GAMBIT GAZES FEARLESSLY AT UNSPEAKABLE PAIN--YET QUAKES AT HIS OWN MOTIVATION?
AS SCRIBE TO APOCALYPSE, I HEAR EVERYTHING. AND I KNOW THAT YOU WILL JOIN US...BECAUSE YOU HAVE COME TO HATE THE X-MEN.

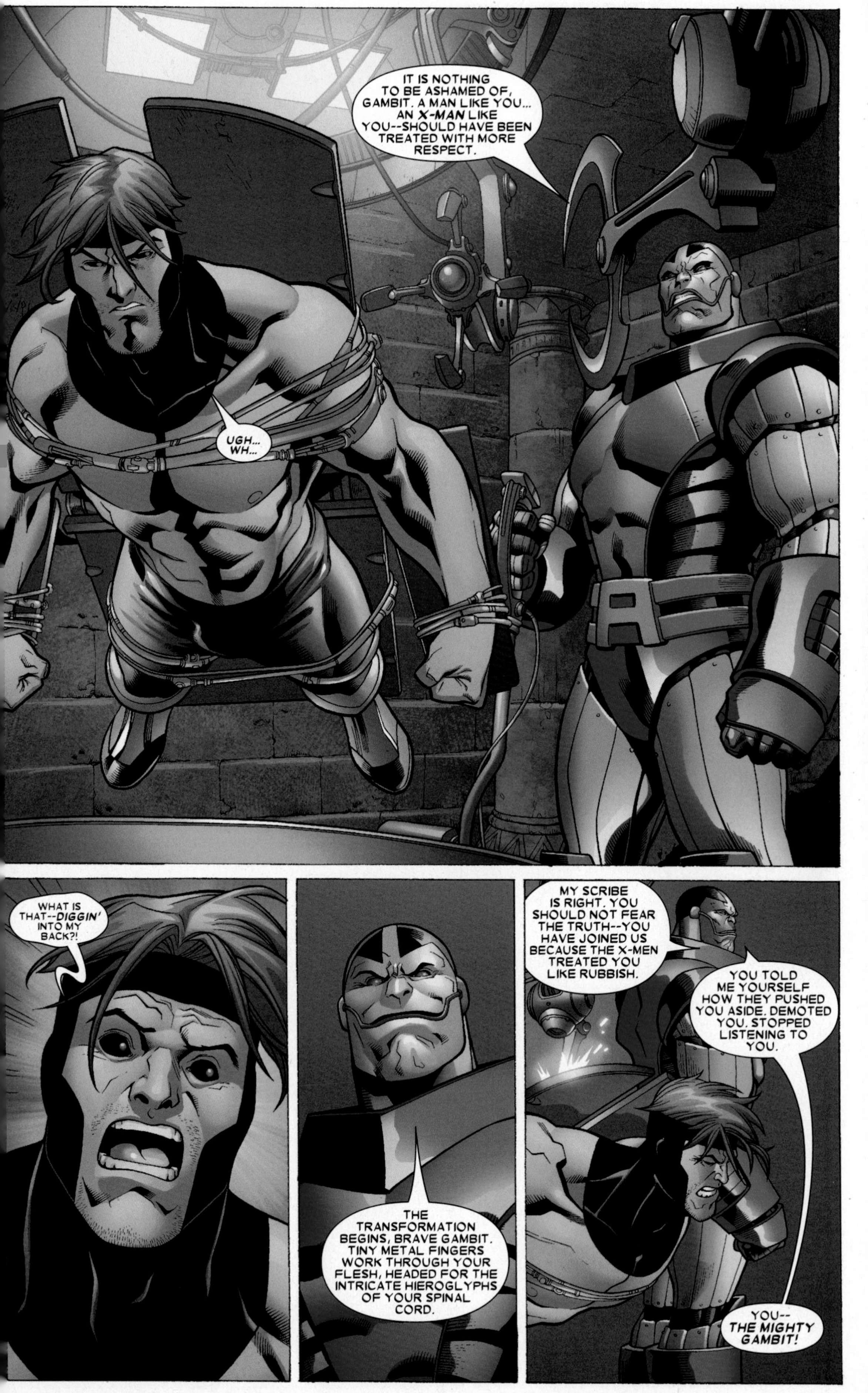

IT IS NOTHING TO BE ASHAMED OF, GAMBIT. A MAN LIKE YOU... AN *X-MAN* LIKE YOU--SHOULD HAVE BEEN TREATED WITH MORE RESPECT.
UGH... WH...
WHAT IS THAT--*DIGGIN'* INTO MY BACK?!
THE TRANSFORMATION BEGINS, BRAVE GAMBIT. TINY METAL FINGERS WORK THROUGH YOUR FLESH, HEADED FOR THE INTRICATE HIEROGLYPHS OF YOUR SPINAL CORD.
MY SCRIBE IS RIGHT. YOU SHOULD NOT FEAR THE TRUTH--YOU HAVE JOINED US BECAUSE THE X-MEN TREATED YOU LIKE RUBBISH.
YOU TOLD ME YOURSELF HOW THEY PUSHED YOU ASIDE. DEMOTED YOU. STOPPED LISTENING TO YOU.
YOU-- *THE MIGHTY GAMBIT!*

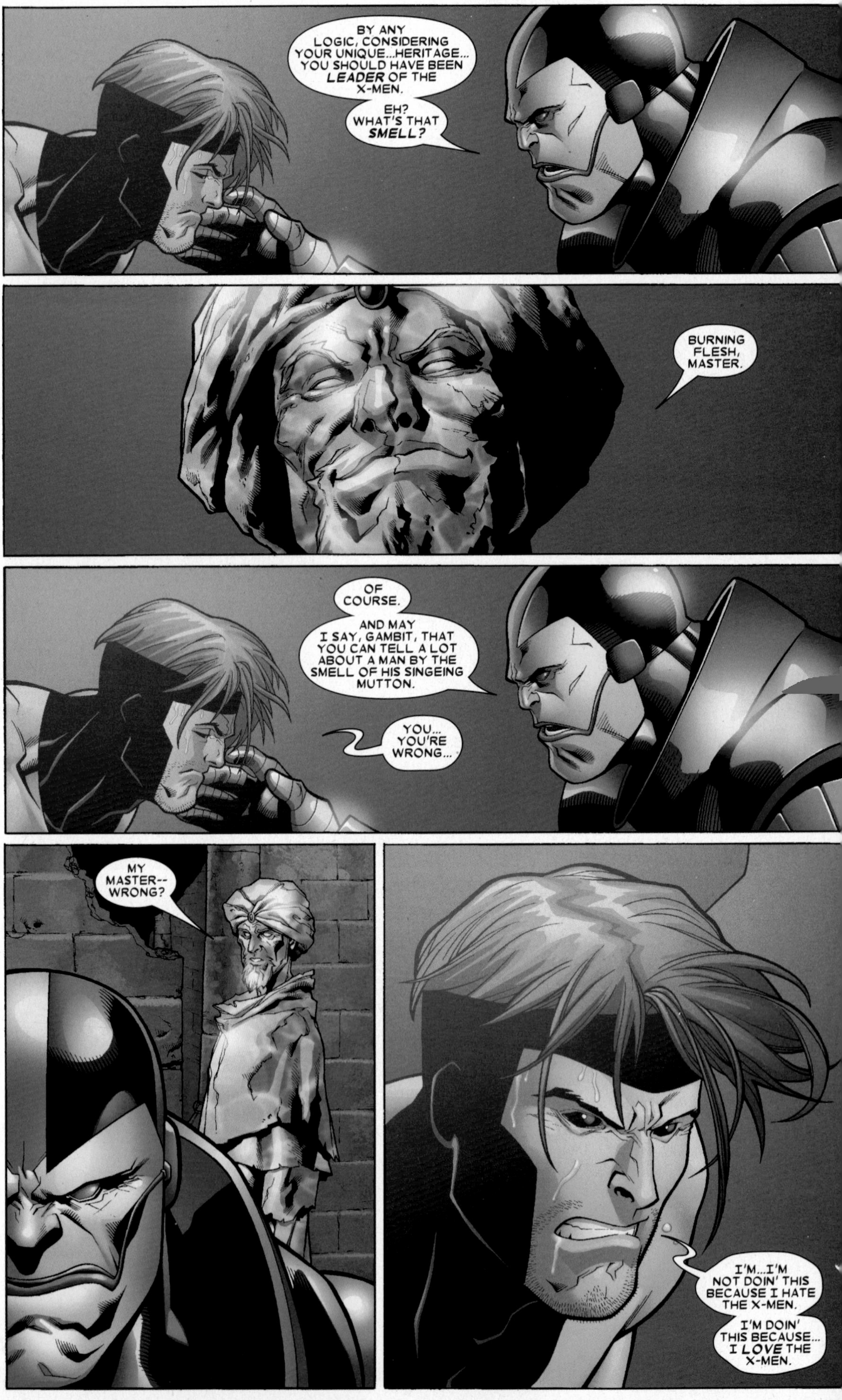
BY ANY LOGIC, CONSIDERING YOUR UNIQUE...HERITAGE... YOU SHOULD HAVE BEEN LEADER OF THE X-MEN.
EH? WHAT'S THAT SMELL?
BURNING FLESH, MASTER.
OF COURSE.
AND MAY I SAY, GAMBIT, THAT YOU CAN TELL A LOT ABOUT A MAN BY THE SMELL OF HIS SINGEING MUTTON.
YOU... YOU'RE WRONG...
MY MASTER-- WRONG?
I'M...I'M NOT DOIN' THIS BECAUSE I HATE THE X-MEN.
I'M DOIN' THIS BECAUSE... I LOVE THE X-MEN.

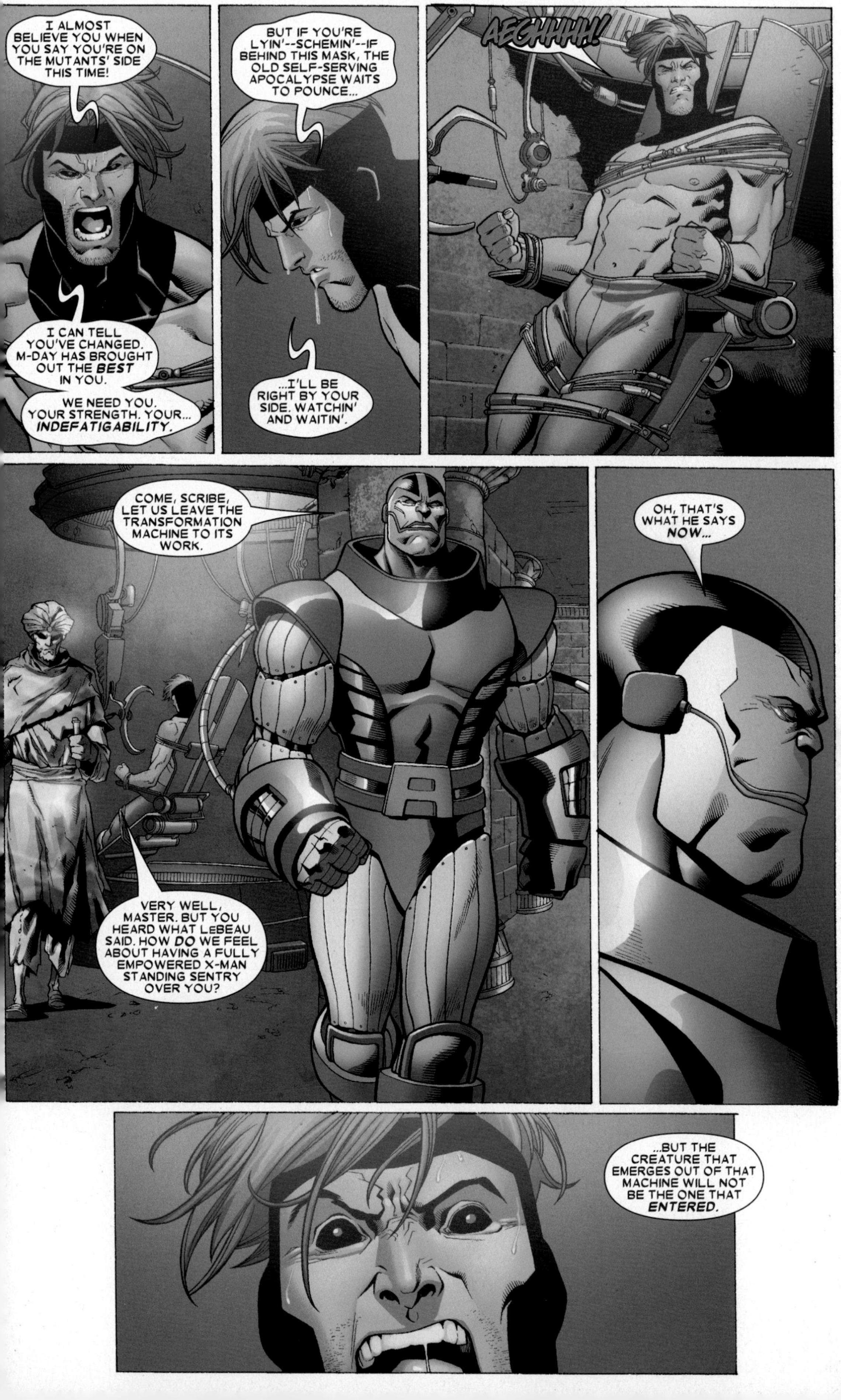
I ALMOST BELIEVE YOU WHEN YOU SAY YOU'RE ON THE MUTANTS' SIDE THIS TIME!
I CAN TELL YOU'VE CHANGED. M-DAY HAS BROUGHT OUT THE *BEST* IN YOU.
WE NEED YOU. YOUR STRENGTH. YOUR... ***INDEFATIGABILITY***.
BUT IF YOU'RE LYIN'--SCHEMIN'--IF BEHIND THIS MASK, THE OLD SELF-SERVING APOCALYPSE WAITS TO POUNCE...
...I'LL BE RIGHT BY YOUR SIDE. WATCHIN' AND WAITIN'.
AEGHHHH!
COME, SCRIBE, LET US LEAVE THE TRANSFORMATION MACHINE TO ITS WORK.
VERY WELL, MASTER. BUT YOU HEARD WHAT LEBEAU SAID. HOW *DO* WE FEEL ABOUT HAVING A FULLY EMPOWERED X-MAN STANDING SENTRY OVER YOU?
OH, THAT'S WHAT HE SAYS *NOW*...
...BUT THE CREATURE THAT EMERGES OUT OF THAT MACHINE WILL NOT BE THE ONE THAT *ENTERED*.

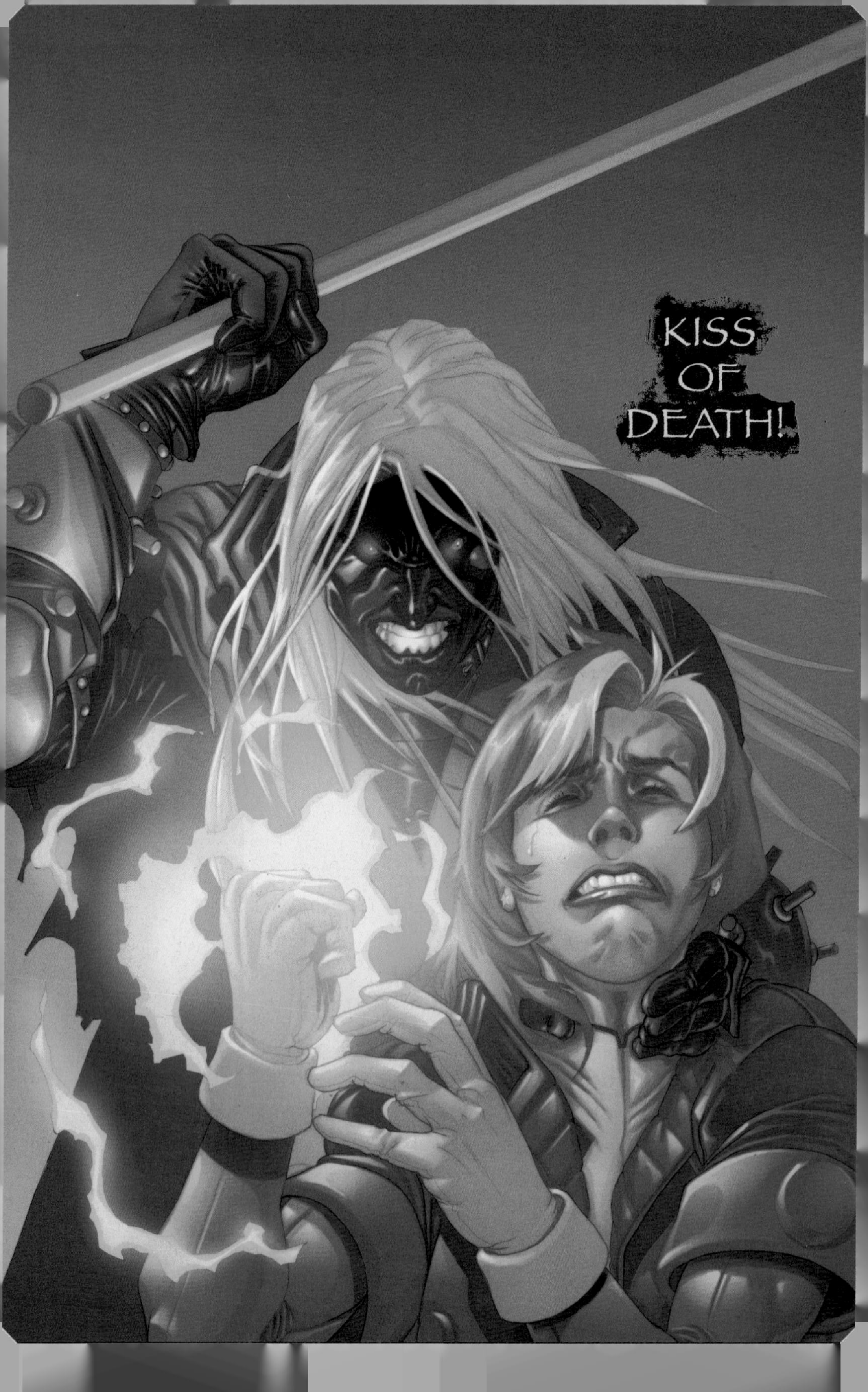
KISS OF DEATH!

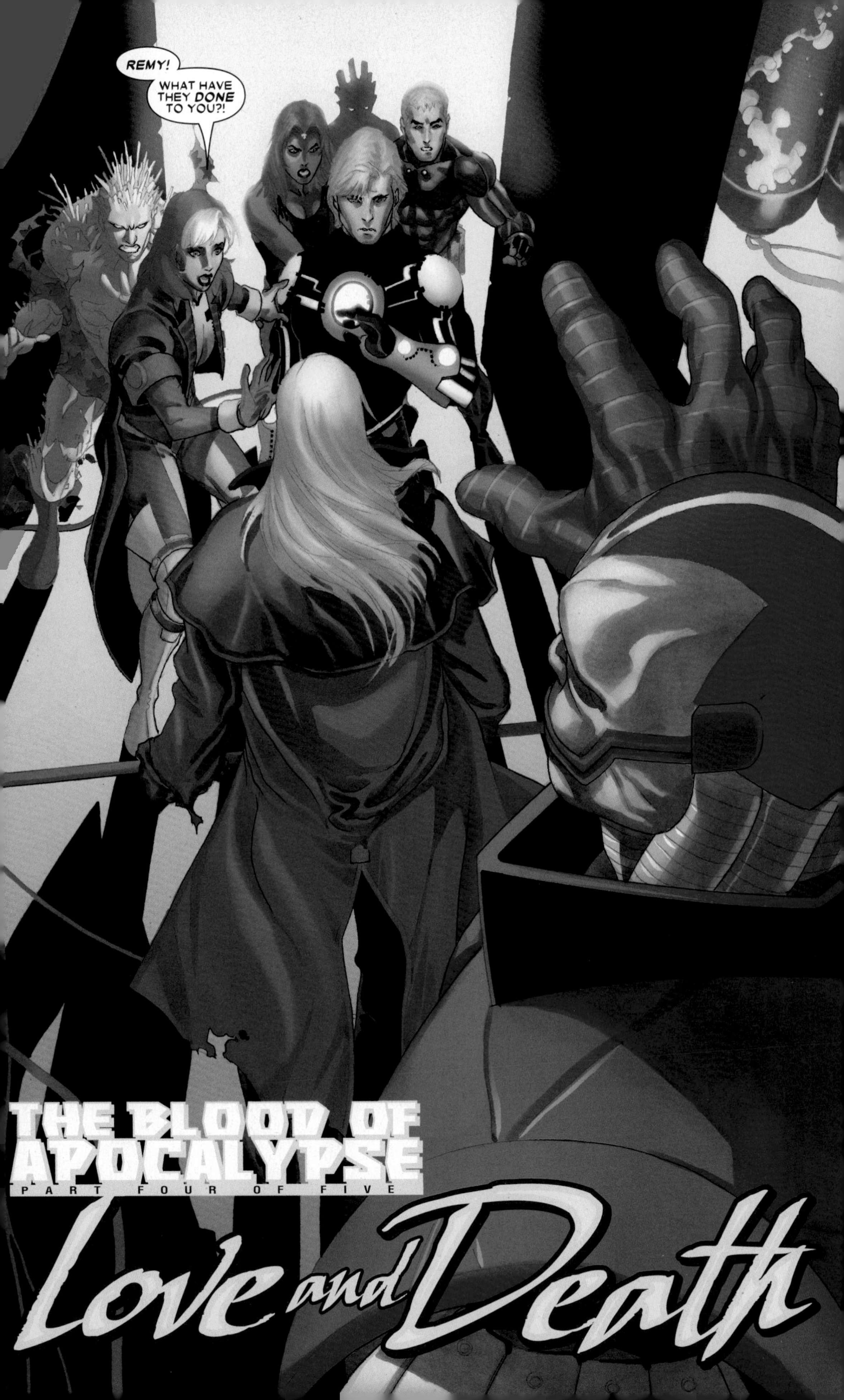
REMY! WHAT HAVE THEY DONE TO YOU?!
THE BLOOD OF APOCALYPSE
PART FOUR OF FIVE
Love and Death

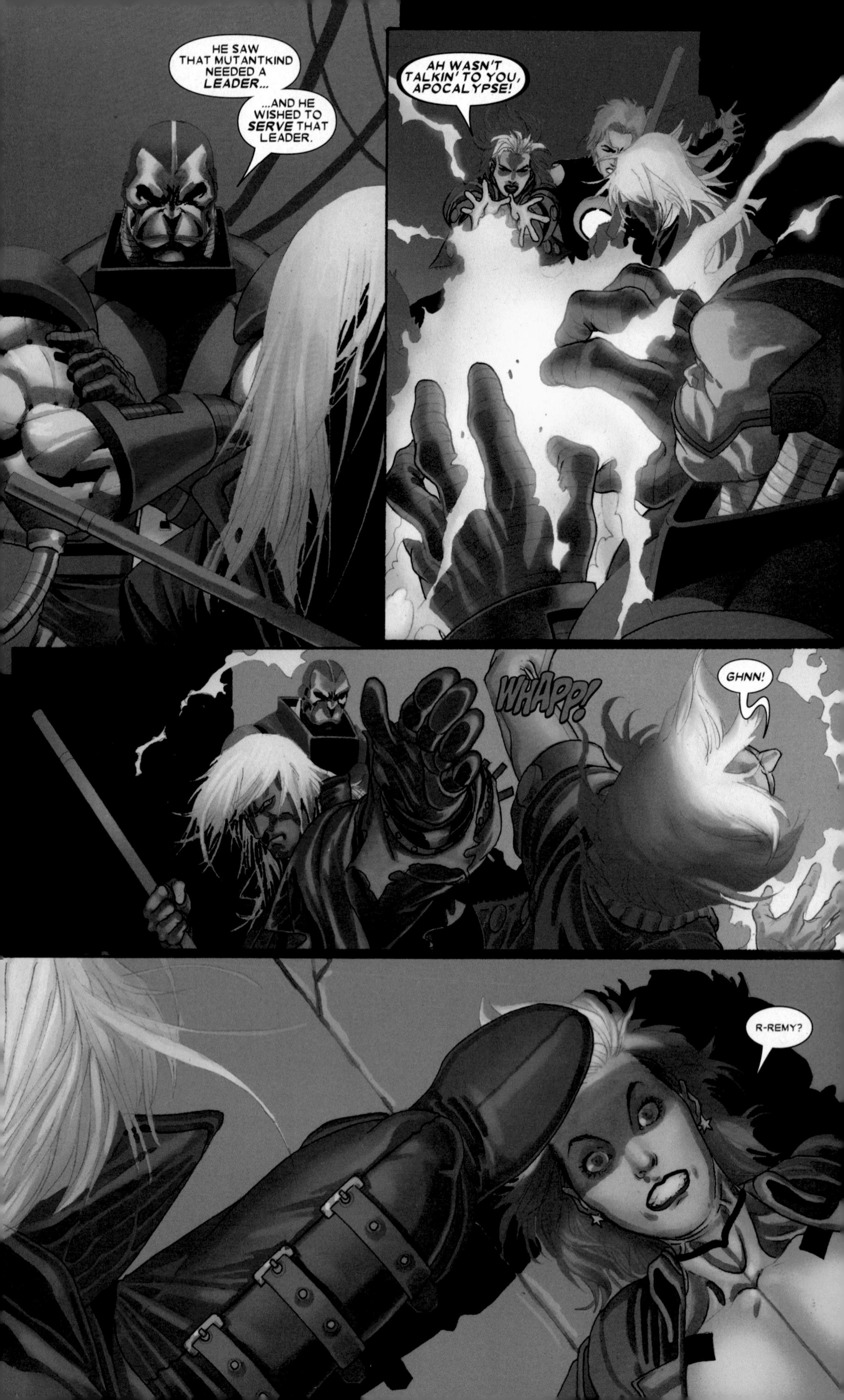
HE SAW THAT MUTANTKIND NEEDED A LEADER...
...AND HE WISHED TO SERVE THAT LEADER.
AH WASN'T TALKIN' TO YOU, APOCALYPSE!
WHAPP!
GHNN!
R-REMY?

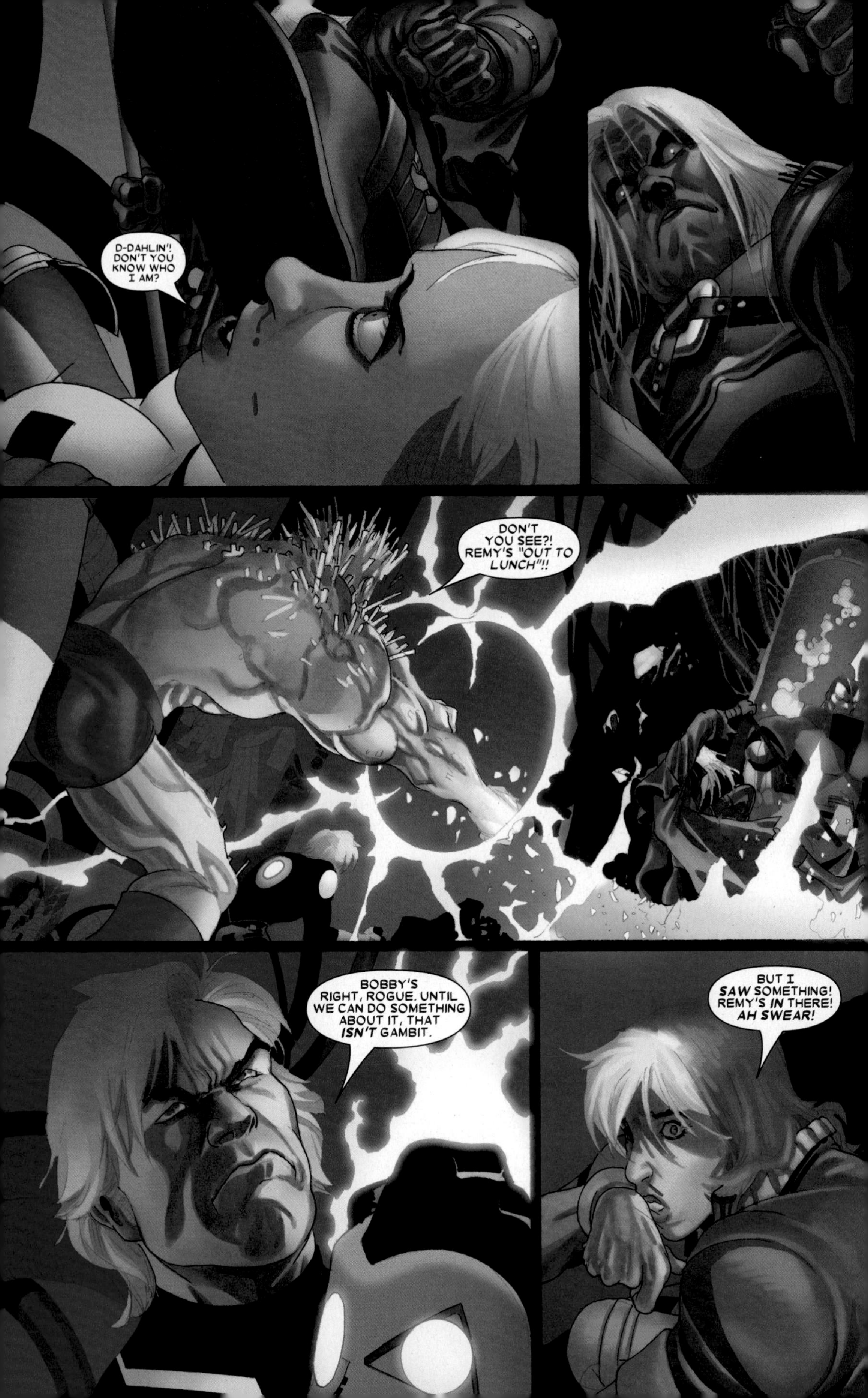
D-DAHLIN'! DON'T YOU KNOW WHO I AM?
DON'T YOU SEE?! REMY'S "OUT TO LUNCH"!!
BOBBY'S RIGHT, ROGUE. UNTIL WE CAN DO SOMETHING ABOUT IT, THAT ISN'T GAMBIT.
BUT I SAW SOMETHING! REMY'S IN THERE! AH SWEAR!

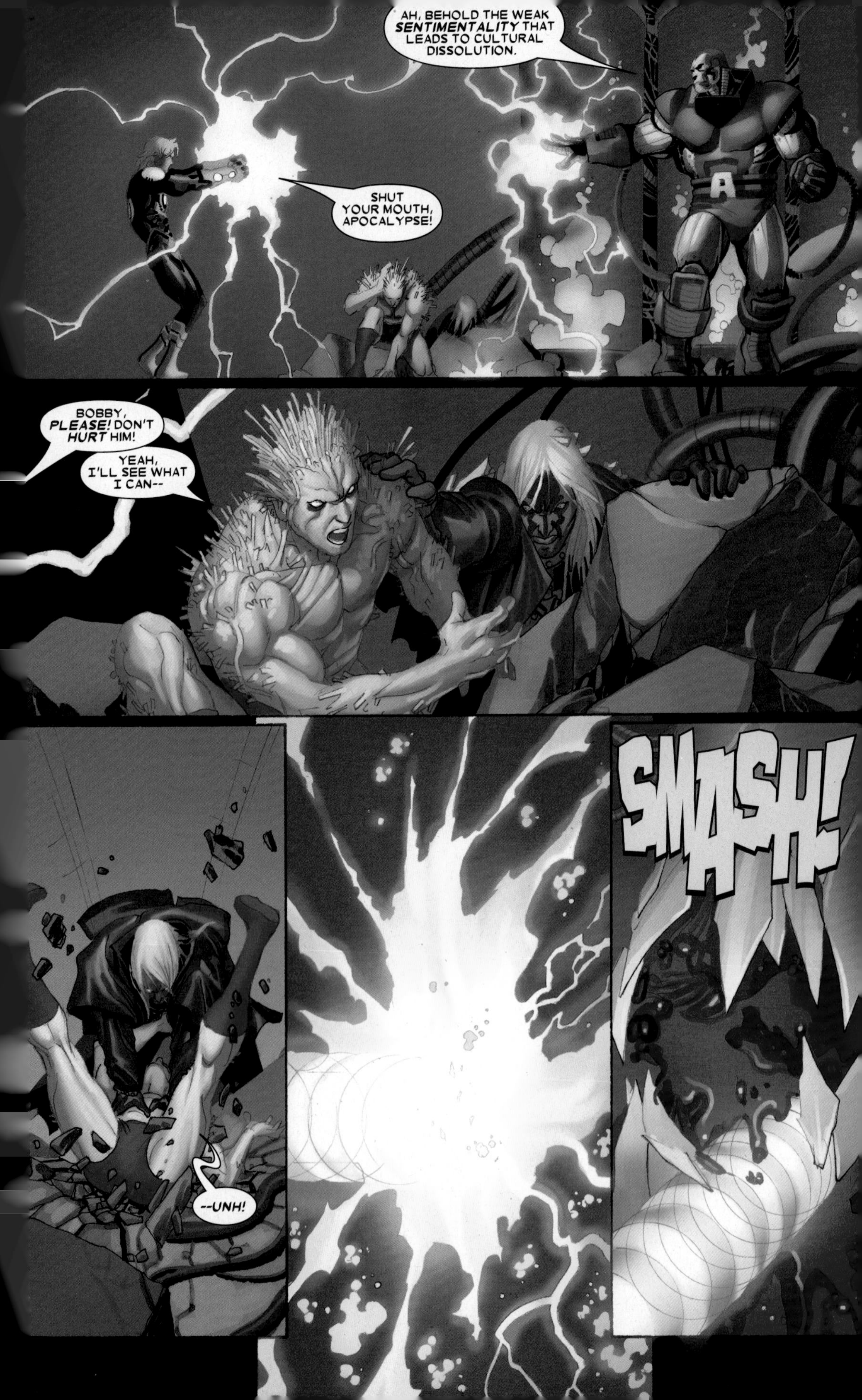
AH, BEHOLD THE WEAK SENTIMENTALITY THAT LEADS TO CULTURAL DISSOLUTION.
SHUT YOUR MOUTH, APOCALYPSE!
BOBBY, PLEASE! DON'T HURT HIM!
YEAH, I'LL SEE WHAT I CAN--
--UNH!
SMASH!

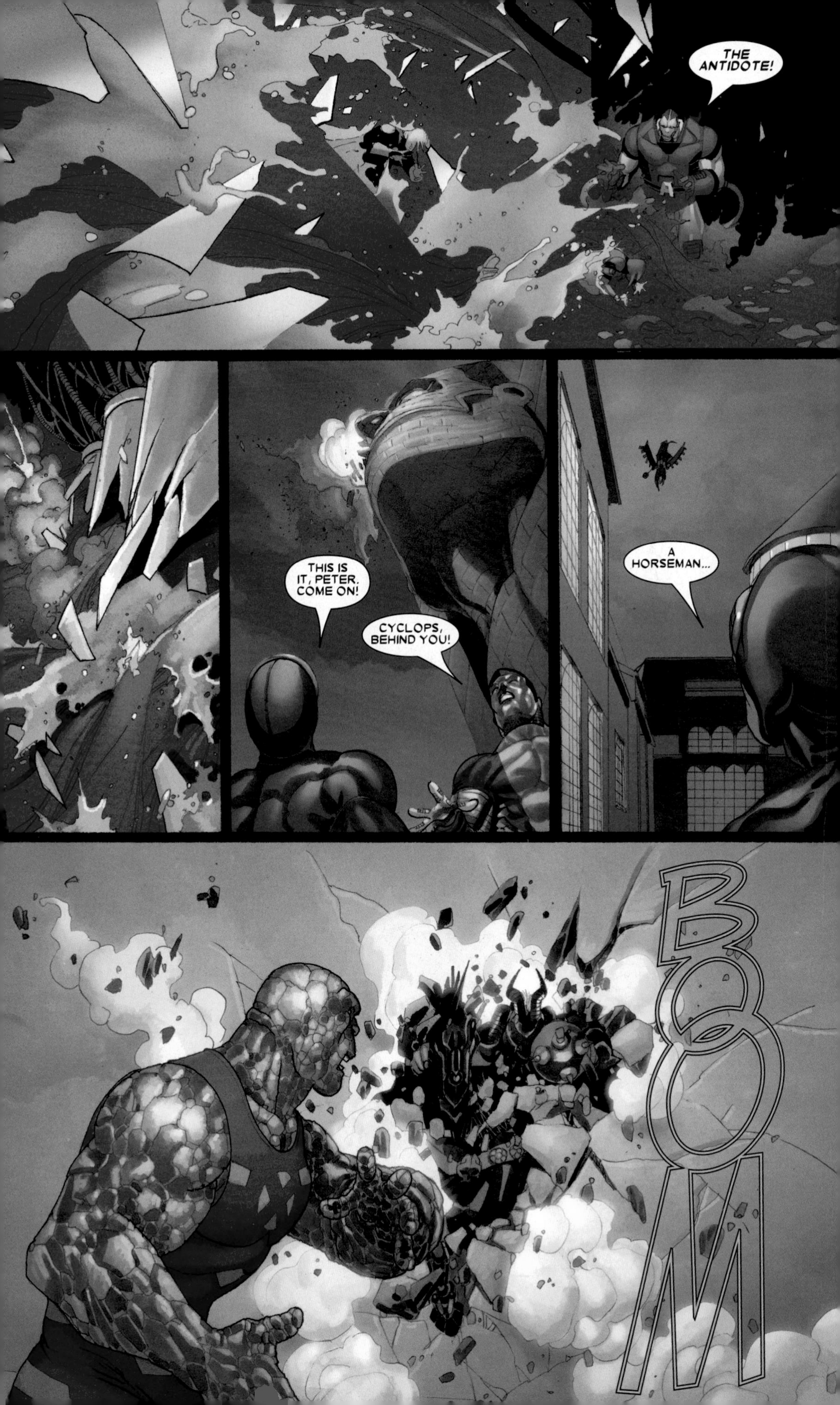
THE ANTIDOTE!
THIS IS IT, PETER. COME ON!
CYCLOPS, BEHIND YOU!
A HORSEMAN...
BOOM

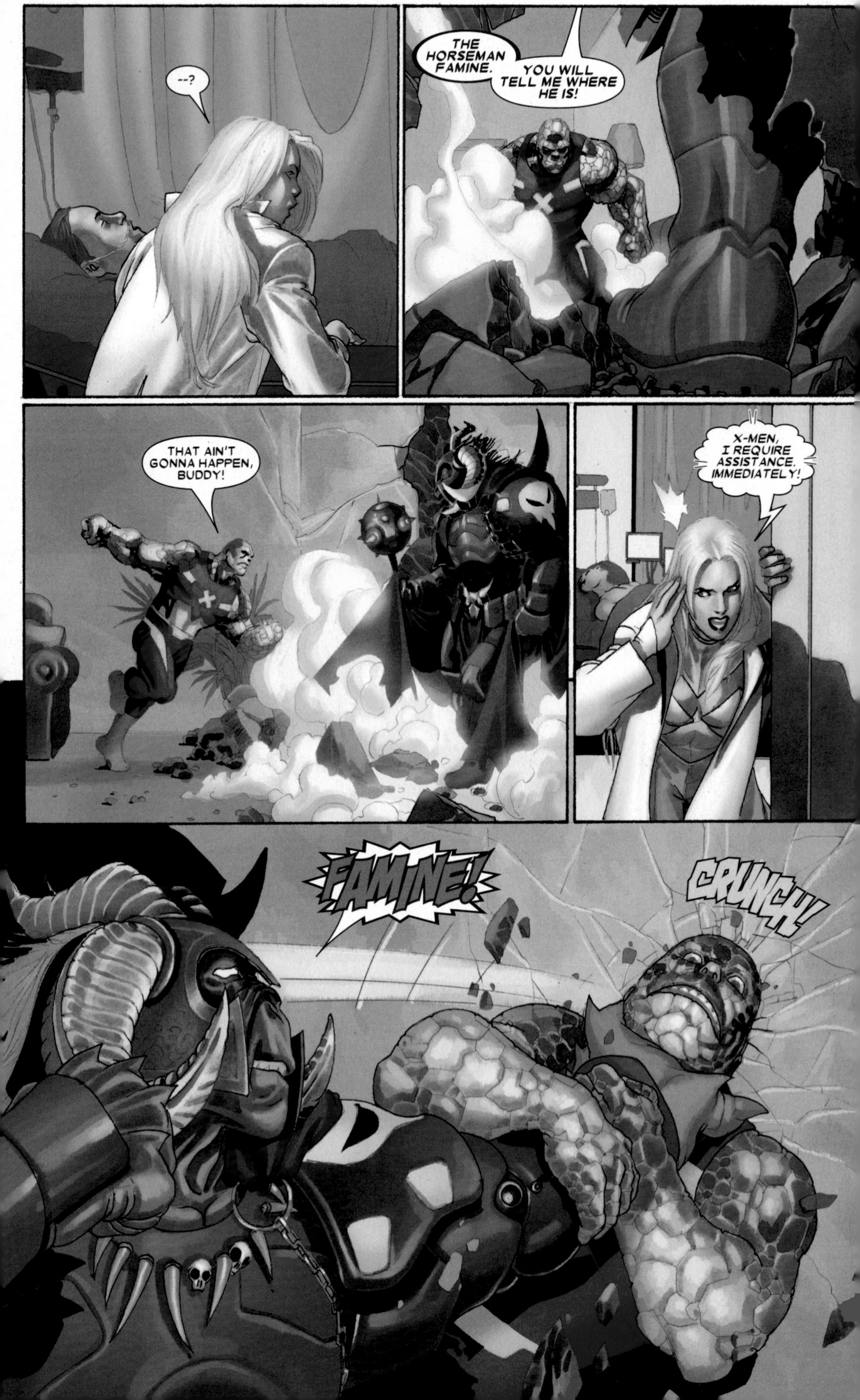
--?
THE HORSEMAN FAMINE.
YOU WILL TELL ME WHERE HE IS!
THAT AIN'T GONNA HAPPEN, BUDDY!
X-MEN, I REQUIRE ASSISTANCE. IMMEDIATELY!
FAMINE!
CRUNCH!

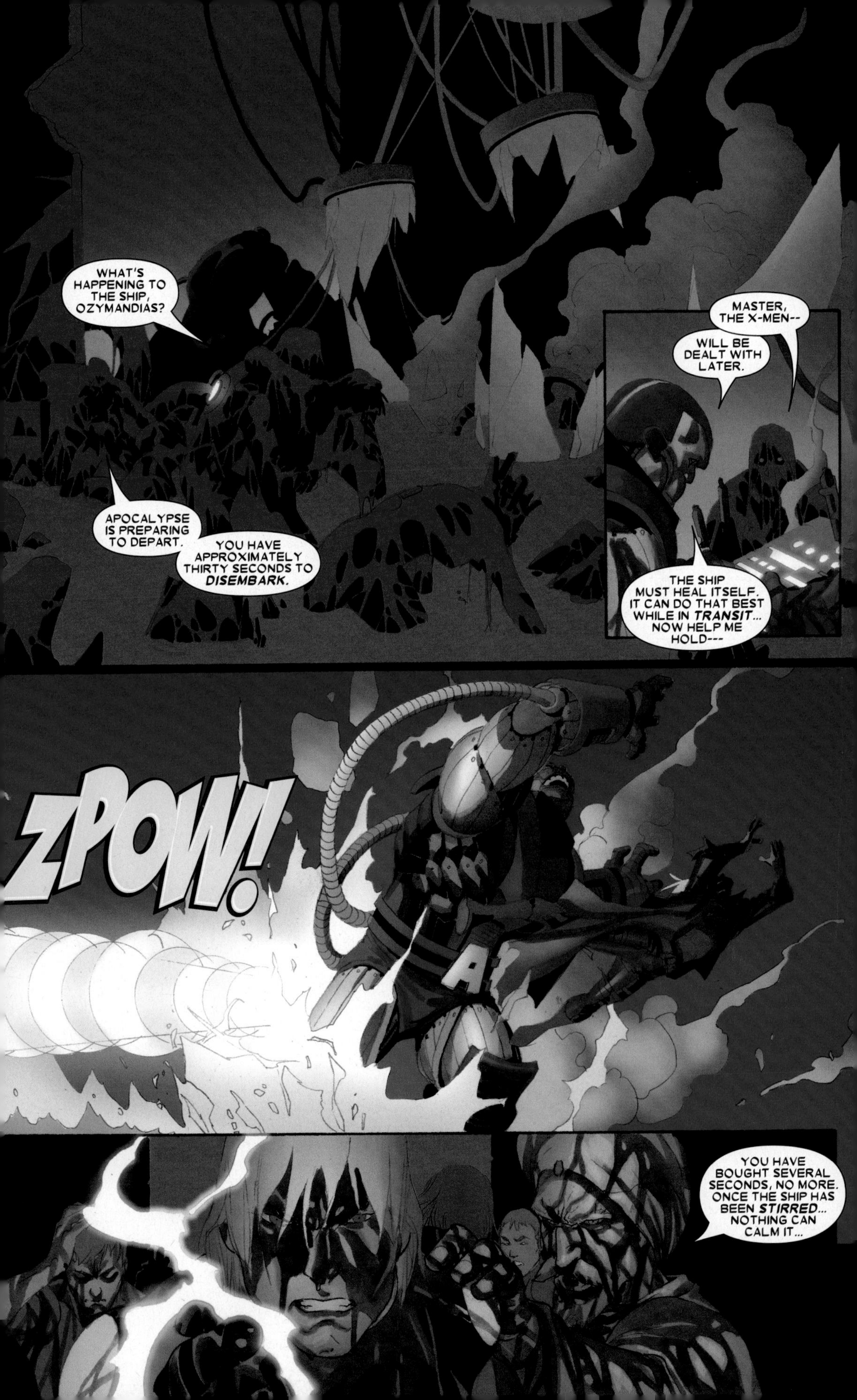
WHAT'S HAPPENING TO THE SHIP, OZYMANDIAS?
APOCALYPSE IS PREPARING TO DEPART.
YOU HAVE APPROXIMATELY THIRTY SECONDS TO DISEMBARK.
MASTER, THE X-MEN--
WILL BE DEALT WITH LATER.
THE SHIP MUST HEAL ITSELF. IT CAN DO THAT BEST WHILE IN TRANSIT... NOW HELP ME HOLD---
ZPOW!
YOU HAVE BOUGHT SEVERAL SECONDS, NO MORE. ONCE THE SHIP HAS BEEN STIRRED... NOTHING CAN CALM IT...

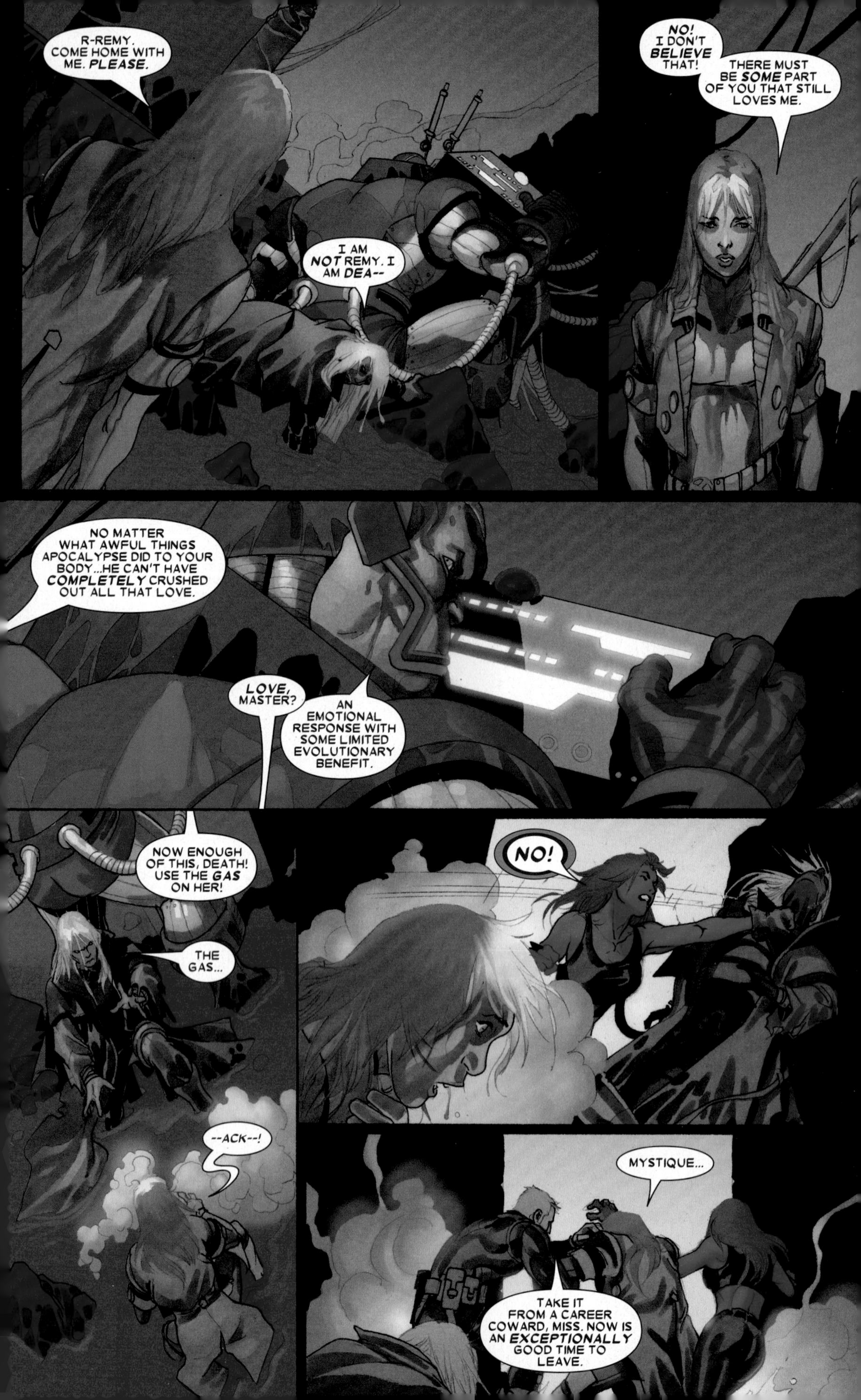
R-REMY. COME HOME WITH ME. PLEASE.
I AM NOT REMY. I AM DEA--
NO! I DON'T BELIEVE THAT!
THERE MUST BE SOME PART OF YOU THAT STILL LOVES ME.
NO MATTER WHAT AWFUL THINGS APOCALYPSE DID TO YOUR BODY...HE CAN'T HAVE COMPLETELY CRUSHED OUT ALL THAT LOVE.
LOVE, MASTER?
AN EMOTIONAL RESPONSE WITH SOME LIMITED EVOLUTIONARY BENEFIT.
NOW ENOUGH OF THIS, DEATH! USE THE GAS ON HER!
THE GAS...
--ACK--!
NO!
MYSTIQUE...
TAKE IT FROM A CAREER COWARD, MISS. NOW IS AN EXCEPTIONALLY GOOD TIME TO LEAVE.

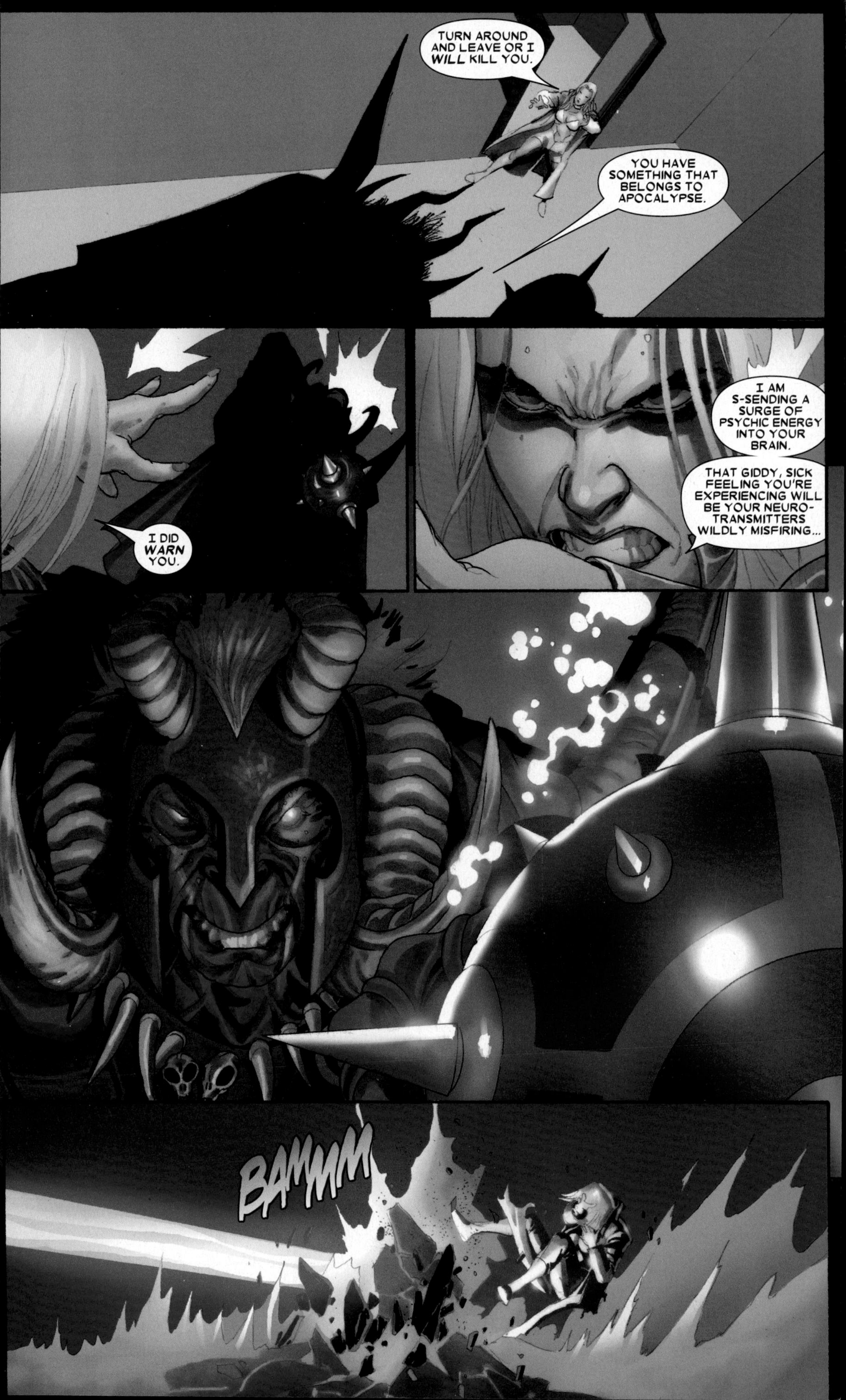
TURN AROUND AND LEAVE OR I WILL KILL YOU.
YOU HAVE SOMETHING THAT BELONGS TO APOCALYPSE.
I DID WARN YOU.
I AM S-SENDING A SURGE OF PSYCHIC ENERGY INTO YOUR BRAIN.
THAT GIDDY, SICK FEELING YOU'RE EXPERIENCING WILL BE YOUR NEURO-TRANSMITTERS WILDLY MISFIRING...
BAMMM

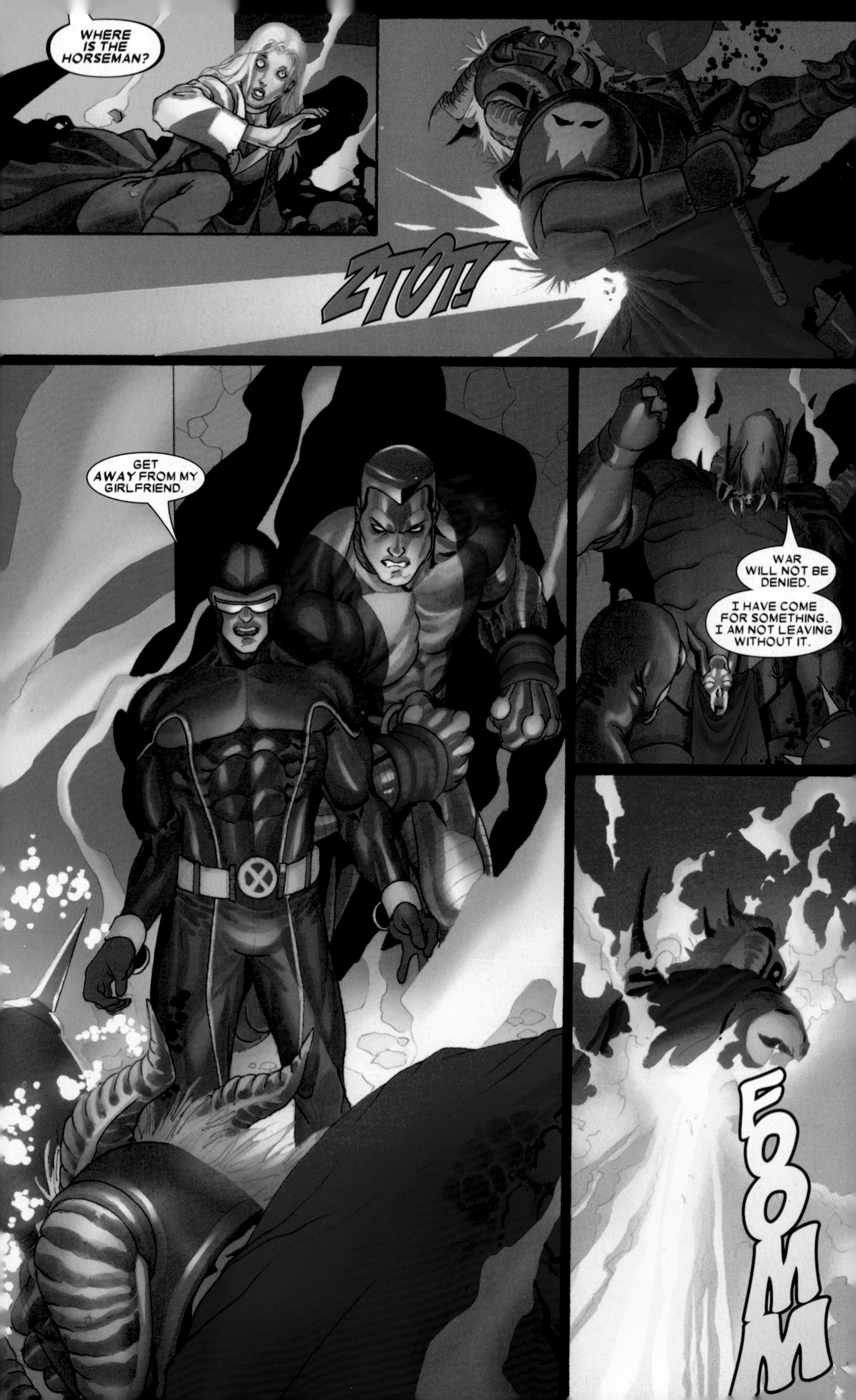
WHERE IS THE HORSEMAN?
ZTOT!
GET AWAY FROM MY GIRLFRIEND.
WAR WILL NOT BE DENIED.
I HAVE COME FOR SOMETHING. I AM NOT LEAVING WITHOUT IT.
FOOMM

T-TELL YOUR MASTER...

...HE HAS *LOST*...A HORSEMAN...

THE BATTLE MAY BE LOST...

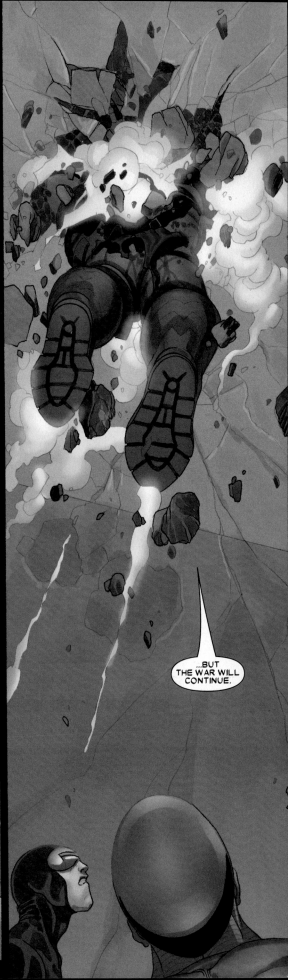

...BUT THE WAR WILL CONTINUE.

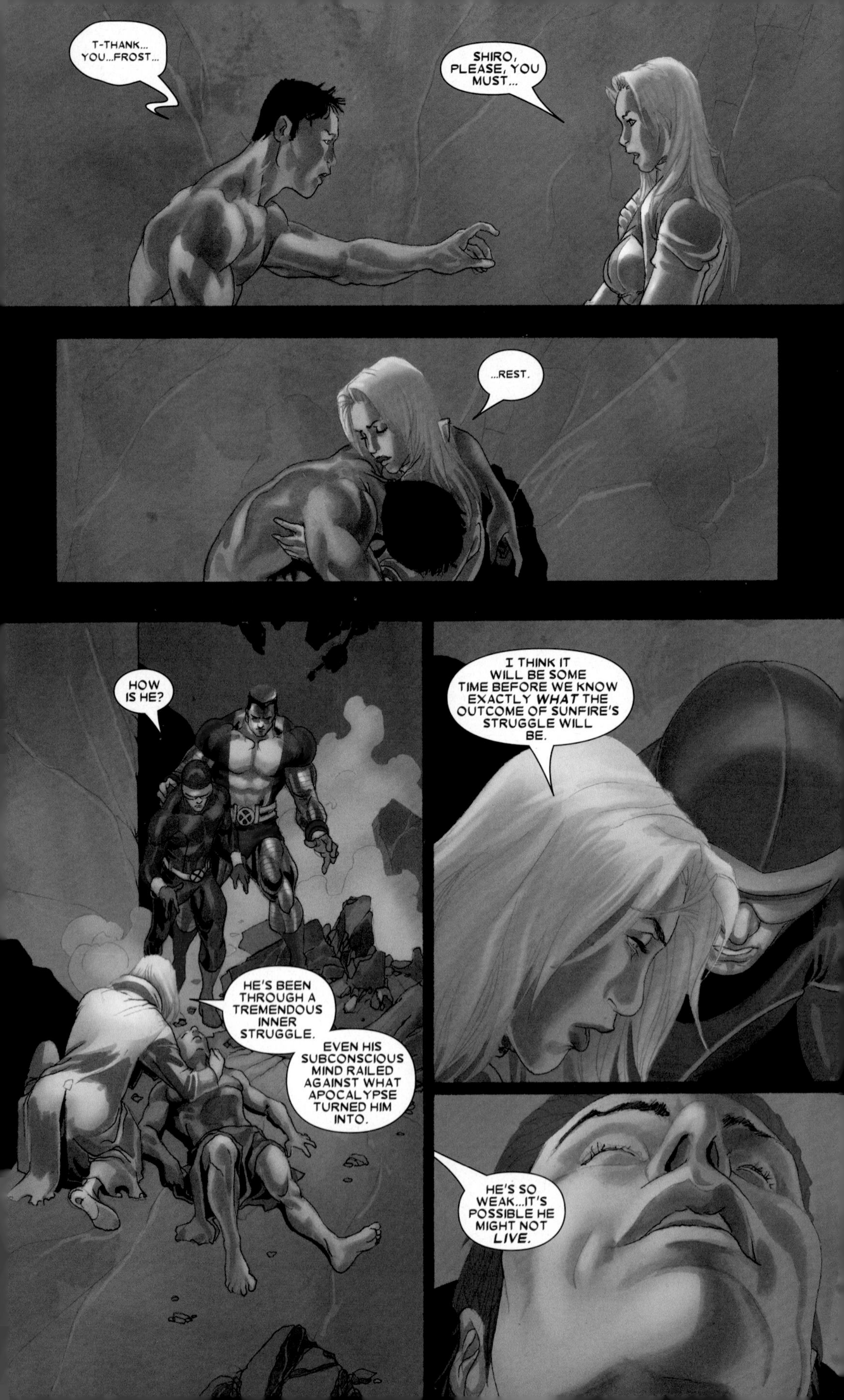

T-THANK... YOU...FROST...
SHIRO, PLEASE, YOU MUST...
...REST.
HOW IS HE?
HE'S BEEN THROUGH A TREMENDOUS INNER STRUGGLE.
EVEN HIS SUBCONSCIOUS MIND RAILED AGAINST WHAT APOCALYPSE TURNED HIM INTO.
I THINK IT WILL BE SOME TIME BEFORE WE KNOW EXACTLY *WHAT* THE OUTCOME OF SUNFIRE'S STRUGGLE WILL BE.
HE'S SO WEAK...IT'S POSSIBLE HE MIGHT NOT *LIVE.*

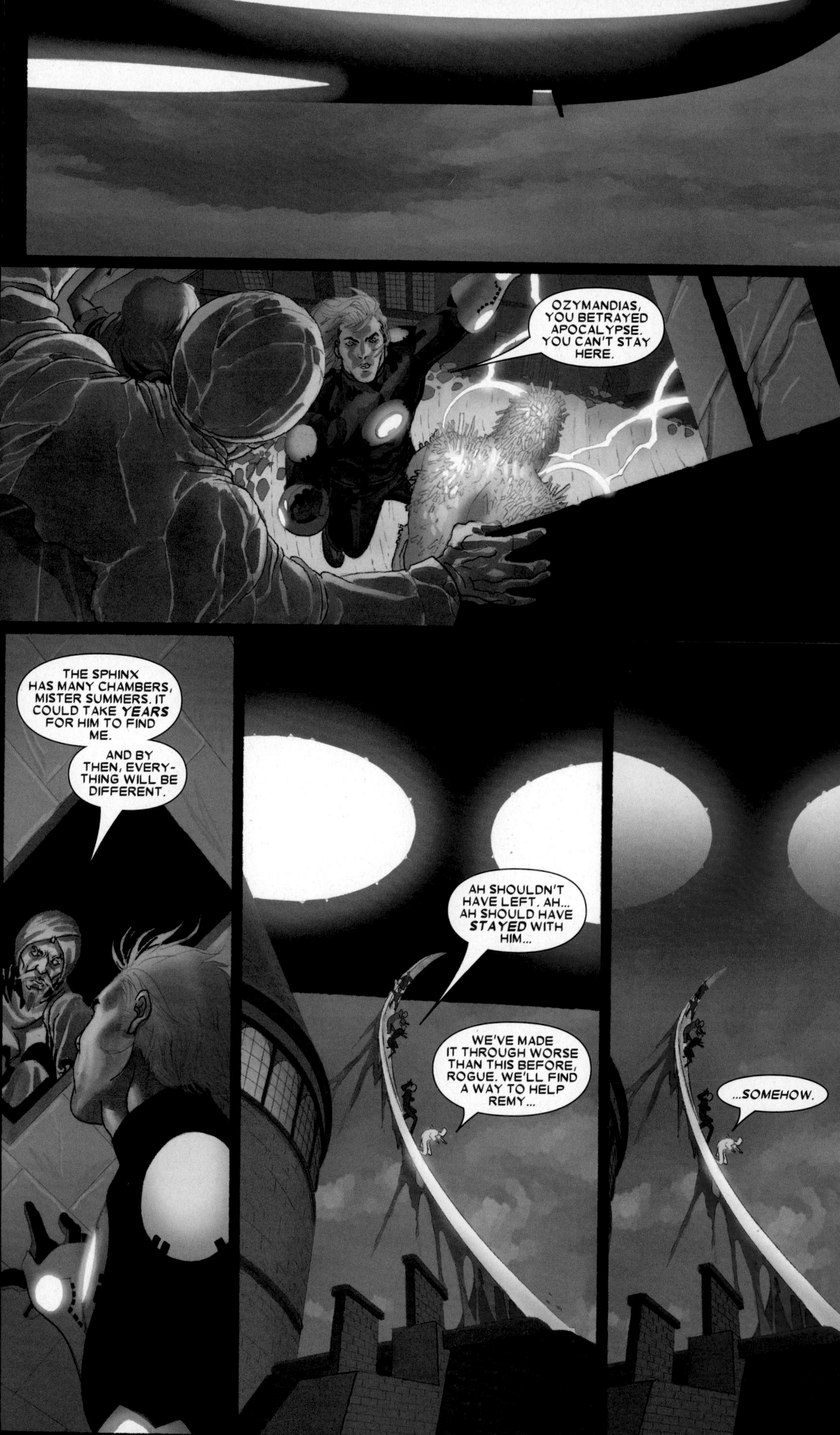
OZYMANDIAS, YOU BETRAYED APOCALYPSE. YOU CAN'T STAY HERE.
THE SPHINX HAS MANY CHAMBERS, MISTER SUMMERS. IT COULD TAKE YEARS FOR HIM TO FIND ME.
AND BY THEN, EVERY-THING WILL BE DIFFERENT.
AH SHOULDN'T HAVE LEFT. AH... AH SHOULD HAVE STAYED WITH HIM...
WE'VE MADE IT THROUGH WORSE THAN THIS BEFORE, ROGUE. WE'LL FIND A WAY TO HELP REMY...
...SOMEHOW.

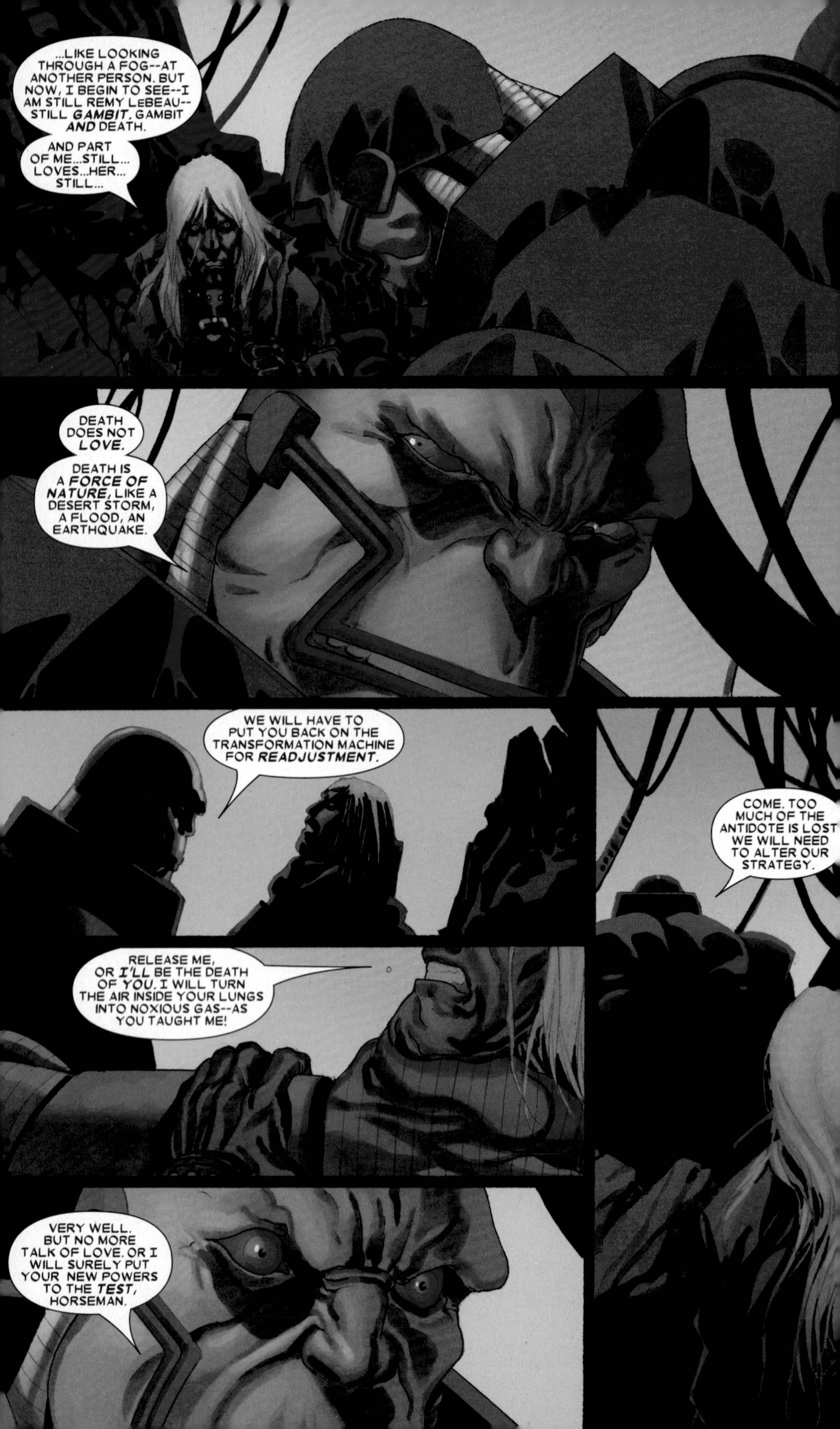
...LIKE LOOKING THROUGH A FOG--AT ANOTHER PERSON. BUT NOW, I BEGIN TO SEE--I AM STILL REMY LEBEAU--STILL GAMBIT. GAMBIT AND DEATH.
AND PART OF ME...STILL... LOVES...HER... STILL...
DEATH DOES NOT LOVE.
DEATH IS A FORCE OF NATURE, LIKE A DESERT STORM, A FLOOD, AN EARTHQUAKE.
WE WILL HAVE TO PUT YOU BACK ON THE TRANSFORMATION MACHINE FOR READJUSTMENT.
RELEASE ME, OR I'LL BE THE DEATH OF YOU. I WILL TURN THE AIR INSIDE YOUR LUNGS INTO NOXIOUS GAS--AS YOU TAUGHT ME!
VERY WELL. BUT NO MORE TALK OF LOVE. OR I WILL SURELY PUT YOUR NEW POWERS TO THE TEST, HORSEMAN.
COME. TOO MUCH OF THE ANTIDOTE IS LOST WE WILL NEED TO ALTER OUR STRATEGY.

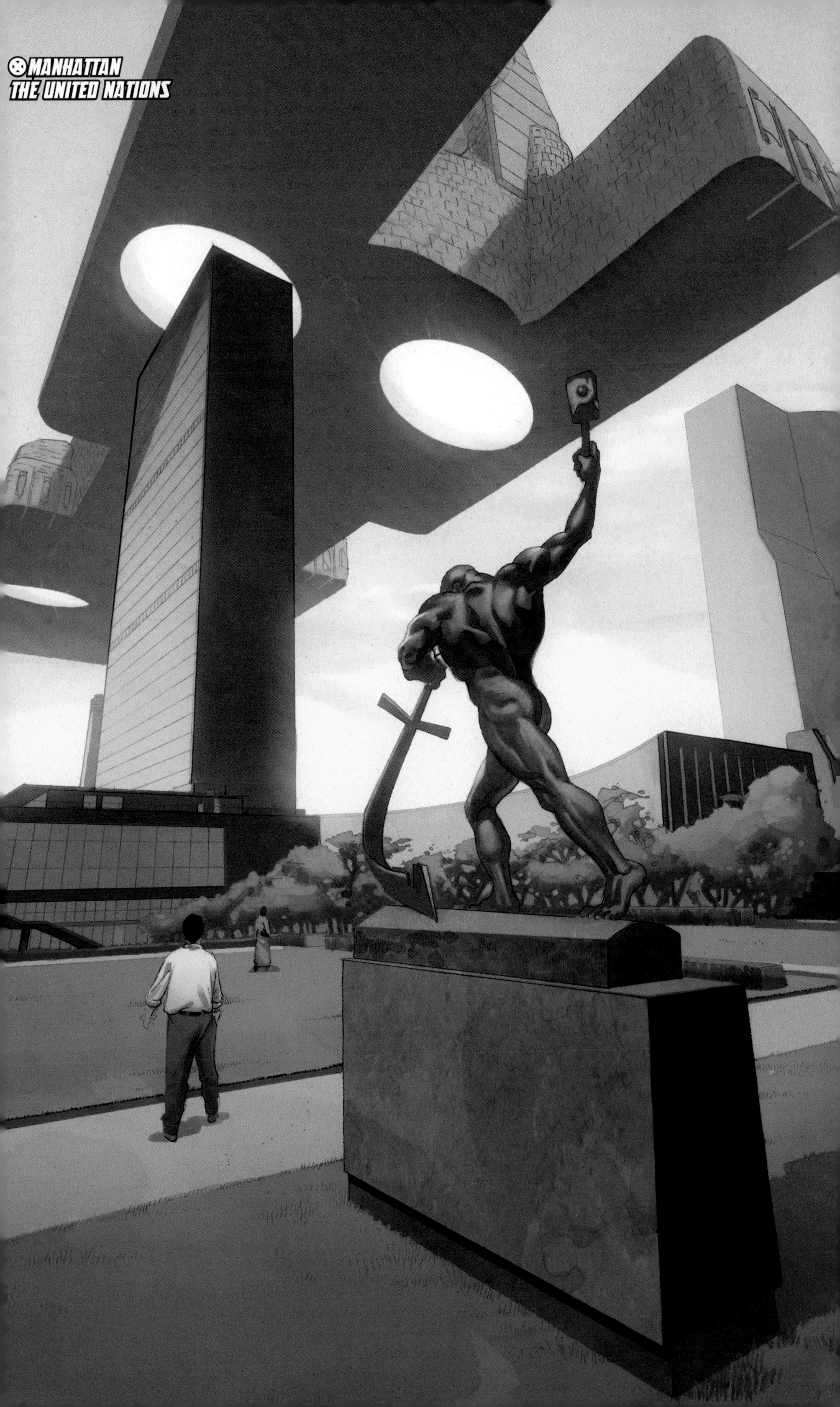
MANHATTAN
THE UNITED NATIONS

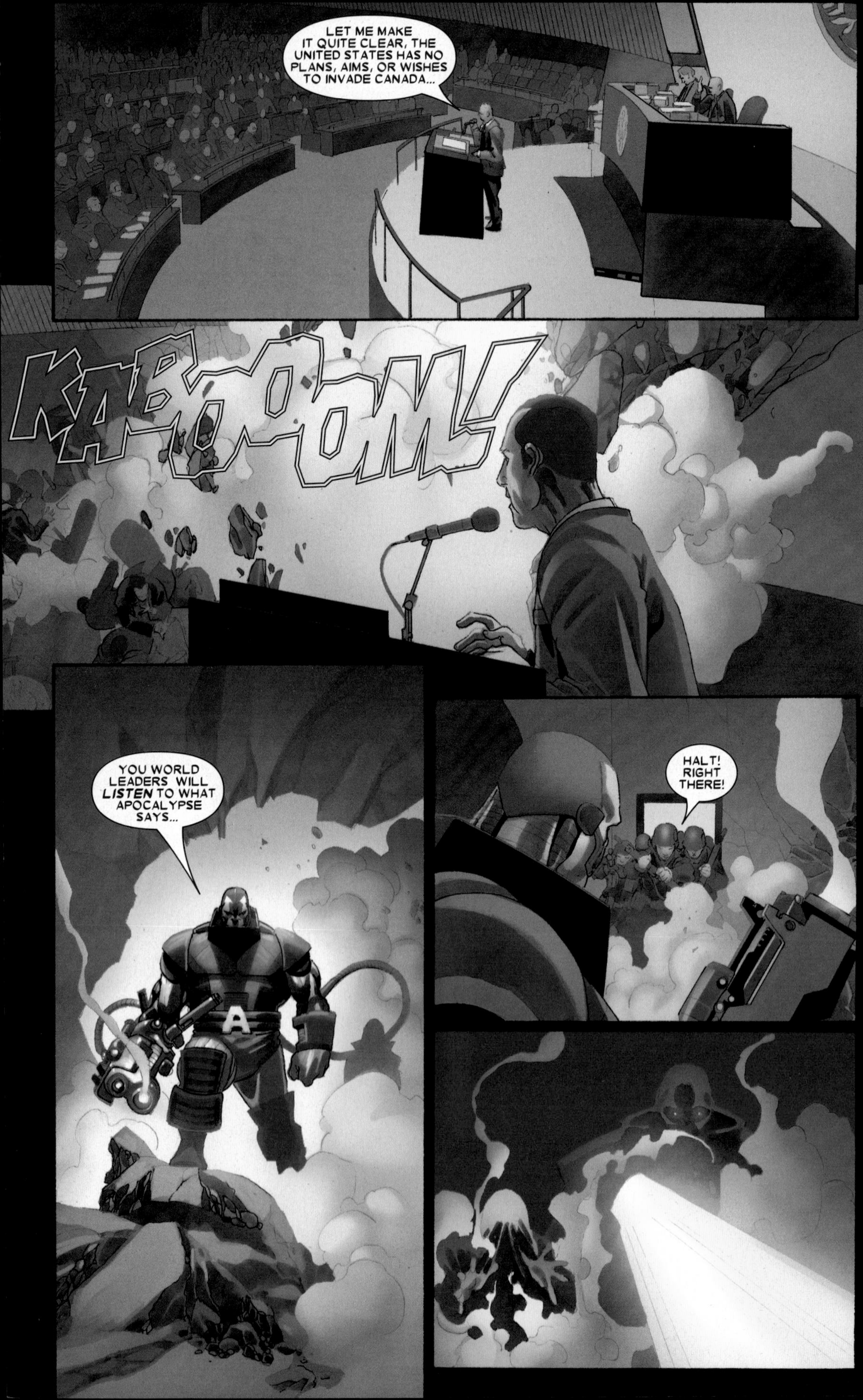
LET ME MAKE IT QUITE CLEAR, THE UNITED STATES HAS NO PLANS, AIMS, OR WISHES TO INVADE CANADA...
KABOOOM!
YOU WORLD LEADERS WILL LISTEN TO WHAT APOCALYPSE SAYS...
HALT! RIGHT THERE!

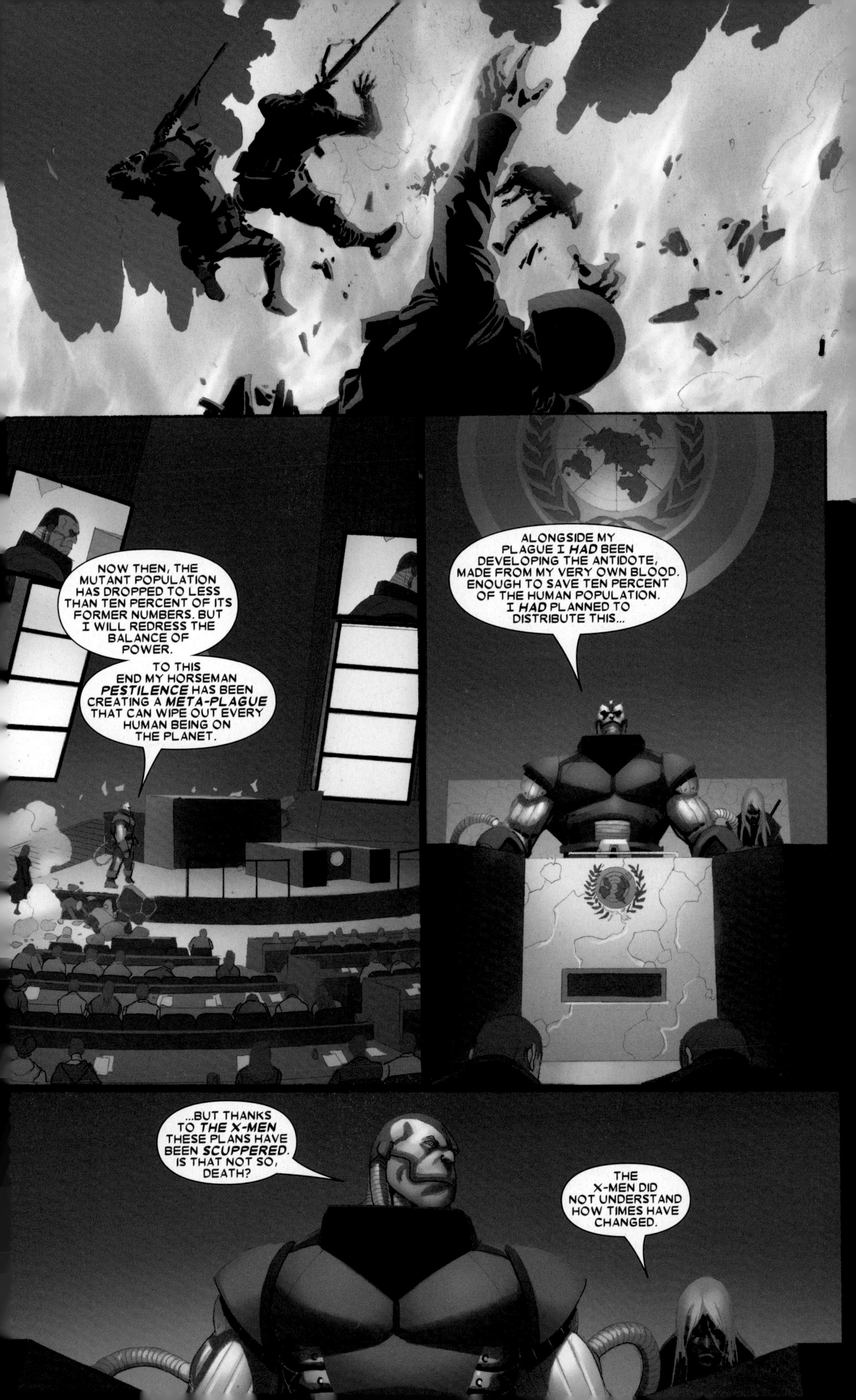
NOW THEN, THE MUTANT POPULATION HAS DROPPED TO LESS THAN TEN PERCENT OF ITS FORMER NUMBERS. BUT I WILL REDRESS THE BALANCE OF POWER.
TO THIS END MY HORSEMAN PESTILENCE HAS BEEN CREATING A META-PLAGUE THAT CAN WIPE OUT EVERY HUMAN BEING ON THE PLANET.
ALONGSIDE MY PLAGUE I HAD BEEN DEVELOPING THE ANTIDOTE, MADE FROM MY VERY OWN BLOOD. ENOUGH TO SAVE TEN PERCENT OF THE HUMAN POPULATION. I HAD PLANNED TO DISTRIBUTE THIS...
...BUT THANKS TO THE X-MEN THESE PLANS HAVE BEEN SCUPPERED. IS THAT NOT SO, DEATH?
THE X-MEN DID NOT UNDERSTAND HOW TIMES HAVE CHANGED.

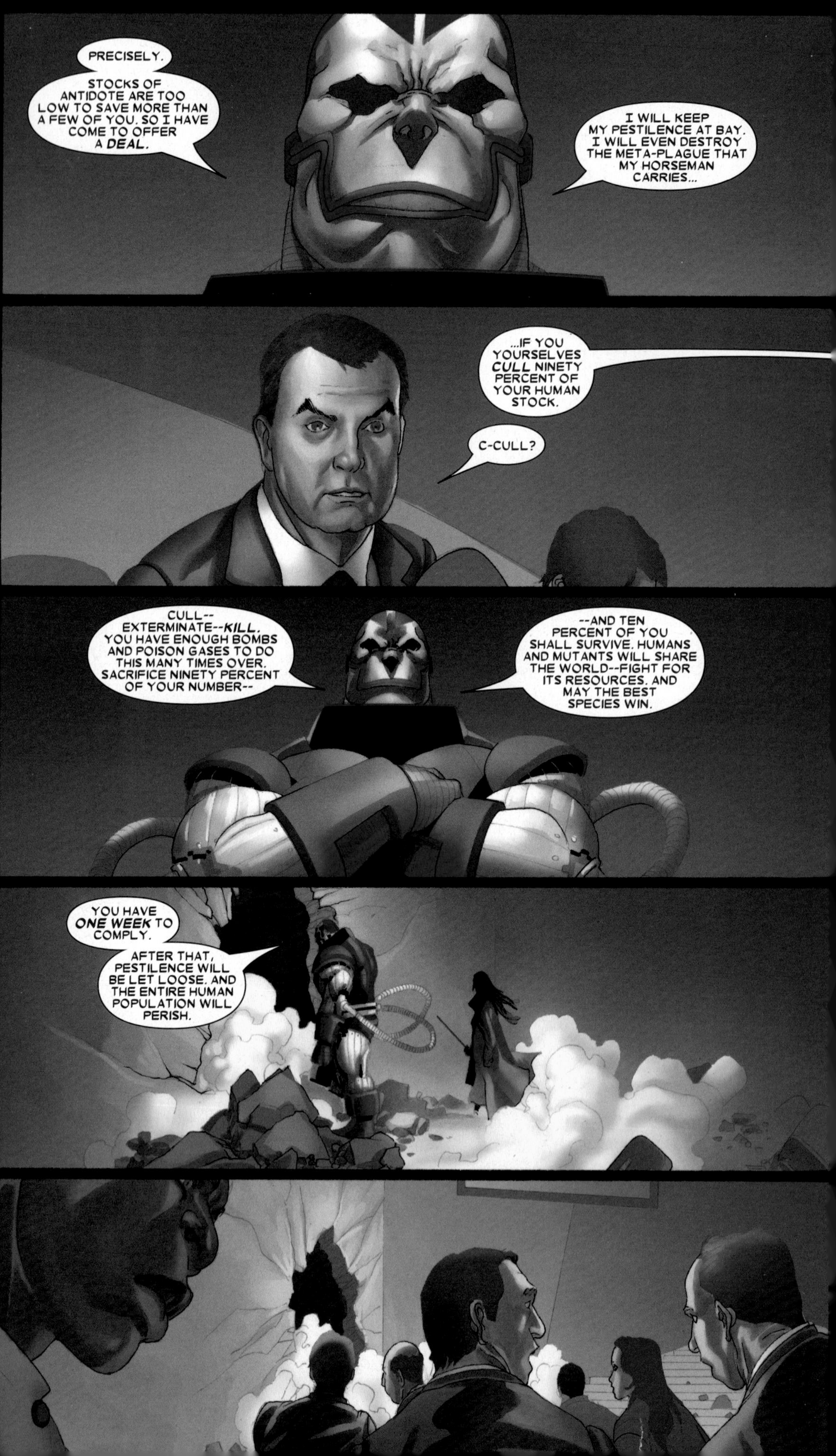
PRECISELY.
STOCKS OF ANTIDOTE ARE TOO LOW TO SAVE MORE THAN A FEW OF YOU. SO I HAVE COME TO OFFER A *DEAL.*
I WILL KEEP MY PESTILENCE AT BAY. I WILL EVEN DESTROY THE META-PLAGUE THAT MY HORSEMAN CARRIES...
...IF YOU YOURSELVES *CULL* NINETY PERCENT OF YOUR HUMAN STOCK.
C-CULL?
CULL--EXTERMINATE--*KILL.* YOU HAVE ENOUGH BOMBS AND POISON GASES TO DO THIS MANY TIMES OVER. SACRIFICE NINETY PERCENT OF YOUR NUMBER--
--AND TEN PERCENT OF YOU SHALL SURVIVE. HUMANS AND MUTANTS WILL SHARE THE WORLD--FIGHT FOR ITS RESOURCES. AND MAY THE BEST SPECIES WIN.
YOU HAVE *ONE WEEK* TO COMPLY.
AFTER THAT, PESTILENCE WILL BE LET LOOSE. AND THE ENTIRE HUMAN POPULATION WILL PERISH.

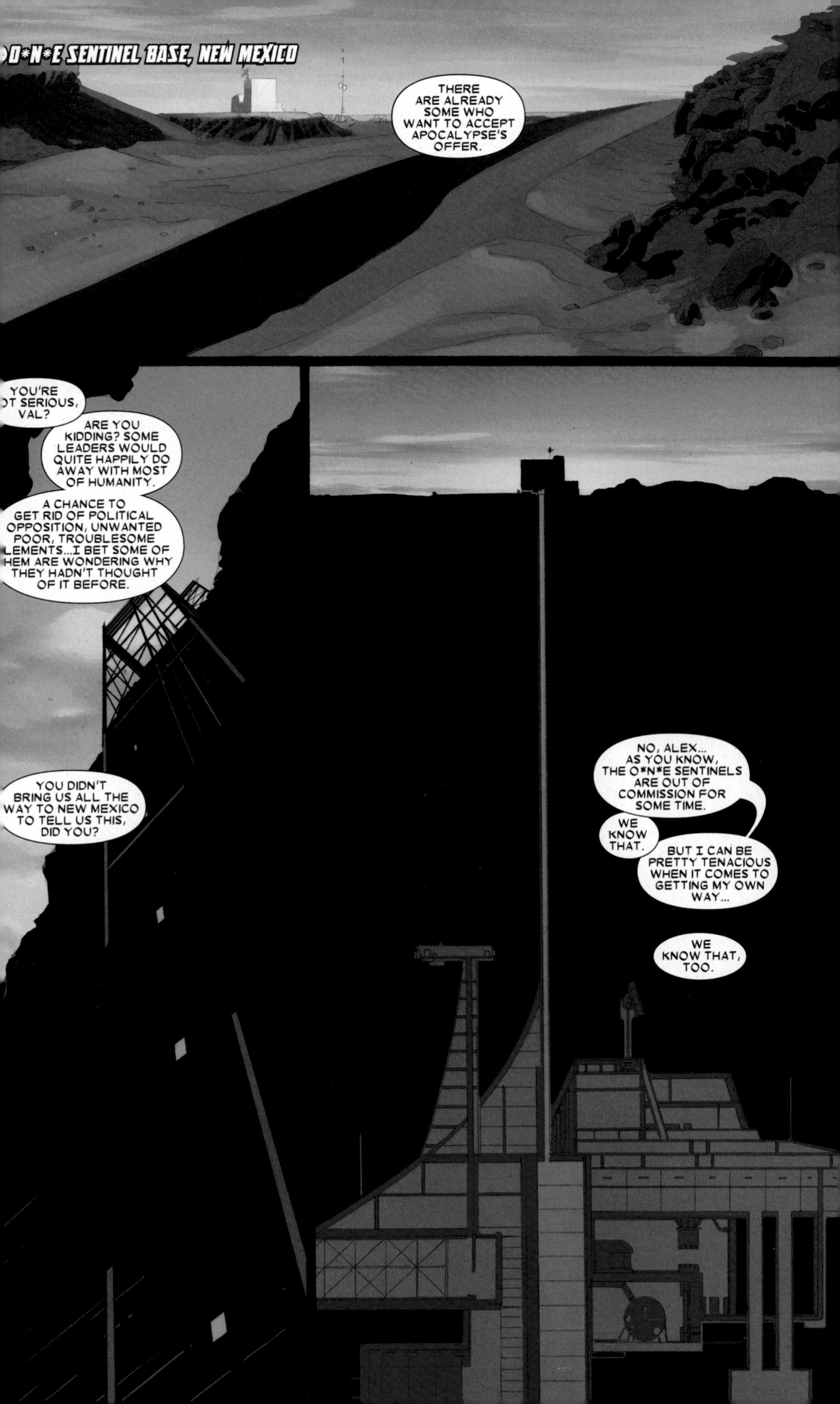
O*N*E SENTINEL BASE, NEW MEXICO
THERE ARE ALREADY SOME WHO WANT TO ACCEPT APOCALYPSE'S OFFER.
YOU'RE NOT SERIOUS, VAL?
ARE YOU KIDDING? SOME LEADERS WOULD QUITE HAPPILY DO AWAY WITH MOST OF HUMANITY.
A CHANCE TO GET RID OF POLITICAL OPPOSITION, UNWANTED POOR, TROUBLESOME ELEMENTS...I BET SOME OF THEM ARE WONDERING WHY THEY HADN'T THOUGHT OF IT BEFORE.
YOU DIDN'T BRING US ALL THE WAY TO NEW MEXICO TO TELL US THIS, DID YOU?
NO, ALEX... AS YOU KNOW, THE O*N*E SENTINELS ARE OUT OF COMMISSION FOR SOME TIME.
WE KNOW THAT.
BUT I CAN BE PRETTY TENACIOUS WHEN IT COMES TO GETTING MY OWN WAY...
WE KNOW THAT, TOO.

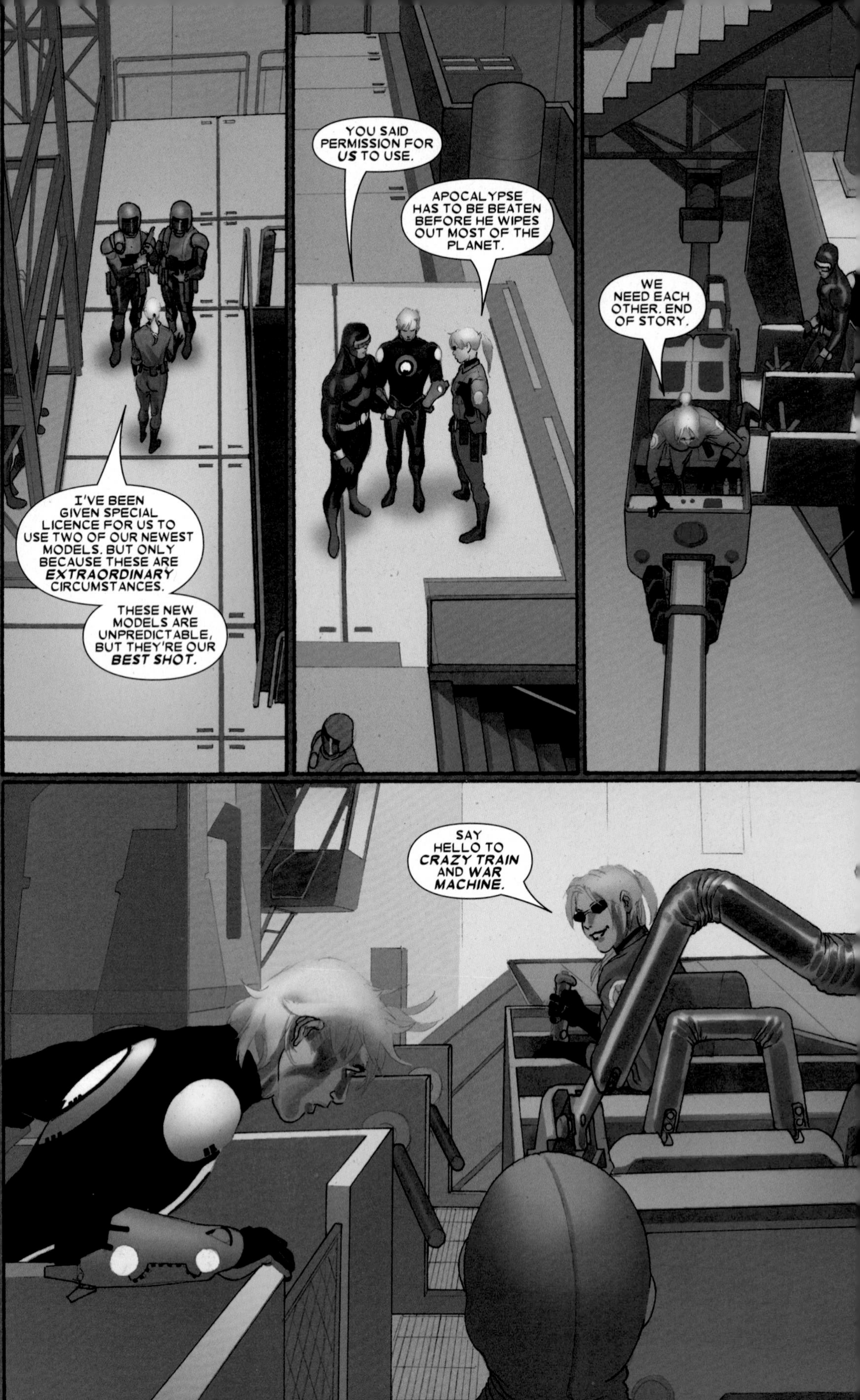

I'VE BEEN GIVEN SPECIAL LICENCE FOR US TO USE TWO OF OUR NEWEST MODELS. BUT ONLY BECAUSE THESE ARE EXTRAORDINARY CIRCUMSTANCES.
THESE NEW MODELS ARE UNPREDICTABLE, BUT THEY'RE OUR BEST SHOT.
YOU SAID PERMISSION FOR US TO USE.
APOCALYPSE HAS TO BE BEATEN BEFORE HE WIPES OUT MOST OF THE PLANET.
WE NEED EACH OTHER. END OF STORY.
SAY HELLO TO CRAZY TRAIN AND WAR MACHINE.

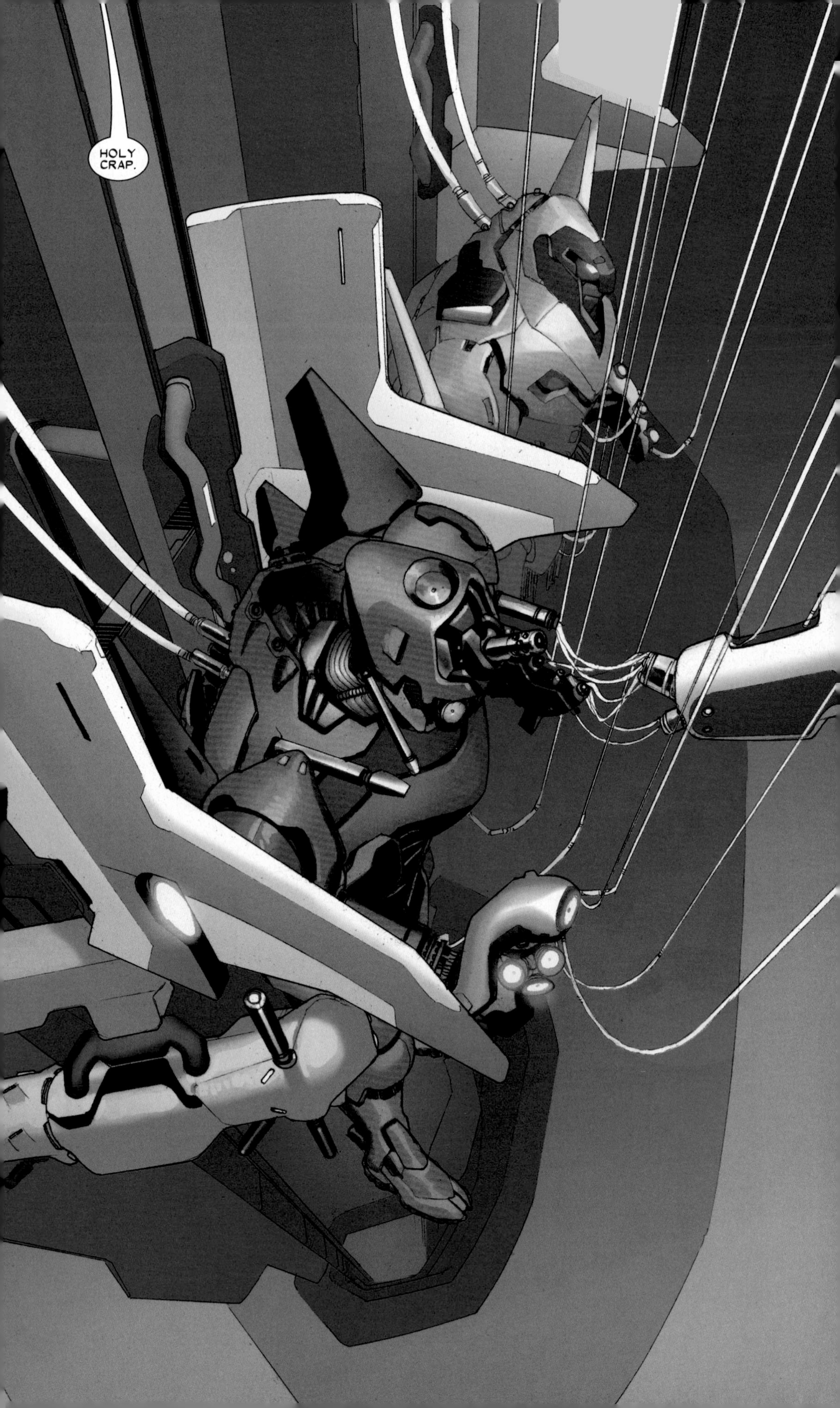
HOLY CRAP.

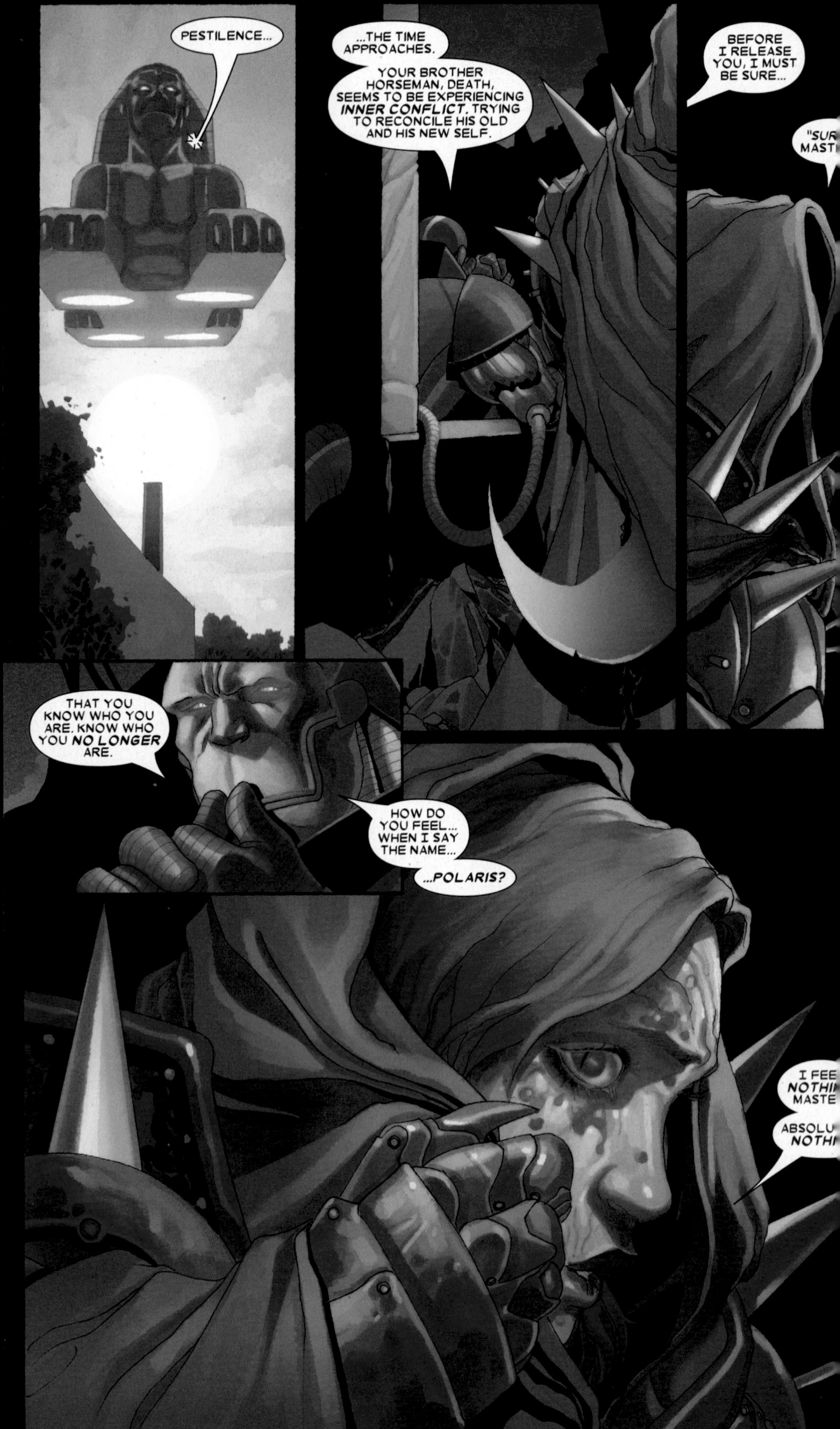
PESTILENCE...
...THE TIME APPROACHES.
YOUR BROTHER HORSEMAN, DEATH, SEEMS TO BE EXPERIENCING INNER CONFLICT. TRYING TO RECONCILE HIS OLD AND HIS NEW SELF.
BEFORE I RELEASE YOU, I MUST BE SURE...
THAT YOU KNOW WHO YOU ARE. KNOW WHO YOU NO LONGER ARE.
HOW DO YOU FEEL... WHEN I SAY THE NAME...
...POLARIS?

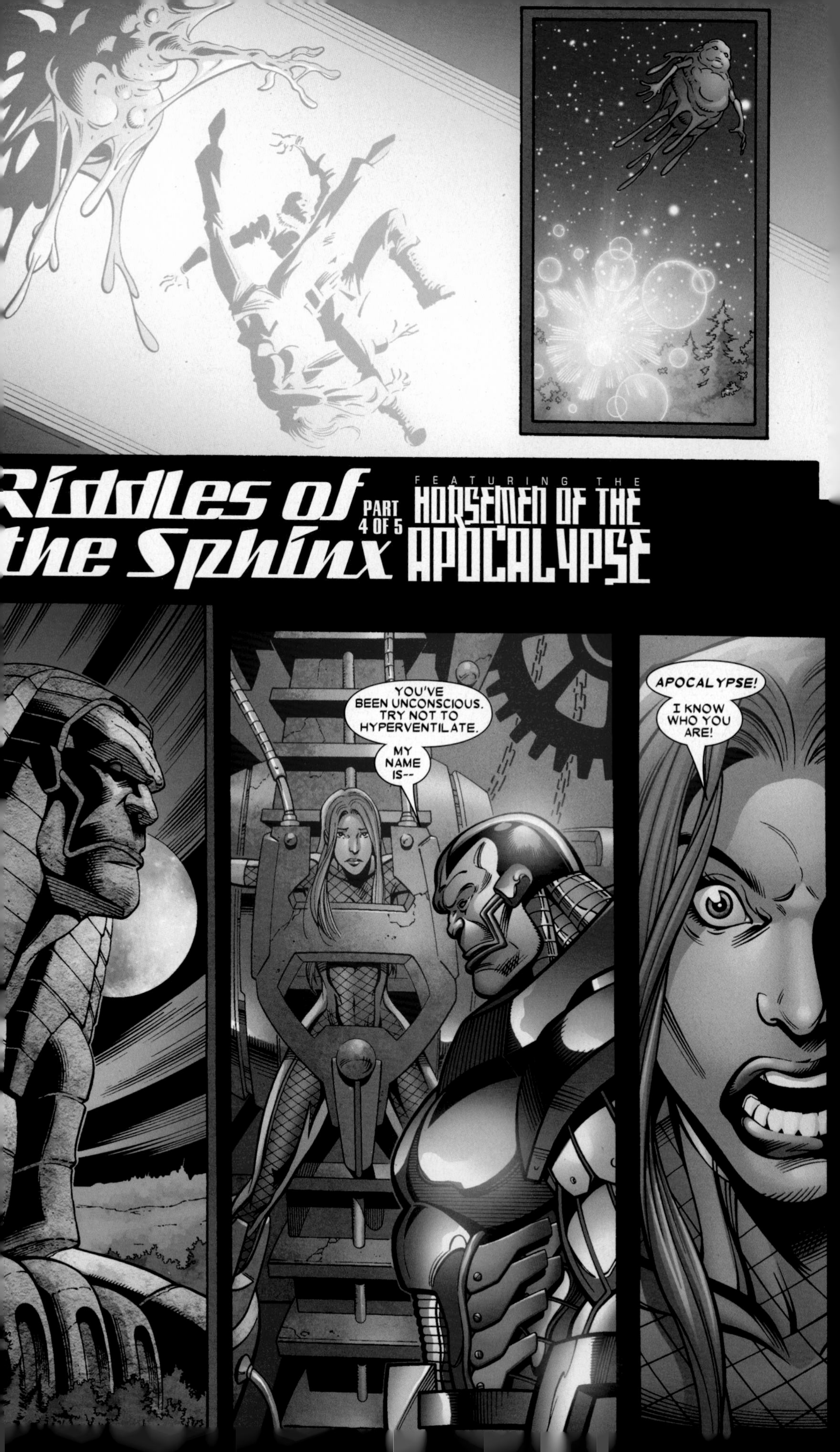

Riddles of the Sphinx
PART 4 OF 5
FEATURING THE HORSEMEN OF THE APOCALYPSE
YOU'VE BEEN UNCONSCIOUS. TRY NOT TO HYPERVENTILATE.
MY NAME IS--
APOCALYPSE!
I KNOW WHO YOU ARE!

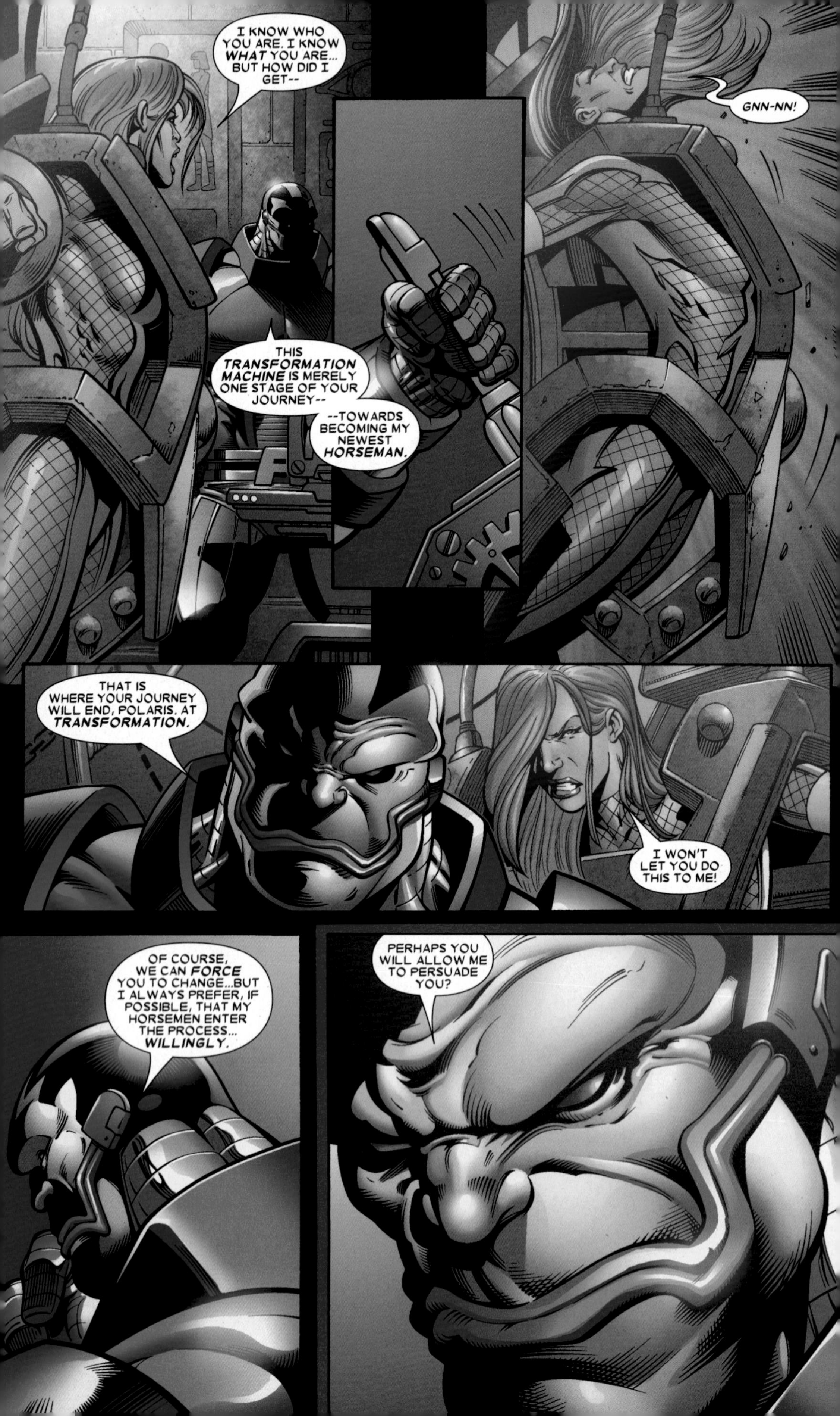
I KNOW WHO YOU ARE. I KNOW WHAT YOU ARE... BUT HOW DID I GET--
THIS TRANSFORMATION MACHINE IS MERELY ONE STAGE OF YOUR JOURNEY--
--TOWARDS BECOMING MY NEWEST HORSEMAN.
GNN-NN!
THAT IS WHERE YOUR JOURNEY WILL END, POLARIS. AT TRANSFORMATION.
I WON'T LET YOU DO THIS TO ME!
OF COURSE, WE CAN FORCE YOU TO CHANGE...BUT I ALWAYS PREFER, IF POSSIBLE, THAT MY HORSEMEN ENTER THE PROCESS... WILLINGLY.
PERHAPS YOU WILL ALLOW ME TO PERSUADE YOU?

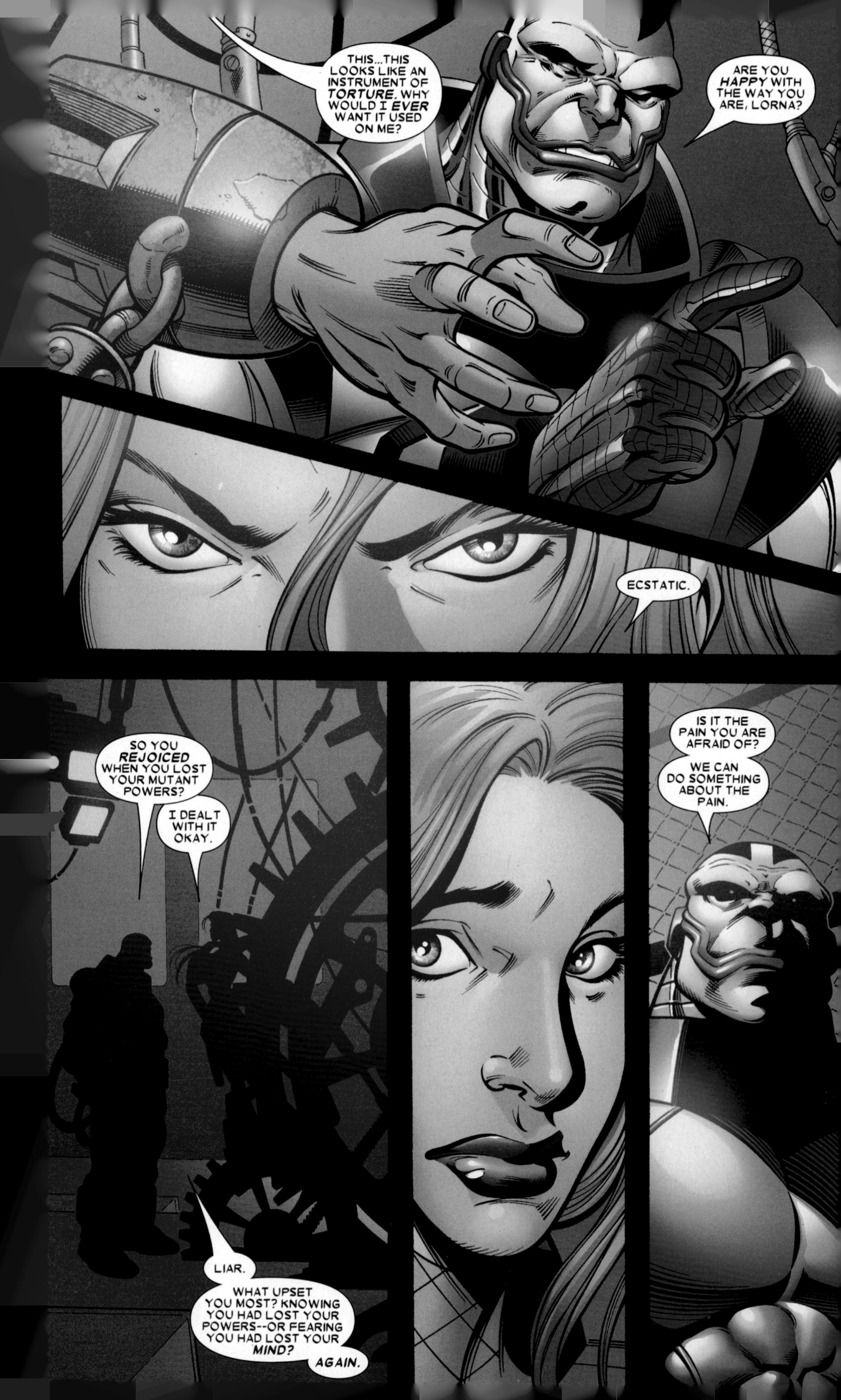
THIS...THIS LOOKS LIKE AN INSTRUMENT OF TORTURE. WHY WOULD I EVER WANT IT USED ON ME?
ARE YOU HAPPY WITH THE WAY YOU ARE, LORNA?
ECSTATIC.
SO YOU REJOICED WHEN YOU LOST YOUR MUTANT POWERS?
I DEALT WITH IT OKAY.
LIAR.
WHAT UPSET YOU MOST? KNOWING YOU HAD LOST YOUR POWERS--OR FEARING YOU HAD LOST YOUR MIND?
AGAIN.
IS IT THE PAIN YOU ARE AFRAID OF?
WE CAN DO SOMETHING ABOUT THE PAIN.

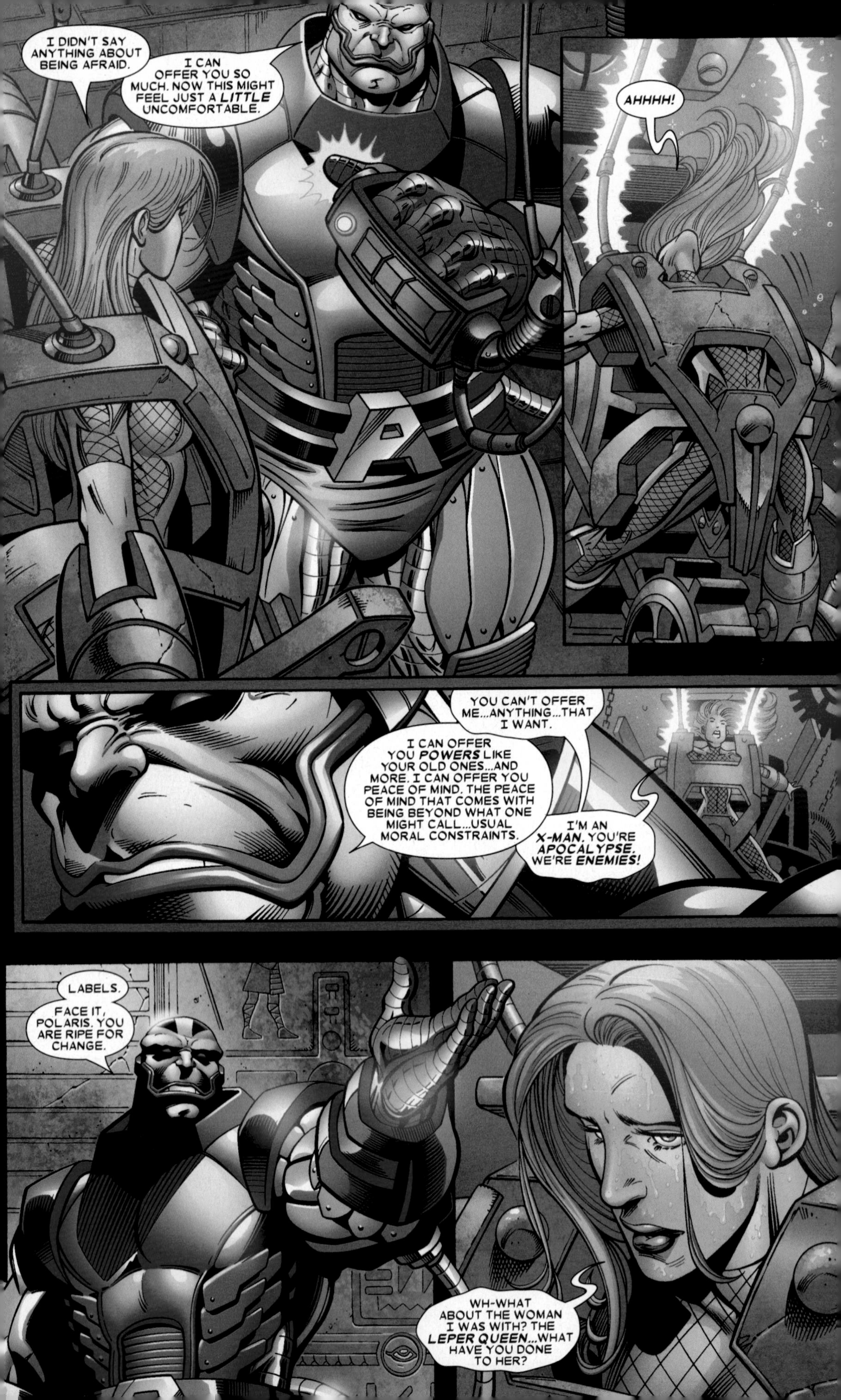
I DIDN'T SAY ANYTHING ABOUT BEING AFRAID.
I CAN OFFER YOU SO MUCH. NOW THIS MIGHT FEEL JUST A LITTLE UNCOMFORTABLE.
AHHHH!
YOU CAN'T OFFER ME...ANYTHING...THAT I WANT.
I CAN OFFER YOU POWERS LIKE YOUR OLD ONES...AND MORE. I CAN OFFER YOU PEACE OF MIND. THE PEACE OF MIND THAT COMES WITH BEING BEYOND WHAT ONE MIGHT CALL...USUAL MORAL CONSTRAINTS.
I'M AN X-MAN. YOU'RE APOCALYPSE. WE'RE ENEMIES!
LABELS.
FACE IT, POLARIS. YOU ARE RIPE FOR CHANGE.
WH-WHAT ABOUT THE WOMAN I WAS WITH? THE LEPER QUEEN...WHAT HAVE YOU DONE TO HER?

SHE WILL BE LOOKED AFTER...UNTIL I HAVE NEED FOR HER. ONLY ONE OF YOU CAN BE MY NEW *PESTILENCE*.

WHILE YOU WERE UNCONSCIOUS, THE LEPER QUEEN WAS INTERVIEWED FOR THE POSITION.

SHE WAS REJECTED.

REJECTED-- WHY?

A CERTAIN DEGREE OF VOLITION IS ADVANTAGEOUS, YES. BUT THAT ONE--THAT ONE WITH THE MASK AND THE RUINED FACE...

"...SHE WANTED IT *TOO BADLY*."

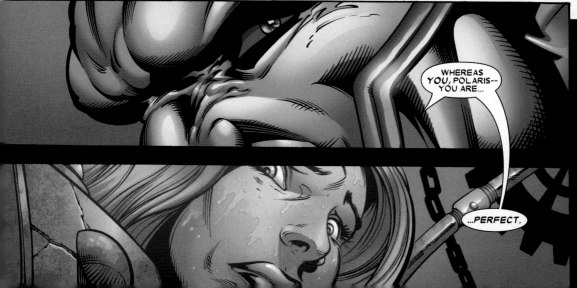

WHEREAS *YOU*, POLARIS-- YOU ARE...

...PERFECT.

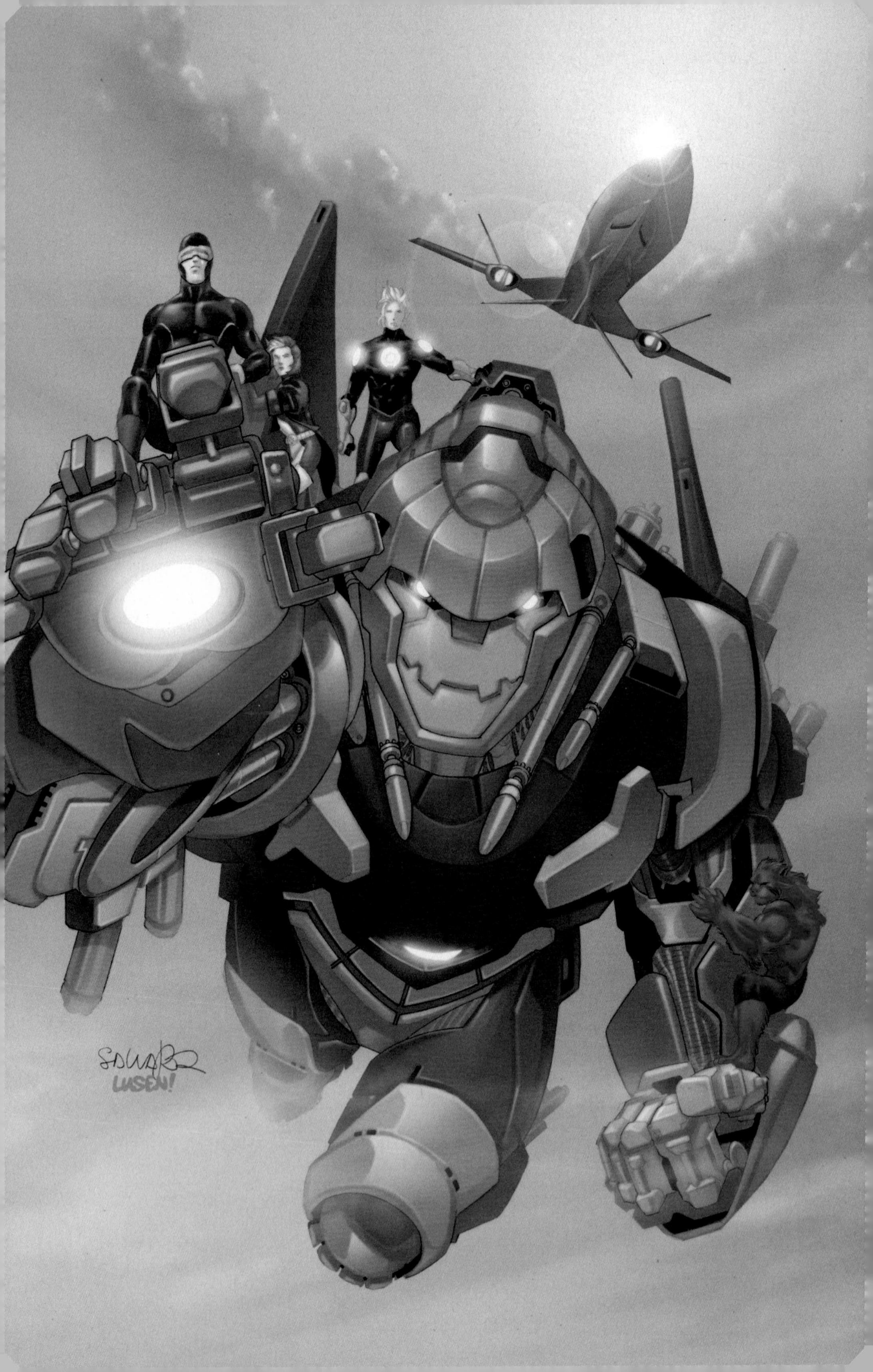

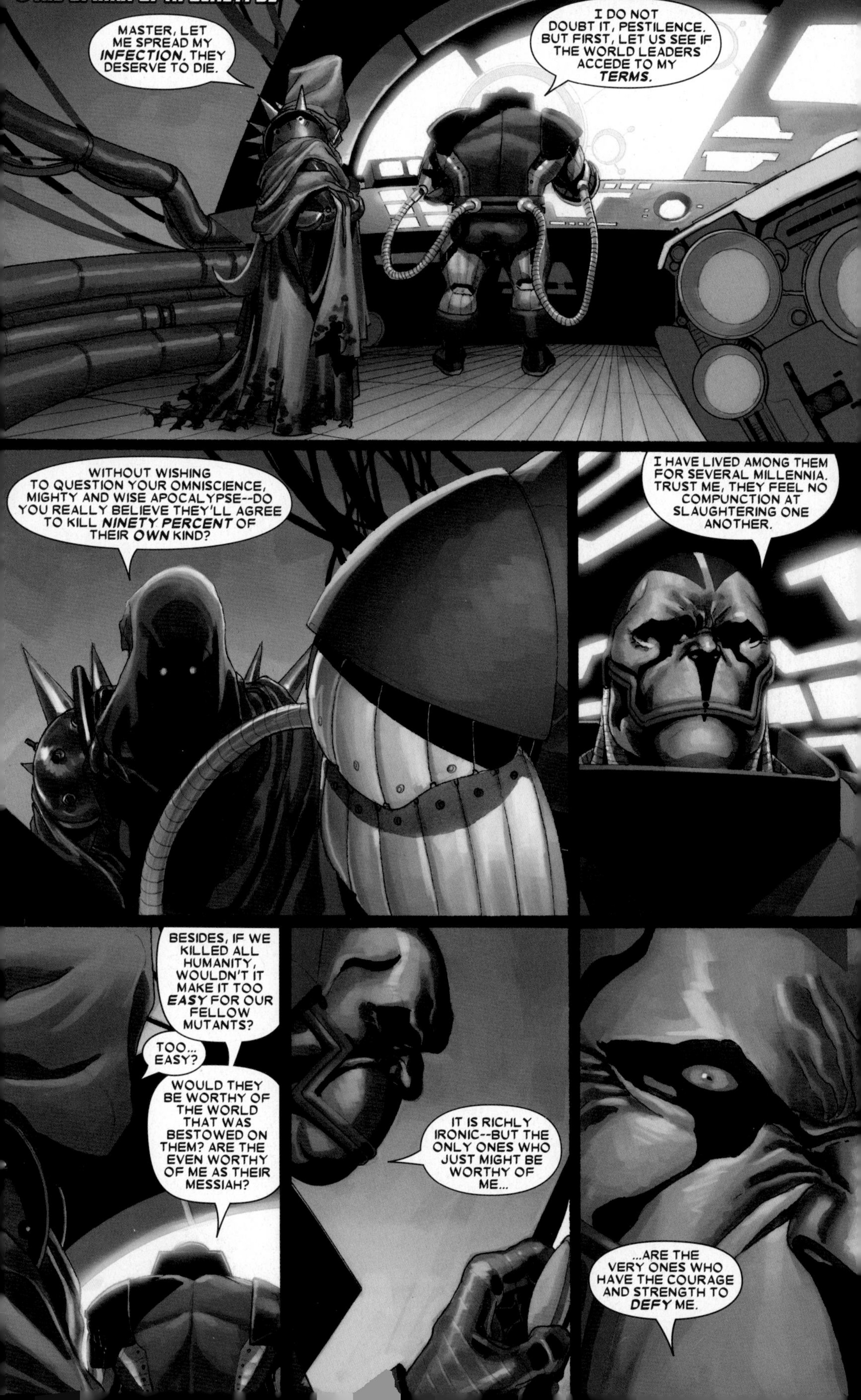
MASTER, LET ME SPREAD MY *INFECTION*. THEY DESERVE TO DIE.
I DO NOT DOUBT IT, PESTILENCE. BUT FIRST, LET US SEE IF THE WORLD LEADERS ACCEDE TO MY *TERMS*.
WITHOUT WISHING TO QUESTION YOUR OMNISCIENCE, MIGHTY AND WISE APOCALYPSE--DO YOU REALLY BELIEVE THEY'LL AGREE TO KILL *NINETY PERCENT* OF THEIR *OWN* KIND?
I HAVE LIVED AMONG THEM FOR SEVERAL MILLENNIA. TRUST ME, THEY FEEL NO COMPUNCTION AT SLAUGHTERING ONE ANOTHER.
BESIDES, IF WE KILLED ALL HUMANITY, WOULDN'T IT MAKE IT TOO *EASY* FOR OUR FELLOW MUTANTS?
TOO... EASY?
WOULD THEY BE WORTHY OF THE WORLD THAT WAS BESTOWED ON THEM? ARE THE EVEN WORTHY OF ME AS THEIR MESSIAH?
IT IS RICHLY IRONIC--BUT THE ONLY ONES WHO JUST MIGHT BE WORTHY OF ME...
...ARE THE VERY ONES WHO HAVE THE COURAGE AND STRENGTH TO *DEFY* ME.

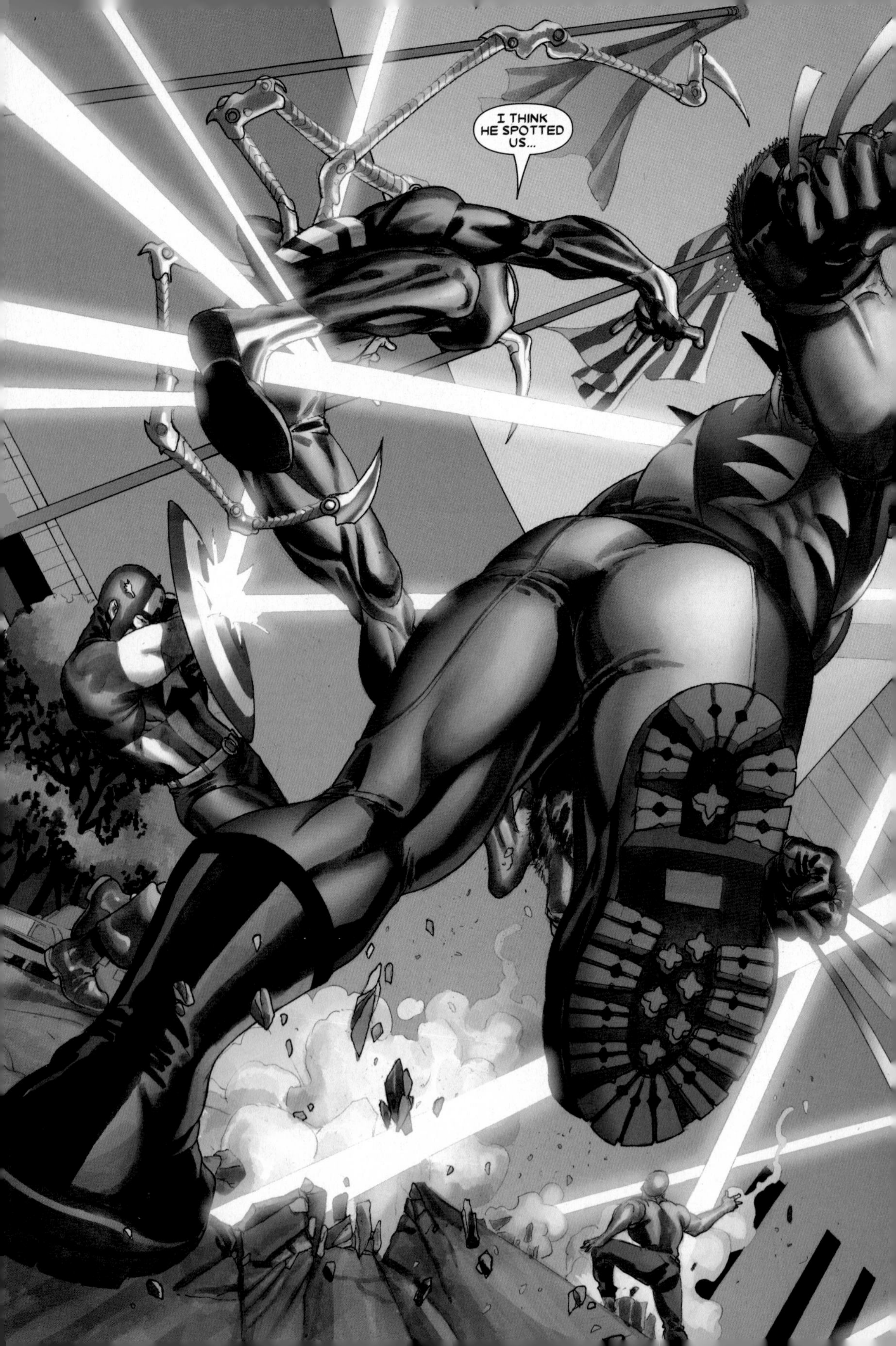
I THINK HE SPOTTED US...

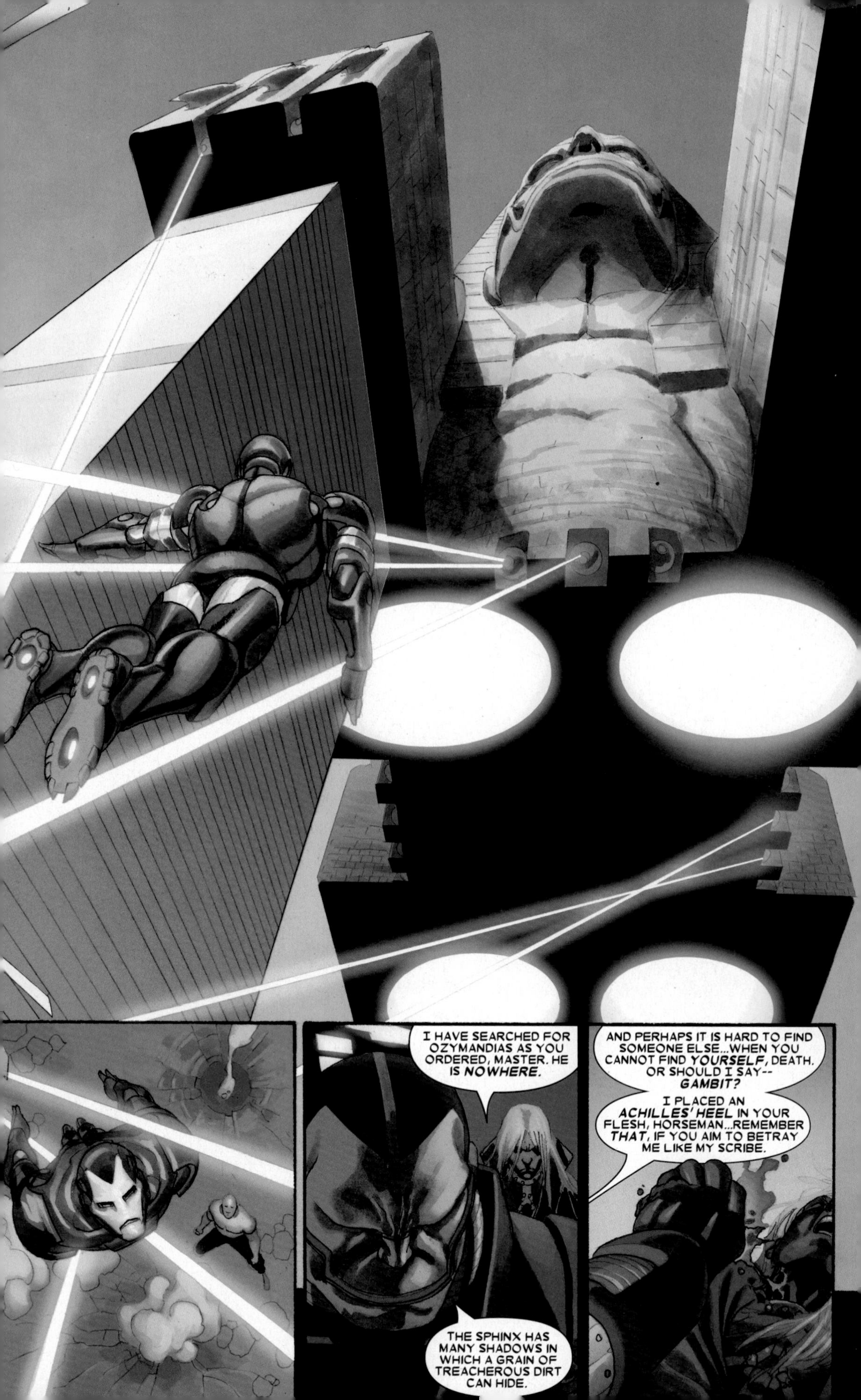
I HAVE SEARCHED FOR OZYMANDIAS AS YOU ORDERED, MASTER. HE IS NOWHERE.
THE SPHINX HAS MANY SHADOWS IN WHICH A GRAIN OF TREACHEROUS DIRT CAN HIDE.
AND PERHAPS IT IS HARD TO FIND SOMEONE ELSE...WHEN YOU CANNOT FIND YOURSELF, DEATH. OR SHOULD I SAY-- GAMBIT?
I PLACED AN ACHILLES' HEEL IN YOUR FLESH, HORSEMAN...REMEMBER THAT, IF YOU AIM TO BETRAY ME LIKE MY SCRIBE.

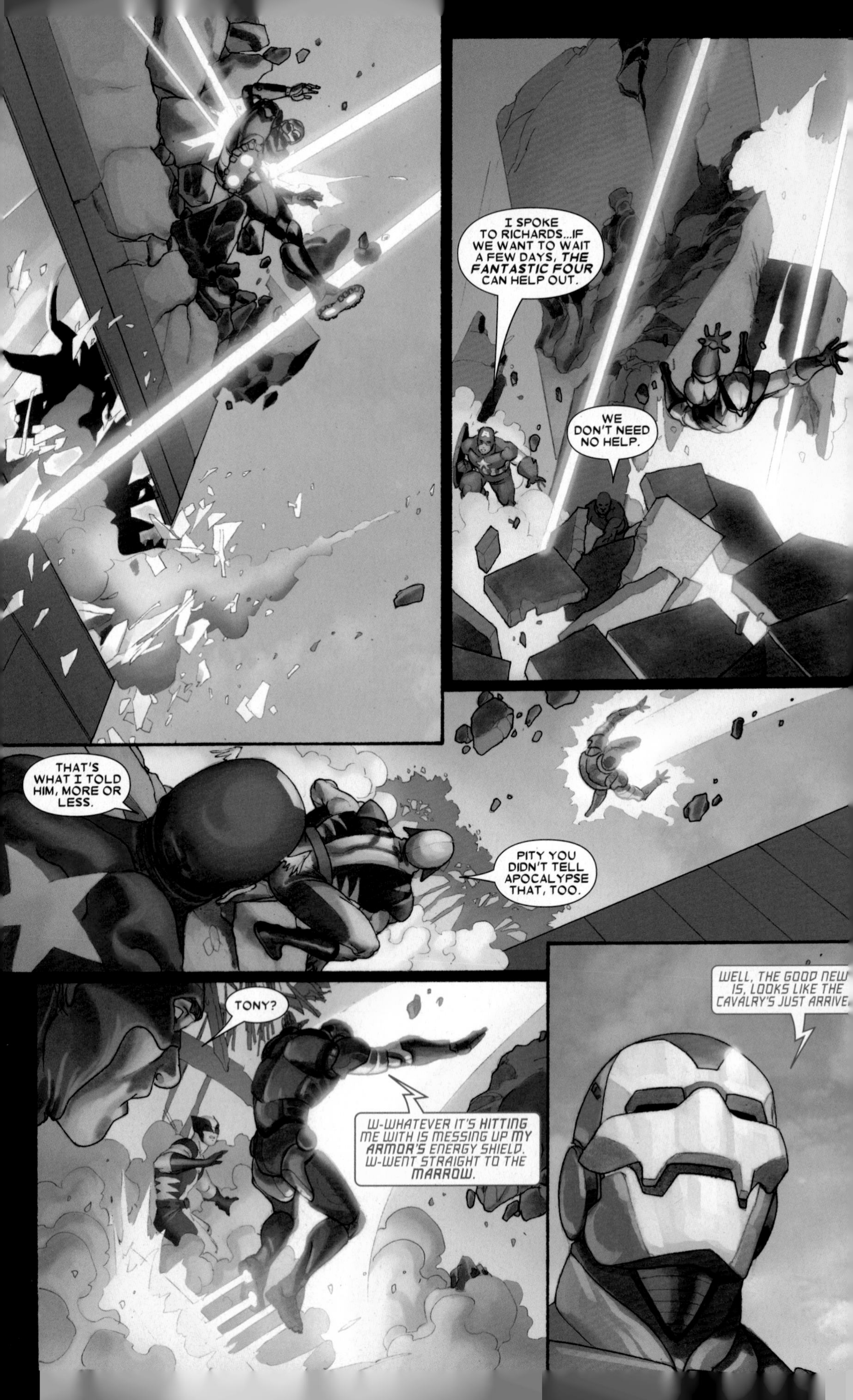
I SPOKE TO RICHARDS...IF WE WANT TO WAIT A FEW DAYS, THE FANTASTIC FOUR CAN HELP OUT.
WE DON'T NEED NO HELP.
THAT'S WHAT I TOLD HIM, MORE OR LESS.
PITY YOU DIDN'T TELL APOCALYPSE THAT, TOO.
TONY?
W-WHATEVER IT'S HITTING ME WITH IS MESSING UP MY ARMOR'S ENERGY SHIELD. W-WENT STRAIGHT TO THE MARROW.

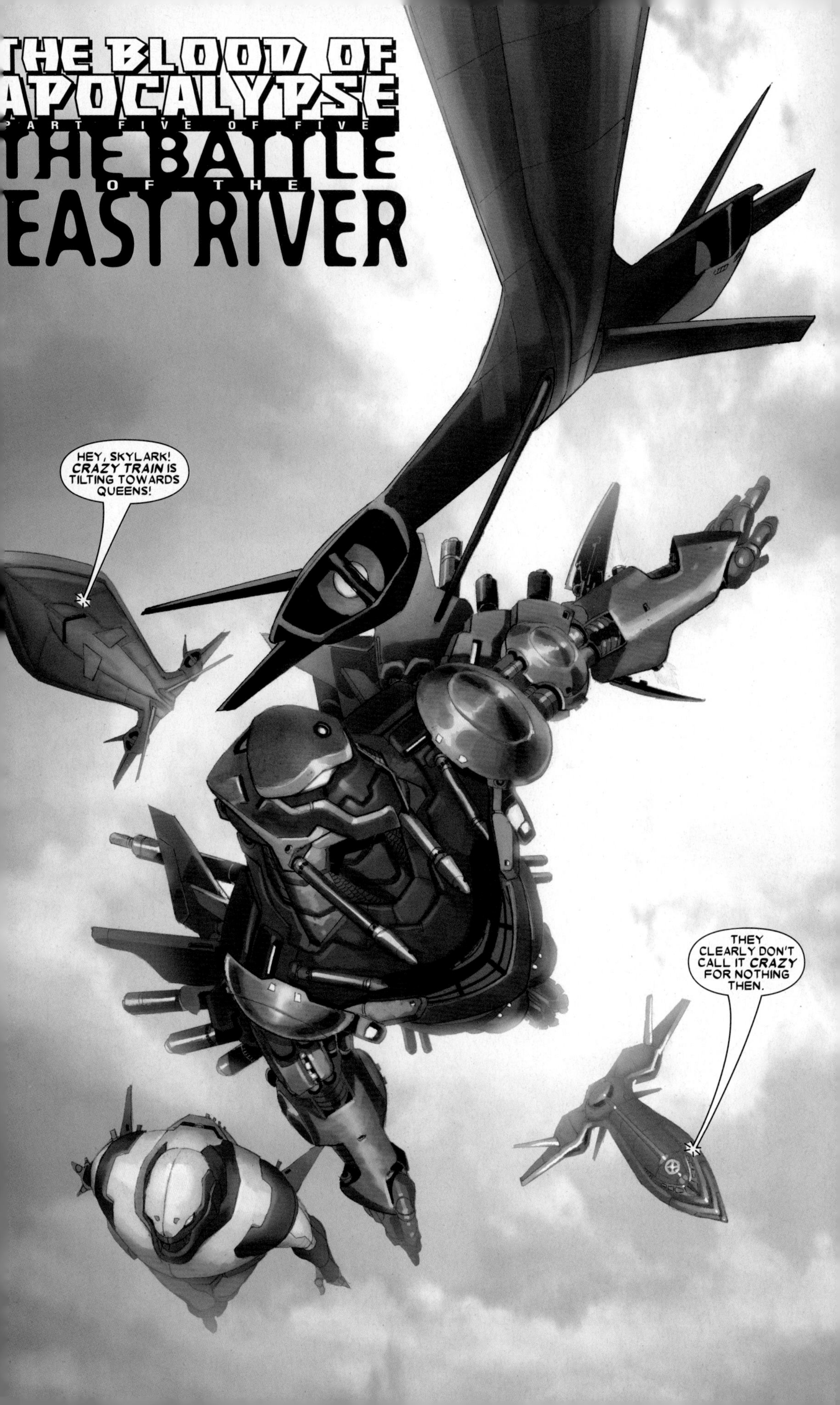
THE BLOOD OF APOCALYPSE
PART FIVE OF FIVE
THE BATTLE OF THE EAST RIVER
HEY, SKYLARK! CRAZY TRAIN IS TILTING TOWARDS QUEENS!
THEY CLEARLY DON'T CALL IT CRAZY FOR NOTHING THEN.

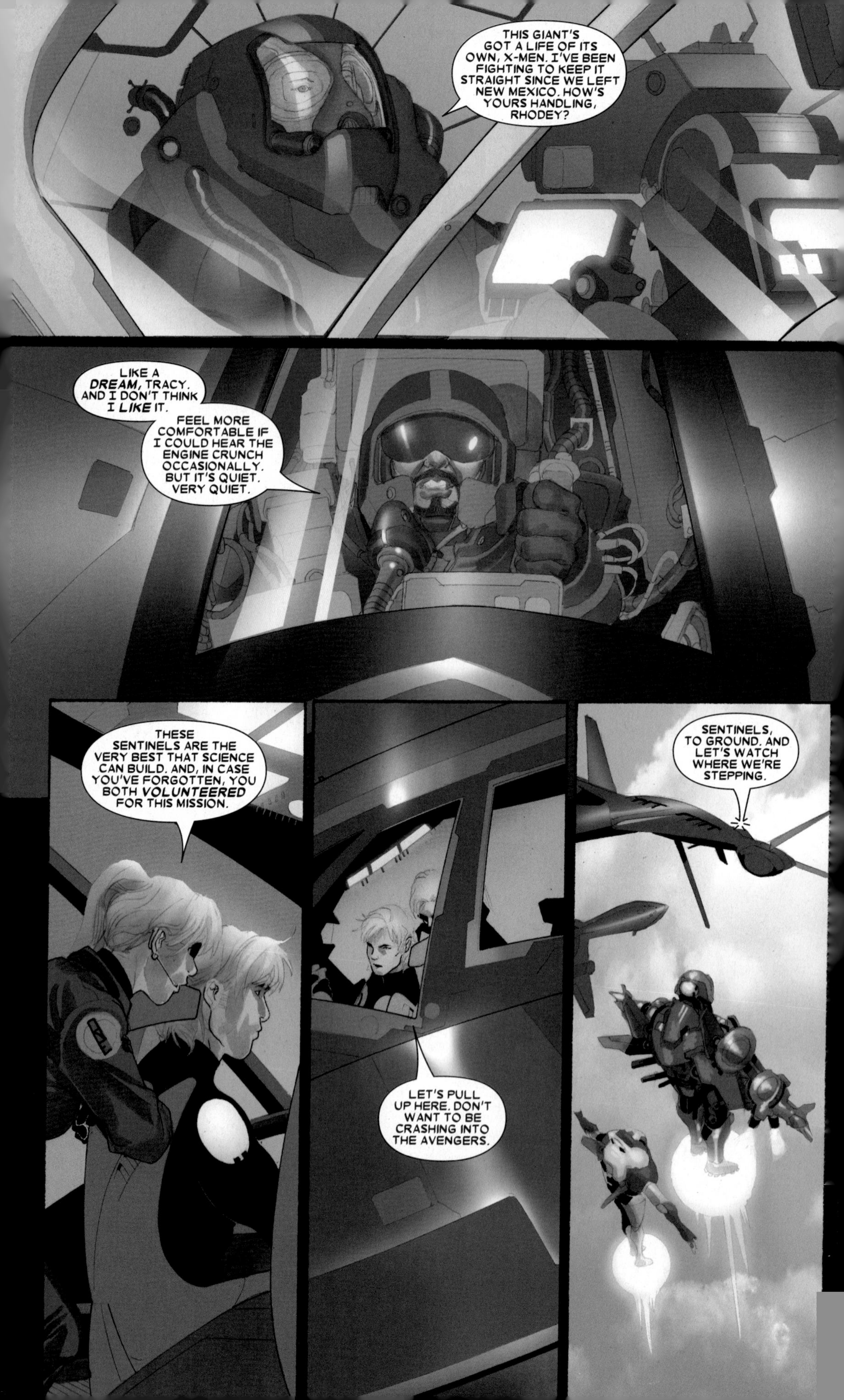
THIS GIANT'S GOT A LIFE OF ITS OWN, X-MEN. I'VE BEEN FIGHTING TO KEEP IT STRAIGHT SINCE WE LEFT NEW MEXICO. HOW'S YOURS HANDLING, RHODEY?
LIKE A *DREAM,* TRACY. AND I DON'T THINK I ***LIKE*** IT.
FEEL MORE COMFORTABLE IF I COULD HEAR THE ENGINE CRUNCH OCCASIONALLY. BUT IT'S QUIET. VERY QUIET.
THESE SENTINELS ARE THE VERY BEST THAT SCIENCE CAN BUILD. AND, IN CASE YOU'VE FORGOTTEN, YOU BOTH ***VOLUNTEERED*** FOR THIS MISSION.
LET'S PULL UP HERE. DON'T WANT TO BE CRASHING INTO THE AVENGERS.
SENTINELS, TO GROUND. AND LET'S WATCH WHERE WE'RE STEPPING.

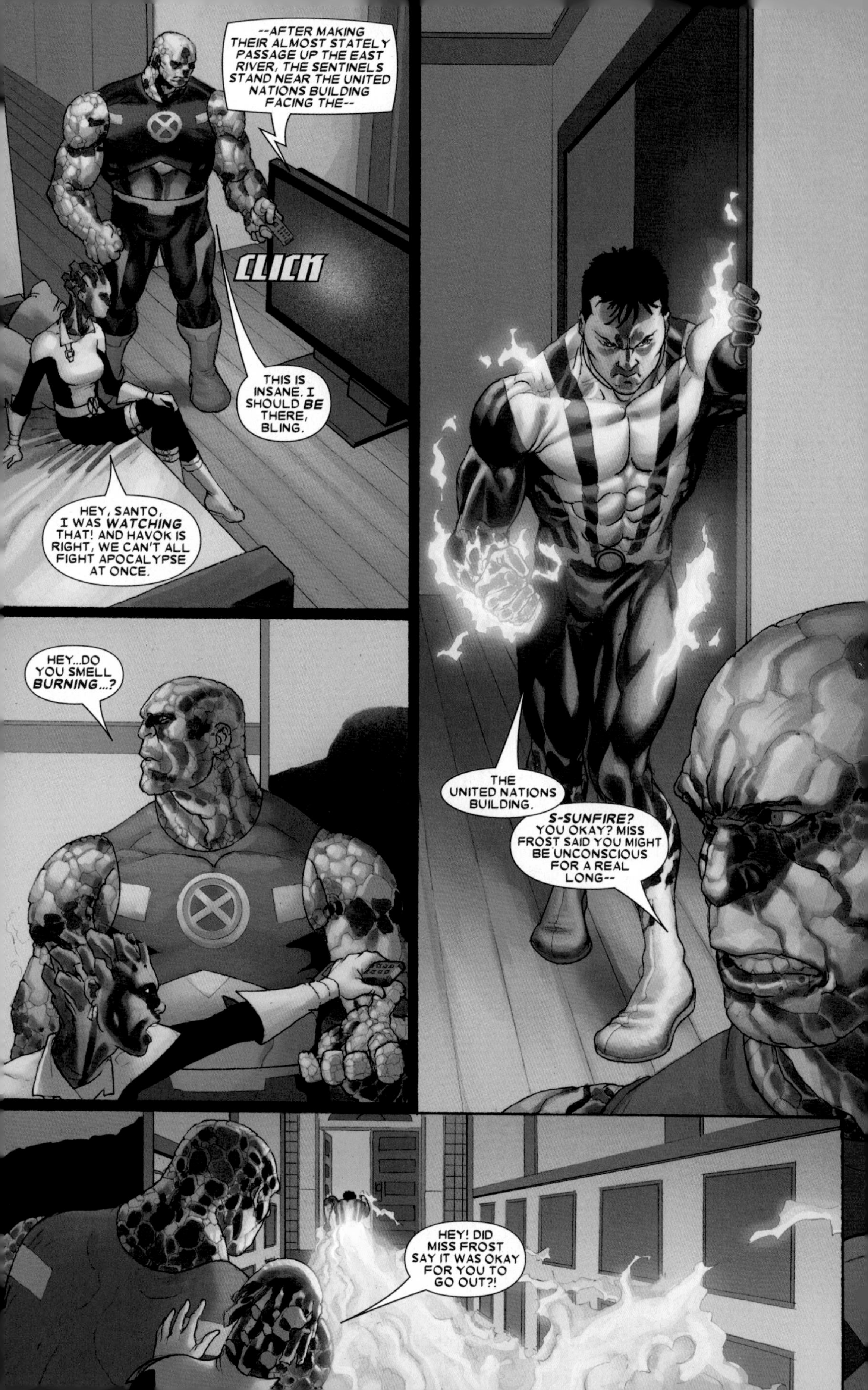
--AFTER MAKING THEIR ALMOST STATELY PASSAGE UP THE EAST RIVER, THE SENTINELS STAND NEAR THE UNITED NATIONS BUILDING FACING THE--
CLICK
THIS IS INSANE. I SHOULD BE THERE, BLING.
HEY, SANTO, I WAS WATCHING THAT! AND HAVOK IS RIGHT, WE CAN'T ALL FIGHT APOCALYPSE AT ONCE.
HEY...DO YOU SMELL BURNING...?
THE UNITED NATIONS BUILDING.
S-SUNFIRE? YOU OKAY? MISS FROST SAID YOU MIGHT BE UNCONSCIOUS FOR A REAL LONG--
HEY! DID MISS FROST SAY IT WAS OKAY FOR YOU TO GO OUT?!

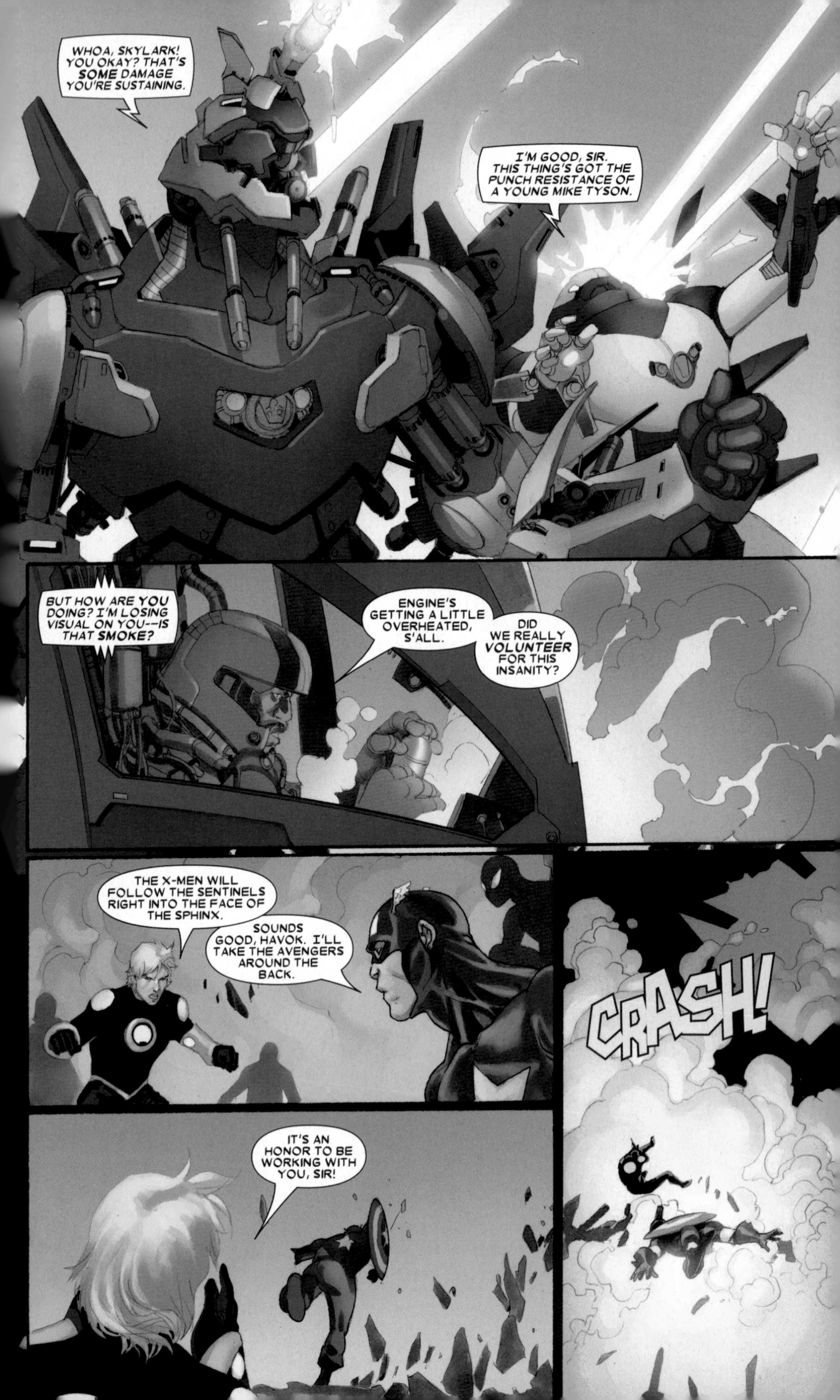

WHOA, SKYLARK! YOU OKAY? THAT'S SOME DAMAGE YOU'RE SUSTAINING.
I'M GOOD, SIR. THIS THING'S GOT THE PUNCH RESISTANCE OF A YOUNG MIKE TYSON.
BUT HOW ARE YOU DOING? I'M LOSING VISUAL ON YOU--IS THAT SMOKE?
ENGINE'S GETTING A LITTLE OVERHEATED, S'ALL.
DID WE REALLY VOLUNTEER FOR THIS INSANITY?
THE X-MEN WILL FOLLOW THE SENTINELS RIGHT INTO THE FACE OF THE SPHINX.
SOUNDS GOOD, HAVOK. I'LL TAKE THE AVENGERS AROUND THE BACK.
IT'S AN HONOR TO BE WORKING WITH YOU, SIR!
CRASH!

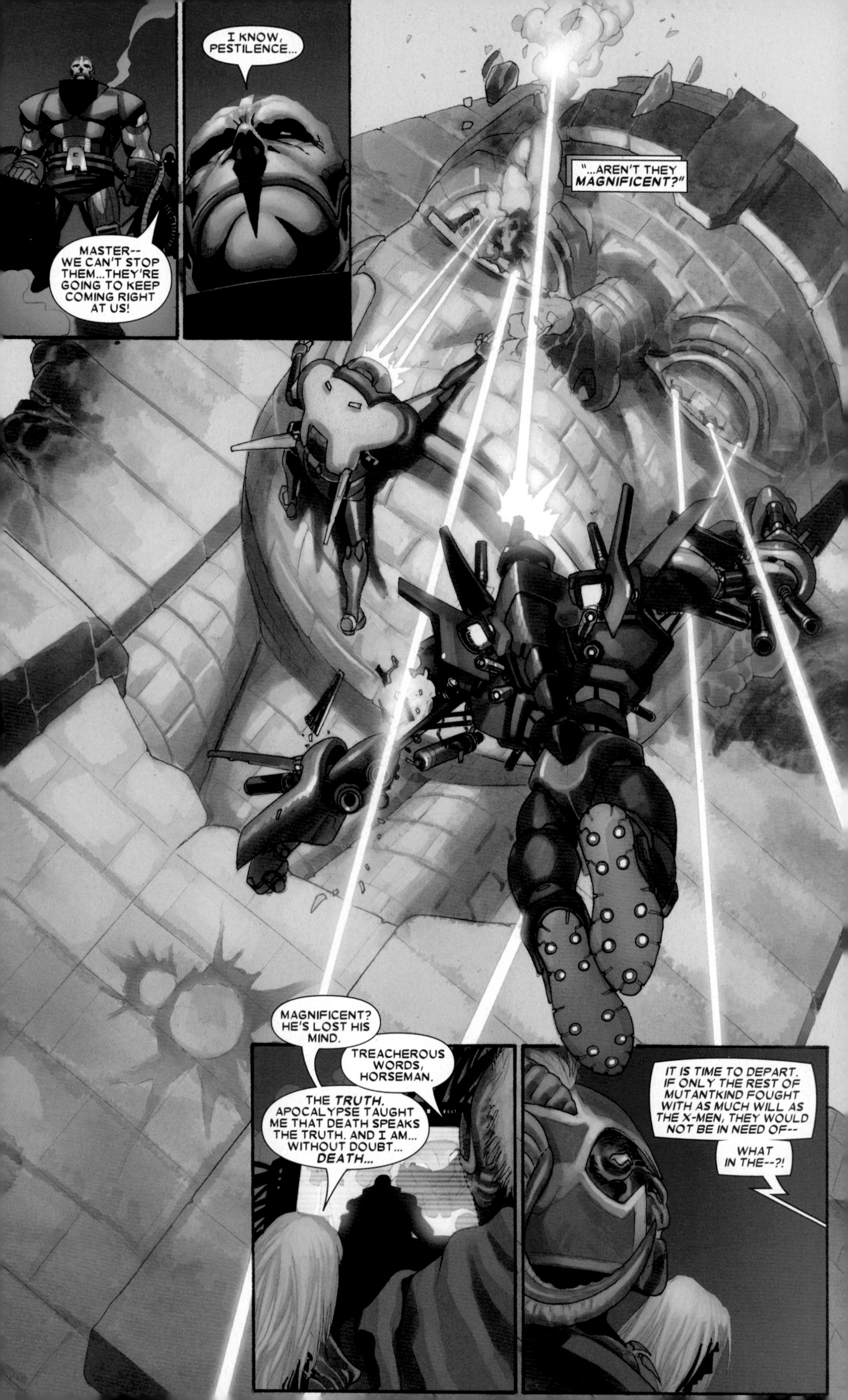
MASTER-- WE CAN'T STOP THEM...THEY'RE GOING TO KEEP COMING RIGHT AT US!
I KNOW, PESTILENCE...
"...AREN'T THEY MAGNIFICENT?"
MAGNIFICENT? HE'S LOST HIS MIND.
TREACHEROUS WORDS, HORSEMAN.
THE TRUTH. APOCALYPSE TAUGHT ME THAT DEATH SPEAKS THE TRUTH. AND I AM... WITHOUT DOUBT... DEATH...
IT IS TIME TO DEPART. IF ONLY THE REST OF MUTANTKIND FOUGHT WITH AS MUCH WILL AS THE X-MEN, THEY WOULD NOT BE IN NEED OF--
WHAT IN THE--?!

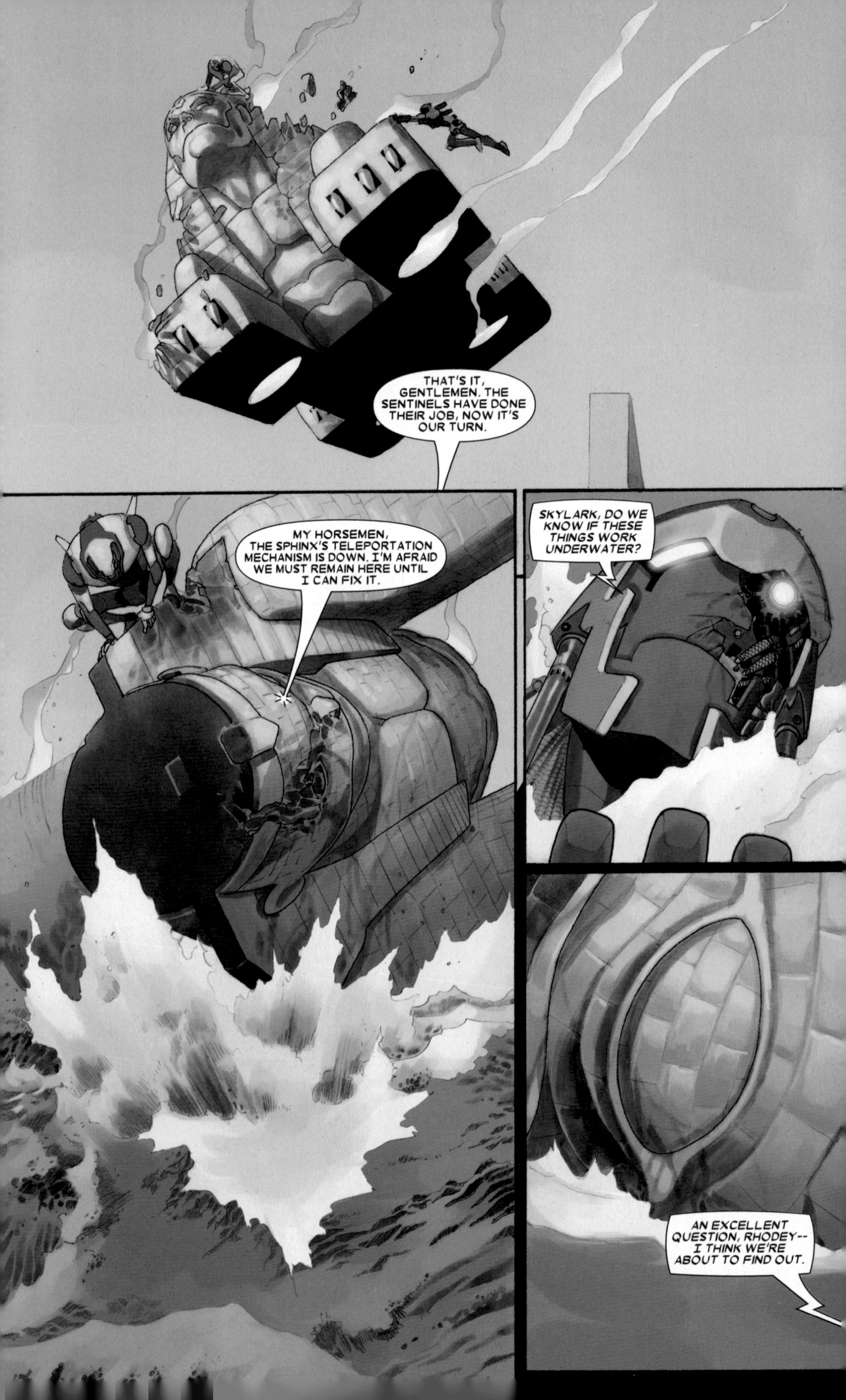
THAT'S IT, GENTLEMEN. THE SENTINELS HAVE DONE THEIR JOB, NOW IT'S OUR TURN.
MY HORSEMEN, THE SPHINX'S TELEPORTATION MECHANISM IS DOWN. I'M AFRAID WE MUST REMAIN HERE UNTIL I CAN FIX IT.
SKYLARK, DO WE KNOW IF THESE THINGS WORK UNDERWATER?
AN EXCELLENT QUESTION, RHODEY-- I THINK WE'RE ABOUT TO FIND OUT.

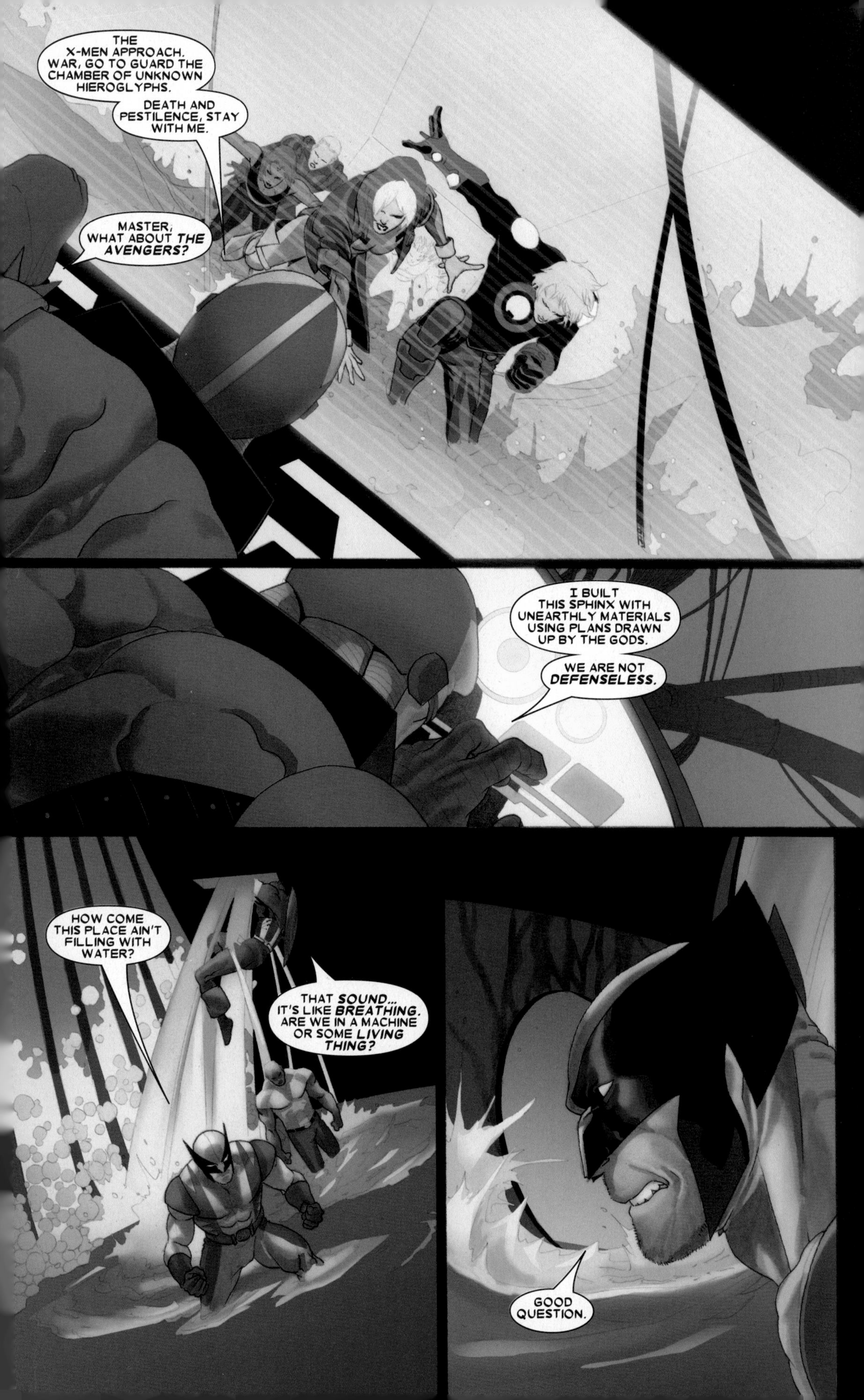

THE X-MEN APPROACH. WAR, GO TO GUARD THE CHAMBER OF UNKNOWN HIEROGLYPHS.
DEATH AND PESTILENCE, STAY WITH ME.
MASTER, WHAT ABOUT THE AVENGERS?
I BUILT THIS SPHINX WITH UNEARTHLY MATERIALS USING PLANS DRAWN UP BY THE GODS.
WE ARE NOT DEFENSELESS.
HOW COME THIS PLACE AIN'T FILLING WITH WATER?
THAT SOUND... IT'S LIKE BREATHING. ARE WE IN A MACHINE OR SOME LIVING THING?
GOOD QUESTION.

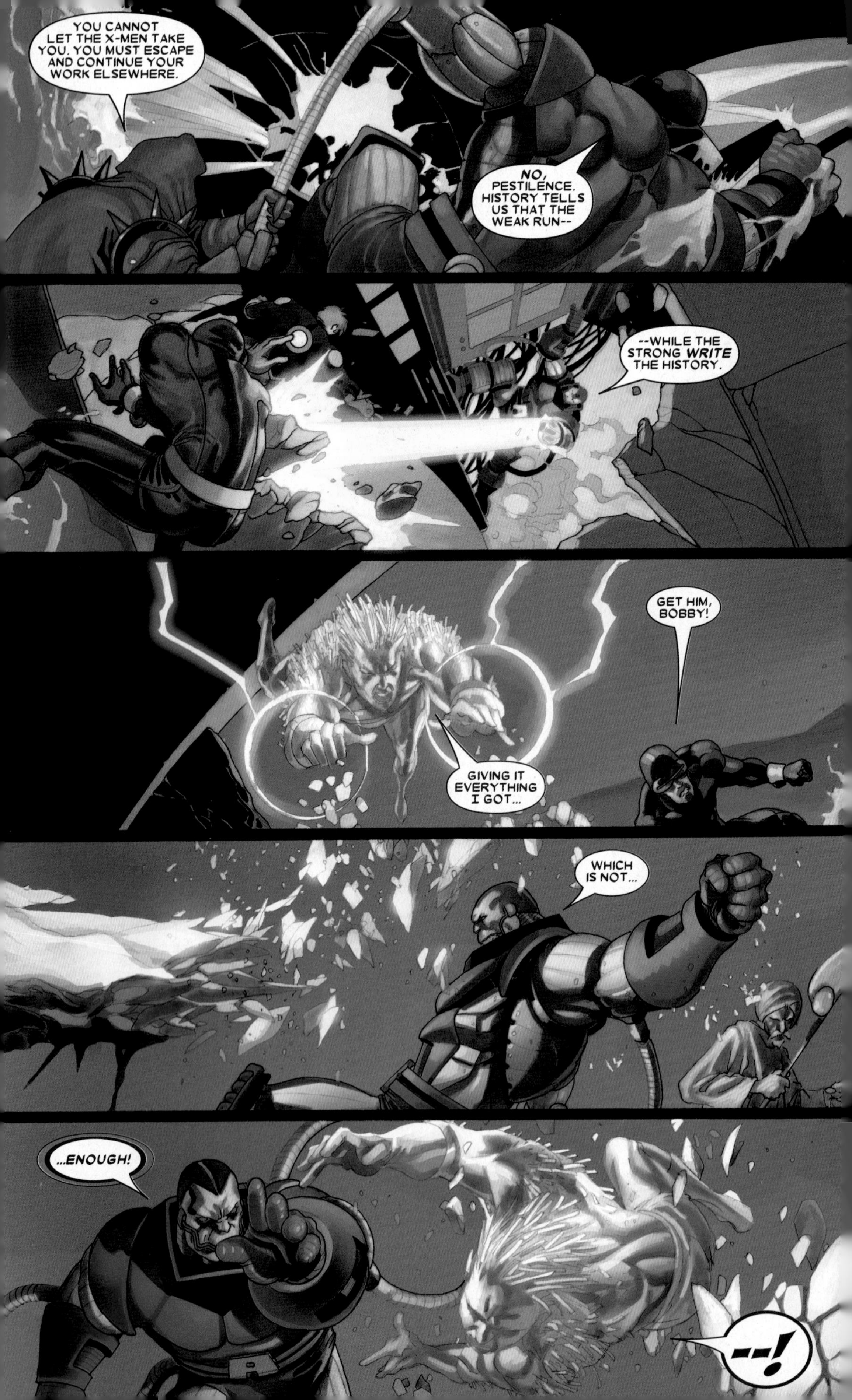
YOU CANNOT LET THE X-MEN TAKE YOU. YOU MUST ESCAPE AND CONTINUE YOUR WORK ELSEWHERE.
NO, PESTILENCE. HISTORY TELLS US THAT THE WEAK RUN--
--WHILE THE STRONG WRITE THE HISTORY.
GET HIM, BOBBY!
GIVING IT EVERYTHING I GOT...
WHICH IS NOT...
...ENOUGH!
--!

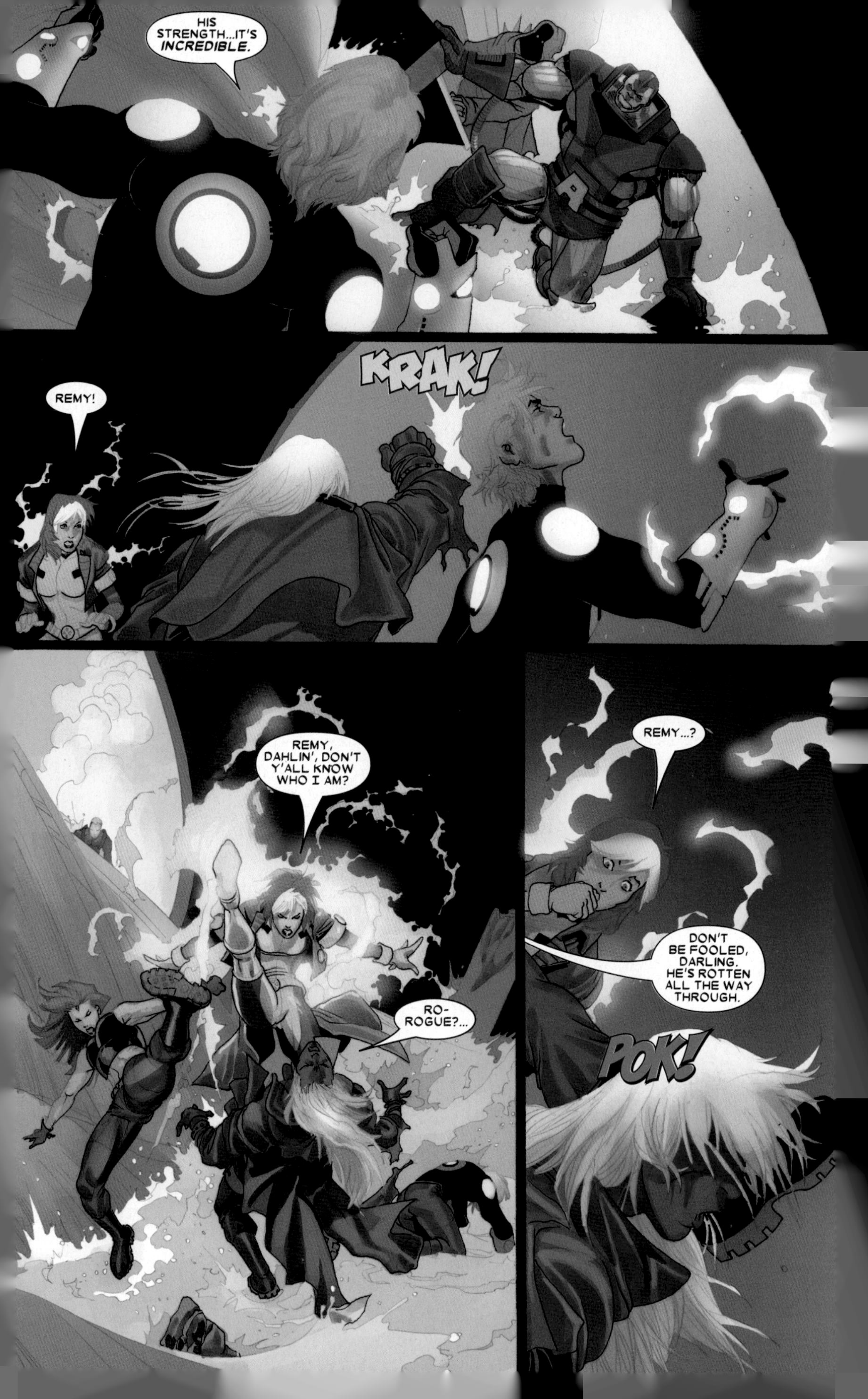
HIS STRENGTH...IT'S INCREDIBLE.
KRAK!
REMY!
REMY, DAHLIN', DON'T Y'ALL KNOW WHO I AM?
RO-ROGUE?...
REMY...?
DON'T BE FOOLED, DARLING. HE'S ROTTEN ALL THE WAY THROUGH.
POK!

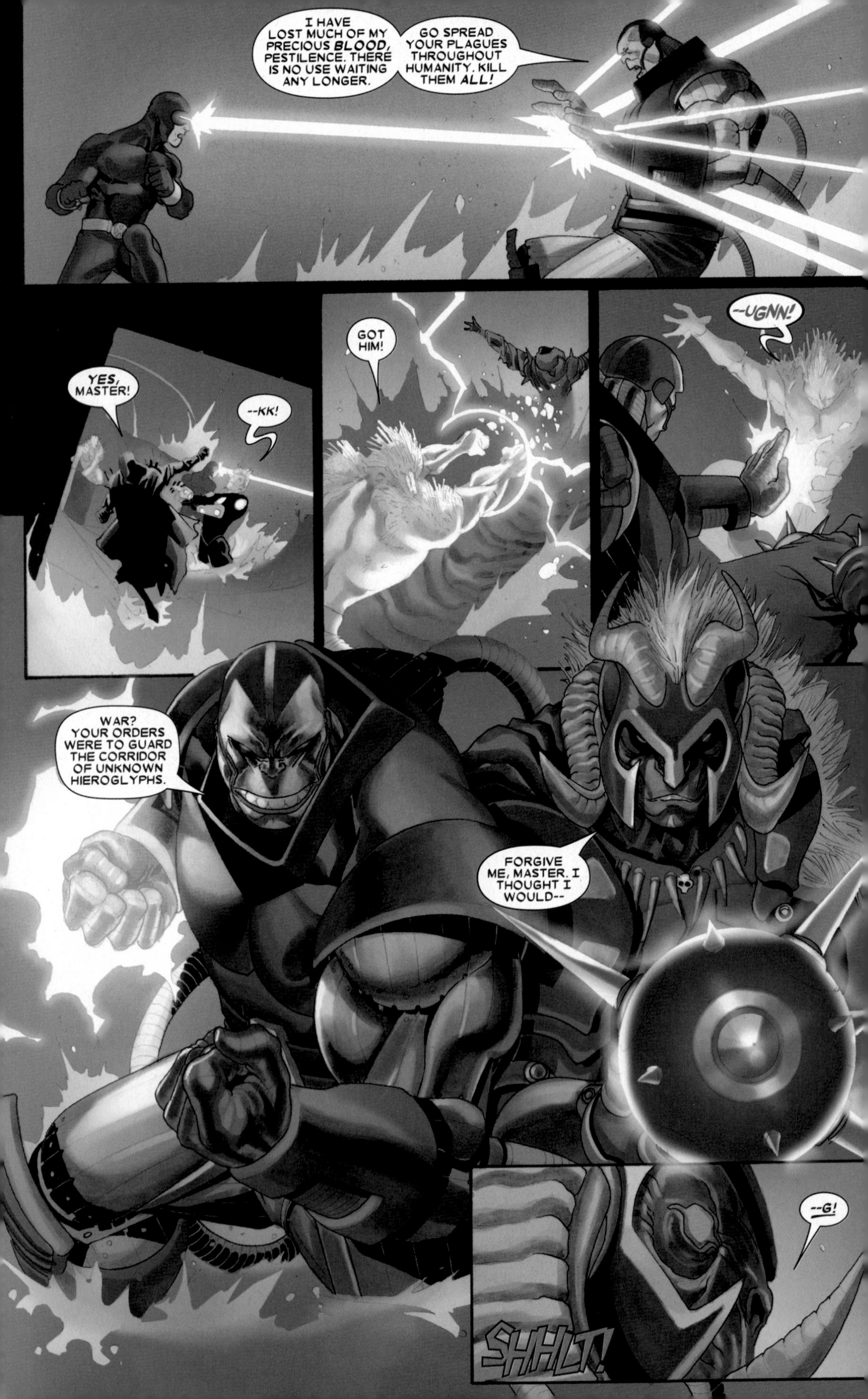
I HAVE LOST MUCH OF MY PRECIOUS BLOOD, PESTILENCE. THERE IS NO USE WAITING ANY LONGER.
GO SPREAD YOUR PLAGUES THROUGHOUT HUMANITY. KILL THEM ALL!
YES, MASTER!
--KK!
GOT HIM!
--UGNN!
WAR? YOUR ORDERS WERE TO GUARD THE CORRIDOR OF UNKNOWN HIEROGLYPHS.
FORGIVE ME, MASTER. I THOUGHT I WOULD--
--G!
SHHLT!

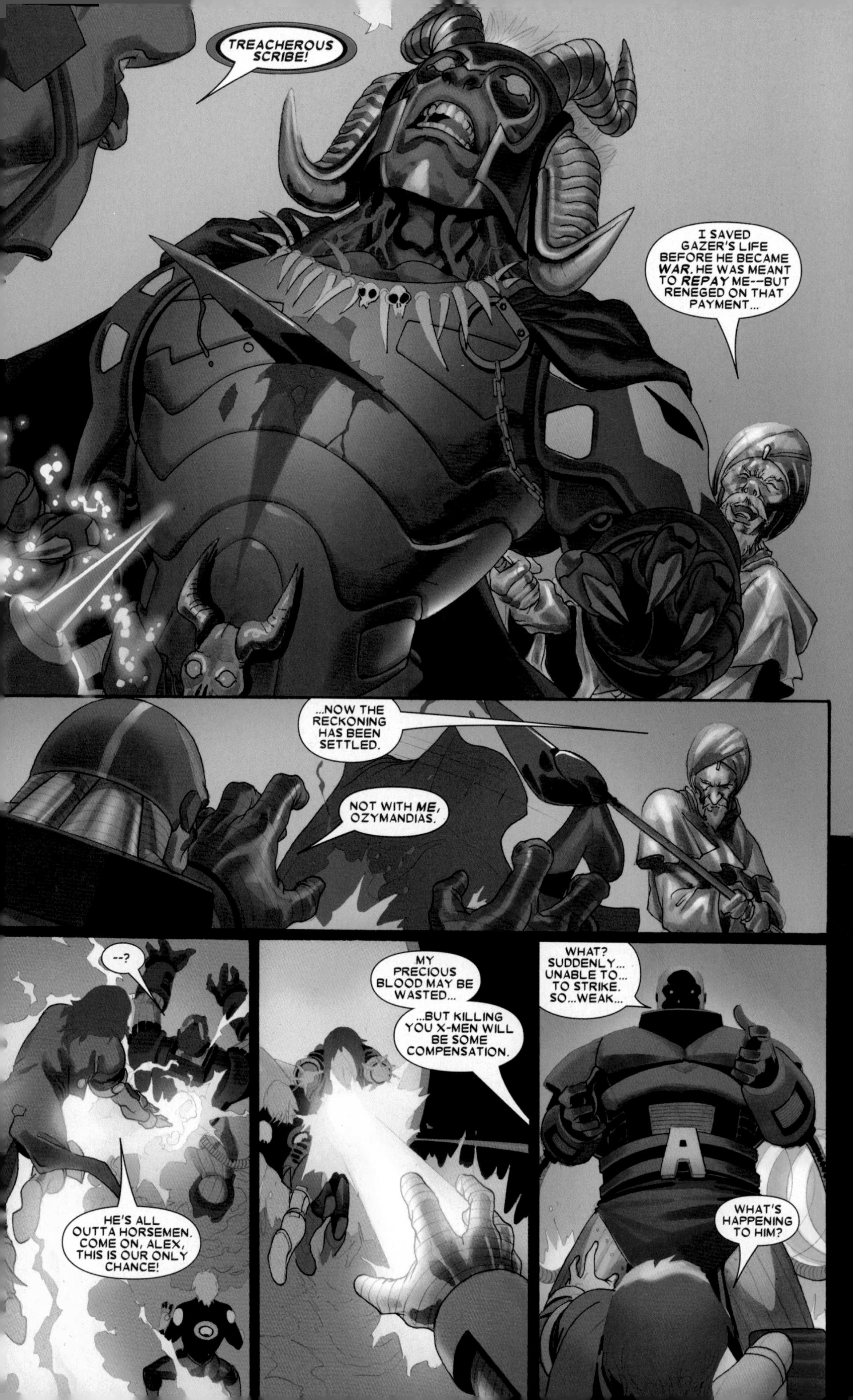
TREACHEROUS SCRIBE!
I SAVED GAZER'S LIFE BEFORE HE BECAME WAR. HE WAS MEANT TO REPAY ME--BUT RENEGED ON THAT PAYMENT...
...NOW THE RECKONING HAS BEEN SETTLED.
NOT WITH ME, OZYMANDIAS.
--?
HE'S ALL OUTTA HORSEMEN. COME ON, ALEX, THIS IS OUR ONLY CHANCE!
MY PRECIOUS BLOOD MAY BE WASTED...
...BUT KILLING YOU X-MEN WILL BE SOME COMPENSATION.
WHAT? SUDDENLY... UNABLE TO... TO STRIKE. SO...WEAK...
WHAT'S HAPPENING TO HIM?

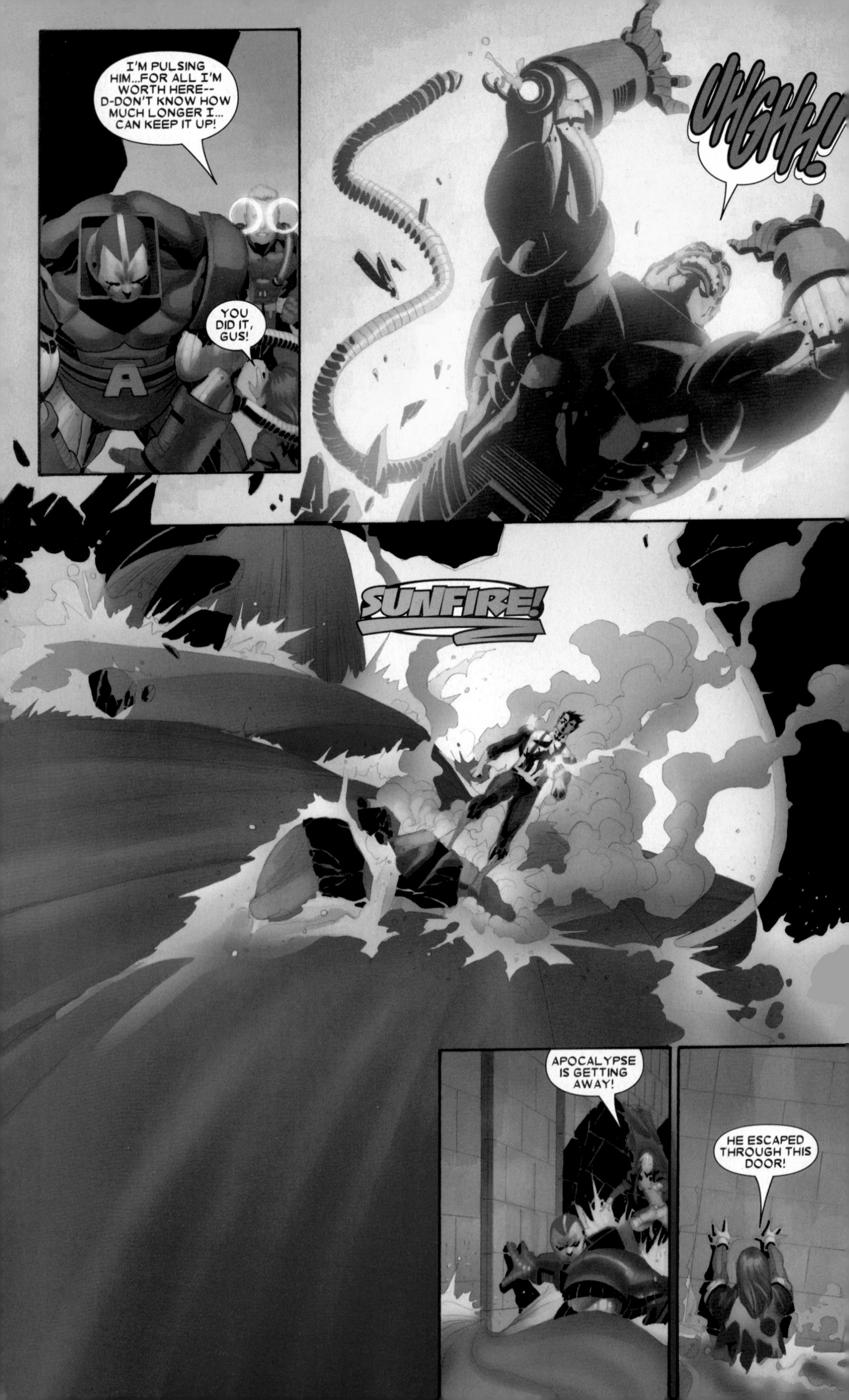
I'M PULSING HIM...FOR ALL I'M WORTH HERE-- D-DON'T KNOW HOW MUCH LONGER I... CAN KEEP IT UP!
YOU DID IT, GUS!
UHGHH!
SUNFIRE!
APOCALYPSE IS GETTING AWAY!
HE ESCAPED THROUGH THIS DOOR!

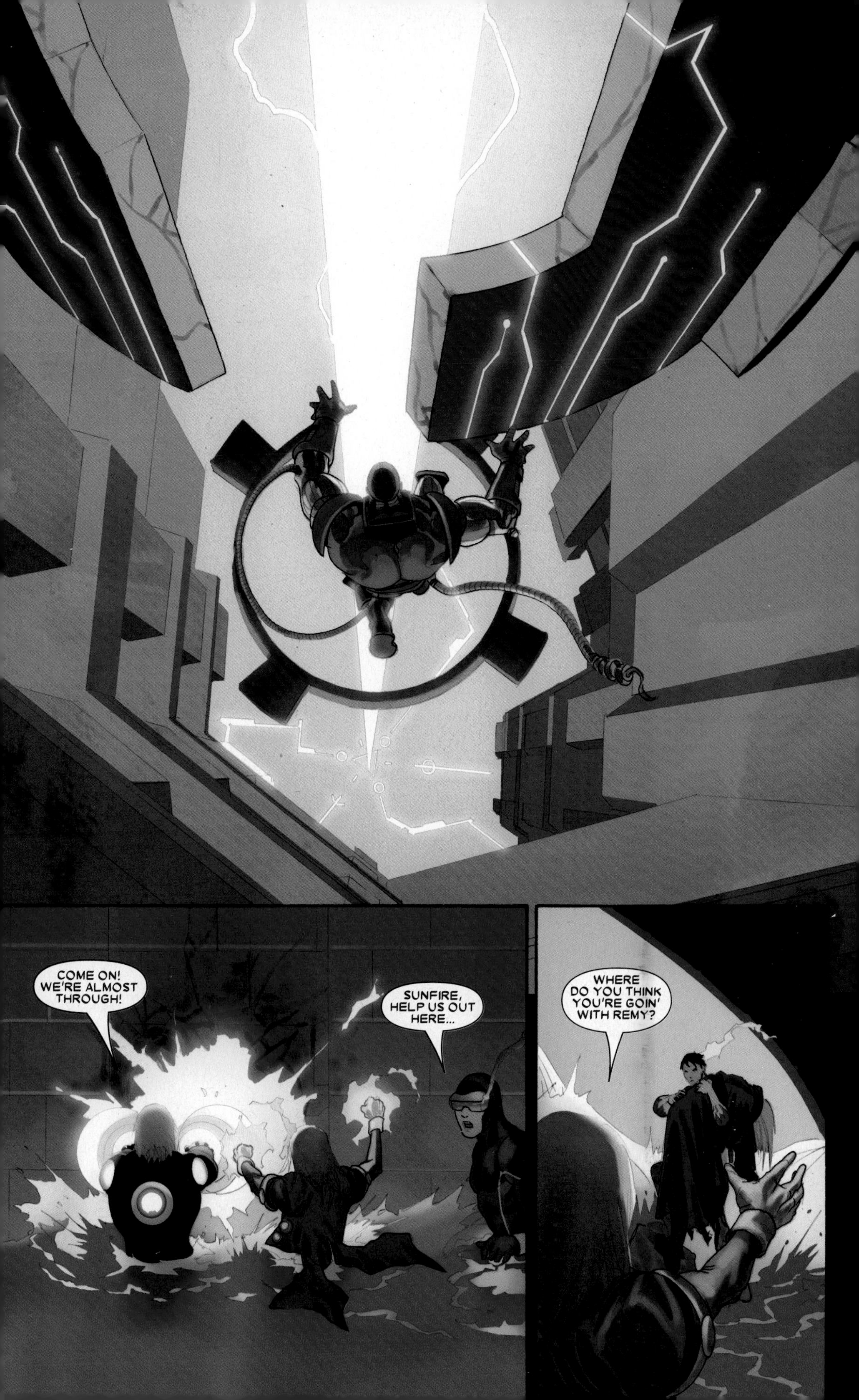
COME ON! WE'RE ALMOST THROUGH!
SUNFIRE, HELP US OUT HERE...
WHERE DO YOU THINK YOU'RE GOIN' WITH REMY?

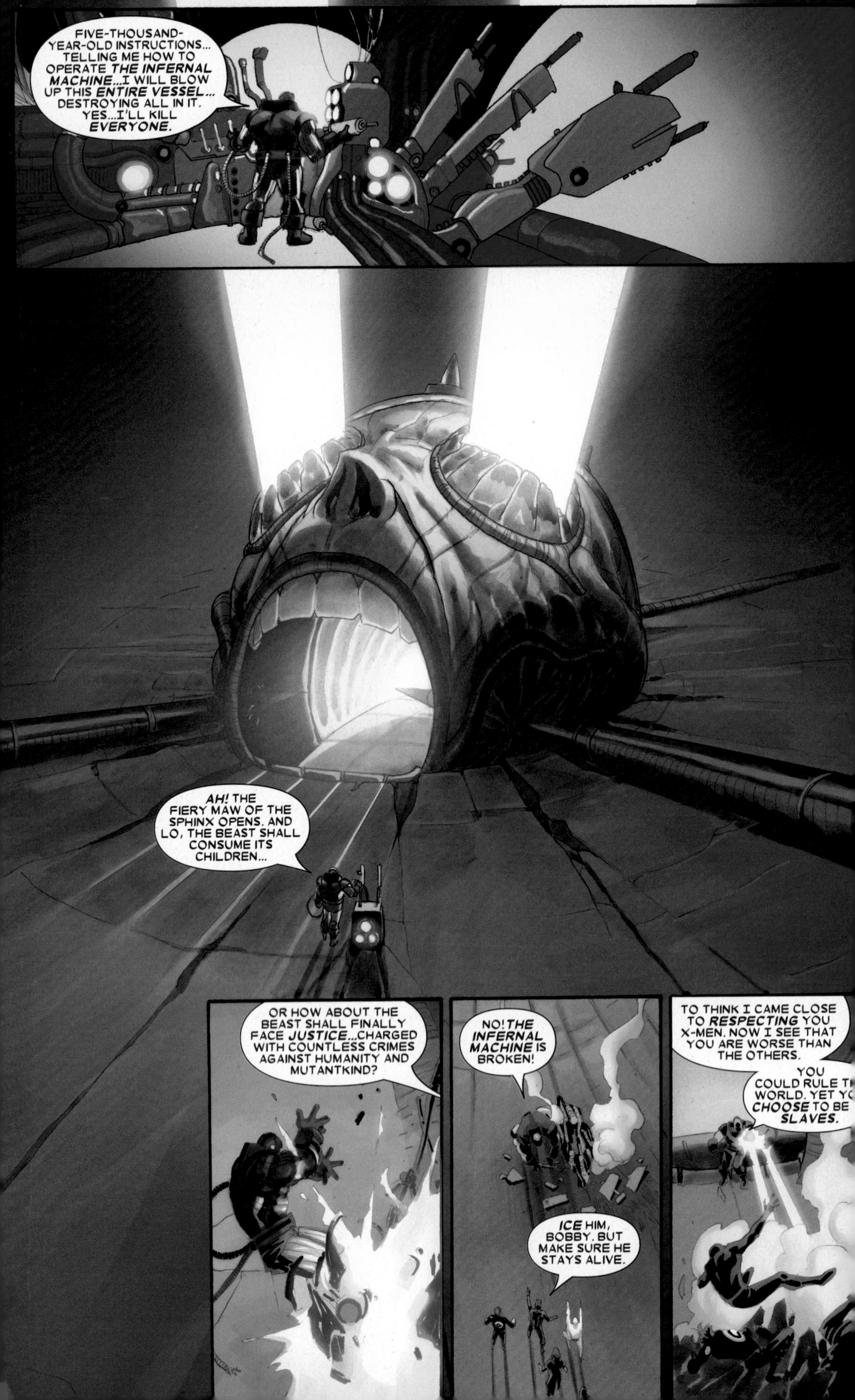
FIVE-THOUSAND-YEAR-OLD INSTRUCTIONS... TELLING ME HOW TO OPERATE THE INFERNAL MACHINE...I WILL BLOW UP THIS ENTIRE VESSEL... DESTROYING ALL IN IT. YES...I'LL KILL EVERYONE.
AH! THE FIERY MAW OF THE SPHINX OPENS. AND LO, THE BEAST SHALL CONSUME ITS CHILDREN...
OR HOW ABOUT THE BEAST SHALL FINALLY FACE JUSTICE...CHARGED WITH COUNTLESS CRIMES AGAINST HUMANITY AND MUTANTKIND?
NO! THE INFERNAL MACHINE IS BROKEN!
ICE HIM, BOBBY, BUT MAKE SURE HE STAYS ALIVE.
TO THINK I CAME CLOSE TO RESPECTING YOU X-MEN. NOW I SEE THAT YOU ARE WORSE THAN THE OTHERS.

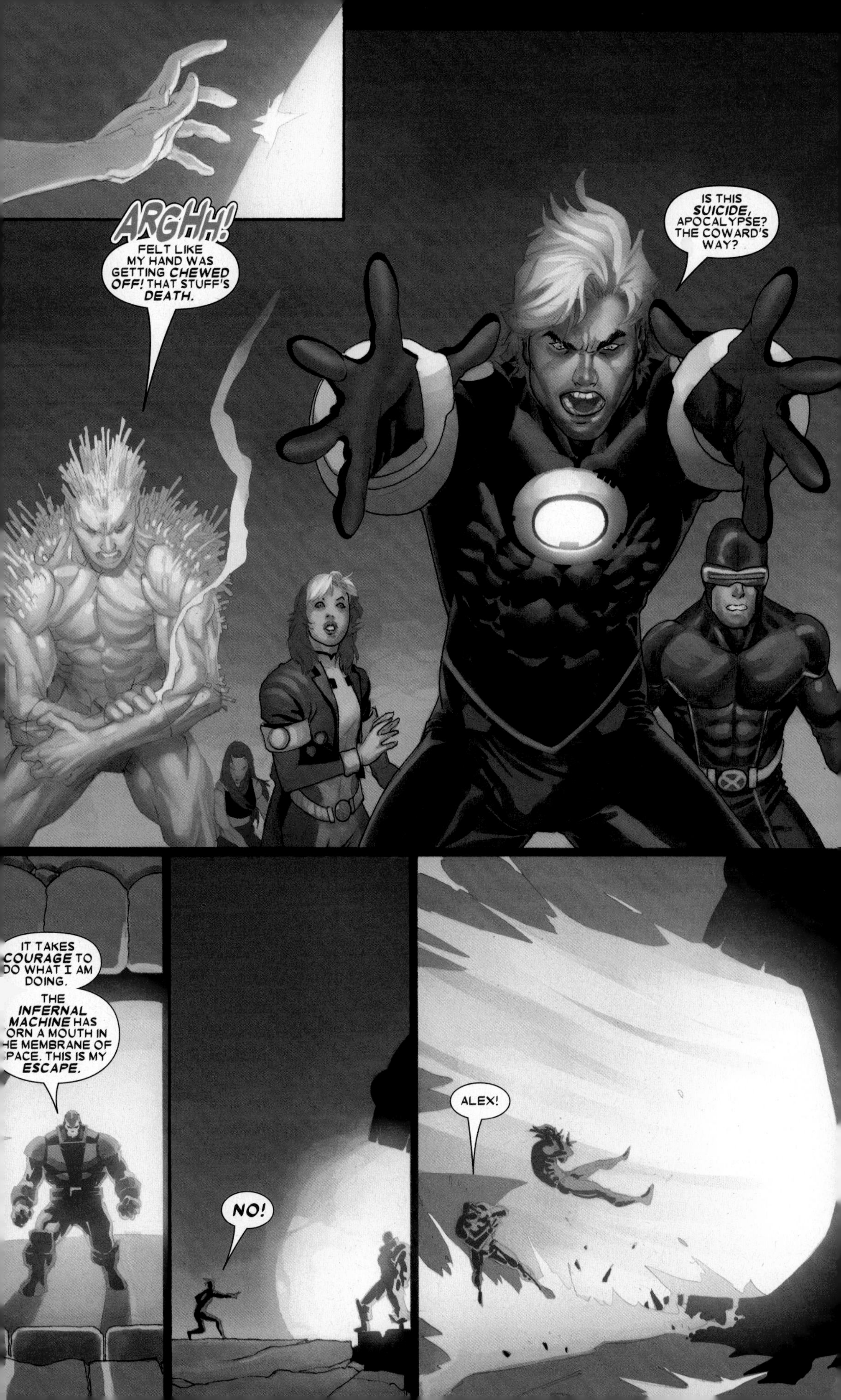
ARGHH!
FELT LIKE MY HAND WAS GETTING CHEWED OFF! THAT STUFF'S DEATH.
IS THIS SUICIDE, APOCALYPSE? THE COWARD'S WAY?
IT TAKES COURAGE TO DO WHAT I AM DOING.
THE INFERNAL MACHINE HAS TORN A MOUTH IN THE MEMBRANE OF SPACE. THIS IS MY ESCAPE.
NO!
ALEX!

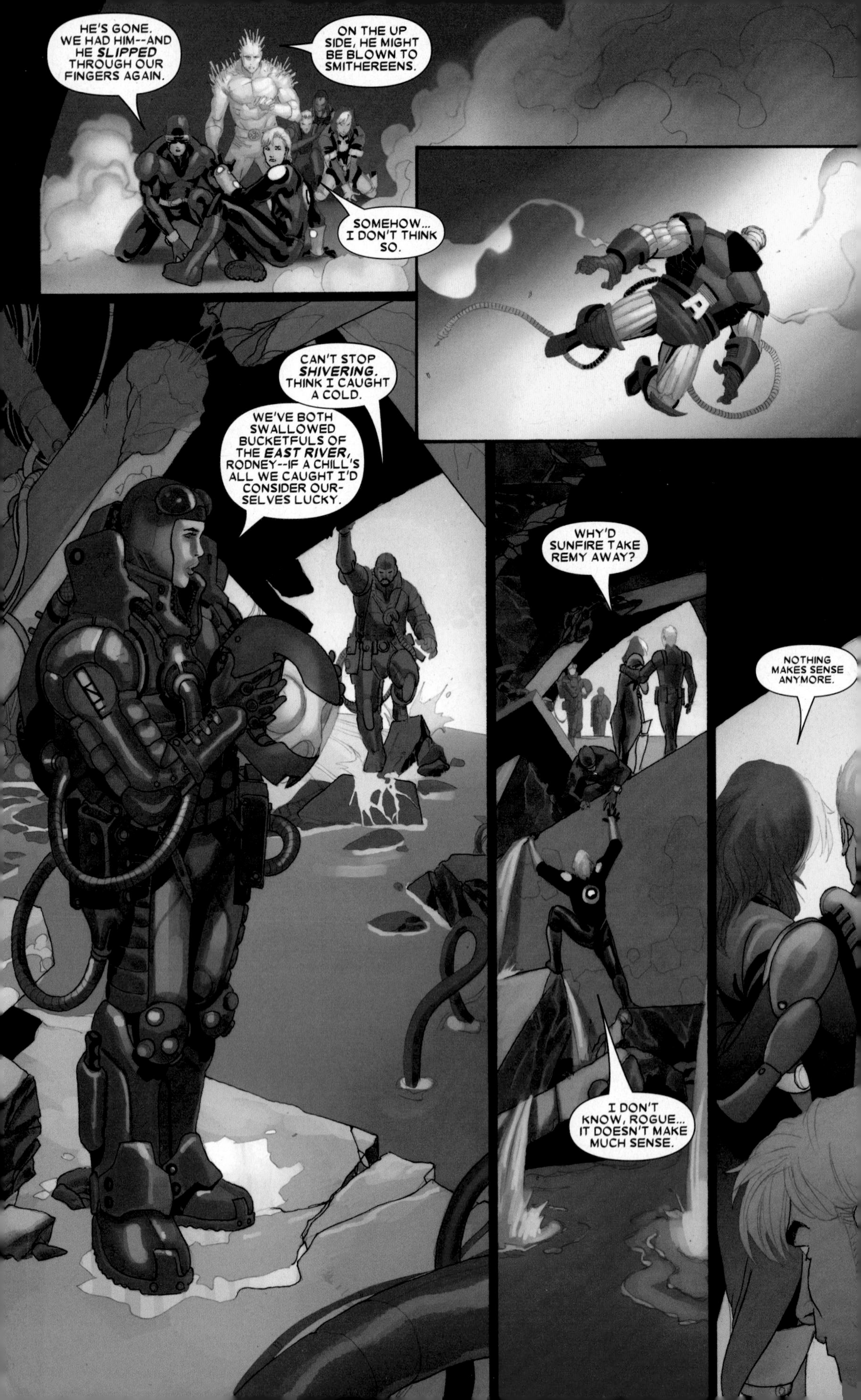
HE'S GONE. WE HAD HIM--AND HE SLIPPED THROUGH OUR FINGERS AGAIN.
ON THE UP SIDE, HE MIGHT BE BLOWN TO SMITHEREENS.
SOMEHOW... I DON'T THINK SO.
CAN'T STOP SHIVERING. THINK I CAUGHT A COLD.
WE'VE BOTH SWALLOWED BUCKETFULS OF THE EAST RIVER, RODNEY--IF A CHILL'S ALL WE CAUGHT I'D CONSIDER OURSELVES LUCKY.
WHY'D SUNFIRE TAKE REMY AWAY?
I DON'T KNOW, ROGUE... IT DOESN'T MAKE MUCH SENSE.
NOTHING MAKES SENSE ANYMORE.

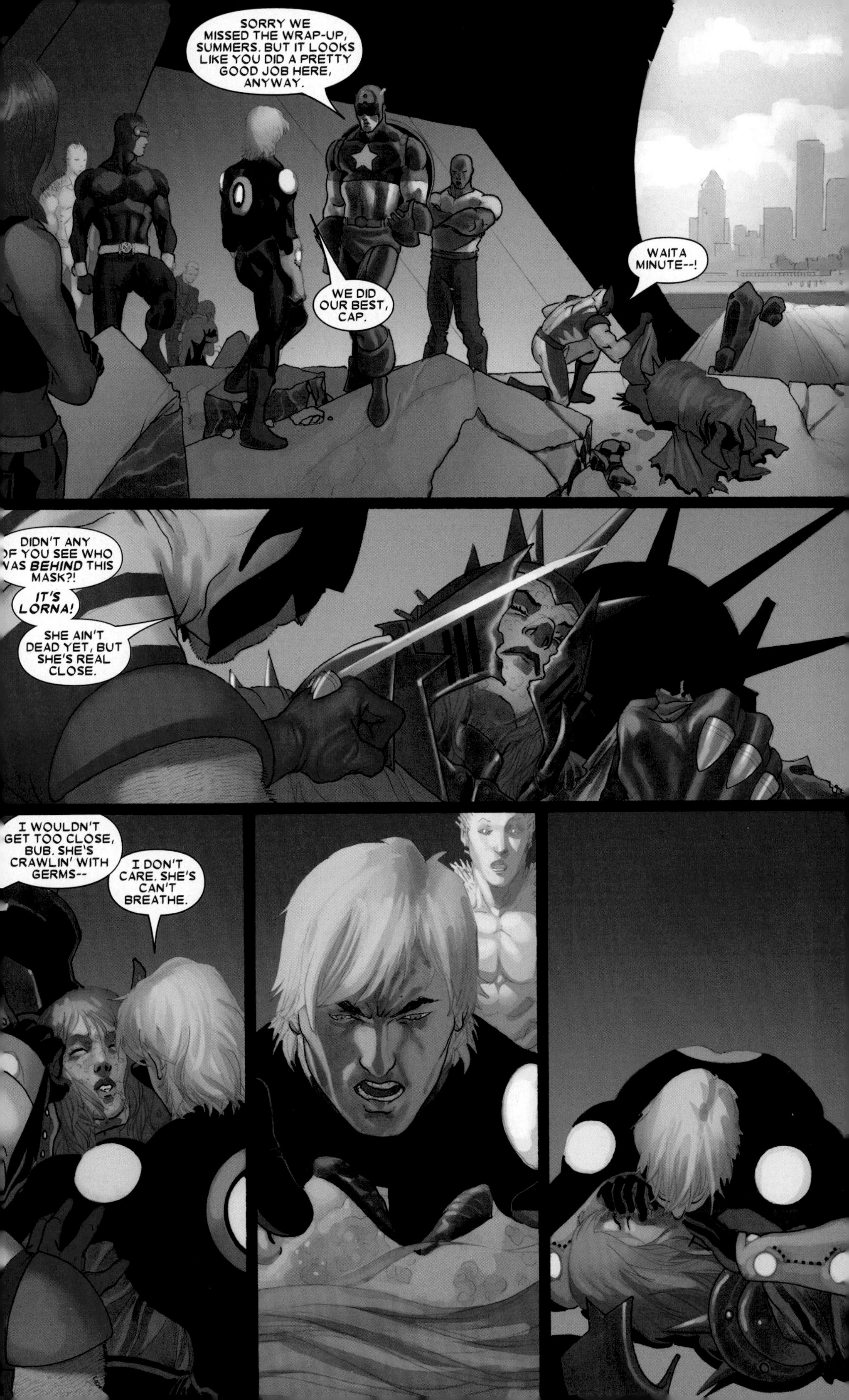
SORRY WE MISSED THE WRAP-UP, SUMMERS. BUT IT LOOKS LIKE YOU DID A PRETTY GOOD JOB HERE, ANYWAY.
WE DID OUR BEST, CAP.
WAITA MINUTE--!
DIDN'T ANY OF YOU SEE WHO WAS *BEHIND* THIS MASK?!
IT'S LORNA!
SHE AIN'T DEAD YET, BUT SHE'S REAL CLOSE.
I WOULDN'T GET TOO CLOSE, BUB. SHE'S CRAWLIN' WITH GERMS--
I DON'T CARE. SHE'S CAN'T BREATHE.

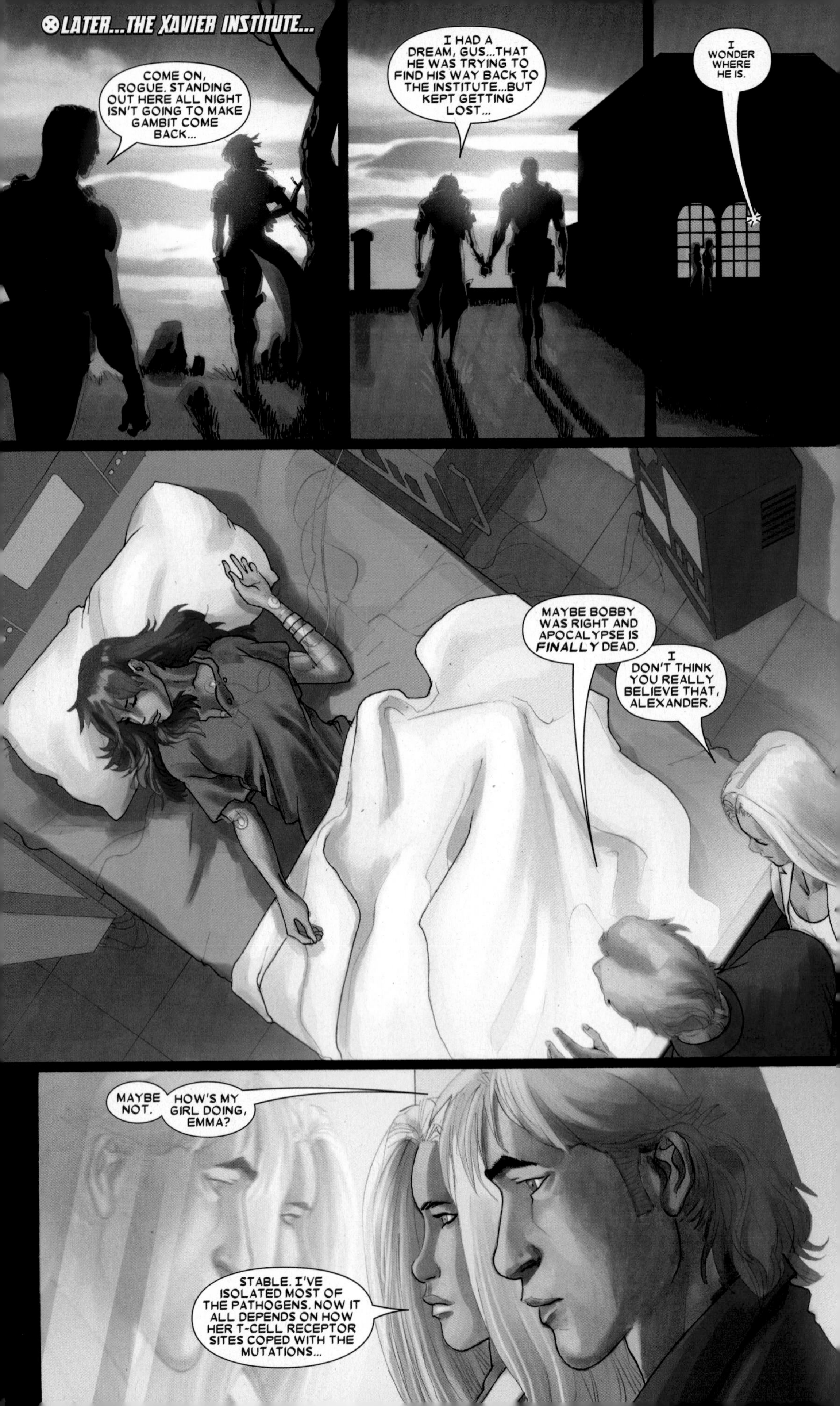
LATER...THE XAVIER INSTITUTE...
COME ON, ROGUE. STANDING OUT HERE ALL NIGHT ISN'T GOING TO MAKE GAMBIT COME BACK...
I HAD A DREAM, GUS...THAT HE WAS TRYING TO FIND HIS WAY BACK TO THE INSTITUTE...BUT KEPT GETTING LOST...
I WONDER WHERE HE IS.
MAYBE BOBBY WAS RIGHT AND APOCALYPSE IS FINALLY DEAD.
I DON'T THINK YOU REALLY BELIEVE THAT, ALEXANDER.
MAYBE NOT.
HOW'S MY GIRL DOING, EMMA?
STABLE. I'VE ISOLATED MOST OF THE PATHOGENS. NOW IT ALL DEPENDS ON HOW HER T-CELL RECEPTOR SITES COPED WITH THE MUTATIONS...

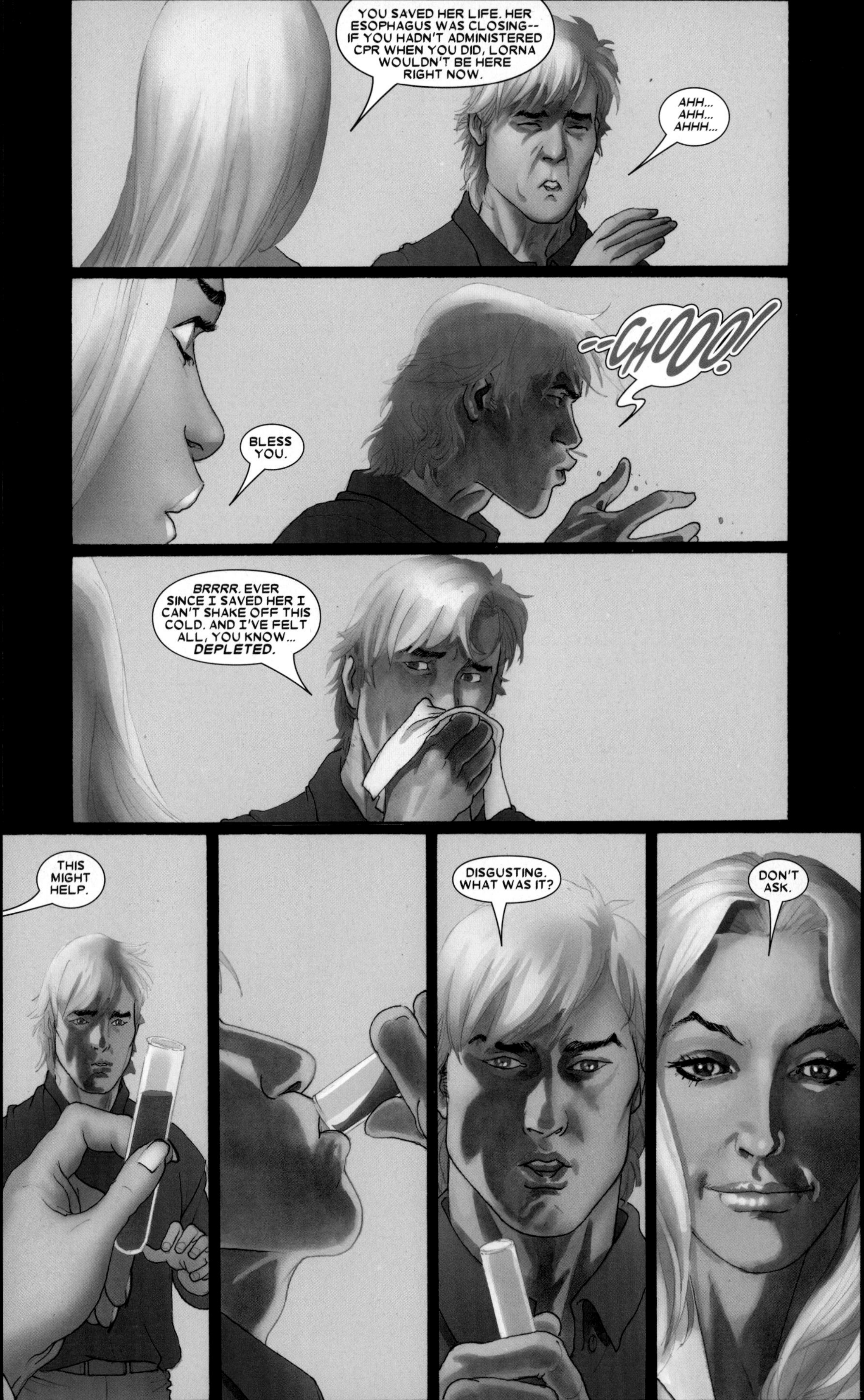
YOU SAVED HER LIFE. HER ESOPHAGUS WAS CLOSING-- IF YOU HADN'T ADMINISTERED CPR WHEN YOU DID, LORNA WOULDN'T BE HERE RIGHT NOW.
AHH... AHH... AHHH...
--CHOOO!
BLESS YOU.
BRRRR. EVER SINCE I SAVED HER I CAN'T SHAKE OFF THIS COLD. AND I'VE FELT ALL, YOU KNOW... DEPLETED.
THIS MIGHT HELP.
DISGUSTING. WHAT WAS IT?
DON'T ASK.

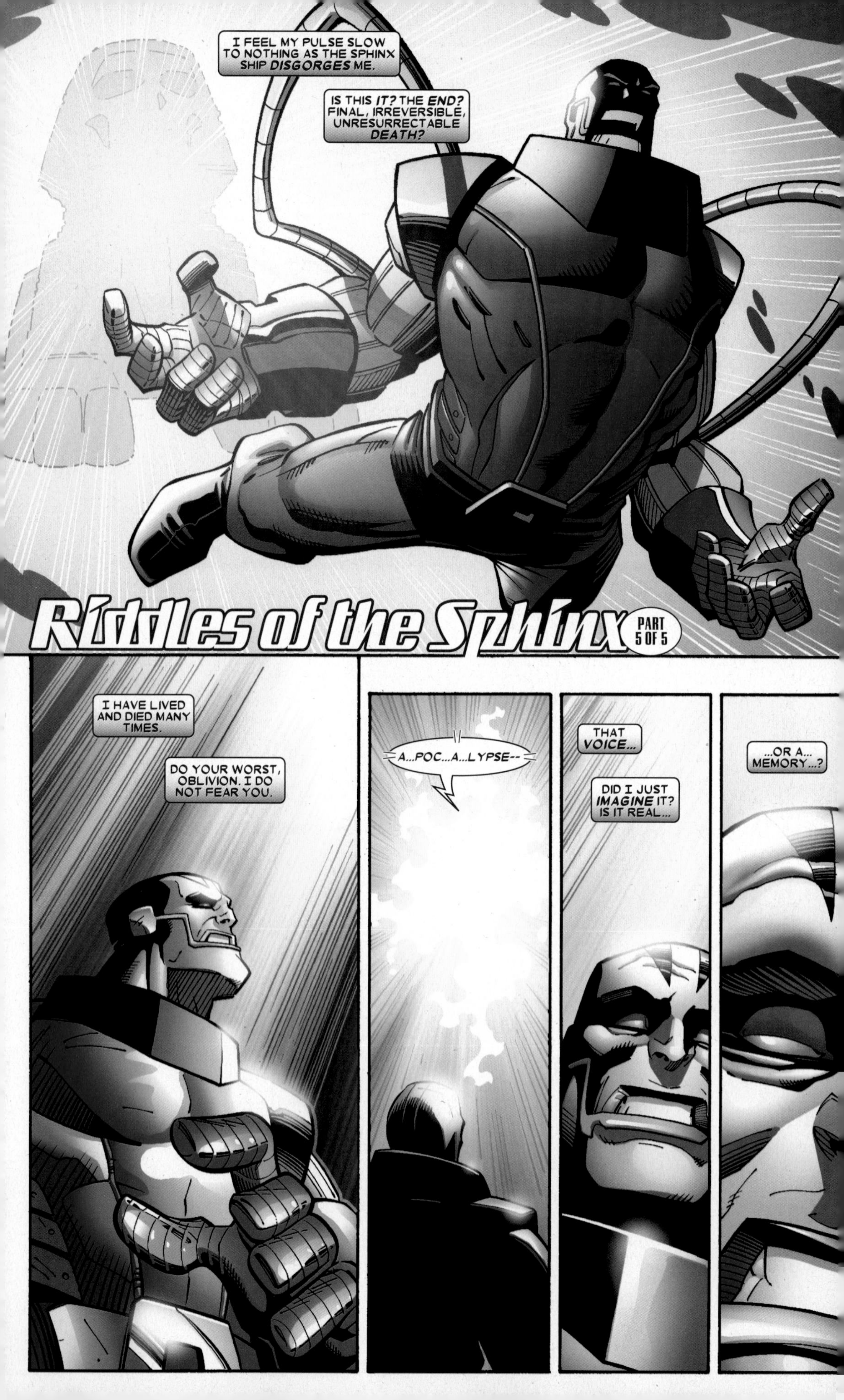

I FEEL MY PULSE SLOW TO NOTHING AS THE SPHINX SHIP DISGORGES ME.
IS THIS IT? THE END? FINAL, IRREVERSIBLE, UNRESURRECTABLE DEATH?
Riddles of the Sphinx
PART 5 OF 5
I HAVE LIVED AND DIED MANY TIMES.
DO YOUR WORST, OBLIVION. I DO NOT FEAR YOU.
A...POC...A...LYPSE--
THAT VOICE...
DID I JUST IMAGINE IT? IS IT REAL...
...OR A... MEMORY...?

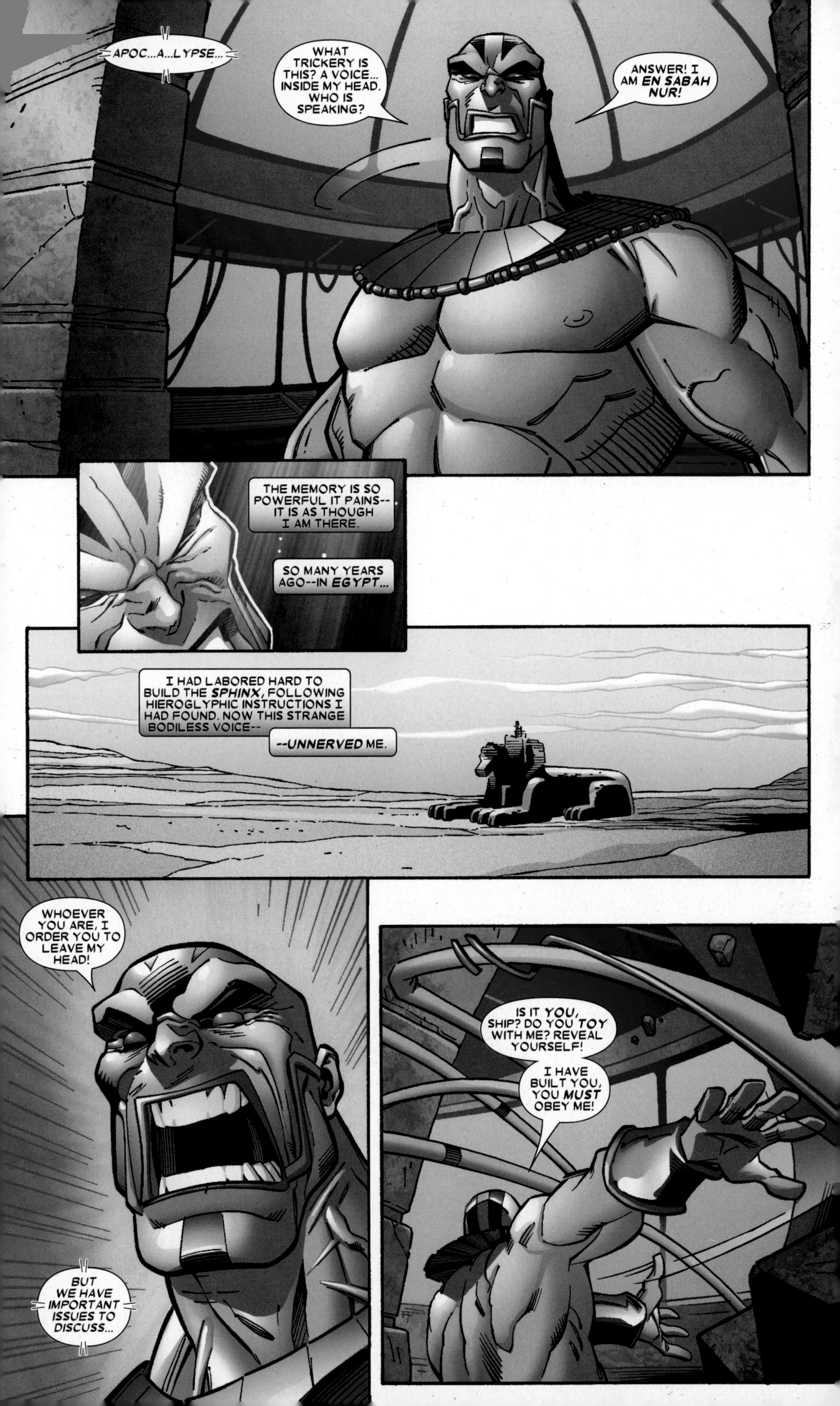

APOC...A...LYPSE...
WHAT TRICKERY IS THIS? A VOICE... INSIDE MY HEAD. WHO IS SPEAKING?
ANSWER! I AM EN SABAH NUR!
THE MEMORY IS SO POWERFUL IT PAINS-- IT IS AS THOUGH I AM THERE.
SO MANY YEARS AGO--IN EGYPT...
I HAD LABORED HARD TO BUILD THE SPHINX, FOLLOWING HIEROGLYPHIC INSTRUCTIONS I HAD FOUND. NOW THIS STRANGE BODILESS VOICE--
--UNNERVED ME.
WHOEVER YOU ARE, I ORDER YOU TO LEAVE MY HEAD!
BUT WE HAVE IMPORTANT ISSUES TO DISCUSS...
IS IT YOU, SHIP? DO YOU TOY WITH ME? REVEAL YOURSELF!
I HAVE BUILT YOU, YOU MUST OBEY ME!

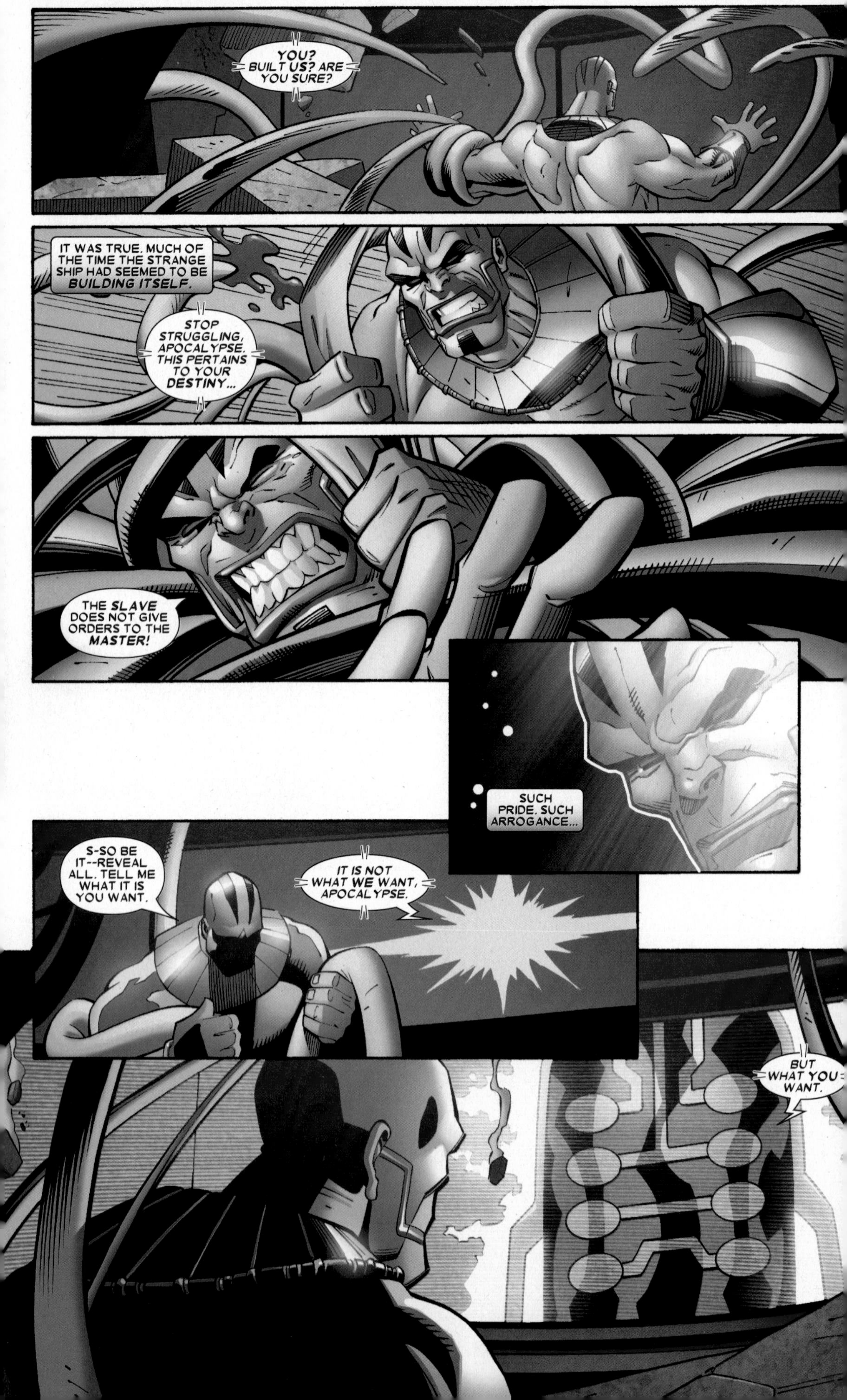
YOU? BUILT US? ARE YOU SURE?
IT WAS TRUE. MUCH OF THE TIME THE STRANGE SHIP HAD SEEMED TO BE BUILDING ITSELF.
STOP STRUGGLING, APOCALYPSE. THIS PERTAINS TO YOUR DESTINY...
THE SLAVE DOES NOT GIVE ORDERS TO THE MASTER!
SUCH PRIDE. SUCH ARROGANCE...
S-SO BE IT--REVEAL ALL. TELL ME WHAT IT IS YOU WANT.
IT IS NOT WHAT WE WANT, APOCALYPSE.
BUT WHAT YOU WANT.

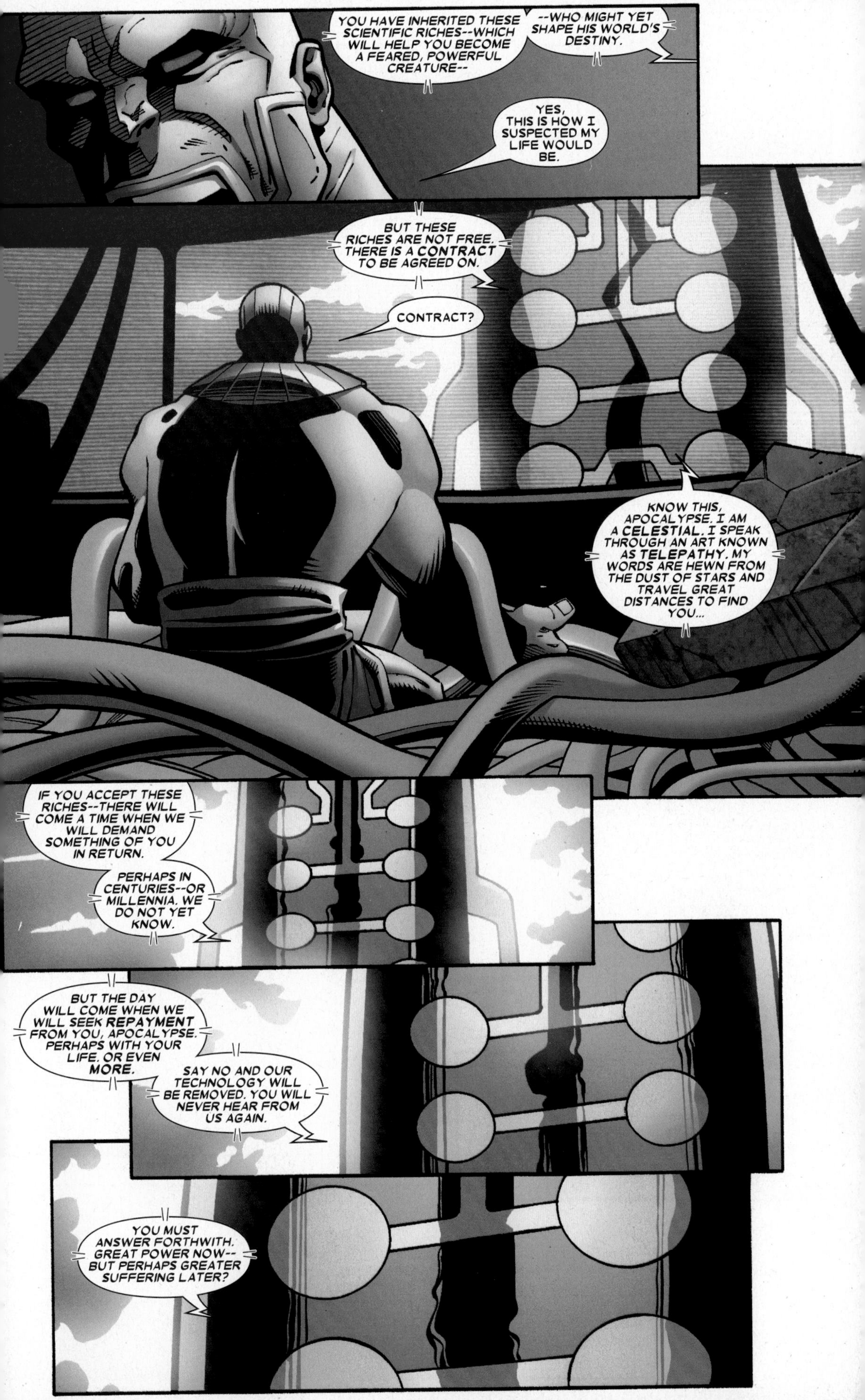
YOU HAVE INHERITED THESE SCIENTIFIC RICHES--WHICH WILL HELP YOU BECOME A FEARED, POWERFUL CREATURE--
--WHO MIGHT YET SHAPE HIS WORLD'S DESTINY.
YES, THIS IS HOW I SUSPECTED MY LIFE WOULD BE.
BUT THESE RICHES ARE NOT FREE. THERE IS A CONTRACT TO BE AGREED ON.
CONTRACT?
KNOW THIS, APOCALYPSE. I AM A CELESTIAL. I SPEAK THROUGH AN ART KNOWN AS TELEPATHY. MY WORDS ARE HEWN FROM THE DUST OF STARS AND TRAVEL GREAT DISTANCES TO FIND YOU...
IF YOU ACCEPT THESE RICHES--THERE WILL COME A TIME WHEN WE WILL DEMAND SOMETHING OF YOU IN RETURN.
PERHAPS IN CENTURIES--OR MILLENNIA. WE DO NOT YET KNOW.
BUT THE DAY WILL COME WHEN WE WILL SEEK REPAYMENT FROM YOU, APOCALYPSE. PERHAPS WITH YOUR LIFE. OR EVEN MORE.
SAY NO AND OUR TECHNOLOGY WILL BE REMOVED. YOU WILL NEVER HEAR FROM US AGAIN.
YOU MUST ANSWER FORTHWITH. GREAT POWER NOW--BUT PERHAPS GREATER SUFFERING LATER?

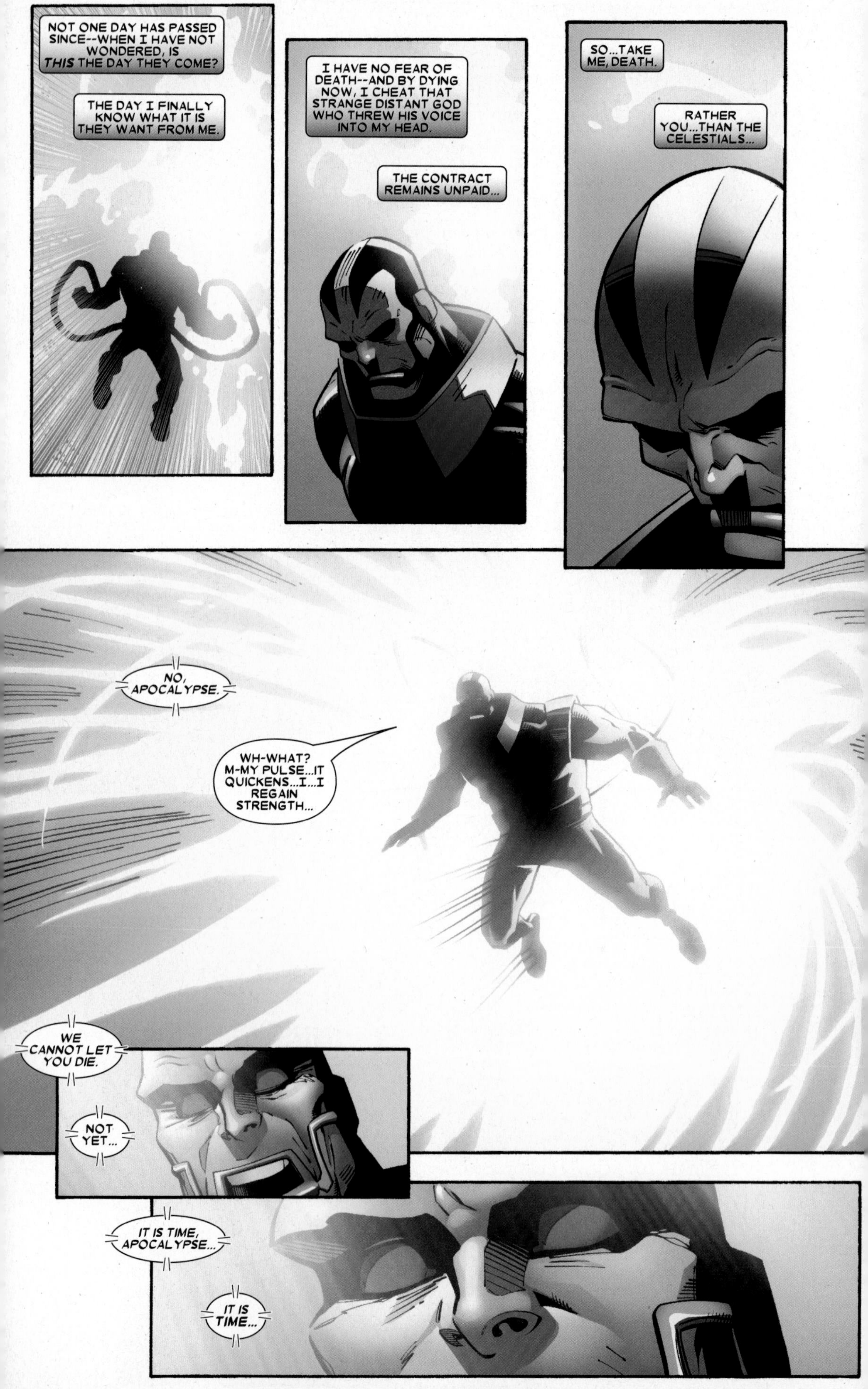
NOT ONE DAY HAS PASSED SINCE--WHEN I HAVE NOT WONDERED, IS *THIS* THE DAY THEY COME?
THE DAY I FINALLY KNOW WHAT IT IS THEY WANT FROM ME.
I HAVE NO FEAR OF DEATH--AND BY DYING NOW, I CHEAT THAT STRANGE DISTANT GOD WHO THREW HIS VOICE INTO MY HEAD.
THE CONTRACT REMAINS UNPAID...
SO...TAKE ME, DEATH.
RATHER YOU...THAN THE CELESTIALS...
NO, APOCALYPSE.
WH-WHAT? M-MY PULSE...IT QUICKENS...I...I REGAIN STRENGTH...
WE CANNOT LET YOU DIE.
NOT YET...
IT IS TIME, APOCALYPSE...
IT IS TIME...

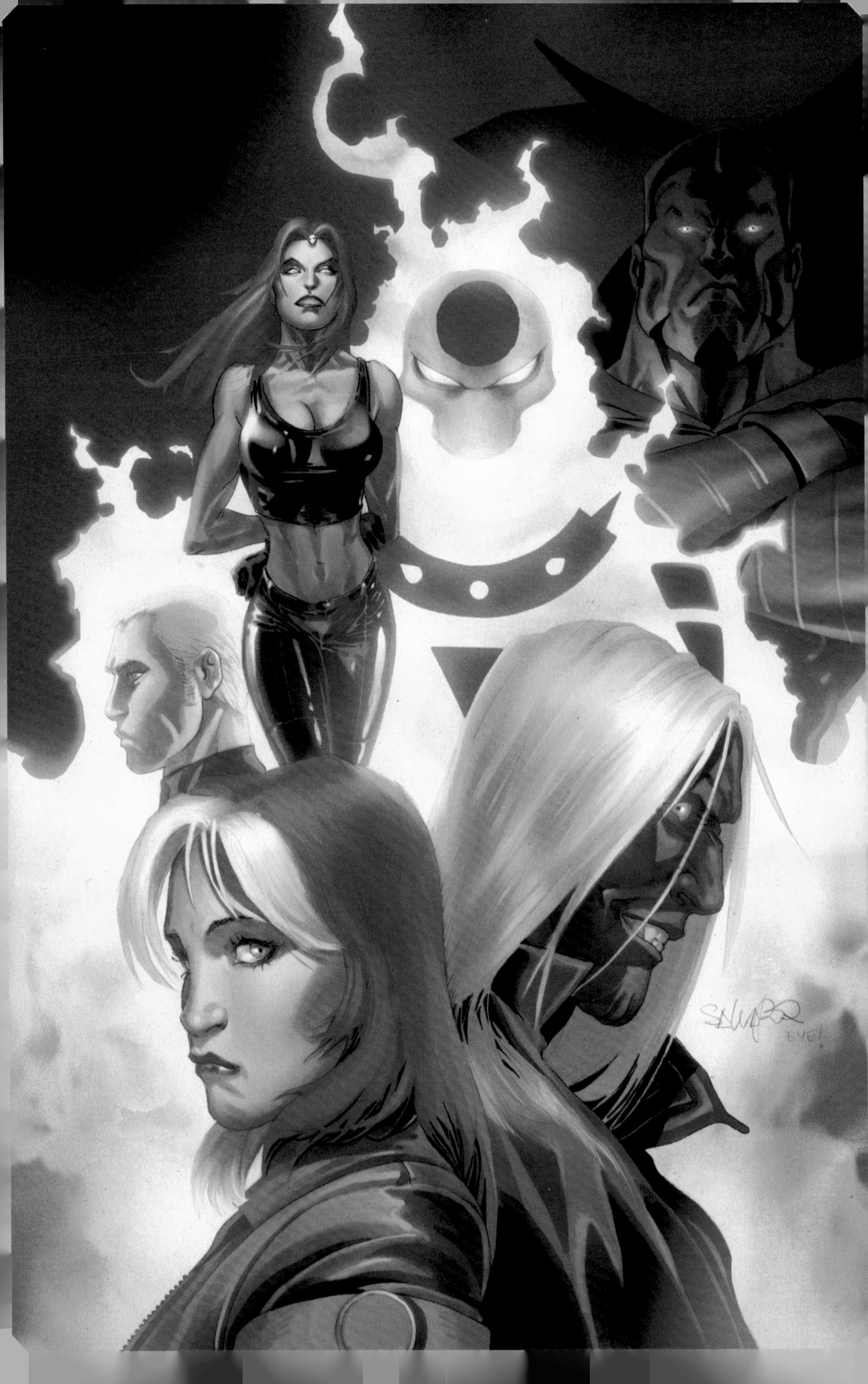

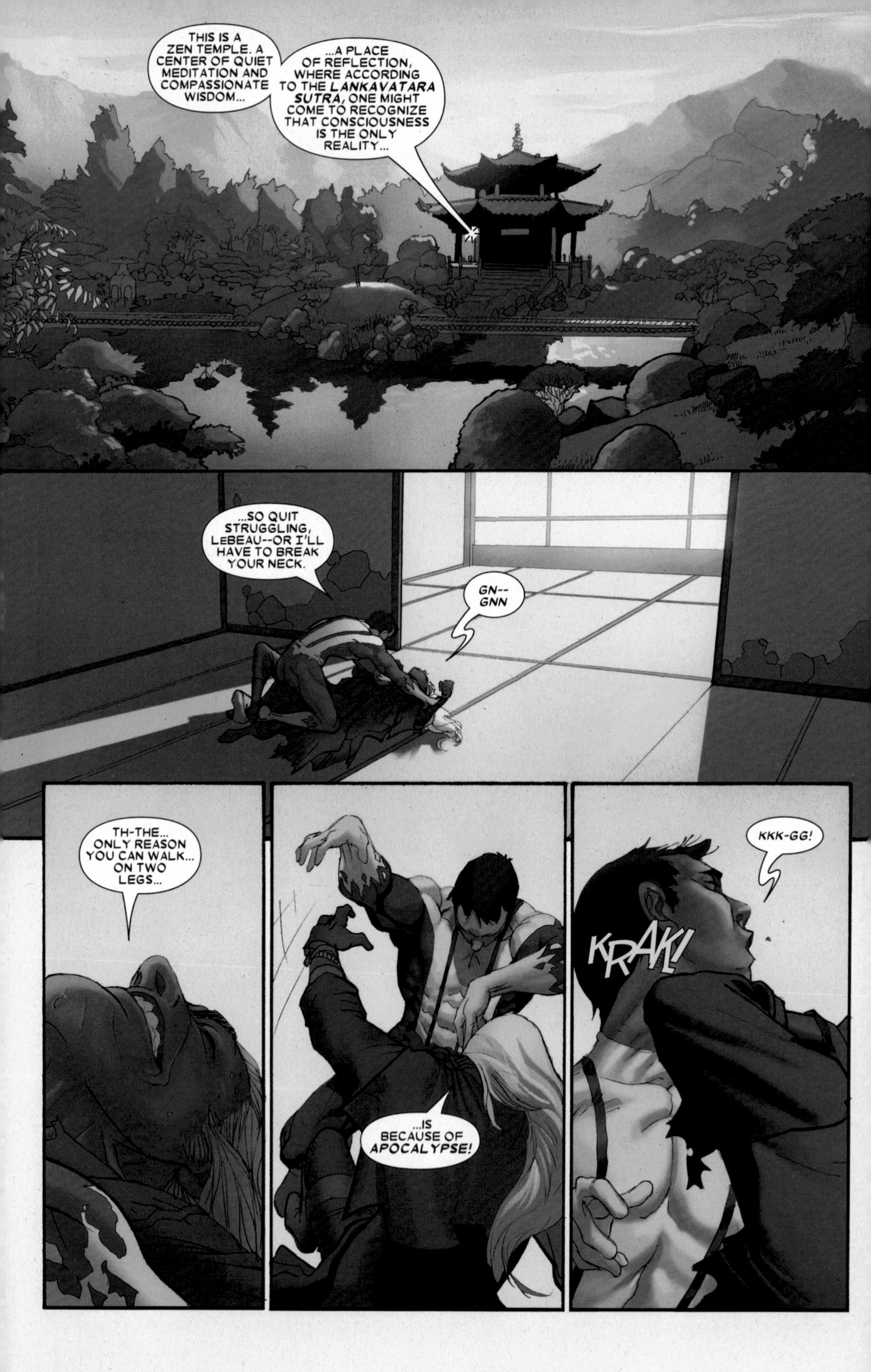
THIS IS A ZEN TEMPLE. A CENTER OF QUIET MEDITATION AND COMPASSIONATE WISDOM...
...A PLACE OF REFLECTION, WHERE ACCORDING TO THE LANKAVATARA SUTRA, ONE MIGHT COME TO RECOGNIZE THAT CONSCIOUSNESS IS THE ONLY REALITY...
...SO QUIT STRUGGLING, LEBEAU--OR I'LL HAVE TO BREAK YOUR NECK.
GN-- GNN
TH-THE... ONLY REASON YOU CAN WALK... ON TWO LEGS...
...IS BECAUSE OF APOCALYPSE!
KRAK!
KKK-GG!

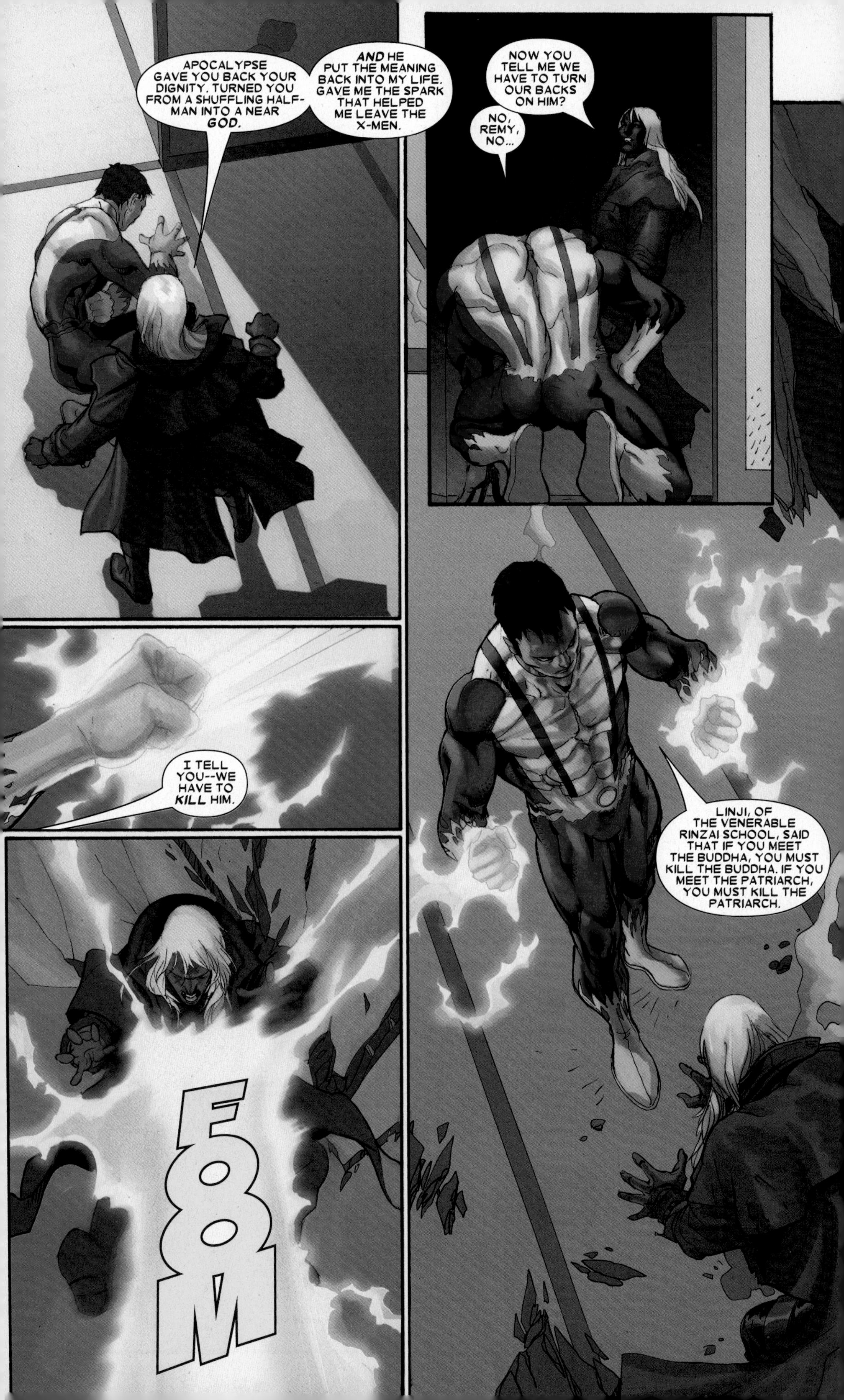
APOCALYPSE GAVE YOU BACK YOUR DIGNITY. TURNED YOU FROM A SHUFFLING HALF-MAN INTO A NEAR GOD.
AND HE PUT THE MEANING BACK INTO MY LIFE. GAVE ME THE SPARK THAT HELPED ME LEAVE THE X-MEN.
NOW YOU TELL ME WE HAVE TO TURN OUR BACKS ON HIM?
NO, REMY, NO...
I TELL YOU--WE HAVE TO KILL HIM.
FOOM
LINJI, OF THE VENERABLE RINZAI SCHOOL, SAID THAT IF YOU MEET THE BUDDHA, YOU MUST KILL THE BUDDHA. IF YOU MEET THE PATRIARCH, YOU MUST KILL THE PATRIARCH.

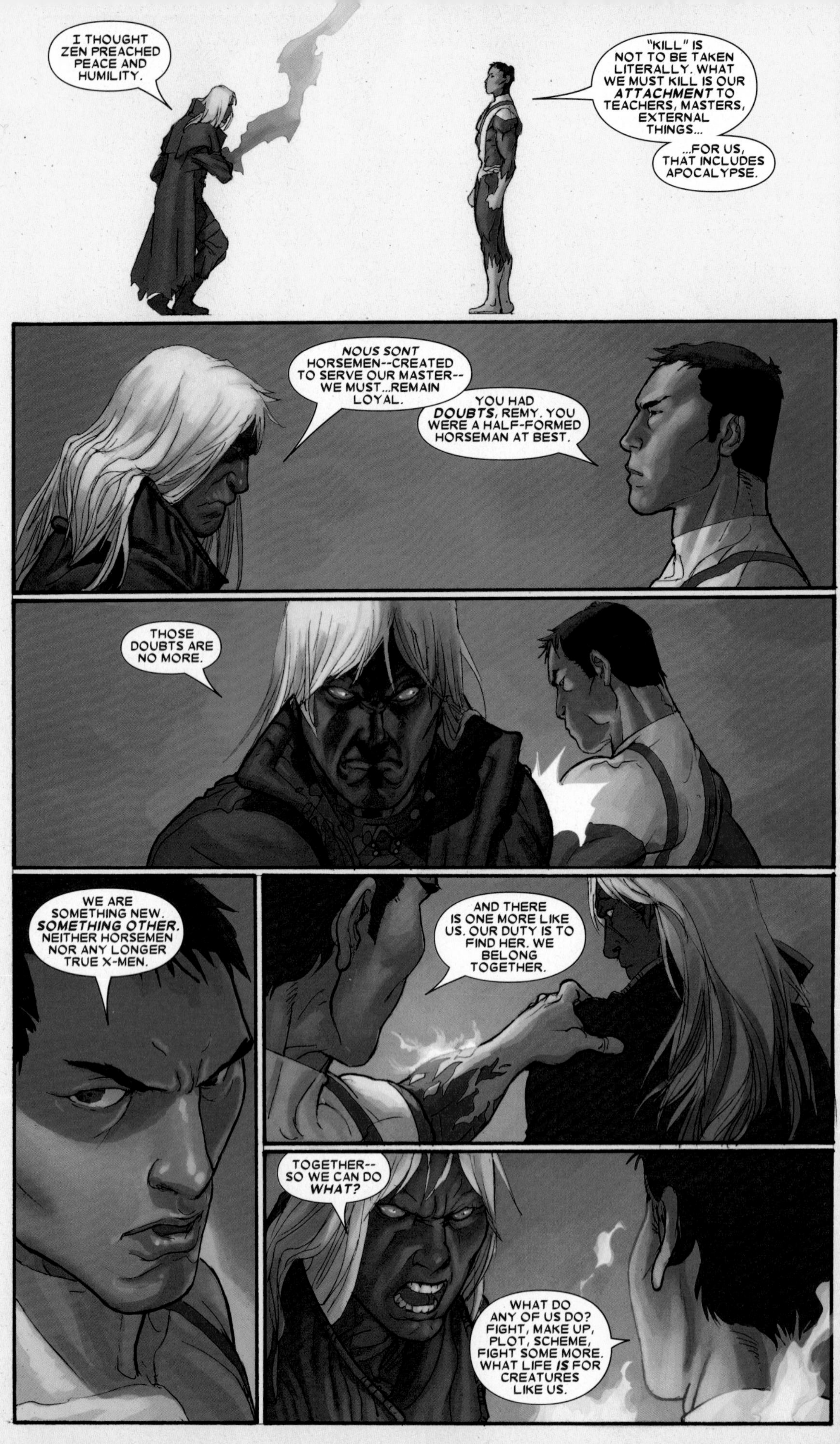
I THOUGHT ZEN PREACHED PEACE AND HUMILITY.
"KILL" IS NOT TO BE TAKEN LITERALLY. WHAT WE MUST KILL IS OUR *ATTACHMENT* TO TEACHERS, MASTERS, EXTERNAL THINGS...
...FOR US, THAT INCLUDES APOCALYPSE.
NOUS SONT HORSEMEN--CREATED TO SERVE OUR MASTER--WE MUST...REMAIN LOYAL.
YOU HAD *DOUBTS*, REMY. YOU WERE A HALF-FORMED HORSEMAN AT BEST.
THOSE DOUBTS ARE NO MORE.
WE ARE SOMETHING NEW. *SOMETHING OTHER.* NEITHER HORSEMEN NOR ANY LONGER TRUE X-MEN.
AND THERE IS ONE MORE LIKE US. OUR DUTY IS TO FIND HER. WE BELONG TOGETHER.
TOGETHER--SO WE CAN DO *WHAT?*
WHAT DO ANY OF US DO? FIGHT, MAKE UP, PLOT, SCHEME, FIGHT SOME MORE. WHAT LIFE *IS* FOR CREATURES LIKE US.

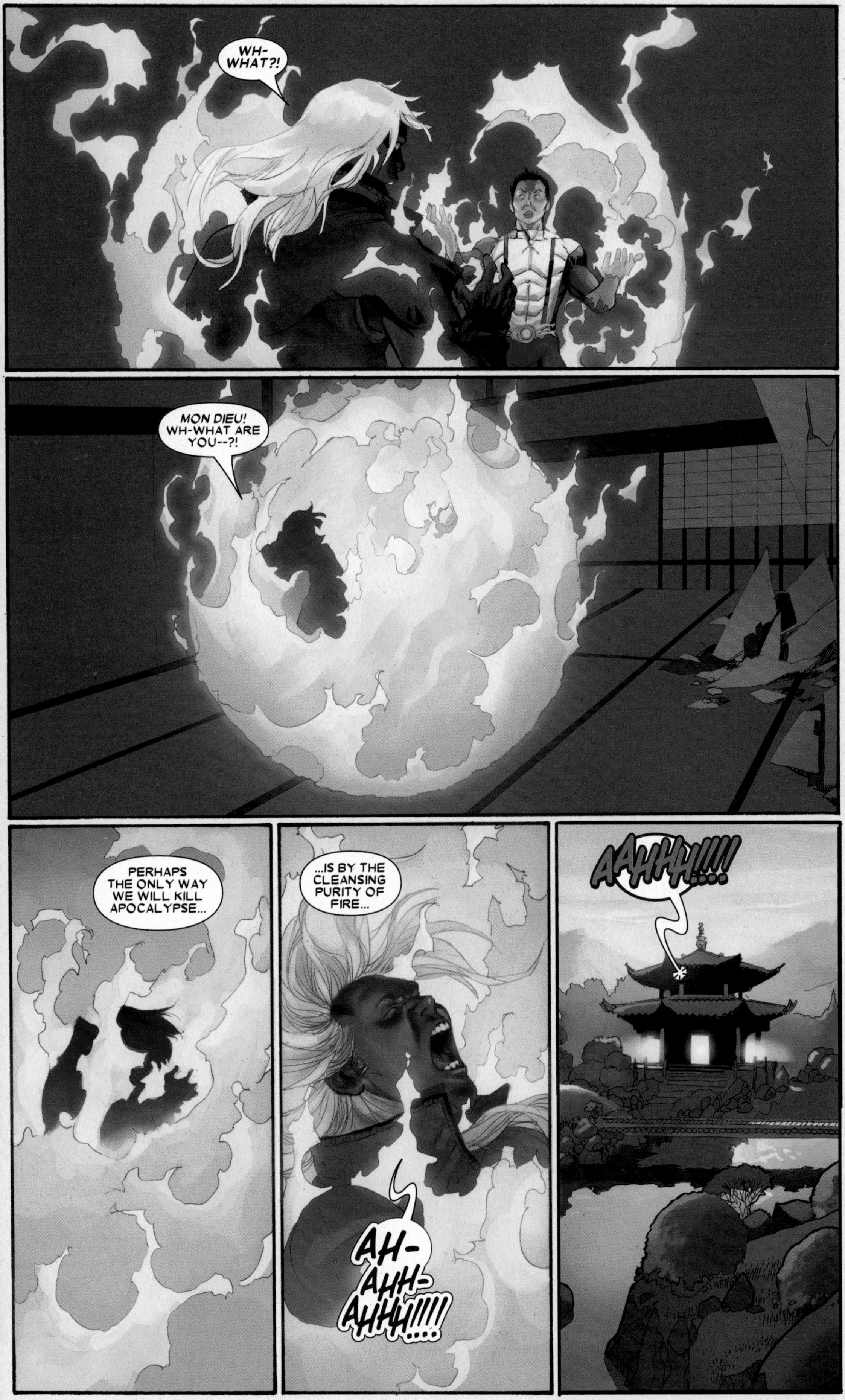

WH-WHAT?!
MON DIEU! WH-WHAT ARE YOU--?!
PERHAPS THE ONLY WAY WE WILL KILL APOCALYPSE...
...IS BY THE CLEANSING PURITY OF FIRE...
AH-AHH-AHHH!!!!...
AAHHH!!!!...

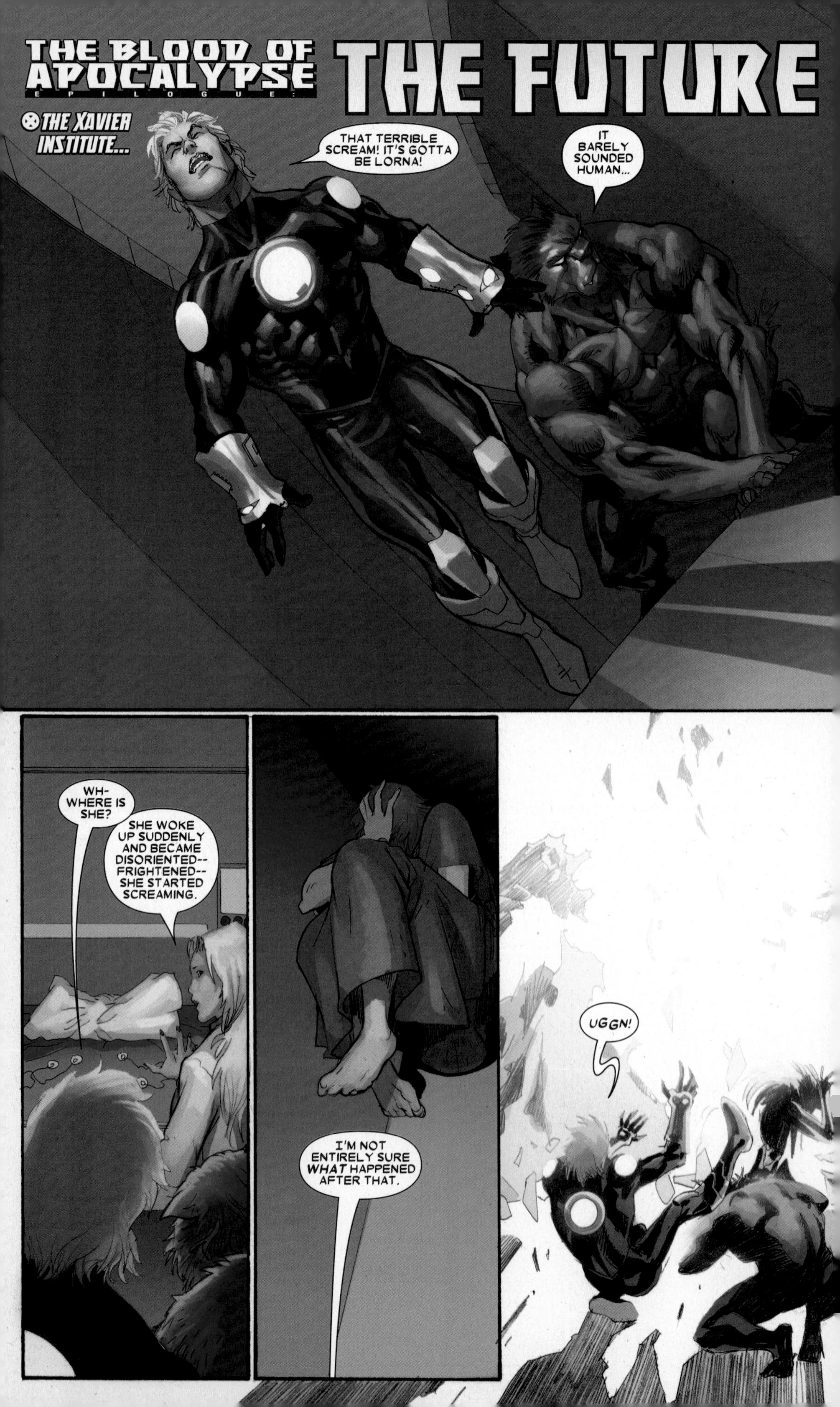

THE BLOOD OF APOCALYPSE
EPILOGUE:
THE FUTURE
THE XAVIER INSTITUTE...
THAT TERRIBLE SCREAM! IT'S GOTTA BE LORNA!
IT BARELY SOUNDED HUMAN...
WH-WHERE IS SHE?
SHE WOKE UP SUDDENLY AND BECAME DISORIENTED--FRIGHTENED--SHE STARTED SCREAMING.
I'M NOT ENTIRELY SURE WHAT HAPPENED AFTER THAT.
UGGN!

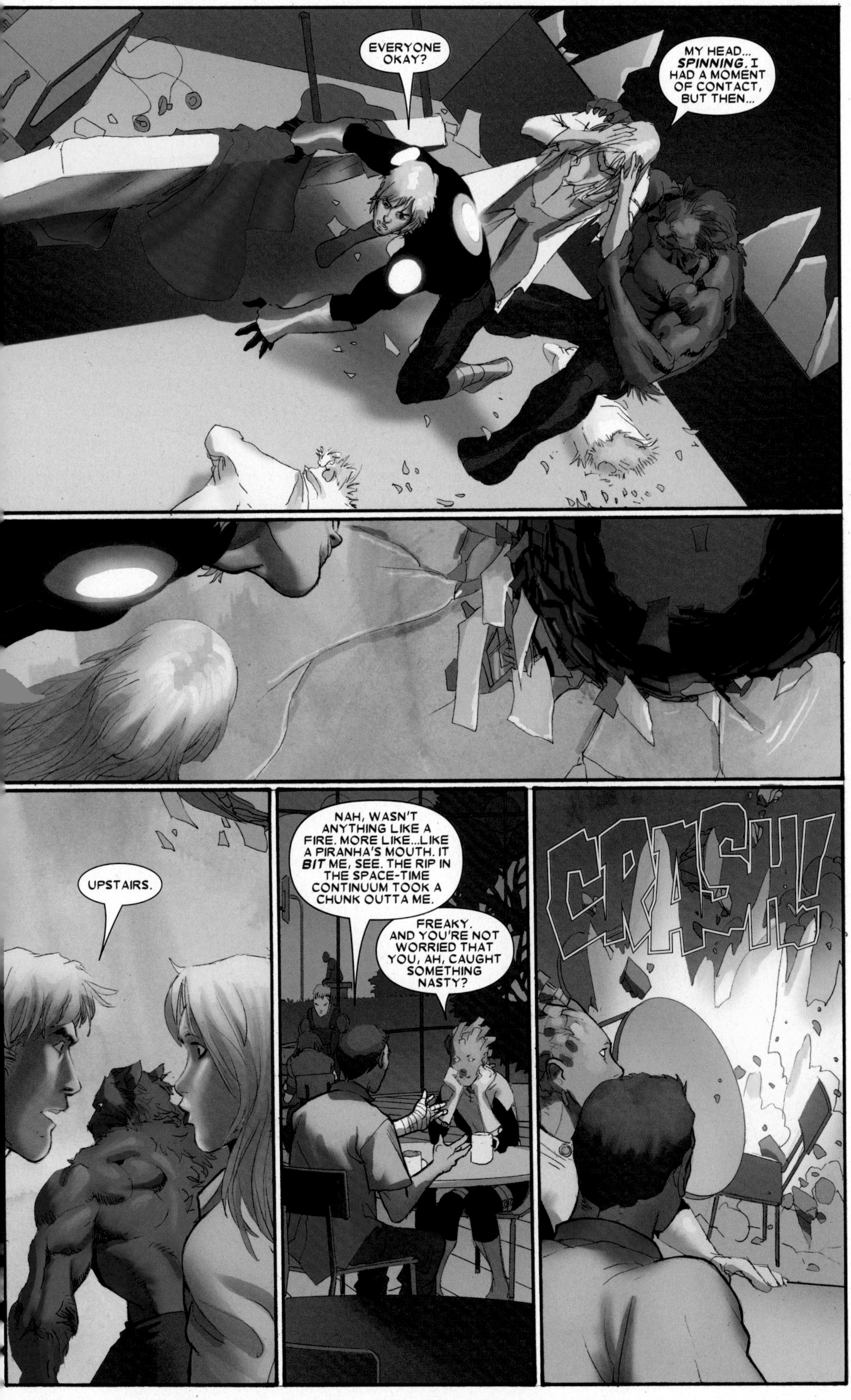
EVERYONE OKAY?
MY HEAD... *SPINNING.* I HAD A MOMENT OF CONTACT, BUT THEN...
UPSTAIRS.
NAH, WASN'T ANYTHING LIKE A FIRE. MORE LIKE...LIKE A PIRANHA'S MOUTH. IT *BIT* ME, SEE. THE RIP IN THE SPACE-TIME CONTINUUM TOOK A CHUNK OUTTA ME.
FREAKY. AND YOU'RE NOT WORRIED THAT YOU, AH, CAUGHT SOMETHING NASTY?
CRASH!

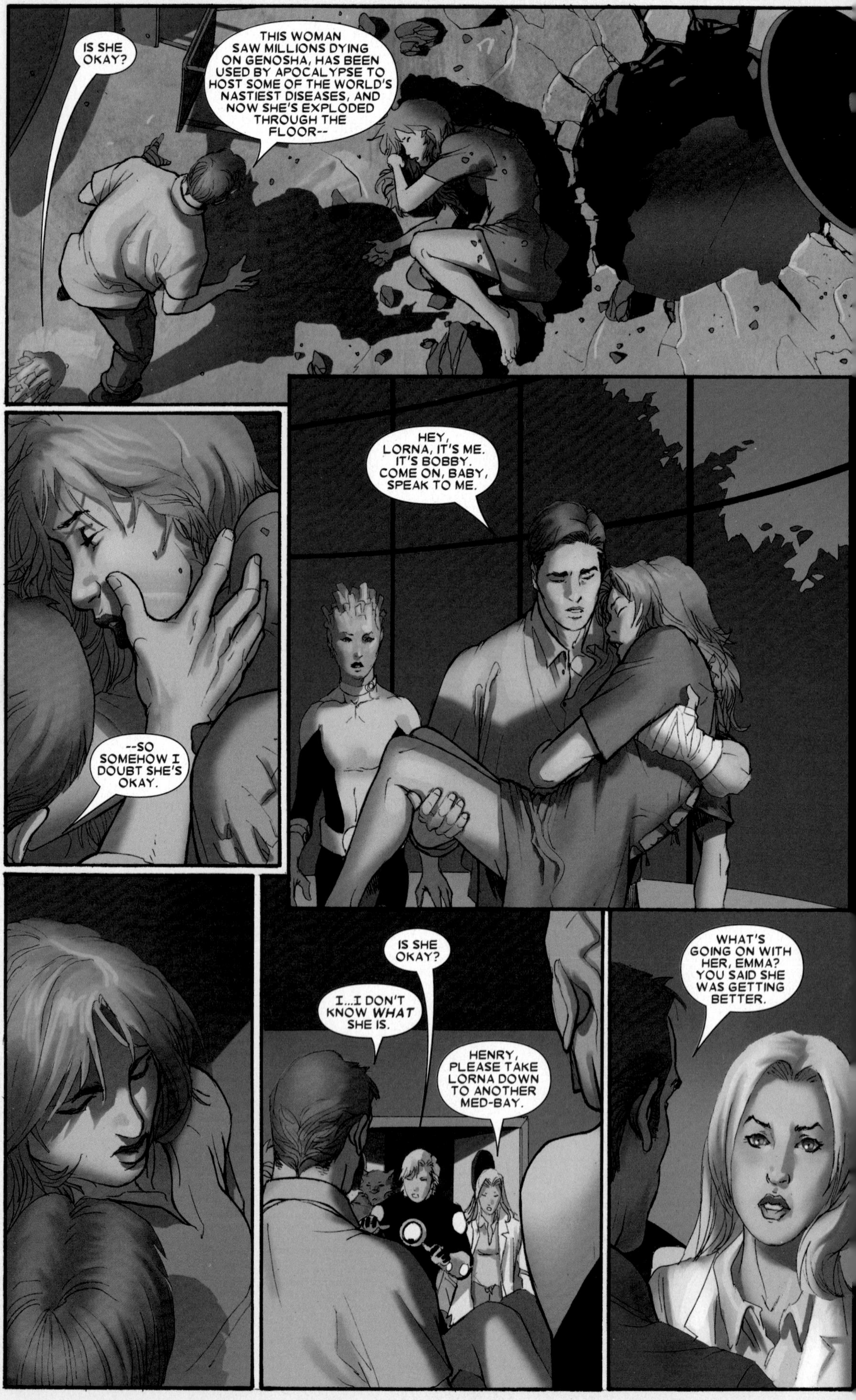
IS SHE OKAY?
THIS WOMAN SAW MILLIONS DYING ON GENOSHA, HAS BEEN USED BY APOCALYPSE TO HOST SOME OF THE WORLD'S NASTIEST DISEASES, AND NOW SHE'S EXPLODED THROUGH THE FLOOR--
--SO SOMEHOW I DOUBT SHE'S OKAY.
HEY, LORNA, IT'S ME. IT'S BOBBY. COME ON, BABY, SPEAK TO ME.
IS SHE OKAY?
I...I DON'T KNOW *WHAT* SHE IS.
HENRY, PLEASE TAKE LORNA DOWN TO ANOTHER MED-BAY.
WHAT'S GOING ON WITH HER, EMMA? YOU SAID SHE WAS GETTING BETTER.

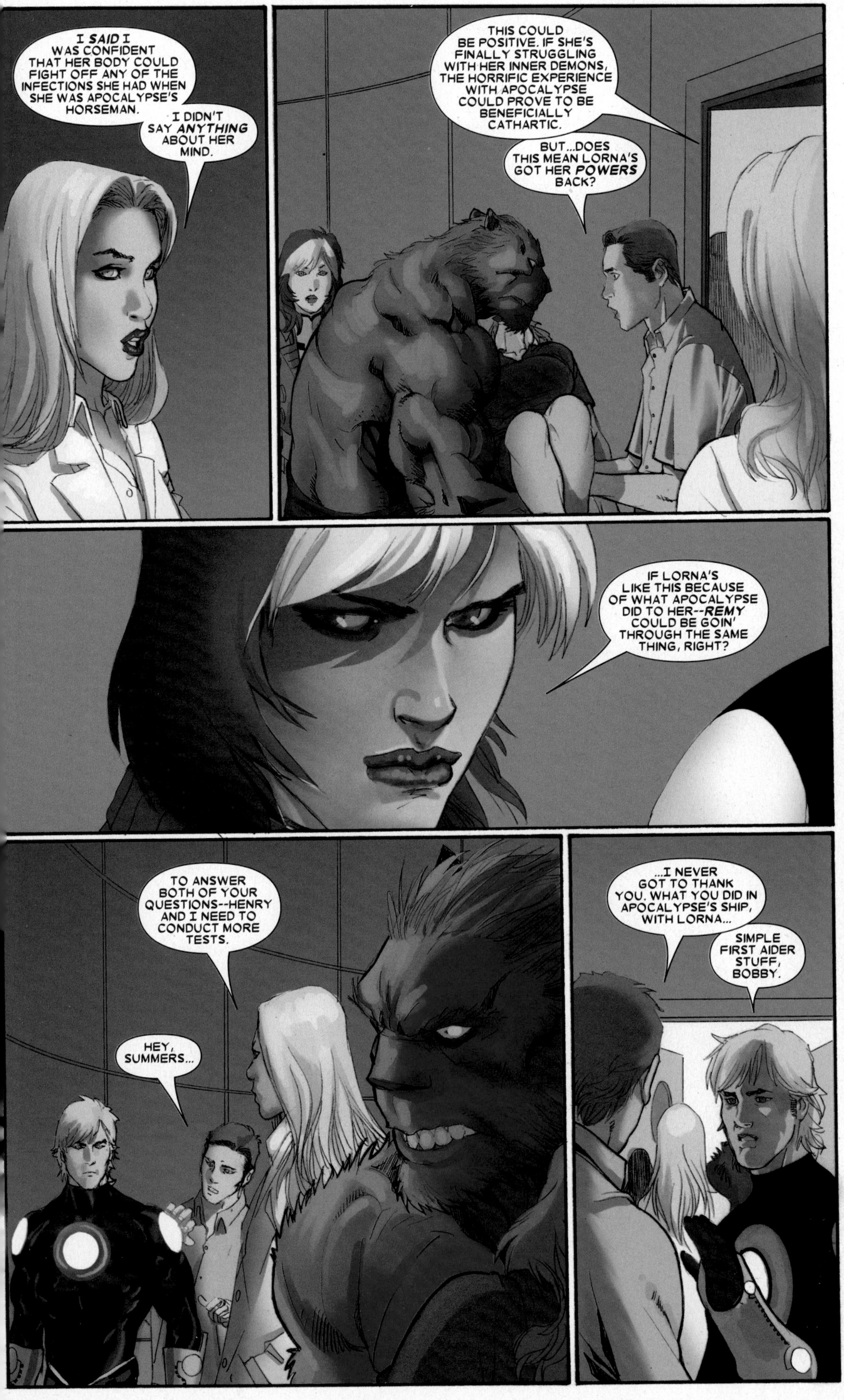
I SAID I WAS CONFIDENT THAT HER BODY COULD FIGHT OFF ANY OF THE INFECTIONS SHE HAD WHEN SHE WAS APOCALYPSE'S HORSEMAN.
I DIDN'T SAY ANYTHING ABOUT HER MIND.
THIS COULD BE POSITIVE. IF SHE'S FINALLY STRUGGLING WITH HER INNER DEMONS, THE HORRIFIC EXPERIENCE WITH APOCALYPSE COULD PROVE TO BE BENEFICIALLY CATHARTIC.
BUT...DOES THIS MEAN LORNA'S GOT HER POWERS BACK?
IF LORNA'S LIKE THIS BECAUSE OF WHAT APOCALYPSE DID TO HER--REMY COULD BE GOIN' THROUGH THE SAME THING, RIGHT?
TO ANSWER BOTH OF YOUR QUESTIONS--HENRY AND I NEED TO CONDUCT MORE TESTS.
HEY, SUMMERS...
...I NEVER GOT TO THANK YOU. WHAT YOU DID IN APOCALYPSE'S SHIP, WITH LORNA...
SIMPLE FIRST AIDER STUFF, BOBBY.

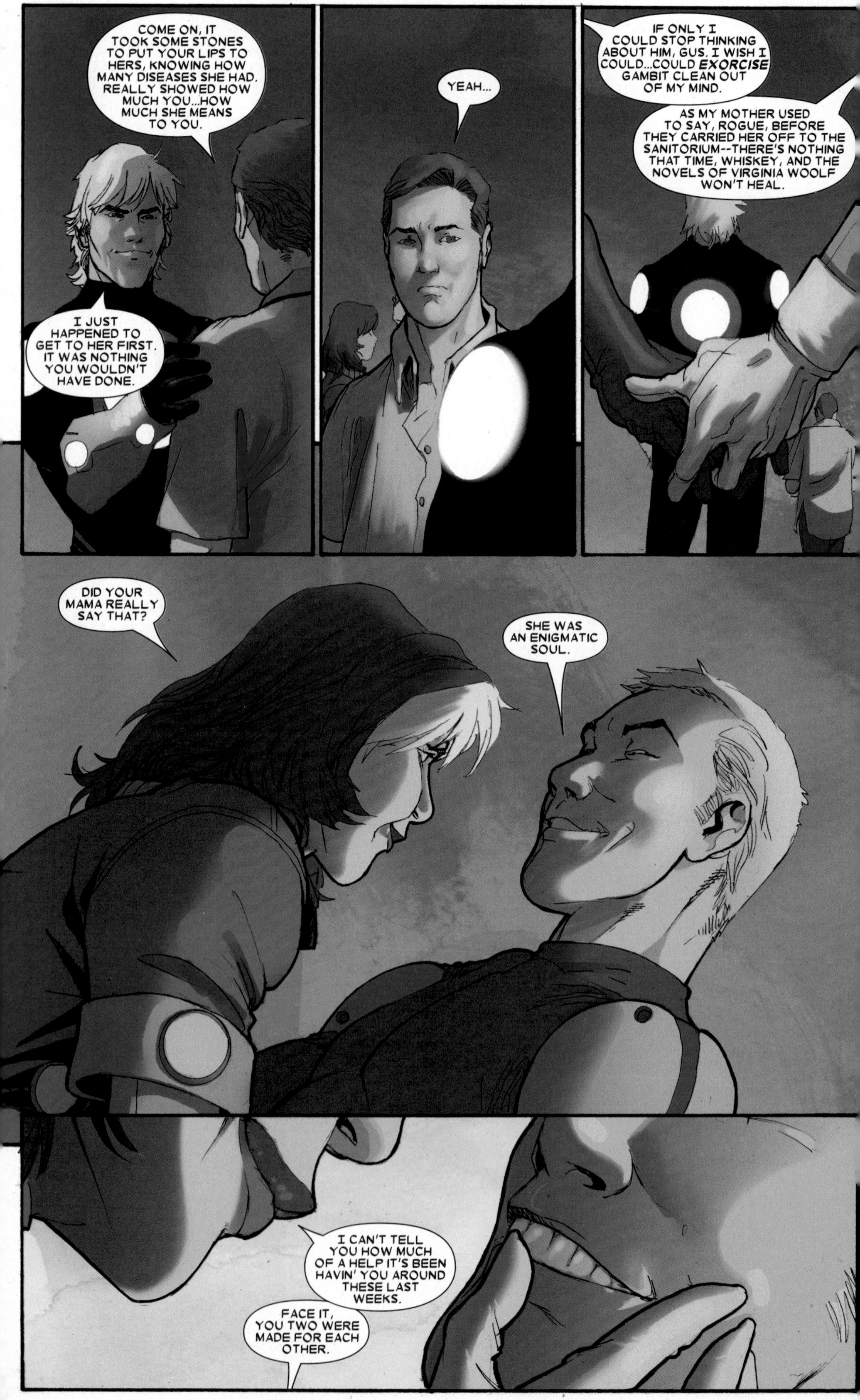

COME ON, IT TOOK SOME STONES TO PUT YOUR LIPS TO HERS, KNOWING HOW MANY DISEASES SHE HAD. REALLY SHOWED HOW MUCH YOU...HOW MUCH SHE MEANS TO YOU.
I JUST HAPPENED TO GET TO HER FIRST. IT WAS NOTHING YOU WOULDN'T HAVE DONE.
YEAH...
IF ONLY I COULD STOP THINKING ABOUT HIM, GUS. I WISH I COULD...COULD EXORCISE GAMBIT CLEAN OUT OF MY MIND.
AS MY MOTHER USED TO SAY, ROGUE, BEFORE THEY CARRIED HER OFF TO THE SANITORIUM--THERE'S NOTHING THAT TIME, WHISKEY, AND THE NOVELS OF VIRGINIA WOOLF WON'T HEAL.
DID YOUR MAMA REALLY SAY THAT?
SHE WAS AN ENIGMATIC SOUL.
I CAN'T TELL YOU HOW MUCH OF A HELP IT'S BEEN HAVIN' YOU AROUND THESE LAST WEEKS.
FACE IT, YOU TWO WERE MADE FOR EACH OTHER.

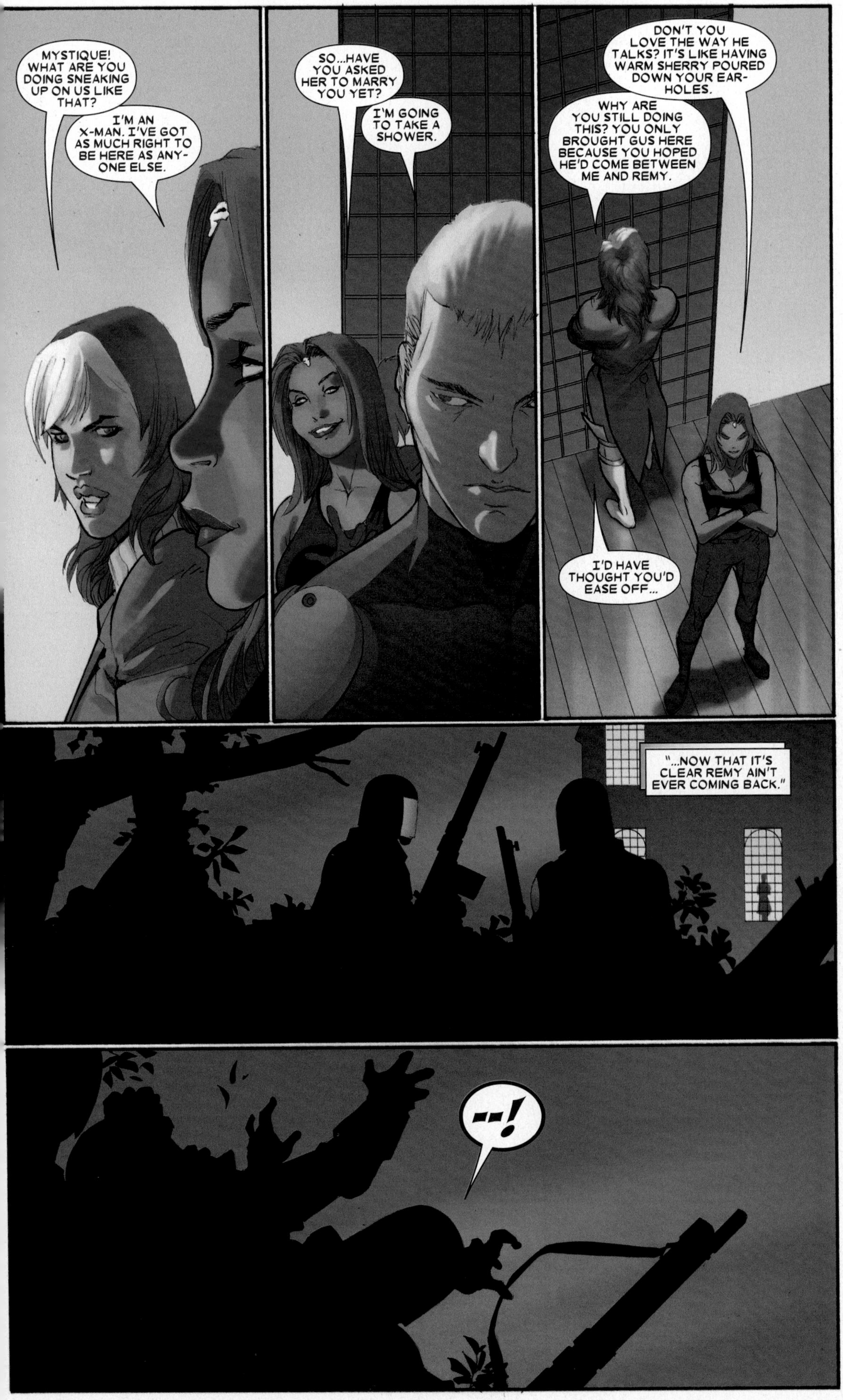

MYSTIQUE! WHAT ARE YOU DOING SNEAKING UP ON US LIKE THAT?
I'M AN X-MAN. I'VE GOT AS MUCH RIGHT TO BE HERE AS ANY-ONE ELSE.
SO...HAVE YOU ASKED HER TO MARRY YOU YET?
I'M GOING TO TAKE A SHOWER.
DON'T YOU LOVE THE WAY HE TALKS? IT'S LIKE HAVING WARM SHERRY POURED DOWN YOUR EAR-HOLES.
WHY ARE YOU STILL DOING THIS? YOU ONLY BROUGHT GUS HERE BECAUSE YOU HOPED HE'D COME BETWEEN ME AND REMY.
I'D HAVE THOUGHT YOU'D EASE OFF...
"...NOW THAT IT'S CLEAR REMY AIN'T EVER COMING BACK."
--!

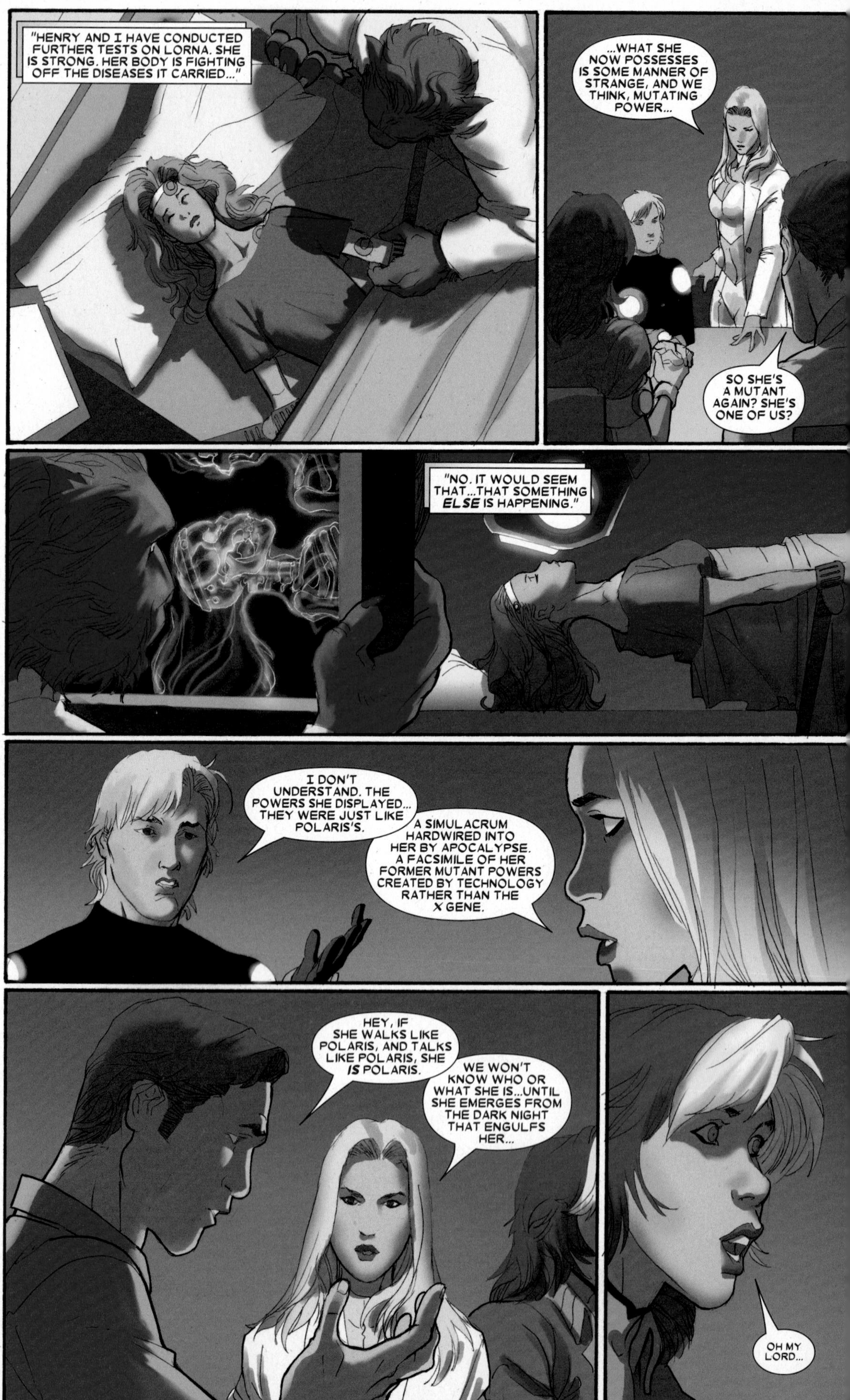
"HENRY AND I HAVE CONDUCTED FURTHER TESTS ON LORNA. SHE IS STRONG. HER BODY IS FIGHTING OFF THE DISEASES IT CARRIED..."
...WHAT SHE NOW POSSESSES IS SOME MANNER OF STRANGE, AND WE THINK, MUTATING POWER...
SO SHE'S A MUTANT AGAIN? SHE'S ONE OF US?
"NO. IT WOULD SEEM THAT...THAT SOMETHING ELSE IS HAPPENING."
I DON'T UNDERSTAND. THE POWERS SHE DISPLAYED... THEY WERE JUST LIKE POLARIS'S.
A SIMULACRUM HARDWIRED INTO HER BY APOCALYPSE. A FACSIMILE OF HER FORMER MUTANT POWERS CREATED BY TECHNOLOGY RATHER THAN THE X GENE.
HEY, IF SHE WALKS LIKE POLARIS, AND TALKS LIKE POLARIS, SHE IS POLARIS.
WE WON'T KNOW WHO OR WHAT SHE IS...UNTIL SHE EMERGES FROM THE DARK NIGHT THAT ENGULFS HER...
OH MY LORD...

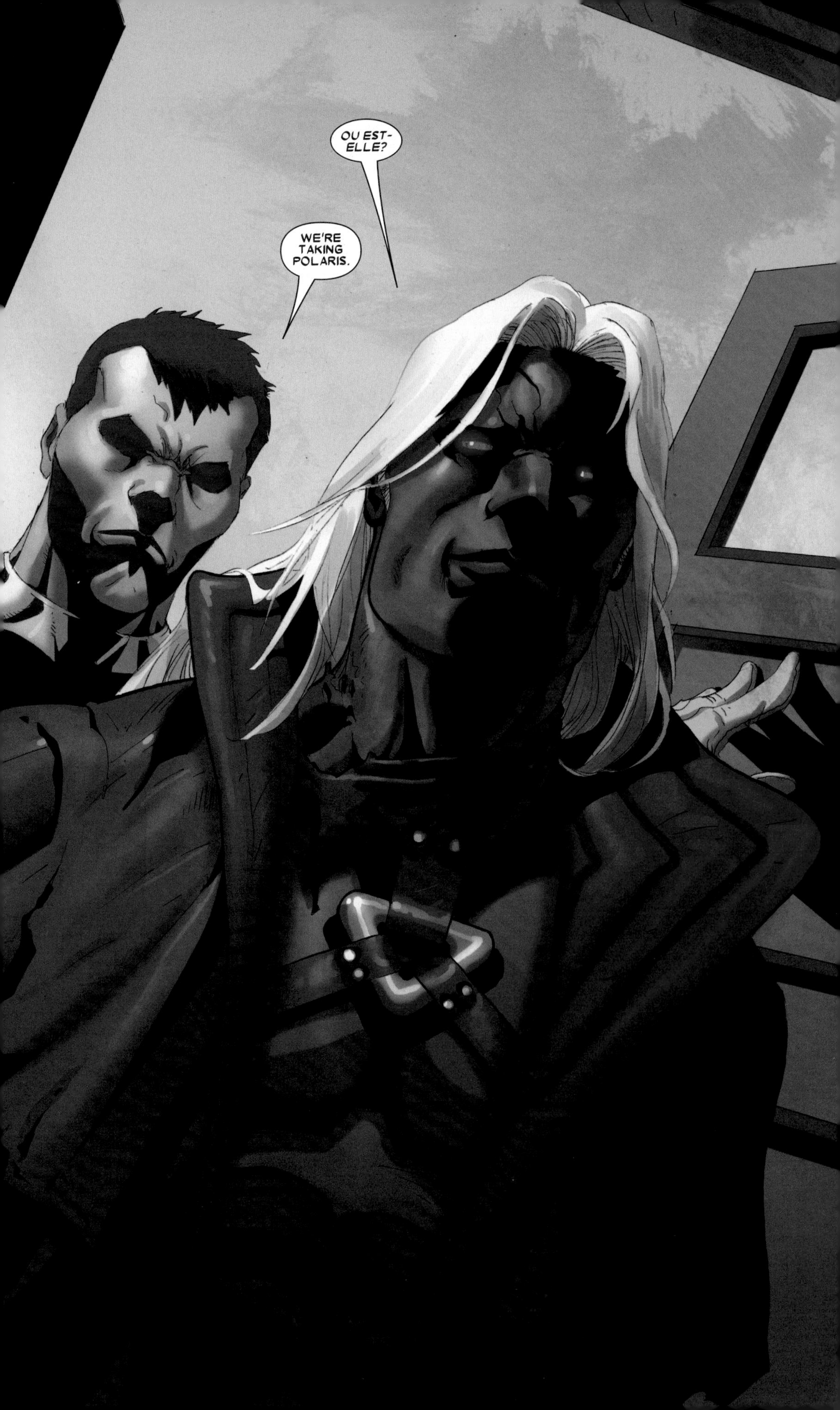
OU EST-
ELLE?
WE'RE
TAKING
POLARIS.

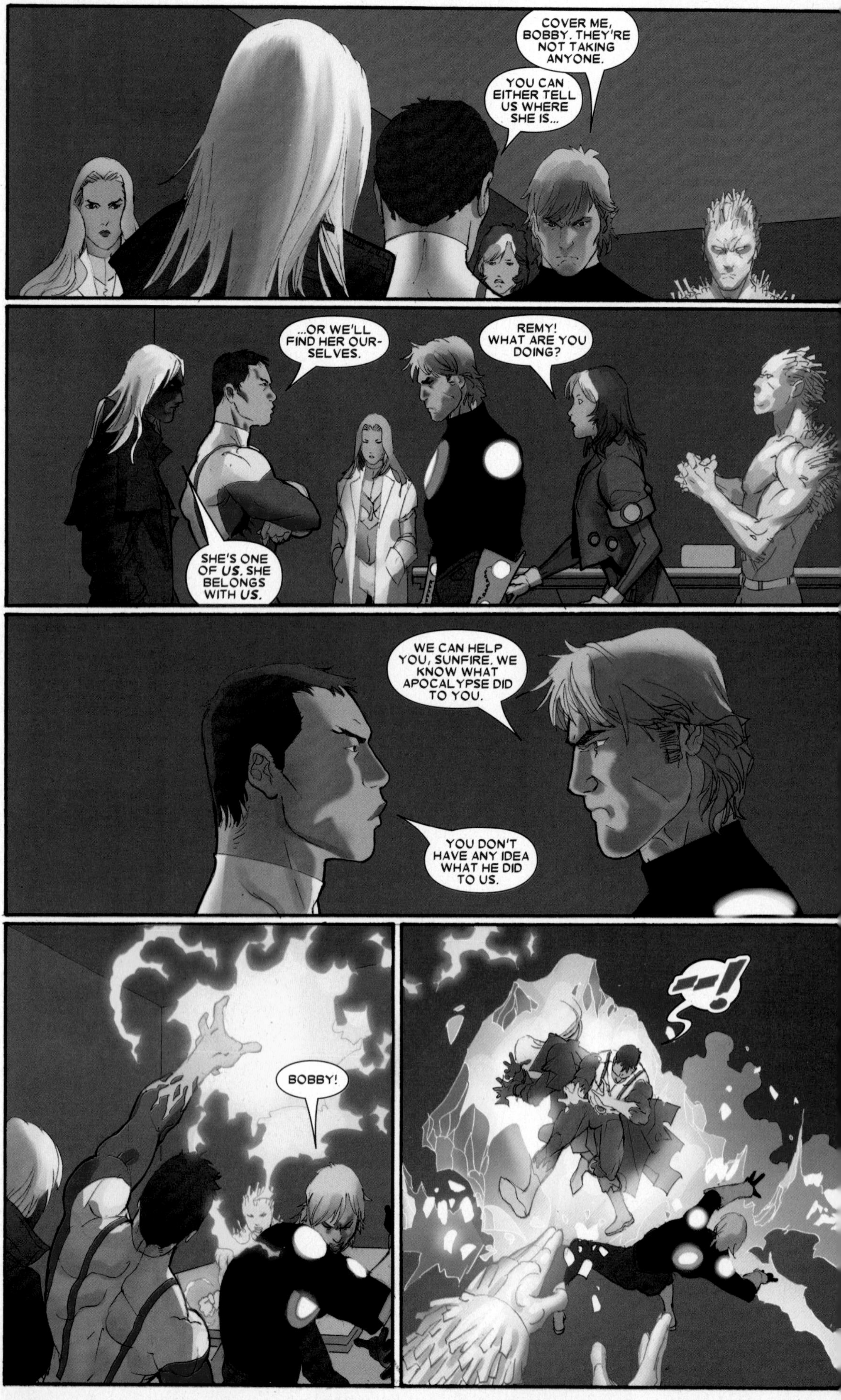

COVER ME, BOBBY. THEY'RE NOT TAKING ANYONE.
YOU CAN EITHER TELL US WHERE SHE IS...
...OR WE'LL FIND HER OUR-SELVES.
SHE'S ONE OF *US*. SHE BELONGS WITH *US*.
REMY! WHAT ARE YOU DOING?
WE CAN HELP YOU, SUNFIRE. WE KNOW WHAT APOCALYPSE DID TO YOU.
YOU DON'T HAVE ANY IDEA WHAT HE DID TO US.
BOBBY!
--!

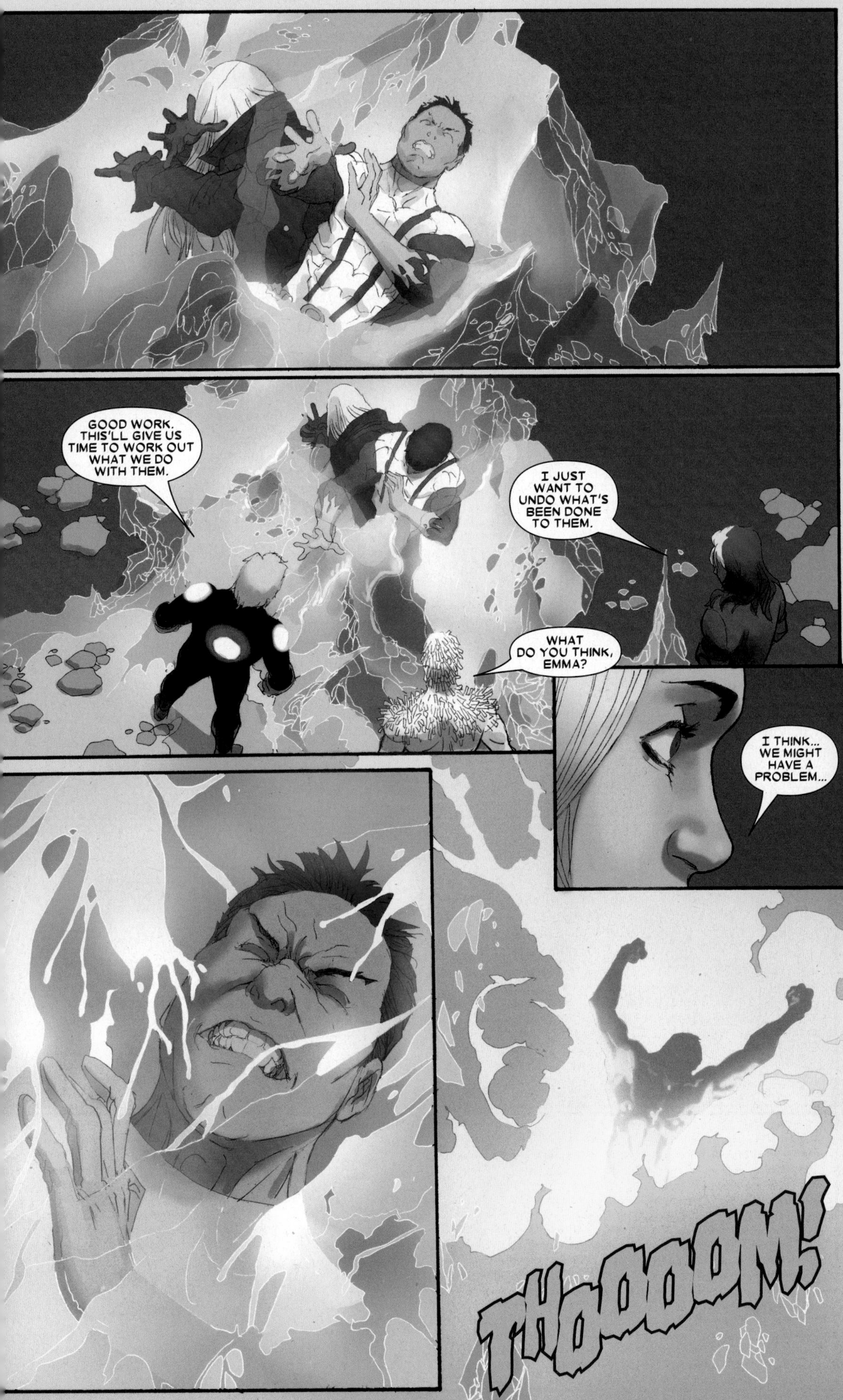
GOOD WORK. THIS'LL GIVE US TIME TO WORK OUT WHAT WE DO WITH THEM.
I JUST WANT TO UNDO WHAT'S BEEN DONE TO THEM.
WHAT DO YOU THINK, EMMA?
I THINK... WE MIGHT HAVE A PROBLEM...
THOOOOM!

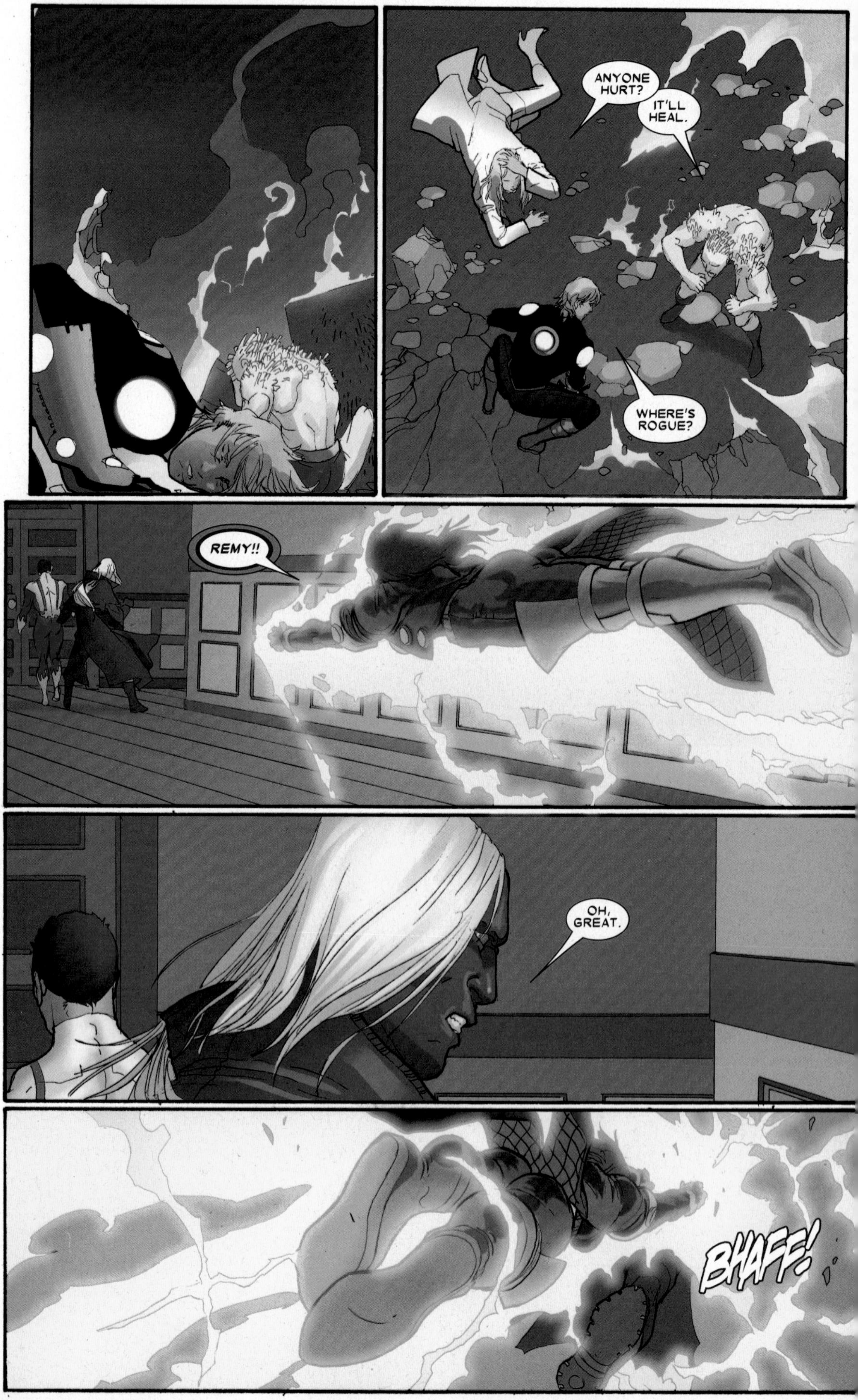
ANYONE HURT?
IT'LL HEAL.
WHERE'S ROGUE?
REMY!!
OH, GREAT.
BHAFF!

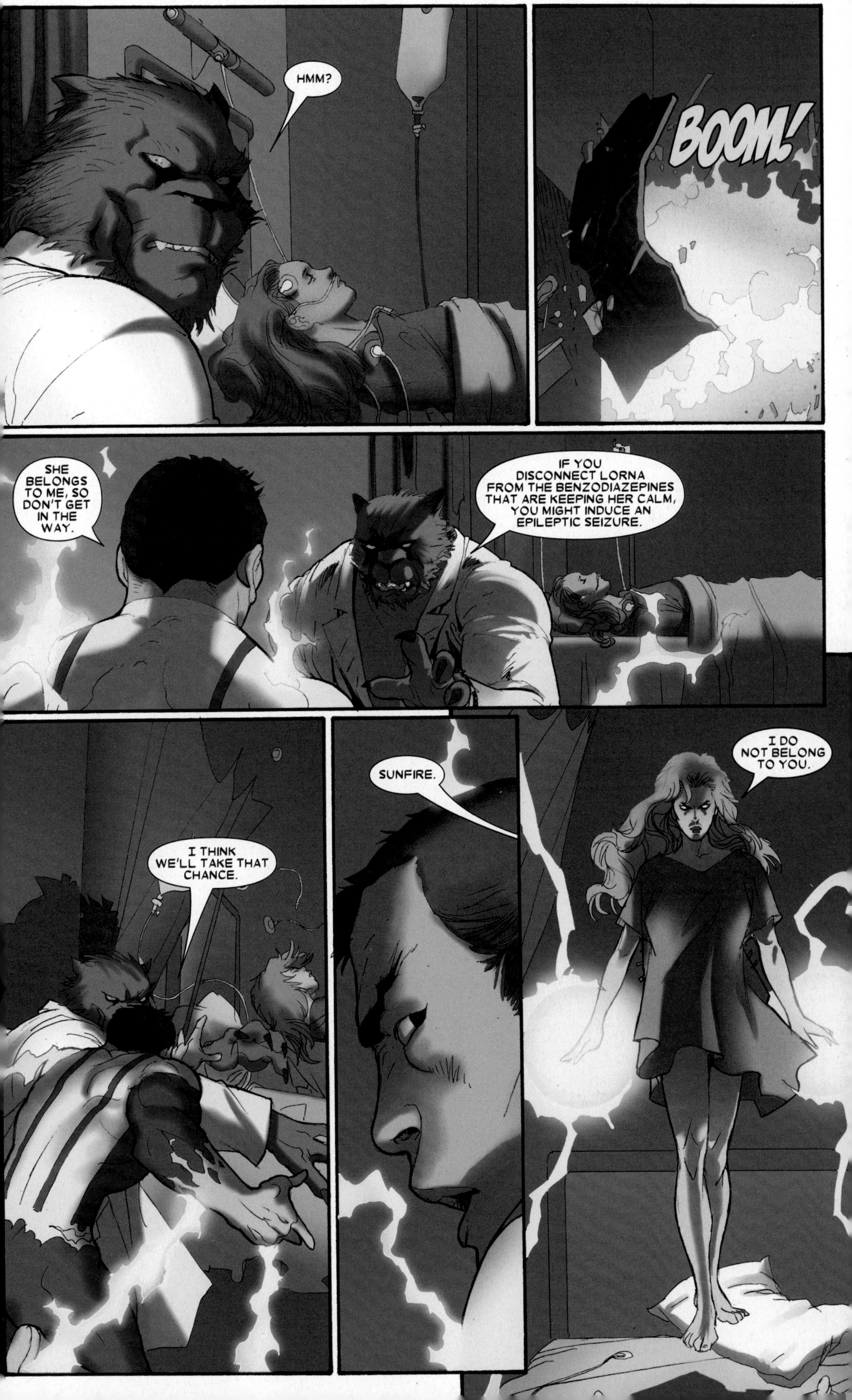
HMM?
BOOM!
SHE BELONGS TO ME, SO DON'T GET IN THE WAY.
IF YOU DISCONNECT LORNA FROM THE BENZODIAZEPINES THAT ARE KEEPING HER CALM, YOU MIGHT INDUCE AN EPILEPTIC SEIZURE.
I THINK WE'LL TAKE THAT CHANCE.
SUNFIRE.
I DO NOT BELONG TO YOU.

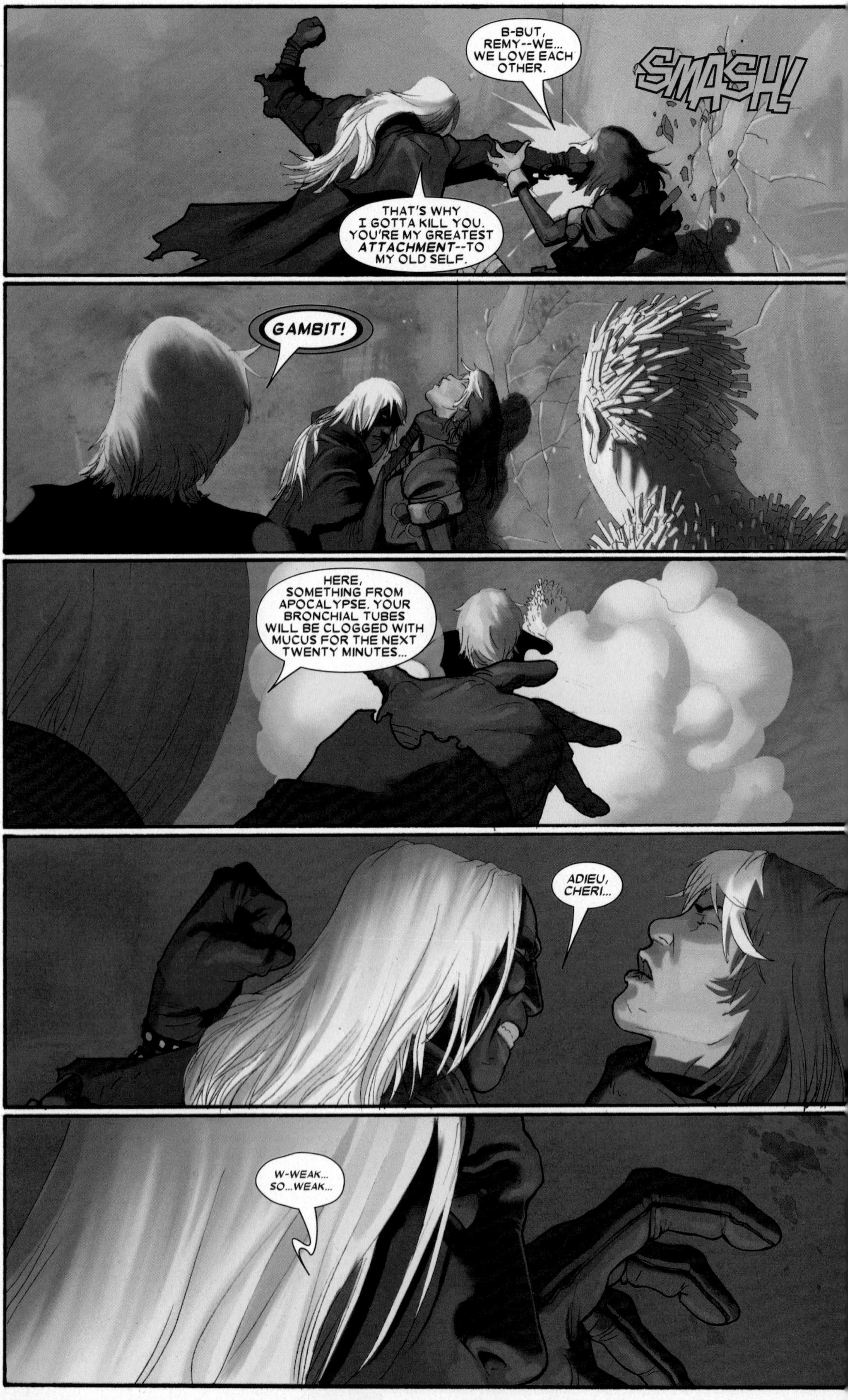
B-BUT, REMY--WE... WE LOVE EACH OTHER.
SMASH!
THAT'S WHY I GOTTA KILL YOU. YOU'RE MY GREATEST ATTACHMENT--TO MY OLD SELF.
GAMBIT!
HERE, SOMETHING FROM APOCALYPSE. YOUR BRONCHIAL TUBES WILL BE CLOGGED WITH MUCUS FOR THE NEXT TWENTY MINUTES...
ADIEU, CHERI...
W-WEAK... SO...WEAK...

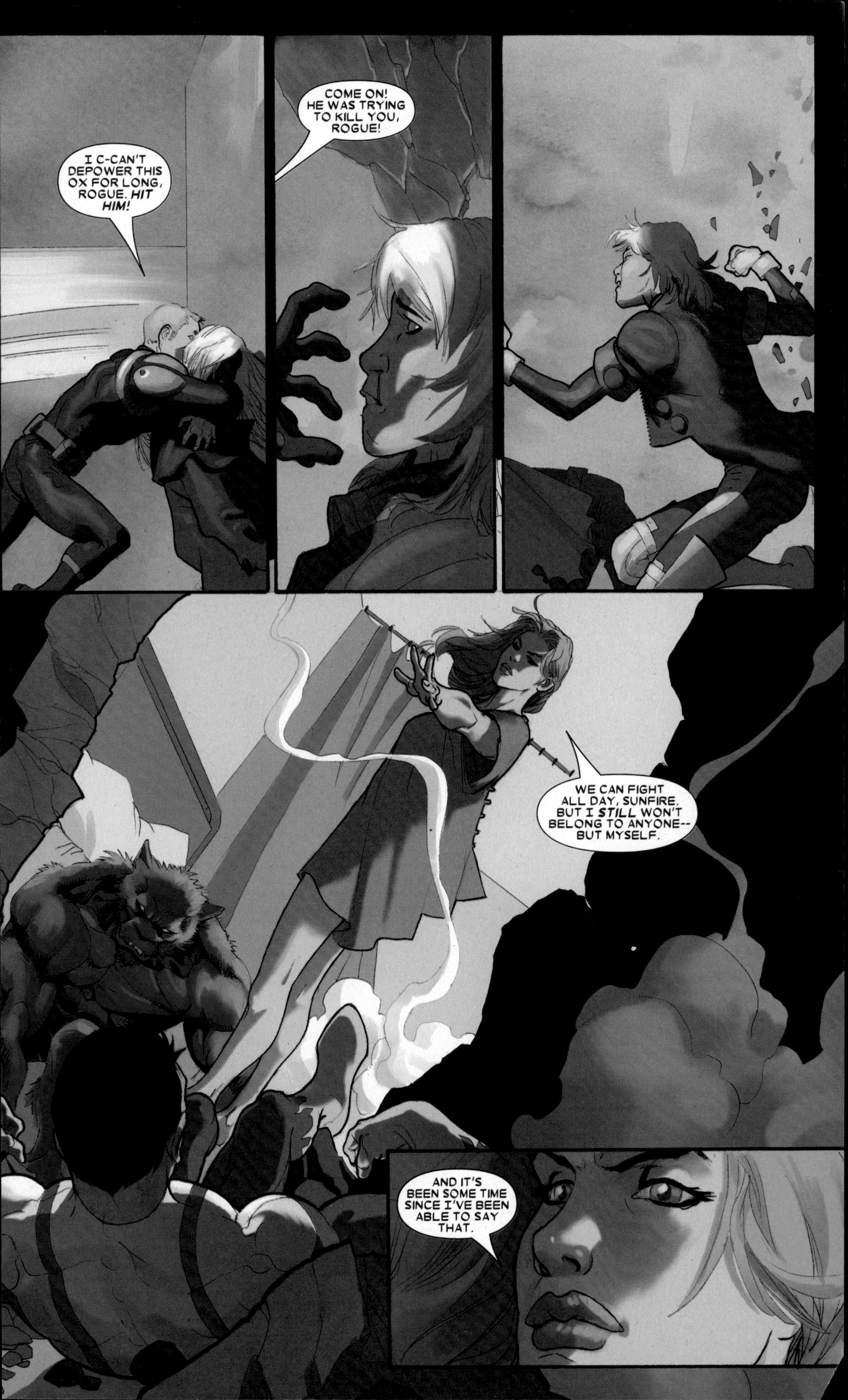

I C-CAN'T DEPOWER THIS OX FOR LONG, ROGUE. *HIT HIM!*
COME ON! HE WAS TRYING TO KILL YOU, ROGUE!
WE CAN FIGHT ALL DAY, SUNFIRE. BUT I *STILL* WON'T BELONG TO ANYONE-- BUT MYSELF.
AND IT'S BEEN SOME TIME SINCE I'VE BEEN ABLE TO SAY THAT.

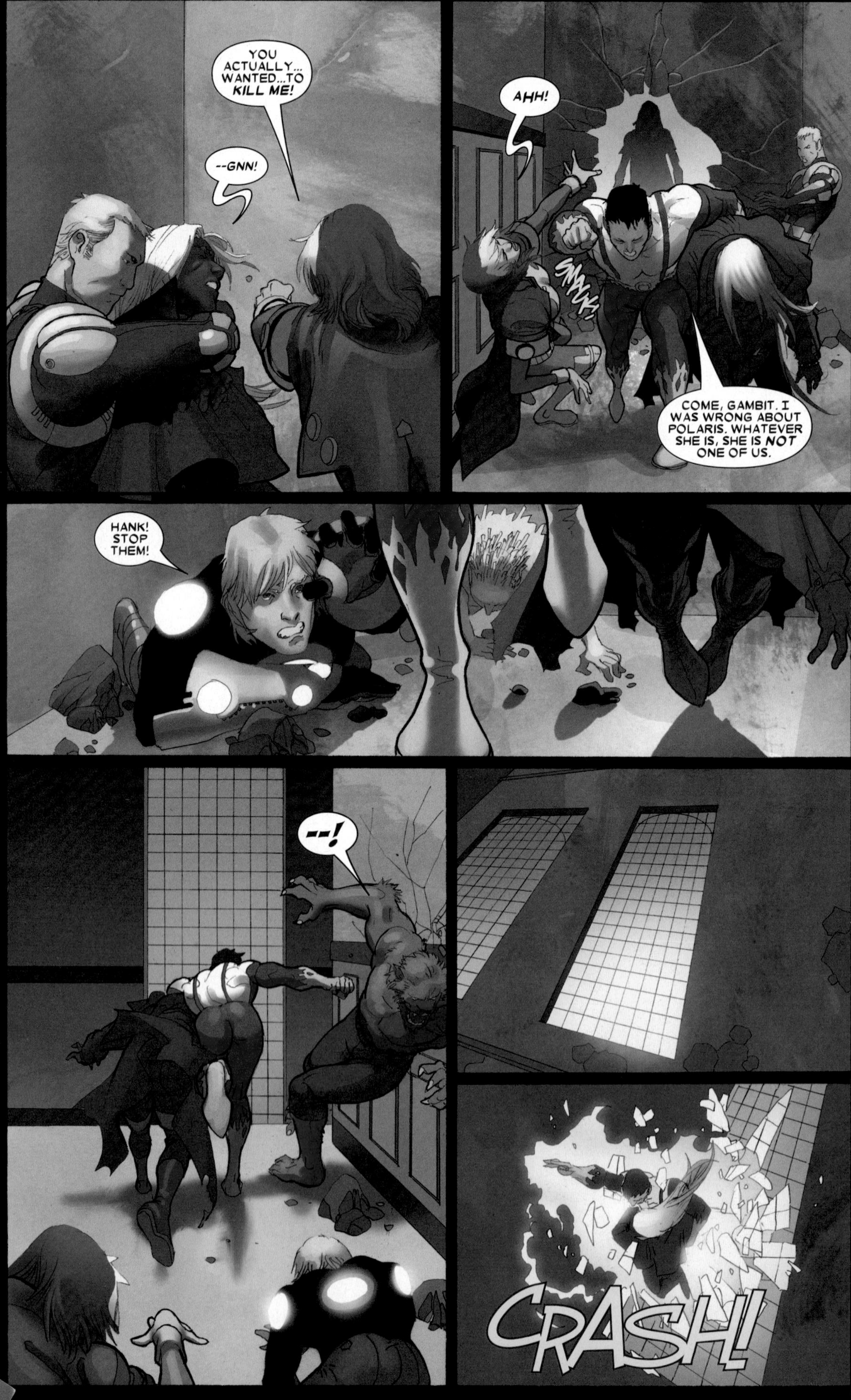
YOU ACTUALLY... WANTED...TO KILL ME!
--GNN!
AHH!
SMACK!
COME, GAMBIT. I WAS WRONG ABOUT POLARIS. WHATEVER SHE IS, SHE IS NOT ONE OF US.
HANK! STOP THEM!
--!
CRASH!

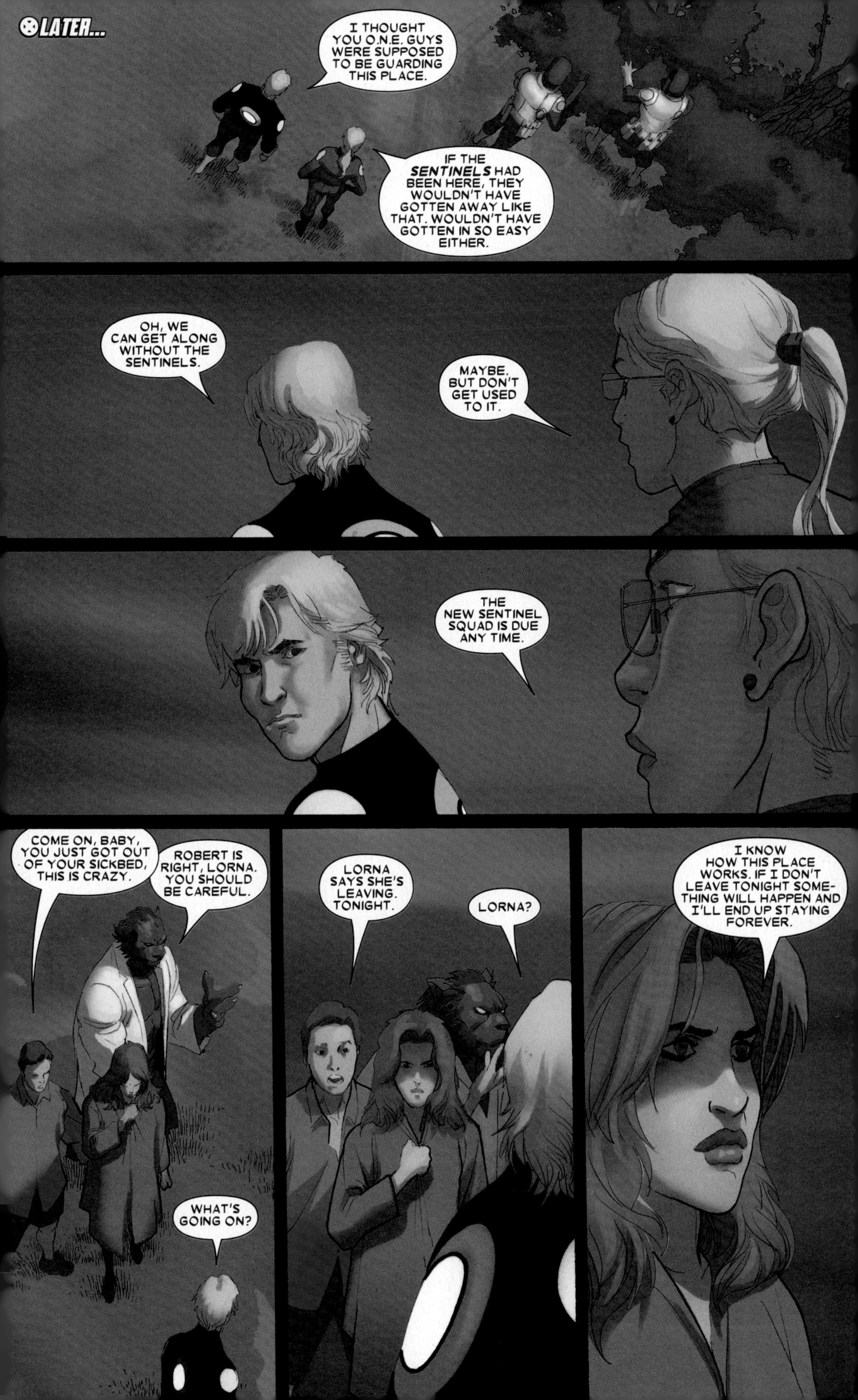
LATER...
I THOUGHT YOU O.N.E. GUYS WERE SUPPOSED TO BE GUARDING THIS PLACE.
IF THE *SENTINELS* HAD BEEN HERE, THEY WOULDN'T HAVE GOTTEN AWAY LIKE THAT. WOULDN'T HAVE GOTTEN IN SO EASY EITHER.
OH, WE CAN GET ALONG WITHOUT THE SENTINELS.
MAYBE. BUT DON'T GET USED TO IT.
THE NEW SENTINEL SQUAD IS DUE ANY TIME.
COME ON, BABY, YOU JUST GOT OUT OF YOUR SICKBED, THIS IS CRAZY.
ROBERT IS RIGHT, LORNA. YOU SHOULD BE CAREFUL.
WHAT'S GOING ON?
LORNA SAYS SHE'S LEAVING. TONIGHT.
LORNA?
I KNOW HOW THIS PLACE WORKS. IF I DON'T LEAVE TONIGHT SOMETHING WILL HAPPEN AND I'LL END UP STAYING FOREVER.

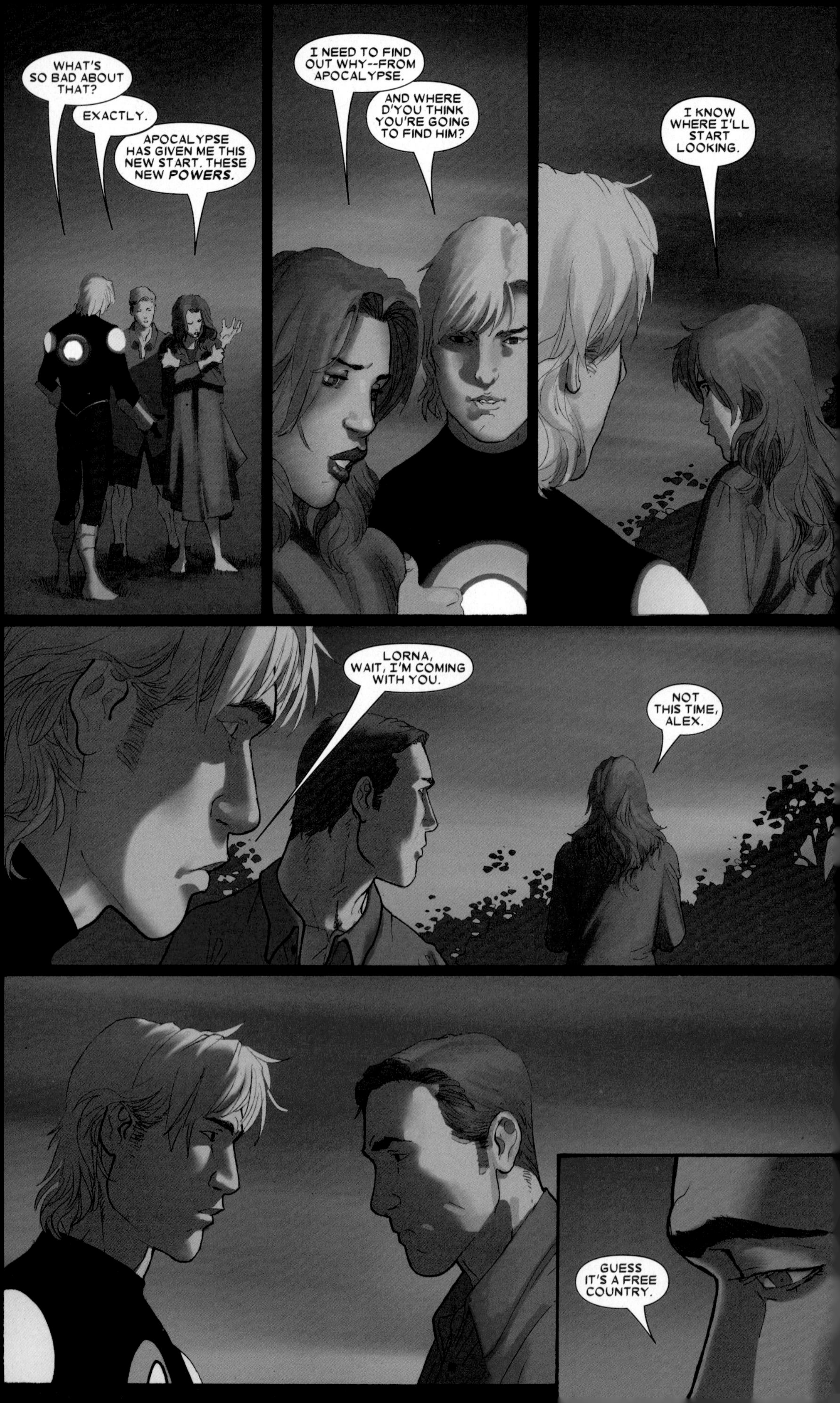
WHAT'S SO BAD ABOUT THAT?
EXACTLY.
APOCALYPSE HAS GIVEN ME THIS NEW START. THESE NEW POWERS.
I NEED TO FIND OUT WHY--FROM APOCALYPSE.
AND WHERE D'YOU THINK YOU'RE GOING TO FIND HIM?
I KNOW WHERE I'LL START LOOKING.
LORNA, WAIT, I'M COMING WITH YOU.
NOT THIS TIME, ALEX.
GUESS IT'S A FREE COUNTRY.

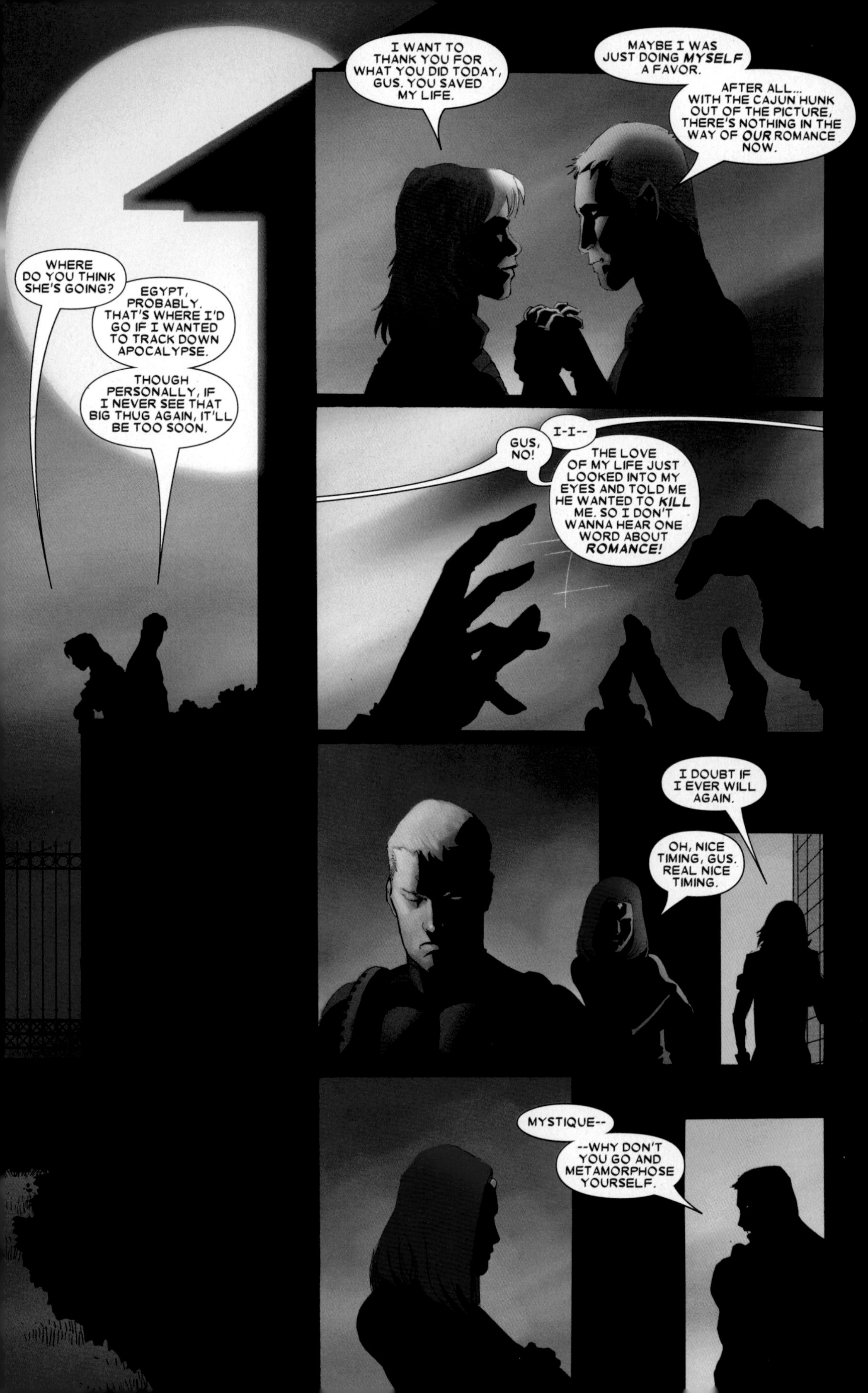
WHERE DO YOU THINK SHE'S GOING?
EGYPT, PROBABLY. THAT'S WHERE I'D GO IF I WANTED TO TRACK DOWN APOCALYPSE.
THOUGH PERSONALLY, IF I NEVER SEE THAT BIG THUG AGAIN, IT'LL BE TOO SOON.
I WANT TO THANK YOU FOR WHAT YOU DID TODAY, GUS. YOU SAVED MY LIFE.
MAYBE I WAS JUST DOING MYSELF A FAVOR.
AFTER ALL... WITH THE CAJUN HUNK OUT OF THE PICTURE, THERE'S NOTHING IN THE WAY OF OUR ROMANCE NOW.
GUS, NO!
I-I--
THE LOVE OF MY LIFE JUST LOOKED INTO MY EYES AND TOLD ME HE WANTED TO KILL ME. SO I DON'T WANNA HEAR ONE WORD ABOUT ROMANCE!
I DOUBT IF I EVER WILL AGAIN.
OH, NICE TIMING, GUS. REAL NICE TIMING.
MYSTIQUE--
--WHY DON'T YOU GO AND METAMORPHOSE YOURSELF.

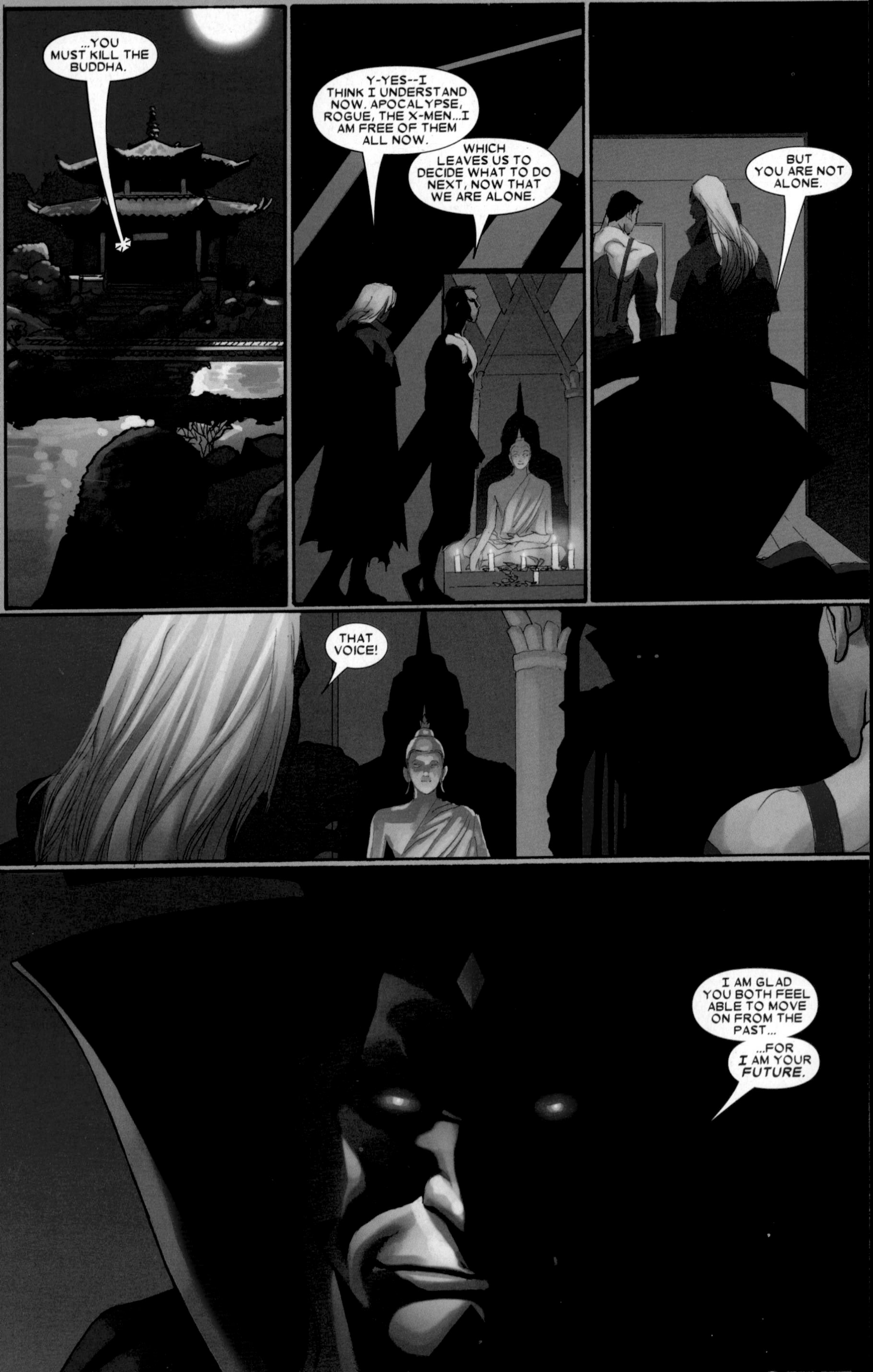
...YOU MUST KILL THE BUDDHA.
Y-YES--I THINK I UNDERSTAND NOW. APOCALYPSE, ROGUE, THE X-MEN...I AM FREE OF THEM ALL NOW.
WHICH LEAVES US TO DECIDE WHAT TO DO NEXT, NOW THAT WE ARE ALONE.
BUT YOU ARE NOT ALONE.
THAT VOICE!
I AM GLAD YOU BOTH FEEL ABLE TO MOVE ON FROM THE PAST...
...FOR I AM YOUR FUTURE.

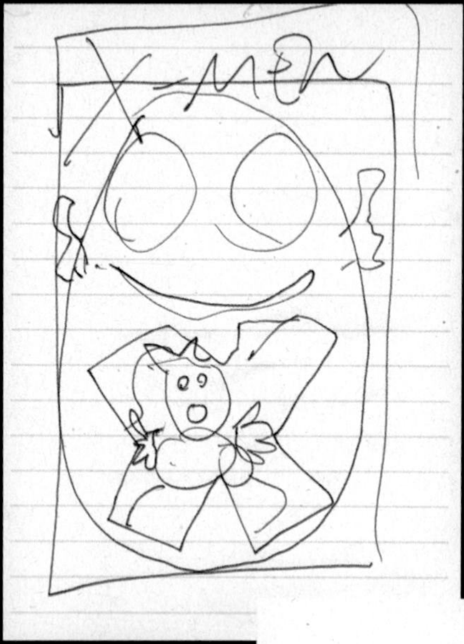
X-MEN

Cover concept by
Nick Lowe

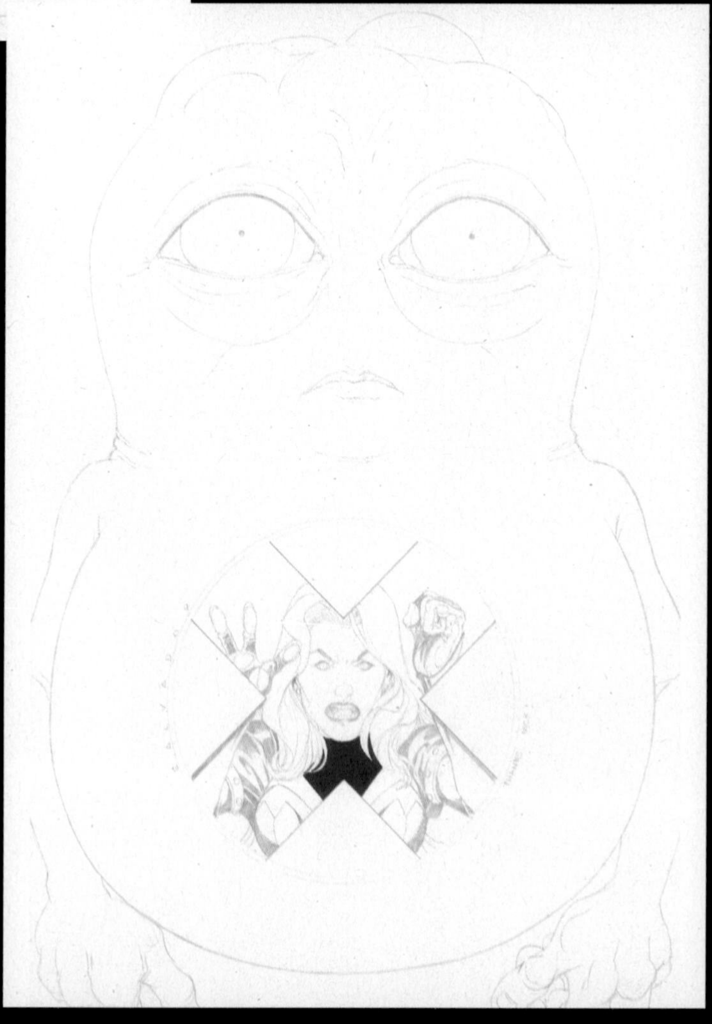

Cover pencils by
Salvador Larroca

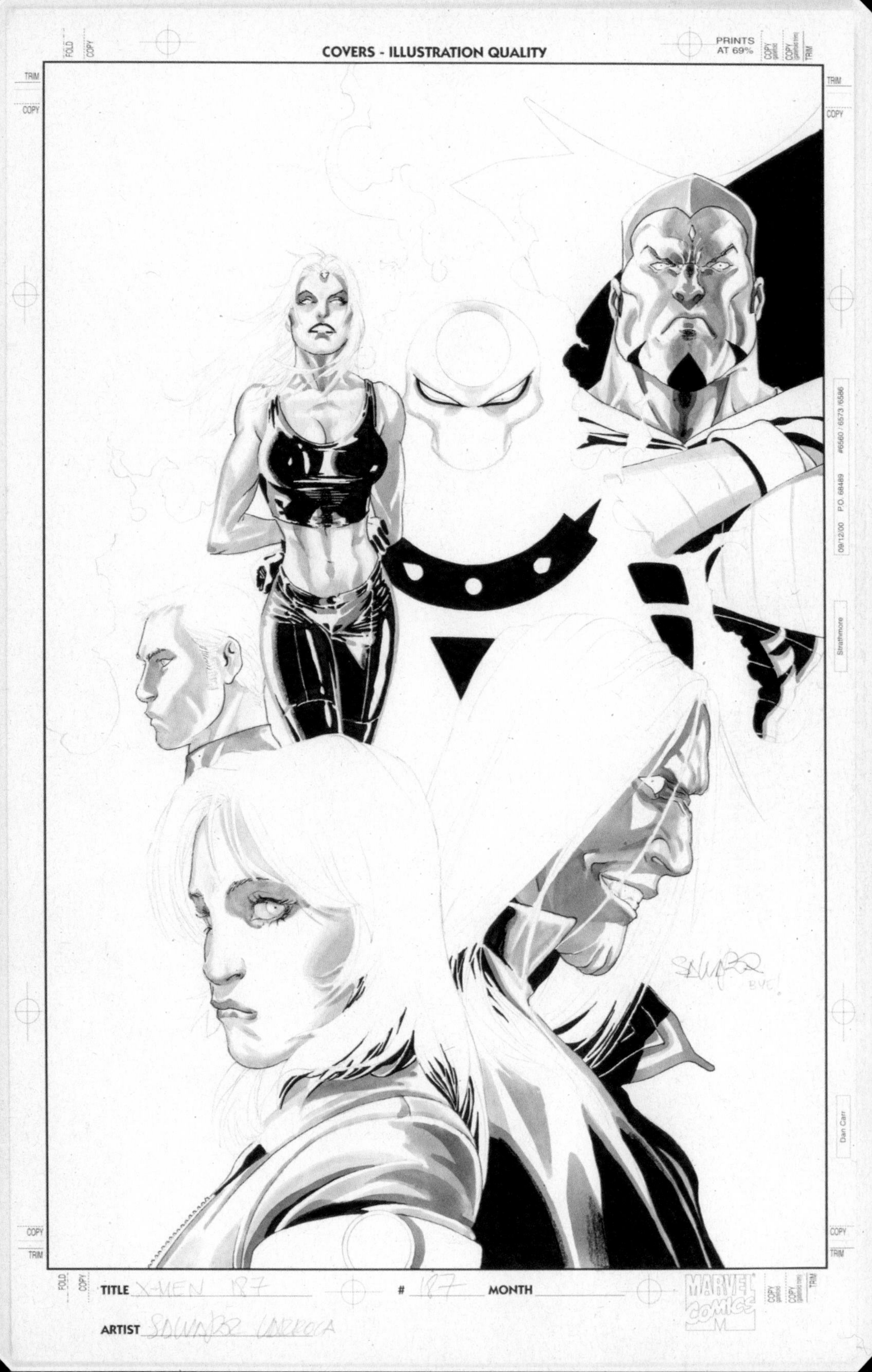
COVERS - ILLUSTRATION QUALITY
PRINTS AT 69%
TITLE X-MEN 187
187
MONTH
ARTIST SALVADOR LARROCA
MARVEL COMICS

X-Men #187 cover art by **Salvador Larroca**

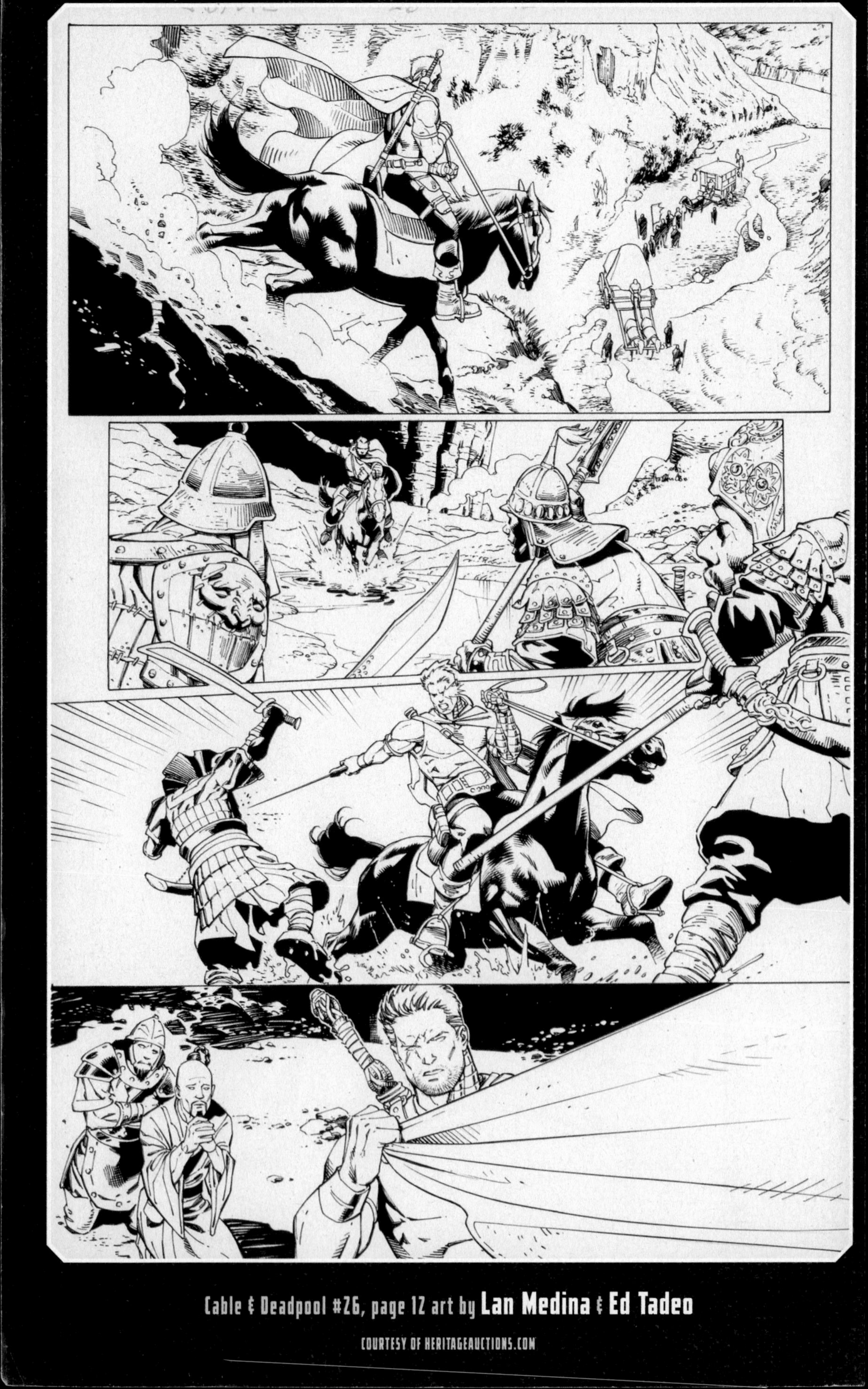

Cable & Deadpool #26, page 12 art by **Lan Medina & Ed Tadeo**

COURTESY OF HERITAGEAUCTIONS.COM